Apocalyptic Fever

Apocalyptic Fever
End-Time Prophecies in Modern America

RICHARD KYLE

CASCADE *Books* • Eugene, Oregon

APOCALYPTIC FEVER
End-Time Prophecies in Modern America

Copyright © 2012 Richard Kyle. All rights reserved. Except for brief quotations in critical publications or reviews, no part of this book may be reproduced in any manner without prior written permission from the publisher. Write: Permissions, Wipf and Stock Publishers, 199 W. 8th Ave., Suite 3, Eugene, OR 97401.

Cascade Books
An Imprint of Wipf and Stock Publishers
199 W. 8th Ave., Suite 3
Eugene, OR 97401

www.wipfandstock.com

ISBN 13: 978-1-61097-697-8

Cataloging-in-Publication data:

Kyle, Richard

Apocalyptic fever : end-time prophecies in modern America / Richard Kyle.

xvi + 372 p. ; 23 cm. Includes bibliographical references and index.

ISBN 13: 978-1-61097-697-8

1. Millennialism—United States—History. 2. Eschatology. 3. End of the world. 4. Popular culture—United States. I. Title.

BL503 K95 2012

Manufactured in the U.S.A.

To my colleagues over many years at Tabor College

Contents

Preface | ix

1 Approaching Doomsday | 1
2 Western Contours of Doomsday | 21
3 The Millennial Nation | 47
4 The End Takes Shape | 80
5 Apocalypse Loud and Clear | 101
6 Millennial Anxieties | 134
7 From 9/11 to 666 | 157
8 Imaging the Apocalypse | 180
9 The Politics of Armageddon | 203
10 Messiahs, Prophets, and End-Time Visions | 228
11 The Godless Apocalypse | 266
12 An Eschatological Hodgepodge | 293
13 The Next Great Turning Point? | 319
14 Why Do We Love Doomsday? | 338

Bibliography | 353
Index |

Preface

AT TIMES PEOPLE HAVE eschatological moments, meaning that they think about end-time events in a more personal way. I am one of those people. On four occasions—the first as a young teenager, the second as a student in divinity school, and the third and fourth as a college professor—I thought more personally about such issues.

The first time came in October 1956. Israeli forces struck swiftly, rolling the Egyptian army back across the Sinai Peninsula. British and French troops seized the Suez Canal. The Soviet Union threatened to intervene on behalf of Egypt. Were these the opening shots of Armageddon? I thought so. At that time I was a young teenager who had been raised in a Plymouth Brethren church. Coming from such a background, I had drunk deeply at the fountains of dispensational premillennialism. I had been reared on the *Scofield Reference Bible*. Thus, I firmly embraced the premillennial beliefs regarding the Antichrist, rapture, tribulation, Armageddon, and millennium.

With great anxiety I went to the house of a leading elder. (Plymouth Brethren do not have paid pastors). He assured me that believers would be raptured before Armageddon. This helped assuage my anxieties. (Still, the thought of the elect consisting of only 144,000 gave me pause for concern. Was I one of the 144,000?) But President Eisenhower did a lot to relieve my anxieties. The American presidential elections loomed on the horizon, and he was not about to allow Armageddon to complicate his re-election. So he pulled the rug out from the Israelis, British, and French. Thus the crisis passed, and Armageddon would have to wait for another day.

But my interest in end-time ideas did not pass. At that young age my eschatology was quite limited. I knew of only one view—dispensational premillennialism. Since then I have learned about the many ways people see the end of the world. My horizons were first broadened in divinity

Preface

school. By means of courses in theology and Christian history, I learned about the variety of ways Christians have viewed the end of the world. At that time I experienced my second eschatological moment. During the summer, as I was touring the Rocky Mountains in my little Volkswagon "Bug," the Six Day War of 1967 broke out. Israel won decisively, capturing east Jerusalem and acquiring large tracks of Arab land. This might be biblical prophecy at work, so I thought. Israel now controlled all of the holy city and much of the land that God had promised them.

In 1991 I had another eschatological encounter. As a college professor I direct an annual trip to Europe. As we prepared to depart, the Persian Gulf War loomed on the horizon. Several parents and students believed the end was at hand. Parents called me attempting to get their children out of the trip. One insisted that Armageddon was imminent and asked if money could be returned. Finding out that I did not share her alarm, she even questioned my orthodoxy and asked if I believed in the Second Coming of Jesus Christ. I assured her that I did but that I did not know the time of this event. Unfortunately, airlines and hotels did not share her beliefs and would not return any money. So two of the parents put their money where their mouth was and still withdrew their children. When the actual war broke out, we were in Switzerland and on the way to Italy. More parents and a few students panicked. One even thought Saddam Hussein's missiles could strike Rome. Some of the students were embarrassed at their parents' actions but most had a good time.

My eschatological horizons continued to be expanded. In teaching courses on fringe religions and doing research on this subject, I encountered the doomsday and millennial ideas of many alternative religions. Such research found its way into two earlier books: *The Religious Fringe: A History of Alternative Religions in America* and *The New Age Movement in American Culture*. Then I widened my search to include the way scientists, filmmakers, and fiction writers have viewed the last days. I combined all of these elements—end-time beliefs from two thousand years of Christian history, fringe religions, science, and fiction into a new book: *The Last Days Are Here Again: A History of the End Times*, published by Baker Books. This volume surveys end of the world ideas through two thousand years of Western history and serves as the background for this current book.

My interest in apocalyptic ideas did not end with this volume. In fact, one can say that I had another eschatological moment. As the world approached the year 2000, a great deal of anxiety was in the air. Some people

Preface

connected the year 2000 with doomsday or at best chaos. The world stared the Y2K problem in the face. Would the computers stop working throwing the developed world into a crisis? Some people believed the global economic, transportation, military, and life-sustaining systems would collapse. Thus they stocked up on food, water, gold, and even weapons.

I was not one of these alarmists. But I was directing another student trip to Europe. In fear of a transportation system breakdown, some colleges and universities put their January 2000 international trips on hold. Tabor College (where I teach) did not do this. Still, I took the precaution of arranging a trip to the more stable countries of Europe and left a few days before January 1. Thus I had twenty-six students in Parliament Square London under Big Ben as the new millennium came in. At the stroke of midnight the crowd—including our students—went wild, hugging and kissing each other. And nothing happened except for the metro system (or the "tube" as the English say) being overburdened. Thus we had to walk back to our hotel.

These previous books and experiences all serve as the backdrop for the current volume. Why write another book on the end of the world? Few serious studies have focused on apocalyptic beliefs in modern America. Those that have usually zero in on dispensational premillennialism, the driving force behind eschatological beliefs in contemporary America. While this volume devotes several chapters to this topic, it covers much more. It surveys eschatology in modern America from a wide range of perspectives—dispensational, Catholic, mainline Protestant, evangelical, science, fringe religions, the occult, fiction, the year 2000, Islam, politics, Pentecostal, Seventh-day Adventist, the Mayan calendar, and more. Of considerable importance, this book relates end-times ideas with the cultural forces and trends in American society.

Doomsday ideas in Western history have been both persistent and adaptable. To be sure, as they ran the course of Western history, they have had their ups and downs, often peaking during times of stress and turmoil and abating during good times. But a fascination with the apocalypse has been persistent in Western thinking. In part, this is because doomsday ideas have been so adaptable. As historical situations have changed, so have apocalyptic ideas, at times demonstrating a chameleon-like quality.

But one should not exaggerate the notion of persistence. Apocalyptic ideas have not constantly pervaded the mainstream of Western culture. Rather, end-time visions can be seen as—to use Peter Stearn's analogy—a dormant virus. They remain quiescent until activated by cultural

Preface

conditions; then they break out, often in smaller sectarian groups. But sometimes apocalypticism can infect the wider culture.

And modern America has been one of these times. Public opinion polls indicate that a substantial number of Americans look for the return of Christ or some catastrophic event. The views of these polls have been reinforced by the market process. Whether the approach has been purchasing paperbacks or watching cable television programs, millions of Americans have expressed an interest in end-time events. Yes, Americans have a tremendous appetite for prophecy, more than nearly any other people in the modern world. This appetite is fed by certain trends in American society: religious freedom, a widespread interest in religion, anti-intellectualism, a populist impulse, an escapist mentality, and a Manichaean and conspiratorial worldview. Because eschatology has a chameleon-like character, it has been able to link and adjust its predictions to current events.

Essentially, this book is an intellectual history. It is the history of an idea, the idea of how the world will end. It focuses on one aspect of what people believe about future events, namely the last days as they are perceived in modern America. This volume also closely connects such ideas with the social and cultural framework from which they arise. Such an approach avoids two pitfalls. First, it makes no pronouncements regarding the future. Doomsday has not arrived, and history must concern itself with the past, not the future. In this case, it measures what Americans have believed about the future. Second, the approach of intellectual history helps minimize value judgments. This study is largely about what others believe about the end of time, not what I believe. While no historian is free of personal biases, I trust I have not pushed my perspective on other people.

Through two thousand years of Western history, millions of people have believed that they were living in the last days. And modern America is no exception to this trend. Millions of Americans are expecting the end in the near future. Adopting a historical perspective toward future events helps one to remain judicious and open to whatever lies in store. Many sincere, devout, and knowledgeable people have seen the end as imminent; they have been people of the Bible, anchoring their beliefs in Scripture. But they have all been wrong. The failure of such prognostications, however, should not dull one's sensitivities to end-time events. Rather, one should such view developments historically. Someday the world will end. But sensible people will not jump at every prediction. Apocalyptic ideas, even those grounded in Scripture, have been shaped by their historical context. None are infallible. Thus Christians must be prepared for Christ's

Preface

return, but they need to realize that such signs indicating the last days are not new—they have been visible for two millennia!

To promote a balanced perspective of how Americans view the end times, I have attempted to write a descriptive history. This study is neither a devotional nor an attack on various eschatological positions. Some readers might be disappointed at not finding a chapter critiquing various end-time views. But this is not the job of the historian. By its very nature, of course, the discipline of history leads to a critical analysis. Such an examination should not, however, turn into a polemic.

This study of end-time thought in modern America follows a pattern. There are fourteen chapters, eleven of which examine apocalyptic ideas in America during the twentieth and twenty-first centuries. Chapter 1, "Approaching Doomsday," describes the current fascination with doomsday and tells why this mindset has persisted through Western history, especially in America. The next chapter, "Western Contours of Doomsday," takes us on a brief journey through Western history. It looks at end-time beliefs in the early church, the Middle Ages, the Reformation era, and into the modern world. Described are the various shifts in apocalyptic and millennial views and how they set the stage for eschatological thinking in America.

Chapter 3, "The Millennial Nation," brings the story of doomsday speculations across the Atlantic Ocean. In America millennial thought has been more pronounced than in Europe. This chapter describes end-time ideas found in mainstream American society from the Puritans to the early twentieth century. But it does not stop there. Chapter 3 also expands upon the millennialism of alternative religions such as the Millerites, Shakers, Mormons, Seventh-day Adventists, and Jehovah's Witnesses.

The next two chapters look at dispensational premillennialism in twentieth-century America. Chapter 4, "The End Takes Shape," describes early dispensationalism and how it took hold in America prior to World War II. World War I and the struggle between fundamentalism and modernism provided a tremendous catalyst for the acceptance dispensationalism. In chapter 5, "Apocalypse Loud and Clear," dispensationalism arrives full blast and ignites a major interest in end-time thinking. Prophets of the apocalypse become almost commonplace and numerous speculations are made. And when these prophecies prove false, new ones are made and adjusted to the shifting sands of current events.

The next two chapters examine end-time anxieties largely as they relate to the year 2000 and the events of the early twenty-first century.

xiii

Preface

Chapter 6, "Millennial Anxieties," views the predictions regarding the year 2000 and the Y2K problem from both a secular and religious perspective. Chapter 7, "From 9/11 to 666," traces the shift in eschatological predictions from the Soviet Union to Islam. Islam is now the great enemy and America has largely disappeared from the prophetic stage.

The apocalyptic scene now switches to fiction and politics, and sometime you cannot tell the difference. Chapter 8, "Imaging the Apocalypse," looks at how doomsday has been portrayed through fiction, especially novels and film. Quite often fiction—both secular and religious—measures the pulse beat of how people feel about a subject, in this case the end of the world. Politics does not escape the influence of end-time thinking. Chapter 9, "The Politics of Armageddon," links politics with eschatology, especially as expressed by the Christian Right, Christian reconstructionism, and Christian Zionism.

But the story of doomsday speculation in modern America is not confined to the premillennial popularizers, as is demonstrated in chapter 10, "Messiahs, Prophets, and End-Time Visions." Numerous messiahs, prophets, and alternative religions have told us that the end is right around the corner. Moreover, it will not come gently; great catastrophes and upheavals are looming on the horizon.

Such predictions go beyond the lunatic fringe of American society. Sober scientists are warning us that both human-caused and natural disasters could destroy us. Chapter 11, "The Godless Apocalypse," describes the secular apocalypse. Some hardheaded scientists paint a dire picture of the future. We may be done in by a nuclear catastrophe, a series of natural disasters, global warming, overpopulation, plagues and pestilence, or by an object from outer space.

As we approach the end of this study, some subjects have not been addressed. And they do not fit into a cohesive package. So chapter 12, "An Eschatological Hodgepodge," resembles a medley and looks at the end-time views of Catholicism, the Marian visitations, mainline Protestantism, the Pentecostal and charismatic movements, and contemporary Seventh-day Adventism.

The last two chapters close out this study. Chapter 13, "The Next Great Turning Point?," looks at the predictions of the early twenty-first century, especially those related to Harold Camping's "WE CAN KNOW" movement, the year 2012, and the Mayan calendar. The last chapter attempts to come to grips with America's fascination with doomsday. "Why Do We Love Doomsday?" builds on material expressed elsewhere in the

Preface

book but zeroes in on the question: Why are Americans—more than other people in the industrial world—interested in end-time predictions?

No one writes a book alone. In the time that this book has been in gestation, I have accumulated debts to several individuals and institutions. I hope that my memory is not short in this regard and that I do not inadvertently omit any thanks that are due. Appreciation must go to the library staff of Tabor College for arranging for the acquisition of many books and articles through interlibrary loan. Without these sources my work would not have been possible. Thanks must go to Max Terman and Chris Dick for reading various chapters of this book. In writing this book, I have discussed issues and ideas with a number of people. A partial list would include Bill Kostlevy, Robert Clouse, Deborah Penner, Deborah Penn, Sara Hill, Robin Ottoson, Doug Miller, and Del Gray. Thanks must go to them.

Several debts also have been incurred in the production of this book. I thank Ellie Rempel for her work in putting this manuscript in its final form. Gratitude is due to the Tabor College administration for providing financial assistance through the Hope Scholars Grant for summer work on this study. Academic publishing entails its own problems. Therefore, much appreciation must go to the staff of Cascade Books for publishing this volume—especially to copyeditor Nathan Rhoads, editor Chris Spinks, assistant managing editor Christian Amondson, and typesetter Ian Creeger.

Finally, my gratitude goes to some who were involved only indirectly with the writing and publishing process. In particular, I am grateful to my wife, Joyce, and son, Brent, for sharing me with this project and for encouraging me in this endeavor. Without their support and patience this book would not have been possible.

Richard Kyle
Hillsboro, Kansas

1

Approaching Doomsday

How will the world end? What does the future hold? In modern America many self-proclaimed prophets have attempted to answer these questions. Most of their answers have not boded well for the future. The authors of the best-selling *Left Behind* fictionalized series say that, "In one cataclysmic moment, millions around the globe disappear. Those left behind face war, plagues, and natural disasters so devastating that only one in four people will survive . . ."[1] As the clock moved toward 2000 many dire predictions surfaced. "Rape, murder, earthquakes and, single parent families, war, AIDS. They're all part of God's plan to destroy Earth within the next 10 years according to Rev. Carl Holland of York, Virginia."[2] While Rev. Holland words were a bit strident, many TV preachers, popular authors, and flamboyant clergy brought a similar message to millions of Americans.

But 2000 came and went, and nothing but a few minor disruptions occurred. Many people believed that we had hit a landmark with the year 2000 and the predictions would cease until the next crisis. Never underestimate America's appetite for prophecy, however. The *Left Behind* series continued to sell by the millions for most of the first decade of the twenty-first century. Then September 11 catapulted the Islamic threat onto the

---

1. Tim LaHaye and Jerry B. Jenkins, *Tribulation Force* (Wheaton, IL: Tyndale, 1996), backcover.

2. Ken Baker, "Preachers Proclaiming 'The End Is Near,'" *Wichita Eagle*, 4 February 1995, 7C.

front burner. In Mark Hitchcock's words, "I believe current events in Iran and the Middle East are part of the stage setting for the end-time drama. We are witnessing a growing alliance of Muslim nations and Russia that is strikingly similar" to the alliances predicted in Ezekiel 38–39. In a similar vein, Joel Rosenberg says Iranian president Mahmoud Ahmadinejad "believes the end of the world is rapidly approaching [and] that the way to hasten the coming of the Islamic Messiah known as the 'Hidden Imam' or the 'Mahdi' is to launch a catastrophic global jihad, first against Israel (the 'little Satan') and then against the U. S. ('the Great Satan')."[3]

Related to the Islamic threat was another question: Is Barack Obama the Antichrist? The Internet vibrated over this issue. Most answers range from affirming Obama to be the Antichrist to saying that the "Man of Sin" will be someone like him. According to one Internet source, "Eerily, the Bible says the Antichrist world leader will come in on a platform of peace before all hell breaks loose. And Obama's whole campaign is PEACE . . . he will END WAR and CHANGE the world . . . and the media [will] portray him as a savior . . . a messiah."[4] While Hal Lindsey does not say Obama is the Antichrist, he does declare that Obama is preparing the world for such a leader. In saying so he is referring to Obama's emphasis on global peace, on bringing the planet together, and that he is a "citizen of the world"—all characteristics of the Antichrist.[5] This is to say nothing about the problems Obama faces: an economic crisis, a broken healthcare system, two wars plus other international tensions. If he can solve them he indeed would be regarded as a messiah.

If the Islamic threat and the prospect of the American president being the Antichrist were not enough, try thinking about December 21, 2012. You can buy T-shirts with "2012: THE END" or "12.21.12" on them. What do they signify? Many people, including evangelical Christians, are intrigued by the prophecies of Nostradamus and the Mayan calendar signifying an end of the world on December 21, 2012. In fact, some evangelical and fundamentalist Christians have Christianized these occult and mystical sources and have tied them in with biblical prophecy. But this is not the first time they have done this.

---

3. Mark Hitchcock, *Apocalypse of Ahmadinejad: The Revelation of Iran's Nuclear Prophet* (Colorado Springs, CO: Multnomah, 2007) preface, 125.

4. "Is Barack Obama the Antichrist? End Times 2012 Election 2008," http://www.youtube.com/?v=rfGWBcyeZDY (accessed 15 November 2008).

5. Hal Lindsey, "How Obama Prepped World for the Antichrist," 1 August 2008, http://www.wnd.com/2008/08/71144/. See also Lisa Miller, "Is Obama the Antichrist?," *Newsweek*, 24 November 2008, 18.

Approaching Doomsday

All hell may break loose on 12/21/12. The book *2012 Predictions* notes environmental disasters, lakes disappearing and rivers flowing backward, social websites recruiting American jihads, economic disasters rendering cash meaningless, diseases, oil and water shortages, global warming, weather changes, and World War III as related to biblical prophecy. Others say "unprecedented catastrophes will precede the end of the world in 2012 . . . such as massive earthquakes, tidal waves and volcanic eruptions, among other calamities."[6]

But if you are into New Age thinking, things may not be all that bad. The year 2012 can be seen as a Y2K for the New Age. "Around . . . 2012, a large chapter of human history will be coming to an end, and a new phase of human growth will commence."[7] Better yet if you are a procrastinator: you can defer the end of the world for another day. Isaac Newton tells us that the world will not end until 2060.[8] So you have plenty of time. People know that Newton was one of the greatest scientists of all time, but few are aware that he also dabbled in theology. He arrived at the year 2060 as many have done, that is, by picking a starting date and adding up biblical chronology.

On a lighter note, there is the old fairy tale about Chicken Little, who, having been hit on the head by something, was convinced that the sky was falling. Chicken Little ran off to tell the king and along the way picked up several followers who were also convinced that the sky was falling.

Through much of human history there have been the Chicken Littles who have dashed about proclaiming that the sky was falling or that some other catastrophe would soon happen. There have also been many people willing to follow these prophets of doom.[9] This book is about the Chicken Littles of contemporary American history and those who have followed them.

Since the 1970s there has been a flood of end-of-the-world predictions. In fact, books on prophecy—whether Christian, occultic, or secular—have been a growth industry. They have become big sellers. Christian fundamentalists insist that the Second Coming of Christ is imminent. They claim to hear louder than ever "the Four Horsemen of the apocalypse—War, Plague, Famine, and Death—galloping toward Armageddon."

6. Christine Brouwer, "Will the World End in 2012?," 3 July 2008, http://www.december212012.com/articles/news/ABCnews-Will_the_World_End_in_2012.htm.

7. Lisa Miller, "2012: A Y2K for the New Age," *Newsweek*, 18 May 2009, 12.

8. Stephen D. Snobelen, "Statement on the Date 2060," online: http://www.isaac-newton.org/update.html.

9. Daniel Cohen, *Waiting for the Apocalypse* (Buffalo: Prometheus, 1983) 7–8.

Occultists tell of great calamities to come in the near future. "New Age astrologers foresee psychic anguish, earthquakes, and economic collapse" before the dawn of the Age of Aquarius. Even down-to-earth scientists have joined in, warning us of impending human-caused disasters.[10]

THE END IS NEAR

Of all the groups that have been infected by this apocalyptic mood, the Christian dispensational premillennialists have operated at a fever pitch. They point to a series of events as confirmation of biblical prophecy. The return of the Jews to Israel in 1948 began the countdown to Armageddon. Following on its heels came other developments—the threat of nuclear destruction, the European Common Market, Israel's seizure of Jerusalem in 1967, the perception of the Soviet Union as the great northern power, the first Persian Gulf War, and the war on terror including the conflicts in Iraq and Afghanistan. Within dispensational circles, the popularizers have aroused far more attention than have the more scholarly elements. (For a study of dispensationalism see chapters 4, 5, and parts of 7 and 9.)

During the 1980s the fixation on doomsday even reached the highest levels of American political power. James Watt, the Secretary of the Interior, declared that this generation might be the last. Secretary of Defense Caspar Weinberger made similar statements.[11] In an interview, President Ronald Reagan indicated that recent events had caused him to think of Armageddon: "You know, I turn back to your ancient prophecies in the Old Testament and the signs foretelling Armageddon and I find myself wondering if we're the generation that is going to see that come about . . . believe me, they certainly describe the times we're going through." Of course, it is the Book of Revelation, not the Old Testament, that speaks of Armageddon. But otherwise the president's ideas came close to the public pulse.[12]

And spurred on by Hal Lindsey's best-selling *Late Great Planet Earth*, a host of fundamentalist preachers, authors, and TV personalities have

---

10. The quotes are from Hillel Schwartz, "Fin-de-Siecle Fantasies: A Brief History of the End of Time," *New Republic*, 30 July and 6 August 1990, 22.

11. Frank Palmeri, "Apocalypse: Then and Now," *Humanist*, January–February 1983, 26.

12. The quote is from Robert Jewett, "Coming to Terms with the Doom Boom," *Quarterly Review* 4/3 (Fall 1984) 9. See also Bill Lawren, "Are You Ready for Millennial Fever?," *Utne Reader*, March–April 1990, 91–92; G. Clark Chapman, Jr., "Falling in Rapture before the Bomb," *Reformed Journal* 37 (June 1987) 13.

Approaching Doomsday

continued to bring an apocalyptic message to millions of Americans. Jack Van Impe, Salem Kirban, Pat Robertson, Jerry Falwell, Tim LaHaye, John Hagee, and Mark Hitchcock, to name only a few, have warned that floods, famines, earthquakes, diseases, wars, and Middle East events will precede the Second Coming of Christ. As we have moved into the twenty-first century, the rhetoric and the publications have not tapered off. The fact that the predictions related to the 1980s and 1990s did not come to fruition did not deter the popularizers. They were not embarrassed. Given the chameleon-like nature of end-time predictions, popular preachers and writers adjusted their prognostications to suit the new circumstances. After all, for the most part, they begin with current events and interpret biblical verses in the light of their beliefs. Thus Islamic terrorism, Iran, Middle East affairs, Barack Obama, and natural disasters come to the forefront.

But Christian fundamentalists were not the only ones caught up with this end-time madness. The same apocalyptic impulse has driven a number of individuals and groups on the fringes of American religion. During the lifetime of its founder, Herbert Armstrong, the Worldwide Church of God (now called Grace Community International) believed that the tribulation would begin in the 1970s. Not to be out done, the Jehovah's Witnesses have made numerous end-of-the-world predictions—the last ones pointing to 1975 and 1984. An "ascended Master" supposedly told Elizabeth Clare Prophet of a nuclear catastrophe to befall the world in the 1990s, so she urged her followers to build large bomb shelters. The Children of God (now called the Love Family), a radical millennial group, had an end-time countdown culminating in the rapture in the early 1990s. Before their fiery end at Waco, the Branch Davidians evinced an intense apocalyptic outlook. While most New Agers view the future through rose-colored spectacles, some foresee future disasters[13] And many fringe groups are glued to the Mayan calendar and look for calamitous events in 2012 and thereafter.

Several famous prophets have had bad vibrations about the late twentieth and early twenty-first centuries. The sixteenth-century French seer Nostradamus foresaw the years 1999 and 2000 as a time of wars, tremendous upheaval, and possible global destruction. He has also predicted cataclysmic events for 2012. Edgar Cayce, the "sleeping prophet," also saw dire events coming for the 1990s and beyond. Jeanne Dixon believed that

---

13. Richard Kyle, *The Religious Fringe: A History of Alternative Religions in America* (Downers Grove, IL: InterVarsity, 1993) 366; Ron Rhodes, "Millennial Madness," *Christian Research Journal* 13/2 (Fall 1990) 39; Michael Barkun, "Reflections after Waco: Millennialists and the State," *Christian Century*, 2–9 June 1993, 596.

the Antichrist was currently alive and would assume great power before 2000. Psychic Ruth Montgomery predicted a cosmic disaster in which the North and South Poles suddenly reverse their positions, thus wreaking incredible havoc. Other prognosticators also speak of a pole shift and reversal in 2012. But before then, other horrible events were predicted for the years 2005, 2006, 2008, and 2111. In particular, June 6, 2006 (6/6/06), evoked the fear of negative events. Some said the "satanic boy" would be born on that day.[14]

The Christian tradition does not have a corner on end-time predictions, however. Several other religions have predicted that the world would end around 2000 and beyond. Some Jewish fundamentalists asserted that Armageddon would occur a generation after the reestablishment of the Jewish state. But this timetable is flexible, especially the length of a generation. Some Buddhists believe that the world will end about 2,500 years after the Buddha's death (ca. 483 BC). Aztec, Hindu, Mayan, and Hopi prophecies suggest that the world is teetering on the brink.[15]

Through history most end-time scenarios have had a religious base. But in recent years apocalyptic thought has undergone at least a partial secularization. It extends beyond religious lines and often reaches the public not in the language of divine revelation, but in the profane dress of science, history, and journalism. "Many who claim the end is near get their inspiration as much from science as from Scripture."[16] In fact some of the most "significant outbreaks of millenarianism in our time have been secular."[17]

For much of human history, the end of the world could have come only at the hands of God or a natural calamity. But now humankind can accomplish it without God's help. We have developed the means to destroy

---

14. Bill Lawren, "Apocalypse Now?," *Psychology Today* 23/5 (May 1989) 42; Dick Teresi and Judith Hooper, "The Last Laugh," *Omni* 12/4 (January 1990) 43; Tony Allen-Mills, "Mothers Expect Damien on 6/6/06," *The Sunday Times*, 30 April 2006, http://www.thesundaytimes.co.uk/sto/news/uk_news/article200645.ece; "End-of-World Prophecies: 20 Predictions between 2007 and 2010," http://www.religioustolerance.org/endwrl14.htm (accessed 5 April 2007); Patrick Geryl, "Pole Shift & Pole Reversal in 2012," http://survive2012.com/ger11.php (accessed 5 April 2007).

15. Cullen Murphy, "The Way the World Ends," *Wilson Quarterly* 14/1 (Winter 1990) 54; Teresi and Hooper, "The Last Laugh?," 43.

16. William F. Allman, "Fatal Attraction: Why We Love Doomsday," *U.S. News and World Report*, 30 April 1990, 13.

17. Charles Krauthammer, "Apocalypse with and without God," *Time*, 22 March 1993, 82 (quote); Samuel McCracken, "Apocalyptic Thinking," *Commentary*, October 1971, 61.

ourselves. The ultimate weapon, of course, is nuclear annihilation. As a result, in recent decades millions of Americans have experienced anxiety attacks about a nuclear apocalypse.[18]

But in 1991 the Soviet Union unraveled and the Cold War ended. Thus, nuclear apocalypticism had to be modified. While the threat from the Soviet Union (now Russia) diminished, September 11 and the war on terror came along. It has been feared that either some terrorist or rogue state might launch a nuclear attack on the United States. This reduced threat, however, has been partially replaced by the "ecocatastrophists." They tell of disasters to be brought on by overpopulation, global warming, ozone depletion, chemical weapons, world hunger, AIDS, and other diseases.[19]

If one prefers a more mundane catastrophe, there is an economic apocalypse. There is no shortage of predictions regarding the economic demise of the American economy or, worse yet, a global economic collapse. In recent decades best-seller lists have included *The Crash of '79*, *The Panic of '89*, *The Great Depression of 1990*, *Bankruptcy 1995*, and *The Coming Economic Earthquake*. The terrible recession of 2008–9 fueled the flames of economic fears. And the massive American deficit has done nothing to quell these anxieties.[20]

Such fears regarding the end of the world are not new. They are as old as human history itself. But until the world does come to an end, such prognostications are merely an idea, a belief. And that is what this book is about—the idea of how the world will end. Many world religions—Islamic, Buddhist, Hindu, Zoroastrian, and Jewish—have legends regarding the end of time. However, we will look at end-time predictions primarily as they relate to contemporary America.

A FEW DEFINITIONS

Before we journey through modern American history to see how people have viewed doomsday, we must define some terms and briefly look at such developments in Western history. This book concerns end-of-the-world predictions, not apocalypticism or millennialism per se. Still, individuals

---

18. Krauthammer, "Apocalypse," 82; Ray Corelli, "Boom Time for Futurists," *World Press Review*, December 1989, 28.

19. Corelli, "Boom Time," 28.

20. For example see Ravi Batra, *Great Depression of 1990* (New York: Simon and Schuster, 1987); Krauthammer, "Apocalypse," 82; Corelli, "Boom Time."

and groups who envision the end of the world often have an apocalyptic or millennial worldview.

As Bernard McGinn notes, apocalypticism "is a highly complex phenomenon." Thus it cannot be reduced to "a clear and distinct idea." Moreover, the meaning of apocalypticism has shifted through time, often acquiring different connotations in different eras. Accordingly, we must see apocalypticism as a tradition embodied primarily in Western culture.[21] To understand its essence, we must come up with a working definition and a list of characteristics.

The word *apocalypse* means "revelation, the uncovering or unveiling of a divine secret. It is eschatological in nature, that is, it is concerned with final things—the end of the present age, the judgment day, and the age to come. Apocalyptic thinking assumes a particular view of history: history is essentially linear. It does not go round and round. Rather, history progresses from event to event, moving toward a final goal at the end of time."[22]

Apocalyptic is a form of literature claiming to reveal hidden things and the future. As a genre popular in Israel from about 200 BCE to 100 CE, it closely reflected the persecution that the Jews experienced during this time. The authors of the apocalyptic writings in the biblical canon have been identified by the Christian tradition. However, other apocalyptic literature is often pseudonymous—it bears a fictitious name. Revealed to seers through dreams and visions, it employs a highly symbolic, imaginative language that is subject to wide interpretation.[23]

Apocalyptic thinking has several characteristics. It is dualistic, viewing human history as a cosmic struggle between absolute good and evil. The apocalyptic outlook is also catastrophic in that it holds that this historical conflict will be settled by battles and disasters in which evil will be defeated. Although the word *apocalypse* is currently used as a synonym for disaster, this is only a half truth. "Apocalypse" concerns both "cataclysm and millennium, tribulation and triumph." Finally, apocalyptic thinking is

---

21. Bernard McGinn, *Visions of the End: Apocalyptic Traditions in the Middle Age* (New York: Columbia University Press, 1979) 3; Stephen D. O'Leary, *Arguing the Apocalypse* (New York: Oxford university Press, 1994) 10.

22. Lois Parkinson Zamora, ed., *The Apocalyptic Vision in America* (Bowling Green, OH: Bowling Green University Popular Press, 1982) 2-3.

23. George E. Ladd, "Apocalyptic," in *Evangelical Dictionary of Theology*, ed. Walter A. Elwell (Grand Rapids: Baker, 1984) 63; H. H. Rowley, *The Relevance of Apocalyptic: A Study of Jewish and Christian Apocalypses from Daniel to Revelation* (Greenwood, SC: Attic, 1980), 54ff.; Lester L. Grabbe, "The Social Setting of Early Jewish Apocalypticism," *Journal for the Study of Pseudepigrapha* 4 (April 1989) 24-47.

deterministic, assuming that the sequence of events in the final conflict is "preset in a heavenly clock."[24]

The great majority of the individuals and groups who envision the end of the world think apocalyptically in one way or another. While some individuals believe that the world will end gradually and on a positive note, most predict a cataclysmic, disastrous end to history. Even the secular apocalyptists share this view. While they may not see the world ending because of divine intervention, they do predict upheavals and catastrophes. Many secular apocalyptists foresee these future disasters without the hope of a future golden age.

The words *apocalyptic* and *eschatological* are often used interchangeably. This is technically incorrect. *Eschatology* means "study of the last things." It is a general term referring to all end-time events and ideas. In contrast, *apocalyptic* is a more narrow term, a specific type of eschatological belief characterized by a sense of impending doom.[25]

Prophecy and apocalypticism have a close relationship, but they are not identical. There are apocalyptic prophets, but some prophets do not proclaim an apocalyptic message. A prophet is "one who foretells the future" or "who seeks to correct a present situation." Generally, prophets receive their message from God apart from visions or dreams. This message, which they proclaim in the name of the Lord, is intended to change a current situation. On the other hand, an apocalyptic seer proclaims a message of doom that offers little opportunity for repentance. This message is usually received through a vision and bears a name other than that of the seer.[26]

Millennialism (or millenarianism) and apocalypticism overlap, but they are not the same. *Millennialism*, derived from the Latin word for a thousand, refers to a belief in a thousand-year period of blessedness (*chiliasm*, drawn from the Greek, has the same meaning). Christian millennialism is based on a literal interpretation of Revelation 20:1–10.[27]

---

24. Zamora, *Apocalyptic Vision*, 3, 14 (quote); Jewett, "Coming to Terms with the Doom Boom," 10; Walter Schmithals, *The Apocalyptic Movement* (Nashville: Abingdon, 1975) 18, 21–24.

25. O' Leary, *Arguing the Apocalypse*, 5–6; Barry Brummett, *Contemporary Apocalyptic Rhetoric* (New York: Praeger, 1991), 7; Frank Kermode, *The Sense of an Ending: Studies in the Theory of Fiction* (New York: Oxford University Press, 1967); Catherine Keller, *Apocalypse Now and Then: A Feminist Guide to the End of the World* (Boston: Beacon, 1996), 20.

26. McGinn, *Visions of the End*, 4 (quote); Ladd, "Apocalyptic," 63.

27. Robert G. Clouse, "Views of the Millennium," in *Evangelical Dictionary of Theology*, ed. Elwell, 714; "Millenarianism," in *Oxford Dictionary of the Christian Church*,

Many apocalyptists are millenarians, believing that cataclysmic events will either precede or follow a millennium. Still, there are apocalyptists who do not speak of a millennium, and millennialists who do not believe the world will experience a catastrophic end. Unfortunately, it is easy to muddle the differences between apocalypticism and millennialism. Many books have done so. Indeed, in describing end-time thinking through history, I probably have fallen into the same trap.

Millennialism falls into three main groups—pre-, post-, and amillennialism.[28] These positions differ as to when Christ will return. But their differences go well beyond the timing of Christ's return. They touch upon attitudes toward life, the way in which Scripture is interpreted, the number of resurrections, and the nature of the millennium itself. Pre-, post-, and amillennialism are relatively modern terms. Thus one must be careful not to impose them on earlier ages. Nevertheless, many of the millennial positions expressed through the course of Western history roughly approximate the outlines of pre-, post-, and amillennialism.

Premillennialists believe that Christ will return before the millennium. They tend to be apocalyptists, believing that the new age will be inaugurated in a cataclysmic and supernatural manner. They also interpret Scripture literally and adopt a somewhat pessimistic attitude toward life. That is to say, they often insist that a catastrophe is on the horizon and reject human schemes for building a heaven on Earth and improving human nature. Rather, they believe that God will intervene, probably in a cataclysmic way, to usher in the new millennium. They are not pessimistic about all aspects of life, however. For example, they are often at the forefront in business ventures and the use of technology. Premillennialists can also be divided into two main categories—pre- and posttribulationalists. Pretibulationalistism is by far the most popular variety, contending that the faithful will be raptured before the tribulation. Conversely, posttribulationists say the church will go through the great time of testing at the end of time.

Conversely, postmillennialists say Christ will not come until the end of a golden age. Many of them are not apocalyptists; they insist that the millennium will come in a gradual, less violent way. Moreover, they tend

---

ed. F. L. Cross (2nd ed.; New York: Oxford University Press, 1974) 916.

28. Stanley J. Grenz, *The Millennial Maze: Sorting Out the Evangelical Options* (Downers Grove, IL: InterVarsity, 1992) 24–26, 149–52; Clouse, "Views of the Millennium," 715; Robert G. Clouse, ed. *The Meaning of the Millennium: Four Views* (Downers Grove, IL; InterVarsity, 1977) 7; Grant Underwood, *The Millenarian World of Early Mormonism* (Urbana, IL: University of Illinois Press, 1993) 4, 6.

Approaching Doomsday

to interpret Scripture spiritually and to view life optimistically, believing that human efforts will help inaugurate the millennium.

For much of human history, amillennialism has been the predominate view. Amillennialists do not interpret Revelation 20 literally—in their opinion, it symbolizes certain present realities. Thus they do not believe that Christ will establish a literal earthly rule before the judgment. Rather, the glorious new heaven and Earth will immediately follow the present dispensation of the kingdom of God.

Like apocalypticism, millennial thinking is not confined to the Christian tradition. Millennial beliefs can be found in non-Christian and non-Western religions. Millennialism can also be secular; in fact, Nazism and communism include millennial strands.

Lastly, we must understand what is meant by the "end of the world." Prophets of doom have given it several meanings. It can mean the destruction of the Earth, the extinction of humanity, or perhaps only a widespread catastrophe. Some prophets have in view merely the end of an era and the coming of a new age—not the actual destruction of the world.

SOME INTERPRETATIONS

Apocalyptic literature is rich in imagery and symbolism and can be interpreted many ways—sometimes with considerable imagination. Throughout history people have read into such writings the events of their own time. In this way nearly every generation has regarded their age as the last, or has seen this or that person as the Antichrist. And many of these end-time visions rest on how apocalyptic writings, especially the Book of Revelation, are interpreted.

There are basically four ways in which the Book of Revelation has been interpreted, three of which have eschatological implications. (The idealist view sees the book simply as a depiction of the continual struggle between good and evil—there is no prediction regarding the future). The preterist view interprets Revelation strictly as a first-century book. John is describing the church's situation in his day. The dreadful symbols are pointing to Nero and the Roman Empire. This interpretation is eschatological in that John sees himself as living in the last days. The end will soon come.[29] A modified version of this view contends that while most of

---

29. Leon Morris, *The Revelation of St. John: An Introduction and Commentary* (Grand Rapids: Eerdmans, 1969) 16–17; David Ewert, *The Church under Fire: Studies in Revelation* (Winnipeg: Kindred, 1988) ii–iii.

Revelation pertains to the first century, parts of the book may apply to the future—especially the coming of trials and tribulation. But this modified preterism does not embrace the details projected by many premillennialists or necessarily a future golden age.

The historicist view sees Revelation as an inspired forecast of human history. Its symbols set forth in broad outline the history of Western Europe from the beginning of the church to the Second Coming of Christ. Some interpreters regard the whole book as presaging Western history. For example, they believe that the opening of the little scroll in Revelation 10 depicts the Protestant Reformation. Other interpreters contend that only the letters to the seven churches (chapters 2–3) portray the Christian church.[30] Whatever the approach, the historicist view is used to make end-time predictions. Because such projections have tended to lock the interpreter to a specific timetable, the historicist approach is not common in the modern world.

The futurist view regards all but a few chapters of Revelation as concerned with what will happen at the end of the age. The futurists see the seven seals and all the rest as portraying the events surrounding the second return of Christ and the end of the world.[31] In the modern world the futurist view has led to many doomsday forecasts. Despite the fact that these predictions have backfired, the futurist approach does not lock one into a timetable as does the historicist approach. Thus it is very popular in contemporary America.

WHY THE WESTERN FASCINATION WITH DOOMSDAY?

Through the centuries humanity has had a huge appetite for apocalyptic thought. Why have people been fascinated with doomsday? What has sustained this interest? These are complex questions that defy simple answers. No one theory can account for the fascination, for it has appeared in all periods of history. Certain ideas in Western culture and conditions in Western history have, however, been particularly influential. Moreover, some specific ideas and conditions are tailor made for American culture—namely, religious freedom, a dynamic religious society, a populist impulse in religion, a tendency to follow prophets and accept new and

---

30. Ewert, *Church under Fire*, ii–iii; Morris, *Revelation of St. John*, 17.
31. Morris, *Revelation of St. John*, 17–18; Ewert, *Church under Fire*, ii–iii.

conspiratorial religious ideas, materialism, and an ignorance regarding serious religious beliefs.

Western Ideas

While nearly all cultures have their doomsday theories, fascination with the end time has been most persistent in the Western tradition. In part, this is result of certain ideas that are readily found in Western culture.

First, the historic Christian faith teaches that Jesus Christ will return to Earth personally and visibly. While Christians may debate the details of Christ's return, they agree on the reality of the Second Advent, which will bring an end to the world as we know it. The failure of Scripture to spell out the when and how of this event has spawned all kinds of wild speculations. While the Second Advent is a non-negotiable truth for the sober Christian community, it has also become fodder for fanatics.

Another biblical teaching—that the world was destroyed by a flood—has encouraged apocalyptic thinking. Most Christians believe that God judged and destroyed the first world by water because of its evil and wickedness. Likewise they are convinced that this world's sin and violence will bring a second divine judgment.[32] Christians are not alone, however, in believing that a deluge destroyed the first world. Many religions and primitive cultures have similar stories about a catastrophic flood.

Also worth mentioning are the ancient legends of the sinking of the continent of Atlantis. True, many people in the ancient world regarded the Atlantis story as a fable. Still, the story has persisted until the present, and many books have been written about Atlantis. The story of Atlantis is grist for many occultists and their cataclysmic predictions for the modern world.[33] Our point here is not to debate the historicity of the Noahic flood, nor even to equate it with the Atlantis story. Rather, the point is that "what we believe is going to happen in the future is profoundly influenced by what we think has already happened in the past." A crucial factor in convincing people that "the world would end catastrophically was their belief that a similar catastrophe had already occurred."[34]

---

32. Russell Chandler, *Doomsday: The End of the World, A View through Time* (Ann Arbor, MI: Servant, 1993) 34–35; Otto Friedrich, *The End of the World: A History* (New York: Fromm, 1986) 17–19.

33. Cohen, *Waiting for the Apocalypse*, 78–82; Friedrich, *End of the World*, 20–21.

34. Cohen, *Waiting for the Apocalypse*, 57.

A third factor encouraging speculation about the end of the world is the Western view of history. There are two classic models of history—cyclical and linear. In the perspective of most Eastern religions and ancient cultures, all human events occur in cycles. While the names, dates, and persons involved will change, the same events will happen again. Although the cyclical worldview is not devoid of cataclysmic thinking, it does not encourage predictions about the end of the world. Moreover, the non-Western cultures that do present ideas about the end of the world do so with less anxiety. They usually do not tie their apocalyptic beliefs to particular dates or periods of time—centuries or millenniums. Thus they avoid the great fear and hopes so characteristic of Western apocalypticism.[35]

The linear view of history, which began with the Hebrews and their neighbors, gained strength in the Christian tradition. While this model allows for some repetitive patterns, it views history as generally moving in one direction. The present is not a replay of the past. Rather, history moves from one event to the next until it reaches its final goal.[36] The apocalyptic worldview assumes such a model of history: history is moving toward the end of time, the final judgment, and the catastrophes that will accompany those events.[37]

Two other characteristics of the Western view of history have encouraged end-time predictions—optimism and determinism. The cyclical model of history is generally pessimistic. The situation may be terrible now. But worse still, events go round and round and there is little hope that they will get better. While Western apocalyptic thinking predicts disasters, there is an optimistic side. Cataclysm will be followed by heaven or a utopia of some sort.

Terminal visions are often deterministic. Most individuals who envision great upheavals or the end of the world see these events as determined by forces beyond their control, usually God. Apocalyptists frequently call individuals to repentance. Yet the die is cast—society is collectively

---

35. Donald V. Grawronski, *History—Meaning and Method* (Glenview, IL: Scott, Foresman, 1975) 24–25; Chandler, *Doomsday*, 15–16; D. W. Bebbington, *Patterns in History: A Christian Perspective on Historical Thought* (Downers Grove, IL: InterVarsity, 1979) 21–42; Keller, *Apocalypse Now and Then*, 12; Stearns, *Millennium III*, 12–13.

36. Brummett, *Contemporary Apocalyptic Rhetoric*, 32–33; Bebbington, *Patterns in History*, 43–67.

37. W. Warren Wagar, *Terminal Visions* (Bloomington, IN: Indiana University Press, 1982) 34–35; Brummett, *Contemporary Apocalyptic Rhetoric*, 32–33; Debra Bergoffen, "The Apocalyptic Meaning of History," in *Apocalyptic Vision in America*, ed. Zamora, 13–29; Catherine Keller, "Why Apocalypse Now?," *Theology Today* 49/2 (1992) 184.

doomed. Evil and wickedness are so great that judgment is inevitable—it will take place according to a divine timetable. Apocalyptic thinkers are not necessarily fatalistic or deterministic on an individual level. But they usually hold to an eschatological determinism, regarding the occurrence of certain end-time events as inevitable.

Also related to the traditional Western concept of history is the notion that the Earth is relatively young. On the basis of chronological references in the Old Testament, Archbishop James Ussher of Ireland (1581–1656) calculated that the world was created in 4004 BCE. This date appeared in the margin of the book of Genesis in the Authorized Version and was accepted by many Christians as the gospel truth. Through the ages many prophets of doom have built their prognostications upon Ussher's date or the belief that the world is young.[38] In fact, even prior to Ussher's calculations many people believed that God had created the world in six days sometime between 6000 and 4000 BCE. According to 2 Peter 3:8, "one day is with the Lord as a thousand years." So for centuries many millennialists based their predictions on the six-day or Sabbath theory. They believed that the world would end at the completion of the sixth day, or six thousand years. The millennial age or Sabbath would then begin. No one has suggested a later date for creation than 4000 BCE. Thus, when no eschatological events occurred around 2000 CE dates had to be adjusted.

Conditions in Western History

The persistence of end-time predictions through Western history is due not only to certain ideas that characterize Western culture, but also to specific social, economic, psychological, and political conditions. Apocalyptic and millennial movements are so complex as to defy any simple cause-and-effect explanations. Yet some social theories do help explain why such movements arose in particular periods in history.

Both John Gager and Gerd Theissen regard early Christianity as a millennial movement. They see the early Jesus movement as having grown out of a socially and politically oppressive environment. This movement, they contend, "contained prophetic promises of an imminent salvation and reversal of the present social order." It first centered on a messianic figure and later on other charismatic leaders.[39]

38. Cohen, *Waiting for the Apocalypse*, 83; Daniel Cohen, *Prophets of Doom* (Brookfield, CT: Millbrook, 1992) 15.

39. D. H. Williams, "The Origins of the Montanist Movement: A Sociological

In his classic book, *The Pursuit of the Millennium*, British historian Norman Cohn attempts to account for the rise of apocalyptic movements in the Middle Ages. He contends that "revolutionary millenarianism drew its strength from a population living on the margin of society"—peasants, journeymen, and unskilled workers. Such people "lacked the material and emotional support afforded by traditional social groups." Because they were in a defenseless position, they reacted "sharply to any disruption of the normal, familiar pattern of life." Cohn goes on to point out that the greatest millenarian activities came against the background of natural disasters, namely, plagues and famines.[40]

Other scholars have questioned Cohn's ideas. Bernard McGinn and Marjorie Reeves, for example, have demonstrated that apocalyptic speculations were more widespread than once believed. They were embraced not only by the people on the margins of medieval society, but also by its more secure members. Indeed, apocalyptic thinking formed an important component of the medieval mentality.[41]

In *Disaster and the Millennium*, political scientist Michael Barkun argues that disasters are the chief factor in producing apocalyptic millennial movements. These disasters "must be multiple rather than single." They are accompanied by "a body of ideas or doctrines of a millenarian cast" shaped by a charismatic leader. Moreover, millenarian movements originate in a rural-agrarian setting rather than in an urban-industrial context. "Only the disaster-prone, homogeneous countryside seems to call forth the pursuit of the millennium."[42] Barkun's ideas need to be modified

---

Analysis," *Religion* 19 (1989) 334 (quote); John G. Gager, *Kingdom and Community: The Social World of Early Christianity* (Englewood, Cliffs, NJ: Prentice-Hall, 1975); Gerd Theissen, *Sociology of Early Palestinian Christianity* (Philadelphia: Fortress, 1978).

40. Norman Cohn, *The Pursuit of the Millennium: Revolutionary Millenarians and Mystical Anarchists of the Middle Ages* (rev. ed.; New York: Oxford University Press, 1974) 281–82.

41. Marjorie Reeves, *The Influence of Prophecy in the Later Middle Ages: A Study in Joachimism* (New York: Oxford University Press, 1969) 314–17. Reeves refers to an earlier edition of *Pursuit of the Millennium*, from 1957 or 1961. McGinn, *Visions of the End*, 2, 36, 145–48; Bernard McGinn, "Introduction: John's Apocalypse and the Apocalyptic Mentality," in *The Apocalypse in the Middle Ages*, ed. Richard K. Emmerson and Bernard McGinn (Ithaca, NY: Cornell University Press, 1992) 11.

42. Michael Barkun, *Disaster and the Millennium* (New Haven, CT: Yale University Press, 1974) 6.

somewhat, for some highly industrial areas experience disasters and thus can fall prey to apocalyptic excitement.[43]

Essentially these theories tell us that apocalyptic movements arise during times of social instability and transition. Such views do not go unchallenged. Yet they do have relevance for explaining apocalyptic movements in Europe and the developing world.

Such theories, however, only partially explain the millennial movements in America. The Millerite premillennial movement in the 1840s did not consist of the socially disinherited. The Millerites lived at a time of profound social change. Yet they were the middling sort, actually slightly better off than the average person.[44] Likewise, the millions who bought the books of Hal Lindsey, Tim LaHaye, and John Hagee, or who watched Pat Robertson or Jerry Falwell on television were not powerless. In fact, many of these individuals are part of the Religious Right, which gained considerable power in the late twentieth century.[45] But while modern Christian fundamentalists are not downtrodden, their spokespersons sound warnings of doom. They declare that our society is on a collision course with disaster. Disturbed by the sin and violence in our society, they sincerely believe that divine judgment is imminent.

There is another factor at work here. The Christian fundamentalists of our day may not be economically downtrodden, but they are a cognitive minority—that is, their ideas no longer fit comfortably into the mainstream of American society. Fundamentalist thinking assumes a literal reading of the ancient writings and a supernaturalist vision—two suppositions that are not at home in the modern world. In addition, many fundamentalists embrace a Manichean worldview. Everything is either black or white, leaving no room for grey or pluralism in respect to ideas and culture. Such a polarization is at odds with postmodern thinking. Moreover, we live in the post-Christian era, when Christianity is no longer the definer of cultural

---

43. For a refinement of Barkun's ideas see his *Crucible of the Millennium: The Burned-Over District of New York in the 1840s* (Syracuse: Syracuse University Press, 1986).

44. James H. Moorhead, "Searching for the Millennium in America," *Princeton University Bulletin* 8/2 (1987) 17-33; Brummett, *Contemporary Apocalyptic Rhetoric*, 29; David L. Rowe, "Millerites: A Shadow Portrait," in *The Disappointed: Millerism and Millenarianism in the Nineteenth Century*, ed. Ronald L. Numbers and Jonathan M. Butler (Knoxville: University of Tennessee Press, 1993) 7-8.

45. O'Leary, *Arguing the Apocalypse*, 9; Robert G. Clouse, "The New Christian Right, America, and the Kingdom of God," *Christian Scholar's Review* 12 (1983) 3-16; Erling Jorstad, *The Politics of Moralism: The New Christian Right in American Life* (Minneapolis: Augsburg, 1981).

values. The Christian faith has been challenged in many quarters. The beliefs and values of Christian fundamentalists have been ridiculed by many. Intellectually and morally the Christian fundamentalists are a minority, so they long for a divine intervention to rectify the current social order.

The views of the Christian fundamentalists are part of a larger apocalyptic mood that has gripped American society in the late twentieth and early twenty-first centuries. To many Christians, the establishment of the Israeli state in 1948 and the seizure of Jerusalem in 1967 were confirmations of prophecy. Among the wider public, a series of natural and unnatural disasters (Bhopal, Chernobyl, AIDS, earthquakes, global warming, hurricanes, September 11, tsunamis, etc.) has heightened an apocalyptic fever. Moreover the rapid social changes of our day are baffling to many people. They are confused and perplexed. They are uncomfortable with the direction of society, but feel powerless to change it.[46]

We should note here that, while sudden change and social chaos create an atmosphere conducive to predictions regarding the end of the world, this change and chaos must seem to be inexplicable. When disruptions have reasonable explanations, apocalyptic visions do not usually arise. But in the view of the disturbed and disorientated people of the late twentieth and early twenty-first centuries, the systems have failed to explain why such changes have come. Although conditions today are not as cataclysmic as they were in the Middle Ages, they can terrify individuals who do not understand them.

To these considerations a few more must be added. Many people are influenced by a "numerological determinism, a deep-seated conviction that years and historical epochs come in tens and groups of ten." Clearly, the end must be near. Also, "there is a growing appetite for the weird."[47] Many people who do not accept the Christian faith will believe almost anything else. Witness the extreme occultic and fanatical groups that have predicted the end of time—the Branch Davidians, Supreme Truth, Children of God, Church Universal Triumphant, Christian Identity, some New Agers, and UFO cultists. Given the social and psychological conditions that exist at the close of the twentieth and beginning of the twenty-first centuries, it is little wonder that apocalyptic thinking is rampant.

---

46. Kenneth A. Myers, "Fear and Frenzy on the Eve of A.D. 2000," *Genesis* 3/1 (January 1990) 1, 3; Curt Suplee, "Apocalypse Now: The Coming Doom Boom," *Washington Post*, 17 December 1989, B1–2.

47. Suplee, "Apocalypse Now."

American Culture

Having said all of this, "America has always been fertile ground for millennialism." Certain cultural trends help to promote and spread end of the world thinking. Religious freedom has produced a free market religious economy, which in turn allows people to believe, worship, organize, and promote their ideas as best they can. People are free to follow sober or traditional expressions of religion, but they also have the liberty to embrace unconventional ideas. In most cases millennial beliefs impact only a few people but at times it has drawn a large following and even penetrated the popular culture. On such occasions, end-of-the-world thinking can go outside the religious community and find secular expressions. For example, after September 11 a Time/CNN poll indicated that about 35 percent of Americans began to think "more seriously about how current events could be leading to the end of the world." Furthermore, "more than one in five expected to live long enough to see the end of the world."[48]

Of great importance, millennial thinking connects with America's populist impulse. Every culture has both an elite and popular culture. In both religion and politics, America is deeply populist, meaning that the wisdom of the common person is superior to that of the so-called experts. Some aspects of millennialism—especially its dispensational premillennial version—reverberate strongly with the popular culture. The belief that Christians will be spared the horrors of the great tribulation has a mass appeal. With religious freedom, Americans have largely been spared hardships and persecution. So it is only natural for people to desire such a pattern to continue. Escaping persecution is more popular than going through it. Escapism and a buy now but pay later attitude is deeply engrained in American culture. Thus dispensationalism simply has a better story to tell than do some versions of millennialism. And the popular fundamentalist TV preachers and writers capitalize on this appeal. Prophecy sermons pack out the sanctuary; end time books make the best-seller lists.[49]

Critically important to the appeal of millennialism is its ability to link prophecy with current events. As Timothy Weber notes, "No millennial

---

48. Timothy P. Weber, "Dispensationalism and Historic Premillennialism as Popular Millennial Movements," in *A Case for Historic Premillennialism: An Alternative to "Left Behind" Eschatology*, eds. Craig L. Blomberg and Sung Wook Chung (Grand Rapids: Baker, 2009) 1, 2.

49. Richard Kyle, *Evangelicalism: An Americanized Christianity* (New Brunswick, NJ: Transaction, 2006) 269–311; Weber, "Dispensationalism and Historic Premillennialism," 2, 21.

movement retains its audience for long unless it is able to do this consistently or else adjust its system when history takes an unexpected turn." Popular dispensational premillennialists have been able to do this remarkable well. And in doing so, this system has demonstrated its chameleon-like character, a necessary trait to sustain a millennial movement.[50]

---

50. Weber, "Dispensationalism and Historic Premillennialism," 17, 18, 21.

2

Western Contours of Doomsday

THE CRY "THE END is upon us" has waxed and waned throughout Western history. At times it has been intense. People literally sat on the edge of their seats waiting for the end to come. In other periods of time, only the eccentrics and people on the religious fringe paid any attention to the notion of the world coming to an end. Such was the pattern of apocalyptic beliefs from the early Christian era to modern times, namely one of advance and decline. Still, apocalyptic thinking and writing has been significant throughout Western history. It has been a "source of hope and courage for the oppressed, but has also given rise, on many occasions, to fanaticism and intolerance." End-time beliefs have been a powerful element in Western religions and have been a source "of both good and evil, and still is today."[1] Thus this chapter will briefly survey the contours of apocalyptic thinking in Western culture, especially Western Europe. In doing so, one can detect the framework for eschatology in modern America.

APOCALYPSE POSTPONED: EARLY CHRISTIANITY

In early and medieval Christianity a pattern of end-time thinking emerged. For the first two hundred years or so, Christians intensely expected Christ to return and usher in a golden age. Over the next two hundred years

---

1. Bernard McGinn, John J. Collins, and Stephen J. Stein, eds., *The Continuum History of Apocalypticism* (New York: Continuum, 2003) xv.

a transition took place. The intense expectancy regarding Christ's return waned, and Christians began to make peace with the world. Official church doctrine declared that the millennium was in progress. Consequently, the breathless anticipation for Christ's return was put on hold for about a thousand years. Yet apocalyptic thinking never died out. In fact, despite being suspect and almost heretical, it penetrated most ranks of medieval society.

End-time thinking is rooted in Jewish apocalyptic literature. Included are the Old Testament books of Ezekiel and Daniel plus many apocalyptic writings penned between 300 BCE and 100 CE that did not make the canon. Building on this apocalyptic literature are many passages in the New Testament found in both the Gospels and epistles. Most important is the Book of Revelation, which has through two millennia of Christian history produced a flood of end-time speculations.

The apocalyptic worldview expressed in various texts of the New Testament has had an important place in the Western intellectual tradition. It has incited revolutions and uprisings; it has inspired poets, artists, sculptures, and composers. The apocalyptic assumption that human activities are being moved by God toward a transcendent goal has also significantly influenced the Western view of history. Until the eighteenth-century Enlightenment, the Bible's apocalyptic texts were taken seriously by people in all ranks of society. Since then their influence has waned in scholarly circles. But at the popular level apocalyptic thinking continues to maintain a vital existence, even surging to high levels of influence during times of uncertainty.[2]

Early Millenarian Movements

The New Testament contains several passages suggesting that Christ might not return as soon as expected. Still, most first-century Christians believed that the world would soon end, probably in their lifetime. But as time went on, these early Christians had to confront the delay in Christ's Second Coming. Some believers still maintained their intense expectation that Christ would soon return and establish his kingdom. Others, however, gradually abandoned their hope for an imminent return.

During the second and third centuries a tension existed in the early church. Some followers of Christ had radical millennial expectations that his earthly kingdom would soon be inaugurated. Other Christians

2. Ibid., x, xv.

were more oriented to the institutionalization of the church. Apocalyptic movements with their charismatic leaders and end-time expectations are usually anti-institutional. Still, if any movement is to survive, it must establish an adequate organizational structure. The need to institutionalize the early church gradually prevailed over its apocalyptic impulse—but not completely. Inasmuch as Christ's return and the expected end of the world are cardinal Christian beliefs, "the apocalyptic vision was not eclipsed as quickly or as completely in the second and third centuries," as some theologians have claimed.[3]

In fact, millennialism in several forms remained strong in the early church. It came in with Jewish apocalypticism, even thriving at times. Conditions in the second and third centuries provided fertile soil for apocalyptic millennialism. Christians experienced sporadic persecutions that fueled their apocalyptic expectations. Moreover, their struggle against Gnosticism, which argued for a purely spiritual notion of salvation, led to an increased emphasis on an earthly millennium.[4] In addition, early Christianity was essentially a movement among the lower orders, and millennial visions are more at home with the lower social classes.[5] Still, the hope for an earthly millennium was not shared by all Christians. "In the post-apostolic era millenarianism was regarded as a mark neither of orthodoxy nor of heresy, but as one permissible opinion among others."[6]

Not all early millennial theories fit into neat packages. In fact, some thinkers combined elements of several views. Two basic approaches, however, were, particularly prominent. In the area of Ephesus (in modern Turkey) there developed a millennial tradition featuring material blessings. This tradition, which shares some features with modern premillennialism, emphasized the physical aspects accompanying the future rule of Christ over the renewed Earth following the resurrection at the end of the present age.[7]

3. Jaroslav Pelikan, *The Emergence of the Catholic Tradition* (Chicago: University of Chicago Press, 1971) 122.

4. J.C. DeSmidt, "Chiliasm: An Escape from the Present into an Extra-Biblical Apocalyptic Imagination," *Scriptura* 45 (1993) 83–84; Lester L. Grabbe, "The Social Setting of Early Jewish Apocalypticism," *Journal for the Study of Pseudepigrapha* 4 (April 1989) 27–47.

5. Michael J. St. Clair, *Millenarian Movements in Historical Context* (New York: Garland, 1992) 65; Robert M. Grant, *Early Christianity and Society* (New York: Harper, 1977) 79–84.

6. Pelikan, *Emergence of the Catholic Tradition*, 125.

7. Stanley J. Grenz, *The Millennial Maze: Sorting Out the Evangelical Options* (Downers Grove, IL: InterVarsity, 1992) 38; Avihu Zakai and Anya Mali, "Time,

The second basic approach to millenarianism is often called the six-day theory or the "creation day-world age" theory. This notion, based on 2 Peter 3:8 ("one day is with the Lord as a thousand years, and a thousand years as one day"), links the seven days of creation with seven millennia of human history. God created the world in six days and rested on the seventh. Thus God will consummate everything in six thousand years. Arising in the area of Antioch, Syria, this approach prompted Christians to try to calculate the date of Christ's return. A common element here was the belief that the world was about 5,700 to 6,000 years old.[8]

While apocalyptic millennialism was strong in the early church, on the whole the early church fathers shied away from specific date setting. However, Hippolytus (170–236) set an exact date for Christ's return. On the basis of the six-day theory and the belief that about 5,500 years separated Adam from Christ, Hippolytus postulated that the world would expire soon. The six days or six thousand years would be up in about 500 CE.[9] Similarly, Sextus Julius Africanus (ca. 160–240), on the basis of a supposed date for creation and a tidy pattern drawn from Revelation, first calculated the end to be 500 CE and then readjusted it to 800. Most church fathers, however, spoke of Christ's impending but unpredictable coming.

Rejecting Millennialism

Not everyone in the early church espoused this exciting brand of apocalyptic millennialism. And as time went on, it became even less fashionable. The decline of millennialism can be attributed to several factors. One, the anticipated events of the final days did not develop. Christ did not return in triumphant glory.[10] Two, the political scene changed dramatically. By

History and Eschatology: Ecclesiastical History from Eusebius to Augustine," *Journal of Religious History* 17/4 (Dec. 1993) 403–4.

8. Russell Chandler, *Doomsday* (Ann Arbor, MI: Servant, 1993) 39; Grenz, *Millennial Maze*, 39; Zakai and Mali, "Time, History and Eschatology," 403.

9. Yuri Rubinsky and Ian Wiseman, *A History of the End of the World* (New York: Morrow, 1982) 56; Justo L. Gonzalez, *History of Christian Thought* (Nashville: Abingdon, 1970) 1:235–37; Jeffery L. Sheler, "The Christmas Covenant," *U.S. News and World Report*, 19 December 1994, 64; Chandler, *Doomsday*, 39; Bernard McGinn, *Visions of the End* (New York: Columbia University Press, 1979) 51; Peter N. Stearns, *Millennium III, Century XXI* (Boulder, CO: Westview, 1996) 16.

10. Grenz, *Millennial Maze*, 42; J. N. D. Kelly, *Early Christian Doctrines* (rev. ed.; New York: Harper, 1978) 464–65; Bernard McGinn, *Antichrist: Two Thousand Years of the Human Fascination with Evil* (San Francisco: Harper, 1994) 70–75; Catherine Keller, *Apocalypse Now and Then: A Feminist Guide to the End of the World* (Boston:

Western Contours of Doomsday

the fourth century, Christianity had moved from being a persecuted sect to the official religion of the empire. No longer did Christians yearn for a glorious earthly millennium—they were now a privileged religion. Next, Christianity became institutionalized both organizationally and doctrinally. The church developed an ecclesiastical hierarchy and doctrinal norms that tended to restrain the excesses of apocalyptic millennialism.[11]

Four, the allegorical approach to interpreting Scripture became dominant. Premillennialism assumes a literal interpretation of Revelation 20. Scholars in the Ephesus and Antioch circles took a literal approach to the Bible and were generally millennialists. By contrast, the theology of Alexandria and Rome favored a more allegorical interpretation of Scripture. This approach tended to spiritualize certain biblical passages, especially Daniel and Revelation. A natural consequence of this development was the demise of millennial expectancy.[12]

The rejection of apocalyptic millennialism must be seen in its proper context. Constantine had been converted to Christianity in 312, thus ending the persecution of Christians. The hope for the imminent return of Christ remained strong as long as Christians were a persecuted minority. But when Christianity became the official religion in the Roman Empire during the fourth century, these millennial aspirations either declined or took new forms.[13]

In the post-Constantinian era, the greatest blow against millennialism came from Augustine (354–430), the bishop of Hippo. This preeminent theologian of the late patristic era rejected the millennialism of his day because of its crass materialism. Some millenarians envisioned an earthly paradise in which Christians enjoyed immoderate leisure and carnal pleasure.[14]

Beacon, 1996) 97.

11. Zakai and Mali, "Time, History, and Eschatology," 406; Kelly, *Early Christian Doctrines*, 464–65; Robert M. Grant, *Augustus to Constantine* (San Francisco: Harper, 1990) 51; Ernest Lee Tuveson, *Millennium and Utopia: A Study in the Background of the Idea of Progress* (New York: Harper, 1964) 14.

12. Kelly, *Early Christian Doctrines*, 41–48; Pelikan, *Emergence of the Catholic Tradition*, 124–25.

13. St. Clair, *Millenarian Movements in Historical Context*, 88–89; Zakai and Mali, "Time, History and Eschatology," 413.

14. Paul Boyer, *When Time Shall Be No More: Prophecy Belief in Modern American Culture* (Cambridge, MA: Harvard University Press, 1992) 48; Grenz, *Millennial Maze*, 42–43; Paula Fredriksen, "Tyconnius and Augustine on the Apocalypse," in *The Apocalypse in the Middle Ages*, eds. Richard K. Emmerson and Bernard McGinn (Ithaca, NY: Cornell University Press, 1992) 24; Keller, *Apocalypse Now and Then*, 102–3.

In his condemnation of millennialism, Augustine was not original. He borrowed heavily from the Donatist thinker Tyconius in interpreting the apocalyptic books of the Bible allegorically. In *The City of God* Augustine saw the Book of Revelation as a description of the history of the church, not as a prophecy of the end of time. The millennium in his view was the present church age.[15]

Actually, Augustine arrived at a position that did not reject outright the concept of a millennium. Rather, he accommodated the millennial idea to suit the current situation of the church. The millennium had begun with Christ's first coming and is now in progress. "The church now on Earth is both the kingdom of Christ and the kingdom of heaven," explained Augustine.[16] In later years such a view became known as amillennialism.

Catholic doctrine had come to regard the church as the vehicle for salvation. Accordingly, Augustine explained the millennium as a spiritual outworking of this the church's preeminent mission. Next on God's schedule was not Christ's return to set up an earthly paradise. Rather, the church would accomplish its mission, Christ would return, and then the judgment would come.

For the chiliasts the decisive culmination of history was to be Christ's Second Coming and his millennial role—both future events. For Augustine the "decisive moment in the history of salvation had already occurred with Christ's first coming."[17] The chiliasts saw the millennium standing outside of history—a future event. Augustine placed the millennium within history—a present event.

Augustine spiritualized the millennial concept in Revelation 20. Although his ideas on the subject were not without some ambiguity, he would have been aghast at how future generations utilized them. Indeed, some people used his ideas to interpret the millennium literally and came to the belief that Christ would return one thousand years after either his birth or death—that is, in the year 1000 or 1033.[18]

15. Peter Brown, *Augustine of Hippo* (Berkeley, CA: University of California Press, 1969) 140, 272; Gerald Bonner, "Augustine's Thoughts on This World and Hope for the Next," *Princeton Seminary Bulletin* Supplementary Issue 3 (1994) 94–99; Grenz, *Millennial Maze*, 45; Fredriksen, "Tyconius and Augustine," 20–24, 136, 140; Bruce W. Speck, "Augustine's Tale of Two Cities: Teleology/ Eschatology in The City of God," *Journal of Interdisciplinary Studies* 8/1–2 (1996) 104–30.

16. Augustine, *City of God*, 20 n. 9 (quote). See Bonner, "Augustine's Thoughts," 102; Fredriksen, "Tyconius and Augustine," 31.

17. Zakai and Mali, "Time, History and Eschatology," 411.

18. Grenz, *Millennial Maze*, 44; Rubinsky and Wiseman, *End of the World*, 59; Robert Lerner, "The Medieval Return to the Thousand-Year Sabbath," in *The Apocalypse in*

Western Contours of Doomsday

But, on the whole, Augustine's non-millenarian theology prevailed well into the Middle Ages. In 431 the Council of Ephesus condemned as superstition the belief in a literal millennium. Steadily, official Catholic doctrine distanced itself from end-time speculations.[19]

The General Pattern

Persecution, anxiety, stress, and poverty often promote apocalyptic thinking. And there were plenty of such troubles to go around in the first few centuries of the Christian era. The Jews struggled to retain their religious identity against Roman oppression and the Hellenistic religions. This atmosphere seeped into the early Christian church, which can be seen as an apocalyptic sect within Judaism. The early Christians fervently believed that the crucified Jesus would soon return. But the present world order did not end as expected. So the early Christians had to come to grips with this delay in Christ's return—a development that caused considerable anxiety in the early church.

Institutionalization usually stifles the apocalyptic mindset. As long as Christianity remained a persecuted sect, the apocalyptic fires burned brightly. But any movement must institutionalize if it is to survive. Gradually apocalypticism moderated and the church developed a hierarchy. Christianity moved from a minor Jewish sect to a world religion. When this happened, its apocalyptic fever declined. With their millennial expectations dampened, some Christians found other outlets for their zeal—monasticism, mystical visions, ascetic practices, and more.

THE SLUMBERING APOCALYPSE: MEDIEVAL CHRISTIANITY

"The apocalypse and the attitude toward history which it represented slumbered as force in Western culture—except for some uneasy tossings—for more than a thousand years," wrote Ernest Lee Tuveson in 1964.[20] More recent scholarship has certainly modified Tuveson's judgment. Still, the Augustinian view that linked the institutional church to the kingdom

---

the Middle Ages, eds. Emmerson and McGinn, 52.

19. Zakai and Mali, "Time, History, and Eschatology," 416–17; Boyer, *When Time Shall Be No More*, 49; St. Clair, *Millenarian Movements*, 87; Grenz, *Millennial Maze*, 44; Fredriksen, "Tyconius and Augustine," 35–36.

20. Tuveson, *Millennium and Utopia*, 21–22.

of God remained the official and dominant eschatology throughout the Middle Ages.

Taking its cue from Augustine, the medieval church assumed the scheme of six days of history, and then a seventh, which was the eternal Sabbath—not the millennium as the chiliasts believed. History was moving in one direction. For six ages God and Satan would engage in a great struggle that would end in divine judgment. However, Augustine and most medieval theologians refused to give any literal significance to such concepts as the millennium, the Antichrist, and Gog and Magog.[21]

Despite the official position there was a continuous flow of interest in apocalyptic eschatology throughout the Middle Ages. While apocalyptic expectations may have been greater among the oppressed of the lower classes, they were widespread. An apocalyptic worldview penetrated the medieval mentality and intrigued people of all social ranks. Though relatively subdued between 400 and 1100, apocalyptic visions soared to greater heights after 1100. Two streams of interpretation of apocalyptic texts flowed through the entire medieval period. The literal-historical interpretation, drawn from the early church, produced most of the end-time predictions. But the symbolic interpretation coming from Tyconius and Augustine was not without its apocalyptic imaginations.[22]

Stirrings in the Early Middle Ages

Tuveson's contention that apocalyptic ideas slumbered during the Middle Ages best applies to the early years—400 to 1100. During this period no forceful apocalyptic movement arose. Rather, there were pockets of apocalyptic voices.

Apocalyptic visions often arise during times of crisis, and there were crises during the early Middle Ages. But the official non-millenarian view of the Western church often muted the voices of doom and prevented the rise of a major apocalyptic movement. Some individuals did, however, see the collapse of the Roman Empire in the West as a sign of the end. They regarded Rome as the force in 2 Thessalonians 2:7 that restrained evil. Now that Rome was gone, the Antichrist would emerge on the scene. The

---

21. Walter Klaassen, *Living at the End of the Ages* (Lanham, MD: University Press of America, 1992) 4–5; J. C. DeSmidt, "Chiliasm: An Escape from the Present into an Extra-Biblical Apocalyptic Imagination," *Scriptura* 45 (1993) 85. See also Beryl Smalley, *The Study of the Bible in the Middle Ages* (Notre Dame, IN: University of Notre Dame Press, 1964).

22. Klaassen, *Living at the End of the Ages*, 5.

Western Contours of Doomsday

collapse of Rome also approximated the year 500, the time Hippolytus had predicted for the end of the world.[23]

In the early Middle Ages, people saw the Antichrist several ways—as evil within, an individual, or a collective entity. Thus invasions or threat of invasions from the Huns, Muslims, Magyars, and after 1100 from the Mongols and Turks prompted visions of the Antichrist and his hordes—the peoples of Gog and Magog. A strong ruler could be viewed two ways. If he was tyrannical, he stirred up images of the Antichrist. If seen as a force for good, he might be viewed as the last world emperor—the one who would do battle with the Antichrist.[24]

End-Time Panic in the Late Middle Ages

Apocalyptic millennialism smoldered on the fringes of early medieval society, only to burst forth after 1100. Previously it existed in popular religion and in many sects. Now apocalyptic millennialism found a home in several of the acknowledged orders of the church. The presence of millenarian ideas in the institutionalized Catholicism presented a serious challenge to the church.[25]

Why did apocalyptic expectations explode in the late Middle Ages? Apocalyptic thinking emerges during times of change, stress, anxiety, and disasters. The years from 1100 to 1500 experienced all of these and more. This was an era of complex political, social, and intellectual changes that eventually led to the Protestant Reformation. The gradual breakup of the religious and political unity of Western Europe produced an atmosphere charged with apocalyptic expectations. As the church's grip on religious beliefs began to loosen, there was an upsurge of radical millenarian movements.[26]

The Crusades beginning in 1095 were not a result of apocalypticism. Instead, they stimulated apocalyptic thinking. The rise of Muslim power after 1000 terrified many Europeans and contributed to Islam's image as the Antichrist. The fact that the holy city of Jerusalem was in Muslim hands

---

23. McGinn, *Visions of the End*, 51.

24. Norman Cohn, *Pursuit of the Millennium: Revolutionary Millenarians and Mystical Anarchists of the Middle Ages* (rev. ed.; New York: Oxford University Press, 1974) 35-36; McGinn, *Antichrist*, 80-81, 87-90; Otto Friedrich, *The End of the World: A History* (New York: Fromm, 1986) 27-64.

25. Grenz, *Millennial Maze*, 46.

26. St. Clair, *Millenarian Movements*, 95-96.

conjured up apocalyptic visions of the last battle. Many medieval Christians believed that heresy—including Islam and Judaism—had to be stamped out before the end. Also, the Crusades dovetailed with the myth of the last emperor. The public identified him with several rulers—Charlemagne, Louis VII, Frederick II—who were expected to rescue Jerusalem.[27]

Several natural disasters also fostered end-time anxieties. Christians in the Middle Ages—as they do today—felt that any widespread disaster could be a precursor of Christ's Second Coming. The Black Death reached Europe in 1347. Its impact on apocalyptic thought has been exaggerated. Nevertheless, "many in Western Europe took the plague to be an eschatological sign." Believing that certain events—such as the reign of the Antichrist—must precede the end of the world, "many thought that the Black Death signaled God's displeasure" and in some way pointed to the end.[28] Other natural disasters such as earthquakes and famines also contributed to apocalyptic fears.

Perhaps the greatest impulse for the rise of millenarianism was the various reform movements. A partial list would include the Great Reform inaugurated by Pope Gregory VII, which settled the issue of leadership in Christian society, and the monastic reform movements—Cluniac, Cistercian, Carthusian, Franciscan, and Dominican. These movements gained a momentum beyond the intentions of their originators. They responded to the spiritual hunger of the masses and in doing so stimulated an interest in eschatology and apocalypticism.[29]

The Millennium and Antichrist

In fact, these reform movements contributed some new wrinkles to millennial thought. On one hand, the medieval millennialists were not premillennialists as were the chiliasts of the early church, who believed

---

27. Ibid., 97; Rubinsky and Wiseman, *End of the World*, 73, 75; Hans E. Mayer, *The Crusades* (New York: Oxford University Press, 1972) 28–31; Friedrich, *End of the World*, 111–42.

28. Robert E. Lerner, "The Black Death and Western European Eschatological Mentalities," *American Historical Review* 86/3 (1981) 534 (quote). See also Philip Ziegler, *The Black Death* (New York: Harper and Row, 1969); Barbara W. Tuchman, *A Distant Mirror: The Calamitous 14th Century* (New York: Ballantine, 1978); Hillel Schwartz, *Century's End* (New York: Doubleday, 1990) 65–74.

29. McGinn, *Visions of the End*, 94; St. Clair, *Millenarian Movements*, 96; Grenz, *Millennial Maze*, 46. See also Steven Ozment, *The Age of Reform*, 1250–1550 (New Haven, CT: Yale University Press, 1980).

that Christ would return before the golden age. Instead, the millennialists of the Middle Ages usually held that Christ would return after the millennium—a view that resembled the postmillennialism of a later era.[30] On the other hand, the medieval people normally did not spiritualize the end-time events as did Augustine. There was to be a literal Antichrist and a golden age (variously believed to be 500, 890, 1,000, or 1,400 years). The medieval millennialists also adopted another feature common to modern premillennialists. The Antichrist was usually seen as a single human being—not a collective evil. Further, they expected the Antichrist to appear before the millennium. But unlike modern premillennialism, the reformers equated the Antichrist with someone who opposed needed religious changes. Modern premillennialism tends to see him more as a political or military figure.[31]

The sense of an impending end gripped the Middle Ages. Yet this imminent doom was not usually associated with the Second Advent. As death stared every medieval person in the face, the end-time event expected by most people was the unveiling of the Antichrist. People in the Middle Ages set dates for the coming of the Antichrist, not Jesus Christ. Based on a variety of calculations, the years 1184, 1229, 1260, 1300, 1325, 1335, 1346, 1365, 1387, 1396, and 1400 were proposed. The passing of the proposed date for the cataclysmic event obviously did not discourage future date setting.[32]

Joachim of Fiore and the New Age

The late Middle Ages witnessed a number of apocalyptic movements and individuals—Merlin the Seer, the Franciscan Spirituals, Frederick II, the Flagellants, the Taborites, Savonarola, and more. But most significant was Joachim of Fiore (ca. 1135–1202). He burst upon the medieval scene and dramatically changed how Western Europeans viewed the end of time. A biblical scholar and Cistercian abbot from Sicily, he was the most original apocalyptic thinker of the Middle Ages. Joachim invented a new prophetic system that proved to be the most influential in Europe until Marxism. He developed one of the most unique theories of history in the Western

---

30. Emmerson, *Antichrist in the Middle Ages*, 56–57; Grenz, *Millennial Maze*, 47.

31. Emmerson, *Antichrist in the Middle Ages*, 7; Grenz, *Millennial Maze*, 47; Robert E. Lerner, "The Medieval Return to the Thousand-Year Sabbath," in *The Apocalypse in the Middle Ages*, 70–71.

32. Emmerson, *Antichrist in the Middle Ages*, 54–55.

tradition.³³ As the fountainhead for most late medieval eschatological speculations, he also indirectly influenced such ideas right down to the present day.³⁴ Abbot Joachim's theory of three ages of historical evolution impacted many future philosophies, including those of Gotthold Lessing, Friedrich Schelling, Johann Fichte, Georg Hegel, Auguste Comte, and Karl Marx. Even the modern New Age movement claims Joachim as their predecessor. New Agers believe that the coming new age will share characteristics with Joachim's third stage.³⁵

Joachim had a complex sense of history, the world, and the end of time—all interpreted through his view of the Trinity. He saw the Trinity as built into the very fabric of time. Thus he divided history into three overlapping ages or *status*—the ages of the Father, the Son, and the Holy Spirit.³⁶ These three ages roughly corresponded with the Old Testament, the Christian era until Joachim's day, and the age to come. But Joachim's scheme was much more complex than this. Not only did these *status* overlap, but they also had long periods of incubation. For example, the incubation period for the third stage began with Benedict of Nursia (ca. 480–547).³⁷ Now, some seven hundred years later, this incubation stage between the ages of the Son and the Holy Spirit was nearing a close. Joachim interpreted the political and religious events of his day as the last gasp of the second stage. The struggle between the church and the empire and the resurgence of Islam convinced him.³⁸

Noting that the Gospel of Matthew recorded forty-two generations from Adam to Christ, Joachim believed that this figure held true for each age. Allowing thirty years for each generation, he placed the end of the second stage between 1200 and 1260. But before the third age would come in, the Antichrist had to reign for three and a half years. In an interview with Richard the Lion-Hearted in 1191, Joachim said that the Antichrist

---

33. Cohn, *Pursuit of the Millennium*, 108; McGinn, *Visions of the End*, 126; Catherine Keller, *Apocalypse Now and Then*, 107.

34. Majorie Reeves, *Joachim of Fiore and the Prophetic Future* (New York: Harper and Row, 1976) i–ii; St. Clair, *Millenarian Movements*, 99.

35. Cohn, *Pursuit of the Millennium*, 109; Marilyn Ferguson, *The Aquarian Conspiracy* (Los Angeles: J.P. Tarcher, 1980); Richard Kyle, *The New Age Movement in American Culture* (Lanham, MD: University Press of America, 1995) 21.

36. Reeves, *Joachim of Fiore*, 1–28; McGinn, *Visions of the End*, 127; Grenz, *Millennial Maze*, 46; Keller, *Apocalypse Now and Then*, 108.

37. Cohn, *Pursuit of the Millennium*, 109–10; Reeves, *Joachim of Fiore*, 6–17.

38. Bernard McGinn, "Angel Pope and Papal Antichrist," *Church History* 47/2 (1978) 160–61; Rubinsky and Wiseman, *End of the World*, 77–78.

had already been born. After the defeat of the Antichrist, the age of the Holy Spirit would be ushered in. This third age would be less rational and institutional and more spiritual. A purified church would rule over a peaceful, contemplative, monastic world. The Holy Spirit would speak to people mystically, and humankind would experience God directly and become like him.[39]

Joachim was neither a revolutionary nor a millennialist in any strict sense. He did not desire the downfall of the Catholic Church. Rather, his thinking was evolutionary. Joachim desired to purify and transform the church from a life of activity to one of contemplation. He envisioned a reformed and purified Christendom as the goal of this evolutionary process.[40] Yet, in respect to end-time thinking, Joachim turned Europe upside down. While he may not have been a radical, he set some revolutionary ideas in motion. Most important, "Joachim broke decisively with the Tyconian-Augustinian tradition of interpreting the Apocalypse allegorically and instead interpreted it historically."[41] In many circles the apocalyptic images of Daniel, Ezekiel, and Revelation—Antichrist, millennium, Gog and Magog—were no longer spiritualized, but were regarded as real people and events.

The General Pattern

In general, during the Middle Ages there were three approaches to the end. The official church position spiritualized the millennium and identified it with the church. The end would come in the form of the last judgment and then the eternal state. The church thus maintained a non-millenarian position. Still, this did not mean that the end of the world was in the distant future. Many who upheld the official church doctrine believed that the world would soon end. Modern observers have described this official church position as amillennialism.[42]

Unofficially, a strong current of apocalyptic millennialism erupted in the late Middle Ages. In general, the chiliasts believed that the Antichrist

39. McGinn, *Visions of the End*, 134; Rubinsky and Wiseman, *End of the World*, 78; Klaassen, *Living at the End of the Ages*, 13; Hillel Schwartz, *Century's End* (New York: Doubleday, 1990) 52–53.

40. E. Randolf Daniel, "Joachim of Fiore: Patterns of History in the Apocalypse," in *Apocalypse in the Middle Ages*, 73.

41. Daniel, "Joachim of Fiore," 87.

42. Robert G. Clouse, ed., *The Meaning of the Millennium: Four Views* (Downers Grove, IL: InterVarsity, 1977) 9–10.

would appear and be defeated. After his defeat and the turmoil associated with it, there would be a golden age of an indefinite length, followed by the return of Christ.

A third strand—the secular apocalyptic—becomes barely discernible during the Middle Ages. The vast majority of Europeans attributed the Black Death to divine judgment. But as time went on, there were repeated outbreaks of the plague, striking both the righteous and evildoers alike. Some people began to wonder: did God do all of this? Very gradually some educated individuals began to seek natural causes for such disasters. To be sure, the exact cause of the Black Death was not determined until the twentieth century. But a new factor emerged in end-time thinking—natural causes.

To a large degree, historical forces determined the shape millennialism took in the Middle Ages. The early Middle Ages were not without chaos. But as long as Christendom remained a unity and the Catholic Church maintained a strong grip on society, the non-millenarian orthodoxy held sway. Fringe groups with their wild-eyed apocalyptic ideas were kept in check.

Augustine's non-millennialism remained the official position of the Catholic Church throughout the Middle Ages. But the apocalyptic groups could no longer be corralled. Apocalypticism erupted with a vengeance. Joachim of Fiore's ideas opened Pandora's box. And millennial thinking has not been the same since. The critical events of the late Middle Ages—persecution, crop failures, the Black Death, social upheavals, and reform movements—all combined to produce a growing sense of apocalypticism in the late Middle Ages.

THE REFORMATION AND BEYOND

"We have reached the time of the white (pale) horse of the Apocalypse. This world will not last any more, if God wills it, than another hundred years," wrote Martin Luther.[43] Luther believed that he was living in the last days. During the sixteenth century and for much of the seventeenth, many Europeans shared this expectancy—some more fervently than Luther. Modified versions of the two medieval eschatological patterns had carried over into the Reformation and beyond. Luther and some other Reformers largely accepted the official non-millenarian eschatology of the Catholic

---

43. Martin Luther, *Dr. Martin Luthers Sammtliche Schriften*, ed. Johann Georg Walch (St. Louis: Concordia, 1881–1910) 22:1334.

Western Contours of Doomsday

Church, but added some apocalyptic dimensions to it. The fervent apocalypticism of the medieval millennialists also spilled over into the sixteenth and seventeenth centuries.

As the seventeenth century wound down, so did the fervent apocalyptic expectancy. To be sure, the eighteenth and nineteenth centuries experienced some lively millennial movements. In addition, many individuals declared that the end was near, and designations of specific individuals as the Antichrist continued to be made. Natural disasters and political upheavals still stirred up apocalyptic imaginations. Terminal visions of the secular sort became more prominent. Nevertheless, when compared to the preceding two hundred years, European society in the years after 1700 experienced fewer end-time anxieties.

Why did apocalyptic eschatology wane in Europe? In part the supernatural worldview of previous centuries underwent a change. The late seventeenth century saw the rise of deism—the religion of many educated Europeans that called into question the supernatural aspects of Christianity. Also, by the late seventeenth century, phenomena such as witchcraft, magic, omens, prophecies, and astrology were generally on the decline. Many educated Europeans now questioned their validity.[44] The Age of Reason had begun to undercut such beliefs. Because millennialism and apocalyptic ideas embrace a supernatural worldview, they too experienced decline. For the apocalyptic mentality to thrive, calamities must appear to be unexplainable. But science could now explain many of the disasters that people encountered.[45]

Among other factors in the decline of apocalypticism, the Industrial Revolution improved the material aspects of life. Famines and disease were less pronounced. The doctrine of progress said that life was getting better, and people believed it. God did not seem interested in destroying the world, and humankind had not yet devised the means to do so. Though millennial movements do exist in such a context, they are usually a variation of postmillennialism, which sees the end of the world only in a distant future.

Consider as well that the secularization of life tends to reduce the sacred apocalyptic. In nineteenth-century Europe, God no longer occupied center stage. People were no longer preoccupied with the world to come—the Antichrist, millennium, and the judgment. To be sure, there

---

44. See Keith Thomas, *Religion and the Decline of Magic* (New York: Scribner, 1971).

45. See Michael Barkun, *Disaster and the Millennium* (New Haven, CT: Yale University Press, 1974).

is such a phenomenon as the secular apocalyptic, but it had not yet come into full swing.[46]

Apocalyptic Visions during the Reformation

Apocalyptic ideas and activities increase during times of stress and upheavals. The sixteenth century was such a time. Beginning with the discoveries of Columbus, the wheels of change spun faster and faster, affecting nearly every area of life—the social, economic, political, and religious. This was a time of great religious experimentation and intense religious activity. Thus many new religious movements were spawned.

As a result, the years from 1500 to 1650 were charged with apocalyptic expectations. Europeans believed that they were living in the perilous last times. When a summer storm approaches, there are signs in the sky—dark rumbling clouds, lightning flashes, and sudden eerie stillness. People read these signs and take appropriate shelter. The same is true with eschatology. The sixteenth century had many "calendarizers"—people who make end-time calculations. They saw the events of their time in the light of Daniel, Revelation, and even astrological predictions. Many Europeans concluded that they were standing on the extreme edge of time.[47]

Each of the three major religious groups in Europe during the sixteenth century—the mainstream Protestants, the Radicals, and Catholics—had their eschatological distinctive. The Radicals produced some violent millennial movements that shocked all of Europe. Some mainstream Protestant Reformers de-emphasized eschatology, but others articulated non-millenarian apocalyptic ideas, especially in their scathing attacks on the papacy. In response, Catholic thinkers countered with their own eschatological perspective.

Radical Upheavals

The Radical Reformation had little cohesiveness. It was largely a group of sects that revolted against Rome but did not fit the Protestant patterns. In general, the Radicals felt that the Lutheran and Zwinglian reforms had not

---

46. See W. Warren Wagar, *Terminal Visions: The Literature of the Last Things* (Bloomington, IN: Indiana University Press, 1982) 54–61; Frank Kermode, *The Sense of an Ending: Studies in the Theory of Fiction* (New York: Oxford University Press, 1967) 93–124.

47. Klaassen, *Living at the End of the Ages*, 20, 23.

gone far enough. Of these groups the Anabaptists and Spiritualists generated the most notable apocalyptic upheavals.[48]

The Anabaptists took Luther's and Zwingli's teachings a step further. To the mainstream Protestant call for religious reforms, the Anabaptists added social and political changes that challenged the very fabric of society. As a result, they experienced persecution at the hands of both Catholics and Protestants alike. While the Anabaptists shared the general apocalyptic mood of the sixteenth century, this persecution intensified their end-time expectations.

"All Anabaptists were united in their conviction that the return of Christ was near" and "that Christ and the Antichrist were locked in the final struggle."[49] Conrad Grebel warned that the Messiah was about to return. The monster persecuting the church would soon be destroyed, said Michael Sattler. Amid intense persecution, Jacob Hutter's letters and Menno Simons's writings indicate that they expected the end to come soon. While the Anabaptists increasingly interpreted their sufferings in apocalyptic terms—as the last onslaught of Satan against the saints—the vast majority quietly waited for Christ to return. There were two exceptions to this peaceful anticipation—Thomas Müntzer and the debacle at Münster.[50]

Thomas Müntzer (ca. 1488–1525) shot across the Reformation sky like a meteor—bright and flashy but short-lived. Müntzer was one of history's pure revolutionaries. Most revolutionaries have some restraints; Müntzer did not. He believed the Holy Spirit spoke directly to him and he was God's instrument for purging the ungodly. Thus Müntzer is best classified as a revolutionary Spiritualist.[51] He was a well-educated, spellbinding speaker with an apocalyptic vision. The end times had become an

---

48. See George H. Williams, *The Radical Reformation* (Philadelphia: Westminster, 1962); George H. Williams and Angel M. Mergal, eds., *Spiritual and Anabaptist Writers* (Philadelphia: Westminster, 1957) 19–38; William R. Estep, *The Anabaptist Story* (Grand Rapids: Eerdmans, 1975); Leonard Verduin, *The Reformers and Their Stepchildren* (Grand Rapids: Eerdmans, 1964).

49. Walter Klaassen, "Apocalypticism," in *The Mennonite Encyclopedia*, eds. Cornelius J. Dyck and Dennis D. Martin (Scottsdale, PA: Herald, 1990) 5:29 (quote); Klaassen, *Living at the End of the Ages*, 20–21.

50. St. Clair, *Millenarian Movements*, 155.

51. Williams and Mergal, eds., *Spiritual and Anabaptist Writers*, 32; Klaassen, *Living at the End of the Ages*, 34; Steven E. Ozment, *Mysticism and Dissent* (New Haven, CT: Yale University Press, 1973) 79–89; Friedrich, *The End of the World*, 156. See also Eric W. Gritsch, *Thomas Muntzer: A Tragedy of Errors* (Minneapolis: Fortress, 1989); Abraham Friesen, *Reformation and Utopia: The Marxist Interpretation of the Reformation and Its Antecedents* (Wiesbaden: F. Steiner, 1974).

obsession with him. The last days were at hand, and Müntzer's program was a war of extermination against the ungodly. While he believed in a future millennium, Müntzer's emphasis was on the violent war that would usher in the golden age.[52] Using apocalyptic language from Daniel and Revelation, Müntzer incited the peasants to new levels of violence. Believing Christ would return and lead them to victory, the peasants revolted. However, the German princes crushed them, and Müntzer was beheaded.[53]

The next episode of violent apocalypticism occurred in the northwestern German city of Münster. But this story begins a little earlier with Melchior Hofmann (ca. 1495-1543), a persistent calendarizer who set several dates for Christ's return. One of his predictions said Christ would come in 1533. After the slaughter of unbelievers, Strasbourg would become the New Jerusalem. When this date failed, he readjusted his calendar, and did so several times thereafter. The Strasbourg authorities put Hofmann in prison, where he died. Yet the end-time expectations did not die with him.[54]

When Strasbourg did not become the New Jerusalem, the scene shifted to Münster. The link was Jan Matthys (d. 1534), who had been baptized by one of Hofmann's followers. Matthys soon became a revolutionary and a fanatic. He quickly dominated Münster and transformed his apocalyptic vision into public policy. He concluded that Hofmann's new age had arrived. Münster would be the New Jerusalem, the refuge for the righteous. Matthys was killed by the Protestant and Catholic forces, but his successor John of Leiden (also known as Jan Bochelson) was even more radical. He proclaimed himself the Messiah of the last days and imposed his absolute authority on the people. Münster became akin to an Old Testament theocracy, even practicing polygamy.[55] The end of the world may

---

52. Hans-Jurgen Goertz, "Thomas Müntzer: Revolutionary between the Middle Ages and Modernity," *Mennonite Quarterly Review* 64/1 (1990) 27-31; Richard Bailey, "The Sixteenth Century's Apocalyptic Heritage and Thomas Müntzer," *Mennonite Quarterly Review* 57/1 (1983) 37-43; Cohn, *Pursuit of the Millennium*, 240-42. See also Abraham Friesen, *Thomas Muentzer: A Destroyer of the Godless* (Berkeley, CA: University of California Press, 1990).

53. James M. Stayer, *Anabaptists and the Sword* (Lawrence, KS: Coronado, 1972) 80-90; Boyer, *When Time Shall Be No More: Prophecy Belief in Modern American Culture*, 58; Williams, *Radical Reformation*, 81-84; Keller, *Apocalypse Now and Then*, 187-88.

54. Klaassen, *Living at the End of the Ages*, 28-29; Stayer, *Anabaptism and the Sword*, 217-22; St. Clair, *Millenarian Movements*, 170-71; Werner O. Packull, "Melchoir Hoffman's First Two Letters," *Mennonite Quarterly Review* 64/2 (1990) 140-59.

55. Stayer, *Anabaptism and the Sword*, 255-74; St. Clair, *Millenarian Movements*,

not have been at hand—but it certainly was for Münster. The besieging army broke through in 1535, massacring this group of extremists.

Mainline Protestantism: The Papacy as Antichrist

The excesses of the Peasant's War and the debacle at Münster influenced the eschatological thinking of the Protestant Reformers. While they made great contributions to the Christian faith, their end-time ideas were shaped by the events of their age. They pulled back from millennialism in stark horror. No major Reformer was a millennialist. Some, such as Calvin and Zwingli, were even antiapocalyptists and said little about end-time events.

Nonetheless, a definite Protestant apocalyptic tradition did develop in the sixteenth century. Several general characteristics of this tradition can be noted. One, the Protestant Reformers either spiritualized the millennium or believed that it had already occurred. Two, nearly all Reformers regarded the papacy as Antichrist. The Turks, who threatened Europe at this time were seen as in league with the Antichrist—perhaps they were to be identified with Gog or Magog. Next, many Protestants used the historicist method to interpret the Book of Revelation; they matched the symbols of Revelation with various periods in church history.

Four, the Reformers usually adopted an apocalyptic view of history, seeing it as a cosmic conflict between the forces of God and Satan. Lastly, the Protestant apocalyptics insisted they were living at the end of time. A few were moderate date-setters, vaguely predicting when the world would end. They believed that the world would last six thousand years—and this time was about up.[56]

Above all most Reformers echoed a non-millenarian apocalypticism. And in doing so, they pushed two themes: the papacy was Antichrist and Christ would return soon. Reformers embracing such ideas would include Martin Luther, Philip Melanchthon, John Knox, and Heinrich Bullinger.[57] In contrast, Calvin said little about eschatology. In fact, Revelation was the only book in the New Testament that he did not write a commentary on.

177–84; Williams, *Radical Reformation*, 371–75; Keller, *Apocalypse Now and Then*, 191–92.

56. Richard Kyle, *The Last Days Are Here Again* (Grand Rapids: Baker, 1998) 60–61.

57. Robin B. Barnes, *Prophecy and Gnosis* (Stanford, CA: Stanford University Press, 1988) 1–3; Schwartz, *Century's End*, 92; Richard Kyle, *The Mind of John Knox* (Lawrence, KS: Coronado, 1984) 227–32.

The Catholic Position: The Antichrist Is in the Future

The Catholic Church obviously rejected the Protestant claim that the papacy was the Antichrist. Some Catholic writers simply reversed the table and designated Luther as the Antichrist. However, most Catholic theologians favored a more sophisticated approach. They insisted that the Antichrist was an individual—not a collective entity—who would appear in the future.

While some Catholics had labeled individual popes as the Antichrist, they could not designate the office of the papacy as the evil one. The church had to distance itself from such thinking, and the Jesuits took the lead in this effort. Among the Jesuits who insisted that the Antichrist was still to come, the approach of the Spaniard Franciscus Ribeira had significant implications for future millennial thought. Both Catholics and Protestants who identified the Antichrist as a contemporary pope or leader generally took a historicist interpretation of John's Revelation. Ribeira reintroduced a somewhat literal approach to the Apocalypse of John. In doing so he concluded that the Antichrist was a future renegade Jew.[58] By means of a similar literal-futuristic reading of revelation, many modern premillennialists have arrived at doomsday conclusions.

Millenarianism in England

For much of the sixteenth and seventeenth centuries, apocalyptic excitement gripped England. End-time expectations gradually grew until they peaked in the 1640s. By then England was drunk on the millennium. Ordinary people, not simply the scholars, made end-time calculations. Talk that doomsday or the millennium would arrive on this day or that became common in England. By the mid-seventeenth century there developed a consensus in England that certain events were imminent: the defeat of the Antichrist, the return of Christ, and the start of the millennium.[59] In fact, the label *Antichrist* became so widespread as almost to lose meaning. Before 1640 nearly everyone—including the Church of England—applied the term to the papacy. After 1640 the Puritans began to designate the hierarchy of the Church of England as Antichrist.[60] In due time, radical

---

58. McGinn, *Antichrist*, 226–29.

59. St. Clair, *Millenarian Movements*, 200.

60. Christopher Hill, *Antichrist in Seventeenth-Century England* (rev. ed.; London: verso, 1990) 9, 13, 31–32, 62, 77, 131.

Western Contours of Doomsday

elements began to label even the Puritan leaders and the entire political structure as Antichrist. At one time or another, many leaders in English society were tagged as the Antichrist.

As noted, apocalyptic expectations often occur during times of turmoil and upheaval. And the England of the sixteenth and seventeenth centuries was just such a time. These centuries witnessed the break from Catholicism, Queen Mary's persecution of Protestants, the defeat of the Spanish Armada, the English Civil War, the beheading of Charles I, and the Thirty Years War on the Continent. Such events were often interpreted in apocalyptic terms and stimulated a millennial explosion in England.

APOCALYPTICISM IN MODERN EUROPE

After the apocalyptic outburst of the sixteenth and seventeenth centuries, end-time thinking continued in Europe. But it was less intense and not as far-flung. Prophecy was still serious business. For the most part, however, the social and political climates were not conducive to widespread millennial movements. The radical excesses of earlier years caused conservatives to pull back. Talk of the Antichrist, the New Jerusalem, and Second Advent no longer dominated everyday conversations.[61]

Yet there were plenty of exceptions to this general trend. Many individuals, including Isaac Newton, continued to speculate on end-time events. Natural, social, and political disasters—the Lisbon earthquake, the persecution of the Huguenots, the French Revolution—still prompted apocalyptic outbursts. Apocalypticism even burst forth in several mass movements—the Old Believers, Camisards, English Prophets, Southcotts, and Darbyites.

In all of this, several future trends could be detected. The lines between pre-and postmillennialism had tended to be murky. By the eighteenth century the contours of these positions took a more definite shape. The premillennialists saw the world as getting steadily worse. Only the Second Coming of Christ could rescue humanity from a catastrophic disaster. Postmillennialism viewed the future in more optimistic terms. Christianity would gradually spread throughout the globe, thus making a thousand-year period of peace and harmony a reality. Christ would return only at the end of this golden age.[62] Of these two views, postmillennialism,

---

61. Hill, *Antichrist in Seventeenth-Century England*, 146–47; MGinn, *Antchrist*, 230–36.

62. Boyer, *When Time Shall Be No More*, 66–69; J. F. C. Harrison, *The Second*

which was embraced by the more liberal and educated elements of society, tended to dominate until about 1850. Premillennialism was often found in popular circles.

Another future trend—a secular eschatology—began to emerge. Premillennialism foresaw saw a catastrophic end to the world. But in a world that was becoming secularized, God was losing his monopoly over disasters. Several seventeen- and eighteenth-century scientists evoked science in defense of prophecy. For example, William Whiston, Newton's successor at Cambridge University, was influenced by Edmund Halley's study on comets. He argued that the close passage of a comet had caused Noah's flood. The Earth's destruction by fire, predicted Whiston, would come by the same means.[63]

Scientists like Whiston did not rule God out as a cause of the end. Still, their scenarios contained no Second Coming or last judgment. A comet would bring a catastrophic end to the world. Modern prophetic writers have a similar dilemma. They speak of a nuclear holocaust or an ecological disaster. But a question is left unanswered: What role does God play in a human-caused calamity?[64]

Postmillennialism also has its secular thrust. In this view, the world will not end until sometime in the distant future, after society has become better and better. Some postmillennialists have secularized the millennium into a utopia to be attained through human progress. Thus postmillennialism has become equated with the idea of progress—the advancement of knowledge and the human condition.[65]

Apocalyptic ideas declined in modern Europe. As noted, however, a number of exceptions existed. A list would include the following: the mass suicides of the Old Believers in Russia, the Camisard prophets in France, Emanuel Swedenborg's vision of a new age, the end-time excitement stirred up by the French Revolution, the predictions of British millenarians, and several reported visitations by the Virgin Mary that had

---

Coming: Popular Millenarianism, 1780–1850 (New Brunswick, NJ: Rutgers University Press, 1979) 3–7.

63. James West Davidson, *The Logic of Millennial Thought* (New Haven, CT: Yale University Press, 1977) 87–88; Boyer, *When Time Shall Be No More*, 67; Tuveson, *Millennium and Utopia*, 131–32.

64. Perry Miller, *Errand into the Wilderness* (Cambridge, MA: Harvard University Press, 1964) 222–32; Boyer, *When Time Shall Be No More*, 67. See also Saul Friedlander, "Themes of Decline and End in Nineteenth-Century Western Imagination," in *Visions of the Apocalypse* (New York: Holmes and Meir, 1985) 61–80.

65. Tuveson, *Millennium and Utopia*, 1; Harrison, *Second Coming*, 6–7.

Western Contours of Doomsday

end-time implications. But as for future eschatological doctrine, most important were the dispensational ideas spawned by of John Nelson Darby.

Darby and the Great Parenthesis

"In a moment, in the twinkling of an eye, at the last trump . . . we shall be changed" (1 Cor 15:52). The notion of the sudden secret rapture of the church has captivated millions of Christians. More than any other eschatological doctrine, premillennial dispensationalism has taught the "any moment" Second Coming of Christ. Dispensationalism also emphasizes that God has dealt differently with humankind through a series of ages or dispensations. Classic dispensationalism divides history into epochs—usually seven. We are currently living in the sixth dispensation—the church age.[66]

Today dispensationalism far exceeds other belief systems in promoting end-time thinking. Where did it come from? Its exact origins are shrouded in mystery. But there can be no question that John Nelson Darby (1800-1882) became its foremost advocate. Born into an Anglo-Irish family, Darby graduated from Trinity College. Ordained three years later, he served in the Church of Ireland. Uneasy about the established church, however, Darby joined the Plymouth Brethren, a separatist sect with an interest in prophecy. As a member of this group, Darby systemized dispensationalism and spread its major principles throughout the English-speaking world.[67]

Premillennialism had surged in Britain during the nineteenth century. But it was the historicist version, which tied itself to a chronology of events predicted in the Bible, especially Revelation. As a result, the premillennialists became "committed at least implicitly to some kind of schedule of expectations." In the process they lost considerable flexibility. With their

---

66. Clarence B. Bass, *Backgrounds to Dispensationalism* (Grand Rapids: Eerdmans, 1960) 19-63; Charles C. Ryrie, *Dispensationalism Today* (Chicago: Moody, 1965) 22-47); David Malcom Bennett, "The Origins of Left Behind Eschatology," PhD diss., University of Queensland, 2008.

67. Timothy P. Weber, *Living in the Shadow of the Second Coming* (New York: Oxford University Press, 1979) 22; Bass, *Backgrounds to Dispensationalism*, 17-18. For more information on Darby and the Plymouth Brethren see Harold H. Rowdon, *The Origins of the Brethren* (London: Pickering and Inglis, 1967); F. Roy Coad, *History of the Brethren Movement* (Grand Rapids: Eerdmans, 1968); George T. Stokes, "John Nelson Darby," *Contemporary Review* 48 (October 1885) 537-52; Henry M. King, "The Plymouth Brethren," *Baptist Review* 3 (1881) 438-65; Thomas Corskery, "The Plymouth Brethren," *Princeton Review*, n.s., 1 (1872) 48-77.

"millennial arithmetic," they often played the "date-setting game," asserts Ernest Sandeen.[68]

Now Darby came along with a new type of premillennialism. Dispensational premillennialism belonged to the futurist school, which held that, except for the first few chapters, Revelation foretells developments taking place in the last days. In taking this position, Darby freed himself from the necessity of tying current events in with Revelation. According to the historicist school, certain events had to happen before Christ would return. But Darby said that no event stood in the way of Christ's return. The teaching of the imminent return of Christ "proved to be one of the greatest attractions of dispensational theology."[69]

Beyond the futuristic approach to prophecy, Darby's eschatology stood on two principles—his doctrine of the church and his method of interpreting the Bible. He sharply separated Israel and the church, insisting that God had a different plan for each. Moreover, Darby interpreted the prophetic passages of the Bible with a rigid literalism.[70] Building on these principles, Darby developed an exact scheme for end-time events. Christians are living in the "Great Parenthesis," the period between the crucifixion and the rapture. Believers will rise to meet Christ in the air. Then the horrors described in Revelation will take place, including the tribulation, the reign of Antichrist, and Armageddon. At this point Christ will return to set up his thousand-year rule. After the millennium Satan will be defeated and the final judgment will take place.

Darby's system was not original. Futurism began with the sixteenth-century Catholics, and elementary forms of dispensationalism can be traced throughout church history. Even the rapture doctrine had earlier precedents, including Increase Mather. Still, Darby combined all of these ideas into a coherent system—one that has significantly influenced modern apocalyptic thought.[71]

---

68. Ernest R. Sandeen, *The Roots of Fundamentalism: British and American Millenarianism, 1800–1930* (Chicago: University of Chicago Press, 1970) 59–60 (quote); Weber, *Living in the Shadow of the Second Coming*, 14–15; "Dates and Date-Setting," *Millennial Prophecy Chart*, May 1994, 9.

69. Sandeen, *Roots of Fundamentalism*, 63–64.

70. Bass, *Backgrounds to Dispensationalism*, 129.

71. Boyer, *When Time Shall Be No More*, 88; Bennett, "The Origins of Left Behind Eschatology," 139–67.

Western Contours of Doomsday

Some Limited Endings

Like much of Western history, post-medieval Europe has witnessed peaks and quiet periods of apocalyptic activity. To a large extent, the ebb and flow of end-time thinking has paralleled the stress and changes in Western culture. In particular, the years from 1500 to 1650 were charged with apocalyptic excitement. The social, economic, and political upheavals of the late Middle Ages spilled over into the Reformation Era. Religious reform spanned several centuries. Such conditions produced an apocalyptic atmosphere that may have peaked in seventeenth-century England.

But in Europe the widespread apocalyptic mood declined after 1650. Talk of end-time events no longer provided the grist for everyday conversations. Still, interest in eschatology was not dead. A number of individuals and groups insisted that the end was at hand. Christ would return and usher in the millennial state. Religious persecution, natural disasters, political upheavals, and social changes encouraged apocalyptic anxieties.

Yet in modern Europe such apocalyptic feelings usually did not become widespread. They did not grip society as they had from 1500 to 1650. Prophetic individuals had their followers, but only a few mass movements arose. Natural disasters and political upheavals still conjured up end-time predictions—but usually on a more limited basis than in centuries past. The modern world with its rational and secular outlook put a damper on apocalyptic activities.

Instead of being widespread, doomsday often had a local face. To those involved in limited catastrophes, their world had ended. For example, the 1775 Lisbon earthquake set the city ablaze and killed sixty thousand people. Entire villages in the area were swallowed up. Bodies were piled six to seven deep. Indeed, their world had ended.[72]

Such limited endings also had a secular look. The Holocaust ended the world of the Jews involved in Hitler's Final Solution. Hitler slaughtered millions of Christians, Jews, gypsies, and dissidents. Perhaps no savagery in history approaches that of the Nazis. But Stalin certainly tried. There was a second, less publicized holocaust. From 1930 to 1947 Stalin murdered ten to thirty million people. Indeed, these natural disasters and secular holocausts were doomsday in microcosm!

---

72. Friedrich, *End of the World*, 179–212; Chandler, *Doomsday*, 115.

SOME CONNECTING POINTS

Our focus is on apocalyptic thinking in modern America. What does this quick journey through two thousand years of Western history have to do with our subject? It lays the foundation for end time visions in contemporary United States. While there are vast differences between how people in previous church ages have viewed the end of time and the visions of modern-day prophets, several future trends can be observed.

First, we can see the Western view of history—so important to end-time thinking—in action. Until modern times, history has been seen as moving toward an end. Modern apocalyptic thinkers still embrace this mentality. Next, as is the case today, divisions on how people interpreted the Second Coming of Christ and the millennium were evident. Third, at times in the medieval and early modern worlds, apocalypticism exploded. While *explode* may be too strong of a word to describe the current situation, there is strong interest in end-of-the-world events. Like today, at times an impending sense of the end has gripped segments of society. Fourth, as we do today, these premodern societies had their "calendarizers," that is, people who predicted the end of the world. Next, and of great importance, Darby systematized dispensationalism, the theology prompting most end-time excitement in modern America. Sixth, apocalyptic views were not confined to Christianity. While only in an embryonic stage, one can see the fingerprints of science and natural causes directing end-time thinking. Lastly, as is the case today, apocalyptic thinking found a ready home with religious groups on the fringes of society.

3

The Millennial Nation

END-TIME EXPECTATIONS GO RIGHT to the heart of American religion. Unlike Europe, where millenarianism usually existed on the fringes of society, in America it has been more central to the religious experience. In various shapes the millennial hope has been an enduring strand in American religion, so much so that Catherine Albanese has described it as the "red thread" in the tapestry of American religion. Similarly, Ernest Sandeen has said that end-time excitement was so strong by the early nineteenth century that America was "drunk on the millennium."[1] Indeed, such millennial thinking has helped to set the stage for end-time ideas in modern America.

For much of the colonial period and well past the Civil War, postmillennialism dominated the American millennial scene. On the whole, this strand of millennialism lacked apocalyptic qualities. It did not see the world ending anytime soon. Rather, the gospel would penetrate society, and life on Earth would gradually improve until Christ's return. Still, there were plenty of exceptions to this general pattern. The early Puritans looked for Christ's imminent return. Even the early postmillennialists used apocalyptic language, insisting that the Antichrist had to be defeated

1. Ernest R. Sandeen, *The Roots of Fundamentalism British and American Millenarianism, 1800–1930* (Chicago: University of Chicago Press, 1970) 42: Catherine Albanese, *America: Religion and Religions* (2nd ed.; Belmont, CA: Wadsworth, 1992); Sidney E. Mead, *The Nation with the Soul of a Church* (New York: Harper and Row, 1975); Ernest Tuveson, *Redeemer Nation: The Idea of America's Millennial Role* (Chicago: University of Chicago Press, 1968).

before the millennium could begin. Historicist premillennialism surged in the early nineteenth century, culminating in the Millerite movement. There were also numerous communal and Adventist groups who believed either the millennium or the Second Advent to be at hand.

THE PURITAN DIVINES

Millennial fever literally gripped seventeenth-century England. Not surprisingly, then, apocalyptic frenzy infected the Puritans migrating to America at this time. As part of their cultural baggage, they brought with them an intense eschatological expectation.[2] For the most part they maintained the millennial ideas prevalent in seventeenth-century England, but tailored them for the American environment.

From the beginning the Puritans endowed America with a millennial mission. The Reformation had broken the grip of the papal Antichrist. But the Europeans failed to build on this good start; they proved unequal to the divine call of restoring the true Christian faith. Thus God selected a small group to go to the New World and set up a New Jerusalem, a "city upon a hill," the holy commonwealth.[3] In various forms this millennial mission has run the course of American history. It has fueled diverse and even contradictory expressions of American culture—revivalism, civil religion, missions, nationalism, sectarian communalism, and social reform movements. Through the years Americans have tended to see themselves as the chosen nation and their enemies as demonic.

The early Puritans were fervent millennialists, insisting that the millennium was coming. Like the English millennialists, they often blurred the distinctions between pre-and postmillennialism. Most Puritans looked for the apocalyptic events surrounding the defeat of the Antichrist and the inauguration of Christ's kingdom. Whether Christ would come before or after the millennium was disputed and unclear.[4]

Some Puritans, however, can best be seen as chiliasts or premillennialists. Increase and Cotton Mather, for example, held Christ's return

2. Ira V. Brown, "Watchers for the Second Coming: The Millenarian Tradition in America," *Mississippi Valley Historical Review* 39 (December 1952) 445.

3. Robert Fuller, *Naming the Antichrist: The History of an American Obsession* (New York: Oxford University Press, 1995) 42–43.

4. James West Davidson, *The Logic of Millennial Thought: Eighteenth-Century New England* (New Haven, CT: Yale University Press, 1977) 75; Ruth H. Bloch, *Visionary Republic: Millennial Themes in American Thought* 1756-1800 (New York: Cambridge University Press, 1985) 12.

The Millennial Nation

to be imminent. Believers would be caught up into the air, and then the disasters and persecutions would begin, followed by the millennium. However, postmillennialism was also common at the end of the seventeenth century.[5]

Before 1660, the Puritans often reflected the same millennial themes as did their English counterparts—notably the defeat of the Roman Antichrist and the Turks.[6] But increasingly the Puritans Americanized the apocalyptic tradition, finding prophetic meaning in their own experience. Increase Mather (1639-1723) saw the millennium as in the future and found apocalyptic meaning in current events. He suggested that the red horse of the Apocalypse foretold the bloodshed of King Philip's War (1675-76), a conflict that pitted the colonialists against the Indians.[7]

Increase's son Cotton (1663-1728) further Americanized the apocalypse. He "inaugurated an era of apocalyptic expectation in America that did not lose its force until after the American Revolution."[8] He focused on the many problems that the Puritans encountered in the wilderness, including Indian massacres. Though he did not go so far as to label the Native Americans as the Antichrist, he did attribute to them a cosmic significance, regarding them as in league with the Antichrist.[9]

Cotton Mather was also a date-setter. On the basis of events involving the Turks and the revocation of the Edict of Nantes, he tentatively calculated the end to come in 1697. When this date passed, he quietly readjusted the time first to 1736 and then back to 1716. Of course he had no doubt where the New Jerusalem would be located—New England.[10]

The Mathers regarded the millennium as a golden age characterized by miracles. It was more than a mere improvement of the human

---

5. Davidson, *Logic of Millennial Thought*, 63, 262, 281; Bloch, *Visionary Republic*, 12.

6. J. F. Maclear, "New England and the Fifth Monarchy: The Quest for the Millennium in Early American Puritanism," *William and Mary Quarterly* 32 (April 1975) 225-26; Brown, "Watchers for the Second Coming," 445; Michael J. St. Clair, *Millenarian Movements in Historical Context* (New York: Garland, 1992) 268.

7. Paul Boyer, *When Time Shall Be No More: Prophecy Belief in Modern American Culture* (Cambridge, MA: Harvard University press, 1992) 69.

8. Robert Middlekauff, *The Mathers: Three Generations of Puritan Intellectuals, 1596-1728* (New York: Oxford University Press, 1976) 323.

9. Fuller, *Naming the Antichrist*, 45-47. See also James Alan Patterson, "Changing Images of the Beast: Apocalyptic Conspiracy Theories in American History," *Journal of the Evangelical Theological Society* 31 (December 1988) 443-44.

10. Davidson, *Logic of Millennial Thought*, 62-63; Boyer, *When Time Shall Be No More*, 69-70; Middlekauff, *Mathers*, 342-43, 346.

condition or the universal preaching of the gospel. We should also note that Increase Mather's perception of the Second Advent foreshadowed that of the dispensationalists—a rapture in which believers are taken into the air.[11]

Much of the date setting done by the Puritans rests on the Book of Revelation's statements that the Antichrist's reign would last 1,260 days (or 42 months). Many people at this and other times extended the 1,260 days to 1,260 years. By adding 1,260 years to what they believed to be the date at which the Antichrist's rule began, they could predict the end of his reign. Some Puritans believing that the Antichrist's rule began in the fifth century, calculated the end to be around 1700.[12]

POSTMILLENNIALISM: THE END IS WAY OFF

Cotton Mather's brew of eschatology and date setting was not to everyone's liking. As the eighteenth century advanced and rationalism gained strength, apocalypticism faded. Progressive postmillennialism held sway until the late nineteenth century.

At first, postmillennialism maintained an evangelical orientation, believing that the gradual improvements would be the fruit of human efforts and the work of the Holy Spirit. In fact, postmillennialism forged a link with another nineteenth-century movement—perfectionism. Christian perfectionism places a strong emphasis on holiness, contending that the believer through God's grace can achieve and maintain a moral perfection in this life.[13] Both postmillennialism and perfectionism promoted evangelicalism, morality, and a better quality of life.

But as the nineteenth century progressed, this evangelical postmillennialism gave way to more secular versions—the idea of progress, civil religion, the social gospel, and the millennial mission of America. In particular, the idea of progress—that humanity is advancing toward a better world—complemented secular postmillennialism. Perfectionism

11. Davidson, *Logic of Millennial Thought*, 62; Boyer, *When Time Shall Be No More*, 75, 88.

12. Brown, "Watchers for the Second Coming, 446–50; Davidson, *Logic of Millennial Thought*, 13–16, 60–63.

13. Timothy Smith, "Righteousness and Hope: Christian Holiness and the Millennial Vision for America, 1800–1900," *American Quarterly* 31/1 (Spring 1979) 21–27; Russel Blaine Nye, *Society and Culture in America, 1830–1860* (New York: Harper and Row, 1974) 36, 289–92; William G. McLoughlin Jr., *Modern Revivalism: Charles Grandison Finney to Billy Graham* (New York: Ronald, 1959) 102–3.

also fueled several humanitarian movements—abolition, suffrage, and temperance—and blended in with secular postmillennialism.[14]

But our concern is with the end of the world. Evangelical postmillennialism addressed this subject. It contained pockets of apocalypticism and even pointed to the end of time, though it be in the distant future. Several eighteenth-century events set off these eschatological speculations—the first being the Great Awakening. The religious revival of the 1740s ignited end-time speculations. Along with a number of other New England ministers, Jonathan Edwards (1703-1758) saw the Great Awakening as a prelude to the millennium.[15] But Edwards's apocalypticism was not that of the Mathers. He was a postmillennialist, mingling human and divine efforts to usher in the golden age. He foresaw the millennium as taking place on Earth within history, and as being "achieved through the ordinary processes of propagating the gospel in the power of the Holy Spirit."[16]

Still, Edwards had his apocalyptic moments. He designated the Roman papacy as Antichrist. The Antichrist had risen gradually, but the Reformation dealt him a blow from which he could not recover. Thus his days were numbered. Believing that the Antichrist had achieved power in 606, Edwards calculated that the beast would fall by 1866 (606 + 1260 years = 1866).[17] He regarded the Great Awakening as an early sign of the approaching millennium. Edwards saw the emotionalism that accompanied these revivals as an outpouring of God's Spirit upon the land—a necessary step toward the millennium. These revivals would transform America.

---

14. See Jean B. Quandt, "Religion and Social Thought: The Secularization of Postmillennialism," *American Quarterly* 25 (October 1973) 390-409; James H. Moorhead, "Between Progress and Apocalypse: A Reassessment of Millennialism in American Religious Thought, 1800-1880," *Journal of American History* 71/ 3 (1984) 524-42; James H. Moorhead, "The Erosion of Postmillennialism in American Religious Thought, 1865-1925," *Church History* 53/1 (1984) 61-77; Rush Welter, "The Idea of Progress in America," *Journal of the History of Ideas* 14 (1955) 401-15.

15. Christopher M. Beam, "Millennialism and American Nationalism, 1740-1800," *Journal of Presbyterian History* 54 (Spring 1976) 182; Boyer, *When Time Shall Be No More*, 70; Nathan O. Hatch, "The Origins of Civil Millennialism in America," in *Reckoning with the Past: Historical Essays on American Evangelicalism from the Institute for the Study of American Evangelicals*, ed. D. G. Hart (Grand Rapids: Baker, 1995) 88, 90.

16. C.C. Goen, "Jonathan Edwards: A New Departure in Eschatology," *Church History* 28/1 (1959) 26 (quote); Leonard I. Sweet, "Millennialism in America: Recent Studies," *Theological Studies* 40 (September 1979) 513; Tuveson, *Redeemer Nation*, 99-101.

17. Fuller, *Naming the Antichrist*, 66-67; Goen, "Jonathan Edwards," 29; Patterson, "Changing Images of the Beast," 444; Perry Miller, *Errand into the Wilderness* (Cambridge, MA: Harvard University Press, 1964) 233.

Religious conditions would gradually improve, allowing the millennium to begin in America by 2000.[18]

But the Great Awakening failed to bring the anticipated results. It came to an end. And to the dismay of Edwards and other revivalists, a new age did not dawn. So the American believers looked for apocalyptic signs in other contemporary events—especially the French and Indian War. Most of the revivalists did not lose their optimism, interpreting these signs in the light of postmillennial eschatology.[19]

Bible expositors in the late 1750s and 1760s explained end-time events in both political and religious terms—a trend that would continue. The war with France provided fresh fodder for eschatological expectations. The colonists politicized their view of the millennium—identifying God's prophetic plan with British interests in North America and associating Catholic France with the Antichrist. Thus Britain's military victories over the French Antichrist signaled the beginning of a millennium of religious and civil liberty. By the end of the French and Indian War, Americans began to blur distinctions between the kingdom of God and the emerging American nation.[20]

With the defeat of Catholic France in North America, the colonists looked for the complete destruction of the Antichrist. But this did not happen. So the colonists, as believers have done throughout Christian history, looked for the Antichrist elsewhere. They had only to look for the nearest enemy—the British government.[21]

The Revolutionary War stimulated all kinds of millennial expectations. Apocalyptic thinking certainly did not cause the War of Independence, but on a popular level it did provide some meaning for the struggle. Colonial ministers used apocalyptic language in support of the patriot cause and as an explanation for the sufferings.[22]

---

18. St. Clair, *Millenarian Movements*, 270; Albanese, *America*, 425.

19. Hatch, "Origins of Civil Millennialism," 91–95; Robert G. Clouse, "The New Christian Right, America, and the Kingdom of God," *Christian Scholar's Review* 12 (1983) 5; Melvin B. Endy Jr., "Just War, Holy War and Millennialism in Revolutionary America," *William and Mary Quarterly* 42 (January 1985) 3–5.

20. Fuller, *Naming the Antichrist*, 68–70; Clouse, "New Christian Right," 5; Hatch, "Origins of Civil Millennialism," 98; Bloch, *Visionary Republic*, 46–48.

21. Clouse, "New Christian Right," 5–6; Hatch, "Origins of Civil Millennialism," 105.

22. Fuller, *Naming the Antichrist*, 71–72; Bloch, *Visionary Republic*, 79–86; Endy, "Just War, Holy War," 15–17; Harry S. Stout, "Preaching the Insurrection," *Christian History* 15/2 (1996) 14–15.

The Millennial Nation

With the Stamp Act crisis, Americans began to change their perception of the Antichrist. Previously they identified the political and religious despotism of Catholicism and the papacy as Antichrist. Now the colonists looked for other forms of tyranny. At first they found it in the British Empire. Then they extended this perception to the Church of England and the episcopacy.[23] By 1773 the Americans even portrayed George III as Antichrist. While the notion had little impact, someone calculated that in Greek and Hebrew the numerical equivalent of the letters in the words "Royal Supremacy in Great Britain" totaled 666.[24]

Many Americans regarded the Revolutionary War as a holy crusade that would usher in the millennium, and with the American victory millennial optimism soared. The Second Great Awakening in the early nineteenth century also brought another wave of postmillennial hope. This evangelical postmillennialism complemented the revivals and perfectionism of that day. Most religious and academic leaders preached a progressive millennialism. For example, Timothy Dwight, president of Yale, predicted that the millennium would come by 2000.[25]

But a different kind of postmillennialism also came to the forefront. Previously the Americans believed that God's people would prepare the world for Christ's kingdom through prayer and preaching. Now they began to equate the kingdom of God with the political and moral destiny of America.[26] Indeed, in the nineteenth century Americans believed that God was smiling on their cause. This new postmillennialism justified American territorial expansion in the West. Religious leaders saw the advances in learning, the arts, science, morality, and religion as signs that the millennium was coming. In pursuit of a Christian commonwealth in America, postmillennialism sparked a number of reform efforts—abolition, temperance, and suffrage. Eventually it developed into a more secular millennium largely devoid of religious impulse.[27]

23. Beam, "Millennialism and American Nationalism," 185; Patterson, "Changing Image of the Beast, 445.

24. Boyer, *When Time Shall Be No More*, 72.

25. N. Gordon Thomas, "The Second Coming: A Major Impulse of American Protestantism," *Adventist Heritage* 3 (1976) 4; Brown, "Watchers for the Second Coming," 449.

26. Clouse, "New Christian Right," 6; Patterson, "Changing Images of the Beast," 445; Bloch, *Visionary Republic*, 103–4; Tuveson, *Redeemer Nation*, 125–31; Richard Kyle, *Evangelicalism: An Americanized Christianity* (New Brunswick, NJ: Transaction, 2006) 23–43.

27. Clouse, "New Christian Right," 6–7; Fuller, *Naming the Antichrist*, 72–73; Dawn Glanz, "The American West as Millennial Kingdom," in *The Apocalyptic Vision*

FRINGE GROUPS AND MILLENNIALISM

The millennial idea powerfully affected both mainstream and fringe religions throughout the course of the nineteenth century. Early nineteenth-century America witnessed an explosion of new religious movements such as had not been seen since the sixteenth century. Many of these bodies combined millennial ideas with beliefs common at that time, especially perfectionism and communalism. In doing so, these fringe groups gave a new twist to end-time thinking.[28]

A wave of communal social orders came about in the early nineteenth century. By their very nature, communal groups separate from society in their quest for the ideal. The perfectionism so prevalent in antebellum (pre–Civil War) America found its way into the communal sects. Even if they did not believe society could be perfected, they endeavored to build for themselves a perfect way of life in their cloistered communities.[29]

To a large extent, most of these groups were millennialists, though their eschatology cannot be neatly categorized as either pre- or postmillennialism. In one form or another, they placed considerable emphasis on the return of Christ or the start of the millennium. Millennialism may not have been a distinctive for which these groups were best known, but it did provide the rationale for some behavior that otherwise would make no sense. Most notably, the belief that the millennium was at hand led some radical sects, including the Society of the Public Universal Friend and the Shakers, to adopt celibacy.

The Public Universal Friend

The Society of the Public Universal Friend was an early indigenous American communitarian movement with some millenarian characteristics. It

---

in America: Interdisciplinary Essays on Myth and Culture, ed. Lois Parkinson Zamora (Bowling Green, OH: Bowling Green University Popular Press, 1982) 141; Albanese, *America*, 426–27; Moorhead, "Erosion of Postmillennialism," 62–72; Moorhead, "Between Progress and Apocalypse," 526–27; Tuveson, *Redeemer Nation*, 131, 162–63; Quandt, "Religion and Social Thought," 391–92.

28. Richard Kyle, *The Religious Fringe: A History of Alternative Religions in America* (Downers Grove, IL: InterVarsity, 1993) 62, 72, 74.

29. Kyle, *Religious Fringe*, 74–75; Rosabeth M. Kanter, *Commitment and Community: Communes and Utopias in Sociological Perspective* (Cambridge, MA: Harvard University Press, 1972) 1–8; Alice Felt Tyler, *Freedom's Ferment: Phases of American Social History from the Colonial Period to the Outbreak of the Civil War.* (New York: Harper and Row, 1944) 108–10.

The Millennial Nation

flourished in New York, Rhode Island, and Connecticut from 1776 to 1863. Founded by Jemima Wilkinson (1752–1819), the daughter of a prosperous Quaker farmer in Rhode Island, this sect bore resemblance to the Shakers in a number of ways, including millennial beliefs.[30]

Unusual circumstances surrounded the beginnings of the Society of the Public Universal Friend. At eighteen Wilkinson seemed to have died of the plague. Her body grew cold but then warmed up, and she began to speak. The voice coming from within her claimed that Jemima Wilkinson had "left the world of time," and henceforth her body would function as a vehicle for the Spirit of Life, which came to be known as the Public Universal Friend.[31]

Wilkinson believed that the Spirit of God's descent to Earth and inhabitation of her body was the Second Coming of Christ, who would reign on Earth for a thousand years. For over forty years the Friend operated from within her body. Among other teachings she proclaimed a message of millenarianism and perfectionism. It was the eleventh hour, the last call of mercy to be made to humankind.[32]

The Shakers

The United Society of Believers in Christ's Second Appearing, better known as the Shakers, was one of America's most successful and enduring communal groups. The Shakers originated in England, where they had connections with the so-called Shaking Quakers. Ann Lee Stanley (1736–84) led the group to America in 1774, where economic problems forced them to organize into a socialist Christian community.[33]

---

30. Robert S. Ellwood Jr., *Alternative Altars: Unconventional and Eastern Spirituality in America* (Chicago: University of Chicago Press, 1979) 70; Tyler, *Freedom's Ferment*, 115–16; Kyle, *Religious Fringe*, 80; Ruth Tucker, *Another Gospel: Alternative Religions and the New Age Movement* (Grand Rapids: Zondervan, 1989) 42.

31. Sydney Ahlstrom, *A Religious History of the American People* (New Haven, CT: Yale University Press, 1972) 495–96; Kyle, *Religious Fringe*, 80–81; Catherine Keller, *Apocalypse Now and Then: A Feminist Guide to the End of the World* (Boston: Beacon, 1996) 234–35.

32. St. Clair, *Millenarian Movements*, 276: Kyle, *Religious Fringe*, 80–81; Catherine Keller, *Apocalypse Now and Then*, 234–35.

33. Edward Deming Andrews, *The People Called Shakers: A Search for the Perfect Society* (New York: Dover, 1963); Henri Desroche, *The American Shakers: From Neo-Christianity to Presocialism* (Amherst, MA: University of Massachusetts Press, 1971); Marguerite Fellows Melcher, *The Shaker Adventure* (Cleveland: Western Reserve University Press, 1968); Stephen J. Stein, *The Shaker Experience in America: A History of*

Developing in the context of the Second Great Awakening, the Shakers maintained doctrines common in revivalistic circles. Still, they articulated some unique teachings. Mother Ann believed that God is a dual personality. The masculine side of that personality had been made visible in Christ. Now in Ann Lee a second incarnation of the Holy Spirit had appeared—the feminine element of God, which continued the work done by Christ. In admitting Ann Lee to the Godhead, the Shakers taught that God was a Father-Mother deity, a bisexual being. They considered Christ to be spirit, appearing first in a masculine form and then much later in Mother Ann.[34]

The Shakers were a millennial church. But it was a curious blend of millennialism and communitarianism that defies classification. According to Michael St. Clair, Shaker millennialism can best be seen as a "mystical and realized eschatology that experienced Christ's second appearing in the present and not at the end of time."[35] For Shakers, the Second Coming of Christ had already occurred, being consummated through Ann Lee, who was the feminine incarnation of God. They also believed that the millennium was at hand, and that they were the vanguard whose prayers and example would direct all humankind into a state of sanctity and happiness. Their mission was to gather in the elect, who could achieve perfection and salvation by denying the flesh.[36]

The Shakers were fanatically anti-sex. Convinced that sin had begun with Adam and Eve's sex act in the Garden of Eden, Ann Lee insisted that sexual relations were the root of all sin. Men and women would achieve

---

the United Society of Believers (New Haven, CT: Yale University Press, 1992).

34. William M. Kephart, *Extraordinary Groups: The Sociology of Unconventional Life-Styles* (2nd ed.; New York: St. Martin's, 1982) 224; Ellwood, *Alternative Alters*, 74; Albanese, *America*, 155–56; Tyler, *Freedom's Ferment*, 146–47; Warren Lewis, "What to Do after the Messiah Has Come Again and Gone: Shaker 'Premillennial' Eschatology and Its Spiritual Aftereffects," in *The Coming Kingdom: Essays in American Millennialism & Eschatology*, eds. M. Darrol Bryant and Donald W. Dayton (Barrytown, NY: International Religious Foundation, 1983) 74.

35. St. Clair, *Millenarian Movements*, 292 (quote); Suzanne Youngerman, "Shaking Is No Foolish Play: An Anthropological Perspective on the American Shakers—Person, Time, Space, and Dance-Ritual," PhD diss., Columbia University, 1983, 78.

36. Lewis, "What to Do," 74; Clarke Garett, *Spirit Possession and Popular Religion: From the Camisards to the Shakers* (Baltimore: Johns Hopkins University Press, 1987) 164–65; Tyler, *Freedom's Ferment*, 146–47; J. F. C. Harrison, *The Second Coming: Popular Millenarianism, 1780-1850* (New Brunswick, NJ: Rutgers University Press, 1979) 166; Lawrence Foster, "Had Prophecy Failed?" in *The Disappointed: Millerism and Millenarianism in the Nineteenth Century*, eds. Ronald L. Numbers and Jonathan M. Butler (Knoxville: University of Tennessee Press, 1993) 177.

The Millennial Nation

salvation only by overcoming this fleshly desire. They could not marry or cohabitate. Married converts were "demarried" in an unusual ceremony. In fact, it was forbidden to watch animals (or even flies) mate.[37]

Taking celibacy to extremes, the Shakers felt that they alone among the world's peoples were carrying out God's will. If this Shaker dogma prevailed, the human race would be eliminated. But such a possibility presented no problem for the Shakers—they believed that since the millennium was at hand there was no real reason for the propagation of humankind.[38]

The Mormons

"We believe in the literal gathering of Israel, and the restoration of the Ten Tribes; that Zion will be built upon this continent [North America]," said Joseph Smith, the Mormon leader.[39] The Church of Jesus Christ of Latter Day Saints, better known as the Mormons, is one of the most successful millennial religions in American history. Many of the millennial groups encountered in this book have long since ceased to exist. Not so with the Mormons—they are still thriving.

Mormonism began in the 1820s in western New York State, an area known as the Burned-Over District because it had experienced numerous religious revivals. Here Joseph Smith (1805–44) had a revolutionary experience: he was led by the angel Moroni to discover the Golden Plates, which developed into the Book of Mormon.[40] Supplementing the Bible as scripture, the Book of Mormon describes the emigration of the lost tribes of Israel to America before the birth of Jesus. According to the Book of Mormon, Jesus appeared to these people after the resurrection and set up a church among them. Thus the Book of Mormon "established the Hebraic

---

37. Lawrence Foster, *Religion and Sexuality: The Shakers, the Mormons, and the Oneida Community* (Urbana, IL: University of Illinois Press, 1984) 21–24; Yuri Rubinsky and Ian Wiseman, *A History of the End of the World* (New York: Morrow, 1982) 110.

38. Kephart, *Extraordinary Groups*, 224–25; Ellwood, *Alternative Altars*, 77–78; Tyler, *Freedom's Ferment*, 146–47.

39. Quoted in Harrison, *Second Coming*, 180.

40. See Klaus J. Hansen, *Mormonism and the American Experience* (Chicago: University of Chicago Press, 1981) 1–44; David Brion Davis, "The New England Origins of Mormonism," in *Mormonism and American Culture*, eds. Marvin S. Hill and James B. Allen (New York: Harper and Row, 1972) 13–28; Leonard J. Arrington and Davis Bitton, *The Mormon Experience* (New York: Knopf, 1979); Jan Shipps, *Mormonism* (Urbana, IL: University of Illinois Press, 1985).

origins of American Indians and supplied America with a biblical past," notes Catherine Albanese.[41]

Having adorned America with a sacred past, the Mormons naturally Americanized the millennium. This millennial belief held up America as the Promised Land and as the place where the New Jerusalem would be erected. After all, America is where the lost tribes of Israel chose to migrate. This emphasis reflected the nationalism and optimism of American society as well as the postmillennialism so prevalent in nineteenth-century religious circles.[42]

Yet Mormon millennialism was not this simple. It evidenced several tensions involving both pre- and postmillennial characteristics. At first Smith taught an apocalyptic, premillennial eschatology. But this seemed to fade as the Mormons began to concentrate more on the building of Zion as a place than on an imminent beginning of the millennial kingdom. Yet the Mormons expected their cause to triumph through a cataclysmic judgment rather than the gradual conversion of the world. They waited anxiously for the fulfillment of the signs of the times, while they also labored mightily to build the New Jerusalem in Utah.[43]

All in all, the premillennial characteristics of the Mormon's eschatology outweighed its postmillennialism. To be sure, they often urged human efforts to build the kingdom. Also, they occasionally waned in their expectation of an imminent millennium. But they maintained an apocalyptic dualism, dividing the world into opposing factions. The Mormons believed that salvation would come swiftly rather than gradually,

---

41. Albanese, *America*, 141–42 (quote); Thomas F. O'Dea, *The Mormons* (Chicago: University of Chicago Press, 1957) 22–40; Robert Flanders, "To Transform History: Early Mormon Culture and the Concept of Time and Space," *Church History* 40/1 (1971) 111; Duane S. Crowther, *The Prophecies of Joseph Smith* (Bountiful, UT: Horizon, 1983) 155–202; Bruce R. McConkie, *The Millennial Messiah: The Second Coming of the Son of Man* (Salt Lake City: Deseret, 1982) 182–205.

42. R. Laurence Moore, *Religious Outsiders and the Making of Americans* (New York: Oxford University Press, 1986) 44–46; Tuveson, *Redeemer Nation*, 179–86; Albanese, *America*, 143–44; Harrison, *Second Coming*, 176–92; Tyler, *Freedom's Ferment*, 95–96.

43. Tuveson, *Redeemer Nation*, 179–86; Albanese, *America*, 143–44. The ambivalence in Mormon millennialism has produced disagreement among scholars. See Grant Underwood, "Early Millenarianism: Another Look," *Church History* 54/1 (1985) 215–29; Timothy L. Smith, "The Book of Mormon in a Biblical Culture," *Journal of Mormon History* 7 (1980) 3–21; Klaus J. Hansen, *Quest for Empire: The Political Kingdom of God and the Council of Fifty* (East Lansing: Michigan State University Press, 1967); McConkie, *Millennial Messiah*, 282–96.

be accomplished with the help of supernatural beings, and completely transform life on Earth.[44]

For the end to come, the Mormons held that three events must transpire. First, "the tribe of Ephraim, the Mormons themselves," must gather in Zion—which they believed to be Independence, Missouri. (Despite their having been chased out of this Zion, this belief is still maintained.) Next, "the tribe of Judah—the Jews—will gather in Palestine." Lastly, "the ten tribes of Israel will be found" and gather in Zion. "At this point, Christ will return" to begin the millennium.[45]

Other Unusual Millennial Groups

Nineteenth-century America witnessed the rise and fall of other unusual millennial bodies. A number of these groups combined perfectionism and millennialism with unorthodox sexual practices. The Universal Friend and the Shakers advocated celibacy, the Mormons polygamy; the Oneida Perfectionists and the Rappites went down similarly diverse paths.

The Oneida Community, founded by John Humphrey Noyes (1811–86), was a very successful and widely publicized communitarian experiment with evangelical roots. The doctrine of perfectionism, that human beings could be without sin, propelled Noyes's innovations, including a new marriage system. Noyes believed that the traditional family relationship bred injustice, competition, and dissension. So he proposed a form of communal marriage in which every male was husband to every woman in the community, and every female was wife to every man.[46]

The basis of Noyes's perfectionism resided in his postulation that Christ's Second Coming had occurred in 70 CE. When the Romans destroyed the temple in Jerusalem, Christ had appeared spiritually to his apostles. Thus, liberation or redemption from sin was an accomplished

44. Grant Underwood, *The Millenarian World of Early Mormonism* (Urbana, IL: University of Illinois Press, 1993) 8–9, 40–41.

45. Rubinsky and Wiseman, *End of the World*, 114 (quote); Underwood, *Millenarian World of Early Mormonism*, 32–33; Harry Benjamin Gray, "Eschatology of the Millennial Cults," ThD diss., Dallas Theological Seminary, 1956, 110–17; McConkie, *Millennial Messiah*, 399–405.

46. Leonard Bernstein, "The Ideas of John Humphrey Noyes, Perfectionist," *American Quarterly* 5 (March 1953) 157–65; Ernest R. Sandeen, "John Humphrey Noyes as the New Adam," *Church History* 40/1 (1971) 83–87: Kephart, *Extraordinary Groups*, 94–95: Ahlstrom, *Religious History of the American People*, 498–99; Foster, *Religion and Sexuality*, 16, 76–78, 90–93; Spencer Klaw, *Without Sin: The Life and Death of the Oneida Community* (New York: Penguin, 1993).

fact for the followers of Jesus, who were potentially perfect beings. But the relationship of Christ's invisible coming in 70 CE to the millennium presented problems for Noyes. Was the millennium now in progress? Or had it been delayed? On these questions Noyes was ambivalent and defensive. He even suggested that Christ would appear a third time in the not-too-distant future.[47]

The Rappites were also a communal group with imminent end-time expectations. Like the Shakers, George Rapp (1757–1847) insisted on rigid self-discipline, including strict celibacy and holding of all property in common. Accordingly, the Rappites regarded themselves as a righteous remnant who would be judged holy when Christ returned in the near future. In fact, Rapp believed that the millennium had recently begun.[48]

Some communal movements with a secular orientation also looked for the millennium. For example, the rationalist Robert Owen (1771–1858) regarded communitarianism as a step toward heaven on Earth. Owen was not even a Christian, let alone a biblical millennialist. Yet he announced the arrival of a secular millennium or utopia.[49] By the word *millennium* Owen meant a society free from crime, misery, and poverty—an ideal he believed to be universally possible. For him, the end was the imminent collapse of capitalist civilization. In the Owenite movement the line between social and religious millenarianism became blurred. Owen began to use religious language, and after 1835 the movement exhibited some trappings of a religious cult.[50]

The Christadelphians are a non-traditional religious group begun by John Thomas (1805–71) during the first half of the nineteenth century. Unlike other movements originating at this time, the Christadelphians are not communal, nor do they have any unusual views on sexual relationships. Rather, they are an anti-Trinitarian millennial group with unusual

---

47. Michael Barkun, *Crucible of the Millennium: The Burned-Over District of New York in the 1840s* (Syracuse: Syracuse University Press, 1986) 64–65; Michael Barkun, "The Wind Sweeping Over the Country," in *The Disappointed*, 156–58; Kyle, *Religious Fringe*, 78–79.

48. St. Clair, *Millenarian Movements*, 285–87; Tyler, *Freedom's Ferment*, 121–28; Daniel Cohen, *Prophets of Doom* (Brookfield, CT: Millbrook, 1992) 21–22; K. J. R. Arndt, *George Rapp's Harmony Society*, 1785–1847 (rev. ed.; Philadelphia: University of Pennsylvania Press, 1972).

49. St. Clair, *Millenarian Movements*, 291; Brown, "Watchers for the Second Coming," 453.

50. St. Clair, *Millenarian Movements*, 290–91; Tyler, *Freedom's Ferment*, 203–4.

The Millennial Nation

doctrinal and social characteristics. They still exist in small pockets in America and in larger numbers in Britain.[51]

Thomas insisted that the central message of Scripture was the hope of the kingdom of God, to come with the Second Advent of Christ, which he believed to be imminent. The Christadelphians hold that the promises of Scripture relate to the Jews and those who voluntarily become Jews. Their eschatology thus has a Hebraic focus. They reject any teaching of a heaven beyond the skies, instead believing that the saved will live on a renewed Earth. Therefore, the Christadelphians emphasize the earthly promises made to Israel and expected the returning Christ to reign permanently in Jerusalem.[52]

THE MIDNIGHT CRY: THE MILLERITES

Nearly every year we hear of some well-publicized prediction regarding the end of the world. Occasionally, a prophet gathers a following, and an end-of-the-world panic results. In the mid nineteenth century, Northeastern and Midwestern America experienced such an event.[53]

"I am fully convinced that somewhere between March 21st, 1843, and March 21st, 1844, according to the Jewish mode of computation, Christ will come," declared William Miller (1782-1849).[54] But March 21, 1844, came and went without the return of Christ. Miller confessed his error and acknowledged his disappointment, but still insisted that Jesus would soon return. Under great pressure Miller and his associates set another date—October 22, 1844.

Such were the predictions of William Miller, a simple farmer and Baptist layman from Low Hampton, New York. Ernest Sandeen has called Miller "the most famous millenarian in American history." Without a

---

51. Bryan R. Wilson, *Religious Sects: A Sociological Study* (New York: McGraw-Hill, 1970) 103, 107; Tucker, *Another Gospel*, 46; Charles H. Lippy, *The Christadelphians in North America* (Lewiston, NY: E. Mellen, 1989).

52. Bryan R. Wilson, *Sects and Society* (Berkeley, CA: University of California Press, 1961) 246-47; Wilson, *Religious Sects*, 103, 106-7; Richard Kyle, "Christadelphians," in *Encyclopedia U.S.A.*, ed. Archie P. McDonald (Gulf Breeze, FL: Academic International, 1989) 11:72; Lippy, *Christadelphians in North America*, 133, 135, 156, 299.

53. Daniel Cohen, *Waiting for the Apocalypse* (Buffalo: Prometheus, 1983) 13.

54. Quoted in J. Gordon Melton, *The Encyclopedia of American Religions* (Wilmington, NC: McGrath, 1978) 1:460.

doubt, his preaching spawned the most popular end-time movement that America has seen.[55]

It is true, of course, that postmillennialism was the dominant end-time perspective until late in the nineteenth century. Increased knowledge, material progress, cultural advances, and the growth of democracy propelled the optimistic vision of America's millennial future. Hopeful Americans even saw the Civil War as but an interlude in which God punished the nation for slavery. Still, premillennialism was not dead in the early nineteenth century. It must be remembered that the line between pre- and postmillennialism was not hard and fast. The distinction in millennial studies between the pessimistic premillennialists, who focused on catastrophe, and the optimistic postmillennials, who focused on progress, does not always hold up. Premillennialists often participated in social reform movements, and some postmillennialists spoke of end-time events as if they were right around the corner. For example, the prominent evangelist Charles Finney had a postmillennial vision of the millennium as beginning in three years.[56]

There were, then, always a number of individuals who taught premillennialism. Some events in the late eighteenth and early nineteenth centuries increased their numbers. In particular the French Revolution fostered an interest in prophecy. The turbulence of the revolution created an apocalyptic mood, causing many to believe that the end was near. The demolition of papal power in France was of special interest to Bible scholars in both Britain and America who believed that the papacy had to be destroyed before the millennium could come.[57]

Other European premillennial ideas reached American shores, especially from Britain, where historicist premillennialism surged in the nineteenth century. While there is no evidence that Miller encountered these ideas, his teachings bore a striking resemblance to British premillennialism. Even Miller's emphasis on 1843 as the year for Christ's return was not too unique, for historicist premillennialists in Britain (and some in America too) believed that something cataclysmic would occur in 1843.

---

55. Sandeen, *Roots of Fundamentalism*, 50. See also Numbers and Butler, eds. *The Disappointed*, x, v; David L. Rowe, *God's Strange Work: William Miller and the End of the World* (Grand Rapids: Eerdmans), 2008.

56. Jonathan M. Butler, "From Millerism to Seventh-day Adventism: 'Boundlessness to Consolidation,'" *Church History* 55/1 (1986) 53–54; Numbers and Butler, eds., *The Disappointed*, xviii; James Moorhead, "Searching for the Millennium in America," *Princeton Seminary Bulletin* 8/2 (1987) 21.

57. Clouse, "New Christian Right," 8; Sandeen, *Roots of Fundamentalism*, 5–11.

The Millennial Nation

Where Miller did disagree with the British premillennialists was over the issue of Israel. In Miller's end-time predictions, there was no place for the conversion of the Jews or their return to Palestine.[58]

Although at this time the revivalism of the Second Great Awakening was producing an optimistic postmillennialism, enough negative events were occurring to encourage premillennialism and its catastrophic view of history. Focusing on Christ's statement that wars and rumors of war would characterize the end times, premillennialists were always on the watch for war between major European powers. The fate of the Ottoman Empire and the advance of Russia into this area—events the Millerites believed were predicted in the Book of Revelation—occupied a special role in their calculations.[59]

On the domestic scene, a number of events generated a premillennial excitement. The influx of Catholic immigrants to America aroused apocalyptic feelings. Premillennialists drew dire inferences from disturbances in the natural world: the early nineteenth century witnessed a solar eclipse, dramatic meteor showers, great storms, fires, earthquakes, and crop failures. Economic problems intensified the end-time anxieties. The prosperity of the Jacksonian years gave way to the Panic of 1837 and the following depression.[60]

The Millerite movement was actually a child of American evangelicalism. In fact, Millerism has been called "evangelicalism with a twist."[61] Except for predicting the exact date of Christ's return, Millerism did not substantially differ from its evangelical neighbors. The major impulses of antebellum evangelicalism—millennialism, perfectionism, voluntarism (emphasis on human choice), and revivalism—all helped shape Millerism. Indeed, even in respect to date setting the Millerites were not unique—others did the same.[62]

58. Sandeen, *Roots of Fundamentalism*, 50–53; Barkun, *Crucible of the Millennium*, 36; Louis Billington, "The Millerite Adventists in Great Britain, 1840–1850," in *The Disappointed*, 59–70.

59. Barkun, *Crucible of the Millennium*, 50, 52; Eric Anderson, "The Millerite Use of Prophecy," in *The Disappointed*, 79–80.

60. Barkun, *Crucible of the Millennium*, 54–56; Fuller, *Naming the Antichrist*, 104; Stephen O' Leary, *Arguing the Apocalypse: A Theory of Millennial Rhetoric* (New York: Oxford University Press, 1994) 93, 98. See also Whitney R. Cross, *The Burned-Over District* (New York: Harper, 1965); David L. Rowe, " A New Perspective on the Burned-Over District: The Millerites in Upstate New York," *Church History* 47/4 (1978) 409.

61. Ruth Alden Doan, "Millerism and Evangelical Culture," in *The Disappointed*, 122.

62. Butler, "From Millerism to Seventh-day Adventism," 53; Sandeen, *Roots of*

This popular movement did not originate with some raging fanatic or silver-tongued demagogue. Rather, Miller was a self-educated farmer with few charismatic qualities. For a while he flirted with deism. But in 1816 he was converted and returned to his Baptist roots. Miller began an intensive study of the Bible, which eventually centered on millennial prophecies and biblical chronology. By 1818 his end-time views were settled. Still, he restudied his conclusions for several years and in 1831 began to publicly present his ideas.[63]

Miller's Calculations

Miller set forth a number of principles for understanding biblical prophecy. But his thinking rested on two basic approaches to Scripture. One, he embraced a historicist interpretation of the Book of Revelation—the prophecies of the Apocalypse relate to various periods in history. This approach to premillennialism tended to lock the interpreter into a specific prophetic timetable. Two, whenever possible, Miller interpreted Scripture literally. Figures, parables, and numbers were exceptions: they have a symbolic meaning. Employing these two approaches, Miller looked for the fulfillment of prophecy in both historical events and future developments.[64] Enlarging on historicist premillennialism—which said that Jesus would return before the millennium and that the millennium would not be ushered in by the gradual reform of human institutions, but by a catastrophic destruction of the world's kingdoms—Miller specified when all of this would happen.[65]

Miller's prophetic calculations were quite elaborate. But the key to his biblical arithmetic can be found in Daniel 8:14: "And he said to me,

---

Fundamentalism, 51-53; Doan, "Millerism and Evangelical Culture," 118-20; Moore, *Religious Outsiders*, 131. See also William G. McLoughlin, "Pietism and the American Character," *American Quarterly* 17/1 (1965) 163-86; Ruth Alden Doan, *The Miller Heresy, Millennialism, and American Culture* (Philadelphia: Temple University Press, 1987).

63. St. Clair, *Millenarian Movements*, 306; Barkun, *Crucible of the Millennium*, 35-36; Tyler, *Freedom's Ferment*, 70; Cohen, *Prophets of Doom*, 23; Rowe, "New Perspective," 411-12.

64. Harrison, *Second Coming*, 200-201; Anderson, "Millerite Use of Prophecy," 78-89; Sandeen, *Roots of Fundamentalism*, 59; Tyler, *Freedom's Ferment*, 71; David T. Arthur, "Millerism," in *The Rise of Adventism: Religion and Society in Mid-Nineteenth-Century America*, ed. Edwin Gaustad (New York: Harper and Row, 1974) 154.

65. O"Leary, *Arguing the Apocalypse*, 100; Sandeen, *Roots of Fundamentalism*, 53-58.

The Millennial Nation

Unto two thousand and three hundred days; then shall the sanctuary be cleansed." Miller believed that this sanctuary cleansing referred to the return of Christ, which would purge the world of evil and usher in the millennium.[66] On the assumption that one prophetic day equals one year, Miller theorized that Daniel's 2,300 days meant that 2,300 years must pass before Christ's return and the final cleansing of the Earth. Using Archbishop James Ussher's chronology, Miller calculated that the 2,300-year period began in 457 BCE, when Ezra and 1,700 Jews returned to Jerusalem. This date in turn reflected Daniel 9:24: "Seventy weeks are determined upon thy people . . . to make an end of sins." Interpreting the "end of sins" to be 33 CE—the time of Christ's crucifixion—Miller went back 490 years ("seventy weeks") to arrive at 457 BCE. Then, beginning the countdown in 457, Miller added 2,300 years (which included Daniel's seventy weeks) to arrive at 1843.[67]

Over the next few years, Miller continued to recalculate his figures, bolstering his conclusion that the end would come in 1843. But because so many changes had been made to the calendar over the previous two thousand years, Miller still hesitated to publicly designate an exact year for Christ's return.[68] In fact, Miller said little about his discovery to anyone. But by 1831—when he was almost fifty—his friends persuaded him to go public with his message. Miller took to the preaching circuit throughout New York and Vermont, delivering eight hundred sermons by 1839.[69]

Millerism Reaches Out

Still, Millerism remained a small rural movement until Miller converted Joshua V. Himes to his biblical chronology. Himes, pastor of Chardon Chapel in Boston, proved to be a gifted publicist and organizer. Himes spread Miller's ideas by the extensive use of newspapers, camp meetings,

66. Harrison, *Second Coming*, 194; C. Marvin Pate and Calvin B. Haines Jr., *Doomsday Delusions* (Downers Grove, IL: InterVarsity, 1995) 93; Brown, "Watchers for the Second Coming," 453–54.

67. St.Clair, *Millenarian Movements*, 306; Anderson, "Millerite Use of Prophecy," 80; Pate and Haines, *Doomsday Delusions*, 93–94; Harrison, *Second Coming*, 194; Russell Chandler, *Doomsday: The End of the World, A View through Time* (Ann Arbor, MI: Servant, 1993) 85.

68. Harrison, *Second Coming*, 194; Chandler, *Doomsday*, 85; St. Clair, *Millenarian Movements*, 306.

69. Barkun, *Crucible of the Millennium*, 36–37; Harrison, *Second Coming*, 192–93; St. Clair, *Millenarian Movements*, 308; Chandler, *Doomsday*, 85–86.

and evangelistic tours. Miller's greatest distinctive was the use of the biggest tents America had seen, seating up to four thousand.[70]

Himes made Miller a national figure and greatly expanded his movement through the Northeast and Midwest. Numbers vary, but the number of followers of Millerism is usually estimated to have ranged from thirty thousand to one hundred thousand. Who were the Millerites? David Rowe defines them as people who not only believed in "the imminent apocalypse but acted on behalf of that belief" to specifically support Miller's ideas. While millennial groups usually draw people from the lower social orders, this was not so with the Millerites. On the whole, they came from the middle classes and were probably better off than the average person. Moreover, the Millerites were generally sober people unmarked by fanaticism.[71]

Until 1842 Miller often qualified his predictions, looking for the Second Advent about 1843. Under some pressure to be more specific, at the beginning of 1843 Miller used the Hebrew calendar to calculate that Christ's return would occur between March 21, 1843, and March 21, 1844. This more specific dating generated excitement and Millerism became more popular.[72]

During 1843 and early 1844 the Millerites stepped up their activities and the crowds increased. Even the secular newspapers took notice of the Millerite doctrines. So did the mainstream clergy, who opposed the Millerite date setting. As the year passed, the Millerites were often mercilessly ridiculed and lampooned for insisting that the end was at hand. Stung by such attacks, the Millerites identified both Catholicism and mainstream Protestantism as Babylon and partisans of Antichrist.[73]

---

70. David T. Arthur, "Joshua V. Himes and the Cause of Adventism," in *The Disappointed*, 39–47; Arthur, "Millerism" 155–56; Barkun, *Crucible of the Millennium*, 38; Tyler, *Freedom's Ferment*, 72; Rowe, *God's Strange Work*, 159–69.

71. Moorhead, "Searching for the Millennium in America," 19; David L. Rowe, "Millerites: A Shadow Portrait," in *The Disappointed*, 4–5, 9 (quote); Rowe, *God's Strange Work*, 129–32; O'Leary, *Arguing the Apocalypse*, 131; Michael Barkun, *Disaster and the Millennium* (New Haven, CT: Yale University Press, 1974) 11–33; St. Clair, *Millenarian Movements*, 311–12.

72. Doan, "Millerism and Evangelical Culture," in Pate and Haines, *Doomsday Delusions*, 95–96; Arthur, "Joshua V. Himes," 43.

73. Wayne R. Judd, "William Miller," in *The Disappointed*, 27; Fuller, *Naming the Antichrist*, 105; St. Clair, *Millenarian Movements*, 313–14; Tyler, *Freedom's Ferment*, 74–75; Butler, "From Millerism to Seventh-day Adventism," Arthur, "Millerism," 162–63.

The Millennial Nation

March 21, 1844, passed and Christ did not return. The Millerites faced a crisis of faith. Miller made no attempt to excuse his mistaken date, but he did not give up his belief regarding Christ's imminent return: "I confess my error and acknowledge my disappointment; yet I still believe the day of the Lord is near."[74] Although the movement was at a low ebb in the spring of 1844, many dedicated followers searched the Scriptures for evidence of a new date.

Psychologically, it would seem that the Millerites were not satisfied with the belief that Christ would return shortly. They needed an exact date—"and they got one."[75] As early as February 1844, one of Miller's followers, Samuel Snow, advanced the seventh-month scheme. According to Snow, the prophetic chronology fixed the date of the Lord's Second Advent at the tenth day of the seventh month of the Jewish sacred year. The Millerites identified this date with October 22 of the Gregorian calendar.[76] At a Millerite camp meeting in August of 1844, this new date became public. It infused the movement with new vigor. At first Miller hesitated to accept this new date for Christ's return, but events had snowballed beyond his control. Despite lingering doubts he endorsed the new date on October 6—two weeks before the end was supposed to come.[77]

The Great Disappointment

The Millerites had now painted themselves into a corner. There was no setting a new date. From about mid August to October, the Millerites engaged in a frenzy of activities. They flooded the country with their periodicals, books, and pamphlets. Many withdrew from their churches in anticipation of the Second Advent. They were instructed to get their affairs in order. Many did—selling their property, closing their stores, resigning their jobs, and abandoning their animals and crops. Even in such a frenzy few Millerites engaged in fanatical activities. To the end they were generally sane people.[78]

74. Quoted in Francis D. Nichol, *The Midnight Cry* (Washington, DC: Review and Herald, 1945) 171.

75. Cohen, *Waiting for the Apocalypse*, 28.

76. L Roy E. Froom, *The Prophetic Faith of Our Fathers: The Historical Development of Prophetic Interpretation* (Washington, DC: Review and Herald, 1946-54) 4:812; O'Leary, *Arguing the Apocalypse*, 106; Tyler, *Freedom's Ferment*, 76.

77. St. Clair, *Millenarian Movements*, 314; Cohen, *Waiting for the Apocalypse*, 28-29; Harrison, *Second Coming*, 194.

78. Harrison, *Second Coming*, 195; Chandler, *Doomsday*, 81-82; St. Clair,

But the Great Disappointment came. When the Lord did not return as expected, massive confusion and disillusionment set in. All millennial movements are disappointed when their predictions fail to materialize. But because the Millerites were so specific in their date setting, their disappointment was even more acute.[79]

The Great Disappointment was the last straw. The Millerite movement fragmented and went in several directions. Some went back to their churches. Others were so disillusioned that they abandoned the evangelical faith. A few retreated to the ultimate refuge—they joined separatist groups such as the Shakers. But most Millerites still believed the Second Advent was near. These people formed various Adventist groups, the largest being the Seventh-day Adventists.[80]

Despite its visibility the Millerite movement had little influence on subsequent end-time thinking. It did, however, have three long-term effects: one, Millerism spawned the Seventh-day Adventist Church; two, it discredited historicist premillennialism, causing it to fade out almost entirely after 1844; and three, the Millerite fiasco demonstrated the perils of setting definite dates for Christ's return.[81]

CLEANSING THE SANCTUARY: THE ADVENTISTS

"Following any apocalyptic failure such as the Millerite disappointment of 1844, there are several options open to the faithful followers," declares Gordon Melton. One alternative is to disband the group and return to normal life. Spiritualization is popular option; this entails "the process of claiming that the prophecy was in error to the extent of its being seen as a visible historical event, and the attempt to reinterpret it as a cosmic, inner, invisible, or heavenly event." A final alternative for the "disappointed apocalyptic is to return to the source of revelation (the Bible, a psychic-prophet, or an analysis of contemporary events) and seek a new date." A

Millenarian Movements, 315.

79. Harrison, *Second Coming*, 195.

80. Lawrence Foster, "Had Prophecy Failed?," 175–84; Jonathan M. Butler, "The Making of a New Order," in *The Disappointed*, 189–205; St. Clair, *Millenarian Movements*, 317; Chandler, *Doomsday*, 88–89; Pate and Haines, *Doomsday Delusions*, 126–27; Rowe, *God's Strange Work*, 192–225.

81. Boyer, *When Time Shall Be No More*, 82.

The Millennial Nation

less committed form of this option is to set a vague new date, such as "in the near future."[82]

Following the First Disappointment of 1843, some minor recalculations of biblical chronology pointed to October 1844. This readjustment satisfied most Millerites. Even after the Great Disappointment of 1844, some Adventist leaders did more of the same. They set new dates for the Second Advent—1845, 1846, 1849, and 1851.[83] But after the Great Disappointment this new arithmetic would not suffice. For most Adventists only a change in end-time thinking could soothe the disillusionment of 1844.

The Seventh-day Adventists did an about-face by resorting primarily to the spiritualization option. In doing so, they developed into a large religious organization. "Millenarians cannot last as *millenarians*," notes Jonathan Butler. "The sooner the group can shed its short-term millenarianism, the sooner it can accommodate to the practical business of life in the world." So the Seventh-day Adventists stopped setting dates for Christ's return and spiritualized the Great Disappointment. By shortening their millenarian phase, they became a stable religious denomination.[84]

Seventh-day Adventist eschatology had many strands. But its end-time thinking focused on two ideas—spiritualization of the Great Disappointment and sabbatarianism. After allegedly receiving a vision, Hiram Edson re-examined Daniel 8:14. With the help from O. R. L. Crosier, he set forth the idea that only the event of October 22, 1844—not the date—had been misinterpreted. Miller had interpreted the cleansing of the sanctuary in Daniel 8:14 as a prophecy that Christ would return to Earth and purge it. The Adventists now believed that on that fateful day in October Christ actually entered into the most holy compartment of the heavenly sanctuary and performed his cleansing work.[85] So the cleansing of the sanctuary referred not to the Second Advent, but to Christ's "investigation of the sins of God's people in preparation for the end of the world."

---

82. Melton, *Encyclopedia of American Religions*, 1:481 (quote); Leon Festinger, Henry W. Riecken, and Stanley Schachter, *When Prophecy Fails: A Social and Psychological Study of a Modern Group That Predicted the Destruction of the World* (New York: Harper, 1964) 3–32.

83. Godfrey T. Anderson, "Sectarianism and Organization, 1846–1864," in *Adventism in America: A History*, ed. Gary Land (Grand Rapids: Eerdmans, 1986) 47; Butler, "From Millerism to Seventh-day Adventism," 59.

84. Butler, "From Millerism to Seventh-day Adventism," 50, 59. See also Wilson, *Religious Sects*, 101.

85. Butler, "Making of a New Order," 200; Kenneth R. Samples, "From Controversy to Crisis," *Christian Research Journal* 11/1 (Summer 1988) 11; Gray, "Eschatology of the Millennial Cults," 156–57.

With this doctrine of investigative judgment the Adventists accomplished two things: they spiritualized the failed prediction of October 1844 and established a framework to order their lives while they waited for the end.[86]

The early Adventists believed Christ had two distinct ministries. He had been forgiving sins since his work on the cross. Yet for the repentant sinner some sin still remained on the heavenly records. So on October 22, 1844, Christ entered the holy compartment of the sanctuary. Here he investigates the lives of those who have been forgiven to see if they merit eternal life. When this investigative judgment has been completed, Christ will leave the sanctuary, return to Earth, and usher in the terrible Day of the Lord. Following this judgment the millennium will begin.[87]

Led by Ellen G. White and others, the Adventists soon began to associate Sabbath observance with the event of October 1844 and their new understanding of Christ's ministry in the heavenly sanctuary. They believed that the message of the third angel in Revelation 14:6–12 forecasted their movement. The angel called forth a people from the fallen churches to obey God's commandments, including Sabbath observance.[88] The reason why Christ did not return in 1844 is that Christians had not kept the Sabbath. The Second Advent will occur only after two events transpire—Christ has to complete his priestly work in the sanctuary and God's people must observe the Sabbath. In fact, because Catholics and Protestants worshipped on Sunday, the Seventh-day Adventists viewed them as the two horned beasts of Revelation 13.[89]

---

86. Butler, "Making of a New Order," 200 (quote); St. Clair, *Millenarian Movements*, 320; Samples, "From Controversy to Crisis," 11; Moore, *Religious Outsiders*, 133; Gray, "Eschatology of the Millennial Cults," 164–65.

87. P. Gerard Damsteegt, "Foundations of the Seventh-day Adventist Message and Mission," *Missiology* 8/1 (1980) 75–76; Samples, "From Controversy to Crisis," 11; Roy Adams, *The Sanctuary Doctrine: Three Approaches in the Seventh-day Adventist Church* (Berrien Springs, MI: Andrews University Press, 1981); Gray, "Eschatology of the Millennial Cults," 173.

88. Douglas Morgan, "Adventism, Apocalyptic, and the Cause of Liberty" *Church History* 63/2 (1994) 237–39; Damsteegt, "Foundations of the Seventh-day Adventist Message," 76–78; St. Clair, *Millenarian Movements*, 320–21; Albanese, *America*, 232; Anderson, "Sectarianism and Organization," 39–40.

89. Jonathan M. Butler, "Adventism and the American Experience," in *The Rise of Adventism*, 180–81; Damsteegt, "Foundations of the Seventh-day Adventist Message," 75–77; Morgan, "Adventism, Apocalyptic, and the Cause of Liberty," 237–39; St. Clair, *Millenarian Movements*, 322; Wilson, *Religious Sects*, 102; E. G. White, *America in Prophecy* (Jemison; AL: Inspirational Books East, 1988).

The Millennial Nation

COUNTDOWN TO ARMAGEDDON: THE JEHOVAH'S WITNESSES

"Ours had been one of the greatest 'Chicken Little' religions in modern history. For over one hundred years the sky has been going to fall shortly. Yet apparently Jehovah hasn't been listening," wrote one disillusioned ex-Jehovah's Witness.[90] The Jehovah's Witnesses may be the most persistent date setters in history. Most such groups make one or perhaps two failed predictions. But the Jehovah's Witnesses will not quit. Their leaders have earmarked the years 1874, 1878, 1881, 1910, 1914, 1918, 1925, 1975, and 1984 as times of eschatological significance.

Although millenarians supposedly cannot last long as millenarians, the Jehovah's Witnesses seem to have defied this conventional wisdom. Indeed, "they have preached millenarianism longer and more consistently than any major sectarian movement in the modern world."[91] The belief that God is going to bring an end to the world in the present generation propels their thinking. "Millions now living will never die," proclaimed Joseph Rutherford, one of their early leaders.[92]

Movements that predict the end of the world in the near future have a short life span. How have the Jehovah's Witnesses explained their prophetic failures? First, they have spiritualized a number of eschatological events, claiming that they occurred invisibly. Second, they recalculate their numbers and insist that their predictions will be fulfilled in the near future. Third, the Jehovah's Witnesses reinterpret their earlier prophecies, downplaying former predictions—even admitting mistakes. Finally, their organization is so autocratic that the rank and file have little choice but to accept the explanations.[93]

---

90. Quoted in M. James Penton, "The Eschatology of the Jehovah's Witnesses: A Short Critical Analysis," in *The Coming Kingdom*, 184.

91. M. James Penton, *Apocalypse Delayed: The Story of the Jehovah's Witnesses* (Toronto: University of Toronto Press, 1985) 7.

92. Chander, *Doomsday*, 91, 96; Melvin D. Curry, *Jehovah's Witnesses: The Millenarian World of the Watch Tower* (New York: Garland, 1992) 5–8; Brown, "Watchers for the Second Coming," 455–56.

93. Joseph F. Zygmunt, "Prophetic Failure and Chiliastic Identity: The Case of Jehovah's Witnesses," *American Journal of Sociology* 75 (1970) 933–34; Gray, "Eschatology of the Millennial Cults," 193.

Russell's Leadership

But the Jehovah's Witnesses have done more than survive. They are one of the most successful and well publicized of the Adventist bodies. In the early twenty-first century official members and affiliates numbered over eleven million worldwide. Actually, the Jehovah's Witnesses are the most prominent of about a dozen "Russellite" groups, the Adventist offshoots of the Bible studies conducted by Charles Taze Russell (1852-1916).[94]

The Jehovah's Witnesses, also called the Watchtower Society, are set off from the Christian tradition by their unorthodox beliefs. They deny most traditional Christian doctrines, in particular the Trinity and the deity of Christ and the Holy Spirit. Their lifestyle also erects some enormous barriers to any meaningful interaction with society. Since Satan dominates the world, especially the institutional aspects of business, politics, and religion, dedicated Jehovah's Witnesses separate themselves from social institutions. In addition, the eschatology of the Jehovah's Witnesses, which has been a basic theme of Watchtower literature from its early years, is confusing and contradictory.[95]

In the years following the Great Disappointment of 1844, Russell came under the influence of several Adventist preachers, especially Nelson H. Barbour. Surpassing their Millerite predecessors, Balfour and Russell began to set dates for Christ's return.[96] Convinced that Archbishop Ussher's chronology contained errors, Barbour developed his own formula. This new biblical arithmetic concluded that 1873 was the six-thousandth year from Adam's creation. Thus the millennial rule of Christ—the seventh day—was about to dawn.[97] When nothing happened in that year, in Adventist style Barbour and Russell spiritualized the return of Christ. Pointing out that *Parousia* (the Greek word used to designate Christ's return) actually meant "presence," they concluded that Christ's presence on Earth had begun in 1874. However, until right before the battle of Armageddon, Christ's invisible presence will be known only to his faithful followers. At

---

94. Melton, *Encyclopedia of American Religions*, 1:481-91; J. Gordon Melton, *Encyclopedic Handbook of Cults in America* (New York: Garland, 1986) 62-67; Kyle, *Religious Fringe*, 155-56; Moore, *Religious Outsiders*, 137.

95. Kyle, *Religious Fringe*, 156; Fuller, *Naming the Antichrist*, 152.

96. Tucker, *Another Gospel*, 123; Penton, "Eschatology of Jehovah's Witnesses," 175-79; Penton, *Apocalypse Delayed*, 18-22; Edward H. Abrahams, "The Pain of the Millennium: Charles Taze Russell and the Jehovah's Witnesses, 1879-1916," *American Studies* 18 (Spring 1977) 57-71.

97. St. Clair, *Millenarian Movements*, 325; Chandler, *Doomsday*, 92; Gray, "Eschatology of the Millennial Cults," 206; Curry, *Jehovah's Witnesses*, 101-3.

The Millennial Nation

Armageddon Christ will appear physically and reveal his wrath to all humanity. Russell also taught that during the period of Christ's invisible presence the saints will be invisibly raptured—a view resembling the teachings of John Nelson Darby and the Plymouth Brethren.[98]

By 1878 Russell began to differ with Barbour, developing his own distinct views. While his ideas resembled those of the earlier Adventists and millenarians, Russell shaped a twisted form of premillennial eschatology; he drew his ideas from a literal, contrived interpretation of Daniel and Revelation, and one non-biblical source—the Great Pyramid of Gizeh. Like certain medieval and Renaissance occultists he believed that God had designated the measurements of the Great Pyramid as an indicator of the end times.[99]

Russell also taught that Christ was choosing a church of 144,000 (Rev 7; 14:1). These spiritual Israelites will rule with Christ as king-priests during the millennium, at which time all of humanity will be raised. They will then learn God's will and have the opportunity to accept or reject it. Those who accept God's teachings will pass through Armageddon and live on the new Earth, the new Eden. At the close of the thousand-year period, Satan again will be loosed to deceive the nations. But God will destroy him.[100]

Russell believed that the harvest or gathering of the elect would be complete by 1881. Because Christ obviously did not return in 1881, Russell had to adjust his dates. Reinterpreting Daniel to his needs, he adjusted his biblical math by forty years—from 1874 to 1914. Russell also added a new wrinkle to his eschatology. In addition to 144,000 king-priests, there will be a second class of heavenly servants, referred to as the great company or sheep.[101]

As the Russellite movement grew after 1890, the date 1914 assumed great importance and continues to be a landmark year. On that date "Christ's active rule began," commencing in his judgment, and "his selecting the Watch Tower organization as his official channel" for governing his

---

98. Kyle, *Religious Fringe*, 156; Tucker, *Another Gospel*, 123; Chandler, *Doomsday*, 123; St. Clair, *Millenarian Movements*, 325; David A. Reed, "Whither the Watchtower?: An Unfolding Crisis for Jehovah's Witnesses," *Christian Research Journal* 16/1 (Summer 1993) 26.

99. Tucker, *Another Gospel*, 124; Penton, "Eschatology of the Jehovah's Witnesses," 178; Penton, *Apocalypse Delayed*, 24–29; Reed, "Whither the Watchtower?" 26.

100. St. Clair, *Millenarian Movements*, 326; Chandler, *Doomsday*, 93.

101. Chandler, *Doomsday*, 93–94; Moore, *Religious Outsiders*, 137; Timothy White, *A People for His Name* (New York: Vantage) 95–96.

earthly interests.[102] Russell predicted that 1914 "would see the destruction of the Gentile nations and the time of troubles that would lead to Armageddon." Thus the saints were to be taken "up to heaven with Christ, and the millennial rule of Christ over the Earth was to be inaugurated." The booming guns of World War I in 1914 convinced Russell that his millennial calendar was on target. His followers grew excited. The end was right around the corner. When it did not come in 1914, Russell slightly adjusted his timetable to 1918.[103]

But Russell did not live to see his prediction fail. He died in 1916. His followers were not prepared to see their leader die before the end of the world. They were even more disillusioned because Christ had not taken him physically up to heaven.[104]

Rutherford and Beyond

After Russell's death a power struggle ensued. Out of this dissension Joseph Franklin Rutherford (1869–1942) emerged as the leader of the Jehovah's Witnesses. Rutherford began a campaign to refigure some of Russell's eschatology, developing predictions of his own. Here we see clear evidence that "Biblical chronology is the play dough of millenarians. It can be stretched to fit whatever timetable is needed, or it can be reduced to a meaningless mass of dates and figures so that future predictions can be molded out of the original lump."[105] Rutherford accounted for the failed predictions regarding 1914 and 1918 by repudiating much of Russell's teachings. He then set forth a new chronology based on his interpretation of Daniel and Revelation. Rutherford argued that Christ has been invisibly present since 1914, not 1874, as Russell has said. The time of the end

---

102. Raymond Franz, *Crisis of Conscience: The Struggle between Loyalty to God and Loyalty to One's Religion* (Atlanta: Commentary, 1983) 343–44 (quote); Gray, "Eschatology of the Millennial Cults," 218; Curry, *Jehovah's Witnesses*, 108–12: White, *A People for His Name*, 86–88.

103. St. Clair, *Millenarian Movements*, 328 (quote); Chandler, *Doomsday*, 95; Penton, "Eschatology of Jehovah's Witnesses," 180; Curry, *Jehovah's Witnesses*," 113–14; Wilson, *Religious Sects*, 112–13; Charles S. Braden, *These Also Believe: A Study of Modern American Cults & Minority Religious Movements* (New York: Macmillan, 1957) 374–75.

104. St. Clair, *Millenarian Movements*, 328–29; Chandler, *Doomsday*, 95; Curry, *Jehovah's Witnesses*, 113–15; Penton, *Apocalypse Delayed*, 44–46.

105. Melvin D. Curry, Jr., "Jehovah's Witnesses: The Effects of Millenarianism on the Maintenance of a Religious Sect," Ph.D. diss., Florida State University, 1980, 243.

The Millennial Nation

had begun in 1914. On the whole, the rank-and-file Jehovah's Witnesses accepted this flip-flop with few murmurings.[106]

Rutherford now pointed to 1925 as a new date for the completion of all things. Inasmuch as the millennium was about to begin, he made his claim that "millions now living will never die." Further, because by 1918 the ranks of the 144,000 king-priests had been filled, he gave added attention to the great company, the second class of servants who would live on Earth and represent the earthly establishment of the kingdom of God.[107]

That the completion of all things did not come in 1925 became a serious problem for the Witnesses. Many had quit their jobs and sold their homes in the expectation that they would soon be living in an earthly paradise. This was another great disappointment, and thousands left the movement. Fifty years later, the Watchtower Society repudiated the 1925 prediction. The society even reported Rutherford's admission "that he made an ass of himself over 1925."[108]

But this debacle did not stop the Jehovah's Witnesses from making future predictions. To be sure, they held off for a while, waiting until 1966 to make another major prediction. In that year the Watchtower Society leaders pointed to 1975 as the probable date for the end of the world. Now declaring 4026 BCE to be the date for creation, they counted forward six thousand years.[109]

But doomsday did not come in 1975. Once again, the disillusioned Jehovah's Witnesses defected in droves. The society's leadership apologized for the misunderstanding over 1975. Still, they picked another date for doomsday—1984. Despite grumblings and defections the movement continues to grow. This growth is driven by the belief that the end of the world is right around the corner. By the late 1990s the Jehovah's Witnesses

---

106. Chandler, *Doomsday*, 96; Penton, "Eschatology of the Jehovah's Witnesses," 182; Penton, *Apocalypse Delayed*, 48–56; White, *A People for His Name*, 221–25.

107. Zygmunt, "Prophetic Failure and Chiliastic Identity," 936–37; Chandler, *Doomsday*, 96; Reed, "Whither the Watchtower," 28; Penton, "Eschatology of Jehovah's Witnesses," 182; Gray, "Eschatology of the Millennial Cults," 225–26; Curry, *Jehovah's Witnesses*, 115–18; White, *A People for His Name*, 251–58.

108. Penton, *Apocalypse Delayed*, 58 (quote); Tucker, *Another Gospel*, 125–28; Kyle, *Religious Fringe*, 157.

109. Chandler, *Doomsday*, 97–98; St. Clair, *Millenarian Movements*, 329; Penton, "Eschatology of the Jehovah's Witnesses," 183; Penton, *Apocalypse Delayed*, 99–101; Curry, *Jehovah's Witnesses*, 119–20; Rick Townsend, "When Christians Meet Jehovah's Witnesses," *Christian Herald*, April 1988, 38; Kenneth L. Woodward, "Are They False Witnesses?" *Newsweek*, 20 July 1981, 75; W.C. Stevenson, *Year of Doom*, 1975 London: Hutchinson, 1975).

appeared to be taking a more fluid approach to eschatology. They still insist that the end is near, but are not making any specific predictions. In fact, the society appears to be retreating from its position that 1914 was the beginning of the end.[110]

NATIVE AMERICAN MILLENNIALISTS

During the nineteenth century, white Christians did not have a corner on apocalyptic thinking. Two non-Caucasian groups—black Americans and Native Americans—experienced severe social dislocation. Among one group the apocalyptic element was significant; with the other it was minimal. Some Native American groups embraced an apocalyptic outlook—in part because they had a long history of millennial beliefs, in part because they had charismatic leaders to nurture such ideas.

With black Americans chiliastic expectations did not flourish. Why? The slave experience deprived blacks of much of their historical past—including African religious traditions with millennial dreams. After emancipation the former slaves focused more on issues of conversion and sanctification, not apocalyptic aspirations. African Americans were not without futuristic hopes, but they usually centered on achieving social justice within the current dimension.[111]

But our concern is with apocalyptic groups. Since early times the world of the Native Americans seemed endless. The dense forests, rolling plains, the majestic mountains of North America were Indian lands. Hunting, fishing, primitive agriculture, and food gathering sustained the Native Americans. But the coming of the Europeans ended all of this. For centuries white people encroached upon Indian lands, dramatically altering the Native American way of life.

With their world in disarray, the Native Americans experienced a cultural apocalypse. Faced with calamity and abandonment by their gods, they sought explanations. Native Americans longed to change the present order. Some looked for a return to an older, happier world; others looked

---

110. Tucker, *Another Gospel*, 140; Chandler, *Doomsday*, 98; Curry, *Jehovah's Witnesses*, 124–26; Penton *Apocalypse Delayed*, 99–101; Kenneth L. Woodward, "Apocalypse Later," *Newsweek*, 18 December 1995, 59; "Sect Postpones Armageddon," *Christianity Today*, 5 February 1996, 106.

111. Charles H. Lippy, "Waiting for the End: The Social Context of American Religion," in *Apocalyptic Vision in America*, 50–51; Keller, *Apocalypse Now and Then*, 200–01.

The Millennial Nation

for saviors to rescue and lead them to an improved future.[112] The shaman had traditionally been the mediator with the supernatural. Prophets and messiahs now came, presenting apocalyptic visions to the Native Americans and promising deliverance from the evil white man.[113]

This cultural apocalypse reached its climax in the last third of the nineteenth century. After 1840 the movement of the white Americans into the lands west of the Mississippi accelerated. As the Native Americans were forced onto reservations and their tribal culture came unraveled, hostility toward white Americans exploded. For these American Indians, the cultural, political, and economic situation was desperate.[114]

The solution was the ghost dance, a millennial movement that arose in 1870 and then again in 1890, primarily among the Rocky Mountain and Midwestern tribes. In both cases, charismatic Indian messiahs received apocalyptic revelations which prompted their followers to recall and expect a return to their history. For example, in 1890 the Paiute Indian "Wovoka taught that the time was coming when whites would be supernaturally destroyed and dead Native Americans would return to Earth." On that day game animals would be "restored to their original numbers, and the old way of life would flourish again on a reconstituted Earth where sickness and old age would be no more."[115] To hasten this great day, Native American messiahs instructed their followers to perform the ghost dance at regular intervals. The participants in this ceremony went into a trance. Visiting the spirit world and returning to the past, they conversed with dead relatives and caught glimpses of the old way of life.[116]

This new religion spread rapidly, encouraging great hostility toward whites. It set in motion a chain of events that culminated in the massacre at Wounded Knee in 1890. The ghost dance pointed to a new age that

---

112. Lippy, "Waiting for the End: The Social Context of American Religion," in *Apocalyptic Vision in America*, 50–51; Keller, *Apocalypse Now and Then*, 200–201.

113. Lippy, "Waiting for the End," 50; Rubinsky and Wiseman, *End of the World*, 103–7.

114. Thomas W. Overholt, *Channels of Prophecy* (Minneapolis: Fortress, 1989) 27; Lippy, "Waiting for the End," 49.

115. Overholt, *Channels of Prophecy*, 27–28; (quote); Overholt, "The Ghost Dance of 1890 and the Nature of the Prophetic Process," *Ethnohistory* 21 (1974) 37–63; Barkun, *Disaster and Millennium*, 15; J. Mooney, "The Ghost-Dance Religion and the Sioux Outbreak of 1890," *Annual Report of the Bureau of American Ethnology* 14 (Washington, DC: Government Printing Office, 1896); William Willoya and Vinson Brown, *Warriors of the Rainbow: Strange and Prophetic Indian Dreams* (Happy Camp, CA: Naturegraph, 1962) 61–64.

116. Overholt, *Channels of Prophecy*, 28; Albanese, *America*, 44.

would bring the destruction of the oppressive white culture. On the whole, however, it represented more a restoration of a past golden age than the introduction of a radically new age. At its core was a yearning for a transformation of the present.[117]

APOCALYPTICISM AMERICAN STYLE

Apocalypticism has reared its head throughout American history. Millennialism in its various forms has been far more central to the American experience than it was in Europe. Still, apocalyptic thinking has not been constant. From the seventeenth through the nineteenth centuries, it had its ups and downs—often in response to social, economic, and political instability.

The interest in apocalyptic matters has frequently been generated by prominent individuals. At times apocalyptic thinking has been stimulated by the pens of theologians such as Cotton Mather and Jonathan Edwards. But more often it has been shaped by prophets or charismatic figures, that is, by individuals whose authority rests on their own rare ability and gifts. Normally, their pronouncements are not recognized by the established ecclesiastical structure. Rather, they often gain their following by oratory, emotional preaching, or a charismatic personality. William Miller's profile does not quite fit this pattern. Still, our generalization does apply to the leaders of most nineteenth-century fringe religions—the Shakers, Mormons, Christadelphians, Seventh-day Adventists, Jehovah's Witnesses, and Native American groups.[118]

From the seventeenth through nineteenth centuries, apocalyptic thinking in America was largely driven by three factors—carryovers from Britain, America's millennial mission, and social change. Seventeenth-century England seethed with apocalyptic activities ideas that the Puritans brought with them to the New World. Thus early Puritan apocalypticism was largely an adaptation of British millennialism adjusted to suit the American scene. This Americanization of apocalyptic thinking continued apace in the eighteenth century, fueled by such events as the Great Awakening and the Revolutionary War. More often than not, optimistic postmillennialism dominated end-time thinking well into the nineteenth century. It furthered the utopian vision of America as God's instrument for ushering in the golden age.

---

117. Lippy, "Waiting for the End," 50; Overholt, *Channels of Prophecy*, 28; Chandler, *Doomsday*, 194–96.

118. Lippy, "Waiting for the End," 37–39.

The Millennial Nation

But events would revive premillennialism with its more catastrophic view of the end. The Lisbon earthquake and the French Revolution were thought to signal some ominous apocalyptic events. In addition, much of the first half of the nineteenth century vibrated with social change. The growth of industrialization, urbanization, democracy, and slavery created an atmosphere conducive to apocalypticism. Revivalism, pietism, perfectionism, romanticism, Darwinism, and fundamentalism all combined to drive apocalyptic ideas to their greatest level of excitement since that reached in seventeenth-century England.

Building on the millennial thinking prior to 1900, contemporary end-time prophets have continued to Americanize the apocalypse. While the image of the United States has been tarnished in recent years, many still embrace America's millennial mission. Often this mission comes in secular clothes, such as spreading democracy and human rights to the world. While diminished, civil religion and the Christian view of America are not dead. As in the years prior to 1900, end-time thinking and speculations are still most identified with evangelical Christianity. Such Christians usually embrace premillennialism, but postmillennialism—the dominant view in the nineteenth-century—is experiencing a revival in some circles in modern America.

4

The End Takes Shape

"And as he sat upon the Mount of Olives, the disciples came to him privately, saying, Tell us . . . what shall be the sign of thy coming, and of the end of the world?" (Matt 24:3). Christ answered this question in general terms—wars, rumors of wars, false teachings, false prophets, and an increase in wickedness. Throughout Christian history apocalyptic thinkers have seen these signs as occurring in their time. In the late twentieth and early twenty-first centuries, this end-time watching may have reached epic proportions. Prophecy buffs have gone to great lengths to match specific contemporary events with texts from Ezekiel, Daniel, and Revelation. In doing so, they have constructed an elaborate prophetic jigsaw puzzle. But unlike most puzzles this one has a chameleon-like character—it has been regularly adjusted to suit the changes in current events.

Millenarian expectations have erupted at the edges of Christian societies since the Middle Ages. However, the doom boom of the late twentieth and early twenty-first centuries has a unique twist. The framework is the twenty and twenty-first centuries' political, military, and religious developments. But most important, as Michael Barkun puts it, "the apparatus of modern communications—cable television, video recording, [the Internet, face-booking,] and mass market paperbacks—has brought apocalyptic themes from the theological and social margins . . . into the main stream of American cultural awareness." Not since the years before

The End Takes Shape

the Civil War have so many Americans been exposed to so many apocalyptic ideas.[1]

In recent times, many Americans have accepted these end-time predictions. As the second millennium wound down, polls confirmed this impression. According to a 1983 Gallup poll, 62 percent of Americans had "no doubt" that Jesus Christ will return. A 1994 *U.S. News and World Report* poll found that 60 percent of Americans believed that the world will end; about a third thought it will end in the near future. Closely related, over 61 percent believe in the Second Coming of Christ. And this sense of an end did not abate with the coming and going of the year 2000. In fact September 11 has encouraged apocalyptic thinking. According to a 2002 *Time*/CNN poll, "since 9/11 more than one-third of Americans have been thinking more seriously about how current events might be leading to the end of the world." Indeed, "59 percent thought that events predicted in Revelation were being fulfilled." Furthermore, "almost one in five expected to live long enough to see the end of the world."[2] Since 9/11 more events have prompted eschatological speculations. A short list would include the election of Barack Obama, Muslim terrorism, and the Mayan calendar. While most of these Americans may not have formulated specific end-time ideas, they sense that history is at a turning point.

Apocalyptic themes today generally rest on the theology of Protestant fundamentalism, especially the dispensational variety. While fundamentalism and dispensationalism overlap substantially, they are not identical. There are fundamentalists who are not dispensationalists and vice versa. Also, not all fundamentalists are premillennialists.[3]

Fundamentalism is a broader movement than dispensationalism. George Marsden has defined it as "militantly anti-modernist evangelical

1. Michael Barkun, "The Language of Apocalypse: Premillennialists and Nuclear War," in *The God Pumpers: Religion in the Electronic Age*, eds. Marshall W. Fishwick and Ray B. Browne (Bowling Green, OH: Bowling Green State University Popular Press, 1987) 159 (quote); Robert Jewett, "Coming to Terms with the Doom Boom," *Quarterly Review* 4/3 (Fall 1984) 18.

2. Timothy P. Weber, "Dispensational and Historic Premillennialism as Popular Movements," in *A Case for Historic Premillennialism: An Alternative to "Left Behind" Eschatology*, eds. Craig L. Blomberg and Sung Wook Chung (Grand Rapids: Baker, 2009) 1-2 (quote); Alvin P. Sanoff, "The Faces of Doomsday," *U.S. News and World Report*, 19 October 1992, 73; Paul Boyer, " A Brief History of the End of Time," *New Republic*, 17 May 1993; Jeffery L. Sheler, "The Christmas Covenant," *U.S. News and World Report*, 19 December 1994, 62.

3. George Marsden, *Fundamentalism and American Culture: The Shaping of Twentieth Century Evangelicalism, 1870–1925* (New York: Oxford University Press, 1980) 44.

Protestantism."[4] It draws from a variety of religious traditions, including dispensationalism.[5] But while fundamentalism is primarily a religious phenomenon, it can also be seen as a social reaction to the forces of modern urbanized, industrialized America. Fundamentalism's confrontational approach to the modern world has promoted an apocalyptic outlook within its ranks.

Dispensationalism is a theology with its own distinctives. One of these features is a particular version of premillennialism, which is built into the system. There are about 18–25 million premillennialists in America, the vast majority being dispensationalists.[6] While these people may not have an in depth understanding of dispensationalism, they embrace its popular concepts and in fact may not even be aware of other perspectives. This dispensational premillennialism has been the primary driving force behind the end-time thinking that has gripped modern America. As the key vehicle since the mid twentieth century for conveying apocalyptic ideas, it deserves serious scrutiny. So the next several chapters will deal with aspects of premillennialism, especially the dispensational variety. Chapter 4 will note the developments before 1945, chapter 5 will focus on what has happened in the late twentieth century, and aspects of several more chapters will place the spotlight on early twenty-first-century activities and beliefs.

CLASSIC DISPENSATION ESCHATOLOGY IN A NUTSHELL

We have already briefly encountered dispensational theology in chapter 2. It began with John Nelson Darby. Classic dispensationalism divides history into ages, contending that God tests humanity differently in each dispensation. It separates Israel from the church, insisting that we are

---

4. George Marsden, "Fundamentalism," in *Eerdmans' Handbook to Christianity in America*, ed. Mark Noll et al. (Grand Rapids: Eerdmans, 1983) 384.

5. Ernest R. Sandeen, "Towards a Historical Interpretation of the Origins of Fundamentalism," *Church History* 36/1 (1967) 82; Ernest R. Sandeen, "Fundamentalism and American Identity," *Annals of the American Academy of Political and Social Science* 387 (January 1970) 57–58; George Marsden, "Fundamentalism as an American Phenomenon: A Comparison with English Evangelicalism," *Church History* 46/2 (1977) 225–26; Marsden, *Fundamentalism and American Culture*, 5, 224.

6. Weber, "Dispensationalism and Historic Premillennialism as Popular Movements," 18–19. See also Timothy P. Weber, "Happily at the Edge of the Abyss: Popular Premillennialism in America," *Ex Auditu* 6 (1991) 87.

The End Takes Shape

currently living in the church age. In respect to eschatology, dispensationalism's distinctive is the secret, "any moment" rapture.

Resting on a literal interpretation of the prophetic passages, dispensational eschatology is overwhelmingly premillennial and pretribulational. The specifics (nations and individuals) have changed since Darby. Yet with classic dispensationalism and those who have popularized this tradition, the outline remains essentially the same.

By means of a secret rapture, millions of Christians will suddenly vanish. Snatched up to heaven to meet Christ in the clouds, they will not have to face the trials that are to come upon the Earth. This disappearing act ushers in the seven-year tribulation. For the first three and a half years, human conditions gradually deteriorate. Meanwhile, political and military power shifts to a European confederacy led by the Antichrist. This strong man miraculously survives a head wound and gains unprecedented power. At a point of crisis he orchestrates a seven-year peace treaty in the Middle East. However, the Antichrist, who bears Satan's mark—666—then demonstrates his true nature. About midway through the tribulation he and his assistant, the false prophet, terrorize the world and compel everyone to bear the mark 666 on their hands or forehead.

At this point the Antichrist moves to Jerusalem from Rome, where he has been ruling. In the rebuilt temple of Jerusalem he blasphemes God, breaks the peace pact and persecutes Israel. All chaos breaks out—looting, famines, pollution, plagues, drug abuse, occultism, demon possession, economic dislocations, and lawlessness are rampant. Natural disasters abound: earthquakes destroy the land, the weather becomes bizarre, and stars fall from the sky.

Then, as history draws to a close, a great battle takes place. Armies from the North, the Far East, and Arab nations meet on the mountain of Megiddo in Israel. The bloody battle of Armageddon rages for about a year, killing millions of people. Jesus Christ now appears, destroying what is left of the armies and throwing the Antichrist and the false prophet into the lake of fire. The long-awaited millennium—the thousand-year utopia—now begins. From Jerusalem, Jesus and his saints will rule the world.

But this is not the end. After the thousand years of peace, Satan is released from the bottomless pit. Organizing an army for the final battle, he challenges God for one last time. Fire comes down from heaven, destroying these satanic forces, and the devil is cast into the lake of fire. The dead are now resurrected for the last judgment. The individuals whose names are not found in the book of life are cast into hell forever. God now creates a new heaven and a new Earth. Peace and joy will now reign forever.[7]

THE RISE OF DISPENSATIONALISM

The last half of the nineteenth century witnessed two significant shifts in respect to end-time thinking. The dominant postmillennialism gave way to premillennialism. And within premillennialism, futuristic dispensationalism supplanted the old historicist version. These two important changes have largely shaped the apocalyptic outlook of evangelical Protestantism—a subculture that has become the dominant eschatological voice in modern America. Dispensational premillennialism also established its dominance over historic premillennialism and its posttribulational view of Christ's return. This cannot be seen as a major shift because historic premillennialism, with its view that Christians will go through the tribulation, has never been popular in the modern world.

In 1860 the majority of Protestants embraced postmillennialism, but by the early twentieth century it had largely disappeared. In part, this change occurred because many evangelicals defected to the growing premillennial ranks. To some extent, the rise of premillennialism and the decline of postmillennialism can be seen as two sides of the same coin. But this is only part of the story. Postmillennialism also gradually receded among the more moderate to liberal Protestants, but they did not embrace premillennialism instead.[8]

Several factors contributed to the erosion of postmillennialism. Evangelical postmillennialism had gradually acquired a secular character. Previously, evangelicals had seen God and humanity as working hand in hand to usher in the thousand-year golden age. Some Protestants now began to equate the kingdom of God with America; others came under the influence of the new biblical criticism associated with theological

---

7. This general information can be found in a number of contemporary dispensational sources: Hal Lindsey, *The Late Great Planet Earth* (Grand Rapids: Zondervan, 1970); John F. Walvoord, *Armageddon, Oil and the Middle East Crisis* (rev. ed.; Grand Rapids: Zondervan, 1990); Jimmy Swaggart, *Armageddon: The Future of Planet Earth* (Baton Rouge, LA: Jimmy Swaggart Ministries, 1987); Billy Graham, *Approaching Hoofbeats: The Four Horsemen of the Apocalypse* (New York: Avon, 1983). Aspects of our summary were taken from Russell Chandler, *Doomsday: The End of the World, A View through Time* (Ann Arbor, MI: Servant, 1993) 228–30.

8. James H. Moorhead, "The Erosion of Postmillennialism in American Religious Thought, 1865–1925," *Church History*, 53/1 (1984) 61.

The End Takes Shape

liberalism. These new biblical studies undercut the supernaturalness of the Christian faith, including the apocalyptic elements of Daniel and Revelation and the Second Coming of Christ.[9]

Changing conditions in the late nineteenth and early twentieth centuries also tarnished postmillennialism. Postmillennialism rests on the premise that the world will get better and better. The Civil War, the decline of evangelicalism, the influx of Catholicism, and the outbreak of World War I cast a shadow across this optimistic outlook. In the eyes of many, the situation was getting worse and worse. Under these circumstances postmillennialism became less believable.[10]

Historicism versus Dispensationalism

Premillennialism's resurgence after the Civil War surprised most American evangelicals. Postmillennialism was still riding high, and premillennialism had been dealt a staggering blow by the Millerite fiasco. But circumstances would soon change, notably within the ranks of premillennialism itself. The Great Disappointment of 1844 had decimated historicist premillennialism, but a futurist premillennialism called dispensationalism soon arrived on the scene. This new perspective not only revived premillennialism, but became the dominant evangelical eschatology in the twentieth century.[11]

Historicist and futurist premillennialism differ at significant points. The historicist version looks back—contending that Revelation describes various periods in Christian history. It locks the interpreter into millennial arithmetic and makes date setting an irresistible temptation. Herein lies a potential for disaster. Many historicists set dates—thereby making themselves the laughing stock of the evangelical movement.[12] By contrast the dispensationalists adopt a futurist interpretation of John's Apocalypse. This approach looks forward—insisting that Revelation points to events

---

9. Moorhead, "The Erosion of Postmillennialism," 63–75; Robert G. Clouse, "The New Christian Right, America, and the Kingdom of God," *Christian Scholar's Review* 12 (1983) 6–8.

10. Timothy P. Weber, *Living in the Shadow of the Second Coming: American Premillenialism (1875–1925)* (New York: Oxford University Press, 1979) 41–42.

11. Douglas W. Frank, *Less Than Conquerers* (Grand Rapids: Eerdmans, 1986) 68–69; Weber, "Dispensational and Historic Premillennialism," 18–19.

12. Ernest Sandeen, *The Roots of Fundamentalism: British and American Millenarianism, 1800–1930* (Chicago: University of Chicago Press, 1970) 54, 59; Stanley D. Walters, "The World Will End in 1919," *Asbury Theological Journal* 44/1 (1989) 29–37.

beyond this current age. Thus no prophecy has to be fulfilled before Christ's return.[13]

Here lies the genius of dispensationalism. It does not lock itself into a specific schedule for the Second Advent. On one hand, it avoids setting exact dates for Christ's return (though some dispensationalists have fallen into this trap). On the other, it maintains an intense expectancy for the secret rapture.[14] Christ could return at any time. Yet he might delay his return for years. While the historicist premillennialists were wedded to an exact millennial arithmetic, the dispensationalists lived with "maybes." They did not dare quit their jobs or sell their homes. Their understanding of prophecy lacked the precision of the Millerites and "forced them to live in the tension of now/not yet."[15]

Nevertheless, the dispensationalists did maintain a countdown for Christ's return. Drawing from passages in Daniel 9, they reckoned from Artaxerxes' decree to rebuild Jerusalem. But their arithmetic was different from that of the Millerites. The Messiah was to return at the end of Daniel's seventieth week (490 years). But the Roman authorities had crucified Christ 483 years (69 weeks) after Artaxerxes' decree.[16] The dispensationalists extricated themselves from this difficulty by devising a postponement theory. When the Jews rejected Christ as their Messiah, God suspended his prophetic schedule at the end of Daniel's sixty-ninth week. Therefore, Christ did not return, and God turned his attention away from Israel to the Gentiles.[17]

With their postponement theory the dispensationalists strictly separated Israel from the church—thereby significantly impacting their eschatology. Given God's postponement of his prophetic timetable, it was understood that none of the prophecies point directly to the Christian church. Instead the church stands in a "mysterious, prophetic time warp, a 'great parentheses.'" The dispensationalists believed that God would not

13. Weber, *Living in the Shadow*, 16–17; Sandeen, *Roots of Fundamentalism*, 62–64. See also George E. Ladd, *The Blessed Hope* (Grand Rapids: Eerdmans, 1956) 35–40.

14. Chandler, *Doomsday*, 103; Sandeen, *Roots of Fundamentalism*, 64.

15. Weber, *Living in the Shadow*, 46–48.

16. Weber, "Happily at the Edge of the Abyss," 89; Weber, *Living in the Shadow*, 19; C. I. Scofield, ed., *Scofield Reference Bible* (New York: Oxford University Press, 1909) 914–15. See also Alva McClain, *Daniel's Prophecy of the Seventy Weeks* (Grand Rapids: Zondervan, 1940) 12–15.

17. Martin Marty, *Modern American Religion: The Irony of It All, 1893–1919* (Chicago: University of Chicago Press, 1986) 224; Daniel Fuller, "The Hermeneutics of Dispensationalism," ThD diss., Northern Baptist Seminary, 1957, 287–337; Weber, *Living in the Shadow*, 19–20.

The End Takes Shape

deal with the church and Israel at the same time; God would remove the church from Earth before proceeding with his final plans for Israel.[18]

The historicists and dispensationalists also differed over the nature of the Second Advent. The dispensationalists taught that Christ's return would be a secret event evident only to the raptured saints. The historicists had insisted that it would be a dramatic public event. In effect, the dispensationalists contended that the Second Coming will occur in two stages: the church will be removed in a secret rapture; then, after the tribulation, Christ will return in a public event.[19]

The Arrival of Darbyism in America

Darby's prophetic views spread throughout Britain and Europe. After the Civil War they also caught on in America, where they had their greatest impact. By World War I dispensationalism had won many adherents among American evangelicals. In a modified form Darby's influence on end-time thinking in America has been immense—perhaps more than that of anyone else in the last two centuries.[20]

Between 1859 and 1872 Darby traveled extensively in the United States teaching his distinctive dispensationalism. He won many prominent ministers and laypersons to his teachings, especially in Presbyterian and Baptist circles. A number of evangelicals embraced most of his dispensationalism, including the secret rapture of Christians. Yet few accepted his views regarding the strict separation from the "apostate" denominations. To his dismay, evangelicals did not regard the denominational structure of the churches as hopelessly corrupt.[21]

Another English prophecy writer, Sir Robert Anderson (1841–1918)—an investigator for Scotland Yard and a staunch Darbyite—influenced American evangelicalism. His book *The Coming Prince* (1882) gained an immediate American audience, going through eleven

---

18. Weber, *Living in the Shadow*, 19–20 (quote); Clarence Bass, *Backgrounds to Dispensationalism: Its Historical Genesis and Ecclesiastical Implications* (Grand Rapids: Eerdmans, 1960) 129–39.

19. Sandeen, *Roots of Fundamentalism*, 62–64; Bass, *Backgrounds to Dispensationalism*, 38–39.

20. J. Gordon Melton, *The Encyclopedia of American Religions* (Wilmington, NC: McGrath, 1978) 1:415–16.

21. Jon R. Stone, *A Guide to the End of the World: Popular Eschatology in America* (New York: Garland, 1993) 34; Sandeen, *Roots of Fundamentalism*, 74–76.

editions—one as late as 1986.²² As an avid prophecy scholar, Anderson added some wrinkles to Darby's system. For example, beginning with the usual assumption that a day equals a year, he argued that Daniel's 69 weeks refers to the period between Artaxerxes' command to restore Jerusalem and the coming of the Messiah Prince. This designation of 483 years (69 x 7 = 483) foretold Christ's triumphant entry into Jerusalem.²³

Moody Promotes Premillennialism

By the 1870s the great evangelist Dwight L. Moody (1837-99) was preaching the premillennial return of Christ. The source of his premillennialism is uncertain. His conversion to this doctrine may have been due to contacts with the Plymouth Brethren on a visit to England. Or Darby may have been persuasive on a trip to Chicago.

Moody's theology can hardly be described as systematic. Thus he made no clear distinction between the nuances within premillennialism—for example, between the pretribulational rapture and the posttribulational coming.²⁴ He did, however, contribute significantly to the rise of dispensationalism. His followers did not shy away from declaring their allegiance to the tenet that the pretribulational rapture could occur at any moment.

Nearly every evangelist after Moody followed in Darby's train. Included would be Billy Sunday, Reuben A. Torrey, W. J. Erdman, J. Wilbur Chapman and George Needham. A number of leaders in the evangelical missions movement also embraced Darbyism. Among them was A. B. Simpson, who founded the Christian and Missionary Alliance, and Robert Speer of Presbyterian missions.²⁵

---

22. Paul Boyer, *When Time Shall Be No More* (Cambridge, MA: Harvard University Press, 1992) 90-91.

23. Sir Robert Anderson, *The Coming Prince* (Grand Rapids: Kregel, 1986 [reprint]) 3, 124, 131; McClain, *Daniel's Prophecy of the Seventy Weeks*.

24. Stanley N. Gundry, *Love Them In: The Proclamation Theology of D. L. Moody* (Chicago: Moody, 1976) 179-89; James F. Findlay Jr., *Dwight L. Moody: American Evangelist, 1837-1899* (Grand Rapids: Baker, 1973) 125-28, 260-61; Stanley N. Gundry, "Demythologizing Moody," in *Mr. Moody and the Evangelical Tradition*, ed. Timothy George (London: T. & T. Clark, 2004) 25.

25. Weber, *Living in the Shadow*, 32-33; Chandler, *Doomsday*, 104, 106, Gundry, *Love Them In*, 180-81; Marsden, *Fundamentalism and American Culture*, 46-47; Roger Martin, *R.A. Torrey* (Murfreesboro, TN: Sword of the Lord, 1976) 88-100.

The End Takes Shape

Promotion by the Networks

Moody and his successors established networks to promote the new premillennialism. A number of Bible schools sprang up, at least fifty of which spread the dispensational message—the most prominent being Chicago's Moody Bible Institute, the Bible Institute of Los Angeles (Biola), and the Northwestern Bible Training School of Minneapolis. Almost without exception these Bible institutes taught the secret pretribulational rapture. So did a number of evangelical magazines, including Arno Gaebelein's *Our Hope*, James Brooke's *The Truth*, and Charles Trumbull's *Sunday School Times*.[26]

Among the institutions spreading the new premillennialism, the Bible conferences loomed large. At a series of Bible prophecy conferences from about 1875 to 1900 the dispensationalists encountered other conservative evangelicals and won many converts to their cause. The dispensationalists gradually came to dominate the other premillennialists, especially the posttribulationists. By addressing issues other than eschatology these meetings forged the new premillennialism into a protodenominational movement with larger doctrinal concerns and much energy.[27]

Fundamentalists and Dispensationalists Close Ranks

In the last half of the nineteenth century, evangelical Protestantism came under attack from several quarters—liberal theology, Darwinsim, and the social gospel.[28] In such a climate the evangelicals circled their wagons. They systematized their beliefs in *The Fundamentals* (1910-15), a series of volumes that set forth what evangelicals believed to be the heart of the

---

26. Boyer, *When Time Shall Be No More*, 92; Weber, *Living in the Shadow*, 33-34; William V. Trollinger Jr., *God's Empire: William Bell Riley and Midwestern Fundamentalism* (Madison: University of Wisconsin Press, 1990) 84; Marsden, *Fundamentalism and American Culture*, 32-39; James Davidson Hunter, *American Evangelicalism*, (New Brunswick, NJ: Rutgers University Press, 1983) 27; David A. Rausch, "Arno C. Gaebelein (1861-1945) Fundamentalist Protestant Zionist," *American Jewish History* 68 (September 1978) 44-55.

27. Sandeen, *Roots of Fundamentalism*, 132-43; C. Norman Kraus, *Dispensationalism in America: Its Rise and Development* (Chicago: Moody, 1965) 71-80; Weber, *Living in the Shadow*, 26-28; Stone, *Guide to the End of the World*, 47-48; Frank, *Less than Conquerers*, 69, 75.

28. See William R. Hutchinson, *The Modernist Impulse in American Protestantism* (Durham, NC: Duke University Press, 1992) 76-110; Kenneth Cauthen, *The Impact of American Religious Liberalism* (New York: Harper & Row, 1962) 209-20.

Christian faith—the inerrancy of Scripture, the virgin birth of Jesus, the resurrection, and the physical return of Christ.[29]

In this struggle against theological liberalism the evangelicals sought allies. At first the new premillennialists were suspect. Most evangelicals did not embrace their teaching of a secret rapture at any moment. But the dispensationalists did staunchly uphold the basic Christian beliefs. So the evangelical mainstream gradually welcomed the new premillennialists into their ranks—a step that did much to legitimize their eschatology. And eventually the dispensationalists won over many evangelicals to their belief in a secret rapture.[30]

Scofield and His Bible

By the early twentieth century, dispensationalism had caught on in a big way among American evangelicals. Cyrus Ingerson Scofield (1843–1921) had a lot to do with this development. Although dispensationalism has no classic statement equivalent to communism's *Das Kapital*, *The Scofield Reference Bible* has done much to shape the movement. James Barr has described it as "perhaps the most important single document in all fundamentalist literature."[31]

In some ways Scofield lived two lives—before and after conversion. He fought for the Confederacy during the Civil War. After the war he married, studied law, and began a practice in Kansas. Scofield then abandoned his wife, who later divorced him. Jailed in 1879 in St. Louis for forgery, he experienced a conversion while in prison. He then fell under the influence of the Darbyite pastor James Brookes and also met Dwight Moody.[32]

---

29. Marsden, *Fundamentalism and American Culture*, 118–23; C. Allyn Russell, *Voices of American Fundamentalism* (Philadelphia: Westminister, 1976) 18–19; Sandeen, *Roots of Fundamentalism*, 188–207. See also Louis Gasper, *The Fundamentalist Movement* (The Hague: Mouton, 1968: S. G. Cole, *The History of Fundamentalism* (New York: R. R. Smith, 1931).

30. Weber, *Living in the Shadow*, 27–42; Marsden, *Fundamentalism and American Culture*, 124–25; Sandeen, *Roots of Fundamentalism*, 162–64; Frank, *Less than Conquerers*, 92–93; "Our Future Hope: Eschatology and Its Role in the Church," *Christianity Today*, 6 February 1987, 6–10.

31. James Barr, *Fundamentalism* (Philadelphia: Westminister, 1977) 45. See also Marty, *Modern American Religion*, 219–20; Robert C. Fuller, *Naming the Antichrist: The History of an American Obsession* (New York: Oxford University Press, 1995) 125–26.

32. For more on Scofield's life see J. M. Canfield, *The Incredible Scofield and His Book* (Vallecito, CA: Ross House, 1988); Charles G. Trumbull, *The Life Story of C. I. Scofield* (New York: Oxford University Press, 1920); William A. BeVier, "C. I. Scofield:

The End Takes Shape

In 1882 Scofield became the pastor of a Congregational church in Dallas. Here he wrote *Rightly Dividing the Word of Truth* (1888), a classic and still in print, and began a monthly publication, *The Believer*. In 1895 he left Dallas to engage in a number of activities, including teaching at Moody's school and participating in Bible conferences. By 1902 he devoted himself full-time to writing and speaking tours.[33]

Scofield's enduring legacy rests on his *Reference Bible*, published in 1909, expanded in 1917, and revised in 1967. Sales of this Bible total about ten million. The Scofield Bible immediately became the standard of dispensationalism, and for ninety years was the major vehicle for distributing dispensational ideas.[34]

Scofield's *Reference Bible* packages dispensationalism in an attractive format. It provides paragraphing, cross-references, and notes to the King James Bible that reflect Darby's dispensationalism. Unlike most commentators, who put some distance between the biblical text and their notes, Scofield placed his notes and the biblical text on the same page.[35] As a result, his comments often acquired the authority of Scripture. *The Scofield Reference Bible* has been "subtly but powerfully influential in spreading [Darby's] views among hundreds of thousands who have regularly read the Bible and who often have been unaware of the distinction between the ancient text and the Scofield interpretation." Readers often fail to remember where they first encountered a particular idea—in Scofield's notes or in the biblical text.[36]

Scofield defines a dispensation as a "period of time during which man is tested in respect of obedience to some specific revelation of the will of God." His seven dispensations refine Darby's basic ages: innocence, conscience, human government, promise, law, grace, and the kingdom.

Dedicated and Determined," *Fundamentalist Journal* 2/9 (October 1983) 37–56.

33. C. I. Scofield, *Rightly Dividing the Word of Truth* (Neptune, NJ: Loizeaux, n.d.) BeVier, "C. I. Scofield," 39; John D. Hannah, "Cyrus Ingerson Scofield," in *Dictionary of Christianity in America*, ed. Daniel G. Reid et al. (Downers Grove, IL: InterVarsity, 1990) 1057–58.

34. Melton, *Encylopedia of American Religions*, 1:416–17; Boyer, *When Time Shall Be No More*, 97–98; C. W. Whiteman, "Scofield Reference Bible," in *Dictionary of Christianity in America*, 1058; Fuller, *Naming the Antichrist*, 125.

35. Sandeen, *Roots of Fundamentalism*, 222; Boyer, *When Time Shall Be No More*, 98; Chandler, *Doomsday*, 106.

36. Sandeen, *Roots of Fundamentalism*, 222 (quote); Stanley J. Grenz, *The Millennial Maze: Sorting Out the Evangelical Options* (Downers Grove, IL: InterVarsity, 1992) 93.

Each age ends in human failure and divine judgment for this shortcoming.[37] Thus a sense of apocalypticism pervades Scofield's thinking. Except for the final dispensation, little progress can be seen in his view of history. Like most premillennialists he regarded human nature as contemptible and held little hope for the betterment of society. Humanity was moving down the road to destruction. Like other premillennialists he also predicted that the Jews would return to Palestine in the last days and identified Russia with Gog of Ezekiel 38. Then will come the final dispensation, which will usher in both destruction and triumph. After Christ raptures the church, the terrible tribulation will begin. Christ will then return and rule for a thousand years.[38]

STANDING AT ARMAGEDDON

During the first fifty years of the twentieth century, the world stood at the brink of Armageddon. The talk of wars and rumors of wars made a particularly deep impression at this time. "All our present peace plans will end in the most awful wars and conflicts this old world ever saw," said Reuben A. Torrey in 1913.[39]

The years after 1914 gave premillennialism a tremendous boost. This era witnessed tragedy after tragedy. But "things were never better for American premillennialism."[40] The basic prophecies of the early dispensationalists in the nineteenth century began to take concrete form in the early twentieth century. In the eyes of the dispensationalists, world war, the return of the Jews to Palestine, the Russian Revolution, the redrawing of the European map, and rise of totalitarianism were all predicted in Scripture. Indeed, most of the major themes so conspicuous in modern popular dispensationalism had taken shape before World War II, the only exceptions being the threat of nuclear annihilation, control of the masses by the Antichrist through television and computers, and the emerging Islamic threat.[41]

37. Scofield, *Scofield Reference Bible*, 5. See also Kraus, *Dispensationalism in America*, 114.

38. Marty, *Modern American*, 220–21; C. I. Scofield, *What Do the Prophets Say?* (Philadelphia: Sunday School Times, 1918) 161; Boyer, *When Time Shall Be No More*, 98–99; Fuller, *Naming the Antichrist*, 128–29.

39. Reuben A. Torrey, *The Return of the Lord Jesus* (Los Angeles: Bible Institute of Los Angeles, 1913) 89.

40. Weber, *Living in the Shadow*, 105.

41. Boyer, *When Time Shall Be No More*, 102; Sandeen, *Roots of Fundamentalism*, 224–26.

The End Takes Shape

The apparent fulfillment of ancient biblical prophecies enabled dispensationalism to take solid root in the evangelical subculture. Within premillennialism the tenet of rapture at any moment had prevailed over the posttribulationists. In Pentecostalism and early fundamentalism dispensational premillennialism had taken hold. Further, the modernist/fundamentalist conflict of the late 1920s fragmented many denominations. What emerged was a separatist fundamentalism with its own churches, schools, mission agencies, and publishing houses. Dispensationalism thus had a subculture and an institutional structure to perpetuate itself.[42]

Armageddon Almost

The guns of August 1914 glued the attention of prophecy buffs to current events. Prophecy was being fulfilled before their very eyes—so they believed. World War I and related events roused interest to a high level of expectancy. The apparent apocalyptic happenings moved the new premillennialism out of its narrow confines. In fact, the war gave premillennialism its widest audience since the rise of dispensationalism.[43]

The new premillennialism had a script for the last days, and remarkably enough, current events seemed to be following it. Premillennialists held fast to their established positions. The prophetic clock, which had stopped since the time of Christ, now began to tick.[44]

Some premillennialsits saw World War I literally as the opening shot of a prophetic Armageddon. They believed Scripture spoke of a terrible war, the secret rapture of believers, and then Armageddon. "We are not yet in the Armageddon struggle proper, but at its commencement, and it may be . . . that Christ will come before the present war closes, and before Armageddon," stated *The Weekly Evangel*. Scofield saw World War I as the death struggle of the world system with the kingdom of God to follow.[45]

---

42. Joel Carpenter, "A Shelter in the Time of Storm: Fundamentalist Institutions and the Rise of Evangelical Protestantism, 1929-1942," *Church History* 49/1 (1980) 62-75; Weber, "Happily at the Edge of the Abyss," 90; Marsden, *Fundamentalism and American Culture*, 192-95; Sandeen, *Roots of Fundamentalism*, 219-22.

43. Dwight Wilson, *Armageddon Now!: The Premillenarian Response to Russia and Israel since 1917* (Grand Rapids: Baker, 1977) 37-39; Boyer, *When Time Shall Be No More*, 100-101; Weber, *Living in the Shadow*, 105-6, 115; Sandeen, *Roots of Fundamentalism*, 233. For a description of the early events of World War I see Barbara Tuchman, *The Guns of August* (New York: Dell, 1962).

44. Weber, *Living in the Shadow*, 105-6.

45. Wilson, *Armageddon Now!*, 36-38; *Weekly Evangel*, 10 April 1917, 3; C. I.

The Balfour Declaration of 1917 aroused even more end-time expectations. With the exception of the Millerites, most premillennialists had placed great importance on the Jews and events in Palestine. In fact, before the end could come, the Holy Land had to be in Jewish hands. This expectation was in keeping with the dispensationalists' belief that God had two distinct peoples—Israel and the church. The Jews disobeyed God and rejected Christ as Messiah. So God suspended his dealings with them and turned to the church. But God was not through with the Jews. At the end of the church age and after the secret rapture, he would again turn his attention to the Jews. They would have a national state in Palestine and endure intense suffering, after which Christ would return and set up his kingdom. The Jews would have a special place in this kingdom and once again enjoy the blessings of God.[46] Clearly, without the return of the Jews to Palestine God's cosmic plan as perceived by the dispensationalists would fail. A key piece in the dispensational eschatological puzzle would be missing.[47]

Accordingly, events in the Middle East captivated the dispensationalists. Here secular forces began to give life to premillennial theology. In the late nineteenth century Theodor Herzl (1860-1904) founded Zionism, a philosophy and movement promoting the return of Jews to Palestine. Most dispensationalists supported this secular Zionism because it embraced a central plank of their eschatology—the return of the Jews to the Holy Land. Most prominent among these Christian Zionists were William E. Blackstone and Arno C. Gaebelein.[48]

Scofield, "The War in the Light of Prophecy," *Weekly Evangel*, 28 October 1916, 6-7.

46. See Clarence Larkin, *Dispensational Truth* (11th ed.; Philadelphia: Larkin, 1918) 86-96; Weber, *Living in the Shadow*, 130-31; Charles C. Ryrie, *Dispensationalism Today* (Chicago: Moody, 1965) 159-61.

47. William E. Blackstone, *Jesus Is Coming* (New York: Revell, 1908) 165, 171-72; William B. Riley, *The Evolution of the Kingdom* (New York: Charles C. Cook, 1913) 48; Weber, *Living in the Shadow*, 131; I. M. Haldeman, *The Coming of Christ* (New York: Charles C. Cook, 1906) 205.

48. David A. Rausch, "Zionism" and "Christian Zionism," in *Evangelical Dictionary of Theology*, ed. Walter A. Elwell (Grand Rapids: Baker, 1984) 1200-1202; David A. Rausch, *Zionism within Early American Fundamentalism, 1878-1919* (Lewiston, NY: E. Mellen, 1980); F. B. Nelson, "Zionism and American Christianity," in *Dictionary of Christianity in America*, 1303-4; Ruth Mouly and Roland Robertson, "Zionism in American Premillenarian Fundamentalism," *American Journal of Theology and Philosophy* 4/3 (1983) 98-102. See also Victoria Clark, *Allies for Armageddon: The Rise of Christian Zionism* (New Haven, CT: Yale University Press, 2007); Stephen Sizer, *Christian Zionism: Roadmap to Armageddon?* (Downers Grove, IL: InterVarsity, 2004) Stephen Sizer, *Zion's Christian Soldiers?: The Bible, Israel, and the Church* (Downers

The End Takes Shape

With anti-Semitism reigning strong in nineteenth-century Europe, especially Russia, Jews began to move back to Palestine. But the big events were to come. In November 1917, Arthur Balfour, the British foreign secretary, established the legal framework for the Jews' return to Palestine: "His Majesty's Government views with favour the establishment in Palestine of a national home for the Jewish people, and will use their best endeavors to facilitate the achievement of this object."[49] That December saw the collapse of the Ottoman Empire, the evil power identified for centuries as being in league with the Antichrist. British forces under General Edmund Allenby captured Jerusalem without a shot being fired. For the first time since the Middle Ages, the Holy City was in Christian hands.

Such events sent shock waves through premillennial circles. Dispensationalists experienced a sense of prophetic ecstasy. Scofield wrote, "Now for the first time we have a real prophetic sign." A response in the *Evangel* was euphoric: "Do not we who are looking for the coming of our Lord . . . feel a thrill go through us as we read of the dry bones coming together (Ezek. 37)?" Leading premillennialist A. B. Simpson sobbed as he read the Balfour Declaration to his church.[50]

Premillennialists also regarded wartime events in Russia as prophecy in action. Ezekiel spoke of a northern power that was to invade Israel in the last days. But prophecy enthusiasts had long differed whether this nation would be Russia or the dreaded Turks. The Russian Revolution and the collapse of the Ottoman Empire combined to settle the issue—it would be Russia. The Soviet Union was now a godless communist state and a foreboding threat—two prominent themes in premillennial thinking for most of the twentieth century.[51]

Also of great interest was the map of Europe. Long before World War I the premillennialists had articulated an end-time geopolitical scenario: The last Gentile power will be a ten-nation confederacy resembling a

---

Grove, IL: InterVarsity, 2007.

49. Quoted in Wilson, *Armageddon Now!*, 42. See also David Bebbington, "The Advent Hope in British Evangelicalism since 1800," *Scottish Journal of Religious Studies* 9/2 (Autumn 1988) 107–8; T. DeCourcy Rayner, "Hidden Hands in Palestine," *Moody Monthly* 48/4 (December 1947) 282.

50. *Weekly Evangel*, 19 May 1917, 17; Wilson, *Armageddon Now!*, 37–46, 67; Charles G. Trumbull, *Prophecy's Light on Today* (New York: Revell, 1937) 67: Larkin, *Dispensational Truth*, 63–64.

51. Wilson, *Armageddon Now!*, 48–50; Boyer, *When Time Shall Be No More*, 102; James M. Gray, *A Text-Book on Prophecy* (New York: Revell, 1918) 192; James Alan Patterson, "Changing Images of the Beast: Apocalyptic Conspiracy Theories in American History," *Journal of Evangelical Theological Society* 32 (December 1988) 449–42.

revived Roman Empire and led by the Antichrist. The Antichrist will forge an alliance with the Jewish state. A northern confederacy dominated by Russia will challenge the Antichrist and enlist the king of the south to fight the Antichrist in Israel. The kings of the east will also join the fray against the Western European confederacy. Thus the great powers of the world will gather in Israel for the battle of Armageddon.[52]

The dispensationalists insisted that Christians would be raptured before the events surrounding Armageddon, and that the end-time political structure would be evident before the rapture. Unfortunately, in 1914 the map of Europe gave few hints that these prophecies were unfolding.[53] However, World War I and its peace treaties redrew the European map—much to the satisfaction of the premillennialists. Germany's defeat, the collapse of Austria-Hungary, and the unraveling of the Ottoman Empire altered the boundaries of Europe and the Middle East. These changes made more feasible the rise of a Western European confederacy resembling the old Roman Empire. Moreover, after the war the Russian bear recovered from revolution, embraced communism, and terminated its alliance with the West—thus placing it in a position to lead the northern confederacy.[54]

On the whole, the war significantly furthered the premillennial cause. It confirmed the claim that the world was getting much worse, not better. It dealt a body blow to the optimism of postmillennialism. Instead of a better tomorrow, the war indicated that the sun was setting on Western civilization. In a remarkable way World War I reordered the map of Europe and the Middle East to conform to the premillennial prophecies.[55]

After Armageddon

The 1920s witnessed a lull in end-time speculations. The fundamentalists and modernists engaged in a bitter conflict not only for the religious soul of America, but for control of several denominations. As a result, prophetic speculations tended to be put aside. Premillennialism did, however, remain alive and well during these years.[56]

52. Scofield, *Scofield Reference Bible*, 1341–52.
53. Weber, *Living in the Shadow*, 108.
54. Wilson, *Armageddon Now!*, 50–54; Weber, *Living in the Shadow*, 112.
55. Stone, *Guide to the End of the World*, 93.
56. Wilson, *Armageddon Now!*, 67–68; Boyer, *When Time Shall Be No More*, 104–5; Weber, *Living in the Shadow*, 160–61.

The End Takes Shape

The two decades between the world wars (1918–39) saw tremendous political, social, and economic turmoil. The dispensationalists interpreted these events prophetically. They viewed the League of Nations as an instrument of the Western European confederacy. Godless communism—and even socialism by extension—was regarded as embodying the spirit of the Antichrist, and the theological liberalism that made major inroads into most mainline denominations was interpreted as the apostasy predicted for the last days. Even Franklin Roosevelt's New Deal drew suspicious scrutiny. (One prophecy enthusiast said that the National Recovery Administration might be the mark of the beast.)[57]

Yet it was the rise of totalitarianism that aroused the most prophetic speculation. Events in Germany, Italy, Russia, and Japan riveted the attention of dispensationalists. Some were so carried away that they violated a golden rule of the new premillennialism—do not make specific predictions. Most prophetic writings focused on the rise of the Antichrist and his role as world dictator in the last days. With a revised version of the Roman Empire taking shape, it now remained to identify the beast of Revelation.[58] The favorite candidates for this position were Mussolini, Hitler, Stalin, the League of Nations, communism, socialism, and the Soviet Union. Because the term *Antichrist* can be used very loosely, declares Dwight Wilson, the "premillenarians could speak of Communism or liberalism as embodying the spirit of Antichrist . . . while at the same time they expected a personal Antichrist."[59]

Still, Benito Mussolini took center stage. Could he be the man of sin? Most premillennialists stopped short of categorically declaring him to be the Antichrist. Instead, they mustered evidence pointing to this conclusion or regarded him as only a type of the Antichrist. Il Duce's personal characteristics, premillennialists argued, matched the biblical criteria for the beast: he was charismatic, dynamic, militaristic, power hungry, and intent on geographical expansion.[60] Furthermore, Mussolini ruled in Rome

---

57. Stone, *Guide to the End of the World*, 93–94; Wilson, *Armageddon Now!*, 77–81; Boyer, *When Time Shall Be No More*, 107; Sandeen, *Roots of Fundamentalism*, 239–69; Marsden, *Fundamentalism and American Culture*, 153–59; Louis S. Bauman, "The Blue Eagle and Our Day as Christians," *Sunday School Times*, 16 September 1933, 583–84; Fuller, *Naming the Antichrist*, 148–60.

58. Stone, *Guide to the End of the World*, 93–94; Boyer, *When Time Shall Be No More*, 108; Wilson, *Armageddon Now!*, 82–85.

59. Wilson, *Armageddon Now!*, 81 (quote); Fuller, *Naming the Antichrist*, 148–60; Stone, *Guide to the End of the World*, 93–94.

60. Weber, *Living in the Shadow of the Second Coming*, 178–81; Boyer, *When Time Shall Be No More*, 108; Wilson, *Armageddon Now!*, 82–83. See also Oswald J. Smith,

and in 1929 signed a concordat with the pope, who had been Protestants' favorite candidate for the Antichrist since the Reformation. What clinched the matter for some people was their belief that the fascist symbol appeared on the American dime. They interpreted this as preparation for the Antichrist's global rule. A number of fundamentalist preachers were obsessed with this line of thinking. For example, Leonard Sale-Harrison, an Australian Bible teacher who held prophetic conferences in North America, predicted that the end would come in 1940 or 1941.[61]

Some prophecy buffs saw Hitler as the Antichrist. Given a predetermined numbering system, they reckoned that the letters in the name Hitler added up to 666. On a more serious level, the Nazi-Soviet non-aggression pact of 1939 electrified end-time watchers. Ezekiel 38 speaks of Gog and its ally Gomer. Dispensationalists interpreted this to mean Russia and Germany, thus making the northern confederacy a reality.[62]

Prophetic forecasters also looked beyond Europe for signs of the times. One force in the battle of Armageddon was to be the kings of the East. In the nineteenth century, premillennialists believed this power to be the Turks or the lost tribes of Israel. "Who are these kings?" asked H. A. Ironside, pastor of Chicago's Moody Church. The answer now given by most dispensationalists was Japan and China. They characterized this rising power of Japan and the growth of communism in China as the "yellow peril."[63]

America also got into the fray. Ezekiel 38:13 speaks of "the merchants of Tarshish, with all the young lions thereof," who will stand up to the power of Gog. Prophecy interpreters agreed that this referred to Great Britain and its former colonies, including the United States. To the relief

---

Is the Antichrist at Hand? (5th ed, Toronto: Tabernacle, 1926); Arno C. Gaebelein, *As It Was—So Shall It Be* (New York: Our Hope, 1937); J. M. Ritchie, *Prophetic Highlights* (New York: Revell, 1935).

61. Robert G. Clouse, "The Danger of Mistaken Hopes," in *Dreams, Visions and Oracles: The Layman's Guide to Biblical Prophecy*, eds. Carl E. Armerding and W. Ward Gasque (Grand Rapids, 1977) 33–35; Boyer, *When Time Shall Be No More*, 108; D. Brent Sandy, "Did Daniel See Mussolini?," *Christianity Today*, 8 February 1993, 34; Leonard Sale-Harrison, *The Resurrection of the Old Roman Empire* (London: Leonard Sale-Harrison, 1939).

62. Wilson, *Armageddon Now!*, 114–17; Boyer, *When Time Shall Be No More*, 109; Arthur I. Brown, *The Eleventh Hour* (Findlay, OH: Fundamental Truth, 1940) 77; Louis S. Bauman, "Russia and Armageddon," *King's Business* 29 (September 1938) 286.

63. H. A. Ironside, "The Kings of the East," *Kings Business* 29 (January 1938) 9; Wilson, *Armageddon Now!*, 118–19; Boyer, *When Time Shall Be No More*, 109; Louis T. Talbot, "The Army of Two Hundred Million," *Kings's Business* 23 (October 1932) 424.

of some premillennialists, the English-speaking nations appeared to be the heroes in the end-time conflict.[64]

For a while, current events seemed to bear out the premillennial interpretations. But not everything went their way. There were obvious disconfirmations—especially Mussolini's fate. Instead of being a type of the Antichrist, he died a humiliating death, and the Roman Empire never revived. And Hitler's invasion of the Soviet Union in June 1941 shattered the prophetic expectation of a great northern confederation of Germany and Russia. How did the premillennialists handle these apparent setbacks? Some were confused, others were dumbfounded. But for the most part there "seemed to be just one big awkward silence."[65] Premillennialists tended to ignore the disconfirmations.

THE APPEAL OF EARLY DISPENSATIONALISM

For most of the twentieth century, the primary vehicle for apocalyptic thinking was dispensational premillennialism. But such a situation did not develop overnight. Dispensationalism came on the American scene after the Civil War. By the early twentieth century it had secured a solid base within the evangelical subculture—the first step in gaining national visibility. How did all of this happen? Why did Darby's ideas appeal to American evangelicals?

Apocalyptic thinking takes hold during times of turmoil. The century from the Civil War to World War II may not have been the most tumultuous time in Western history, but it did bring considerable stress and change. Industrialization and urbanization proceeded apace in the late nineteenth century. Immigrants from southern, central, and eastern Europe poured into America. Many of these immigrants brought with them their Roman Catholic, Eastern Orthodox, or Jewish faith, so the Protestant empire came under serious challenge. There was the additional problem of minorities—notably blacks and Native Americans—who experienced discrimination. Then came World War I and the Great Depression. Such events provided fertile soil for apocalyptic ideas.

But more important was the volatile religious climate. Thanks to Darwin's ideas and theological liberalism, the historic Christian faith faced tremendous challenges. Such intellectual developments contested the

---

64. Boyer, *When Time Shall Be No More*, 108.

65. Wilson, *Armageddon Now!*, 146 (quote); Sandy, "Did Daniel See Mussolini?" 34; Weber, *Living in the Shadow*, 183.

authority of Scripture and the supernatural character of Christianity. Fundamentalism confronted these challenges head-on. It affirmed the historic Christian faith and looked for allies in this struggle. The dispensationalists joined the fray and became part of the fundamentalist subculture, thus receiving considerable acceptance within the evangelical community. In the process they established networks and institutions that furthered their end-time ideas.

The turn of world events played an even greater role in solidifying the credibility of dispensational eschatology. Dispensationalism abandoned the emphasis on America's millennial mission and made the Jews preeminent in God's future plans. World War I, the Balfour Declaration, and the redrawing of the European map sent dispensationalism's stock soaring. These events made possible the return of the Jews to Palestine, the rise of Russia, and a European political structure compatible with premillennial predictions. Nothing fuels the creditability of prophecy more than its apparent fulfillment. And in the minds of many evangelicals this is just what happened. Such developments set the stage for the explosion of apocalyptic ideas that would take place after the 1960s.

All of this emphasis on world events takes nothing away from dispensational eschatology itself. Not only did dispensational predictions appear to reflect current events, but they also allowed for Christ's immediate return without setting a timetable. In doing so, dispensationalism solved the problem that had plagued historicist premillennialism.

5

Apocalypse Loud and Clear

WORLD WAR I AND its aftermath catapulted premillennialism to a strong position within the evangelical community. But outside of this subculture few people knew much about it. In part, this can be explained by the fact that dispensationalism was housed within separatist fundamentalism. By the 1930s fundamentalism had its own churches, schools, and publishing agencies; dispensationalism could then perpetuate itself within this framework with little outside help.[1]

But all of this would change by the 1970s and 1980s. Evangelical publishers cranked out prophecy books right and left. Hal Lindsey's *The Late Great Planet Earth* sold over twenty-five million copies—prompting the *New York Times* to declare him the best-selling author of the 1970s. Bumper stickers read "In Case of Rapture, This Car Will Be Driverless" and "Beam Me Up, Jesus." For use in churches and schools dispensationalists produced a number of Hollywood-like films with end-time themes: *The Rapture, A Thief in the Night, The Road to Armageddon,* and *Image of the Beast.*[2]

Premillennialists also jumped into the television business in a big way. Nearly all of the electronic church's big names preached the premillennial

1. Timothy Weber, "Happily at the Edge of the Abyss: Popular Premillennialism in America," *Ex Auditu* 6 (1991) 90; Joel Carpenter, "Fundamentalist Institutions and the Rise of Evangelical Protestantism, 1929–1942," *Church History* 49/1 (1980) 63–75.

2. Joe Maxwell, "Prophecy Books Become Big Sellers," *Christianity Today,* 11 March 1991, 60: Timothy Weber, *Living in Shadow of the Second Coming* (rev. ed.; Chicago: University of Chicago Press, 1987) 211; Weber, "Happily at the Edge of the Abyss," 92.

message—Jerry Falwell, Jimmy Swaggart, Pat Robertson, Jim Bakker, Oral Roberts, Kenneth Copeland, Paul Crouch, and Rex Humbard. Networks and cable stations carried Christian programs that analyzed current events from a dispensational perspective: Paul Crouch's Trinity Broadcasting Network, *Jack Van Impe Presents*, Pat Robertson's *700 Club*, Charles Taylor's *Today in Bible Prophecy*, and Ray Brubaker's *God's News behind the News*.[3]

Premillennialism even reached the highest levels of the American government. In a 1981 appearance before Congress, Secretary of the Interior James Watt questioned whether humanity had many more generations left before the Lord returns. In 1984 President Reagan had several discussions with reporters in which his quasi-dispensational views came out. Of course, the news media pounced on these opportunities, running programs and articles about "Ronald Reagan and the Politics of Armageddon."[4]

How did dispensationalism come out of its subculture into the national spotlight? Most obvious is the use of modern media. The premillennialists became masters of mass communication. They skillfully expressed their views to a popular audience through mass-market paperbacks, radio, television, movies, videocassettes, and eventually DVDs and the Internet.[5]

Most important, while apparent confirmations of prophecy have throughout history added fuel to the millenarian fire, in the twentieth century events appeared to jibe with biblical prophecy as never before. The long awaited divine promise was fulfilled—Israel became a state in 1948. The premillennialists were handed a prophetic windfall of unprecedented proportions. They also saw the atomic bomb as bringing the end-time cataclysm predicted in Scripture. The total destruction of planet Earth now became a real possibility. Russia had long been eyed by premillennialists

---

3. Michael Barkun, "The Language of Apocalypse: Premillennialists and Nuclear War," in *The God Pumpers: Religion in the Electronic Age*, eds. Marshall W. Fishwick and Ray B. Browne (Bowling Green, OH: Bowling Green State University Popular Press, 1987) 159; Weber, "Happily at the Edge of the Abyss," 92; Jeffery L. Sheler, "The Christmas Covenant," *U.S. News and World Report*, 19 December 1994, 62; Erik Davis, "Spiritual Warfare: Televangelists Stay Tuned for the End," *Village Voice*, 19 February 1991, 49–50; Richard G. Kyle, "The Electronic Church: An Echo of American Culture," *Direction* 39/2 (2110) 162–76.

4. Robert Jewett, "Coming to Terms with the Doom Boom," *Quarterly Review* 4/3 (Fall 1984) 9; G. Clark Chapman Jr., "Falling in Rapture Before the Bomb," *Reformed Journal* 37 (June 1987) 13; Weber, "Happily at the Edge of the Abyss," 93–94; David Douglas, "God, the World and James Watt," *Christianity and Crisis*, 5 October 1981, 258, 269–70; Ronnie Dugger, "Does Reagan Expect a Nuclear Armageddon?," *Washington Post*, 8 April 1984, C1, C4.

5. Barkun, "Language of Apocalypse," 159; Weber, "Happily at the Edge of the Abyss," 92–93; Maxwell, "Prophecy Books Become Big Sellers," 60.

Apocalypse Loud and Clear

as the great northern power, and now the Soviet Union had become a superpower with the capability of invading Israel.

Another factor energizing eschatological speculations was the cultural climate. The 1960s and 1970s witnessed an occult revival. The occult arts took on a new life. Americans dabbled in witchcraft and spiritualism; they speculated about UFOs and about psychic phenomena. In their quest to know the future, Americans turned to astrology, tarot cards, and Ouija boards. While there is a great gulf between premillennial theology and the occult, the curiosity regarding the future spilled over into the evangelical community. In their zeal to know when Christ will return, some evangelicals went too far. Spurred on by *The Late Great Planet Earth*, they engaged in a flood of predictions concerning the Second Coming and events of the last times. This preoccupation with "Christian tea leaves" became a fad among many conservative Christians.[6]

THE VARIETIES OF DISPENSATIONALISM

In the twentieth century, dispensationalism has been at the forefront in pointing to Christ's return. But dispensationalism is not a monolithic theology; not all dispensationalists are the same. Some pursue end-time events in a rabid fashion, others are more moderate.

Darrell Bock describes three types of dispensationalism in the twentieth century—Scofieldian, revised, and progressive. The Scofieldian and revised versions are often lumped together and called classic dispensationalism. In fact, all three stripes are alike in holding to the essentials of dispensational eschatology—namely, a separation between the church and Israel, premillennialism, and the secret rapture—but there are differences.[7]

Scofieldian dispensationalism, best represented by C. I. Scofield and Lewis Sperry Chafer, rigidly separates Israel and the church. Revised dispensationalism, which developed in the mid-twentieth century, allows for more continuity between Israel and the church and between the various dispensations. Scholarly representatives of revised dispensationalism

6. Richard Kyle, *The Religious Fringe: A History of Alternative Religions in America* (Downers Grove, IL: InterVarsity, 1993) 258–63; Terry Tremaine, "Global Fortune-Telling and Bible Prophecy," *Skeptical Inquirer*, Winter 1994, 166–69.

7. Darrell L. Bock, "Charting Dispensationalism," *Christianity Today*, 12 September 1994, 26–29. See also Timothy P. Weber, "Dispensational and Historic Premillennialism as Popular Movements," in *A Case for Historic Premillennialism: An Alternative to "Left Behind" Eschatology*, edited by Craig L. Blomberg and Sung Wook Chung (Grand Rapids: Baker, 2009) 21, 22.

include John Walvoord, Charles Ryrie, and J. Dwight Pentecost.[8] However, this version of dispensationalism has also produced individuals who have popularized the apocalyptic books of Scripture. These popular authors have often sensationalized eschatology and yielded to date setting or something close to it. The remainder of this chapter and several others will largely focus on these popularizers.

The third type, progressive dispensationalism, is even more moderate. It sees considerable continuity in God's plan for humanity and avoids wild prophetic speculations. In fact, many progressive dispensationalists regard Hal Lindsey's views as an eccentric deviation from dispensationalism. Even more so, they regard the *Left Behind* series as breaking from traditional dispensationalism. But because progressive dispensationalism has not yet filtered down to the churches and the laity, the popular authors still exert the greatest influence over end-time thinking.[9]

PROPHETS OF THE APOCALYPSE

"There are now in the United States almost as many prophets of doom as could ever be found in the cities of medieval Europe.... The fear—and more often the hope—that the world will come to a quick and violent end is still very much with us today," wrote Daniel Cohen in the 1980s.[10] In the last fifty years or so, the number of end-time prophets has increased geometrically. Most, but not all, have proclaimed a premillennial message or a twisted version thereof. Some of these self-designated prophets have taken a scholarly approach to the matter, but many have engaged in pure sensationalism.

---

8. Bock, "Charting Dispensationalism," 27–28. For examples of revised dispensationalism see J. Dwight Pentecost, *Things to Come: A Study in Biblical Eschatology* (Grand Rapids: Zondervan, 1958); Charles C. Ryrie, *Dispensationalism Today* (Chicago: Moody, 1965); John F. Walvoord, *Armageddon, Oil and the Middle East Crisis* (rev. ed.; Grand Rapids: Zondervan, 1990).

9. Sheler, "Christmas Covenant," 70; Bock, "Charting Dispensationalism," 28–29; Stanley J. Grenz, *The Millennial Maze: Sorting Out the Evangelical Options* (Downers Grove, IL: InterVarsity, 1992) 94; C. Marvin Pate and Calvin B. Haines Jr., *Doomsday Delusions: What's Wrong with Predictions about the End of the World* (Downers Grove, IL: InterVarsity, 1995). See also Craig A. Blaising and Darrell L. Bock, *Progressive Dispensationalism: An Analysis of the Movement and Defense of Traditional Dispensationalism* (Wheaton, IL: Victor/Bridgepoint, 1993); Robert L. Saucy, *The Case for Progressive Dispensationalism: The Interface between Dispensational & Non-Dispensational Theology* (Grand Rapids: Zondervan, 1993).

10. Daniel Cohen, *Waiting for the Apocalypse* (Buffalo: Prometheus, 1983) back cover.

Apocalypse Loud and Clear

A large number of the end-time thinkers—especially the more scholarly version—have either a direct or indirect connection with Dallas Theological Seminary. Founded in 1924 as Evangelical Theological College, Dallas Seminary became the hothouse for dispensational thought in America. According to Timothy Weber, "Dallas Seminary has been the academic and ideological 'Vatican' of the movement." It has provided the scholarly basis for dispensationalism and has been the training ground for many Bible college teachers and pastors at independent churches. Some of the ill-educated popularizers have attended a Bible college where the Dallas brand of dispensationalism has held sway.[11]

Another common trait is that, remembering the Millerite fiasco, the majority of premillennial prophets have shied away from exact date setting. The postponement theory allows the dispensationalists to avoid setting dates while they continue to hold that Christ could return at any moment. Still, some come very close to making specific predictions. They may pick a time frame, but hedge their statements by using words such as "probable," "could," "perhaps," and "suggest." In this way they can extricate themselves from a corner when a chronological prediction fails.[12]

Most modern prognosticators range from the sensible to the ludicrous. Most scholarly would be the late John F. Walvoord (1910–2003), long-time president of Dallas Seminary and the author of about thirty books. Best known is his *Armageddon, Oil and the Middle East Crisis*, which sold over a million copies. Walvoord did not suggest any dates for Christ's return. But he believed that most events on the end-time calendar have been fulfilled and that the rapture is at hand. Except for a few nuances, Walvoord does not break new turf. Rather, he presents a good general picture of classic dispensationalist eschatology.[13]

Venerable evangelist Billy Graham is a premillennialist. His *Approaching Hoofbeats* best expresses his end-time views. While he has avoided the date-setting trap, he is also convinced that humanity is living in the last days. Humankind is headed for an unprecedented cataclysm brought on by nuclear holocausts, biological warfare, chemical contamination, and pestilence.[14]

11. Weber, *Living in the Shadow*, 238–39. See also John D. Hannah, "Dallas Theological Seminary," in *Dictionary of Christianity in America*, ed. Daniel G. Reid et al. (Downers Grove, IL: InterVarsity, 1990) 338.

12. Russell Chandler, *Doomsday: The End of the World, A View through Time* (Ann Arbor, MI: Servant, 1993) 253.

13. Walvoord, *Armageddon, Oil and the Middle East Crisis*, 17–30.

14. Billy Graham, *Approaching Hoofbeats: The Four Horsemen of the Apocalypse*

Pat Robertson—1988 presidential candidate and founder of the Christian Broadcasting Network—has made some doomsday predictions, and he continues to do so. (These will be noted in future chapters). He once implied that the tribulation would be brought on in 1982 by the Soviet Union's invasion of Israel. The Middle East would explode, with two billion people being killed at Armageddon. But Robertson's apocalypticism was tempered by his political ambitions. While he embraced a premillennial eschatology, he espoused something resembling the postmillennial optimism. Peace, freedom, and prosperity can be achieved in the here and now. Strictly speaking, Robertson is a premillennialist but not a dispensationalist.[15]

The late Jerry Falwell (1933-2007), the founder of the Moral Majority, was a thunderous voice for biblical prophecy: "I believe in the premillennial, pretribulational coming of Christ." Prophecy, he claimed, is crucial because there is no hope in this world's system. Nuclear war is inevitable. Humankind is headed for utter destruction—except for Christians, who will be raptured before the tribulation. The greatest indicator of these coming events "is the restoration of the nation of Israel."[16]

By any estimate Hal Lindsey must be regarded as the king of the popularizers during the twentieth century. A Dallas Seminary graduate, he did perhaps more than anyone else during the late twentieth century to bring premillennialism to the non-evangelical popular culture. Through a flood of books, tapes, and lectures he has exerted tremendous influence on American thinking. He has brought his message of biblical prophecy regarding global events to college campuses, Congress, the State Department, the Pentagon, and foreign governments. It all began with *The Late*

(New York: Avon, 1983). See also Billy Graham, *World Aflame* (Garden City, NY: Doubleday, 1965).

15. See Pat Robertson, *Perspective* (newsletter), February-March 1980, 5; Pat Robertson, *The New World Order* (Dallas: Word, 1991); Pat Robertson, *The New Millennium* (Dallas: Word, 1990); Mark G. Toulouse, "Pat Robertson: Apocalyptic Theology and American Foreign Policy," *Journal of Church and State* 31/1 (Winter 1989) 73-99; Stephen D. O'Leary and Michael McFarland, "The Political Use of Mythic Discourse: Prophetic Interpretation in Pat Robertson's Presidential Campaign," *Quarterly Journal of Speech* 75/4 (November 1989) 431-52; Andrew G. Lang, "Armageddon: The Religious Doctrine of Survivable Nuclear War," *Japanese Christian Quarterly* 5 (Spring 1987) 106.

16. Jerry Falwell, "The Twenty-first Century and the End of the World," *Fundamentalist Journal* 7/5 (May 1988) 10-11 (quote); Jerry Falwell, *Nuclear War and the Second Coming of Jesus Christ* (Lynchburg, VA: Old Time Gospel Hour, 1983).

Apocalypse Loud and Clear

Great Planet Earth, which was followed up by numerous other books—all building on the same themes.[17]

In *The Late Great Planet Earth* Lindsey contributes little to standard dispensational eschatology. He simply packages it in an exciting format and adds urgency by connecting biblical prophecy with recent events—especially the return of Israel and the 1967 Six-Day War. He also comes close to setting a date for the end on the basis of the parable of the fig tree in Matthew 24: 32-33: "Now learn a parable of the fig tree; When his branch is yet tender, and putteth forth leaves, ye know that summer is nigh: So likewise ye, when ye shall see all these things, know that it [the return of the Son of man] is near." Lindsey equates the fig tree with Israel: "When the Jewish people, after nearly 2,000 years of exile . . . became a nation on May 14, 1948, the 'fig tree' put forth its first leaves."[18] In v. 34 Jesus continues: "Verily, I say unto you, This generation shall not pass, till all these things be fulfilled." Lindsey contends that Jesus is here connecting his Second Coming with the rebirth of Israel. Noting that a biblical generation was about forty years, he goes on to say that "within forty years or so of 1948, all these things could take place."[19]

Most people understood Lindsey to have predicted that the rapture would occur in or about 1988. Later on he did some backtracking, saying he suggested 1988 as a general time frame. In *Planet Earth—2000 A.D.* he reminded readers that he had conditioned his earlier forecast with several ifs and maybes. He also pointed out that "all these things" in Matthew 24:34 could be the return of Israel in 1948 or the 1967 Six-Day War. Moreover, he redefined the biblical generation as "somewhere between 40 to 100 years." Nevertheless, Lindsey does maintain that the current generation will witness the end. He expects Christ to come at any moment—"probably in your lifetime."[20]

---

17. Chandler, *Doomsday*, 248-49. See Hal Lindsey, *The Late Great Planet Earth* (Grand Rapids: Zondervan, 1970); Hal Lindsey, *The Road to Holocaust* (New York: Bantam, 1989; Hal Lindsey, *1980s: Countdown to Armageddon* (New York: Bantam, 1981); Hal Lindsey, *There's a New World Coming* (New York: Bantam, 1973); Hal Lindsey, *Planet Earth—2000 A.D.* (Palos Verdes Estates, CA: Western Front, 1994); Chapman, "Falling in Rapture before the Bomb," 12.

18. Lindsey, *Late Great Planet Earth*, 53-58.

19. Ibid. 54.

20. Chandler, *Doomsday*, 251; Roy Rivenburg, "Is the End Still Near?," *Los Angeles Times*, 30 July 1992, E1-2; Russell Chandler and John Dart, "Visions of Apocalypse Rise Again: Prophets of Doom Link Bible Predictions to Current Events," *Los Angeles Times*, 26 July, A14; Jewett, "Coming to Terms with the Doom Boom," 17; Lindsey, *Planet Earth*, 3, 6.

A host of other prophets have made a splash in modern America. (Some have been active in both the twentieth and twenty-first centuries, and their later writings will be encountered in subsequent chapters). In *Rapture under Attack* (1992), for instance, Tim LaHaye, a conservative activist, while cautioning about date setting, envisions a pretribulational rapture that causes great havoc. When Christian drivers and pilots are snatched up to heaven, global chaos will occur.[21]

But some others boldly set dates. According to Grant R. Jeffrey in *Armageddon: Appointment with Destiny* (1988), the Bible makes it clear that the end of the world is near—it will probably occur around the year 2000.[22] And Chuck Smith, long-time pastor of Calvary Chapel in southern California, can be regarded as a converted date-setter. In *Future Survival* (1978), he declared that "the Lord is coming for his church before the end of 1981." But ten years later Smith repented of his mistake and then condemned date setting: "Date setting is wrong, and I was guilty of coming close to that."[23]

A more sensational end-timer is Jack Van Impe, the self-styled Walking Bible. In a 1975 newsletter he insisted that the "Soviet flag would fly over Independence Hall in Philadelphia by 1976." This prophetic misfire did not stop him. Van Impe began to address large audiences through his TV program (*Jack Van Impe Presents*), videos, cassettes, and literature. One of his 1992 videos conveyed the message that the rapture, World War III, and Armageddon would occur in about eight years.[24] (Van Impe is still making many predictions, but that is a subject for future chapters).

Well-known end-time specialist Salem Kirban may not have set any dates, but he has inched very close to this pitfall. The invasion of the

21. Tim LaHaye, *Rapture under Attack: Can We Still Trust the Pre-Trib Rapture?* (Sisters, OR: Multnomah, 1992). See also Tim LaHaye, *No Fear of the Storm* (Sisters, OR: Multinomah, 1992); Tim LaHaye, *The Beginning of the End* (Wheaton, IL: Tyndale, 1972).

22. Grant R. Jeffrey, *Armageddon: Appointment with Destiny* (Toronto: Frontier Research, 1988) 193.

23. Chuck Smith, *Future Survival* (Costa Mesa, CA: Calvary Chapel, 1978); Chuck Smith, *The Last Days, the Middle East, and the Book of Revelation* (Tarrytown, NY: Chosen, 1991); William A. Alnor, *Soothsayers of the Second Advent* (Old Tappan, NJ: Revell, 1989) 41–42.

24. Jack Van Impe, *Has Russia Really Changed?: America's Next President—and World War III?* (Troy, MI: Jack Van Impe Ministries, 1992); Ed Hindson, "The End is Near . . . or Is It?" *World*, 24 November 1990, 12; Gary DeMar, *Last Days Madness* (Brentwood, TN: Wolgemuth and Hyatt, 1991) 38; Kenneth L. Woodward, "The Final Days Are Here Again," *Newsweek*, 18 March 1991, 55; Jack Van Impe, *2001: On the Edge of Eternity* (Dallas: Word, 1996).

Apocalypse Loud and Clear

African killer bees galvanized him. As they moved through Mexico into the southern United States, he saw these insects as the locusts of Revelation 9. In the judgment sounded by the fifth trumpet, everyone without the seal of God is subjected to painful stings for five months.[25]

In the late twentieth century, John Hagee made some big waves, and he still continues to do so. His book *Beginning of the End* has been described as a *Late Great Planet Earth* for the 1990s. Hagee did not pinpoint the time when Christ will rapture his people. But he did insist that contemporary events fit into God's time table for the end. In particular, he contended that the assassination of Yitzhak Rabin would trigger a series of events leading to Christ's return. The prophetic clock is ticking fast, said Hagee. "The moment that Yigal Amir pulled the trigger will stand as a defining moment in world history."[26]

Things start to get even more bizarre. In 1983 Mary Stewart Relfe claimed that God spoke to her through dreams. On his instructions she released a chart spelling out the divine time table: World War III would break out in 1989, the great tribulation would begin in 1990, the United States would be totally destroyed several years before Armageddon, and Christ would return in 1997 after Armageddon. A noteworthy feature was Relfe's mid-tribulationism—the church is to witness the rise of the Antichrist before being raptured midway through the tribulation.[27]

Not to be outdone, Edgar Whisenant made even more precise predictions. He did not hedge his bets with "abouts" or "shoulds" as do most prognosticators. Instead he painted himself into a prophetic corner. His *88 Reasons Why the Rapture Will Be in 1988*, which sold two million copies, dated the rapture between September 11 and 13, 1988. Jesus' statement that no one knows the day or hour of his return does not mean that we cannot know the month or the year, reasoned Whisenant. He even dated the beginning of World War III (October 3, 1988) and other eschatological

---

25. Salem Kirban, *Countdown to Rapture* (Irvine, CA: Harvest House, 1977) 33; Tom Gorman, "San Diego Prepares Tactics to Battle Killer Bee Swarms," *Los Angles Times*, 10 September 1992, A1, A19; Chandler, *Doomsday*, 255. See also Salem Kirban, *666* (Wheaton, IL: Tyndale, 1970); Salem Kirban, *Guide to Survival* (Chattanooga: AMG, 1990).

26. John Hagee, *Beginning of the End* (Nashville: Nelson, 1996) 4. See also H. Wayne House, "A Summary Critique: Beginning of the End," in *Christian Research Journal* 19/3 (1997) 50.

27. Mary Stewart Relfe, *Economic Advisor* (newsletter), 28 February 1983; Alnor, *Soothsayers of the Second Advent*, 35; Weber, *Living in the Shadow*, 225.

events. When 1988 came and went, he pushed his predictions ahead by several years.[28]

"This could be the year," Charles Taylor said repeatedly. Taylor, a popular teacher of prophecy for years, may be America's ultimate date-setter. But because he has misfired so many times, his ministry has declined. Also, Taylor qualified his predictions, calling them suggestions, not date setting. Nevertheless, he suggested eleven dates from 1975 to 1989 for the rapture. These suggestions center on the main theme of his preaching—just before the tribulation Jesus will rapture the church during the Jewish Feast of Trumpets.[29]

The vast majority of doomsday prophets are premillennialists. In many cases, they take great liberties with dispensational theology, even distorting it at times. But Harold Camping (b. 1921) is an exception. He is a Reformed amillennialist. (Many amillennialists say the millennium is symbolic or spiritual). Camping, the president of Family Radio, predicted the world would end in September 1994. His book 1994? and its sequel, *Are You Ready?*, presented an elaborate system of dating, numerology, and allegory pointing to 1994. The arithmetic is not based on the usual dispensational scenario, but is his own unorthodox system. Despite the obvious disconfirmation, Camping believes that Christ will return very soon and has continued to make predictions for the twenty-first century, especially for 2011.[30]

The late twentieth century witnessed many more popular prophets. While they may not have set dates for Christ's return, they have made other

---

28. Edgar C. Whisenant, 88 *Reasons Why the Rapture Will Be in 1988* (rev. ed.; Nashville: World Bible Society, 1988) 3, 36, 56; Edgar C. Whisenant, *On Borrowed Time: The Bible Dates of the 70th Week of Daniel, Armageddon, and the Millennium* (Nashville: World Bible Society, 1988) 48; Edgar C. Whisenant, *The Final Shout: Rapture Report* (Nashville: World Bible Society, 1989) 24; Paul Boyer, *When Time Shall Be No More* (Cambridge, MA: Harvard University Press, 1992) 130; Alnor, *Soothsayers of the Second Advent*, 35–36; Dean C. Halverson, "88 Reasons: What Went Wrong," *Christian Research Journal* 11/2 (Fall 1988) 15–16.

29. Charles R. Taylor, *Get All Excited—Jesus Is Coming Soon* (Redondo Beach, CA: Today in Bible Prophecy, 1975) introduction, 89, 93; Charles R. Taylor, *Those Who Remain* (Orange, CA: Today in Bible Prophecy, 1980) 70–71; Alnor, *Soothsayers of the Second Advent*, 134–35.

30. Harold Camping, *1994?* (New York: Vantage, 1992); Joe Maxwell, "End-times Prediction Draws Strong Following," *Christianity Today*, 20 June 1994, 46–47; Joe Maxwell, "Camping Misses End-times Deadline," *Christianity Today*, 24 October 1994, 84; Perucci Feraiuolo, "Could '1994' Be the End of Family Radio?" *Christian Research Journal* 16/1 (Summer 1993) 5–6. See also Harold Camping, *Time Has an End* (New York: Vantage Press, 2005).

prophetic statements—often about the identity of the Antichrist. Most of these prognosticators have common characteristics. Since 1945 premillennialism has produced serious thinkers—Donald Grey Barnhouse, Wilbur Smith, George Ladd, John Walvoord, Dwight Pentecost, Charles Ryrie, and more. But the "prophecy popularizers were rarely trained theologians, denominational leaders, or settled ministers, but were freelance writers, evangelists, or TV preachers."[31] Modern prophecy has often been done by amateurs. Some have training in science or engineering, but not in theology or history. Despite their disdain for traditional higher education, these popularizers are eager for intellectual respectability. Whenever possible, they claim scientific or historical authority for their pronouncements. Despite deriding academia, they often fashion themselves as educated people—sometimes with honorary or even bogus doctorates.[32]

END-TIME THEMES

After World War II, dispensational eschatology did not change substantially. To be sure, in the late twentieth century the progressive dispensationalists have taken the apocalyptic edge off dispensational end-time ideas. They reject the mentality of many popularizers that insisted on setting the date for doomsday. Yet the main outlines of dispensational eschatology have been in place since the nineteenth century. World War I and the decades thereafter simply fleshed out these themes as current events appeared to be fulfilling prophecy.

Still, end-time prophecy underwent some modifications, both in substance and tone. As noted earlier, in the late twentieth century only two new themes could be detected—nuclear destruction and the Antichrist's use of television and computers to control the masses. But the tone changed. The more scholarly and thoughtful prophetic interpreters have taken a backseat to the popularizers, who are usually not restrained by external institutions. Many have their own organizations, television programs, and publishing houses. Therefore, as the twentieth century moved to a close, the popularizers became increasingly reckless. Their predictions were often irresponsible and even laughable.

31. Boyer, *When Time Shall Be No More*, 304–5.

32. Ibid. 305, 310–11. For a broader view of anti-intellectualism in evangelical circles see Mark A. Noll, *The Scandal of the Evangelical Mind* (Grand Rapids: Eerdmans, 1994); Mark Noll, "The Scandal of the Evangelical Mind," *Christianity Today*, 25 October 1993, 29–32; Os Guinness, *Fit Bodies, Fat Minds: Why Evangelicals Don't Think and What to Do about It* (Grand Rapids: Baker, 1994).

Millennialism has always evidenced a chameleon-like character. As predictions fail, the prophets adjust their prognostications to suit another current event. This tendency has accelerated since World War II. Prophecy is now big business. And to make a big splash, a popularizer must make sensational predictions. Invariably, this reckless approach to prophecy backfires, and the interpreter usually comes up with a different prediction to match the new circumstance.

Another hallmark of premillennialism is its tendency to be pessimistic. It sees history ending in a catastrophe. And as the popularizers preached the coming doom, the pessimism has thickened. For example, Hal Lindsey has never been an optimist in respect to world affairs. Yet in *Planet Earth—2000 A.D.* (1994) his alarm accelerated. He addressed every conceivable topic—the crime explosion, unprecedented earthquakes and natural disasters, berserk global weather, AIDS, drug abuse, ethnic conflicts, and environmental damage.[33]

In this same vein most premillennialists saw humanity on the path to perdition. The present age is under the control of Satan and is rapidly approaching a crisis point. Yet Christians need not despair—they will be raptured before the world goes up in smoke. "We see no hope in politics, in the business world, in education, in the world of medicine. But there is hope, and it is in the Second Coming of Christ," said the late Jerry Falwell.[34]

By the Bomb's Early Light

Among the major themes of dispensational eschatology is worldwide destruction. The Earth has already been destroyed by water. For most of the Christian era, biblical interpreters have pointed to a second and final cataclysm—this time by fire. According to 2 Peter 3:10, "the heavens shall pass away with a great noise, and the elements shall melt with fervent heat, the Earth and the works that are therein shall be burned up." Prior to 1945 most prophecy scholars interpreted this catastrophe in natural terms—comets, volcanic eruptions, and earthquakes. Other interpreters saw it as an eschatological event attributable to God but beyond human comprehension. All of this changed with the atomic bomb: the nuclear

---

33. Lindsey, *Planet Earth—2000 A.D.* See also John M. Werly, "Premillennialism and the Paranoid Style," *American Studies* 18 (Spring 1977) 39–55.

34. Falwell, "Twenty-first Century," 10. See also Lang, "Armageddon," 107.

destruction of Hiroshima and Nagasaki set off a tidal wave of apocalyptic prognostications both secular and biblical.[35]

The awesome destructive power of nuclear weapons riveted the attention of many segments of society: scientists, the popular culture, mainstream theologians, and premillennialists. Linking the atomic bomb with biblical prophecy, the popularizers added a new wrinkle to the premillennial scenario—nuclear destruction. They combed the Scriptures for evidence that nuclear annihilation is prophesied and inevitable. In the process they faced some puzzling interpretative problems. Would this coming holocaust be a nuclear war between nations? Or would God punish humankind by using nuclear weapons? Some premillennialists— Hal Lindsey among them—worked out a detailed scenario for World War III. Others felt the need to preserve God's transcendence. John Walvoord hardly mentioned nuclear weapons. Jack Van Impe said that God does not need humankind's modern inventions to fulfill his will. A few premillennialists straddled the fence. They suggested two nuclear events—World War III and God's destruction of Earth at the end of time.[36]

A second interpretative problem concerned the nature of the warfare. Would World War III actually involve the weapons envisioned by the apocalyptic writers—mounted warriors, bows and arrows, and spears? Remember, a literal interpretation of Scripture is a hallmark of dispensationalism! Some, following this principle explicitly, envisioned a disarmament or some other circumstance that will necessitate the use of primitive weapons. Salem Kirban describes the battlefield of Armageddon as "a scene from a Middle Ages history book. Bows, arrows, shields, spears everywhere. Crude weaponry but highly sophisticated nuclear explosives for close-up fighting."[37] Others adopted a more figurative approach, what they

---

35. Wilbur M. Smith, *This Atomic Age and the Word of God* (Boston: Wilde, 1948) 45, 52; Boyer, *When Time Shall Be No More*, 115–16. See also Paul Boyer, *By the Bomb's Early Light* (New York: Pantheon, 1985).

36. Merrill F. Unger, *Beyond the Crystal Ball* (Chicago: Moody, 1973) 113,115; LaHaye, *Beginning of the End*, 9; Jack Van Impe, *Signs of the Times* (Royal Oak, MI: Jack Van Impe Ministries, 1979) 66; Boyer, *When Time Shall Be No More*, 131; Harold Lindsell, *The Armageddon Spectre* (Westchester, IL: Crossway, 1984) 16, 18; G. Clarke Chapman Jr., "American Theology in the Shadow of the Bomb," *Union Seminary Quarterly Review* 41/3-4 (1987) 25–38.

37. Kirban, 666, 136. See also Boyer, *When Time Shall Be No More*, 132; Richard W. De Haan, *Israel and the Nations in Prophecy* (Grand Rapids: Zondervan, 1968) 140–41.

called "word pictures." Lindsey, for example changed the spears, swords, and chariots into modern weapons, including atomic bombs.[38]

How did the premillennialists view the threat of nuclear disaster? Though opinions varied, most premillennialists said it was inevitable. The rank-and-file agreed with Jerry Falwell—nuclear war is inescapable for everyone except believers, who will be raptured. But the imminent conflict will not destroy humanity; the ultimate nuclear catastrophe will come only after the millennium. Meanwhile, nuclear conflict can be delayed by evangelism and diplomacy.[39]

Pat Robertson's position evidenced more ambivalence. In the late 1970s he predicted a holocaust by 1982. But as time went on he retreated from the abyss: "God does not want to incinerate the world," he commented. Reflecting something of a dominion theology, he urged Christians to take more responsibility for creation. Billy Graham also wavered in this regard. Though he had earlier embraced the standard premillennial fatalism, by the 1980s he was addressing the issues of social justice and world peace.[40]

The advent of the atomic age has given new meaning to apocalypticism. All people must come to grips with the chilling possibility of a nuclear holocaust. For premillennialists the key is the secret rapture. They face the coming holocaust with a degree of confidence, in some cases even smugness. After all, they will be snatched up to heaven before the nuclear catastrophe.[41]

---

38. Lindsey, *Late Great Planet Earth*, 146–68; Boyer, *When Time Shall Be No More*, 133; S. Maxwell Coder, *The Final Chapter* (Wheaton, IL: Tyndale) 97.

39. Falwell, *Nuclear War and the Second Coming of Jesus*; Falwell, "Twenty-first Century," 11; Boyer, *When Time Shall Be No More*, 137; Barkun, "Language of Apocalypse," 160.

40. Robertson, *Perspective*, 5; Toulouse, "Pat Robertson," 73–99; Boyer, *When Time Shall Be No More*, 138–40; Danny Collum. "Armageddon Theology as a Threat to Peace," *Faith and Mission* 4/1 (1986) 63–64; David Edwell Herrell Jr., *Pat Robertson: A Personal, Religious, and Political Portrait* (San Francisco: Harper, 1987); Graham, *World Aflame*, 246–52; Graham, *Approaching Hoofbeats*, 127–59.

41. Charles B. Strozier, *Apocalypse: On the Psychology of Fundamentalism in America* (Boston: Beacon, 1994); Stephen O'Leary, *Arguing the Apocalypse: A Theory of Millennial Rhetoric* (New York: Oxford University Press, 1994) 141; Michael R. Cosby, "The Danger of Armageddon Theology," *Covenant Quarterly* 51/3 (1993) 40–41; Chapman, "Falling in Rapture before the Bomb," 11.

The Greatest Sign

"There isn't the slightest doubt but that the emergence of the nation Israel among the family of nations is the greatest piece of prophetic news that we have had in the 20th century," said William W. Orr of the Bible Institute of Los Angeles.[42] Israel is the very linchpin of premillennial eschatology. Without the establishment of the state of Israel in 1948, dispensational thinking would make little sense.

For more than a century, dispensationalists had predicted the return of the Jews to Palestine. Prophecy now came true, a process that validated premillennial eschatology. "Perhaps the single most significant event that solidified in the minds of many the correctness of the dispensational scheme of the end times was the 'rebirth of the state of Israel.'"[43] The related developments of the twentieth century—the Balfour Declaration, the British capture of Jerusalem, and then the return of the Jews—gave great credibility to dispensationalism.

Israel became a state in 1948—about the same time the Soviet Union gained great power. Many dispensationalists had long seen Russia as the great northern power. According to Dwight Wilson, "the juxtaposition of events in 1948 brought in the succeeding months a sense of expectation that would not be equaled again." Since 1948 the central assertion of dispensationalism has been the return of Israel. This key event is seen as a divine act starting the prophetic clock and the countdown to the final days.[44]

"The existence of Israel revitalized premillennialism and gave it, at least in its own eyes, undeniable credibility," said Timothy Weber.[45] But more was to come. In June 1967 the Arabs and Israelis fought the Six-Day War. Israel won a resounding victory. It captured the Sinai Peninsula, the Gaza Strip, the Golan Heights, the West Bank, and most important of all, Jerusalem. The Six-Day War sent further chills down the prophetic spines of premillennialists. The Jews were now in a position to rebuild the temple destroyed in 70 CE—an event many believed would occur during the tribulation. Bible teacher Wilbur Smith declared, "Christians believe that the events of these recent days are part of God's plan for the ages." John

---

42. Louis T. Talbot and William W. Orr, *The Nation of Israel and the Word of God!* (Los Angeles: Bible Institute of Los Angeles, 1948) 8.

43. Grenz, *Millennial Maze*, 92.

44. Dwight Wilson, *Armageddon Now!: The Premillennial Response to Russia and Israel since 1917* (Grand Rapids: Baker, 1977) 123. See also Grenz, *Millennial Maze*, 92–93; Hagee, *Beginning of the End*, 91–94.

45. Weber, *Living in the Shadow*, 204.

Walvoord called the conquest of Jerusalem "one of the most remarkable fulfillments of biblical prophecy since the destruction of Jerusalem in A.D. 70."[46]

Of course, interest in the Jews was not new. For much of Christian history, interpreters of prophecy have looked to the Jews and often linked them to end-time events. Some believed that the Jews had to be converted before the end could come; others insisted that Israel had to be restored before the Second Advent. Darby built on this tradition by placing the Jews at the center of his theological system. Other dispensationalists continued this line of thought. Then came World War I, the Balfour Declaration, the rebirth of Israel, and the Six-Day War.[47] All of these events produced a flood of interest in the Jews. Israel became the focus of prophetic speculation. As Jerry Falwell put it, "the restoration of the nation of Israel . . . is the single greatest sign indicating the imminent return of Jesus Christ." Falwell went even further: "Since the Ascension of our Lord Jesus Christ to the right hand of His Father nearly two thousand years ago, the most important date we should remember is May 14, 1948. On that day . . . Israel became a nation again." According to other popularizers, "The Jew is God's time clock, and all prophetic truth revolves around the Jews."[48]

The restoration of Israel in 1948 became the springboard for date setting, or something close to it. As noted earlier, the parable of the fig tree in Matthew 24 was pivotal. Dispensationalists equated the budding of the fig tree with the restoration of Israel and declared that the generation alive at the time would not pass away until the end-time events began. Most popularizers regarded a biblical generation as about forty years and did an arithmetic computation: 1948 + 40 = 1988. Or, on the assumption that the rapture would occur just before the seven-year tribulation: 1948 + 40 − 7 = 1981. Other popularizers, equating the tree's budding with the Six-Day War, offered the calculation 1967 + 40 = 2007.[49]

---

46. Wilbur M. Smith, *Israeli/Arab Conflict and the Bible* (Glendale, CA: Regal, 1967) preface; John F. Walvoord, "The Amazing Rise of Israel," *Moody Monthly*, October 1967, 22. See also John F. Walvoord, *Israel in Prophecy* (Grand Rapids: Zondervan, 1962); John F. Walvoord, *Armageddon, Oil and the Middle East Crisis*, 31–51.

47. Boyer, *When Time Shall Be No More*, 181–84; David Dolan, *Holy War for the Promised Land: Israel's Struggle to Survive* (Nashville: Nelson, 1991).

48. Falwell, "Twenty-first Century," 10; Jack Van Impe with Roger F. Campbell, *Israel's Final Holocaust* (Nashville: Nelson, 1979) 9.

49. Lindsey, *Late Great Planet Earth*, 53–58; David Webber and Noah W. Hutchings, *Is This the Last Century?* (Nashville: Nelson, 1979) 45–47; Wim Malgo, *Russia's Last Invasion* (West Columbia, SC: Midnight Call, 1980) 59; Boyer, *When Time Shall Be No More*, 190.

Apocalypse Loud and Clear

The premillennialists went on to insist that God had much more in store for Israel. The events of 1948 gave the Jews a homeland; those of 1967 expanded their territory. Yet even these lands fell far short of what dispensationalists believed God had promised the Jews. As Tim LaHaye noted, "the Jews today occupy only a small portion of what God intended for them to enjoy." Most interpreters believed that a vast territory would be acquired during the millennium. Though this lies in the future, most premillennialists in America today are staunchly pro-Israeli, supporting their territorial expansion and dominance of the Palestinians.[50]

However, Israel's future also has a dark side in the view of the premillennialists. Terrible events lie ahead; Israel is destined for horrendous suffering. As if the Nazi persecution were not enough, the Jews will face a more horrible ordeal during the tribulation—Satan will pour out his hatred on them. On the other hand, many Jews will be converted during the tribulation. And during the millennium they will experience a glorious future.[51]

Satan's Global Lineup

With their attention centered on Israel, the premillennialists constructed a prophetic geopolitical scenario for the last days. Drawing from Ezekiel 38 and Daniel 2 and 7, they predicted the end-time drama. The main actors were Russia, the European confederacy, and Israel. The supporting cast would include the kings of the east and the king of the south. If the United States had a role, it was to be a minor one.

This prophetic outline first emerged during the nineteenth century among the early dispensationalists. In the opinion of most premillennialists, World War I confirmed this outline. They regarded the events of this era—the Balfour Declaration, the defeat of the Turks, the Russian

---

50. Walvoord, *Israel in Prophecy*, 63–79; Boyer, *When Time Shall Be No More*, 194–97; Tim LaHaye, *The Coming Peace in the Middle East* (Grand Rapids: Zondervan, 1984) 26; Robert G. Clouse, "The New Christian Right, America, and the Kingdom of God," *Christian Scholars Review* 12 (1983) 11–12. See also Steven R. David, "Bosom of Abraham: America's Enduring Affection for Israel," *Policy Review* 55 (Winter 1991) 57–59; Moishe Rosen, *Overture to Armageddon* (San Bernardino, CA: Here's Life, 1991) 114–16; Timothy P. Weber, *On the Road to Armageddon* (Grand Rapids: Baker, 2004); John Hagee, *In Defense of Israel* (Lake Mary: FL: Frontline, 2007).

51. Walvoord, *Israel in Prophecy*, 101–4; Walvoord, *Armageddon, Oil and the Middle East Crisis*, 169–75; Pentecost, *Things to Come*, 275–313.

Revolution, and the new map of Europe—as prophecy in action. Prophecy had been fulfilled, at least in part.

World War II and the years immediately following saw some equally striking developments—the atomic bomb, the Cold War, the United Nations, the North Atlantic Treaty Organization (NATO), and the European Economic Community (the Common Market, and now the European Union or EU). The premillennialists wove these developments into their prophetic scenarios. And any current events that ran counter to their prophetic projections they either ignored or explained away.[52]

Long before the Cold War, writers on prophecy had identified Gog with Russia. Ezekiel 38 is a prophecy against "Gog, the land of Magog, the chief prince of Meshech and Tubal." While dispensational scholars identified these locations as cities in Russia, other academics disagreed. Yet a similarity does exist: *Rosh* (the Hebrew word for "chief") resembles Russia; Meshech connects with Moscow. But most striking is that, according to Ezekiel, in the last days invading armies will come against Israel from the north. Geography clinches the argument, said John Walvoord: "The reference is to Russia . . . there is no other reasonable alternative."[53]

From 1945 to the end of the Cold War, dispensational scholars and popularizers pushed the belief that Russia would invade Israel in the final days. In the 1940s Harry Rimmer and Harry Ironside said that Russia would invade Israel for its mineral wealth. Writers on the subject have valued the mineral riches in the vicinity of the Dead Sea at between one and two trillion dollars.[54] To the contrary, Salem Kirban, pointing to the Soviet Union's chronic food shortages, argued that famine will motivate Russia's invasion.[55] To other premillennialists, oil will be Russia's incentive. Conquest of Israel will be part of Russia's strategy for controlling the oil of the Middle East. Thus Walvoord's *Armageddon, Oil and the Middle East Crisis* saw oil drawing many nations to the Middle East for a great conflict.

---

52. Boyer, *When Time Shall Be No More*, 159–60; Wilson, *Armageddon Now!*, 152.

53. John Walvoord, "Russia: King of the North," *Fundamentalist Journal* 3/1 (January 1984) 37. See Boyer, *When Time Shall Be No More*, 155; Wilson, *Armageddon Now!*, 152; Tim LaHaye, "Will God Destroy Russia?" in Tex Marrs et al., *Storming toward Armageddon* (Green Forest, AK: New Leaf, 1994) 260–64.

54. Harry Rimmer, *Shadow of Coming Events* (Grand Rapids: Eerdmans, 1946, 42–44; Boyer, *When Time Shall Be No More*, 163; Harry A. Ironside, *Expository Notes on Ezekiel the Prophet* (Neptune, NJ: Loizeaux, 1949) 267.

55. Kirban, *Guide to Survival*, 181; Boyer, *When Time Shall Be No More*, 163; LaHaye, "Will God Destroy Russia?," 265–66.

Apocalypse Loud and Clear

In *The Coming Oil War* (1980) Doug Clark similarly contended that an energy shortage will precipitate a crisis leading to war.[56]

According to Ezekiel, Gog will have allies when it attacks Israel. Foremost among them is Gomer. What is Gomer? The role of Germany has perplexed prophecy buffs. A part of Germany was in the old Roman Empire and thus a candidate for the Western confederacy that will confront Gog. The division of Germany into East and West solved this problem. East Germany fell into the Soviet orbit and thus was Gomer. But most popularizers, including Lindsey, would identify Gomer only as "part of the vast area of modern Eastern Europe."[57]

Russia has other allies. Daniel 11 mentions the kings of the south. Some interpreters regarded this as referring to Africa as a whole. Others saw it as a pan-African alliance led by Egypt. According to Lindsey, "many of the African nations will be united and allied with the Russians in the invasion of Israel."[58]

The kings of the east will also invade Israel in the last days. Before and during World War II, premillennialists generally interpreted these kings to be Japan. But with the defeat of Japan and China's embrace of communism, China came to the forefront. The Sino-Soviet alliance of the 1950s fueled this interpretation. Revelation 9:16 speaks of an army of two hundred million marching on Israel. When China boasted of its ability to assemble an army of this exact size, premillennialists took notice. In 666 Salem Kirban portrayed the Chinese troops marching on the Middle East. Hal Lindsey spoke of the vast hordes of the Orient, the Yellow Peril, and the Red Chinese war machine.[59]

But Russia and its allies will be confronted by another power bloc—the revived Roman Empire. Daniel 2 and 7 record two visions, which have impacted prophecy interpreters through the centuries and carry particular weight in dispensational circles. These chapters describe

---

56. Walvoord, *Armageddon, Oil and the Middle East Crisis*, 26–29; Doug Clark, *The Coming Oil War: Predictions of Things to Come* (Irvine, CA: Harvest House, 1980). See also Charles H. Dyer, *World News and Bible Prophecy* (Wheaton, IL: Tyndale, 1993) 115–23.

57. Lindsey, *Late Great Planet Earth*, 70; Boyer, *When Time Shall Be No More*, 166; Wilson, *Armageddon Now!*, 180; Walvoord, *Russia: King of the North*, 37.

58. Lindsey, *Late Great Planet Earth*, 68; Lindsey, *Planet Earth*, 171–83; Boyer, *When Time Shall Be No More*, 166–67; Walvoord, *Armageddon, Oil and the Middle East Crisis*, 179; James M. Boice, "Are We Nearing the Last Holocaust?," *Eternity*, December 1972, 59.

59. Kirban, 666, 234; Boyer, *When Time Shall Be No More*, 167–69; Lindsey, *Late Great Planet Earth*, 81–87; Lindsey, *1980s*; Lindsey, *There Is a New World Coming*, 124.

Nebuchadnezzar's and Daniel's visions of five future world governments. The first four governments were the Babylonian, Medo-Persian, Greek, and Roman empires. Emerging from the Roman Empire, a fifth empire is represented as having ten toes, ten horns, and ten kings—signifying a ten-nation confederacy. One horn, which is interpreted as the Antichrist, dominates the confederation.[60]

Dispensationalists had long looked for a ten-nation European confederacy to arise. In fact, a united Europe had been a dream since Charlemagne's days, a vision that never went away. The events of post-World War II Europe convinced prophetic interpreters that European unity was right around the corner. With considerable excitement they watched the establishment of the Western European Union (1948), NATO (1959), and the European Economic Community or Common Market (1957). That the treaty paving the way for the Common Market was signed in Rome, the center of the old Roman Empire, jarred the premillennialists.[61] All of these developments caused a flutter of interpretive activity, most of it linking some European institution with Daniel's fifth empire. Arno Gaebelein interpreted NATO to be the ten kings of the revived Roman Empire. Referring to NATO and the United Nations, Harry Ironside said that "the ten kingdoms are already in process of organization."[62]

As the Common Market took a definite shape, the prophetic voices grew louder. In the 1960s and 1970s the Common Market stood at fewer than ten members. Still, prophetic interpreters saw this as the probable beginning of the revived Roman Empire of the last days. As Hal Lindsey stated in 1970, "we believe that the Common Market . . . may well be the beginning of the ten-nation confederacy predicted by Daniel and the Book of Revelation." Referring to the Common Market, Edgar C. James similarly claimed that "for the first time since the fall of Roman Empire, a great new power is emerging in Europe—just as the Bible has long declared it would."[63]

---

60. This view is common in dispensational circles. See C. I. Scofield, *Scofield Reference Bible* (New York: Oxford University Press, 1909) 900-902, 909-11; LaHaye, *Beginning of the End*, 156-58; Lindsey, *Late Great Planet Earth*, 94-97; Clarence Larkin, *Dispensational Truth* (11th ed.; Philadelphia: Clarence Larkin, 1918) 119-21; Steve Terrell, *The 90's: Decade of the Apocalypse* (South Plainfield, NJ: Bridge, 1994) 1-26.

61. Herbert H. Ehrenstein, "The Common Market and Bible Prophecy," *Eternity*, March 1962, 18-20, 34; Boyer, *When Time Shall Be No More*, 126-77.

62. *Our Hope* 55 (1948-49) 673; H.A. Ironside, "Setting for the Last Act of the Great World Drama," *Our Hope* 56 (1949-50) 20. The quote is from Wilson, *Armageddon Now!* 157.

63. Lindsey, *Late Great Planet Earth*, 94; Edgar C. James, "Prophecy and the

In January 1981 the Common Market membership reached the magic number of ten. Prophecy buffs leaped for joy. However, by the 1990s the Common Market had fifteen members, which caused another problem. Bible interpreters addressed this dilemma by citing the statement in Daniel 7:8 that the little horn destroys three horns on the beast, that is to say, the Antichrist will smash some of the nations. Other nations, Britain in particular, will probably drop out of the European Union.[64] (That the European Union currently stands at twenty-seven and is still growing presents an even greater problem, but this will be addressed in a subsequent chapter).

In the 1990s the unification of Europe has continued apace. The popularizers believed that if implemented, the Maastricht Treaty would forge something close to a United States of Europe. Heading this confederacy would be the Antichrist. Based in Western Europe, he will dominate the world. For the United States will decline, Russia will be destroyed—some say by the Antichrist, others say by God's supernatural power. Then God will demolish the Antichrist at Armageddon.[65]

The Demonic World Order

A theme related to dispensational eschatology is that there will be a new world order in the last days. Satan will orchestrate a political structure to persecute God's people, and after the rapture his demonic world order will take hold. This frightening new order will destroy all aspects of individual autonomy—the traditional family, religious liberty, personal privacy, and economic freedom. Instead, it will impose a universal religion,

---

Common Market," *Moody Monthly*, March 1974, 24; Ehrenstein, "Common Market," 18–20, 34; Boice, "Are We Nearing the Last Holocaust?" 18–20, 59; J. Vernon McGee, "The Prophetic Word in Europe," in *The Prophetic Word in Crisis Days*, ed. Paul Bauman (Findlay, OH: Durham, 1961) 78.

64. Lindsey, *Planet Earth—2000 A.D.*, 225–35; Boyer, *When Time Shall Be No More*, 277; Jack Van Impe, *11:59 and Counting* (Royal Oak, MI: Jack Van Impe Ministries, 1983) 106; William R. Goetz, *Apocalypse Next and the New World Order* (Camp Hill, PA: Horizon, 1991) 117–27; Terrell, *The 90's*, xx–xxi, 11–15; Noah W. Hutchings, *The Revived Roman Empire* (Oklahoma City: Hearthstone, 1993).

65. Kirban, *Guide to Survival*, 16–62; Boyer, *When Time Shall Be No More*, 254–55; Robertson, *New World Order*, 26–34; Robertson, *New Millennium*, 163–80; LaHaye, *Beginning of the End*, 87–134; Lindsey, *Planet Earth*, 11–25; Dyer, *World News and the Bible Prophecy*, 185–206; John Ankerberg and John Weldon, *One World: Biblical Prophecy and the New World Order* (Chicago: Moody, 1991) 21–28; Fiammetta Rocco, "The Antichrist of the Berlaymont," *Spectator*, 19 September 1992, 15–17.

a standardized economy, and totalitarian political control—all dominated by impersonal global structures. Indeed, many believed George Orwell's *1984* was on the horizon.[66]

But before this new world order is in place, the old one has to collapse. A transition must take place. Premillennialists in the late twentieth century insisted that signs of the new political order were visible—the Common Market, Russian power, and the rise of China. Likewise, they were examining the cultural landscape for indications of the new demonic order. For the premillennialists insisted that Scripture has predicted not only the end-time political scenario, but cultural developments as well.

What were these prophetic signs? Premillennialists saw civilizations literally disintegrating before their eyes; the disordered cosmos described in Revelation was under way. The family structure was unraveling; teenagers rebelled against their parents. Violence and immorality ran rampant. In religion apostasy loomed large. Premillennialists regarded the National Council of Churches, the World Council, and ecumenical movement as demonic forerunners of the apostate universal religion. Theological liberalism and Roman Catholicism also came under attack.[67]

Moreover, dispensationalists have earmarked the emerging global economy for special denunciation. The Antichrist will consolidate the world's economy by controlling energy, the financial system, and the food supply. Collectivism, socialism, and the welfare state are signs of things to come. Premillennialists pointed to the International Monetary Fund, the World Bank, the Federal Reserve Board, and the Common Market as forerunners of the new global economic order.[68]

---

66. Boyer, *When Time Shall Be No More*, 254–55; Edgar Z. Friedenberg, "George Orwell's Neglected Prophecy," *Dalhousie Review* 69/1 (1989) 270–75; Van Impe, 2001, 85–92; Hagee, *Beginning of the End*, 117–20.

67. For these general conditions see William T. James, "Characteristics of End-Time Man," in *Storming toward Armageddon*, 21–45; Ray Brubaker, "The Unmistakable Evidence Mounts: Christ's Return is Imminent," in *Storming toward Armageddon*, 47–62; Kirban, *Guide to Survival*, 48–91; Robertson, *New Millennium*, 183–200; Graham, *World Aflame*, 1–49; Graham, *Approaching Hoofbeats*, 83–105; LaHaye, *Beginning of the End*, 125–33; Robert Van Kempen, *The Sign* (Wheaton, IL: Crossway, 1992) 145–56; Dave Hunt and T. A. McMahon, *The Seduction of Christianity* (Eugene, OR: Harvest House, 1985).

68. For these general conditions see Mary Stewart Relfe, *When Your Money Fails: The 666 System Is Here* (Montgomery, AL: Ministries, Inc., 1981); Dave Hunt, *Peace, Prosperity and the Coming Holocaust* (Eugene, OR: Harvest House, 1983) 155–86; Texe Marrs, *Millennium: Peace, Promises and the Day They Take Our Money Away* (Austin, TX: Living Truth, 1990) 115–75; Grant R. Jeffrey, *Prince of Darkness* (Toronto: Frontier Research, 1994) 146–56; "Signs of Times," *This Week in Bible Prophecy*, June 1994, 4–5.

Premillennialists contended that Scripture predicts a one-world government, so the United Nations is particularly suspect. They fiercely denounced any attempt to reduce national sovereignty and place American interests under UN control. Prophecy interpreters regarded the Trilateral Commission—that shadowy international organization comprising the United States, Japan, and Western Europe—as the ultimate conspiracy. Its membership consisted of some of the world's most powerful political and economic leaders. Behind the scenes they pull the puppet strings, exercising immense global control.[69]

The vehicle for political and economic control is modern technology. Computers, communications satellites, credit cards, money machines, laser-read price markings, fax machines, the Internet, and much more will soon make a global system a reality. For the first time in history, global control can be achieved—so the premillennialists say. Computers will "dictate that every man, woman, and child in the world lives, works, buys, and sells under a system of code marks and numbers," says William Goetz.[70]

Basic to premillennial thinking, then, is "the belief that a demonic world order lies ahead, and that its beginnings may be discerned in contemporary world trends."[71] Through TV, radio, videos, the Internet, and mass paperbacks premillennialists have communicated this worldview to millions of people.

Will the Real Antichrist Please Stand Up!

The new demonic world order presupposes two things: the collapse of the old order and the appearance of the Antichrist. In premillennial thinking both concepts jumped to the forefront. Western society must face a

---

69. Marrs, *Millennium*, 35–66; Joseph R. Chambers, "The Rise of Babylon," in *Storming toward Armageddon*, 100–102; Lindsey, *Planet Earth*, 47–63; Hunt, *Peace, Prosperity and the Coming Holocaust*, 47–60; Robertson, *New World Order*, 95–115; Goetz, *Apocalypse Next*, 191–220; Jeffrey, *Prince of Darkness*, 103–11; Gary H. Kah, *En Route to Global Occupation* (Lafayette, LA: Huntington House, 1992) 120–40; Norman N. Franz, "One World Government," *Monetary Economic Review*, March 1993, 1, 11–13; Larry Bates, "New World Order—Phase II," *Monetary and Economic Review*, May 1993, 1, 11–13.

70. Goetz, *Apocalypse Next*, 202; Relfe, *When Your Money Fails*, 115–29; William T. James, "The Computer Messiah Comes Forth!," in *Storming toward Armageddon*, 71–92; Jeffrey, *Prince of Darkness*, 91–102; Robertson, *New Millennium*, 209–23.

71. Boyer, *When Time Shall Be No More*, 266, 268–70 (quote); Hagee, *Beginning of the End*, 117–30; Van Impe, 86–90.

political and economic crisis of unprecedented proportions, and then the Antichrist will take power. Signs of decay of the old order already abound, especially in the economy. Larry Burkett's *Coming Economic Earthquake* contended that America stands on the brink of economic collapse. While Burkett passed away in 2003, the "Great Recession" beginning in 2008 reinforced this thinking and other evangelicals picked up on the same theme.[72] Moral, social, and political anarchy will compound this crisis and push the old order over the edge.

The premillennialists have a scenario to accommodate this crisis. They did not invent the idea of the Antichrist, but in a secular world that tends to make light of such ideas, dispensationalism has accentuated it — sometimes in a very serious way and sometimes by reducing "it to a child's plaything."[73]

The concept of the Antichrist rests on several passages in Daniel, Revelation, Mark, 2 Thessalonians, and 1 and 2 John. Daniel 7:8 speaks of the "little horn" that sprouts from the beast. Revelation 13 portrays the Antichrist as a seven-headed beast that emerges from the sea and performs great wonders. In Mark 13:22 Jesus warns of false Christs arising in the last days, and the Apostle Paul speaks of the "man of sin" or "lawless one" in 2 Thessalonians 2:3. 1 and 2 John contain the only specific references to the Antichrist in Scripture. But John speaks of the Antichrist only as an evil force, not as an individual. Premillennialists insist that the Antichrist is a person and thus ironically do not emphasize these verses.[74]

For nearly two thousand years Christians have interpreted these passages in various ways. The result is a diverse tradition that alternately construes Antichrist as an individual, an institution, a movement, and evil in general. Some have even believed in two Antichrists—perhaps a force of evil or a blasphemous person labeled a type of the Antichrist, and then the final enemy. Before World War II a number of individuals and

---

72. Larry Burkett, *The Coming Economic Earthquake* (Chicago: Moody, 1991). See also Norman N. Franz, "The World Financial System," *Monetary and Economic Review*, April 1994, 1, 9, 15; John Hagee, *Financial Armageddon* (Lake Mary, FL: Frontline, 2008).

73. Bernard McGinn, *Antichrist: Two Thousand Years of Human Fascination with Evil* (San Francisco: Harper, 1994) 253.

74. The key biblical passages on the Antichrist include Dan 2:41; 7:7; 8:24; 9: 26–27; 11:31; Matt 24:15–16, 23–24; Mark 13:32; 2 Thess 2:3; 1 John 4:3; 2 John 1:7; and Rev 13:1, 5; 17:12. See D. A. Hubbard, "Antichrist," in *Dictionary of Theology*, ed. Walter A. Elwell (Grand Rapids: Baker, 1984) 55–56; Paul Lee Tan, *Interpretation of Prophecy* (Winona Lake, IN: BMH, 1974); Walter K. Price, *The Coming Antichrist* (Chicago: Moody, 1974).

Apocalypse Loud and Clear

institutions made the list of potential Antichrists or types of the beast: Antiochus Epiphanes, Nero, a Jew from the tribe of Dan, Judas Iscariot, the papacy as an institution, individual popes, Frederick II Hohenstaufen, Napoleon, Mussolini, and Hitler. The most enduring identification of the Antichrist through history has been the papacy.[75]

After 1945 the quest for the Antichrist produced some amazing theories. Throughout history the search has often focused on finding evidence of conspiracy.[76] During the last fifty years or so, however, this pursuit may have risen to new heights in premillennial circles. Some dispensationalists are tenaciously seeking the identity of the beast, for they believe that he is now alive somewhere in the world.

The vast majority of premillennialists believe that the Antichrist is an individual. So the popularizers have come up with name after name. But some dispensationalists see the Antichrist as a system or a movement. Other premillennialists muddy the waters. While they may hold to an individual Antichrist, they tend to see certain systems as in league with the beast. They often regard these movements and systems as demonic and make them synonymous with the Antichrist. The consensus among premillennialists in the late twentieth century seemed to be that the Antichrist will be "a European, as yet unknown, who [will] rule a ten-nation revived Roman Empire, then extend his domain worldwide," says Paul Boyer.[77]

The more sober dispensationalists were content with the Antichrist's anonymity. They did not feel the necessity to name him. But the prophetic popularizers felt no such restraints—they were reckless and discredited premillennialism in the process. The list of potential Antichrists reads like a who's who. Since 1945 the suggestions have included Pope Pius XII, John

75. See Bernard McGinn, *Antichrist*; Bernard McGinn, *Visions of the End: Apocalyptic Traditions in the Middle Ages* (New York: Columbia University Press, 1979); James Alan Patterson, "Changing Images of the Beast: Apocalyptic Conspiracy Theories in American History," *Journal of the Evangelical Theological Society* 31 (December 1988) 443-52; Norman Cohn, *Pursuit of the Millennium* (rev. ed.; New York: Oxford University Press, 1974); Walter Klaassen, *Living at the End of the Ages* (Lanham, MD: University Press of America, 1992); Michael J. St. Clair, *Millenarian Movements in Historical Context* (New York: Garland, 1992).

76. See Brooks Alexander, "The Final Threat: Apocalypse, Conspiracy, and Biblical Faith," *SCP Newsletter*, January-February 1984, 7-8; Patterson, "Changing Images of the Beast," 447-49; William T. Still, *New World Order: The Ancient Plan of Secret Societies* (Lafayette, LA: Huntington House, 1990).

77. Boyer, *When Time Shall Be No More*, 276 (quote). See Jimmy Swaggart, *Armageddon: The Future of Planet Earth* (Baton Rouge, LA: Jimmy Swaggart Ministries, 1987) 130-34.

F. Kennedy, Pope John XXIII, Henry Kissinger, Moshe Dayan, Pope John Paul II, Anwar Sadat, Jimmy Carter, Ronald Reagan, Pat Robertson, King Juan Carlos of Spain, Sun Myung Moon, Mikhail Gorbachev, and Saddam Hussein.[78] (New names have been added in the early twenty-first century).

The popularizers seemed to use one or two criteria to determine the identity of the Antichrist—the number 666 (Rev 13:18) and evidence of a deadly wound (Rev 13:3).[79] A person is really suspect if both criteria apply. In efforts to decipher the meaning of 666, letters of the alphabet are assigned numerical equivalents. Of course, the numbers will vary according to the language employed, and an interpreter can arbitrarily assign a particular value to each letter. As a result, if one works at it, one can find some way of associating a good many names with the number 666.

Henry Kissinger became a favorite candidate for the Antichrist. He was a Jew who orchestrated several peace initiatives. Also, ways were devised to make the letters in his name total 666. Another proposal alleged that tanks in Jimmy Carter's secret force were stamped 666. Other individuals met both tests. There are six letters in each of Ronald Wilson Reagan's names, and his house address in California was 666. Moreover, as president he was shot. When President Sadat of Egypt reopened the Suez Canal in 1975, his ship had 666 on the bow. In addition, he later received a mortal wound.[80]

Some candidates for the Antichrist primarily met the deadly wound test. Moshe Dayan, the hero of the Six-Day War, had previously lost his eye in action. Not only did John F. Kennedy's Roman Catholic faith arouse fears of the Antichrist, but he fell to an assassin's bullets. Some expected him to rise from the dead. Other individuals denounced Pope John Paul II as Antichrist, partly because of the attempt on his life, partly because of his endorsement of greater European economic and administrative cooperation.[81]

---

78. See William Martin, "Waiting for End," *Atlantic Monthly*, June 1982, 35–36; McGinn, *Antichrist*, 259–61; Raymond L. Cox, "Will the Real Antichrist Please Stand Up!," *Eternity*, May 1974, 15–17, 60; Boyer, *When Time Shall Be No More*, 275–78; Robert Faid, "Gorby the Antichrist," *Harper's Magazine*, January 1989, 24–26. Other candidates have included Kurt Waldheim, Willy Brandt, and Muammar el-Qaddafi.

79. Cox, "Will the Real Antichrist Please Stand Up!," 15–16.

80. Martin, "Waiting for the End," 35; Cox, "Will the Real Antichrist Please Stand Up!," 17; Robert C. Fuller, *Naming the Antichrist: The History of an American Obsession* (New York: Oxford University Press, 1995) 166; Relfe, *When Your Money Fails*, 31, 138; Tom Sine, "Bringing Down the Final Curtain," *Sojourners* 13/6 (June–July 1984) 12–13.

81. Fuller, *Naming the Antichrist*, 160; Boyer, *When Time Shall Be No More*, 274–77;

Apocalypse Loud and Clear

Many dispensationalists are fundamentalists who tend to regard the world system and even culture in general as demonic. Thus they identify a variety of elements in the global order as forces of the Antichrist. Frequently targeted were Roman Catholicism, liberal Protestantism, the global economic system, modern technology, Jews, socialism, communism, the New Age movement, Islam, environmentalism, the Common Market, the Soviet Union, feminism, peace organizations, and rock music.[82]

The criteria most often employed by premillennialists to determine the forces in league with the Antichrist have been the number 666 and global control. As in identifying individuals, popularizers have devised ingenious mathematical formulas and applied them to particular institutions or movements. For example, elaborate schemes have associated both New York City and computers with 666. Premillennialists have also warned that certain international economic, political, and cultural institutions have the potential for global dominance. Such organizations will band together and enable the Antichrist to control the world.[83]

The targeting of Roman Catholicism largely subsided after 1945. Indeed, many fundamentalists now praise Catholicism's stance against communism, feminism, homosexuality, and abortion, and its support of family values. Still, the old anti-Catholicism has not completely died out. Dave Hunt implied that the Catholic Church is the false prophet who will assist the Antichrist, and John Ankerberg and John Weldon connected the pope with the Antichrist's message.[84]

What was most denounced in the late twentieth century as a force of the Antichrist is the global economic system. It was pointed out that, according to Scripture, a revived Roman Empire will wield great economic power; the beast will have absolute control. In order to buy and sell, in order to receive basic services, one will need to have the mark of the beast, probably an invisible mark implanted in the body. The Antichrist will control a global credit system, which in fact is currently in place. Thus Mary

---

Cox, "Will the Real Antichrist Please Stand Up!," 15–16; "Paisley and the Pope," *Time*, 24 October 1988, 62.

82. Fuller, *Naming the Antichrist*, 134–90.

83. Relfe, *When Your Money Fails*, 15–40; Boyer, *When Time Shall Be No More*, 282–83; Fuller, *Naming the Antichrist*, 179–84; Hutchings, *Revived Roman Empire*, 121–30.

84. Dave Hunt, *Global Peace and the Rise of the Antichrist* (Eugene, OR: Harvest House, 1990) 99–111; Ankerberg and Weldon, *One World*, 19. See also Lindsey, *Planet Earth—2000 A.D.*, 231; Boyer, *When Time Shall Be No More*, 275; Fuller, *Naming the Antichrist*, 145–48; Ken Klein, *The False Prophet* (Eugene, OR: Winterhaven, 1993).

Relfe said, "The 666 system is here." The World Bank code number is 666. J.C. Penney prefixes its accounts with 666. And by using three languages Visa can be construed to equal 666: VI is the Roman numeral for six; "six" in classical Greek looks like the letter S; and in Babylonian the letter A has the value of six.[85]

In the last days there will also be a global religion controlled by the Antichrist and the false prophet. The New Age movement with its pantheism and mysticism embodies this end-time religion, said some premillennialists. According to Dave Hunt, when the end comes, "millions of New Agers in thousands of network groups around the world will be sincerely implementing the Antichrist's programs in the name of peace, brotherhood, and love."[86] Similarly, in *The Hidden Dangers of the Rainbow* (1983), Constance Cumbey portrayed the New Age movement as a gigantic satanic conspiracy designed to control the world and force the universal worship of the Antichrist. She asserted that "for the first time in history there is a viable movement—the New Age Movement—that truly meets all scriptural requirements for the Antichrist and the political movement that will bring him on the world scene."[87]

The popularizers earmark many other institutions as in league with the Antichrist, and the list is long and growing. But most important is the issue of control. These institutions and modern technology were viewed as enabling the beast to enforce his will on the entire world. Individuality and freedom in all forms will be stamped out. In fact, some popularizers have even gone so far as to suggest that the Antichrist might be a computer. Jack Van Impe theorized that the "Antichrist will enslave and control Earth's billions through a sophisticated computer fashioned in his likeness."[88]

85. Relfe, *When Your Money Fails*, 18–22; McGinn, *Antichrist*, 261; Patterson, "Changing Images of the Beast," 451: Fuller, *Naming the Antichrist*, 185; Marrs, *Millennium*, 84–87; 177–80; Jeffrey, *Prince of Darkness*, 103–9; Sylvia J. Michaelson, *The New World Order: The Mark ($) of the Beast* (Helena: MT: Ministering Angel, 1991); Van Impe, 2001, 123–29.

86. Hunt, *Peace, Prosperity, and the Coming Holocaust*, 35, 52, 68, 80, 108, 122, 145, 180, 198, 232. See also Boyer, *When Time Shall Be No More*, 233–34; Fuller, *Naming the Antichrist*, 183–84; Marrs, *Millennium*, 181–82.

87. Constance Cumbey, *The Hidden Dangers of the Rainbow: The New Age Movement and Our Coming Age of Barbarism* (rev. ed.; Layfayette, LA: Huntington House, 1983) 7. See also Richard Kyle, *The New Age Movement in American Culture* (Lanham, MD: University Press of America, 1995) 202.

88. James, "Computer Messiah Comes Forth!," 71–92; Boyer, *When Time Shall Be No More*, 283; Van Impe, 11:59 *and Counting*, 119, 121, 208; Van Impe, 2001, 124–28; Relfe, *When Your Money Fails*, 115–29; Ankerberg and Weldon, *One World*, 141–48; Jeffrey, *Prince of Darkness*, 110–11.

Apocalypse Loud and Clear

THE SHIFTING SANDS OF PROPHECY

The late twentieth century witnessed a number of earthshaking events. Some seemed to disrupt the dispensational end-time scenario—especially the collapse of communism in Eastern Europe, the unraveling of the Soviet Union, the end of the Cold War, and the reduction of the nuclear threat. On the other hand, the Persian Gulf War and the continuing move toward European unity reinvigorated dispensationalism.

How did the prophetic popularizers respond to these events? For the most part, they continued to maintain their traditional themes. After all, the main outline of their prophetic predictions remained intact. But when disconfirmations arose, the chameleon-like quality of popular dispensationalism came to the forefront. Interpretations were adapted to the shifting sands of world events.[89]

The popularizers could feel good about a number of things. Israel still existed and struggled against the Arab world. Although some observers looked with concern on Israel's peace overtures to the Palestine Liberation Movement, the centerpiece of premillennial eschatology—the Israeli state—remained intact. Further, in the 1990s European unification proceeded apace. Accordingly, some popularizers shifted their attention from the Soviet Union to an apparent prophetic confirmation—the European Union. On the economic side, globalization accelerated. A worldwide financial system, multinational corporations, and a global information network drew the world closer. On the social ledger, human wickedness increased and morals declined—key ingredients in any last-days scenario.[90]

The Persian Gulf War of 1991 shot adrenaline into the veins of the premillennial world. The popularizers felt right at home. A flood of end-time publications rolled off the press; prophecy books boomed in sales. Some popularizers saw Saddam Hussein's invasion of Kuwait as the beginning of the end: "The nations of the world are drifting into their final formation of alliances for the Tribulation Period," declared Salem Kirban.

89. Boyer, *When Time Shall Be No More*, 325–26.
90. See "As it Was in the Days of Noah," *Midnight Call*, September 1992, 4–10; "Signs of the Times," 4–6; Norman N. Franz "The Truth about NAFTA," *Monetary and Economic Review*, July 1994, 13–15; Franz, "World Financial System," 1,9,15; Norman N. Franz, "PLO Wants Israel," *Monetary and Economic Review*, September 1993, 1, 7, 13; Arno Froese, "Europe: Beyond 2000—the USA," *Midnight Call*, May 1994, 7–15; Jeffrey, *Prince of Darkness*, 103–21, 142–43; Dyer, *World News and Prophecy*, 185–206; Dave Breese, "Europe and the Prince That Shall Come," in *Storming toward Armageddon*, 173–201.

Focusing on Revelation 18 and its predictions of the destruction of Babylon, some premillennialists believed that Saddam Hussein was about to rebuild ancient Babylon. "The Bible makes it clear that Babylon will be rebuilt," said Charles Dyer.[91] Although Iraq's rapid defeat by the United States took much of the steam out of this interest in eschatology, most popularizers viewed Saddam Hussein as a type of the Antichrist and the Persian Gulf War as a dress rehearsal for Armageddon.[92]

Still, dispensationalism's view of the end encountered some rough water—especially the collapse of the Soviet Union and the end of the Cold War. How did the prophetic popularizers respond to this apparent disconfirmation? After all, the belief that Gog will invade Israel is central to popular premillennial eschatology. There were three basic responses.

Some premillennialists ignored these world happenings. Instead, they focused on apparent fulfillments of prophecy, especially European unity. They also took notice of global problems with apocalyptic dimensions—environmental disasters, world famine, and plagues.

Most common was the second response. Many popularizers regarded the events in Eastern Europe and the Soviet Union as temporary glitches. The bear has not been declawed, they said; it will be back. Russia's "land and naval forces remain strong" and the country "still has basic resources to rebuild her tattered economy," warned Charles Dyer. Or, as Hal Lindsey put it, "Yes, the Evil Empire may be gone, but Russia's role in the end times scenario remains the same."[93] A more radical version of this second response was Grant Jeffrey's discussion of what he called "the Great Russian Deception." Supposedly, communism is dead and Russia is weak both militarily and economically. But "the KGB and Communist Party have embarked upon the greatest deception plan in history ... Glas-

91. Kenneth L. Woodward, "The Final Days Are Here Again," *Newsweek*, 18 March 1991, 55; David Jeremiah, "Prophecy and the Persian Gulf," *Christian Herald*, November 1990, 8; Peter Steinfels, "Gulf War Proving Bountiful for Some Prophets of Doom," *New York Times*, 2 February 1991, 1, 10: Jeffery L. Sheler, "A Revelation in the Middle East," *U.S. News and World Report*, 19 November 1990, 67–68; Boyer, *When Time Shall Be No More*, 328 (Kirban quote); Charles H. Dyer, *The Rise of Babylon: Sign of the End Times* (Wheaton, IL: Tyndale, 1991) cover: John F. Burns, "New Babylon Is Stalled by a Modern Upheaval," *New York Times*, 11 October 1990.

92. Molly Guthrey, "Prelude to Armageddon?," *Minnesota Daily*, 16 January 1991, 1, 14; Russell Chandler, "Persian Gulf Threat Inspires Warnings of Fiery Armageddon," *Minneapolis Star Tribune*, 21 September 1990, 17A; Sheler, "Revelation in the Middle East," 67–68; Dyer, *World News and Bible Prophecy*, 140.

93. Dyer, *World News and Bible Prophecy*, 104; Lindsey, *Planet Earth*, 190. See also Scot Overbey, *Vladimir Zhirinovsky: The Man Who Would Be God* (Oklahoma City: Hearthstone, 1994); Van Impe, 2001, 41–53.

Apocalypse Loud and Clear

nost, perestroika and democracy are simply disinformation designed to deceive the West."[94]

A third response seriously questioned the identification of Russia with Gog. Mark Hitchcock contended that the northern power that will invade Israel is actually an Islamic confederation. The real threat to Israel comes from Islam, not Russia. The southern republics of the former Soviet Union are now independent Muslim nations. They will form an alliance with other Islamic nations, including Turkey, and become the northern confederacy that attacks Israel.[95] (Versions of the Islamic threat to Israel become even more pronounced in the twenty-first century and will be the subject for a future chapter).

Premillennialists also noted other developments in late-twentieth-century events. Although the Soviet nuclear menace is diminished, the spread of nuclear technology to smaller nations means that the threat was not over. The rise of German and Japanese economic power has also not gone unnoticed. Germany was seen as the dominant power in the western confederacy, and Japan may join China as the Asian powers that threaten Israel.[96] Whatever events occur in the future, premillennialism will probably continue to demonstrate a remarkable ability to adjust its predictions to the reality of world affairs.

THE PROPAGATION OF PREMILLENNIALISM

By the late twentieth century, premillennial eschatology had captured the interest of millions of Americans. Why? A number of factors have contributed to this development—some religious, others political and cultural. To start, premillennialism had become entrenched within the evangelical subculture before World War II. While the evangelical faith has always occupied a significant place in American religion, since World War II it has experienced a surge in growth. By the end of the twentieth century, about 25–30 percent of the American population could be categorized as evangelical. Further, in the 1970s evangelicals became politically active, and

94. Jeffrey, *Prince of Darkness*, 161.

95. Mark Hitchcock, *After the Evil Empire: The Fall of the Soviet Union and Bible Prophecy* (Oklahoma City: Hearthstone, 1992) 6–7.

96. Dominique Lagarde, "The Highest Bidder Gets the Weapons," *World Press Review*, December 1991, 11; "Germany: The Next Super Power?," *Midnight Call*, June 1992, 15; "End-Time Destruction," *God's News Behind the News*, July–August 1994, 6–7; "Hands of Doomsday Clock Are Moved Up Three Minutes," *Wichita Eagle*, 9 December 1995, 7A.

one of their own (Jimmy Carter) even became president. By the 1990s they constituted an important power bloc in American politics. The mere fact that premillennialists constitute a notable presence within evangelicalism has given their end-time ideas a boast. Indeed, the vitality of the evangelical faith has provided a vehicle for promoting premillennial eschatology in the late twentieth century.[97]

Closely related was the use of the mass media by premillennialists. During the 1930s and 1940s they began to propagate their ideas by means of the radio. This small beginning turned into a flood after World War II. Along with other evangelicals the premillennialists became quite adept at using the mass media—especially television and paperback books. Premillennialist popularizers frequently preach their end-time message on television. But most important, they have mass-produced countless paperbacks for an eager audience that has gobbled them up by the millions. Indeed, the premillennial message has gotten out in a big way.

Still, there must be an audience for such ideas. And, in fact, the cultural and political climate of the late twentieth century had produced an audience with an apocalyptic mindset. Throughout the twentieth century the dominant mood in Western society has been one of pessimism. Successive military conflicts, the specter of nuclear annihilation, energy shortages, regional famines, threats to the environment, and financial crises have cast a foreboding shadow across the future of humanity. In such an environment the premillennialist doomsday predictions appear quite credible.[98]

Of crucial importance, specific dispensational predictions appeared to be coming true right before people's eyes. This, of course, gave early dispensationalism much credibility. And the trend increased after World War II. The establishment of the Israeli state in 1948, the capture of Jerusalem in the Six-Day War, the growth of Soviet power, the development of nuclear weapons, and the organization of the European Common Market were seen as prophecy in action. And nothing gives prophecy more weight than its apparent confirmation. One confirmation carries more weight than do several disconfirmations.

Finally, the psychological makeup of many evangelicals, especially the fundamentalist variety, may be a factor in the growth of dispensational eschatology. Throughout history socially deprived people have been

---

97. Boyer, *When Time Shall Be No More*, 293–94; Richard Kyle, *Evangelicalism: An Americanized Christianity* (New Brunswick, NJ: Transaction, 2006) 167–209.

98. Grenz, *Millenial Maze*, 20–22.

vulnerable to apocalyptic ideas. But most of the contemporary premillennialists do not come from the lower social orders. They are not the powerless. In fact, they often have considerable political and economic clout. Why then do they embrace apocalyptic ideas? One theory contends that they are a cognitive minority. Premillennialists embrace a supernatural worldview, a perspective that is out of step with the modern mindset. Whether they are actually oppressed as a result is less important than how they feel. Many fundamentalists feel tyrannized by society and thus are alienated from the world. Their eagerness to embrace apocalypticism, then, is not surprising.[99]

99. O'Leary, *Arguing the Apocalypse*, 8–10; Boyer, *When Time Shall Be No More*, 293.

6

Millennial Anxieties

As THE SECOND MILLENNIUM moved to a close, many asked if the end was near? Yes said widely dissimilar categories of people—dispensational fundamentalists, UFO cultists, and interpreters of Nostradamus and the Mayan calendar. The last thirty years of the twentieth century witnessed a surge of predictions from several quarters—Christians, New Agers, psychics, environmentalists, and Native Americans. Yes, apocalyptic thinking was in the air.[1]

As Hillel Schwartz noted, the end of a century prompts an apocalyptic stir. So much more so for 2000. It stood at the end of a millennium, not just another century. Ted Daniels, editor of *Millennial Prophecy Report*, accurately predicted that "When the world's odometer ticks over to three zeros, it will have cosmic significance."[2] According to Richard Erdoes, people were speaking of the "Second Coming—the coming of Christ, of the anointed Messiah, of the Tenth Imam, of the Mahdi, even of Buddha." Some neo-Nazis were eagerly awaiting the reappearance of the Fuhrer from outer space. A collection of individuals and groups on the margins of society, including "Neo-Nostradamians, Paracelsians, Cagliostroans,

1. Stephen D. O'Leary, *Arguing the Apocalypse: A Theory of Millennial Rhetoric* (New York: Oxford University Press, 1994) 3; Gary DeMar, *Last Days Madness: The Folly of Trying to Predict When Christ Will Return* (Brentwood, TN: Wolgemuth and Hyatt, 1991) 209.

2. Hillel Schwartz, "Fin-de Siecle Fantasies," *New Republic*, 30 July and 6 August 1990, 22 (quote); Jeffery L. Sheler, "The Christmas Covenant," *U.S. News and World Report*, 19 December 1994, 62.

Millennial Anxieties

Saucerians, Pyramidians, followers of Edgar Cayce the sleeping Prophet, of Wanda the Ultra-Aquarian, of Joseph the Hairstyling Augur, and of other sooth-or-gloomsayers," predicted that some cosmic cataclysm would destroy the world or a portion of it.[3]

But it was not only the eccentrics walking the streets with placards "proclaiming the end of the world who [thought] that this planet of ours might not survive the twentieth century." Perfectly rational people, including scientists and Nobel laureates, "predict humankind's demise due to overpopulation, famines, deforestation, pollution, depletion of the Earth's ozone layer, or simply the collapse of civilization due to the exhaustion of essential, non-renewable raw materials."[4] Perhaps most pervasive was the fear of the Y2K bug, that is, the global computer system would malfunction on January 1, 2000 and create widespread chaos. An apocalyptic mentality was pervasive in the minds of both strange and sane individuals. On the other hand, the collapse of communism and the diminished possibility of a nuclear holocaust have encouraged a degree of optimism. Such a positive outlook fits into the predictions of many New Age groups, which anticipate not the end of the world but a new and improved age.

WHY 2000?

Why the frenzy over 2000? It was a subjective date with no significance in the Bible, ancient writings, or science. In fact, the third millennium began in 2001, not 2000. Yet the world went wild on December 31, 1999. Millennial parties were completely booked years in advance. Major gatherings took place at Stonehenge, the Great Wall of China, the Great Pyramid, the Eiffel Tower, the Taj Mahal, the Acropolis, Red Square, and aboard the *Queen Elizabeth II*.[5]

---

3. Richard Erdoes, *A.D. 1000: Living on the Brink of the Apocalypse* (New York: Harper and Row, 1988) x. See also Curt Suplee, "Apocalypse Now: The Coming Doom Boom," *Washington Post*, 17 December 1989, B1-2; Ron Rhodes, "Millennial Madness," *Christian Research Journal* 13/2 (Fall 1990) 39; Richard Kyle, *The Religious Fringe: A History of Alternative Religions in America* (Downers Grove, IL: InterVarsity, 1993) 376.

4. Erdoes, *A.D. 1000*, x; (quote); Kyle, *Religious Fringe*, 377.

5. Schwartz, "Fin-de Siecle Fantasies," 23; Leslie Savan, "The Biggest Party Ever!," *Working Woman*, January 1991, 72; Jill Smolowe, "Tonight We're Gonna Party Like It's 1999," *Time*, Fall 1992 (special issue), 10-11; William David Spencer, "Does Anyone Really Know What Time It Is?," *Christianity Today*, 17 July 1995, 29.

Other dates have inspired end-of-the-world excitement—999, 1013, 1300, 1600, 1666, 1844, and 1914. Still 2000 was different. It excited perhaps unparalleled passion. A nice round number, 2000 marked the end of a century and a millennium and had tremendous psychological appeal. And thanks to the global calendar and modern technology, nearly the whole world celebrated the dawn of a new millennium simultaneously. The year 2000 just seemed like a time when something momentous would happen, something like the end of the world.[6]

Beyond the usual eschatological frenzy that a string of zeroes could arouse, there existed several other psychological factors. Curt Suplee listed five of them. One, in the twenty years preceding 2000 there have been a lot of natural and unnatural disasters—perhaps not more than in past years, but we were more aware of the them. Two, a deep numerical determinism griped many people; they saw historical epochs coming in tens and groups of tens. Next, people have a growing appetite for the weird, especially in religion; witness the strange activities in many fringe religions. Four, in the decades before 2000 America had experienced tremendous social change, and social change often prompts people to expect a great cosmic change. Lastly, American society was gripped with a sense of inadequacy; the problems seemed overwhelming. In such a climate people looked for some ultimate calamity.[7]

Also of tremendous importance was the view of the date of creation. Through the centuries Christians have believed that God created the world in six days and rested on the seventh. And according to 2 Peter 3:8, a day with the Lord is as a thousand years. Thus the millennium or the end of time must come six thousand years after creation. Such a scenario has provided the grist for much date setting. When the world was created, however, is a matter of speculation. Thus prophets have considerable flexibility—at least until 2000. Inasmuch as no one has claimed a date for creation later than 4000 BCE, 2000 CE was somewhat of a dead end.[8]

Events in the late twentieth century also pointed to 2000—so some thought. "Since 1945 it began to be technologically feasible to end life on

6. Schwartz, "Fin-de-Siecle Fantasies," 23–24; Daniel Cohen, *Waiting for the Apocalypse* (Buffalo: Prometheus, 1983) 247; Dick Teresi and Judith Hooper, "The Last Laugh?" *Omni* 12/4 (January 1990) 43.

7. Suplee, "Apocalypse Now," B1–2. See also Kenneth A. Myers, "Fear and Frenzy on the Eve of A.D. 2000," *Genesis*, January 1990, 1, 3.

8. Daniel Cohen, *Prophets of Doom* (Brookfield, CT: Millbrook, 1992) 15; Cohen, *Waiting for the Apocalypse*, 83; Schwartz, "Fin-de-Siecle Fantasies," 25: William A. Alnor, *Soothsayers of the Second Advent* (Old Tappan, NJ: Revell, 1989) 99–107.

Millennial Anxieties

this planet," noted philosopher Michael Grosso.[9] Either a nuclear holocaust or an environmental disaster could do us in. "It is an age of terror," wrote Ulrich Kortner. "The catastrophic possibilities have obtained hitherto unimagined dimensions in our century."[10] While conditions did not lock people into the year 2000, they made it appear likely as an approximate date.

The overall irrationality of the age also pointed to 2000. There existed no rational basis for endowing the year 2000 with end-time significance. Apocalyptic thinking, however, involves a certain amount of irrationality, which the focus on 2000 raised to another level. Predictions regarding 2000 had no biblical or scientific basis. Rather, they rested largely on psychic vibrations, dreams, astrological projections, and so forth.

CHRISTIAN PROPHETS AND 2000

What predictions pointed to the year 2000? Actually, there were fewer than one might suppose. Rather, there existed more of an apocalyptic mood than a rash of specific predictions. Christians have made many end-time predictions for the late twentieth century, but few earmarked the year 2000. Still, while Christian prophets hesitated to predict a specific date for Christ's return, surveys indicated that many evangelicals believed that the Second Coming would occur around 2000. A number of scientists, economists, and sociologists saw 2000 as a benchmark year, but they usually did not endow it with any apocalyptic significance. Actually, the vast majority of prophecies regarding 2000 came from fringe religions—astrologers, freelance prophets, soothsayers, New Agers, and psychics—many of whom based their end-time scenarios on a combination of sources, including the occult, ancient writings, and the Bible.[11]

Most of the Christian references to 2000 or thereabouts came several centuries before that date. A noteworthy example occurred in the early Protestant apocalyptic tradition, which rested on three sources: the books of Daniel and Revelation and the Prophecy of Elias. This prophecy divided history into three periods: before the law, under the law, and of

9. Quoted in Teresi and Hooper, "Last Laugh?," 43.

10. Ulrich H. J. Kortner, *The End of the World* (Louisville: Westminster John Knox, 1995) 265–66.

11. See A. T. Mann, *Millennium Prophecies* (Rockport, MA: Element, 1992; Robert W. Thompson, "2001: A Millennial Odyssey?," *Military Chaplain's Review* 18/4 (Fall 1989) 42; Daniel Wojcik, *The End of the World as We Know It: Faith, Fatalism, and Apocalypse in America* (New York: New York University Press, 1997) 212.

the Messiah. Each period was allotted two thousand years, and thus the duration of the world was six thousand years. If creation came about 4000 BCE, as many suggested, the end would be about 2000 CE.[12]

But most Protestant apocalyptic thinkers in the sixteenth and seventeenth centuries believed that God in his mercy would shorten the last age. This old world is so evil that it could not last another four or five hundred years—so they thought. This led them to set dates much earlier than 2000, often close to their own day. For example, Martin Luther initially mentioned 2000, but later believed that the end would come around 1600.[13]

In early modern Europe most references to the end were more immediate. But at least two individuals pointed to the end of the millennium. Archbishop James Ussher—famous for dating creation at 4004 BCE—believed the duration of the world to be six thousand years. This placed the world's end in 1996. Jansenism, an austere version of French Catholicism, produced a radical apocalyptic group—the Convulsionaries. Most Convulsionaries looked for an immediate doomsday, but one of their ranks, Jaques-Joseph Duguet (d. 1733), set 2000 as the date for Christ's Second Coming. He believed that many developments—including the conversion of the Jews—had to occur before that event.[14]

Colonial and early national America heard at least two references to 2000. Most premillennialists at that time looked for a much earlier date for the Second Advent, but the postmillennialists felt that more time was needed for the world to be ready for the millennium. Jonathan Edwards regarded his own age, the First Great Awakening, as the vanguard of the millennium. Given the conversions during that period of revival, conditions would improve and the world would be ready for the millennium to begin by 2000.[15] Timothy Dwight made a similar prediction. Living during the Second Great Awakening, he regarded the revivals and perfectionism

---

12. Katharine R. Firth, *The Apocalyptic Tradition in Britain, 1530-1645* (Oxford: Oxford University Press, 1979) 5, 17, 21, 113, 196, 216, 228.

13. Ibid. , 195; Schwartz, "Fin-de-Siecle Fantasies," 25; Schwartz, *Century's End*, 90; T.F. Torrance, "The Eschatology of the Reformation," *Scottish Journal of Theology, Occasional Papers* 2 (1953) 43-44; John M. Headley, *Luther's View of Church History* (New Haven, CT: Yale University Press, 1963) 240-65.

14. Michael J. St. Clair, *Millennial Movements in Historical Context* (New York: Garland, 1992) 228, 306; Clarke Garrette, *Spirit Possession and Popular Religion: From the Camisards to the Shakers* (Baltimore: Johns Hopkins University Press, 1987) 10-11.

15. C.C. Goen, "Jonathan Edwards: A New Departure in Eschatology," *Church History* 28/1 (1959) 33; St. Clair, *Millenarian Movements*, 272; Catherine Albanese, *America: Religions and Religion* (2nd ed.; Belmont, CA: Wadsworth, 1992) 425.

Millennial Anxieties

of his day as preparation for the millennium, which he too saw as beginning by 2000.[16]

One would expect the premillennial popularizers to be gushing with proclamations about the year 2000. Many were in fact in a state of intense expectancy as the twentieth century wound down, but few made specific predictions regarding 2000. Why? First, as Timothy Weber notes, premillennialists live in "the tension of the now/not yet." Whereas no event needs to be filled before the Second Advent, they take us to the very edge of the now. But they usually hold up and do not make a specific prediction about the not yet. However, some popularizers have yielded to this temptation and made predictions. Others have "suggested" a date for the end. These "suggesters" attach qualifiers to their predictions, e.g., "very soon," "near," or "possibly by." But in the popular evangelical mind, the date-suggesters are virtually indistinguishable from the date-setters.[17]

Second, many premillennial popularizers had already shot their prophetic cannon and had less than spectacular results. Their suggestions regarding the 1980s and 1990s have already misfired. Two factors set off these prognostications. Hal Lindsey "suggested" that Christ would come one generation (forty years) after the establishment of the state of Israel (1948). Many prognosticators followed in the train of Lindsey's "suggestion" and made predictions for the 1980s and 1990s. Then, too, the long arm of Ussher's influence reached the late twentieth century. If the duration of human history is six thousand years and creation took place in 4004 BCE, then the end, it was reasoned, would come in 1996. Subtracting seven years for the tribulation yielded a date in the late 1980s or the early 1990s.[18]

Among the popularizers who mentioned 2000 as a time of eschatological significance, if not the end of the world, was Lester Sumrall of LE-SEA Broadcasting. In his book *I Predict 2000 A.D.* he declared, "I predict the absolute fullness of man's operation on planet Earth by the year 2000

---

16. N. Gordon Thomas, "The Second Coming: A Major Impulse of American Protestantism," *Adventist Heritage* 3 (1976) 4; St. Clair, *Millenarian Movements*, 271: Ira V. Brown, "Watchers for the Second Coming: The Millenarian Tradition in America," *Mississippi Valley Historical Review* 39 (December 1952) 449.

17. Timothy P. Weber, *Living in the Shadow of the Second Coming* (New York: Oxford University Press, 1979) 48; Richard Abanes, *End-Time Visions: The Road to Armageddon?* (Nashville: Broadman and Holman, 1998) 100.

18. Alnor, *Soothsayers of the Second Advent*, 30, 35–39, 99–107; Peter N. Stearns, *Millennium III, Century XXI* (Boulder, CO: Westview, 1996) 59.

C.E. Then Jesus Christ shall reign from Jerusalem for 1000 years."[19] Relying on the six-thousand-year theory and Ussher's dates, other popularizers inched toward 2000. In his *End Times News Digest* James McKeever said that Christ could return anytime between 1983 and 2030.[20] That the two-thousand-year messianic age could have begun with Christ's resurrection in 29 CE accounts for the *terminus ad quem* of 2030. Canadian Grant Jeffrey argued that the early church accepted the six-thousand-year theory and believed Christ would return around 2000. He also noted that 2000 is the target that groups like the New World Order and New Agers have set for the imposition of a new one-world government.[21] In his book, *2001: On the Edge of Eternity*, Jack Van Impe said Christ would return "right around 2000." The sixth day will not "conclude until the year 2000, and perhaps as far ahead as the year 2012."[22]

Other popularizers also "suggested" that apocalyptic events would occur around the year 2000. In *Seven Years of Shaking: A Vision*, Pentecostal preacher Michael D. Evans told of an end-time vision from God. This vision pointed to a number of events, which would occur by 2000. He saw the inauguration of Bill Clinton as marking an era of depravity and decadence. Worse than Clinton, the Russians will point their military might toward Washington, worldwide plagues will erupt, famines will engulf the globe, and America will become bankrupt. J. R. Church, host of the television show *Prophecy in the News*, took a unique approach to prophecy. In his best-seller, *Hidden Prophecy in the Psalms*, he claimed that Psalms contained a code connecting each psalm with a year in the twentieth century (e.g., Psalm 1 = 1901, Psalm 40 = 1940, Psalm 65 = 1965). For example, Church contended the following: Psalm 48 told of Israel becoming a state in 1948 and Psalm 88 "suggested" the rapture in 1988. While his 1988 "suggestion" failed to materialize, Church jumped on the year 2000 bandwagon. The rapture "might" occur in 2000 and then the tribulation. "Once we come to Psalms 101–107 [2001–2007], we then have what appears to be a period of tribulation."[23]

19. Lester Sumrall, *I Predict 2000 A.D.* (South Bend, IN: LESEA, 1987) 74; Alnor, *Soothsayers of the Second Advent*, 39.

20. *End Times Digest*, February 1983, 5; Alnor, *Soothsayers of the Second Advent*, 102.

21. Grant R. Jeffrey, *Prince of Darkness* (Toronto: Frontier Research, 1994) 85; Grant R. Jeffrey, *Armageddon: Appointment with Destiny* (Toronto: Frontier Research, 1988); Alnor, *Soothsayers of the Second Advent*, 106–7.

22. Jack Van Impe, *2001: On the Edge of Eternity* (Dallas: Word, 1996) 16.

23. Abanes, *End-Time Visions*, 96–98, 102–5.

Millennial Anxieties

The year 2000 rang a bell in other ways for some evangelicals. Reflecting Reconstructionist tendencies, Pat Robertson saw major changes by 2000. For example, one of his many predictions dated 2007 as the time for the Earth's destruction. And when you subtract seven years of tribulation from 2007, you wind up with the year 2000.[24] A number of mission groups were targeting 2000 for completion of the task of world evangelization, which is regarded by many as a prerequisite for the return of Christ.[25] To others the German reunification in 1990, the collapse of the Soviet Union in 1991, and the furtherance of European unification all point to an apocalyptic event—the establishment of a single European currency by 2000.[26]

One evangelical, however, did pinpoint 2000 as the time for Christ's return. In *The Final Victory: The Year 2000?* Marvin Byers gave a new twist to Daniel's seventieth week. Most dispensationalists see time suspended at the sixty-ninth week and that the church is now living in the parenthesis, that is, the church age or the time between the first and second return of Christ. Byers is a premillennialist but held to something resembling the posttribulational position. He believed "that by correctly interpreting Daniel's prophecy, we can discover the year of the Second Coming of Christ and the time of His 'launch.'" Instead of suspending Daniel's seventieth week at Christ's first coming, he added up the years Israel has been independent since Daniel's time. Seventy times seven is 490 years, the exact time he contended Israel has been independent from Daniel's prophecy, to 2000. Thus in his calculations Christ was to return in 2000.[27]

Not everyone pointed to 2000 as a time for apocalyptic events. The year 2000 was an important initiative in charismatic Christianity for global evangelization. Its official statement said, "A Church for Every People and the Gospel for Every Person by the Year 2000." While the movement

---

24. Pat Robertson, *The New Millennium* (Dallas: Word, 1990); Pat Robertson, *The New World Order* (Dallas: Word, 1991); Abanes, *End-Time Visions*, 137–38.

25. David B. Barrett and Todd M. Johnson, *Our Globe and How to Reach It: Seeing the World Evangelized by AD 2000 and Beyond* (Birmingham, AL: New Hope, 1990) 130: Robert M. Bowman Jr., "Mission for the Third Millennium," *Christian Research Journal* 14/4 (Spring 1991) 37; Russell Chandler, *Doomsday: The End of the World, A View through Time* (Ann Arbor, MI: Servant, 1993) 279; David A. Lewis, *Prophecy 2000* (6th ed.; Green Forest, AK: New Leaf, 1990) 12.

26. Steve Terrell, *The 90's: Decade of the Apocalypse* (South Plainfield, NJ: Bridge, 1994) xv–xvi; Chandler, *Doomsday*, 280; Chuck Freadhoff, "Europeans Squabble over Unity," *Investor's Business Daily*, 9 September 1992, 1; Lewis , *Prophecy* 2000, 14.

27. Marvin Byers, *The Final Victory: The Year* 2000? (Shippensburg, PA: Treasure House, 1994) 179–88, 245–48, 251–52, 265–70, 281–82, 295–96, 301–2, 337–38.

never officially linked its efforts with the Second Coming of Christ, many of its followers got caught up in end-time excitement. In a different way, the Roman Catholic world pointed to 2000 and the Great Jubilee. In 1997, Catholics were asked to focus on Jesus Christ and the mystery of salvation. In 1998, people were to develop a "renewed appreciation of the presence and activities of the Holy Spirit." Next, in 1999 the theme became appreciation for God the Father. And finally, after this preparation, 2000 would be the year to celebrate. While the Catholic Church did not intend this event to have eschatological expectations, some Catholics got caught up in the apocalyptic mood of the time. In fact, some Catholics believed the Marian apparitions included predictions that the world would end in 1999 or 2000.[28]

SECULAR PROPHETS AND 2000

Secular doomsdayers had even less to say about the year 2000, although there was no shortage of secular doomsday predictions. Scientists told us that humanity could be destroyed by a nuclear war or an environmental catastrophe. Economists pointed to a global financial collapse. Still, most of these secularists did not earmark 2000. A few scientists like Paul Ehrlich had issued warnings that pointed to years prior to 2000. Others gave humanity another seventy-five to one hundred years. And while the predicted economic disasters may be catastrophic, it was not believed that they would bring the end of the world. Even the feared Y2K meltdown only pointed to widespread chaos and not doomsday.

Yet a few secular prognosticators did mention the years around 2000 or told us what the new millennium would bring. Their visions of the future were not always negative; in fact, some were utopian. About a hundred years ago, several prognosticators said a secular millennium would dawn by 2000. Edward Bellamy looked forward to a cooperative utopia, Winnifred Cooley to a feminist welfare state, Friedrich Bilz to a universal nature cure, William Morris to a socialist revolution, and Edward Berwick to a vegetarian farmers' paradise.[29]

28. Damian Thompson, *The End of Time: Faith and Fear in the Shadow of the Millenium* (Hanover, NH: University Press of New England, 1996) 152–54, 167–168, 183(quote); Wojcik, *The End of the World as We Know It*, 212; Joseph Gallagher, "Don't Count On the Millennium to Be the End," *National Catholic Reporter*, 11 August 1995, 21; Lisa McMinn, "Y2K, the Apocalypse, and Evangelical Christianity: The Role of Eschatological Belief in Church Responses, *Sociology of Religion* 62/2 (2001) 6–7.

29. Edward Bellamy, *Looking Backward: 2000–1887* (Garden City, NY: Dolphin,

Millennial Anxieties

As humanity approached the end of the millennium, other secularists were caught up with end-ism. In 1960 socialist Daniel Bell paved the way when he proclaimed *The End of Ideology*. Other such books included *The End of Affluence*, *The End of Capitalism*, and *The End of Nature*. Francis Fukuyama set Washington abuzz with his article "The End of History?" and a subsequent book, *The End of History and the Last Man*. In these writings Fukuyama was not predicting the end of the world, but argued that liberal democracy had triumphed over all other ideologies—monarchy, fascism, and communism. As a result, "history understood as a single, coherent, evolutionary process" had come to an end.[30]

Charles Berlitz's *Doomsday 1999 A.D.* (1981) was not for the faint of heart. His brew of scientific, occultic, and psychic elements pointed directly to doomsday. He spoke of nuclear annihilation and environmental suicide. Pseudoscientist Berlitz was different from most secular prophets in that he said all of this could happen by 2000. He placed great emphasis on the direct alignment of Jupiter, Saturn, Uranus, Neptune, the sun, and the moon with the Earth. This alignment, which occurred in 1982, could produce all kinds of geological changes by the year 2000—tidal waves, earthquakes, a polar flip, and a collision with a planetoid.[31]

Several economists forecasted financial disasters around 2000. Most of these predictions, however, fell short of an economic apocalypse. Most specific and pessimistic was Peter Jay and Michael Stewart's *Apocalypse 2000*, which spoke of a catastrophic economic breakdown and the suicide of democracy by 2000. In the United States poverty, despair, and violence would become endemic. "Life in America in 2000 [will be like] Lebanon in the mid-1980s." Conditions in Europe were not to be much better.[32]

Some other economists used apocalyptic language but did not earmark 2000. In *The Great Depression of 1990* Ravi Batra forecast a global financial Armageddon. However, this catastrophe would be followed by a

---

1951); Hillel Schwartz, *Century's End: A Cultural History of the Fin de Siècle—from the 990s through the 1990s* (New York: Doubleday, 1990) 269; Martin Ebon, *Prophecy in Our Time* (New York: New American Library, 1968) 181–91.

30. Francis Fukuyama, "The End of History?," *The National Interest* 16 (Summer 1989) 3–18; Francis Fukuyama, *The End of History and the Last Man* (New York: Free Press, 1992) xi–xii. See also Cullen Murphy, "The Way the World Ends," *Wilson Quarterly* 14/1 (Winter 1990) 51–52; Catherine Keller, *Apocalypse Now and Then: A Feminist Guide to the End of the World* (Boston: Beacon, 1996) 85–86.

31. Charles Berlitz, *Doomsday: 1999 A.D.* (Garden City, NY: Doubleday, 1981) 1–5. See Also Murphy, "Way the World Ends," 54–55.

32. Peter Jay and Michael Stewart, *Apocalypse 2000: Economic Breakdown and the Suicide of Democracy, 1989–2000* (New York: Prentice Hall, 1987) 234–46.

moral regeneration in which people came to their senses and condemned immorality and great wealth.[33] Robert Heilbroner used some Frankensteinian language to describe the future—sprawling urban blight, starving masses, revolution, and war.[34]

While not pointing to doomsday, some other economic forecasters noted serious problems beginning around 2000. In *Millennium* Jacques Attali saw the United States in a decline and a world dominated by Europe and Japan.[35] Paul Kennedy predicted a similar future for America. In *The Rise and Fall of the Great Powers* he argued that America might be a great military power, but its economic base was rotting away. In *Preparing for the Twenty-First Century* he addressed global issues—scarce resources, food production, AIDS, and an exploding population.[36] C. Owen Paepke's *Evolution of Progress* told us that the age of economic growth was over.[37]

THE PSYCHICS AND 2000

The psychics told us that all kinds of disasters would happen by 2000. Ruth Montgomery, for example, described a polar shift: "After a period of churning seas and frightful wind velocities the turbulence will cease, and those in the north will live in a tropical clime, and vice versa. Before the year 2000 it will come to pass."[38] Other expected disasters include earthquakes, wars, pestilence, and collisions with celestial bodies. Many said that a new age of peace and tranquility would emerge after such calamities.

---

33. Ravi Batra, *The Great Depression of* 1990 (New York: Simon and Schuster, 1987). See also Ray Corelli, "Boom Time for Futurists," *World Press Review*, December 1989, 28; Barry Brummett, "Popular Economic Apocalyptic: The Case of Ravi Batra," *Journal of Popular Culture* 24/2 (1990) 153-63.

34. Robert L. Heilbroner, *An Inquiry into the Human Prospect* (rev. ed.; New York: Norton, 1980). See also Paul D. Hanson, "The Apocalyptic Consciousness," *Quarterly Review* 4/3 (1984) 26.

35. Jacques Attali, *Millennium: Winners and Losers in the Coming World Order* (New York: Times Books, 1991).

36. Paul Kennedy, *The Rise and Fall of the Great Powers: Economic Change and Military Conflict from* 1500 *to* 2000 (New York: Random House, 1987); Paul Kennedy, *Preparing for the Twenty-First Century* (New York: Random House, 1993).

37. C. Owen Paepke, *The Evolution of Progress: The End of Economic Growth and the Beginning of Human Transformation* (New York: Random House, 1993).

38. Quoted in John Hogue, *The Millennium Book of Prophecy* (San Francisco: Harper, 1994) 83. See also Leo M. Braun, *Apocalypse 1998: Revelations of Forthcoming Worldwide Catastrophes* (New York: Vantage, 1993) 73-74.

Millennial Anxieties

While the year 2000 had no apocalyptic importance for the Bible or science, it had magical appeal for psychics, soothsayers, and astrologers, who expected momentous happenings around 2000. The source of their knowledge was usually dreams, trances, visions, ancient writings, or channeling sessions. Some occultists regarded the Great Pyramid as a source of prophecy. Western esoteric schools have long regarded its dimensions and the symbols found in its passageways as keys to the future. One inch, for example, is regarded as equal to a year of time. Interpretations of the pyramid vary. According to occultist Max Toth, a kingdom of the spirit will emerge between 1995 and 2025. The year 2040 will see Christ's physical reincarnation, and great human achievements will mark the years between 2055 and 2080. The predictions go on until 2979, the last date indicated by the pyramid.[39]

A number of seers, mystics, and psychics have told stories of disaster and triumph for the end of the millennium. Heading the list was Nostradamus. Some of his interpreters said his quatrains predicted disasters for the year before 2000. Close behind was Edgar Cayce, who predicted cataclysmic upheavals for the years 1998 and 2001. Jeane Dixon foresaw natural disasters, Armageddon, and Christ's return before 2000. The list also included Ruth Montgomery, Rudolf Steiner, Elizabeth Clare Prophet, Carl Jung, Madame Blavatsky, Djwhal Khul, Sun Bear, Alice Bailey, and Jose Arguelles. Of course, their individual predictions differed. But most of them would agree that the years around 2000 would experience floods, a polar shift, earthquakes, catastrophes brought on by a planetary alignment, famine, pestilence, droughts, fires, overpopulation, political repression, international terrorism, wars, and other horrors. "Great afflictions will come. . . . Nations will end in flames, and famine will annihilate millions," said Princes Billante of Savoy in the early twentieth century. Prominent among the seers who pinpointed 2000 for worldwide disaster was Richard Noone, the author of *5/5/2000: Ice, the Ultimate Disaster*. This book argued that on May 5, 2000, a planetary realignment would dislodge the South Pole ice, thereby causing a polar shift and the destruction of Earth.[40]

---

39. Mann, *Millennium Prophecies*, 44–49; Joey R. Jochmans, *Rolling Thunder: The Coming Earth Changes* (Santa Fe, NM: Sun, 1980) 117–19: Alnor, *Soothsayers of the Second Advent*, 174–87.

40. Quoted in Hogue, *Millennium Book of Prophecy*, 69. See also Braun, *Apocalypse 1998*, 71–90; Jochmans, *Rolling Thunder*, 135–37; Berlitz, *Doomsday*, 1–9; Moira Timms, *Prophecies and Predictions: Everyone's Guide to the Coming Changes* (Santa Cruz, CA: Unity, 1980) 173–84; Peter Lorie, *Nostradamus: The Millennium and*

Still, in true apocalyptic fashion triumph usually follows disaster. Many occultists saw a new age dawning sometime after 2000. Humankind would survive the unprecedented upheavals. The world would be ushered into an era of peace, justice, and spiritual harmony. Because Christianity has lost its influence, inspiration would be drawn from various spiritual sources including Eastern wisdom and Native American religions. Spiritually, philosophically, economically, politically, scientifically, and artistically, all people would be integrated into a new world order.[41]

Along with this coming new age would be the arrival of a world savior or avatar. The major world religions all pointed to the coming of such an individual. Hindus awaited Kalki, Buddhists Maitreya, the Jews the Messiah, the Muslims Madhi, and Christians the Christ. According to many psychics, he would arrive at the beginning of the twenty-first century and inaugurate a true golden age. But before this new age the world would be purged by many catastrophes. Many occult prophets did not in fact conceive of an absolute end of the world, but "merely a kind of purification" that was to come during the 1990s.[42]

Many seers saw the future of humankind hanging in the balance. According to John Hogue, "all prophetic cycles throughout history pinpoint the 1990s as a turning point." Their collective vision foresaw "humankind either destroyed by an outer fire or transformed by an inner one." From Nostradamus and Edgar Cayce to the Spirit Guides of Ruth Montgomery and the Center for Strategic and International Studies, "saints, seers, and authorities have indicated that our present historical movement is at the crossroads of utter doom or utopian splendor."[43]

It is intriguing that while the Bible did not endow the year 2000 with any particular significance, many psychics and seers employed the basic outline of Christian eschatology—impending catastrophes, a period of purging, the deeds of an Antichrist or an evil one, the arrival of a great religious leader, and the coming of a golden age. Psychics adapted these concepts to their own situation and said that they would come to fulfillment around 2000.[44]

Beyond (New York: Simon and Schuster, 1993) 194–217; Wojcik, *The End of the World as We Know It*, 213.

41. Mann, *Millennium Prophecies*, 122–28; Braun, *Apocalypse 1998*, 92–111; Rhodes, "Millennial Madness," 39; *Millennial Prophecy Report*, May 1994, 12–15; John Naisbitt and Patricia Aburdene, *Megatrends 2000* (New York: Avon, 1990).

42. Jochmanns, *Rolling Thunder*, 52, 107–8; Mann, *Millennium Prophecies*, 122.

43. Hogue, *Millennium Book of Prophecy*, back cover.

44. For examples see Jochmans, *Rolling Thunder*, 185–94; Hogue, *Millennium Book*

Millennial Anxieties

Y2K: A SECULAR APOCALYPSE

"Disaster," "crisis," "catastrophe," "chaos," "time bomb," and "calamity" were words used to describe the coming Y2K computer meltdown. (Y stands for "year," 2K is the acronym for 2000.) Some consumer journals employed such expressions to depict the impending computer malfunctions that would occur worldwide on January 1, 2000, and beyond. A worst-case scenario said the year 2000 would end the use of most computers. At best companies would have to spend from $300–600 billion worldwide to make their computers function in the twenty-first century.[45]

The Problem

What was this problem? It concerned two little digits. To save space, COBOL computer programmers used just six digits to specify the date—two for the day, two for the month, and two for the year. Thus calculations that employed dates would be incorrect. The meaning of dates would also be ambiguous. For example, a computer would not be able not tell whether 1/10/01 refers to the year 1901 or 2001. Such a system was designed in the middle of the twentieth century and nobody cared much about what would happen with the turn of the millennium. Few computers were used at that time. But by 2000 the world ran on computers and a crisis loomed.[46]

Unfortunately, few people noted this computer problem. In 1979 Robert Bemer, a one-time IBM employee, sent out the first warnings. But no one wanted to rock the boat. In 1993, a young Canadian named Peter de Jager raised the issue in his article "Doomsday 2000," which appeared in *Computerworld*. Starting in 1995, people began to catch on to the problem and the Y2K awareness reached a critical mass. The White House, Congress, and the media got wind of the millennial bug and made a big thing out of it. In 1996, Senator Daniel Patrick Moynihan wrote the first report on Y2K and warned President Clinton of the "year 2000 time

---

of Prophecy, 45–47, 87, 99, 103, 125; Mann, *Millennium Prophecies*, 23–39; Abanes, *End-Time Visions*, 64–66.

45. Sandra Schanzer, "The Impending Computer Crisis of the Year 2000," in *The Year 2000: Essays on the End*, eds. Charles B. Strozier and Michael Flynn (New York: New York University Press, 1997) 263.

46. Chris Taylor, "The History and the Hype," *Time*, 18 January 1999, 72; Schanzer, "The Impending Computer Crisis," 263; Katie Hafner, "The Day the World Shuts Down," *Newsweek*, 2 June 1997, 54.

bomb." So a problem that people had ignored for forty years came to the forefront and sent many people into a tizzy.⁴⁷

The alarmists went into high gear. Computers are the engines of modern society, and their malfunction, it was believed, would precipitate a global crisis of unimaginable proportions. Nearly every aspect of the modern world is regulated, monitored, or made more efficient by computers. Thus their failure, some believed, would present society with the most disruptive crisis it ever faced—the worst since World War II.⁴⁸

What specific areas would the computer bug impact? According to doomsday proponents, nearly every area of life would be affected. Most all computers contain embedded microchips and many of these chips would fail causing widespread systems to malfunction. The electrical power grid would crash. Almost everything in modern society depends on reliable electricity, thus the chaos would be spread throughout the globe. Water and sewage utilities could fail. Worldwide telecommunications would breakdown. Telephones would not work. Banks, the stock markets, and the entire financial system would grind to a halt. Personal savings might not be protected because the Federal Deposit Insurance system might not function.⁴⁹

The Y2K crisis would significantly harm the United States military. As a military superpower with no draft, the Department of Defense substantially relies on sophisticated weapons systems. This dependence may place the United States at an extreme disadvantage come the year 2000. The DOD has over six million computers throughout the globe and their malfunction would create a national security nightmare. ICBM missiles might not fire, warplanes might not fly, and communication systems would come to a standstill. More specifically, the Global Positioning Satellite (GPS) system, which guides within a few yards ships, troop carriers, missiles, and

---

47. Taylor, "The History and the Hype," 73; Schanzer, "The Impending Computer Crisis, 264; McMinn, "Y2K, the Apocalypse, and Evangelical Christianity," 2.

48. Grant R. Jeffrey, *The Millennium Meltdown: The Year 2000 Computer Crisis* (Toronto: Frontier Research, 1998) 9–10; Donald S. McAlvany, *The Y2K Tidal Wave: Year 2000 Economic Survival* (Toronto: Frontier Research, 1999) 9–10; Richard D. Wiles, *Judgment Day 2000!: How the Coming Worldwide Computer Crash Will Radically Change Your Life* (Shippensburg, PA: Treasure House, 1999) preface.

49. Michael S. Hyatt, *The Millennium Bug: How to Survive the Coming Chaos* (Washington, DC: Regnery, 1998) 59–156; Hafner, "The Day the World Shuts Down," 56–57; Jeffrey, *Millennium Meltdown*, 55–93; McAlvany, *The Y2K Tidal Wave*, 111–68; Steven Levy, "Will the Bug Bite the Bull?," *Newsweek*, 4 May 1998, 62; Wiles, *Judgment Day 2000*, 161–213; Steve Farrar, *Spiritual Survival during the Y2K Crisis* (Nashville: Nelson, 1999) 75.

Millennial Anxieties

planes to specific places may not function. Moreover, our Western allies would experience similar problems. As a result of the above, some people believed this vulnerability would embolden our enemies (especially Russia and China) to attack us. It was said that these nations depended less on computer technology than did the Western powers.[50]

The government had more computer problems than national defense. If the governments—national, state, and local—failed to solve the Y2K bug the impact would be enormous. About 30 percent of the national economy depended on some level of government. You name it—Social Security, commerce, the IRS, the welfare system, treasury, labor, interior, agriculture, justice, education, energy, transportation, and health services are all dependent on computers and they were not prepared for 2000. As mentioned, Senator Patrick Moynihan notified President Clinton regarding the problem. On February 4, 1998, the president signed an executive order requiring every department to take steps to solve the computer problem. But many people regarded this as too little too late and insisted that the government did not fully grasp the enormity of the problem.[51]

If you thought the federal, state, and local governments in America were in bad shape, most other nations had worse problems. And their unpreparedness might have consequences for the U.S. While the millennial bug would impact the entire globe, the levels of preparation varied from country to country. The nations with the best preparation were the U.S., Canada, and Australia. Western European nations and Japan were on the next level. The news regarding Y2K compliance in Russia, Eastern Europe, South America, Asia, and Africa was not encouraging. Their only solace was that these societies were not as computer dependent as was the West.[52]

The Solutions

Many rational people went to work to solve the problem. But how did the alarmists react to the millennial bug? Many pushed the panic button and advocated measures common to the survivalist or militia culture. Others capitalized on this hysteria and made considerable money: they

50. Jeffrey, *The Millennium Meltdown*, 103–11; McAlvany, *The Y2K Tidal Wave*, 179–207; Hyatt, *The Millennium Bug*, 125–33; Wiles, *Judgment Day 2000*, 141–60.

51. Hafner, "The Day the World Shuts Down," 56; Jeffrey, *The Millennium Meltdown*, 113–38; Hyatt, *The Millennium Bug*, 103–24; McAlvany, *The Y2K Tidal Wave*, 169–78; Wiles, *Judgment Day 2000*, 261–70.

52. Jeffrey, *The Millennium Meltdown*, 135–38; McAlvany, *The Y2K Tidal Wave*, 209–17.

wrote books telling people how to survive the coming catastrophe or sold materials designed to help them live through this chaos. Michael Hyatt and others envisioned three levels of problems—"Scenario 1: Brownout," "Scenario 2: Blackout," and "Scenario 3: Meltdown."[53]

"Scenario 1: Brownout" concerned projected isolated system failures. There would be local electrical outages, problems with water treatment resulting in some unsafe water, confusion with all levels of transportation, higher gasoline and food prices, and interruptions in telecommunications. The brownout phase would last from two weeks to three months. "Scenario 2: Blackout" said multiple systems would fail and there would be social upheavals. The power grid would be totally out for an extended period, water would not be treated or pumped, disease would spread, all levels of transportation would come to a standstill, basic food and fuel products would be unavailable, and all communication systems would be disrupted. The blackout phase would last four months to three years. "Scenario 3: Meltdown" pointed to extreme disruption. The power grid would totally fall apart, nuclear meltdowns would occur, water would not be able to be pumped so sickness would result, food would not be able to be distributed so starvation would result in some places, and communication systems would completely fail. The meltdown phase would last four to ten years. In all three of these scenarios, there would be rioting and strife, the worse coming in the last two projections.[54]

Hyatt and others urged people to take specific survival steps. The instructions were largely the same, but the amount of what one did would depend on the scenario they anticipated. Hyatt believed the crisis would be somewhere between the brownout and the blackout possibilities

He listed thirteen preparations. One, "secure hard copies of all important documents." Two, "build an emergency preparedness library." Three, "evaluate your current location" and imagine what your community would be like with out basic supplies. Cities are not good places to live. Four, "determine your self-defense philosophy," and if it does not conflict with your values get a firearm and practice with it. Five, "find an alternative source of water." Six, "stockpile food and common household goods." Seven, "purchase adequate clothing." Eight, "develop an alternative source of heat and energy." Nine, "prepare an emergency medical kit." Ten,

---

53. Michael S. Hyatt, *The Y2K Personal Survival Guide: Everything You Need to Know to Get from This Side of the Crisis to the Other* (Washington, DC: Regnery, 1999) 285–87; Hyatt, *The Millennium Bug*, 162–74.

54. Hyatt, *The Y2K Personal Survival Guide*, 285–87; Hyatt, *The Millennium Bug*, 176–79; Farrar, *Spiritual Survival*, 76–77.

Millennial Anxieties

"determine how you will depose of waste." Eleven, "secure an alternative form of currency." Twelve, "develop an alternative communications system." Lastly, "acquire a basic selection of hand tools."[55]

Y2K: A CHRISTIAN APOCALYPSE

Though the looming Y2K problem had a secular origin, Christians, especially evangelicals, soon recast it in religious terms. While not necessarily predicting the end of the world, TV preachers boomed dire warnings from their pulpits and urged their listeners to prepare for the worst. Evangelical books, videos, and websites with similar admonitions sprang up like weeds. While the specifics differed, the general messages were similar: America was condemned for its immorality and the Y2K crisis was the first step toward the one-world government and the rise of the Antichrist.[56]

Government and business leaders and the secular media expressed much concern over the Y2K problem. Still, evangelical Christians were the most persistent "Chicken Littles" regarding the Y2K crisis. There were several reasons for this development. One, most evangelicals have some knowledge of biblical prophecy and—despite differences in regard to eschatology—many expect some kind of apocalyptic disaster.[57] More specifically, the dispensational variety is accepted by many as "gospel truth" and this version of eschatology has spawned speculations regarding a one-world government controlled by the man of sin.

Two, evangelical Christians have traditionally maintained a strong populist approach to religion. They often do not think critically and tend to value the opinions of popular preachers and writers. As a result, evangelicals have been significantly influenced by the sensationalists and alarmists who capitalized on the Y2K bug. Three, several varieties of Christians, including Roman Catholics, suggested that the Y2K problem could be an opening for the church to minister to people and demonstrate the love of Christ.[58]

55. Hyatt, *The Millennium Bug*, 185-202; Hyatt, *The Y2K Personal Survival Guide*, 61ff.; Jeffrey, *The Millennium Meltdown*, 213-24.

56. Mark A. Kellner, "A Secular Apocalypse?," *Christianity Today*, 11 January 1999, 56; W. Scott Poole, *Satan in America: The Devil We Know* (Lanham, MD: Rowman and Littlefield, 2009) 188; McMinn, "Y2K, the Apocalypse, and Evangelical Christianity," 3-4.

57. Dave Hunt, *Y2K: A Reasoned Response to Mass Hysteria* (Eugene, OR: Harvest House, 1999) 129; McMinn, "Y2K, the Apocalypse, and Evangelical Christianity, 3-4.

58. Richard Kyle, *Evangelicalism: An Americanized Christianity* (New Brunswick,

Who Were Their Leaders?

For the most part, the individuals who spread the Y2K hysteria could be regarded as sensationalists who pandered to the evangelical urge for the bizarre. But some of the more mainline leaders were not immune to this pressure, and they jumped on the bandwagon, even embracing the thinking of the alarmists.

Heading the list of fear mongers was *New York Times* best-selling author Michael Hyatt. His two books, *The Millennium Bug* and *The Y2K Personal Survival Guide*, fed on the evangelical and survivalist thirst for paranoia. He was quoted by other sensationalists and even mainline evangelicals. He told his readers that the results of Y2K "will be catastrophic" and then proceeded to list specifics. They ranged from the stopping of social security checks to bank failures, failure of military systems, food shortages, and more. But his business did not end with his books. On his website, Hyatt used high-pressure sales pitches: "Panic buying may occur in late 1999 as the year 2000 crisis worries increase, stressing the food supply chain to the breaking point from which it may never recover." He then proceeded to offer a one-year, four-person food supply for only $3,395 plus shipping. This price, he noted, was much less than other offers, which ran over $6,500.[59]

Another merchant peddling fear was Don McAlvany. In *The Y2K Tidal Wave* he contended "that a power hungry Clinton administration could use the [Y2K] crisis to try to usurp a tremendous amount of financial and political power, much as Franklin Roosevelt did in 1933 in the midst of the Great Depression." In most of his literature, he railed against the government and used unsubstantiated information to stir up fears about the new world order. Like Hyatt, McAlvany also had some self-serving motives. To deal with the coming crisis, he urged people to buy gold and silver from International Collectors Associates—his own gold, silver, and rare coin brokerage firm. He also sold "Self-Sufficiency Food ... Good as Gold," and thus recommended that people should have about a one-year supply of freeze-dried or dehydrated food.[60]

NJ: Transaction, 1996) 318–20; Hunt, *Y2K*, 129–30.

59. Quote from Hank Hanegraaff, *The Millennium Bug Debugged* (Minneapolis: Bethany House, 1999) 42–43; Hyatt, *The Millennium Bug*, back cover; Hyatt, *The Y2K Personal Survival Guide*, 1–8.

60. McAlvany, *The Y2k Tidal Wave*, 11 (quote) 234–35, 247; Abanes, *End-Time Visions*, 142–46.

Millennial Anxieties

More fear mongers capitalized on the Y2K hysteria. Chuck Missler fueled Y2K fears with several irrational implications: America would have no elections in 2000; it was the U.S. government that blew up the federal building in Oklahoma City in 1995; and control of the U.S. military would pass to the United Nations. Jack Van Impe regarded Y2K as a very serious topic, even as a clever satanic plot, and saw it as possibly a prelude to the coming of Christ. In *The Millennium Meltdown*, Grant Jeffrey regarded the Y2K problem as preparation for many of the prophecies found in Revelation—namely, the cashless society, the mark of the beast, and the one-world government.[61]

Perhaps under the influence these sensationalists—especially Michael Hyatt—some mainstream evangelical figures jumped on the Y2K bandwagon. Several of these evangelicals were not dispensationalists and thus did not necessarily regard the Y2K crisis as preparation for the coming of Christ. Still, they saw a disaster coming.

James Kennedy believed the Y2K dilemma as nearly insurmountable and thus urged his followers to start stockpiling as soon as possible. Jerry Falwell viewed the problem to be without historical precedent and as judgment upon America. While he did not regard the crisis as the end of the world, he said the faithful should prepare as they would for the worst hurricane. James Dobson insisted Y2K would have enormous implications. Clearly under Hyatt's influence, he believed the crisis would fall within one of the brownout, blackout, or meltdown scenarios. He also foresaw terrorist activity against the U.S., massive civil disobedience, a global economic crisis, and that our current political leaders would not relinquish political power.[62]

What Were Their Beliefs?

Most fear mongers—but not all—placed the coming Y2K crisis in the context dispensational eschatology. In his book *When Time Shall Be No More*, Paul Boyer detailed the rise of dispensationalism. According to him, the belief that the tribulation could begin with the Y2K collapse "fits very closely into what the popularizers have been saying for years: the increasing reliance of society on technology and global electronic transfers

---

61. Jeffrey, *The Millennium Meltdown*, 149–71; Hanegraaff, *The Millennium Bug Debugged*, 41–49; Hunt, *Y2K*, 5–6, 40–42.

62. Hanegraaff, *The Millennium Bug Debugged*, 23–32; Lacayo, "The End of the World as We Know It," 62; Hunt, *Y2K*, 23–25.

of capital and information are paving the way for the Antichrist's global control." Because the Y2K problem focused on the dependence of modern society on technology, it reinforced that specific strand of interpretation. There existed a long history of people who connected eschatology with technology. And because this line of thinking has an element of sensationalism, it has had a popular appeal.[63]

Not all dispensationalists connected the Y2K crisis with biblical prophecy. But many of the popularizers did. In the words of N. W. Hutchings and Larry Spargmino, "It is hard to believe that the Bible does not say anything about the Y2K problem."[64] They and other dispensational alarmists saw Y2K as fulfilling the prophecies found in Daniel and Revelation for the end times. Some alarmists simply regarded Y2K as God's judgment on America. Still, most saw Y2K as precipitating the crisis that would set in motion the standard elements of dispensational eschatology: totalitarian rule, one-world government, a cashless economy, the mark of the beast, and the rise of the Antichrist.[65]

The Y2K problem could produce worldwide distress including a financial depression, riots, widespread crime, and famines. Modern conveniences such as utilities, water, social security checks, bank services, and ATMs would be gone. Who could solve such a problem? Only a totalitarian state with unlimited powers would able to cope with such a crisis. Such political regimes are unpopular, but under dire circumstances people would surrender their liberties and turn to such a government. But the crisis would be global so these unlimited powers must go beyond national boundaries. Such a need would be a catalyst for the one-world government. Indeed, the confusion generated by the millennial bug may create such a desire for order that people turn to a "strong man," a charismatic leader, to unite the world.[66]

While few people speculated that Bill Clinton would be this strong man, many saw him using the Y2K crisis as a pretext to seize power and

---

63. Kellner, "Secular Apocalypse?," 60 (quote); McMinn, "Y2K, the Apocalypse, and Evangelical Christianity," 3–4.

64. N. W. Hutchings and Larry Spargimino, *Y2K = 666?* (Oklahoma City: Hearthstone, 1998) 65.

65. Some examples include the following: Jeffrey, *The Millennium Meltdown*; Hutchings and Spargimino *Y2K = 666?*; McAlvany, *The Y2K Tidal Wave*; Wiles, *Judgment Day 2000*; Farrar, *Spiritual Survival during the Y2K Crisis*.

66. Jeffrey, *The Millennium Meltdown*, 141–71; McAlvany, *The Y2K Tidal Wave*, 269–83; Wiles, *Judgment Day 2000*, 213; Lacayo, "The End of the World As We Know It," 62–68.

Millennial Anxieties

promote the one-world government. The story went something like this. President Clinton has deliberately done or even said little about the Y2K problem, thus allowing the crisis to explode. He and his leftist administration were intentionally setting the stage for a panic and thus a reason to declare a national state of emergency and martial law late in 1999. A number of emergency executive orders would allow President Clinton or any other president to seize power. "It should not be forgotten that Clinton, Gore, [and] Hillary are dedicated leftists (socialists) who aspire to great power . . . and control over the people. They are also globalists who dream of a world government in which they are major players," wrote Donald McAlvany.[67]

Another scenario envisioned a revival of Russia. According to some popularizers, Russian leaders wanted their nation to regain its dominant power. And this could only be done if the United States and NATO were demolished. The U.S. nuclear arsenal utilizes GPS to guide its missiles to the target, and this system would malfunction on August 22, 1999, when it rolls back "to produce erroneous navigational data." Russia used an older system known as gravitational mapping, which would not experience Y2K problems. So from August 22 to December 31, 1999, there would be a window of opening for a Russian nuclear attack. Some doomsday prophets believed Russia would exploit this situation and wipe out the United States.[68]

Not all Y2K alarmists linked their predictions to dispensational eschatology. Calvinist Reconstructionist Gary North made so many dire predictions that he acquired the nickname "Scary Gary." His website noted nearly every kind of disaster imaginable—famine, pestilence, financial chaos, no legal or educational systems, anarchy, and more. In sum, he predicted "the end of Western civilization as we know it." Even worse, he seemed to want it that way. He believed "its part of his duty to bring [America] down, to be replaced by a Bible-based Reconstructionist state that will impose the death penalty on blasphemers, heretics, adulterers, gay men and women who have had abortions or sex before marriage."[69]

Turning back the clock to a new millennium evoked both religious and secular anxieties. In doing so, the three streams of end-time ideas noted in this book—Christian, occult, and secular—flowed together.

67. McAlvany, *The Y2K Tidal Wave*, 234 (quote); Farrar, *Spiritual Survival*, 199–200.

68. Jeffrey, *The Y2K Meltdown*, 204–6; Wiles, *Judgment Day 2000*, 283–90.

69. Hunt, *Y2K*, 15, 30–31, 33, 37; Hanegraaff, *The Millennium Bug Debugged*, 17, 39 (quote); McMinn, "Y2K, the Apocalypse, and Evangelical Christianity," 7.

Apocalyptic Fever

While not important in itself, the year 2000 had nearly a magical appeal, and when this combined with the Y2K threat all kinds of emotions were aroused. Most of these feelings were irrational, but irrationality is closely related to apocalyptic thinking. Such fears proceeded down two paths—religious and secular. Some self-styled prophets saw the projected chaos sufficient enough to set in motion the biblical prophecies regarding the Antichrist, who would rescue humanity from a global crisis. Other individuals did not regard the Y2K problem as the end of the world, but as a crisis of unprecedented portions—one that would result in catastrophic changes to planet Earth.

7

From 9/11 to 666

THE LATE TWENTIETH CENTURY WITNESSED SEVERAL DISCONFIRMATIONS OF PROPHECY. THE "SUGGESTIONS" MADE BY HAL LINDSEY AND OTHERS FOR THE 1980s did not come to fruition. Jesus did not rapture up the saints nor did the tribulation begin. In 1989 communism collapsed in Eastern Europe. The Soviet Union, seen as the northern power destined to invade Israel, came unraveled in 1991. The danger of a nuclear confrontation between major powers thus has been diminished. The first Gulf War (1991) did not turn out to be Armageddon. Saddam Hussein is dead and buried and not the Antichrist. The European Union has grown well beyond the predicted ten nations and now stands at twenty-seven. Moreover, the Y2K bug did not create the chaos necessary to bring on the "man of sin" and the one-world government.

But to be certain, end-time prophecy has been extremely resilient throughout history and it continues to be so in our day. The chameleon-like character of apocalyptic literature allows it to be interpreted to fit current events. And the popular prophets have made the most of this characteristic. While some have maintained their traditional "suggestions," most have adjusted them to the events of the late twentieth and early twenty-first centuries. But most important, the centerpiece of dispensational prophecy—the return of Israel as a state in the Middle East—is still in place. As long as this is the case, apparent disconfirmations will not shake the faithful.

PROPHETIC ADJUSTMENTS

Taking center stage in the business of making predictions were the dispensational popularizers. How did they adjust to the post-Cold War world? In general they maintained their familiar approach to prophecy but with some different emphases. They de-emphasized some themes while highlighting others. Still, they still saw the pieces of the prophetic puzzle coming together. At first some of the popularizers sought to preserve the traditional approach to the end times. As noted in chapter 5, they regarded the collapse of the Soviet Union as either a temporary glitch or a trick to lull the United States to sleep. To support this view, they pointed to the following biblical warning: "When they shall say peace and safety, then sudden destruction cometh upon them."

The events of the twenty-first century, however, did force many of the popularizers to adjust their prognostications. Some prophets made minimal alterations to their prophetic thinking while others made major shifts. In general the controlling theme was not the Russian threat to the Jews but the Islamic menace. Earlier in *The Rise of Babylon* (1991), Charles Dyer focused on Saddam Hussein and the rebuilding of Babylon.[1] The events of the early twenty-first century then propelled the Islamic motif to the forefront. The attacks of September 11, the war against terrorism, the rise of Islamic fundamentalism, the wars in Iraq and Afghanistan, and the threat of a nuclear Iran all pushed the Islamic threat to the forefront. The election of Barack Hussein Obama to the presidency even fueled some people's paranoia. His father was a Muslim and he even has a Muslim middle name. So some people regarded him as a "closet Muslim."[2]

In the early twenty-first century, most of the events that have excited the faithful concern Islam. Eager watchers for "signs of the times" can log on to www.raptureready.com for an assessment of just how close we are to the rapture. This Rapture Index was founded in 1995 by Todd Strandberg and calls itself the Dow Jones of end-time activities. It monitors forty-five trends on a scale of one to five. The higher the score, the sooner people believe the world is coming to an end. In calculating the imminence of the

---

1. Paul Boyer, "The Growth of Fundamentalist Apocalyptic in the United States," in *The Continuum History of Apocalypticism*, eds. Bernard McGinn, John J. Collins, and Stephen J. Stein (New York: Continuum, 2003) 541–42; Charles H. Dyer, *The Rise of Babylon: Sign of the End Times* (Wheaton, IL: Tyndale, 1991).

2. Lisa Miller, "Is Obama the Antichrist?," *Newsweek*, 24 November 2008, 18; Hal Lindsey, "How Obama Prepped World for Antichrist," http://www.wnd.commentary.com; "Is Barack Obama the Antichrist? End Times 2012 Election 2008," http://youtube.com/?v=rfGWBcyeZDY (accessed 15 November 2008).

rapture, the prophetic categories include the following: technology, wars and rumors of wars, marks of the beast, earthquakes, famines, pestilence, apostasy, ecumenism, immorality, tensions in the Middle East and more. According to Strandberg, any score higher than 145 means "Fasten your seat belts." The index hit a record high of 182 immediately after 9/11. At the onset of Israeli-Hezbollah conflict in July of 2006, the site jumped from 180,000 hits to 250,000. On August 7, 2006 with the second Gulf War dominating the headlines, the Rapture Index soared to an exciting 158.[3]

The Muslim menace, however, was an old theme in Christian eschatology. For centuries, Christians had identified the power of the north and the demonic power of the end times with the Ottoman Empire, sometimes allied with Russia but usually standing alone. But when the Ottoman Empire collapsed in 1917, the popularizers downplayed the role of Islam and accentuated that of the Soviet Union.[4]

Currently, some writers do the opposite. They do not ignore Russia and say it still has a major role in the end-time events, but one closely allied with Islamic nations. Other popularizers, however, focus on the Islamic menace while minimizing Russia's end-time activities. In his 1994 book *Planet Earth—2000 A.D.*, Hal Lindsey identified the Muslim world with Ishmael, Abraham's illegitimate son, and pointed to the rising Islamic threat. He said, "Islam has replaced Marxism as the No. 1 ideology and power in the world to destroy Western civilization."[5] Numerous books published in the twenty-first century move further down this path and emphasize Islamic fundamentalism as the demonic force in the end days. A few examples include: *Islam in the End Times*; *Christianity and Islam: The Final Clash*; *The Apocalypse of Ahmadinejad*; *From 9/11 to 666*; *Antichrist: Islam's Awaited Messiah*; *Showdown with Nuclear Iran*; *Epicenter*; *Iran: The Coming Crisis*; *The Final Move Beyond Iraq*; and *Countdown to Crisis: The Coming Nuclear Showdown with Iran*.

Ironically, the opposite is also happening. Islam has its apocalyptic literature and its popularizers have constructed an end-time scenario reflecting the influence of popular Christian eschatology. They have their

---

3. Timothy P. Weber, *On the Road to Armageddon: How Evangelicals Became Israel's Best Friend* (Grand Rapids: Baker, 2004) 211-12 (quote); Victoria Clark, *Allies for Armageddon: The Rise of Christian Zionism* (New Haven, CT: Yale, 2007) 161.

4. Paul Boyer, "The Apocalyptic in the Twentieth Century," in *Fearful Hope: Approaching the New Millennium*, eds. Christopher Kleinhenz and Fannie J. LeMoine (Madison: University of Wisconsin Press, 1999) 160.

5. Hal Lindsey, *Planet Earth—2000 A.D.* (Palos Verdes, CA: Western Front, 1994) 172.

returning messiah, "the Mahdi who—with the aid of Jesus—will fight the demonic forces of the Dajjal, the Islamic antichrist figure," notes Michael Baigent. Like their Christian counterparts, Muslim fundamentalists expect this final struggle to come soon. As has also happened with Christians, such apocalyptic beliefs have affected their view of the world, especially their politics.[6]

In the post-Cold War era, end-time watchers have also modified their view of America. Throughout much of its history, America has been viewed as a nation favored by God and perhaps even destined to lead the world into the millennial age. With the collapse of godless communism, America was not needed as a check on the "evil empire." So now a bleaker view of America took center stage. What was the role of America in prophecy? Except as a supporter of Israel, most popularizers surmised that it had none. The emphasis was now on America's "dark side"—materialism, secularism, abortion, homosexuality, same-sex marriage, and radical feminism. Consequently, America has become apostate and no longer a force for good in the end times.[7]

While not new, several other shifts in emphasis could be seen in the post–Cold War era. The nuclear confrontation between the United States and Russia receded but the nuclear danger did not. End-time watchers still believe the Book of Revelation describes an atomic cataclysm. Now the perpetrators are not so much the major nuclear powers but either Iran or terrorists who have acquired such horrific weapons. Advanced technology and computers are not new to the dispensational view of the end times, but in the post Cold War era greater emphasis has been placed on them. The same can be said regarding globalization. As the world becomes more connected, the one-world economic and political systems have come to the forefront.[8]

As dispensationalists further broadened and updated their scenario, they made more of environmental issues. The Book of Revelation can be interpreted as describing the ultimate ecological disaster: "the sun and moon darken; the seas become 'as the blood of a dead man;' earthquakes, searing heat, monstrous insects, and hideous sores make life a torment."

---

6. Michael Baigent, *Racing toward Armageddon: The Three Great Religions and the Plot to End the World* (New York: HarperCollins, 2009) xix; David Cook, *Contemporary Muslim Apocalyptic Literature* (Syracuse, NY: Syracuse University Press, 2005).

7. Mark Hitchcock, *The Late Great United States* (Colorado Springs, CO: Multnomah, 2009); Boyer, "The Apocalyptic in the Twentieth Century," 158.

8. Daniel Wojcik, *The End of the World As We Know It* (New York: New York University Press, 1997) 149–74.

From 9/11 to 666

John's apocalyptic vision can easily connect with ozone depletion, global warming, toxic pollution, and radioactive waste.[9]

In *Planet Earth—2000 A.D.*, Lindsey pointed to this developing emphasis on environmental issues. He believed earthquakes and volcanoes were increasing and also noted deforestation, global warming, and ozone depletion. He acknowledged the changes in his thinking: "The physical tribulations of the Earth and its environment has been one of the most significant development[s]—prophetically speaking—since I authored *The Late Great Planet Earth* 25 years ago."[10] (These issues shall be the subject of a subsequent chapter, however.)

ISLAMIC ESCHATOLOGY: A BRIEF LOOK

To understand what inroads the Muslim menace has made into end-time thinking in America, some knowledge is needed regarding Islamic eschatology. Like Christianity and Judaism, Islam has an apocalyptic and messianic tradition. And in all three traditions, such strands of belief are not regarded as mainstream. These three religions have apocalyptic literature both within their holy books and in extracanonical literature. In the case of Islam, most of the apocalyptic writings lie outside of the Qur'an. Along with Christianity and Judaism, Islam has its popularizers who take great liberties with this apocalyptic literature and interpret these writings in the light of current events.[11]

Still, aspects of the Islamic apocalyptic tradition have been important to Muslims at all times, namely, the belief that the world will eventually come to an end. Like Christians, Muslims are told that this time is in the hands of God and they are not to speculate on the when and how of this event. Yet their apocalyptic writers engage in end-of-the-world predictions despite admonitions to the contrary.[12]

As with Christians, Islamic apocalypticists see the world in terms of a conflict between good and evil, that is, Islam and other religions. Both Christian and Muslim apocalyptic writers have made much of Samuel Huntington's book *The Clash of Civilizations and the Remaking of the*

---

9. Boyer, "The Apocalyptic in the Twentieth Century," 161.

10. Lindsey, *Planet Earth—2000 A.D.*, 90.

11. David Cook, *Contemporary Muslim Apocalyptic Literature* (Syracuse, NY: Syracuse University Press, 2005) 1–7; Jean Filiu, *Apocalypse in Islam* (Berkeley: University of California Press, 2011) xix–xxi.

12. Ibid., 84.

World Order. His controversial thesis has divided the world into seven or eight civilizations that will inevitably conflict because of differing religious and cultural values. The West and Islam are two of these civilizations and both Christian and Muslim apocalyptic writers regard this confrontation as unavoidable for two reasons: these civilizations are in total opposition, and such a conflict is ordained of God and part of the end time events.[13]

Islam has two main divisions, the Sunnis and the Shiites, plus a number of minor sectarian groups. Muhammad's death in 632 triggered a rupture over the issue of who has the right to rule and interpret Islamic scriptures. The Shiites maintain that only the direct descendants of Muhammad have this right while the Sunnis are more flexible. Rulers can come from a broader group so long as there is a consensus among the religious scholars. While the formal split came in 666, the issue of succession came to a head in a battle near Karbala in 680. The Shiites chose Hussein—the son of Ali, who was a descendent of Muhammad—to lead them. During the battle he was decapitated. Rather than end the dispute, Hussein's death provided the Shiites with a martyr whose death is still observed.[14]

Even within Shiite Islam there are divisions, the most popular and the official religion of Iran is the Ithna Ashari or Twelvers. Shiites believe the title *imam* is reserved for the male descendants of Muhammad. Born in 868, Abu'l-Qasium Muhammad became the twelfth descendant of Muhammad or the twelfth imam. But as a boy he disappeared. As a child he had no sons and thus the Shiites had no successor to Muhammad's line. To explain this major dilemma and the boy's disappearance, Shiite tradition holds that he did not die but went into occultation or hiding. Twelvers believe that this boy (Muhammad) is the twelfth or Hidden Imam and he will return as the Madhi.[15]

Both the Sunnis and Shiites have their apocalyptic literature and traditions. And there are differences. While the Sunnis are by far the largest Islamic body, because of the rise of Iran and their more pronounced

---

13. See Samuel P. Huntington, *The Clash of Civilizations and the Remaking of World Order* (New York: Simon and Schuster, 1996); Filiu, *Apocalypse in Islam*, 121–99.

14. Neil MacFarquhar, "Iraq's Shadow Widens Sunni-Shiite Split in U.S.," *New York Times*, 4 February 2007; Bobby Ghosh, "Why They Hate Each Other," *Time*, 5 March 2007, 32.

15. Moojan Momen, *An Introduction to Shi'i' Islam: The History and Doctrines of Twelver Shi'ism* (New Haven, CT: Yale University Press, 1985) 159–66; Mark Hitchcock, *The Apocalypse of Ahmadinejad* (Colorado Springs, CO: Multnomah, 2007) 37–38; Oliva Tulley, "12th Imam, Key Facet of Islamic Prophecy, Fueling Middle East Turmoil, Experts Say," http://www.sbcbaptistpress.org/bpnews.asp?ID=23746; Filiu, *Apocalypse in Islam*, 23–29.

From 9/11 to 666

apocalyptic tradition the Shiites get the most attention. Nevertheless, some general statements regarding Islamic eschatology can be made that apply to both versions of Islam.

The Madhi

End-time events in Islamic eschatology can be divided into two categories: the Minor and Major Signs. The Minor or Lesser Signs have been visible throughout much of Islamic history and can be found in most societies: natural disasters, wars, moral decay, crime, ignorance, and apostasy. Apocalypticists employ these signs to arouse the faithful. The Major or Greater Signs speak of more significant events and are regarded as a map of the future. They especially include the coming of Islam's dominant end-time figures: the Madhi (the Muslim messiah), a Muslim Jesus, and the Dajjal (the Muslim Antichrist).[16]

The coming of the Madhi is established doctrine for both Sunni and Shiite Muslims. Who is he? He is the Islamic Messiah, a great spiritual and military leader—the one foreordained to purify religion, create a just social order, and free the world from oppression. Muslims believe the Madhi will rule not only all of Islam but also the non-Islamic world. He will lead a global revolution that will establish a new Islamic world order throughout the entire Earth. The Madhi will accomplish this global rule primarily by multiple military conquests or holy wars (jihad).[17]

A particular objective will be Israel. The Mahdi's army will slaughter the Jews until very few are left and then establish Jerusalem as the location for his worldwide rule. Extreme anti-Semitism is prominent in Islamic eschatology. Muslims believe that Jews run the Western power structures and are the force behind American global dominance. Moreover, Muslims are still smarting because of their humiliating defeat at the hands of Israel in the 1967 War.[18]

---

16. Cook, *Muslim Apocalyptic Literature*, 8–9; Joel Richardson, *Antichrist: Islam's Awaited Messiah* (Enumclaw, WA: Pleasant Word, 2006) 37–39.

17. Shaykh Muhammad Hisham Kabbani, *The Approach of Armageddon?: An Islamic Perspective* (Washington, DC: Islamic Supreme Muslim Council of America, 2003) 228; Sideeque M. A. Veliankode, *Doomsday Portents and Prophecies* (Toronto: Al-Attique, 2001) 277; Richardson, *Antichrist*, 41–48; Abdulrahman Kelani, *The Last Apocalypse: An Islamic Perspective* (Arlington, TX: Fustat, 2003) 34–35; Filiu, *Apocalypse in Islam*, 141–64.

18. Cook, *Muslim Apocalyptic Literature*, 59, 223–25.

The Madhi will bring about what Muslims yearn for, namely, the restoration of a worldwide Caliphate. The Caliph is the supreme religious and political leader of all Muslims and the Caliphate is his office or dominion. This is the closest Islam gets to a millennium or golden age as found in Christian eschatology. As Christians await the return of Jesus, Muslims are waiting for the Madhi and his reinstatement of the global Caliphate. In this final Caliphate Islam will be the only religion practiced on Earth, justice will prevail throughout the globe, and wealth will be distributed. As a result, the Madhi will be loved by all people on the Earth.[19]

Jesus Christ and the Dajjal

Among the Major Signs, the return of Jesus Christ is second in importance only to the coming of the Madhi. Yes, Muslims are anxiously awaiting the return of Jesus but he is dramatically different from the Jesus of Christianity. Muslims reject the idea that Jesus was or is the son of God. Moreover, Islam denies that Jesus ever died for the sins of humanity. In fact, he never experienced death. Rather, Allah miraculously rescued Jesus from death and took him alive into heaven. He is now with Allah and awaits his opportunity to return to Earth and complete his ministry. Instead of being the savior for humanity, Jesus was an important prophet. And when he returns, he comes back as a radical Muslim.[20]

While Jesus is clearly subordinate to the Madhi in both rank and mission, he does have very important work to do. He is to convert many Christians to Islam and abolish all other religions. In fact, non-Muslims will have the choice of accepting Islam or dying. In the process, Jesus is to institute and enforce Islamic Shariah law throughout the globe. After Jesus abolishes Christianity his next job is to kill the Dajjal, the Muslim version of the Antichrist. Not only does he slay the Dajjal, but he kills the Dajjal's followers, who for the most part are Jews and women. After completing these tasks, Jesus lives on Earth for forty years, during which time he marries, has children, and then dies.[21]

---

19. Ibid., 226–29; Richardson, *Antichrist*, 43–44; Mark Evans, *Showdown with Nuclear Iran* (Nashville: Nelson Current, 2006) 8, 13; Filiu, *Apocalypse in Islam*, 153–55.

20. Cook, *Muslim Apocalyptic Literature*, 216–17; Richardson, *Antichrist*, 71–72.

21. Cook, *Muslim Apocalyptic Literature*, 9, 22, 193,196–98, 127; Richardson, *Antichrist*, 73–79; Michael Baigent, *Racing toward Armageddon* (New York: HarperCollins, 2009) xix.

The third major figure in Islamic eschatology is the Dajjal, the Muslim Antichrist. He is described as a great deceiver who temporarily will have great powers over the entire Earth. His miraculous works come from Satan and allow him to deceive and thus convert Muslims into unbelief. He claims to be the Islamic Jesus Christ and this deception is believed by many as he travels the Earth performing false miracles and recruiting many followers. The bulk of the Dajjal's followers consist of Jews, who are the great enemy, and women, who are regarded as ignorant and easily misled.[22]

The biblical Antichrist is described as physically attractive. Contrary to this, the Dajjal is blind in one eye and rather unattractive. He is believed to be a Jew and, in the Islamic mind, the Jewish Messiah. At any rate, he is the defender of the Jews and assembles a great army at the end of time. The real Islamic Jesus returns and, along with the Mahdi, attacks Israel and kills the Dajjal.[23]

End-Time Events

The Islamic end-time scenario resembles the pattern found in Christian eschatology, but the details are dramatically different. In the last days, the Mahdi—who has unprecedented political, economic, and religious power—will emerge. His sidekick will be the Islamic Jesus and together they will have a powerful army that attempts to subdue and dominate the entire world. The Muslim Jesus forces the world to convert to Islam and executes everyone who will not submit. The Mahdi and the Muslim Jesus now establish a new world order, which changes times and the laws. The Gregorian calendar (AD) is replaced with the Islamic calendar (AH). Friday displaces Saturday and Sunday as the official day of worship. Islam will become the universal and only religion on Earth. And Shariah law will be imposed on the entire world.[24]

All of this will be done by force and deceit. The Mahdi and the Muslim Jesus will kill anyone who fails to submit to Islam, and these executions will be done by beheading. More specifically, Jews will be the target

22. Cook, *Muslim Apocalyptic Literature*, 184–90; Richardson. *Antichrist*, 89–92; Kabbani, *Approach of Armageddon*, 223; Filiu, *Apocalypse in Islam*, 5–18, 168–73.

23. Cook, *Muslim Apocalyptic Literature*, 184–95; Richardson, *Antichrist*, 72–77; Ayatullah Baqir al-Sadr and Ayatullah Muratda Mutahhari, *The Awaited Savior* (Karachi: Islamic Seminary Publications, n.d.) prologue, 4–5.

24. Cook, *Muslim Apocalyptic Literature*, 126–42; Richardson, *Antichrist*, 187–91; Filiu, *Apocalypse in Islam*, 184–96.

and many will be killed. In the process, the Mahdi and the Muslim Jesus will attack and reconquer Jerusalem for Islam. From Jerusalem, the final Islamic Caliphate will be established. Both the Madhi and the Muslim Jesus will perform miracles that impress large numbers of people. The Madhi makes a peace treaty for exactly seven years. Confronting him will be the Dajjal, who gathers a great following of Jews and claims to be Jesus Christ and does battle against the Madhi and the Muslim Jesus. But he is defeated and killed.[25]

While only a few examples can be noted, Islamic popular writers have read all kinds of contemporary events into their apocalyptic literature. In this endeavor they have been significantly influenced by Christian ideas and sources. But there is a big difference. The Islamic forces, strengthened by the power of Allah, emerge victorious in these struggles.

The dominance of America in the modern world has found its way into Islamic apocalyptic literature. As the principal center of Jewish power, America is hated and experiences a downfall. Some writers see the Antichrist ruling America or most modern American presidents either being the Antichrist or his agents. Henry Kissinger plus some cultural figures such as Clint Eastwood and Burt Lancaster have also been labeled as Antichrist. At the end, however, the appearance of the Madhi changes things. He liberates the Islamic world from American occupation and a tremendous earthquake destroys much of America, including New York.[26]

Some Islamic writers have even read the events of September 11, 2001, into their apocalyptic literature. This "war on terror" is thus interpreted through Islamic lenses. Osama bin Laden is viewed as serving Allah and the Taliban are regarded as the Mahdi's followers. The Taliban are initially defeated by the American forces in Afghanistan. How is this explained? Islam was not unified and not all Muslims supported the Islamic cause. But this will change because the Muslim forces will eventually be victorious. These few examples demonstrate the malleability of Islamic apocalyptic literature. The Islamic apocalyptic tradition—much like its Christian counterpart—has had the ability to deal with new situations and to reinterpret the classic apocalyptic literature in a new and convincing manner.[27]

---

25. Cook, *Muslim Apocalyptic Literature*, 9, 22, 193; Richardson, *Antichrist*, 188.

26. Cook, *Muslim Apocalyptic Literature*, 150–71; Filiu, *Apocalypse in Islam*, 186–96.

27. Cook, *Muslim Apocalyptic Literature*, 163–71; Filiu, *Apocalypse in Islam*, 194–96.

From 9/11 to 666

THE BEAR AND THE CRESCENT

During the early years of the twenty-first century, doomsday prophets—whether they be Christian dispensationalists, other evangelicals, or even secularists—began to focus on the Muslim menace as the major threat facing the Western world. More specifically, the spotlight was on Iran, its erratic leader Ahmadinejad, and Islamic fascism. The only question was the degree of this emphasis. Most dispensationalists linked Iran and Islamic fascism with the revived Russian threat. Other evangelicals and secularists largely ignored the Russian component in their end-time scenarios.

Most Christian dispensationalists maintained the typical picture of the last days that has been briefly described in chapters 5 and 6. But some timeline is necessary at this point. While the details differ among the dispensationalists, their chronology generally looks something like this.

World tensions continue to mount and Israel, Islam, and oil become the focus of world interest. People cry out for peace, stability, and security. At that time Jesus returns to rapture out his church. This event greatly impacts the United States, which loses millions of its citizens and shifts global power to Europe and Asia. Fulfilling the prophecy of Ezekiel 38 and 39, at the end of history four great power blocs will emerge: the revived Roman Empire, and the kings of the north, south, and east. The revived Roman Empire represents the west in the form of the European Union and becomes the power base for the Antichrist.

Out of the chaos and from his European headquarters, the Antichrist launches a career that acquires great political, economic, and military power and he becomes a global dictator. At the start of the tribulation, he signs a seven-year treaty with Israel guaranteeing their security. The world utters a collective sigh of relief because this treaty brings a temporary peace and assures the flow of oil. The Antichrist will be hailed as a great peacemaker. At midpoint during the tribulation, he is assassinated but is brought back to life by the power of Satan. This imitation of Christ's resurrection allows the Antichrist and his partner the false prophet to implement the mark of the beast (666) and a totalitarian police system. People lose their freedom, personal identity, and must submit to the Antichrist.

But the Antichrist's global dominion will be challenged by the three remaining power blocks. The Middle East, with its mineral wealth and religious importance, becomes the place of a series of wars, culminating in the cataclysmic battle of Armageddon. The northern power is Russia, who links up with a number of Islamic nations (the king of the south) and swoops down on Israel. The western army, led by the Antichrist, meets the

Russian and Islamic forces and decisively defeats them. At this point, the nations of the east unite and march on the Holy Land. This massive two-hundred-million-man Asian army will meet the forces of the Antichrist in the final battle of Armageddon. The devastation and carnage of this battle will be unprecedented.

Christ now returns to Earth to rescue his chosen people. He defends Israel by defeating the western and eastern armies, who are pitted against God's people. Christ defeats the Antichrist and banishes Satan to the bottomless pit for a thousand years. With this act Christ begins his thousand year messianic kingdom on Earth.[28]

Islamic Fascism and Iran

"We're now at the dawn of an era in which extreme fanatical religious ideology, undeterred by the usual calculations of prudence and self-preservation, is wielding state power and will soon be wielding nuclear power," states political commentator Charles Krauthammer.[29] He is referring to Iran, and a number of Christian dispensationalists concur with this opinion. Some examples would be Mark Hitchcock, John Hagee, and Joel C. Rosenberg. They speak of Iran and its leader Ahmadinejad not in secular terms, as has Krauthammer, but as a prophetic signpost signaling the end of the world.

In two books, *Iran: The Coming Crisis* (2006) and *The Apocalypse of Ahmadinejad* (2007), Mark Hitchcock presents his views regarding the potential Iranian menace. "The world today faces the greatest crisis in human history. Yes . . . Greater than Nazi Germany. Greater than Soviet communism." This crisis, he says, officially began when Iran restarted its nuclear program. It was only a matter of time before Ahmadinejad, Iran's anti-Semitic president, would have his finger on the nuclear button.[30]

Thus Hitchcock concludes, "One would be very hard-pressed to find another time in history when there was more at stake—or when the major prophetic signposts were lined up pointing to the end." In fact, he argues that the rise of Iran has set the stage for end-time events. "Iran must

28. Parts of this summary have been drawn from Grant T. Jeffrey, *Countdown to the Apocalypse* (Colorado Springs, CO: Waterbook, 2008) 14–16; and Mark Hitchcock, *Iran: The Coming Crisis* (Sisters, OR: Multnomah, 2006) 192–93.

29. Quoted in Hitchcock, *Iran: The Coming Crisis*, 15.

30. Hitchcock, *Iran: The Coming Crisis*, 15–16. For similar statements regarding Iran's menace to the United States and Israel, see Mike Evans, *The Final Move beyond Iraq* (Lake Mary, FL: FrontLine, 2007) and Mike Evans, *Showdown with Nuclear Iran*.

become a key player in the Middle East for the ancient prophecy of Ezekiel 38 to be fulfilled." More specifically, a militant Islam is setting the stage for Ezekiel's prophecy in two ways. It is contributing to worldwide instability and globalism—two factors necessary for the rise of the Antichrist. Second, Iran's ascendancy is preparing the way for the invasion of Israel.[31]

What frightens Hitchcock and many others is Ahmadinejad's eschatology. He is motivated not by secular goals but by "an apocalyptic, end-of-days Messianism . . ." A number of his comments suggest that "he believes the apocalypse will occur in his own lifetime" and that his administration is "destined to bring about the end times." But for this to occur the long expected twelfth Imam, the Mahdi, must return. More alarming than this, Ahmadinejad is connected with the Hojatieh society, which believes that "only great tribulation, increased violence, and conflict will bring about his coming." And some believe Ahmadinejad would not hesitate to trigger the events necessary for the return of the Mahdi.[32]

What happens if Ahmadinejad does not remain president? Does this scenario change? No! says Hitchcock. Ahmadinejad himself notes that the nation's supreme leader is Ayatollah Mohammed Ali Khamenei. So Ahmadinejad's apocalyptic visions will not end with his passing. They are state policy. Even without Ahmadinejad, Iran's current nuclear policy would continue.[33]

John Hagee has written a number of books from the perspective of dispensational eschatology. Two of them penned in the early twenty-first century, *Jerusalem Countdown* (2007) and *In Defense of Israel* (2007), say much about the Islamic threat and are similar to Hitchcock's perspective. While Hagee regards the rise of a nuclear Iran as a step toward the return of Christ, he places much emphasis on the danger Iran presents toward the United States and Israel. He believes Islamic fascism hates the West, desires to exterminate Christians and Jews, and intends to establish a "one-world Islamic government and religion." Thus there can be no appeasement or compromise with Islamic fascism.[34]

---

31. Hitchcock, *Iran: The Coming Crisis*, 53–54, 67. See also Kenneth R. Timmerman, *Countdown to Crisis: The Coming Nuclear Showdown with Iran* (New York: Three Rivers, 2006). Timmerman argues that the only way to deal with Iran is to encourage the democratic movements within the country. Both appeasement and military action will be counterproductive.

32. Ibid., 75.

33. Hitchcock, *The Apocalypse of Ahmadinejad*, 108.

34. John Hagee, *Jerusalem Countdown* (Lake Mary, FL: FrontLine, 2007) 1–2, 23; John Hagee, *Can America Survive?* (New York: Howard Books, 2010) 21–60.

Hagee places great emphasis on Islamic fascism's anti-Semitic character and compares Ahmadinejad with Adolf Hitler. The Iranian president has denied that the Holocaust ever happened and has threatened to wipe Israel off the face of the Earth. Hagee even harkens back to the pre–World War II days when the West appeased Hitler and compares some American political leaders (especially liberals) to the weak-kneed Europeans. His hero of course is Winston Churchill, and he urges American leaders to follow in his footsteps.[35]

Hagee also brings nuclear terrorism to the center stage. Iran may be able to develop the missile capacity to reach Israel. But America is probably out of range in the foreseeable future. Still, the United States is not out of danger. "If Iran gets nuclear weapons, America will see nuclear suitcase bombs that will have the ability to kill 1–1.5 million people per atomic blast." And according to the FBI, "there are seven U.S. cities targeted by Islamic terrorists for nuclear suitcase bombs."[36]

Hagee does not see these developments only in secular terms. He regards the rise of global terrorism and tensions in the Middle East as "part of a much bigger picture—that of God's plan for the future of Israel and the entire world." What is occurring in the Middle East is part of a countdown—"a countdown that will usher in the end of the world."[37]

In *Epicenter* (2006), Joel Rosenberg draws a close connection between the rise of Iran and its alliance with Russia—a subject that will be noted shortly. According to Rosenberg, Ahmadinejad told his colleagues that he believed "the end of the world was just two or three years away." Being driven by his messianic complex, he also stated that he believed himself "chosen by Allah to become Iran's leader at this critical hour to hasten the coming ... of the Madhi by launching a holy war against Christians and Jews." Ahmadinejad also "boasts that the Imam gave him the presidency for a single task: provoking a clash of civilizations" in which Islam led by Iran defeats the infidel West. So according to this perspective, Ahmadinejad's actions are not driven by secular considerations but by the desire to hasten the coming of the Islamic Messiah.[38]

---

35. Hagee, *Jerusalem Countdown*, 12–13, 32–35; John Hagee, *In Defense of Israel* (Lake Mary, FL: FrontLine, 2007) 2–3; Hagee, *Can America Survive?*, 21–60.

36. Hagee, *Jerusalem Countdown*, 35.

37. Ibid., 37.

38. Joel C. Rosenberg, *Epicenter* (Carol Stream, IL: Tyndale, 2006) x, 123; Evans, *Showdown with Nuclear Iran*, 119.

The Russians Are Still Coming

Has the bear been declawed? Did the collapse of the Soviet Union in 1991 mean that Russia will no longer be the "king of the north" who attacks Israel in the last days? No say a majority of the prophecy writers. As Joel Rosenberg states, "While it may be tempting to believe that the Russian Bear is dead and buried and poses no threat to Israel, the U.S. or anyone else, Ezekiel makes it clear that the Bear is only hibernating and will soon be back with a vengeance."[39] Despite some disconfirmations, most dispensational students of prophecy still identify Gog of the land of Magog with Russia. The difference is that they now emphasize Russia's alliance with Islamic nations, especially Iran.

According to Rosenberg, chapters 38–39 of Ezekiel speak of a period of security for Israel followed by a military alliance between Russia, Iran, and other Islamic nations. In fact, nearly all of the nations mentioned in Ezekiel as Russia's allies are predominately Islamic. These nations attack Israel and bring the world to the brink of the apocalypse of the last days.[40]

Numerous changes, he contends are currently underway in Russia that strongly point to the fulfillment of prophecy. In particular, Rosenberg stresses the role Vladimer Putin has had in restricting freedoms and moving the nation in an autocratic direction. Putin has been rebuilding the Russian military and is forging a close relationship with Iran. In fact, Russia is assisting Iran in the development of its nuclear program, which could produce the "Islamic Bomb" called for by Rafsanjani. What does Russia want in this relationship with Iran and other Islamic nations? It desires to restore the old Soviet Union, make money, acquire more oil, and gain increased access to warm weather ports.[41]

Hagee maintains the traditional dispensational interpretation of Ezekiel, namely, the four military powers—the kings of the west, north, south, and east—rise at the end of time. Russia, of course, is the king of the north and its anti-Semitic dictator leads a coalition of Arab nations to invade Israel. Hagee regards Russia's courtship of Iran, especially being its main partner in the development of nuclear weapons, as a fulfillment of prophecy. In Hagee's eyes, this marriage has benefits for both sides. Russia's payoffs have already been noted. As for the Muslims, they realize it will take Russia's assistance to realize their great goals—namely, exterminating

39. Ibid., 139–40.
40. Ibid. 24.
41. Ibid. 91–92, 113–14. Putin was *Time* magazine person of the year in 2007. See the various articles in the January 7, 2008 issue.

the Jews and gaining absolute control of Jerusalem as the capital of a new Palestinian state.[42]

In reference to Gog, Ezekiel 38:4 says God will "put hooks in your jaws" and call you to arms for an invasion of Israel. Hitchcock interprets this verse and others in the chapter as God pulling "a reluctant Russia down into the land of Israel in the latter years." According to him, Russia's geopolitical strategy to strengthen its relations with several Islamic nations could be "what will pull them into Israel in the end times as Ezekiel predicted." As Hitchcock notes, Russia's close ties with Iran and other Muslim nations could be the hook that drags them into events in the Middle East at the end of history.[43]

In *Prophecy 20/20* (2006), Chuck Missler points to a potential new wrinkle regarding the Russian and Islamic relationship. The key player, he believes, might be Turkey. While the king of the north is still Russia, Turkey becomes one of its allies. This would represent a major turn of events. Turkey is a Westernized secular state, an important nation in NATO, and an ally of Israel. Turkey applied to the European Union and received an associate membership in 1963. Since then it has become obvious that most EU nations do not want Turkey to have full membership. As a consequence of this apparent rejection and strains with Israel, Turkey has experienced a rising Islamic influence. If these trends continue, Missler suggests that Turkey would turn toward Eurasia and the Islamic Middle East. He believes such a direction would be setting the stage for the events of Ezekiel 38.[44]

Besides nuclear destruction, Missler also believes many other weapons of mass destruction are described in the Book of Revelation. An electromagnetic pulse (EMP) can be produced by nuclear and non-nuclear weapons. Such a blast would interact with the Earth's atmosphere, ionosphere, and magnetic field thus significantly impacting electrical and electronic systems over a widespread area. Since America is greatly dependent on computers and other electrical systems, an EMP attack could cripple the U.S.—and both Russia and China are capable of such attacks. The prophets and the four horseman of Revelation speak of widespread diseases in the later days. Missler contends that diseases such as tuberculosis, cholera, and malaria have become more drug-resistant and present

42. Hagee, *Jerusalem Countdown*, 137, 143; John Hagee, *Final Dawn over Jerusalem* (Nashville: T. Nelson, 1998) 144–46.

43. Hitchcock, *Iran: The Coming Crisis*, 94–95.

44. Chuck Missler, *Prophecy 20/20* (Nashville: T. Nelson, 2006) 171–73. See also Hitchcock. *Iran: The Coming Crisis*, 186.

a global threat. In addition, there are the new diseases such as the Ebola virus. If this were not enough, rogue nations and terrorists are capable of cheaply producing a range of biological weapons.[45]

ISLAM AS ANTICHRIST

As previously noted, Christian and Islamic eschatology bear a superficial resemblance. In fact, many parallels exist between the two views. "Muslims use much the same language, similar portents, and a corresponding time frame in discussions about the end of the age."[46] Several evangelical Christian writers reject the standard dispensational end-time scenario, namely, that the Antichrist will emerge from the revived Roman Empire based in Western Europe, and Russia is the northern power who attacks Israel. Rather, they contend that Islam will be the revived Roman Empire (not Western Europe) and the Mahdi will be the Antichrist. In various ways, Joel Richardson, Robert Livingston, and Ralph W. Stice take this approach.

According to Richardson, the Bible's description of the Antichrist bears strong resemblance to the Muslim depiction of the Mahdi. Both individuals will be supreme political, military, and religious leaders. In such capacities, the Antichrist and the Madhi will dominate the world, establish a New World Order, and even change the laws and the times. Moreover, both will institute a universal religion (Islam) and execute anyone who does not submit to it. Jews become a particular target. They are to be killed and Jerusalem will be the center of this universal religion. Richardson also draws parallels between the Muslim Jesus and the false prophet as described in the Book of Revelation. They both perform miracles and force people to worship the Antichrist.[47]

Most important, Richardson argues that the specific nations making up the revived Roman Empire are all Muslim countries, not European nations. Thus he concludes, "the future Antichrist Empire will be an Islamic empire" and "students of eschatology [should] at least consider the role of Islam in the last days very seriously."[48]

Livingston makes similar arguments, contending that the Antichrist's Empire is Islamic. He also notes the parallels between the Antichrist and

45. Missler, *Prophecy 20/20*, 107–25.
46. Ralph W. Stice, *From 9/11 to 666* (Nashville: ACW, 2005) 130.
47. Richardson, *Antichrist*, 187–91.
48. Ibid., 98–99. See also Daniel Botkin, "Islam in Prophecy?," http;//www.endtimeinsights.com/site/v2-3/content/view/63/63/.

the Madhi and the Islamic composition of the nations mentioned in Ezekiel. But he gives a different twist to the latter point. He says the Roman Empire was more than Western Europe. It stretched into what became Islamic nations. Furthermore, he points out what many secular prophets say about Europe. Europeans are having few children while the Muslim population is growing rapidly by childbirth and immigration. Thus, as some secular forecasters are doing, Livingston speculates that even Western Europe might become Islamic.[49]

Like Richardson and Livingston, Stice contends for an Islamic Antichrist. In doing so, he employs the same arguments—the similarities between the Antichrist and the Madhi and the makeup of the nations found in Ezekiel 38. But he does so with more gusto. In his opinion, "a preponderance of evidence, both biblical and historical," exists to advance the thesis that the Antichrist will be a Muslim. To use Stice's words: "Muslims will play a key role in the End Times," which are soon approaching. "If the antichrist is not a Muslim, surely the titanic clash of Islam versus the West will set the stage for a world dictator who tries to bring resolution to this tremendous battle of cultures and faiths."[50]

Stice even offered us a possible timetable for these forthcoming events. By 2010 a civil war in Saudi Arabia overthrows the repressive monarchy. The new government favors Wahhabism, a version of Islamic fundamentalism. Because of the threat of nuclear terrorism and a possible cut off of oil, the United States must intervene. Aroused Muslims see this attempt to secure the Saudi oilfields as a crusader invasion. So in 2011 terrorists unleash nuclear weapons on the American forces. Because of our previous invasions of Iraq and Afghanistan, this attack receives nearly universal approval among Islamic nations. What will the U.S. do? To use our nuclear weapons would destroy much of the world's oil supply. By 2012 the Western world is frozen by this monumental dilemma. So the

---

49. Robert Livingston, *Christianity and Islam: The Final Clash* (Enumclaw, WA: Pleasant Word, 2005) 143. A number of secular sources make the same point. They suggest that Islam could become the dominant religion in Western Europe. See Bruce Bawer, *While Europe Slept: How Radical Islam Is Destroying the West from Within* (New York: Broadway, 2006); Mark Steyn, *America Alone: The End of the World as We Know It* (Washington, DC: Regnery, 2008); Walter Laqueur, *The Last Days of Europe: Epitaph for an Old Continent* (New York: Thomas Dunne, 2007); Philip Jenkins, *God's Continent: Christianity, Islam, and Europe's Religious Crisis* (New York: Oxford University Press, 2007).

50. Stice, *From 9/11 to 666*, 9, 173. For another rejection of traditional dispensationalism and its eschatology see Ellis Skolfield, *Islam in the End Times* (Ft. Myers, FL: Fish House, 2007).

From 9/11 to 666

world now seeks a peacemaker who could bridge the gap between the West and the Islamic nations. Thus they turn to the Madhi—a charming Muslim who can "straddle the worldviews in conflict." In projecting such a scenario, Stice clearly rejected a centerpiece of dispensational eschatology, namely, the pretribulational rapture. The church is still here when these events occur.[51]

Several writers including Livingston, Stice, and Ellis Skolfield point to a numerical possibility in identifying Islam as the Antichrist. How one divides the verses in the Qur'an is up for debate. Thus scholars count the verses in the Qur'an differently. One count says there are 6,666 verses while another notes 6,616. The designation of 666 in Revelation 13:18 as the mark of the beast has led to countless and humorous speculations as to who or what the numbers might designate. The above writers do not do this, but they do note that if one number were removed from either calculation it would be 666 and perhaps the Islamic Jesus could be the Antichrist.[52]

WHERE IS AMERICA IN PROPHECY?

Where is the United States to be found in these last-time scenarios? According to the contemporary prophets, the world sits on the edge of a precipice. Unprecedented events are about to happen. But where is the world's only superpower? Does the United States play a role in these apocalyptic events? If so, what is it? The Bible, as interpreted by many, speaks of four power blocs at the end of history. Where does America fit in this lineup? Does the Bible mention the United States in its description of the last days? Some self-proclaimed prophets say yes. But a majority say no.

America in Prophecy

"The United States is involved in Bible prophecy, even if many students have neither discovered nor explored the fact," says Douglas B. MacCorkie.[53] As is the case with most nations, America is never specifically

---

51. Stice, *9/11 to 666*, 40, 155–69.

52. Livingston, *Christianity and Islam*, 198; Stice, *9/11 to 666*, 141; Skolfield, *Islam in the End Times*, 111.

53. Quoted in Hitchcock, *Late Great United States*, 11. See "The United States in Prophecy," http://goodnewschristianministry.org/unitedstates.htm (accessed 21 February 2007).

mentioned in prophecy. But a number of prophecy writers claim they can identify the United States.

Four reasons are usually given in support of this view. America, especially New York City, is Babylon as described in Revelation 17–19. Writing in 1968, Franklin Logsdon says, "it is unthinkable that the God who knows the end from the beginning would pinpoint such small nations as Libya, Egypt, Ethiopia and Syria in the prophetic declaration and completely overlook the wealthiest and most powerful nation on the Earth." Jack Van Impe concurs with this view. Both of these writers look to Jeremiah 50–51 and Revelation 17–19 and point out the parallels between Babylon and modern America. America, not the literal city of Babylon, is being described. And like Babylon, it is sinful and will be destroyed.[54]

Second, America is seen as the unnamed nation in Isaiah 18. This passage refers only to an unspecified great nation whose "people are fierce and enterprising" and is a "great maritime power."[55] Next, America is the ten lost tribes of Israel. This view is called British Israelism or Anglo-Israelism and contends that many of the inhabitants of Britain are descendants of the ten tribes of Israel. When Samaria fell to the Assyrians in BCE 722, large numbers of the ten tribes were enslaved but a number of them fled to northern Europe and eventually to Britain. Since then they have made their way to the United States and other nations of the former British Empire. And since God favored Israel, he has since then looked kindly on America. Such a position has scant biblical evidence but was promoted by Herbert Armstrong of the Worldwide Church of God.[56]

Four, America is the "young lions of Tarshish" in Ezekiel 38:13. Ezekiel 38–39 lists the nations that descend upon Israel in the last days. A small group of nations—"Sheba, Dedan, and the merchants of Tarshish"—weakly protest this invasion. Sheba and Dedan have been identified as Saudi Arabia, Oman, Yemen, and the Gulf States. Tarshish is not as easy to pinpoint. Some people believe it refers to western European nations and the colonies that they founded, including the United States. Other

---

54. S. Franklin Logsdon, *Is the U.S.A. in Prophecy?* (Grand Rapids: Zondervan, 1968) 9; Jack Van Impe, *The Great Escape* (Nashville: Word, 1998) 207; Hitchcock, *Late Great United States*, 13–15; Jack Van Impe, *2001: On the Edge of Eternity* (Dallas: Word, 1996) 179. See also Edward Tracy, *The United States in Prophecy* (Pine Grove, CA: Convale, 1969).

55. Van Impe, *The Great Escape*, 206; Hitchcock, *Late Great United States*, 21–23.

56. Herbert W. Armstrong, *The United States and Britain in Prophecy* (Pasadena: Worldwide Church of God, 1980) 98; Hitchcock, *Late Great United States*, 23–25; Carl G. Howie, "British-Israelism and Pryamidology," *Interpretation*, 11 (1957) 307–23.

prophets are more specific, contending that Tarshish is England and the young lions refer to its colonies, especially the United States. Of the four views arguing for an American role in the events of the last days, this one has the most support.[57]

The Late Great United States

"The world has shifted from anti-Americanism to post-Americanism.... The distribution of power is shifting, moving away from American dominance," says Fareed Zakaria. (Zakaria is not actually arguing for America's absolute decline, but for the rise of other nations. A number of nations will catch up to America). Many of the end-time prophets would agree with Zakaria, but to his emphasis on secular factors they would add a moral and biblical dimension and see America in more of an absolute decline.[58]

A number of reasons are given for this majority opinion. Despite some veiled references, most dispensationalists would say America is not mentioned in biblical prophecy. And this is no accident they say. By the last days America has declined significantly. The only reasonable explanation for Europe's preeminent position in the last days is that the United States is no longer a super- or even first-rate power. Most dispensational scholars would contend that America has been absorbed into the Western power block dominated by the Antichrist.[59]

America, however, does remain reasonably strong until the rapture. Why? The United States is Israel's primary protector and friend. Scripture says God will bless the nation that blesses Israel. So until the rapture, America serves God's purpose in its support of Israel. In fact, Missler and others contend that when America has not supported Israel as it should, the United States has been judged. For example, he believes that because America pressured Israel into withdrawing from Gaza, it experienced Hurricane Katrina. The view that America maintains strength until the rapture rests on Ezekiel 38, which portrays Israel as peaceful and thriving in the end times. So logically, a powerful America must be supporting it.[60]

57. Ed Hindson, *Is the Antichrist Alive and Well?* (Eugene, OR: Harvest House, 1998) 127; Hitchcock, *The Late Great United States*, 27–31.

58. Quoted in Hitchcock, *The Late Great United States*, front page. See also Fareed Zakaria, *The Post-American World* (New York: Norton, 2009); David S. Mason, *The End of the America Century* (Lanham, MD: Rowman & Littlefield, 2009).

59. Hitchcock, *The Late Great United States*, 32, 34, 39–41; Hitchcock, *Iran: The Coming Crisis*, 120–21.

60. Hitchcock, *Iran: The Coming Crisis*, 126; Missler, *Prophecy 20/20*, 130–36, 249.

What causes America's eventual decline in the last days? John Hagee argues that America will elect a president who promotes a "retreat in defeat" foreign policy. After fighting long wars in Iraq and Afghanistan, the American public has grown tired of war. Thus they now support an isolationist or appeasement mentality and elect political leaders who favor such policies.[61]

Other writers believe America becomes the victim of a nuclear attack, most likely from terrorists. A suitcase-sized nuclear weapon is smuggled into the United States and destroys a major city, killing millions. In addition to the economic and human impact, such an attack would shock America into an isolationist position. Many political leaders, both Republican and Democratic, agree that the greatest threat America faces is a nuclear terrorist attack. If the terrorists cannot smuggle a nuclear bomb into the United States, they have a fall back option: a dirty bomb. A dirty bomb is an ordinary explosive device wrapped in radioactive material. Such an explosion would contaminate an area for years, kill many people, and have devastating psychological effects.[62]

Many forecasters, some of them serious scholars, believe America will experience a substantial economic decline in the future. Some popularizers latch on to this and believe America's absence from biblical prophecy is because the nation is no longer economically strong. They point to our dependency on imported oil, which is over 70 percent of our supply. Being so critically dependent on imported oil, a petroleum crisis could cause an economic crash. To compound this problem, the Unites States already has a huge deficit, much of it funded by foreign nations, especially the Chinese and Japanese. When all economic factors are considered, America could be facing a "perfect storm."[63]

Another factor is America's moral decay. In the past God has judged nations for their immorality and such may happen to the United States. End-time prophets say that since the 1960s America has slid into a serious

---

See Hagee, *In Defense of Israel.*

61. John Hagee, *Financial Armageddon* (Lake Mary, FL: FrontLine, 2008) 34.

62. Hitchcock, *Iran: The Coming Crisis,* 121–26; Hagee, *Financial Armageddon,* 35–36; Hitchcock, *Late Great United States,* 72–83; Evans, *Final Move beyond Iran,* 97–115, 149–66; "The Fall of the United States," http://www.endtimeinsights.com/site/v2-3/contnet/view/63/63 (accessed 2 March 2007); Mark Lawrence, "The Bible Scenario—Is the United States in the Bible? Cheney: Nuclear Attack on U.S. Cities Very Real—Is This Biblical?," http://www.secretsofsurvival.com/survival/bible-scenario.html (accessed 1 May 2007); Hagee, *Can America Survive?,* 16–19.

63. Hitchcock, *The Late Great United States,* 63–72; Hagee, *Financial Armageddon,* 35–36; Missler, *Prophecy 20/20,* 193–210; Hagee, *Can America Survive?,* 7–15; 75–103.

moral decline and is rotting from within. They point to a number of factors: acceptance of homosexuality, abortion, pervasive pornography, alcoholism, drug use, sexual immorality, and the unraveling of the family. America is seen as hemorrhaging from within. Thus America may not be active at the end of history because it has experienced God's judgment in the last days.[64]

The most important reason why America will not be a major "prophetic superpower" centers on the rapture. About 40 percent of Americans claim to be "born again." While such figures may be an exaggeration, millions of people would be raptured, more than in any nation on Earth. The economic, military, and political impact would be incalculable. Every segment of American society would suffer a staggering blow. Writing in the 1990s, Charles Dyer says, "the economic fluctuations of the eighties and even the Great Depression will pale in comparison to the political and economic collapse that will occur when our society suddenly losses individuals who were its salt and light." Or as Mark Hitchcock puts it, "the Rapture may well be the end of America as we know it."[65]

End-time ideas usually rest on apocalyptic literature, which is highly symbolic. Thus such writings can be interpreted many ways. This situation contributes to the chameleon-like quality of eschatology. Consequently, in the late twentieth and early twenty-first centuries, a shift in the way dispensationalists viewed eschatological events became evident. With the collapse of the Soviet Union and the decline of communism, a major pillar in the dispensational scenario regarding the end of time vanished. How did the prophets of the apocalypse handle this apparent disconfirmation? Never fear, they adjusted their prognostications. In doing so, they followed two paths. While still regarding Russia as the northern power, they closely linked the Russian bear with the Islamic crescent. The two powers would work closely and move on Israel. A second path said no. The enemy was Islamic fascism and some even regarded Islam as the Antichrist. What happened to America? Most end-time speculators relegated the United States to a minor role in these end-of-the-world events.

---

64. Hitchcock, *The Late Great United States*, 91–93; Evans, *Final Move beyond Iran*, 33–45.

65. Dyer, *Rise of Babylon*, 168; Hitchcock, *Iran: The Coming Crisis*, 127–29; Hagee, *Financial Armageddon*, 34–35.

8

Imagining the Apocalypse

MOST OF THE IDEAS on how the world will end have come from the Bible, science, or the occult. But eschatology—both secular and Christian—has also been conveyed through fiction, especially novels and films. This is not totally surprising, for the imagination is not pure invention. It connects with one's perception of reality, or what one believes reality will be in the future. Perception fuels the imagination, and in turn imagination fuels ideas. So as perception changes, the imagination and ideas also change. Novels and films with end-time themes signal something about their writers and audiences—they believe the world will come to a disastrous end in the future. Indeed, declares Warren Wagar, "the bulk of eschatological fictions . . . can be read as indicators of a growing consciousness within modern Western culture that its end is in view" and that a new civilization will replace it.[1]

Why have end-time novels and films been so popular? In the late twentieth and early twenty-first centuries, there has been a tremendous appetite for them—especially in America. They are a reflection of popular culture. They say something about both the writers and their audiences. Popular culture is a two-way street. In analyzing popular culture, an important principle is that "popular culture both reflects us and shapes us."

---

1. W. Warren Wagar, *Terminal Visions* (Bloomington: Indiana University Press, 1982) 204 (quote); Yuru Rubinsky and Ian Wiseman, *A History of the End of the World* (New York: Morrow, 1982) 136. See also Frank Kermode, *The Sense of an Ending* (New York: Oxford University Press, 1967).

Imagining the Apocalypse

Most often people think of the influence of popular culture as shaping us, for better or for worse. Still, what does popular culture tell us about ourselves? How does it reflect us? Why do we choose what is popular? In one sense, "looking at popular culture is like holding up a mirror in which the general public sees itself: its needs, its desires, its beliefs, its yearnings," writes Bruce Forbes.[2]

End-time novels and films must be seen in the larger context of the broad themes found in American popular culture. And conservative Christians do not have a corner on such subjects. For example, the struggle between good and evil is not limited to Christian writings and films. Rather, they pervade nearly all aspects of American culture. Such themes can be found in westerns, science fiction stories, comic books, and most action and adventure novels or films. Sometimes the struggle between good and evil occurs on a cosmic level. Other times such conflicts develop in more personal and human situations.[3]

The struggle between good and evil, which pervades apocalyptic thought—whether secular or Christian—contains a number of sub themes. First is the notion that "evil comes from the outside." This evil could be a natural disaster, a nuclear attack, or the Antichrist. But because the evil or problem comes from without provides people with psychological comfort: "we are not the problem." Next, "people are either good or evil, not both." The culprit could be an earthquake, a terrorist attack, or a villain with a black hat in a western movie. The good people could be those saving humankind from a natural disaster or the cowboy wearing a white hat. Such a clear-cut distinction between good and evil makes decisions easier and resonates better with popular culture, which does not prefer ambiguity.[4]

Third, "the solution is the destruction of the evil-doers." When no doubt exists as to who are good and bad, the answer is simple: destroy the enemy. After all, such bad people are usually beyond redemption. Lastly, good wins. Unless a sequel is planned, people do not prefer ambiguous

---

2. Bruce David Forbes, "How Popular Are the Left Behind Books . . . and Why?," in *Rapture, Revelation, and the End Times: Exploring the Left Behind Series*, eds. Bruce David Forbes and Jeanne Halgren Kilde (New York: Palgrave, 2004) 22–23 (quotes); James Poniewozik, "Postapocalypse Now," *Time*, 23 October 2006, 94; Mark Moring, "It's the End of the World and We Love It," *Christianity Today*, March 2010, 44.

3. Forbes, "How Popular Are the Left Behind Books," 23; Robert Jewett and John Shelton Lawrence, *Captain America and the Crusade against Evil* (Grand Rapids: Eerdmans, 2003) 131–46.

4. Forbes, "How Popular Are the Left Behind Books" (quotes). See also John Shelton Lawrence, *The Myth of the American Superhero* (Grand Rapids: Eerdmans, 2002).

endings. While the good guys may struggle and get bloodied up, they usually win.⁵

While such themes may not always connect with Christian theology or science, they are embraced by most segments of American popular culture, including the evangelical community. Consequently, they are a factor in the popularity of apocalyptic fiction. In addition, life in the modern world has filled people with many anxieties: wars, terrorism, and economic collapse have turned their thoughts to the question of death and the afterlife. Moreover, people through the centuries have craved to know the future and while apocalyptic literature may be fiction, it helps to meet this need.⁶

SECULAR ESCHATOLOGICAL FICTION

By the late seventeenth century the notion of progress had pushed end-of-the-world ideas into the background. But during the nineteenth century things began to change. The Romantic Movement cherished nature and resented what the industrial world was doing to it. Forms of irrationalism reared their heads and embraced apocalyptic ideas. Economist Thomas Malthus painted a dire picture regarding overpopulation and humankind's future. Charles Darwin's theory of evolution shook everyone's beliefs and in the mind of some people diminished God's power. Prominent philosophers such as Arthur Schopenhauer and Friedrich Nietzsche expressed pessimistic and irrational ideas. Following the boom in science came a rapid growth of science fiction, the major genre for eschatological fiction. Then World War I provided a real apocalypse for the imagination to feed on.⁷

---

5. Forbes, "How Popular Are the Left Behind Books," 24.

6. Moring, "It's the End of the World," 44; Forbes, "How Popular Are the Left Behind Books," 25; Heather Hendershot, *Shaking the World for Jesus: Media and Conservative Evangelical Culture* (Chicago: University of Chicago Press, 2004) 176–209.

7. For general sources see Roland N. Stromberg, *An Intellectual History of Modern Europe* (2nd ed.; Englewood Cliffs, NJ: Prentice-Hall, 1975); W. Warren Wagar, *World Views: A Study in Comparative History* (Hinsdale, IL: Dryden, 1977); Franklin L. Baumer, *Modern European Thought* (New York: Macmillan, 1977); Crane Brinton, *The Shaping of Modern Thought* (Englewood Cliffs, NJ: Prentice-Hall, 1950).

Imagining the Apocalypse

Novels

Eschatological fiction began to pop up during the nineteenth century. For "it was in the nineteenth century in the West, that the vision of the total end of man appeared for the first time in a systematic and repeated fashion."[8] And fiction served as a major vehicle for communicating these end-time ideas. Prior to 1914 it was the forces of nature, not humankind, that were depicted as causing the collapse of civilization: "the world most often ended in imagination because of some natural catastrophe."[9]

In 1805 a French priest, Jean-Baptiste Cousin de Grainville, published *Le Dernier Homme* (The Last Man). The world ends by a natural catastrophe—soil exhaustion and human sterility. Mark Shelley published *The Last Man* in 1826, the story of a plague that begins in Eastern Europe and kills off all of humanity except four people. They make their way to Italy where one of them dies of typhus and two drown, leaving only Lionel. He makes his way to Rome where he lives until 2100. Then he sails off throughout the world searching in vain for other humans. When the end comes, it is not "a gateway to a new world, nor a judgment, but simply an end, produced by the cold necessity of natural causes." *The Last Man*, indeed, has "a strong claim to be the first major example of secular eschatology in literature."[10]

In the first half of the nineteenth century end-time themes crossed the Atlantic. During this time several comets excited America, including the most famous of them all, Halley's Comet. Inspired by these and other events, Edgar Allan Poe wrote three end-time stories. In "The Conversation of Eiros and Charmion" (1839), a comet strikes the Earth, and humankind perishes in great agony. In "The Masque of the Red Death" (1842), a plague—which causes people to bleed profusely at their pores—is the vehicle for destruction. The last humans are led in vain by a prince named Prospero. Just as he is about to plunge a dagger into a red-masked figure who symbolizes death, he collapses. Once again, human efforts are "frustrated by cosmic forces." Finally, in "The Colloquy of Monos and Una" (1850), Poe saves his sharpest indictment of human pride. The world

---

8. Saul Friedlander, "Themes of Decline and End in Nineteenth-Century Western Imagination," in *Visions of Apocalypse*, ed. Saul Friedlander et al. (New York: Holmes and Meier, 1985) 61.

9. Wagar, *Terminal Visions*, 24.

10. Wagar, *Terminal Visions*, 13-15 (quotes); I.F. Clarke, *The Pattern of Expectation, 1644-2001* (New York: Basic, 1979) 43-44; Chris H. Lewis, "Science, Progress, and the End of the Modern World," *Soundings* 75/2 (Summer-Fall 1992) 316.

ends because humankind, obsessed with the idea of progress, attempts to control nature instead of obeying natural law. The result was unyielding and constant decay.[11]

During the middle decades of the nineteenth century few secular eschatological works were written. But apocalyptic excitement heated up by the 1890s. From the 1890s to the early twentieth-first century, Western civilization has been embroiled in serious problems—wars, economic crises, totalitarianism, terrorism, natural disasters, epidemics, and even psychological issues that damage self-esteem. Such a climate lends itself to doomsday thinking.[12]

The king of apocalyptic writers was English novelist H. G. Wells (1866–1946). He published numerous novels and stories regarding the future, many of them pointing to doomsday. In *The Time Machine* (1895), the world ends in three ways: biological degeneration, class conflict, and the dying of the sun. The short story "The Star" (1897) tells about a runaway star causing great havoc on Earth, killing all but a few people. In *The War of the Worlds* (1898), humankind is nearly obliterated by technologically superior Martian invaders. An early atomic bomb ends civilization in *The World Set Free* (1914), and *All Aboard for Ararat* (1941) describes a modern Noah and a gentle, lovable God. Wells continued to write books with terminal endings until the sunset of his life. In his last book, *Mind at the End of Its Tether* (1945), he does abandon one of his earlier themes, namely a post-holocaust utopia.[13]

In eschatological fiction before 1914, natural forces were the usual means of destroying humankind. However, around 1900 a shift could be detected. Nature continued to perform its evil deeds, but more often humanity became the chief cause of world-ending catastrophes. Of these human made disasters, most were brought on by world wars fought with doomsday weapons.[14] Wells' *Shape of Things to Come* (1933) envisioned a new order after a global war that wrecked civilization. Wells had previously

---

11. Burton R. Pollin, *Discoveries in Poe* (Notre Dame, IN: University of Notre Dame Press, 1970) ch. 5; Wagar, *Terminal Visions*, 17 (quote); Lewis, "Science, Progress, and the End of the Modern World," 316.

12. Wagar, *Terminal Visions*, 19–20.

13. Wagar, *Terminal Visions*, 20; Rubinsky and Wiseman, *End of the World*, 140–41. See also W. Warren Wagar, ed., *H. G. Wells: Journalism and Prophecy*, 1893–1946 (Boston: Houghton Mifflin, 1964) 441–42; H. G. Wells, *The War of the World* (New York: Harper, 1898); H. G. Wells, *The Time Machine* (New York: New American Library, 1984); H. G. Wells, *All Aboard for Ararat* (New York: Alliance, 1941).

14. Wagar, *Terminal Visions*, 24; Friedlander, "Themes of Decline," 80.

Imagining the Apocalypse

said similar things in *The War in the Air* (1908). In Edward Shank's *People of the Ruins* (1920), the cause of humanity's downfall is a series of socialist revolutions. Shaw Desmond's *Ragnarok* (1926) and Stephen Southwold's *Gas War of 1940* (1931) focus on the horrors of modern weaponry. In *Public Faces* (1933) Harold Nicolson predicted the destruction of New York by a single atomic bomb delivered by a rocket from Europe. At the last minute, however, disaster is averted by heroic diplomatic efforts. In J. B. Priestley's Doomsday (1938), a mad scientist nearly blows up the world.[15]

The post–World War II era has brought a deluge of speculative fiction—too much for this study to note. And much of it has dealt with apocalyptic subjects. As during the time from 1920 to 1945, human-made disasters predominate over the natural variety by perhaps two to one. As before, many human endings come from people fighting with the latest weapons. But many catastrophes occur by accident, rather than by intention—especially ecological disasters or technology run amok. Another difference is that many of the eschatological writings contain psychological themes.[16]

A few examples will suffice. In John Wyndham's *The Day of the Tiffids* (1951), humans are attacked by mobile killer plants and by a freak meteor. In the mid 1960s, J. G. Ballard published four books that spoke of humanity being assaulted by the four classical elements—air, water, fire, and earth. The novels are *The Wind from Nowhere*, *The Drowned World*, *The Drought*, and *The Crystal World*. In the 1960s and 1970s, Edgar Pangborn's novels—*Davy*, *The Judgment of Eve*, and *The Company of Glory*—portrayed a post-nuclear America.[17] A number of other novels addressing similar subjects have been made into movies but that subject will be addressed shortly.

Films

The late twentieth and early twenty-first centuries have also witnessed a surge of apocalyptic films, many of which were based on novels. Granted, eschatological fears have rarely been out of fashion in America. Still, the events and circumstances of the modern era have worked overtime to

15. Wagar, *Terminal Visions*, 24–25; H. G. Wells, *The Shape of Things to Come* (New York: Macmillan, 1933); Edward Shanks, *The People of the Ruins* (New York: Stokes, 1920); Shaw Desmond, *Ragnarok* (London: Duckworth, 1926); Stephen Southwold, *The Gas War of 1940* (London: Partridge, 1931); J. B. Priestley, *The Doomsday Men* (New York: Harper, 1938).

16. Wagar, *Terminal Visions*, 24–25.

17. Ibid.; Rubinsky and Wiseman, *End of the World*, 142.

stimulate end-time imaginations. Annihilation by war became the subject of many films, especially in the 1950s and 1960s. Nikita Khrushchev's threat to bury the United States precipitated a flurry of movies. Several wars broke out in the Middle East, all of which called up the image of Armageddon. The civil rights movement, the burning of cities, the birth of the drug culture, assassinations of several political leaders, the Vietnam War, and Watergate made people feel insure and paranoid. Then came terrorism and a severe economic crisis. If this were not enough, technological fears arose. People imagined that their technological creations might turn on them. And on top of this, humankind is creating an environmental apocalypse: poisoning our water, polluting our air, and defoliating our land. Last but not least, according to some interpretations of the Mayan calendar, the world will end on December 21, 2012.[18]

Numerous films conveyed these fears and anxieties and millions of people flocked to see them. *On the Beach* (1959) shows us an Australia where people wait for a nuclear war's radiation to reach them. It shows the anxieties of the time as the United States and the Soviet Union competed for nuclear supremacy. *On the Beach* differs from Christian accounts in two senses: God is not involved in the disaster and there are no survivors. In *The Day the Earth Caught Fire* (1962), accidental nuclear detonations by the United States and the Soviet Union knock the Earth into a lower orbit around the sun. *Dr. Strangelove* (1963) satirically portrays the absurd way in which the final war begins. A demented scientific genius holds out hope for humanity by starting a new post-nuclear Earth, but in the end there are no survivors.[19]

Both *The Planet of the Apes* (1967) and *Beneath the Planet of the Apes* (1969) carry this theme further. In the former movie, a nuclear war has wiped out civilization on a future Earth, reducing humans to a primitive existence while apes rule. The latter film extends the total destruction of Earth by a superbomb, assembled by mutant scientists. These films are almost devoid of hope for survival. Occasionally, human remnants survive

---

18. John Wiley Nelson, "The Apocalyptic Vision in American Popular Culture," in *The Apocalyptic Vision in America* (Bowling Green, OH: Bowling Green University Popular Press, 1982) 173–74; Harvey Elliot, "Apocalypse Eventually," *Video*, 3 June 1986, 77–79, 150–51; Ramin Setoodeh, "Apocalypse Now," *Newsweek*, 7 December 2009, 70; James Poniewozik, "Postapocalypse Now," *Time*, 23 October 2006, 94.

19. Jonathan Kirsch, *A History of the End of the World* (San Francisco: HarperSanFrancisco, 2006) 211–12.

as in *A Canticle for Liebowitz* (1960). Here as the final catastrophe occurs, a few people escape to other planets on a spaceship.[20]

Several other films follow the theme of nuclear destruction but take a different approach, largely focusing on mistakes. In some, atomic radiation from a nuclear mishap enlarges animals and insects to monster proportions and they terrorize humanity. In *Them* (1954) humans encounter gigantic ants, mutated by atomic radiation to the size of automobiles. *Night of the Lepus* (1976) describes how people in a small Arizona town battle thousands of mutated, carnivorous killer rabbits. In *The Food of the Gods* (1977) wasps, worms, chickens, and rats feed off of an icky, gooey substance that causes them to grow to gigantic proportions and then terrorize people.[21]

A number of films describe life in a post-apocalyptic world and several of them do not note the cause of the catastrophe. The three *Mad Max* movies (1979, 1981, 1985) portray a post-apocalyptic world in which individuals must defend themselves against marauders. In *Waterworld* (1995), after the doomsday event of flooding, caused by melting icecaps, the remnants of the human race who survived now live in large floating constructs made of debris. The television series *Jereicho* describes life in a Kansas town after a nuclear strike cripples America.[22]

More recent post-apocalyptic films are *The Road* (2009) and *The Book of Eli* (2010). In *The Road* a father and his young son struggle to survive a number of years after an unspecified, devastating cataclysm has destroyed civilization—including all plant and animal life—and reduced the remnants to cannibalism. The father and son travel south, hoping to find warmer weather while scavenging for food and avoiding bands of cannibals. In the end the father dies but the boy joins another family. *The Book of Eli* describes life thirty-one years after an apocalyptic event. Eli travels toward the west coast of America with two rare commodities—the ability to read and a Bible. He must do many things to survive but eventually

---

20. Nelson, "Apocalyptic Vision in American Popular Culture, 173–74; Elliot, "Apocalypse Eventually," 77–79, 150–51; Rick Marin, "Alien Invasion! *Newsweek*, 8 July 1996, 48–53; Russell Chandler, *Doomsday* (Ann Arbor, MI: Servant, 1993) 276–77; Kirsch, *History of the End of the World*, 213.

21. Nelson, "Apocalyptic Vision in American Culture," 173; Kirsch, *History of the End of the World*, 213.

22. Amy Lennard Goehner and Rebecca Winters Keegan, "Apocalypse New," *Time*, 28 January 2008, 112–13.

reaches a community on the West coast that reproduces the Bible, much like the monks did during the Middle Ages.[23]

A number of apocalyptic films fit into diverse categories. *Independence Day* (1996) is about a hostile alien invasion of Earth, focusing on a disparate group of individuals and families as they converge in the Nevada desert. They meet with the remaining human survivors and plan a last chance retaliation against the invaders on July 4. *Asteroid* is a 1997 NBC TV movie about the United States government trying to stop an asteroid colliding with the Earth. In *Invasion of the Body Snatchers* (1978), people are being replaced by replicas grown from plant-like pods. The pod people then work together with the objective of eliminating the entire human race.

Outbreak (1995) is a disaster movie focusing on the spread of a fictional Ebola virus strain called Motaba, which threatens the existence of humanity. In *I Am Legend* (2007), a virus is also the culprit. It kills most humans and turns others into vampire-like monsters. *The Omen* (1976 and 2006) tells the story of the birth and childhood of Damien, the long-prophesied Antichrist. With interpretations of the Mayan calendar telling the world of dire consequences, there had to be a movie regarding these events. The film *2012* (2009) describes a world of upheavals in which nearly everything comes crashing down. But a number of special ships serve like modern Noah's arks and save a remnant. Apocalyptic themes can be found in many other films also. A partial list would include *Lord of the Flies*, *Star Wars*, *The Poseidon Adventure*, *Battlestar Galactica*, *Earthquake*, *The Towering Inferno*, *The Terminator*, *Judgment Day*, *Rise of the Machines*, *Terminator Salvation*, *Escape from New York*, *Cloverfield*, and *The World Without Us*.

EVANGELICAL PROPHECY FICTION

In evangelical thinking, reading fiction has undergone a serious change—from being regarded as worldly to becoming a vehicle of popular entertainment. Evangelicals have published many serious and scholarly books and have demonstrated considerable intellectual vitality. But the skyrocketing evangelical book market rests more on popular publications—both fiction and non-fiction—and prophecy fiction is a major component in this surge. In fact, of all the subjects launching the soaring evangelical

---

23. Poniewozik, "Postapocalypse Now," 94; Setoodeh, "Apocalypse Now," 70; Moring, "It's the End of the World," 44–45.

book market, prophecy books rank first, including fictional accounts of the last times.²⁴

Actually, fiction has replaced non-fiction as the primary vehicle for promoting end-time teachings. Why is this so? Prophecy fiction can make predictions without being wrong as have Hal Lindsey's "suggestions." Prophecy writers have much more latitude because after all, they are writing fiction and do not have many constraints. Second, prophecy novels are entertaining. When Lindsey wrote *The Late Great Planet Earth* in a popular style, he blurred the line between "prophetic entertainment and biblical interpretation." In doing so, he "defined the mood of the 1970s and 1980s" for much of North American fundamentalism. Popular dispensationalism, as its critics would say, became "dispen-sensationalism" and its writers have increasingly turned to entertaining fiction to convey their ideas.²⁵

Evangelicals struggle with many of the issues that concern the general public in modern America—wars, terrorism, economic crises, environmental disasters, rapid changes on almost every level, and a general fear of the future. But they have an additional agenda. They view the world through a different lens. Evangelicals have at least a vague understanding concerning the end-time prophecies found in Ezekiel, Daniel, and Revelation. On a popular level, many accept the dispensational script for the last days and they view current events in the light of this interpretation. Dispensational eschatology, of course, in a popular way is the theology that is propagated in prophecy fiction.

Two other issues are lurking beneath the surface—modernity and populism. At face value prophecy novels concern the future but in reality they are "very much about the present." Evangelicals, especially the fundamentalist variety, have struggled with modernity and the values it represents. Many evangelicals have found it difficult to cope with the social, technological, and culture changes that have emerged in the post–World War II era. "The explosive growth of new technologies, a global economy, and an increasingly free-flow of information" have "erased borders" and threatened the fundamentalist subculture. Such developments are seen as marks of the rising "Beast system."²⁶

24. Richard Kyle, *Evangelicaslism: An Americanized Christianity* (New Brunswick, NJ: Transaction, 2006) 275–76; Steve Rabey, "No Longer Left Behind," *Christianity Today*, 22 April 2002, 26–31.

25. Crawford Gribben, *Writing the Rapture: Prophecy Fiction in Evangelical America* (New York: Oxford University, 2009) 8–9.

26. Glenn W. Shuck, *Marks of the Beast: The Left Behind Novels and the Struggle for*

On one hand, evangelicals desire to erect boundaries between themselves and the modern world, that is, this "Beast system." One the other, they enjoy the good life and the material benefits of modern progress. Thus fundamentalists struggle with a dilemma. They desire to remain a separate subculture but separatism is no longer tenable in the modern world. Prophecy fiction thus has an escapist orientation. While its believers cannot physically leave the world, they can leave it psychologically. Prophecy novels help its readers to maintain a tension between themselves and the mainstream while still enjoying the material fruits of the world. They can read about conflicts in the Middle East and what they regard as the sins of liberal America and know that they will be raptured out of the world. For the most part, the prophecy novels demonstrate conservative political and social values and most of its readers connect with this agenda, thus giving them some comfort.[27]

In fact, this tension dispensational fundamentalism has had with the world is changing because of the tremendous success experienced by the prophecy novels. Many millions have been sold. On one hand, prophecy fiction has been deeply influenced by American culture. Indeed, apocalypticism is as American as McDonald's. On the other, these novels have had an impact on American culture. Many non-evangelicals have read them and to some extent have connected with their views. Thus, prophetic fiction has helped dispensational fundamentalism make a transition through three stages. It has moved dispensational fundamentalism from a subculture to being countercultural to having an influence on the mainstream culture.[28]

Second, evangelicals—especially the writers and readers of prophetic fiction—are deeply and profoundly populist. Despite having many respected scholars, on the whole, the thinking and behavior of the evangelical community is driven by uneducated popularizers. Millions of evangelicals accept as gospel truth the ideas found in the books and messages of the evangelical gurus. Their books sell by the millions and they are regarded as the last word on many subjects. They claim to have some new insight into Scripture. The voices of evangelical scholars have indeed been largely drowned out by a deluge of popular opinions.[29]

Evangelical Identity (New York: New York University Press, 2005) 1–2.

27. Shuck, *Marks of the Beast*, 1–3; Gribben, *Writing the Rapture*, 1, 4, 10. Amy Johnson Frykholm, *Rapture Culture* (New York: Oxford University Press, 2004).

28. Gribben, *Writing the Rapture*, 24–25; Hendershot, *Shaking the World for Jesus*, 190–93.

29. Kyle, *Evangelicalism*, 317–18.

Imagining the Apocalypse

What has been said about the evangelical populist impulse in general is even more applicable to prophecy fiction. On the whole, trained theologians and ministers have not engaged in prophecy writing, especially fiction. This has been the domain of amateurs, staunch in their faith, often uneducated or at best trained in scientific methods but not in theology or history. Some claim God has given them a special insight into end- time matters. Others come from decentralized denominations or independent churches where there is little control or ministerial credentialing. As Paul Boyer notes, prophecy writing usually evidenced the following characteristics: simple writing, "often in large type with short paragraphs" and with an emphasis on "the universal accessibility of prophetic truth."[30]

Earlier Novels

While it has captivated a wide audience, by no means did the *Left Behind* series invent prophetic fiction. It has had many precursors. Still, the *Left Behind* books embody the traits found in the wider genre of prophetic fiction—a rejection of modern values, an assault on liberal America, escapism, political conservatism, and deeply populist. Like the *Left Behind* series, the earlier novels speak about the future but they really tell the reader much about the present and the worldview of many fundamentalists. While prophecy fiction is responding to present conditions, it is adaptable. As with apocalyptic literature in general, it has a chameleon-like character. Originally, prophecy fiction was born in the context of early-twentieth-century dispensational fundamentalism. But since then such novels have reflected the changes encountered by the movement giving it birth.[31]

Moreover, prophecy fiction is not always orthodox in the dispensational-fundamentalist meaning of the word. Fiction writers have many liberties that the authors of non-fiction do not have. As a result, the novels do not always toe the dispensational line. Dispensational premillennialism says the rapture will take place prior to the tribulation. But some fictional accounts have it occurring in the middle or end of the tribulation. Other novels have people being left behind and they become the main

30. Paul Boyer, *When Time Shall Be No More: Prophecy Belief in Modern American Culture* (Cambridge, MA: Harvard University, 1992) 305–7.

31. Melani McAlister, "Prophecy, Politics and the Popular: *Left Behind* Series and Christian Fundamentalism's New World Order," *South Atlantic Quarterly* 102/4 (2003) 782; Gribben, *Writing the Rapture*, 3–4; Amy Johnson Frykholm, "What Social and Political Messages Appear in the Left Behind Books?," In *Rapture, Revelation, and the End Times*, 167–69.

characters of the book. Still, some fictional accounts completely reject the dispensational scenario regarding the last days. Others prophecy fictions have been written by Catholics and non-fundamentalists. Most important, market forces have impacted prophecy novels. Book sales reflect cultural trends and often dictate the contents of a book. Thus, while prophecy fiction grew out of dispensationalism, in the late twentieth and early twenty-first centuries it is "increasingly attempting to reshape it."[32]

The earliest prophecy novels in America appeared at the beginning of the twentieth century. They developed in the context of immigration struggles and the developing confrontation between conservative and liberal Christianity. One of the first prophecy novels was *Titan, Son of Saturn: The Coming World Emperor: A Story of the Other Christ* (1905) written by Joseph Birbeck Burroughs. *Titan* concerns the rise of a great king who becomes the Antichrist and persecutes Christians. There is also a struggle involving race and faith for world domination. Another early prophecy novel is Milton H. Stine's *The Devil's Bride: A Present Day Arrangement of Formalism and Doubt in the Church and in Society, in the Light of Holy Scriptures: Given in the Form of a Pleasing Story* (1910). In *The Devil's Bride*, Stine has moved from postmillennialism to a dispensational premillennial position. He now questions the future glory of a Christian America because of immigration, criticizes theological liberalism, and warns of the coming apostasy as the end times approach.[33]

In the years from 1905 to World War II, prophecy fiction continued to be written, and like all forms of this literary genre these novels reflected contemporary issues. From a religious perspective, the fundamentalist-modernist fight held center stage. Liberalism, in the mind of many fundamentalists, acquired an eschatological dimension, being linked with the rise of the one world religion and the Antichrist. Conspiracies, especially by the communists, found their way into prophecy fiction. Also evident was the perceived threat presented by immigration and its challenge to Anglo-Saxon cultural superiority. Moreover, dispensational premillennialism had clearly supplanted postmillennialism in evangelical ranks and this shift could be found in the novels of the period.[34]

Lord of the World (1907) by Robert Hugh Benson spoke of liberalism as paving the way for the rise of the Antichrist and demonstrated fears

---

32. Gribben, *Writing the Rapture*, 19–21 (quote); Shuck, *Marks of the Beast*, 1–3.

33. Gribben, *Writing the Rapture*, 27–45.

34. See George M. Marsden, *Fundamentalism and American Culture* (New York: Oxford University Press, 1980) 3–7; Kyle, *Evangelicalism*, 100–113.

Imagining the Apocalypse

regarding international conspiracies, e.g. Freemasonry and communism. *The Judgment Day: A Story of the Seven Years of the Great Tribulation* (1910) by Joshua Hill Foster was the first novel in English to clearly articulate the dispensational eschatological scheme of events and in doing so established the prophecy fiction genre. Sydney Watson wrote a trilogy—*Scarlet and Purple* (1913), *The Mark of the Beast* (1915), and *In the Twinkling of an Eye* (1916)—which promoted the standard dispensational paradigms and were widely distributed in America. All of these early novels were written as the dominance of the old white Anglo-Saxon world was coming to an end and revealed the anxieties of this cultural group.[35]

Tensions mounted as the world moved toward World War II and some of these issues emerged in the prophecy novels. Because of the Scopes Trial, fundamentalists retreated into their subculture and were thus becoming marginalized. The anti-Semitism and anti-Catholicism of these years became apparent. Communism became something to be feared and it was associated with the Jews and liberalism. And of course, the economic difficulties of the Great Depression could not escape notice.

Forrest Loman Oilar published *Be Thou Prepared for Jesus Is Coming* (1937). This novel displayed great hostilities toward modernism, market capitalism, and Catholicism. And most unusual, it demonstrated a concern for animals and pets after the rapture. *They That Remain: A Story of the End Times* (1941) by Dayton A. Manker is the first novel to demonstrate a concern for non-religious America. What would happen to those left behind—a subject that gets much attention in later novels? Would there be widespread accidents because of the rapture? Manker also evidences great fear of communism, which has been orchestrated by the Jews. Both of these authors preferred small government and can be seen as preparing the prophecy fiction genre for many of the geopolitical concerns of the modern world.[36]

Mid- and Late-Century Novels

The Cold War years prompted some new twists to prophecy fiction. The world had entered the atomic age and now the fear that the entire world could be destroyed became realistic. Indeed, doomsday had a new meaning. Communism continued to arouse considerable eschatological concern. Of great importance were the events of the Middle East, especially

35. Gribben, *Writing the Rapture*, 54–62.
36. Ibid., 69–85.

the birth of the Israeli state and the 1967 War. Then came the arrival of "pop dispensationalism" in the form of *The Late Great Planet Earth*. While not intended to be fiction, this and other such books stimulated an interest in prophecy and thus a market for prophetic fiction. In addition, America experienced many changes in the 1960s and beyond—feminism, a sexual revolution, recreational drugs, a Catholic president, student riots, and the Vietnam War. These changes and the concerns they aroused, especially the moral decline of America, found their way into prophecy novels.[37]

Raptured (1950) by Ernest W. Angley attacked liberalism and encouraged pious political apathy and social withdrawal. In doing so it mirrored the separatist, fundamentalist ethos of the mid twentieth century. It also spoke of the chaos resulting from the rapture, namely, trains crashing, auto accidents, and missing people. John Myer's *The Trumpet Sounds* (1965) laments the ungodly America of the 1960s and longs for a return to the 1940s. Like other fundamentalists he attacks liberalism, materialism, ecumenism, and communism. But he was a mid-tribulationist, insisting that the church would not go unscathed in the tribulation. Most of Frederick Albert Tatford's writings were exegetical but he wrote one prophecy novel, *The Clock Strikes* (1971). This novel and some of his other writings connected eschatology with the political developments of the Cold War years, e.g., the Common Market and United Nations.[38]

The best-selling prophecy novel prior to the mid 1970s was 666 (1970) by Salem Kirban. He followed this with a sequel, 1000 (1973). Kirban downplayed the significance of the return of Israel because he was an Arab. But he condemned a number of trends in contemporary America—elitist thinking, worldly engagement, and watering down of the gospel. The remarkable sales of 666 served notice that prophecy fiction had become a major instrument to promote pop dispensationalism.[39]

Gary Cohen, a converted Jew and a professor, wrote a number of non-fiction prophecy books. He followed these with *Civilizations Last Hurrah: A Futuristic Novel about the End* (1974). This was republished as *The Horseman Are Coming* (1979). This novel emphasized the imminent rapture of the church and represented classic dispensationalism. It also portrayed Americans as stanch backers of Israel. Cohen directed his

---

37. Shuck, *Marks of the Beast*, 4–5; Gribben, *Writing the Rapture*, 89–90.

38. Gribben, *Writing the Apocalypse*, 91–104.

39. See Salem Kirban, 666 (Wheaton, IL: Tyndale, 1973) 88–103; Salem Kirban, 1000 (Chattanooga, TN: Future Events, 1973); Robert Price, "The Paperback Apocalypse," *Wittenburg Door* 63 (October–November 1981) 3–8; Philip Melling, *Fundamenalism in America* (Edinburgh: University of Edinburgh Press, 1999) 95.

Imagining the Apocalypse

novel toward Cold War geopolitical issues—a fear of communism, a weak United Nations, great hostility toward modernism, and the rising power of the European confederation.[40]

The 1970s also witnessed a flurry of end-time films. Especially influential were those produced by Donald W. Thompson. Operating on a low budget and with second-rate acting, he created an apocalyptic phenomenon. The four part series included *A Thief in the Night, A Distant Thunder, Image of the Beast,* and *The Prodigal Planet.* These four films dramatized to evangelical audiences the familiar themes of dispensational eschatology. They raised awareness of individuals regarding end-times issues and encouraged them to accept the gospel. They differed from later films and novels, however, in that they did not encourage any resistance to the Antichrist's forces.[41]

The 1970s and 1980s vibrated with eschatological excitement, thanks to Hal Lindsey's "suggestions" in *The Late Great Planet Earth* and Edgar Whisenant's outright predictions in 88 *Reasons Why the Rapture Will Be in 1988.* But with the failure of these "suggestions" and the collapse of communism, one can detect a change in the direction of the prophecy novels. These decades prompted alterations that continued into the 1990s. Domestic issues now came to the forefront. One can notice a modification in the attitude of evangelicals toward Catholicism, in part because Catholics often agreed with evangelicals regarding social issues. Also, evangelicals had moved out of their cultural ghetto and were now politically engaged. New enemies were now needed and they could be found in the New Age movement, satanic cults, the New World Order, and the spiritual decline of America. Such subjects acquired an eschatological dimension in prophecy novels.[42]

The two novels garnering the most attention during this time frame were produced by Frank Peretti and Pat Robertson. Peretti wrote *This Present Darkness* (1986) and its sequel, *Piercing the Darkness* (1989). *This Present Darkness* was a fantasy novel focusing on the conflict between angels and demons in small-town America. This book ranked in the top-ten-selling Christian novels in the late 1980s and early 1990s and earned Peretti the title "the Stephen King of evangelical culture." Spurred on by Constance E. Cumbey's *The Hidden Dangers of the Rainbow: The*

40. Gribben, *Writing the Rapture*, 101–2; Price, "The Paperback Apocalypse," 3–8.
41. Shuck, *Marks of the Beast*, 6–7.
42. See Richard Kyle, *The Last Days Are Here Again* (Grand Rapids: Baker, 1998) 115–37; Richard Kyle, *The New Age Movement in American Culture* (Lanham, MD: University Press of America, 1995) 65–74; Kyle, *Evangelicalism*, 167–209.

New Age Movement and Our Coming Age of Barbarism (1985), spiritual warfare became the subject for a number of best-selling fiction and nonfiction books.⁴³

While Peretti's books barely note the dispensational rapture of believers, they had an eschatological dimension and had a major "impact on the apocalyptic imagination of evangelicals," states Crawford Gribben. They also had a political dimension. In *Piercing the Darkness*, New Age adherents were attempting to take over a small college and believers were encouraged to resist them. Peretti presents New Age religion as the final threat and the beginning of the one-world religion. This book provides an argument against "prophetic pessimism" and "political passivity" and encourages believers to confront evil rather than wait for the rapture. It also provides a distinctive supernaturalism, which many future prophecy novels tended to imitate.⁴⁴

In prophecy fiction, Pat Robertson expanded the theme of political involvement. This development came naturally because he ran for president in 1988 and two of his earlier non-fiction books—*The New Millennium* (1990) and *The New World Order* (1991)—pointed in that direction. In *The End of the Age* (1995), Robertson's only fiction work, he is torn between his premillennialism and his desire to bring reforms found in postmillennialism. During the tribulation, the saints do not meekly submit to ungodly rule but organize themselves into resistance groups. Such a theme resonated with the goals of the Religious Right, which encouraged cultural engagement as a means to reform America.⁴⁵

While Robertson's book clearly has prophetic elements, it abandons the typical dispensational model and nowhere does he speak of the rapture as an imminent event. But he does make predictions, "suggesting" that the end of the Gentile age would be fulfilled "around 2007," forty years after the 1967 War. This date would also signify the demise of America.⁴⁶

---

43. Gribben, *Writing the Rapture*, 108–17 (quote); Constance E. Cumbey, *The Hidden Dangers of the Rainbow: The New Age Movement and Our Coming Age of Barbarism* (Lafayette, LA: Huntington House, 1985); Steve Rabey, "No Longer Left Behind," *Christianity Today*, 22 April 2002, 26.

44. Frank Peretti, *This Present Darkness* (Eastbourne, UK: Minstrel, 1986) 34–382; Frank Peretti, *Piercing the Darkness* (Eastbourne, UK: Minstrel, 1989); Gribben, *Writing the Rapture*, 113–18; Kyle, *Evangelicalism*, 277; W. Scott Poole, *Satan in America: The Devil We Know* (Lanham, MD: Rowman and Littlefield, 2009) 185.

45. See Pat Robertson, *The New Millennium* (Dallas: Word, 1990); Pat Robertson, *The New World Order* (Dallas: Word, 1991); Gribben, *Writing the Rapture*, 120–25.

46. Pat Robertson, *The End of the Age* (Nashville: Word, 1995); Gribben, *Writing the Rapture*, 126–27.

Imagining the Apocalypse

The End of the Age also revised the apocalyptic status of Roman Catholicism, a development continued by other prophecy novels. It depicted John Paul II as a true believer and focused on the beastly nature of the state, not the church. In fact, false religion at the end of the age was Asian, not European. Robertson was also writing about his own importance and one can identify aspects of his career in the novel.[47]

The Left Behind Series

Leading this surge in evangelical prophecy books—whether fiction or non-fiction—is the *Left Behind* series, coauthored by Tim LaHaye and Jerry Jenkins. The first novel, *Left Behind: A Novel of the Earth's Last Days*, appeared in 1995 and the series continued at a pace of a little more than one sequel per year. Volume 12, *The Glorious Appearing*, came out in 2004. This was the final volume but by 2007 a prequel and sequel were published. By this time sales had skyrocketed to over sixty-five million in thirty different languages. In of terms sales, Tim LaHaye and Jerry Jenkins had indeed become some of the most successful authors in the history of American literature and prophecy novels were quite popular. In fact, during this time period the entire market for Christian fiction quadrupled.[48]

The *Left Behind* series aroused so much interest that it produced numerous spinoffs and related end-time projects—other novels, films, children's books, novels in comic book style, apocalyptic CDs, a television series, board games, and video games. *Left Behind: The Kids* consists of forty additional volumes for young people between ten and fourteen, who might be too immature for the regular series but could benefit from the author's perspective of the end times.[49]

In 2001 a film version of *Left Behind* came out but had little box office appeal. Thus LaHaye unsuccessfully sued the filmmaker, believing it was their fault because they had broken "their promise to provide a lavish production budget." In fact, *Left Behind* could not match the success

---

47. Gribben, *Writing the Rapture*, 124–27.

48. Kyle, *Evangelicalism*, 277; Gribben, *Writing the Rapture*, 130–31; Barbara R. Rossing, *The Rapture Exposed* (New York: Basic, 2004) 40; David Gates, "The Pop Prophets," *Newsweek*, 24 May 2004, 45–50; D. G. Hart, *That Old-Time Religion in Modern America* (Chicago: Ivan Dee, 2002) 187–88.

49. Kirsch, *A History of the End of the World*, 244; Shuck, *Marks of the Beast*, 11; Gribben, *Writing the Rapture*, 130; Karen Springen, "Unhappily Ever After," *Newsweek*, 21 July 2008, 58; John Cloud, "How an Evangelist and Conservative Activist Turned Prophecy into a Fiction Juggernaut," *Time*, 1 July 2002, 50–53.

of *The Omega Code* (1999), a low-budget end-times thriller produced by the Trinity Broadcasting Network (TBN). The video game, *Left Behind: Eternal Forces*, created a storm of protest on both sides of the Atlantic. The game's commentators suggested that rewards could come for killing Jews, Muslims, and other enemies of the Christian faith. While the original *Left Behind* series encouraged spiritual resistance, here such activity became violent when the remaining believers were faced with the choice of joining or combating the Antichrist. Critics said it fosters intolerance. On the other hand, Focus on the Family gave it a good review.[50]

Evangelical prophecy novels often begin with some earth-shaking event. The *Left Behind* series commences with the rapture occurring while the main characters are on a transatlantic flight. The "true" Christians are taken away and the remaining passengers awake to find many empty seats, clothing, glasses, jewelry, and more. The captain, Rayford Steele, his chief flight assistant, Hattie Durham, and a journalist, Cameron "Buck" Williams, attempt to calm the fears of the remaining passengers. The plane is rerouted to Chicago, Captain Steele's hometown. Here he finds out that his family—except for his rebellious daughter Chloe—has also disappeared. To his shock, Steele finds out that his lukewarm associate pastor, Bruce Barnes, is still there. But these people have a second chance. They accept Christ as their personal savior and form the nucleus of the Tribulation Force.

The loss of so many people leads to widespread panic, thus enabling the rise of a charismatic leader with plans for rebuilding damaged cities and chaos-ridden nations. He is Nicolae Jetty Carpathia, president of Romania, who becomes the Secretary General of the United Nations. Possessing great charm, he is proficient in many languages and is a person of incredible powers, including the ability to control the minds of non-Christians. He has the right answers and comfort for all the disappearances and offers hope for rebuilding the world from its current crisis. As he rises to power, members of the Tribulation Force find themselves working for him. But they soon discover that he is the Antichrist and are determined to resist him even if it means their death.

In order to facilitate global recovery, people eagerly grant Carpathia wide-sweeping emergency powers. After gaining control of the global media, he proceeds to amalgamate political boundaries and unify the world's

50. Michael R. Smith, "Author LaHaye Sues *Left Behind* Film Producers," *Christianity Today*, 23 April 2001, 20 (quote); Shuck, *Marks of the Beast*, 12; David, Crary, "In Video Game, Christians Slay the Infidels," *Wichita Eagle*, 13 December 2006, 9A; Poole, *Satan in America*, 190–92; Hendershot, *Shaking the World for Jesus*, 176–80.

Imagining the Apocalypse

currencies and religions. In these endeavors, he is aided by his trustworthy assistants—the false prophet, Leon Fortunato, and the mysterious Viv Ivins. Carpathia makes a seven-year treaty with Israel and offers the world unprecedented peace and prosperity in the face of global crises.

The remaining novels portray both his expanding power and the deterioration of his image. These books also chronicle the Tribulation Force's resistance to his plans. They know they cannot defeat him but they hope to convince people that he is an evil deceiver. In opposing the Antichrist, they employ the latest technology to monitor the moves of Carpathia and communicate with believers worldwide. They never lack technical expertise, pilots, medical staff, economists, and spiritual authorities.

The Tribulation Force is also joined by Rabbi Tsion Ben-Judah, a converted Jew and evangelist, who replaces Bruce Barnes as the leader of the group. Rabbi Ben-Judah has the difficult task of opposing the forces of the new worldwide religion, Enigma Babylon One World Faith. The leader of this one-world religion is Pope Pontifex Maximus Peter Matthews, who believes the Book of Revelation is to be interpreted symbolically. But the Tribulation Force toughs it out and struggles with the forces of the Antichrist. Volume 12, *The Glorious Appearing*, which brings the series to a culmination, includes the return of Christ, the battle of Armageddon, and the final judgment.[51]

Who are the people reading these books? Seventy percent have been sold in the Red States, the Republican areas of the Midwest and the South, and the average readers are born-again Christian women in their forties. But two things have modified this information. The evangelical subculture is expanding, both in respect to its numbers and its cultural influence. Evangelicalism has been heavily impacted by the cultural mainstream and in turn it has influenced the wider culture. Apocalyptic and end-time ideas are no longer the domain of evangelicals and evangelicalism is no longer a marginalized subculture.[52]

Second, the readership of the *Left Behind* series has expanded well beyond the evangelical subculture. The books have been sold at Wal-Mart,

---

51. This brief summary regarding the plot of the *Left Behind* series has been drawn from several sources. See Shuck, *Marks of the Beast*, 12–15; Robert G. Clouse, "Fundamentalist Theology," in *Oxford Handbook of Eschatology*, ed. Jerry Walls (New York: Oxford University Press, 2007) 274.

52. Kyle, *The Last Days Are Here Again*, 136; Kyle, *Evangelicalism*, 277–78; Gates, "The Pop Prophets," 47–48. See also Johnson Frykholm, *Rapture Culture in America*; Timothy P. Weber, *On the Road to Armageddon: How Evangelicals Became Israel's Best Friend* (Grand Rapids: Baker, 2004).

Target, and Barnes & Noble. For example, the publisher, Tyndale House, reports that 11 percent of the *Left Behind* readers are Roman Catholic. The Catholic readership has been enough to prompt two Catholic authors to write books refuting the *Left Behind* teachings but it was not until 2003 that Catholic bishops wrote a critical statement regarding the LaHaye-Jenkins books. Moreover, a Barna Research survey indicated that about 10 percent of the readers were atheists, agnostics, or had no religious affiliation. Also, about two million claimed to be Christians but had not accepted Jesus Christ as their savior.[53]

Why are so many people buying these books? Earlier in this chapter, a number of cultural reasons have been noted regarding the popularity of prophecy fiction in general and they will not be repeated here. On the surface, the *Left Behind* series appears to differ little from other prophecy novels. But there are subtle differences. LaHaye and Jenkins have been able to perceive "the cultural changes around them, sense the anxieties of a significant number of Americans, and build novels around such fears . . ." The authors offer their readers more than fear of the future and even hold out hope for those "left behind."[54]

Another difference is that populism is carried to a new level. Of great importance, LaHaye and Jenkins connect with evangelicalism's populist impulse. Their commonsense reading of Scripture and lay language speak to multitudes of average people. As Jenkins says, "I write to pedestrians. And I am a pedestrian. . . . I do not claim to be C. S. Lewis. . . . I wish I was smart enough to write a book that's hard to read . . ." LaHaye and Jenkins are outsiders and populists—and proud of it. They grew up this way. Both have blue-collar backgrounds and LaHaye has a particular disdain for the educated elite. He graduated from Bob Jones University and Jenkins has no college degree. LaHaye also has strong right-wing political views, which emerge at times.[55]

---

53. Kilde and Forbes, :Rapture, Revelation, and the End Times," in *Rapture, Revelation, and the End-Times*, 1; Forbes, "How Popular Are the Left Behind Books . . . and Why?," in *Rapture, Revelation, and the End Times*, 8–9, 21–22; Carl E. Olson, *Will Catholics Be "Left Behind"?* (San Francisco: Ignatius, 2003); Cathleen Falsani, "Bishops Warn Catholics about "Left Behind" Books," *Chicago Sun-Times*, 6 June 2003, 5.

54. Shuck, *Marks of the Beast*, 10–11.

55. Kyle, *Evangelicalism*, 279–80; Gates, "The Pop Prophets," 47–49 (quote).

Imagining the Apocalypse

After Left Behind

While the *Left Behind* series dominated the evangelical fiction market for over a decade, it was by no means the only evangelical novels to dabble in eschatological subjects. A number of other end-time novels came out in the late twentieth and early twenty-first centuries. As noted earlier, the *Left Behind* series produced many spinoffs, including more prophetic novels. While coming off different plots, some of these novels followed the general cultural themes of the *Left Behind* series. Others, however, differ substantially and even rejected some of the *Left Behind* refrains.[56]

Most important, like *Left Behind*, many of these novels reflected the paradox of dispensational eschatology. In recent years evangelicals have achieved considerable political and cultural power. They are no longer marginalized and in many ways they are at the height of their influence. Yet the pessimism of their dispensational eschatology contradicts this cultural ascendancy and is more reflective of their old separatist past with its dualistic worldview. And this paradox becomes evident in many of the post–*Left Behind* novels. This disconnect is especially obvious because of the immense market success achieved by the *Left Behind* series.[57]

Two new series—Mel Odom's *Apocalypse Dawn* (2003) and Neesa Hart's *End of State* (2003)—are political and military thrillers and follow the *Left Behind* scenario. But by suggesting the possibility of salvation through water baptism, *Apocalypse Dawn* does challenge some of the basic evangelical theological assumptions found in the *Left Behind* books. Robert Van Kampen's *The Fourth Reich* (1997) rejects the pretribulation rapture and describes it as a false hope. Hal Lindsay's *Blood Moon* (1996) reflects the author's growing political concerns. Michael Hyatt and George Grant produced the anti-rapture novel *Y2K: The Day the World Shut Down* (1998). Here they argued that the pop dispensationalism of Hal Lindsey and others like him have retarded evangelical cultural engagement. In fact, they contend for the preterist interpretation of Revelation, meaning that its prophecies were fulfilled in the first century. In the *Last Disciple* (2004) and *The Last Sacrifice* (2006), Hank Hanegraaff and Sigmund Brouwer also adopted the preterist approach.[58]

56. Gribben, *Writing the Rapture*, 145–46.

57. Crawford Gribben, "After *Left Behind*—The Paradox of Evangelical Pessimism," in *Expecting the End: Millennialism in Social and Historical Context*, eds. Kenneth G.C. Newport and Crawford Gribben (Waco, TX: Baylor University Press, 2006) 113–14.

58. Gribben, *Writing the Rapture*, 146–47. See Mel Odom, *Apocalypse Dawn* (Wheaton, IL: Tyndale, 2003); Hal Lindsey, *Blood Moon* (Palos Verdes, CA: Western

Perhaps the most significant revision of the *Left Behind* scenario came from its coauthor Jerry Jenkins. *Soon* (2003) is a futurist thriller that imagines what things would be like if Christ does not return in the near future. Jenkins describes evangelicalism in the context of a series of religious wars spurred on by the September 11 attacks. These conflicts become nuclear wars that bring America to the brink of destruction. A coalition of Muslim nations destroys Washington, DC. A North Korean missile demolishes the Pentagon.[59]

Then because of earthquakes and tidal waves the world experiences unprecedented disasters: tsunamis swamp Honk Kong, Taiwan, Japan, Indonesia, Hawaii, California, and the American Northwest. Millions of lives are lost and these disasters end the religious wars. What is left of America is reorganized into seven regions. The world then experiences an extremely repressive time in which religion is banned and governments now have the technology to enforce such a ban. But by now the nation-state takes a backseat to a United Nations–sanctioned new world order.[60]

Apocalyptic thinking reflects more than what people believe about the future—it portrays their present anxieties. Such a statement is especially true for prophetic fiction, whether it comes in the form of novels or films. In apocalyptic fiction—religious and secular—beliefs and fears flow together. In prophecy fiction, as with most apocalyptic expressions, there is a clash between good and evil and the old Manichaean worldview raises its head. Current apprehensions boil over. Potential catastrophes, whether environmental, nuclear, economic, or social, come to the forefront. Or, perhaps Christians are resisting evil trends in contemporary society. Fiction—more than any other expression of end-time thinking—is grounded in popular culture. Fiction must sell and thus it reflects the demands, aspirations, and fears of the people, especially those in the evangelical subculture.

Front, 1996); Michael Hyatt and George Grant, *Y2K: The Day the World Shut Down* (Nashville: Word, 1998); Robert D. Van Kampen, *The Fourth Reich* (New York: Dell, 2000).

59. Gribben, "After *Left Behind*," 119–20; Gibben, *Writing the Rapture*, 158–62.

60. Gribben, "After *Left Behind*," 119–20; Gibben, *Writing the Rapture*, 158–62; See Jerry Jenkins, *Soon* (Wheaton, IL: Tyndale, 2003).

The Politics of Armageddon

CHAPTER 5 HAS MENTIONED some political issues as they related to eschatology. Included would be the developing European Union, the threat of communism and the Soviet Union, the Cold War, the fear of nuclear annihilation, and the coming one world government. But some political subjects related to end-time ideas still remain. They do not form a neat package but nevertheless they should be addressed. Thus this chapter speaks to three subjects pertaining to politics and apocalyptic thinking: the Christian Right, Christian Reconstructionism, and Christian Zionism. The first two topics connect best with domestic issues while the last impacts American foreign policy.

The Christian Right manifests inconsistencies in its eschatology. What are they and why do they exist? What is the Christian Reconstruction movement and how has it influenced these contradictions? How does the vision of a Christian America relate to these issues? Does America have a role in biblical prophecy? In what ways have end-time views impacted American domestic and foreign policy? What is Christian Zionism? What are its aims and how influential has it been? Why are evangelicals Israel's best friend? What are some problems in this cozy relationship?

ESCHATOLOGY AND THE CHRISTIAN RIGHT

What is the Christian Right? Clyde Wilcox defines the Christian Right as a "social movement that attempts to mobilize evangelical Protestants and other orthodox Christians into political action." Some people prefer the broader term "Religious Right." This term would encompass not only conservative Protestants—who would still be the dominant element—but also conservative Catholics and Mormons. Supporters of the Christian Right praise the movement as an attempt to return America to its founding principles. The opponents of the Christian Right see it as "baptizing" a political ideology in the name of Christianity.[1]

Actually, the new Christian Right should be seen as one of the two traditions emerging from the Revolutionary War era that dealt with religion and politics. The Christian Right represents a tradition going back to the Puritans, which attempts to formulate the moral standards of the nation according to its vision. This conservative perspective tends to sanctify America, legitimizing its form of government, economy, and military activities. A second tradition goes back to at least Roger Williams. It recognized that even then America had deep religious and cultural divisions. So in respect to public life—once some basic standards designed to allow civilization to survive were established—explicit religion should be separate from politics. This tradition also tends to be more critical of the American political, economic, and social systems. Contemporary evangelicals have adopted both positions. Jerry Falwell, Pat Robertson, Tim LaHaye, and the Christian Right represent the first tradition, while Jimmy Carter and the evangelical Left upheld something resembling the second.[2]

---

1. Clyde Wilcox, *Onward Christian Soldiers?: The Religious Right in America Politics* (Boulder, CO: Westview, 1996) 5 (quote); Richard Kyle, *Evangelicalism: An Americanized Christianity* (New Brunswick, NJ: Transaction, 2006) 167; Erling Jorstad, *The Politics of Moralism: The New Christian Right in American Life* (Minneapolis: Augsburg, 1981) 108; Michael Lienesch, "Right-Wing Religion: Christian Conservatism as a Political Movement," *Political Science Quarterly* 97/3 (Fall 1982) 407-9.

2. George M. Marsden, *Understanding Fundamentalism and Evangelicalism* (Grand Rapids: Eerdmans, 1991) 96-97; Kyle, *Evangelicalism*, 167-68; Robert Wuthnow, "Divided We Fall: America's Two Civil Religions," *Christian Century* 20 (April 1988) 398; Robert Wuthnow, *The Restructuring of American Religion* (Princeton, NJ: Princeton University Press, 1988) 191-203; Sidney Blumenthal, "The Righteous Empire," *New Republic*, 22 October 1984, 20; Wesley G. Pippert, "Jimmy Carter: My Personal Faith in God," *Christianity Today*, 4 March 1993, 14-20.

The Politics of Armageddon

Bedrock Theology

The Christian Right and dispensational premillennialism are not one and the same. Still, most adherents of the Christian Right do embrace— whether explicitly or implicitly—the dispensational premillennial view regarding end-time events. The Christian Right, however, is much more than an eschatological movement and has several bedrock beliefs, many of which impact its eschatology but some that do not.

The Christian Right's explicit source of authority is an inerrant Bible interpreted literally. Its meaning is clear so there is no need for an interpretation by the educated elite. Because Scripture is accessible to all, this leads to a populist approach to politics and eschatology. Political philosophies and end-time theologies come from fallen human beings and are thus fallible. The evangelical Christian armed with Scripture, however, has direct access to God's will and his plan for the future. Thus, they need no human authorities for their political, social, and eschatological insights. Not only is the Bible the rule for personal morality and worship, but it is the authority for politics, social organization, and end-time events. An essential factor in apocalyptic thinking in modern America is the literal reading and interpretation of Scripture.[3]

The Christian Right also has some implicit authorities and they are important. The old Manichaean worldview, which pervades the evangelical subculture, encourages them to interpret the Bible and much else in black-and-white terms. Consequently, world events are viewed as part of the conflict between good and evil and one is either on God's side or the devil's. This view obviously discourages compromise, which is essential to political discourse.[4]

Such a Manichaean worldview also fosters an intense apocalyptic view of present and future events. Prevailing theologies such as dispensationalism are accepted by millions of evangelicals as synonymous with the Word of God and not just another approach to Scripture. Growing out of this theology is a sense of an impending end to history, a situation that also impacts one's political and social views. Christianity in the United States has been so Americanized that at times it is difficult to tell

---

3. Gabriel Fackre, *The Religious Right and the Christian Faith* (Grand Rapids: Eerdmans, 1982) 31–33; Kyle, *Evangelicalism*, 177–78; D.G. Hart, *That Old-Time Religion in Modern America: Evangelical Protestantism in the Twentieth Century* (Chicago: Ivan Dee, 2002) 145; Mark Noll, *American Evangelical Christianity: An Introduction* (Oxford: Blackwell, 2001) 190.

4. Kyle, *Evangelicalism*, 177.

God's Word from American culture. The Christian Right believes it has adopted a literal approach to Scripture, but in reality it is interpreting the Bible through a "glass darkly," that is, the prism of American culture. This situation has dramatically influenced the Christian Right's stance on both domestic politics and international events.[5]

The evangelical distinctive centers on the conversion experience and informs one's view of politics, social issues, and eschatology. As D. G. Hart notes, conversion is a "great leveler of privilege and rank because it results in a sanctified person who is capable of intuiting what is just or right in social and international affairs." Thus, evangelicals often find it difficult to understand how a truly converted person can oppose the political and social agenda of the Religious Right or embrace "liberal" views. Moreover, evangelicals wonder how one can be confused regarding God's plan for the end times. And conversion is a prerequisite for one being raptured out of the trials that will come upon the world.[6]

Conversion is also able to produce a sanctified and pietistic person. This personal piety is broadened beyond the self to the wider society. It orientates evangelicals toward public issues that have more moral significance on a pietistic level but frequently blinds them to social problems. For example, evangelicals are often preoccupied with sexual sins while they ignore social evils such as poverty and racism. Conservative Protestants, indeed, believe that if religion is truly spiritual it will shape "the behavior of citizens" and order "the affairs of nations."[7]

The Christian Right embraces a number of other bedrock beliefs that have little bearing on eschatology. So they will be noted only briefly. Creationism is a big issue with the Christian Right. Believing in the literal interpretation of an inerrant Bible, in various degrees they are faithful to the Genesis account. Consequently, most reject evolution and this fuels a major issue for the Christian Right. They also accept literally the Genesis account regarding the fall of humanity and the consequences of this original sin.[8]

---

5. Ibid.

6. Hart, *That Old-Time Religion*, 86, 146 (quotes); Kyle, *Evangelicalism*, 177; Fackre, *The Religious Right*, 81–82.

7. Hart, *That Old-Time Religion*, 81–82; Kyle, *Evangelicalism*, 177; Richard V. Pierard, *The Unequal Yoke: Evangelical Christianity and Political Conservatism* (Philadelphia: Lippincott, 1970) 38–39; Robert Ellwood, *1950: Crossroads of American Life* (Louisville: Westminster, 2000) 191.

8. Fackre, *The Religious Right*, 36–38, 81–82; Kyle, *Evangelicalism*, 177–78; Pierard, *Unequal Yoke*, 38. See Shelton Lawrence and Robert Jewett, *The Myth of the American*

The Politics of Armageddon

While the covenant receives little attention from evangelical pulpits, it has major implications for the Christian Right. What are they? God had a covenant with Israel, which entailed moral injunctions. Would God bless or punish Israel? This depended on Israel's obedience to the covenant. The Puritans transferred the covenant to America. Since then American civil religion has viewed the United States as a "chosen nation" with a unique role to play in God's plan for the world. But America must be faithful to the divine commands. And since the 1960s, it has not been. This will bring God's judgment, such as the nation experienced on September 11. Moreover, it may be the reason why many fail to see a role for America in the end-time events.[9]

The Christian Right has applied this chosen-nation concept to many aspects of American life — prayer in the schools, foreign policy, resistance to moral decadence, and support for military action. Gabriel Fackre writes that "the greatest departure from Christian doctrine" is the Religious Right's transfer of the divine covenant with Israel to America. What we have is a "functional elevation of America to the place of a chosen nation . . ." This breeds intense nationalism and military adventurism in foreign affairs while dampening internal criticism of such policies. America's "covenant status makes loyalty" to the nation an aspect of "loyalty to God."[10]

The end is coming, say many evangelicals. This preoccupation plays an important but paradoxical role in the Christian Right's political and social views. While the Christian Right embraces several eschatological views, most hold to the premillennial, pretribulational doctrine. Such a position says that the world will get worse until Christ returns to rapture out believing Christians. Current events are watched closely and interpreted in the light of an impending end. The premillennialists believe that the world must get worse and worse. But they still have a moral reform program for America.[11]

Superhero (Grand Rapids: Eerdmans, 2002).

9. Kyle, *Evangelicalism*, 178.

10. Fackre, *The Religious Right*, 59, 62 (quotes); Kyle, *Evangelicalism*, 178. See Robert Jewett and John Shelton Lawrence, *Captain America and the Crusade against Evil: The Dilemma of Zealous Nationalism* (Grand Rapids: Eerdmans, 2003); Tony Carnes, "The Bush Doctrine," *Christianity Today*, 9 May 2003, 38-40; Howard Fineman, "Bush and God," *Newsweek*, 10 March 2003, 23-30; George Wills, "Paradoxes of Public Piety," *Newsweek*, 15 March 2004, 80. See Robert G. Clouse, "The New Christian Right, and the Kingdom of God," *Christian Scholar's Review*, 12 (1983) 3-16.

11. Kyle, *Evangelicalism*, 178-79. See Malise Ruthven, "Rapture and the American Right," *The Times Literary Supplement*, 29 January, 4 February 1988, 110, 120-22; Peter Stiglin, "Apocalyptic Theology and the Right," *The Witness* 69/10 (October 1986) 6-8.

While many evangelicals believe the end is very near, they have moved up the social ladder and are planning to continue the good life for the foreseeable future. The Christian Right's view of the end closely relates to its dualistic worldview. What is going on right before their eyes is a cosmic battle between the forces of light and darkness—and they are on God's side. Of considerable importance and as result of its eschatology, the Christian Right has a great interest in Israel. The return of the Jews to Palestine set the divine clock ticking. Nothing else needs to be fulfilled before the end. Thus, in respect to American foreign policy, the Christian Right staunchly supports Israel's interests.[12]

Some Inconsistencies

Evangelicalism has manifested a number of paradoxes but one concern is its preoccupation with the end of the world and its political activism. Conservative Protestants are largely premillennialists and believe that they are living at the end of time. They interpret many events, especially those in the Middle East, as pointing toward the return of Christ. Still, they are determined to remake America according to Christian principles. In doing so, they act as if the end is not in sight, and they behave like postmillennialists.[13]

Through much of the nineteenth century, conservative Protestants were politically active and involved in many reform movements. But they were also postmillennialists, an eschatology that is friendly toward redressing society's ills. While many modern fundamentalists still embrace an implicit or residual postmillennialism, it is not an explicit doctrine but a "mixture of piety and powerful American folklore." The fundamentalist movement is indeed torn between two traditions. On one hand, its dispensationalist theology says that the end is near and that things will get worse. On the other, they share in the Puritan heritage that sees America as the "New Israel" and a "city on a hill."[14]

---

12. For an overview of such materials see Richard Kyle, *The Last Days Are Here Again: A History of the End Times* (Grand Rapids: Baker, 1998) 115–37; Timothy P. Weber, *On the Road to Armageddon: How Evangelicals Became Israel's Best Friend* (Grand Rapids: Baker, 2004).

13. Kyle, *Evangelicalism*, 169.

14. Marsden, *Understanding Fundamentalism and Evangelicalism*, 112 (quote); George Marsden, *Religion and American Culture* (New York: Harcourt Brace) 268; Harvey Cox, "The Warring Visions of the Religious Right," *Atlantic Monthly*, November 1995, 64–66; Randall Balmer and Lauren F. Winner, *Protestantism in America*

The Politics of Armageddon

Many contemporary evangelicals desire to remake and reform America. What fuels this passion? A central motivation is their vision of a Christian America. They believe America was established on Christian principles and that it is a Christian nation with a special mission. They also insist that in recent years the vision of a Christian America has been hijacked by secularists and feminists.[15]

Despite cynicism regarding America's status as a Christian nation, many evangelicals maintained this idea and it became an article of faith by the 1980s. So long as fundamentalists separated politics from religion, they could believe the end was imminent and still uphold their belief in a Christian America. But when the Christian Right became heavily involved in politics and attempted to reshape America, the contradiction became more acute. They entered the political arena with a vengeance. But as Robert Clouse notes, they "do not have an eschatological base for such activities. In essence, they want to support a certain type of postmillennial vision for America while maintaining a premillennial eschatology."[16]

Another inconsistency concerns the Christian Right's view regarding Israel and America. While maintaining the view of a Christian America, the Christian Right's dispensational theology "teaches that God's purpose is not centered in America but in Israel." Dispensational eschatology has two centerpieces: the rebirth of Israel as a nation and the rejection of replacement theology, namely, that God's promises to Israel have been fulfilled in the church. Despite these beliefs, many dispensationalists speak of America in postmillennial terms, even while they condemn this approach to eschatology. This development is ironical: many premillennial dispensationalists have adopted a postmillennial view of America without even being aware that they have done so.[17]

When the Christian Right became involved in politics they articulated positions regarding foreign and domestic policy. As noted, in respect to foreign policy they advocate staunch support for Israel. In addition, they would increase the defense budget thus enabling America to maintain the

---

(New York: Columbia University Press, 2002) 67.

15. Kyle, *Evangelicalism*, 179.

16. Robert Clouse, "Fundamentalist Theology," *Oxford Handbook of Eschatology*, ed. Jerry L. Walls (Oxford: Oxford University Press, 2007) 269. See Stephen O'Leary and Michael McFarland, "The Political Use of Mythic Discourse: Prophetic Interpretation in Pat Robertson's Presidential Campaign," *Quarterly Journal of Speech* 75 (1989) 433–52; David Edwin Harrell Jr., *Pat Robertson: A Life and Legacy* (Grand Rapids: Eerdmans, 2010).

17. Clouse, "Fundamentalist Theology," 270.

world's most powerful military. On a domestic level, to return America to its Christian heritage would entail significant changes. The Christian Right would like a strong authoritarian president who reduces welfare spending and programs.[18]

But their major changes would come in the social and moral areas. They would reverse what they perceive as the evil humanist and feminist tide that has engulfed America. They desire to "restore the traditional family, defeat feminism, guarantee child discipline, stop abortion, restrict homosexuals, stamp out child abuse, and stop drug abuse." In essence the Christian Right's implicit postmillennial vision for America would make "it a very conservative place where one group's traditional values would hold sway." With both a strong military and a more moral society, America would be well positioned for what dispensationalists believe is America's primary role in the last times: the defense of Israel.[19]

As can be seen, much of the Christian Right's domestic program is inconsistent with its eschatology. Moreover, the Christian Right has encouraged "civil religion," which also presents problems for its dispensational end-time views. Civil religion is a very vague and controversial subject, which will not be investigated at this point. Suffice it to say that it is a nebulous form of civic or public religion that connects with a nation's history and destiny. Such a heritage is usually perceived as sacred and endows a nation with religious principles accepted by most ranks of society. Civil religion and its embrace of America's Christian and religious past obviously resonates best with postmillennial eschatology. The Christian Right, however, has embraced both civil religion and this sacred past while still upholding a premillennial view of end-time events.

CHRISTIAN RECONSTRUCTIONISM

Further to the right exists a group that goes by several names: Christian Reconstructionism, theonomy, dominion theology, and kingdom theology. By no means is it a cohesive movement but consists of several subgroups. While its roots are in Calvinist theology, it is an uneasy alliance of fundamentalists, charismatics, and miscellaneous evangelicals on the Christian Right. It consists of Christian splinter groups that are postmillennial and desire to take America and the world back to an Old Testament ethic. As used by the Reconstructionists, the term *theonomy* refers to

18. Ibid., 271.
19. Ibid.

The Politics of Armageddon

the abiding validity of God's law throughout history. Dominion theology points to Genesis 1:28 where Adam and Eve were to have dominion over every living creature. Christians thus are entitled to dominate the world's institutions until Christ returns and rules the Earth.[20]

The leaders of this movement include Rousas John Rushdoony (1916-2001), Gary North, Gary DeMar, David Chilton, George Grant, and Greg Bahnsen. While they may quarrel among themselves, they come together over the big picture, namely, the need to restore the nations of the world to Old Testament principles. Or from another perspective, many of these adherents regard Christian Reconstructionism as a resurrected Puritan movement. There are several Christian Reconstructionist organizations but the key centers are as follows: Rushdoony's Chalcedon Foundation in Vallecito, California; his son in-law Gary North's Institute of Christian Economics in Tyler, Texas; and Gary DeMar's American Vision organization in Atlanta, Georgia.[21]

Many people see the Reconstructionist movement beginning in 1960 under the thinking of Cornelius Van Til (1895-1987). (Van Til, nevertheless, denied being a Reconstructionist.) It did not gain an intellectual following, however, until 1973, when Rushdooney published his massive *Institutes of Biblical Law*. Several factors played a part in the rise of this movement. The potential contradiction between the Christian Right's political activism and the eschatological fatalism of premillennialism contributed to the emergence Christian Reconstructionism. Second, they perceived that the Christian Right has either failed to reform the nation or has been willing to compromise its principles. Thus, a more radical and determined movement was necessary.[22]

20. Bruce Barron, *Heaven on Earth?: The Social and Political Agendas of Dominion Theology* (Grand Rapids: Zondervan, 1992) 13-16; Anson Shupe, "The Reconstructionist Movement on the New Christian Right," *Christian Century*, 4 October 1989, 880-81; Anson Shupe, "Prophets of a Biblical America," *Wall Street Journal*, 12 April 1989, sec. 14, col. 3; William Martin, *With God on Our Side* (New York: Broadway, 1996) 353; Michelle Goldberg, *Kingdom Coming: The Rise of Christian Nationalism* (New York: Norton, 2006) 37-38.

21. Anson Shupe, "Christian Reconstructionism and the Angry Rhetoric of Neo-Postmillennialism," in *Millennium, Messiahs, and Mayhem*, eds. Thomas Robbins and Susan J. Palmer (New York: Routledge, 1997) 197-98.

22. Richard John Neuhaus, "Why Wait for the Kingdom?: The Theonomist Temptation," *First Things* 3 (May 1990) 13-14; Kyle, *Evangelicalism*, 204; David A. Rausch and Douglas E. Chismar, "The New Puritans and Their Theonomic Paradise," *Christian Century*, 3-10 August 1983, 712-13; Cox, "Warring Visions of the Religious Right," 66; Shupe, "Christian Reconstructionism and the Angry Rhetoric of Neo-Postmillennialism," 196-97. See also Robert P. Lightner, "Theonomy and Dispensationalism,"

Their Program

The Reconstructionists want nothing less than a complete transformation of the world, beginning first in America. Their program centers on six points. They are postmillennialists and see the Second Coming of Christ way into the future. Thus, they allow for a long gradual transformation of human society that will come largely by peaceful means. While theonomy focuses on many social and political issues, its structure has a great deal to do with eschatology. Postmillennialism has been nearly totally eclipsed since the early twentieth century. Reconstructionism represents a return to postmillennialism and insists that the kingdom is now and comes in the form of the "Church *Very* Militant."[23]

They do not deny the doctrine of the Second Coming but represent a "realized eschatology." Neither do they reject the concept of a future millennium, as do the amillennialists, but say the millennium is now. Humankind is not living in the end times, but in the middle times and it may take hundreds or even thousands of years for the righteous kingdom to be established. Christians thus are not to pray for Christ's return but for the world to be ready for this event.[24]

Two, every human institution of every nation must be reclaimed from the Satanists and humanists. In this they will not compromise, as they believe the Christian Right has done. Thus, in their mind, Christian Reconstructionism is not one option but the only choice. "Our goal is world dominion under Christ's lordship, a 'world takeover' if you will," says David Chilton. "We are the shapers of world history."[25]

Next, the theonomists regard the Bible, especially the Mosaic Law, as the blueprint for this reconstructed society. They believe an absolute God has created a consistent ethical system for all people for all time, not just for the Hebrews. In this there are some differences among the theonomists. Strict Reconstructionists argue that the Mosaic Law must be implemented as it stands. More moderate theonomists, however, say that

---

Bibliotheca Sacra, January–March 1986, 26–36.

23. Shupe, "Reconstructionist Movement," 880; Martin Durham, *The Christian Right, the Far Right, and the Boundaries of American Conservatism* (Manchester: Manchester University Press, 2000) 109; Barron, *Heaven on Earth?* 23–38; Kyle, *Evangelicalism*, 204–5; Neuhaus, "Why Wait for the Kingdom?," 17. See Gary DeMar, *Last Days Madness: Obsession of the Modern Church* (Atlanta: American Vision, 1997).

24. Neuhaus, "Why Wait for the Kingdom?," 17.

25. David S. Katz and Richard H. Popkin, *Messianic Revolution* (New York: Hill and Wang, 1998) 245 (quote).

the entire Bible, including the Mosaic Law, must be applied in consideration of New Covenant principles.[26]

Four, Reconstructionism is a grassroots movement and is not something imposed from above by some religious or political authority. Societal transformation will come from conversion and self-regeneration and will be a majority, non-violent movement. Consequently, such changes may take centuries. But make no mistake, Reconstructionism is not a democratic ideology. It looks with admiration to some past governments with an autocratic character—Calvin's Geneva, Cromwell in England, and the Puritans in colonial America. Moreover, theonomy is a "top-down" intellectual movement with the ideas being generated by a few individuals. Furthermore, the theonomists have little time for democracy and when their goals are implemented, there will be few freedoms—political, religious, or personal. Still, what modifies Reconstructionism's dogmatism and its autocratic demeanor is its organizational structure. It is more of an alliance of like-minded individuals than a tight-knit movement. And they frequently quarrel with each other, sometimes in an acrimonious manner.[27]

Five, Christians should be involved in politics for this is one avenue for transforming society. While politics may be dirty, Christians should be engaged and reform the process. Given Christian Reconstructionism's postmillennialism and its optimism, political involvement is not a contradiction as it is for the more pessimistic premillennialists. In fact, theonomists condemn Christians who focus on inward holiness and make little attempt to reform society. They are derisively referred to as "pietists." To advocate political involvement, however, does not mean that Reconstructionists favor democracy. Democracy is but a means to an end—that is, the complete transformation of society according to divine law. In fact, Rushdoony condemned democracy as heresy and rejected legally protected political and religious pluralism. While some theonomists downplay this strong language, what they have in mind is a theocratic system. (But they prefer the term *Christocracy* to theocracy).[28]

---

26. Shupe, "Reconstructionist Movement," 880; Kyle, *Evangelicalism*, 205; Neuhaus, "Why Wait for the Kingdom?," 14.

27. Shupe, "Reconstructionist Movement," 880; Neuhaus, "Why Wait for the Kingdom?," 18; Shupe, "Christian Reconstructionism and Angry Rhetoric," 198–203.

28. Shupe, "Reconstructionist Movement," 880; Neuhaus, "Why Wait for the Kingdom?," 14–18; Michael Baigent, *Racing toward Armageddon: The Three Great Religions and the Plot to End the World* (New York: HarperCollins, 2009) 155–56.

Lastly, God established a covenant with America and he will be faithful to this nation so long as there exists a remnant obedient to him. (They, of course, see themselves as this remnant). Contrary to the dispensational premillennialists, they do not accord Israel a special place in their postmillennial theology. Rather, the United States occupies such a position. But if America disregards the covenant, God will revoke his blessing. The United States is only one of several nations and avenues through which God can achieve his will. If this country is unfaithful, other nations will become the distributors of Christianity.[29]

Its Implementation

If the Christian Reconstructionists had their own way, nearly every aspect of American life would be dramatically transformed. Society will not be reformed. It will be razed to the ground and rebuilt. All government props will be gone: social security, welfare, minimum wages, government regulation of business, public education, and all taxes except a ten percent income tax. What will replace this government assistance? Private schools and home schooling will provide education. The elderly would be cared for by their children and a private retirement plan. After the harvest has been completed, the poor would be allowed to glean from the fields. America would return to a gold-and-silver monetary standard and, because the Bible prohibits usury, loans would be valid for only seven years. Labor unions would be abolished. The Reconstructionists desire to take America back to the world of radical libertarian economics, a decentralized political system, and social Darwinism.[30]

In respect to morals and religion, the transformation will be just as radical. The family will be run by strict patriarchal principles. Women will be removed from the workforce to stay at home. In some cases they may lose their citizenship. Indentured servitude will solve many problems: unemployment, prison overcrowding, and idle teenagers. Old Testament laws will be strictly enforced. Homosexuals, adulterers, blasphemers, Sabbath breakers, habitual criminals, and disobedient children will be harshly punished—perhaps by stoning. Religious pluralism and toleration will be a thing of the past. There will be no place

---

29. Shupe, "Reconstructionist Movement," 880–81; Kyle, *Evangelicalism*, 205.

30. Shupe, "Reconstructionist Movement," 881; Martin, *With God on Our Side*, 352; Barron, *Heaven on Earth?*, 135–49; Shupe, "Prophets of a Biblical America," sec. 1, p. 14; Rausch and Chismar, "The New Puritans and Their Theonomic Paradise," 723.

in America for Jews, Muslims, Hindus, Buddhists, atheists, humanists, feminists, secularists, and even non-Reconstructionist Christians. The First Amendment guaranteeing such freedoms will be gone and the government will not be neutral toward religion. Rather, it will enforce a biblical faith based on the Old Testament.[31]

Its Influence

Christian Reconstructionists are few in number and it is unlikely that they will ever take over America, let alone the world. Still, their influence is significant, especially among conservative Christians. And this impact is a factor in shaping American social and political policy. Their ideas have less influence, however, on foreign policy largely because Israel does not occupy a meaningful place in their postmillennial eschatology. In fact, a number of theonomists have demonstrated animosity toward Judaism. Still, Reconstructionists desire a strong military in order for America to dominate the world for Christ. Yet, their belief in a decentralized political system would present problems for this objective.

Still, it is difficult to access the influence of Christian Reconstructionism with any accuracy. Because the movement is genuinely radical, the Christian Right has had a mixed reaction toward it. On one hand, conservative Christians and Christian Reconstructionism share a major objective, namely, to restore America to what they regard as its Christian principles. On the other hand, Christian Reconstructionism is so radical that most members of the Christian Right distance themselves from it. Also, the theonomist embrace of postmillennialism presents a huge problem. But as Gary North says, many in the Christian Right are "abandoning premillennialism psychologically if not officially."[32]

For example, Pat Robertson has flirted with some of Reconstructionism's ideas and made use of dominion language. In fact, Gary North has described him as a "halfway house" between the two movements. Gary DeMar referred to Robertson as an "operational Reconstructionist." But because of Reconstructionism's postmillennialism, Robertson has dissociated himself from the movement. George W. Bush's Attorney General

31. Shupe, "Reconstructionist Movement," 881; Martin, *With God on Our Side*, 352; Shupe, 'Prophets of a Biblical America," sec. 1, p. 14; Kyle, *Evangelicalism*, 205; Baigent, *Racing toward Armageddon*, 153; Chris Hedges, *American Fascists: The Christian Right and the War on America* (New York: Free Press, 2006) 12.

32. Martin, *With God on Our Side*, 354; Neuhaus, "Why Wait for the Kingdom?," 19 (quote).

John Ashcroft appeared to have his thinking colored by Reconstructionist ideas. The late Jerry Falwell and the late D. James Kennedy pushed the Christian America concept and endorsed Reconstructionist books but held up at that point.[33] Jay Grimstead does not call himself a Reconstructionist, but he has said, "There are a lot of us floating around in Christian leadership . . . who don't go all the way with the theonomy thing, but who want to rebuild America based on the Bible."[34]

On a practical level, theonomist ideas can be felt in several quarters. A number of political leaders and judges, who consciously or unconsciously share Reconstructionist beliefs, have gained office and this has impacted the legislative and judicial process in America. Several groups oppose abortion, but Rushdoony provided conservative Protestants with a theology for this opposition. As Randall Terry of Operation Rescue grew impatient with moderate methods to oppose abortion, he evidenced an affinity with theonomist ideas. Reconstructionists oppose the separation of church and state in America and, along with other religious conservatives, they have gradually been chipping away at the First Amendment.[35]

Christian Reconstructionism may have had its greatest effect in the home schooling movement. Home schooling has many sources, both religious and secular. But its largest impulse has come from those who feared the influence of a secular approach to education. Thus was born home schooling, which desires to raise and educate the young from a godly perspective, largely outside reaches of secular humanism. In this endeavor the theonomists have helped shape a version of the prepackaged home schooling curriculum. As Gary North states, "we must use the doctrine of religious liberty to gain independence for Christian schools until we train up a generation of people who know that there is no religious neutrality, no neutral law, no neutral education, and no neutral civil government."[36]

---

33. Kyle, *Evangelicalism*, 205; Shupe, "Reconstructionist Movement, 882; Mark G. Toulouse, "Pat Robertson: Apocalyptic Theology and American Foreign Policy," *Journal of Church and State* 31/1 (Winter 1989) 73–99; Katz and Popkin, *Messianic Revolution*, 243 (quote).

34. Baigent, *Racing toward Armageddon*, 158 (quote); Martin, *With God on Our Side*, 354; Phillips, *American Theocracy*, 244; Paul Boyer, *When Time Shall Be No More* (Cambridge, MA: Harvard University Press, 1992) 303–4.

35. Baigent, *Racing toward Armageddon*, 170–72; Goldberg, *Kingdom Coming*, 157–60; Martin, *With God on Our Side*, 355.

36. Baigent, *Racing toward Armageddon*, 172–74 (quote); Gary North, "The Intellectual, Schizophrenia, of the New Chrisitian Right," *Christianity and Civilization* 1 (1982) 25.

The Politics of Armageddon

While a number of Christian Right leaders also want to rebuild America, they do not want to go as far as the theonomists. Their premillennialism presents a barrier. They see culminating events close at hand and not in the distant future. Many Christian Right leaders will compromise and desire a place at the political table, not total domination as do the theonomists. Still, Reconstructionism has had a definite appeal for many conservative Protestants and its ideas have penetrated the Christian Right's wider agenda for moving America in the direction of a theocracy. As one conservative Christian said, "Though we hide their [the Christian Reconstructionists] books under the bed, we read them just the same."[37]

CHRISTIAN ZIONISM AND DISPENSATIONALISM

In looking at the Christian Right and Christian Reconstructionism, the focus has been on eschatology and its connection with American domestic affairs. Now the spotlight will shift to eschatology and foreign affairs, especially as it relates to Christian Zionism and dispensationalism. The Christian Right is not synonymous with dispensationalism or Christian Zionism. Still, there exists considerable overlap. Most followers of the Christian Right embrace some form of dispensationalism, whether serious or on a popular level. And nearly all Christian Zionists are dispensationalists. The difference, however, lies in this: Christian Zionism is a movement that grew out of a theological system called dispensationalism. Thus the terms will be used interchangeably.

But all evangelicals certainly do not accept the dispensational scheme regarding the end times. Sources estimate the total number of evangelicals in America to range between seventy-five and one hundred million with dispensationalists making up about twenty-five million of that total. Yet, the impact of dispensational ideas has been widespread, especially through popular literature, radio, and televangelism. In fact, as George Marsden notes, "Even most of those neo-evangelicals who abandoned the details of Dispensationalism still retained a firm belief in Israel's God-ordained role."[38]

The dominant form of Christian Zionism in America is the dispensational variety. This form, with its teaching of the sudden rapture,

---

37. Baigent, *Racing toward Armageddon*, 158 (quote); Martin, *With God on Our Side*, 154.

38. Donald E. Wagner, "Marching to Zion," *Christian Century*, 28 June 2003, 20; Marsden, *Understanding Fundamentalism and Evangelicalism*, 77.

staunch support of Israel, the rebuilding of the Jerusalem temple, and the soon-coming battle of Armageddon is pervasive. It can be found within the ranks of many evangelical bodies: mainline evangelicalism, Pentecostalism, charismatic bodies, Southern Baptist churches, and independent churches from small Bible churches to megachurches. Dispensational Christian Zionism is especially strong in the Bible Belt, that area stretching from Virginia to Texas. But beyond the evangelical community, dispensational ideas have impacted the broader American culture. Wars, political and economic unrest, the breakdown of morals, natural disasters, and epidemics are often seen as signs of the times. People then tend to look to charismatic leaders to solve or explain such problems.[39]

Dispensationalism has been defined earlier in this study. But what is Christian Zionism? "Christian Zionism centers upon the belief that the emergence of a Jewish state in Palestine in 1948 was a fulfillment of Biblical prophecy [and] that event is somehow linked to God's plan for the fulfillment of human destiny."[40] Christian Zionism has, along with the Middle East in general, received considerable scholarly and popular attention since September 11. At least four scholarly books have focused on this subject or related issues. They are as follows: *On the Road to Armageddon* by Timothy Weber, *Christian Zionism* and *Zion's Christian Soldiers?* both by Stephen Sizer, and *Allies for Armageddon* by Victoria Clark. In addition, several books have looked at Christian Zionism along with similar movements in the Middle East.

In 2010 two popular level documentaries regarding Christian Zionism came out. Both *Waiting for Armageddon* and *With God on Our Side* "explore problems with believing that God has a special plan for ethnic Israel and thus politically advocating on behalf of the modern state of Israel." The first film comes from an insider's perspective and examines the powerful alliance between evangelicals and Israel. Evangelical interviewees take a matter-of-fact approach and explain that the Jews must occupy all of Israel before Christ can return to Earth. *With God on Our Side* looks at the situation from more of a Palestinian viewpoint and asks Zionists to reevaluate their support of Israel.[41]

---

39. Stephen Sizer, *Christian Zionism: Road-Map to Armageddon?* (Leicester, UK: InterVarsity, 2004) 23; Timothy Weber, "How Evangelicals Became Israel's Best Friend," *Christianity Today*, 5 October 1998, 40.

40. Ronald R. Stockton, "Christian Zionism: Prophecy and Public Opinion," *Middle East Journal* 41 (1987) 234.

41. Tim Avery, "Christian Zionism in the Dock," *Christianity Today*, July 2011, 56.

Basic Tenets

Christian Zionists insist on six basic tenets. What are they? Most basic, all of historic Palestine occupied during the 1967 War, including the land west of the Jordan, must be controlled by Israel. This is one of the steps necessary for the Second Coming of Christ. Two, God's covenant with Israel is eternal, exclusive with them, and cannot be abolished. Next, Scripture refers to two distinct and parallel covenants. One is between God and Israel, the other between God and the church. God's covenant with Israel supercedes the one with the church. Rather, the church lives in the parenthesis between Christ's death and the rapture, when God will remove the church from history. At this point, Israel will once again become God's primary instrument on Earth.

Four, Genesis 12:3, which states, "I will bless those who bless you and curse those who curse you," must be interpreted literally. This, of course, will result in America granting substantial military, political, financial, and moral support for the modern state of Israel and the Jewish people. Five, the apocalyptic texts in Scripture such as the books of Daniel and Revelation and passages in Ezekiel and I Thessalonians must be interpreted literally and refer to future events.

Lastly, there are several signs pointing to the final eschatological events such as the battle of Armageddon, Christ's return, and his millennial reign. They include the establishment of the Israeli state, the rebuilding of the Third Temple, the rise of the Antichrist, and the formulation of the coalitions of nations for the attack on Israel. Christian Zionism looks for the increase of satanic forces as they ally with the Antichrist to do battle with Israel and the nations assisting it. And judgment will befall any nation or individual who does not "bless Israel." To support and aid Israel is America's primary role in the eschatological events that are soon to come upon the Earth.[42]

Events to 1967

Stephen Sizer defines Zionism as "the national movement for the return of the Jewish people to their ancient homeland and the resumption of Jewish political sovereignty in the land of Israel . . ." While aspects of Zionism existed in the sixteenth century as a religious movement, it is

---

42. These six tenets have been summarized from Donald E. Wagner, "Marching to Zion," *Christian Century*, 28 June 2003.

usually associated with a nineteenth-century figure, Theodor Herzl. With the publication of his *Der Judenstaat* (The Jewish State) in 1896, political Zionism was born. Herzl's thinking was purely secular for he was an agnostic. But many of his followers were religious and this situation forced Herzl to make some concessions to religious interests.[43]

While political and Christian Zionism have some similar goals, they are not the same. In fact, Christian Zionism predates political Zionism. As premillennialism gained steam during the nineteenth century, many of its adherents not only believed the Jews would return to Palestine but supported their right to do so. Prior to the publication of Herzl's *Der Judenstaat*, fundamentalist-evangelical William E. Blackstone supported the establishment of a Jewish state and even petitioned the United States government to use its influence toward that end. Numerous outstanding Christian and Jewish leaders signed the Blackstone Petition of 1891 and the State Department circulated it throughout much of the globe.[44]

At first, Christian Zionism attracted widespread support from many religious groups and they influenced political action, even the Balfour Declaration. Nevertheless, as time went on, because of their premillennial eschatology, fundamentalist groups came to dominate the drive to return the Jews to Palestine. In his periodical *Our Hope*, from 1894 to 1945 Arno C. Gaebelein advocated for both the return of the Jews to Palestine and their inherent right to that land. Other prominent dispensationalists including Harry Ironside, Reuben Torrey, and M. R. DeHaan also insisted on the biblical basis for the restoration of Israel.[45]

When Israel became a state in 1948, Christian Zionists regarded it as a miracle and the movement gained new momentum. Most fundamentalists viewed the restoration of the Jewish nation as a sign that prophecy was right on target and the end was near. Moreover, they viewed the events of the early Cold War years through the prism of fulfilled prophecy, especially Ezekiel 38–39. The Soviet Union and its allies were seen as in league with the Antichrist. The early development of the European Union raised

---

43. Stephen Sizer, *Zion's Christian Soldiers?* (Nottingham, UK: InterVarsity, 2007) 175; D. A. Rausch, "Zionism," in *Evangelical Dictionary of Theology*, ed. Walter A. Elwell (Grand Rapids: Baker, 1984) 1200.

44. Sizer, *Christian Zionism*, 70–77; D. A. Rauch, "Christian Zionism," in *Evangelical Dictionary of Theology*, 1201; Victoria Clark, *Allies for Armageddon: The Rise of Christian Zionism* (New Haven, CT: Yale University Press, 2007) 93–97; Weber, *On the Road to Armageddon*, 102–6; Weber, "How Evangelicals Became Israel's Best Friends," 41–42.

45. Sizer, *Christian Zionism*, 77–80; Rauch, "Christian Zionism," 2001; Clark, *Allies for Armageddon*, 116–22.

The Politics of Armageddon

suspicions. Was this the beginning of the ten-nation confederation spoken of in Scripture? Many thought so. In the mind of numerous people, all of these events pointed to the invasion of Israel and the culmination of history.[46]

The 1967 War as a Turning Point

The Six Day War of 1967 marked a watershed for evangelicalism's interest in Zionism and Israel. When Israel captured Jerusalem in 1967, dispensationalists exploded with excitement and believed the end to be at hand. By the early 1970s numerous books, films, radio programs, and television specials pushed the premillennial dispensational perspective regarding the end of time. Leading this charge of course was *The Late Great Planet Earth*. This book's influence went well beyond the popular level and reached the highest levels of the American government—Congress, the Pentagon, and the Reagan presidency.[47]

By the 1970s five developments came together promoting Christian Zionism and its support for Israel. One, while mainline Protestantism and Catholicism declined, evangelicalism and charismatic movements grew significantly. And large numbers within these groups embraced premillennialism and its support of Israel. Two, in 1976 Jimmy Carter, a Southern Baptist, became president. Having an evangelical in the White House increased the visibility of a once marginalized movement. While Carter and many evangelicals were not Zionists, the mainline media missed this and linked evangelicalism with a support for Israel.[48]

Next, Israel's occupation of Palestinian lands created tensions between the Jewish and Catholic, Eastern Orthodox, and mainline Protestant

---

46. Wagner, "Evangelicals and Israel: Theological Roots of a Political Alliance," *Christian Century*, 4 November 1998, 1021; Rauch, "Christian Zionism," 2001; Weber, "How Evangelicals Became Israel's Best Friend," 44–45; Hans-Lukas Kieser, *Nearest East: American Millennialism and Mission to the Middle East* (Philadelphia: Temple University Press, 2010) 112–35.

47. Weber, *On the Road to Armageddon*, 188–89, 213; Wagner, "Evangelicals and Israel, 1021; Clark, *Allies for Armageddon*, 213–14; Angela M. Lahr, *Millennial Dreams and Apocalyptic Nightmares* (New York: Oxford University Press, 2007) 134. See also Tom Segev, *1967: Israel, the War, and the Year That Transformed the Middle East* (New York: Metropolitan, 2005); Melanie McAlister, "An Empire of Their Own," *Nation*, 22 September 2003, 31–36.

48. Wagner, "Evangelicals and Israel," 1021; Kyle, *Evangelicalism*, 199, 312–15; Weber, "How Evangelicals Became Israel's Best Friend," 46–47; Weber, *On the Road to Armageddon*, 196–98.

communities. As a result, many Jewish organizations—especially lobbying groups such as the American Israel Political Affairs Committee (AIPAC)—turned to the expanding evangelical community for support. All kinds of Jewish agencies and government officials began to focus on building relationships with evangelical groups. Even the Israeli minister of tourism eyed this growing evangelical market for business.[49]

Four, the election of Menachem Begin as Israel's prime minister stimulated the Christian Zionist political agenda. Before his election in 1977, Israeli politics had been dominated by the left-of-center secular Labor Party. Conversely, Begin's Likud Party contained hardline military figures and allied itself with other right-wing elements such as the settler movement and Orthodox religious parties. Likud's constituencies referred to the West Bank in biblical terms such as Judea and Samaria and believed Israel had a divine right to these lands. Christian Zionists in America concurred and welcomed these Israeli hardliners with open arms.[50]

Lastly, President Carter's March 1977 statement that he supported Palestinian human rights, including their "right to a homeland," hastened the alliance between Likud and the Christian Right. Likud came to power shortly thereafter and immediately began to court the evangelical community. Likud had a simple plan of action: separate evangelical and fundamentalist Christians from Carter's political base and encourage conservative Christians to support Israel. This included opposing the United Nation's Middle East Peace Conference.[51]

Within weeks advertisements flooded American papers supporting Israel. Some read like this: "The time has come for evangelical Christians to affirm their belief in biblical prophecy and Israel's divine right to the land." Fearful of Soviet participation at the UN conference, other articles said, "We affirm as evangelicals our belief in the promised land to the Jewish people. . . . We would view with grave concern any effort to carve out of the Jewish homeland another nation or political entity."[52]

Jerusalem's Institute for Holy Land Studies, an evangelical organization with Christian Zionist ties, financed such ads. This advertising campaign was the first public expression of the Likud-evangelical

---

49. Weber, "How Evangelicals Became Israel's Best Friend," 47–48; Wagner, "Evangelicals and Israel," 1021; Clark, *Allies for Armageddon*, 165, 222, 236–37; Weber, *On the Road to Armageddon*, 214.

50. Weber, *On the Road to Armageddon*, 218–19, 222; Clark, *Allies for Armageddon*, 190–92; Wagner, "Evangelicals and Israel," 1021.

51. Wagner, "Evangelicals and Israel," 1021–22.

52. Ibid., 1022, (quote); Kieser, *Nearest East*, 137–49.

The Politics of Armageddon

alliance. But it was not always a smooth marriage. The Israelis recognized that evangelicals were their source of political and economic strength in America. Moreover, Jewish organizations and evangelicals agreed at many points. But the Christian Right's drive to convert Jews remained a point of tension.[53]

Reagan and Beyond

For a variety of reasons, evangelical and Jewish organizations supported Reagan in the 1980 presidential contest against Carter. With the election of Ronald Reagan, Christian Zionists now had a kindred spirit in the Whitehouse. His knowledge of biblical prophecy was scant at best, but he was familiar with the general dispensational outline of end-time events. So from both a religious and strategic perspective he embraced the Christian Zionist cause.[54]

Through AIPAC, Likud could now aggressively pursue its policy both in Congress and the Reagan administration. Begin developed a close relationship with Reagan and several fundamentalist leaders, especially Jerry Falwell. For example, Israel gave Falwell several perks including a Learjet and the prestigious Jabotinsky Award. And when Israel attacked Iraq's nuclear plant in 1981, Begin called Falwell before he notified Reagan. He asked Falwell to "explain to the Christian public the reasons for the bombing." In turn, Falwell promoted the Zionist cause within the fundamentalist community and on Capitol Hill.[55]

For its part, the Reagan administration conducted briefing sessions and seminars for conservative Christians. Pro-Likud organizations, such as AIPAC and Americans for a Safe Israel, plus over 150 fundamentalist leaders participated in these meetings. Some prominent names include

53. Wagner, "Evangelicals and Israel," 1022; Weber, "How Evangelicals Became Israel's Best Friend," 48.

54. Kyle, *The Last Days Are Here Again*, 17, 116; Robert Jewett, "Coming to Terms with the Doom Boom," *Quarterly Review* 4/3 (Fall 1984) 9; G. Clark Chapman Jr., "Falling in Rapture before the Bomb," *Reformed Journal* 37 (June 1987) 13; Timothy P. Weber, "Happily at the Edge of the Abyss: Popular Premillennialism in America," *Ex Auditu* 6 (1991) 93–94; Ronnie Dugger, "Does Reagan Expect a Nuclear Armageddon?," *Washington Post*, 8 April 1984, C1, C4; Richard N. Ostling, "Armageddon and the End Times," *Time*, 5 November 1984, 73.

55. Wagner, "Evangelicals and Israel," 1022–23 (quote); Clark, *Allies for Armageddon*, 165, 190; Stephen D. O'Leary, *Arguing the Apocalypse: A Theory of Millennial Rhetoric* (New York: Oxford University Press, 1994) 180–83.

Tim and Bev LaHaye, Jim and Tammy Bakker, Jimmy Swaggart, Pat Robertson, and Hal Lindsey.[56]

The Christian Zionist and pro-Israel alliance solidified during the Reagan administration. Still, it declined somewhat during the George H. W. Bush and Bill Clinton administrations. Clinton had ties with the secular Labor Party led by Shimon Peres and Yitzhak Rabin. Because of this alliance, Clinton supported the Oslo peace accords, which called for modest reductions in the expansion of Jewish settlements and requested Israel to withdraw from portions of the West Bank, Gaza, and Jerusalem. Likud and the Christian Zionists, of course, opposed these projected moves.[57]

Shortly after Rabin's assassination (which Pat Robertson regarded as an act of God), Likud and Benjamin Netanyahu returned to power. Long a favorite of the Christian Zionists, he took several steps to reinvigorate the evangelical-Israeli alliance. He spoke to several groups of influential evangelicals including the Israel Christian Advocacy Council and invited many of them for a tour of the Holy Land. After they returned to the United States, they issued a statement closely resembling the Likud policies. Included was a rejection of any kind of pressure on Israel to return the land occupied in the 1967 War.[58]

With major advertisements, the Israel Christian Advocacy Council also launched a campaign entitled "Christians Call for a United Jerusalem." Such advertisements echoed the theme that "Israel's biblical claim to the land" was "an eternal covenant from God." Signers for such statements included many prominent evangelicals: Ralph Reed, then director of the Christian Coalition; Pat Robertson of CBN; Don Argue, president of the National Association of Evangelicals; Ed McAteer of the Religious Roundtable; and Jerry Falwell. These advertisements were a direct response to a campaign began in April 1997 by the Catholic, Orthodox, and mainline Protestant churches for a "shared Jerusalem." Moreover, Christian Zionist groups matched this political advocacy for Likud with substantial financial support.[59]

---

56. Wagner, "Evangelicals and Israel," 1023. See also Kenneth L. Woodward, "Arguing Armageddon," *Newsweek*, 5 November 1984, 91; R. Dugger, "Reagan's Apocalypse Now," *Manchester Guardian Weekly*, 6 May 1984, 17.

57. Weber, "How Evangelicals Became Israel's Best Friend," 47; Wagner, "Marching to Zion," 21; Sizer, *Christian Zionism*, 89–91.

58. Wagner, "Marching to Zion," 21; Sizer, *Christian Zionism*, 251; Clark, *Allies for Armageddon*, 229; Ilene R. Prusher, "Israel's Unlikely Ally: American Evangelicals," *Christian Science Monitor*, 24 March 1998, 1.

59. Wagner, "Marching to Zion," 21 (quotes); Sizer, *Christian Zionism*, 214; Clark,

The Politics of Armageddon

In the late twentieth and early twenty-first centuries, Christian fundamentalist and Zionist support for Israel also converged with that of the neoconservatives. William Kristol, editor of the *Weekly Standard*; syndicated journalists Charles Krauthammer and William Safire; and key advisors in the George W. Bush administration—Richard Perle, Paul Wolfowitz, Elliot Abrams, and Douglas Feith—agreed substantially with the Christian Zionists' agenda. But for the most part, the neoconservatives had economic and geopolitical motives for aligning themselves with conservative Christians. Like historian Samuel P. Huntington in *The Clash of Civilizations and the Remaking of World Order*, they viewed Islam as the most dangerous threat to United States. This perspective also set well with both the Christian Zionists and the Bush administration.[60]

Political support for the Christian Zionist agenda did not end here. Vice President Dick Cheney, Secretary of Defense Donald Rumsfeld, their advisors, and several members of Congress also shared a worldview compatible with that of Christian Zionism. In fact, some of them advocated the "transfer" concept. Under this thinking, Palestinians would be transferred to Jordan, which would become the Palestinian state. At the very least, such political leaders resisted the call for Israel to surrender land settlements for a future Palestinian state.[61]

The marriage of the Christian Right and Christian Zionism reflects political realities. Many believe that to be an evangelical is to be a Republican. Estimates say the Christian Right makes up about 25 percent of the Republican Party. Moreover, about 80–85 percent of evangelicals voted for Bush in the elections of 2000 and 2004. While evangelicals voted for Bush for several value issues, support of Israel was one of them. And Bush was very aware of his political debt to Christian conservatives.[62]

How this political pressure impacted American policy is a matter of debate. After September 11 an evangelical-Islamic dialogue began. Still,

---

Allies for Armageddon, 193–94. Reinforcing such views were the many writings of John Hagee. See John Hagee, *Final Dawn over Jerusalem* (Nashville: T. Nelson) 1998; John Hagee, *Jerusalem Countdown* (Lake Mary, FL: FrontLine, 2007); John Hagee, *In Defense of Israel* (Lake Mary, FL: FrontLine, 2007.

60. Wagner, "Marching to Zion," 22; Samuel P. Huntington, *The Clash of Civilizations and the Remaking of World Order* (New York: Simon & Schuster, 1996) 209–18; Clark, *Allies for Armageddon*, 191.

61. Wagner, "Marching to Zion," 22; Clark, *Allies for Armageddon*, 199.

62. Kyle, *Evangelicalism*, 167; Wagner, "Marching to Zion," 22–23; Bruce Forbes, "How Popular Are the Left Behind Books . . . and Why?," in *Rapture, Revelation, and the End Times*, eds. Bruce David Forbes and Jeanne Halgren Kilde (New York: Palgrave, 2004) 28.

several conservative evangelical leaders countered this initiative with attacks on Islam. Christian Right leaders such as Franklin Graham, Pat Robertson, and Jerry Falwell have portrayed Islam as an evil force in league with the Antichrist and destined to attack Israel. All of this sat well with President Bush's "Axis of Evil" doctrine, which earmarked three nations, two of which were Islamic.[63]

Beyond the rhetoric, in the late twentieth and early twenty-first centuries, Christian Zionism has taken concrete steps to support Israel. They have facilitated immigration for Jews from several parts of the world to Israel. Settlement programs in the West Bank and East Jerusalem have been supported. Christian Zionists have lobbied international organizations and nations to recognize Jerusalem as the capital of Israel. Carrying this thinking even further, some have been attempting to secure funding for the rebuilding of the temple in Jerusalem. Other Christian Zionists have actively opposed the peace process, which has aggravated relations with the Arab world and increased the prospects of war in the Middle East.[64]

This cozy relationship between Christian Zionism and Israel is not without its problems and contradictions. On one hand, the dispensational premillennial doctrine is the driving force propelling many conservative Christians to support Israel and their claim to the Holy Land. On the other hand, this belief system offers the Jews only two options—either be converted before the rapture or slaughtered during the tribulation period. Neither of these options are appealing to the Jews. They know that the Christian Right's theological agenda and aspects of its political program conflicts with Judaism. But as Israel's director of religious communications once said, "Of course we know all this, but we will take support wherever we can get it, and their numbers are significant. We do keep them on a short leash, however."[65]

In broad terms, politics and eschatology intersect in three related and overlapping movements—the Christian Right, Christian Reconstructionism, and Christian Zionism. Yet there are clear differences between these

---

63. Paul Boyer, "John Darby Meets Saddam Hussein: Foreign Policy and Bible Prophecy," *Chronicle of Higher Education*, 14 February 2003, B11; Sizer, *Christian Zionism*, 247–49; Wagner, "Marching to Zion," 24.

64. Sizer, *Christian Zionism*, 206; Malcom Couch, "When Will the Jews Rebuild Their Temple?," *Moody Monthly*, December 1973, 34–35, 85–92.

65. Wagner, "Marching to Zion," 23 (quote). See Stephen Sizer, *Zion's Christian Soldiers?: The Bible, Israel and the Church* (Nottingham, UK: InterVarsity, 2007); Prusher, "Israel's Unlikely Ally," 1–4; Brent Castillo, "Why Are Evangelicals Supportive of Israel?," *Wichita Eagle*, 20 July 2006, 7A.

movements, especially in their view of the millennium. Moreover, the eschatology of one of these groups—the Christian Right—contradicts its domestic policy. The Christian Right's premillennialism points to an imminent and disastrous end of history. At the same time, it attempts to remake America as do the postmillennialists. Such a paradox has prompted the rise of Christian Reconstructionism—a postmillennial movement desiring to take America back to an Old Testament ethic. Reconstructionism is consistent in its postmillennialism and aspiration to remake America and eventually the entire world. The Christian Right, however, embraces a paradox: it is explicitly premillennial but implicitly postmillennial. Where does Christian Zionism come in? While most Christian Zionists are part of the Christian Right, they have a more narrow focus—support for Israel.

10

Messiahs, Prophets, and End-Time Visions

JUST BEFORE DAWN ON April 19, 1993, the loudspeaker blared, "This is not an assault! Do not fire!" Many of the Branch Davidians, however, "thought it was the last day of the world," and for most of them it was.[1] This type of apocalyptic thinking is not limited to the Branch Davidians. Since 1945 a host of fringe religions have paraded across the American religious landscape, some of them with end-time visions.

Indeed, marginal religions elsewhere in the world have held apocalyptic ideas. In 1992 about twenty thousand members of the Dami sect in Korea were convinced that Christ would return on either October 20 or 28. Scores of them quit their jobs, sold their homes, and left their families; some women even underwent abortions in preparation for their trip to heaven. By 12:10 a.m. on October 29, they were disappointed. Irate members of the sect attacked those responsible for the predictions, and the leader, Lee Jang Rim, was arrested for fraud. Then in October 1994 forty-eight members of the apocalyptic Order of the Solar Temple committed suicide in Switzerland. They expected doomsday to be coming soon.

The Supreme Truth, a Japanese doomsday cult, would strike in March 1995. They set off nerve gas in a Tokyo subway as the opening shot of the final war, which they expected between 1997 and 2000. The members of the cult believed that they would be the sole survivors in this final battle

---

1. Barbara Kantrowitz, "Day of Judment," *Newsweek*, 2 May 1993, 22.

Messiahs, Prophets, and End-Time Visions

in which the West attempts to destroy Japan. An even worse case of end-time related suicides or murders (depending on your view), however, occurred in Uganda in 2000. Members of the Movement for the Restoration of the Ten Commandments believed the world would end on December 31, 1999. When January 1 passed without incident, they adjusted the date to March 17. Doomsday did not come and on March 19 over 775 people committed suicide. The authorities, however, claim tests before they were buried indicated they were poisoned.[2]

AN OVERVIEW OF FRINGE RELIGIONS IN MODERN AMERICA

Throughout Western history most apocalyptic groups have existed on the margins of society and exhibited unusual theological or social characteristics. However, in some ways America has had a millennial mission, and accordingly, apocalyptic bodies have been closer to the mainstream. Nonetheless, nineteenth-century America witnessed a number of fringe groups with a millennial orientation—the Shakers, Mormons, Oneida Community, Seventh-day Adventists, and Jehovah's Witnesses.

In this study, we will use two criteria to categorize fringe religions: their orientation toward society and their point of origin. There are world-rejecting and world-affirming movements.[3] The culture-rejecting groups, usually called sects or cults, clearly state that the majority religion is inadequate or downright heretical. Such groups often exhibit apocalyptic tendencies. To them, the world is hopelessly corrupt and must experience an apocalyptic purging.[4] On the other hand, the world-affirming religions, often associated with the New Age and human potential movements, view the social order less contemptuously than do the world-rejecting groups.

---

2. "South Koreans Disappointed by a New Day," *Wichita Eagle*, 29 October 1992, 1A, 7A; "So Much for Doomsday, South Koreans Find," *Wichita Eagle*, 3 November 1992, 3A; Tom Post, "Mystery of the Solar Temple," *Newsweek*, 17 October 1994, 42-44; Steven Strasser, "A Cloud of Terror—and Suspicion," *Newsweek*, 3 April 1995, 36-37; David Van Biema, "Prophet of Poison," *Time*, 3 April 1995, 28-33; "Death Toll Rises in Uganda Suicide Cult Inferno," AANEWS, 21 March 21 2000, http://www.hartford-hwp.com/archives/36/427.html.

3. Max Weber, *The Sociology of Religion* (Boston: Beacon, 1963) 46-117, 166-83; Ernst Troeltsch, *The Social Teaching of the Christian Churches* (New York: Harper, 1960) 1:331-43; J. Milton Yinger, *Religion, Society, and Individual* (New York: Macmillian, 1957).

4. Bryan R. Wilson, *Religion in Sociological Perspective* (New York: Oxford University Press, 1982) 101-5, 121ff.

While the world must be improved, humanity has enormous potential to bring such change about. World-affirming movements often have a millennial mission. Looking forward to a new age, they maintain that it will not be inaugurated by a catastrophe, but will evolve gradually.[5]

Broadly speaking, the points of origin of fringe religions fall into three categories: Western Christian, occult-mystical, and Eastern.[6] Of these three, Western fringe groups are the most apocalyptic and millennial, Eastern bodies the least. Somewhere in between, occult bodies have their prophets of doom, but often foresee a golden age evolving in the near future.

In this chapter we will categorize apocalyptic fringe religions in modern America as Western, occult, or racist. Most of the racist groups have Christian origins, but we will treat them in a separate category. Many of the occult bodies also incorporate Western apocalyptic elements.

Unfortunately, there is no clear thread that ties these diverse groups together. Unlike most dispensationalists, they do not share common themes; nor do their end-time ideas neatly fit into the pre-, post-, and amillennial categories. They even see the end differently. Some groups view it as an impending cataclysm; others see a new age evolving.

The one element that many fringe apocalyptic movements in modern America do have in common is the context in which they arose—the counterculture and its aftermath. The same atmosphere that fueled the apocalypticism of many premillennialists ignited the fringe groups. The years from the election of John F. Kennedy in 1960 to 1975, when Gerald Ford inaugurated the bicentennial era, were tumultuous and traumatic. These years witnessed several political assassinations. Violence erupted in the civil rights and anti-war movements. Feminism and environmentalism challenged some of the most fundamental assumptions of Western culture, namely, that men have the right to dominate women and that humanity can act with impunity toward nature. Urbanization, science, and technology brought incredible change. Indeed, American society was severely shaken and in many ways permanently transformed.[7]

---

5. Roy Wallis, *The Elementary Forms of the New Religious Life* (Boston: Routledge, 1984) Roy Wallis, *The Rebirth of the Gods: Reflections on the New Religions in the West* (Belfast: University of Belfast, 1978) 6–10.

6. For more detailed ways to classify fringe religions see Richard Kyle, *The Religious Fringe* (Downers Grove, IL: InterVarsity, 1993) 29–30; Ron Enroth, *The Lure of the Cults* (Chappaqua, NY: Christian Herald, 1979) 23–35; J. Gordon Melton and Robert L. Moore, *The Cult Experience* (New York: Pilgrim, 1982) 19–20.

7. Richard Kyle, "The Cults: Why Now and Who Gets Caught?," *Journal of the American Scientific Affiliation* 33/2 (1981) 95; Kyle, *The Religious Fringe*, 183–84; Sydney E. Ahlstrom, "The Traumatic Years: American Religion and Culture in the 60's and

Messiahs, Prophets, and End-Time Visions

The supreme catalyst for all the challenges to the American system was Lyndon Johnson's decision to escalate the Vietnam War. Cynicism toward the political establishment erupted into violence. College students and others agitated for nearly half a decade. To cap off this period, America experienced a series of traumas: Watergate, the resignation of President Nixon, and the collapse of the American-backed regime in Vietnam.[8]

All of these developments helped to foster an apocalyptic mentality in American society at large. "The invention of the atomic bomb began the ... apocalyptic mood," which became very strong in both secular and religious sectors during the 1960s and 1970s. Widespread concern with environmental pollution was a manifestation of the apocalyptic mindset. Apocalypticism was political as well. During the 1960s and 1970s many believed "that the American government [was] beyond reforming and must be destroyed in order for something new and better to take its place."[9]

While the apocalyptic mood could be discerned within many groups, "it was perhaps the strongest in the counterculture." As a consequence, the religious groups that emerged from the counterculture in the West tended to be radical and apocalyptic.[10] Yet by the mid-1970s the counterculture had declined and along with it many fringe religions with their end-time ideas. The new religions that arose in the 1970s and 1980s were world-affirming groups. In particular, the human potential and New Age movements were less apocalyptic and tended to view the coming new age more in evolutionary terms.[11]

WESTERN FRINGE GROUPS

Of the many groups in post-World War II America that can be regarded as fringe religions, that is, sects or cults, we will look first at those that

---

70's," *Theology Today* 36/4 (1980) 510–11; Sydney E. Ahlstrom, "The Radical Turn in Theology and Ethics: Why It Occurred in the 1960s," *Annals of the American Academy of Political and Social Science* 387 (January 1970) 9, 12; Ronald B. Flowers, *Religion in Strange Times* (Macon, GA: Mercer University Press, 1984) 1–27.

8. Ahlstrom, "Radical Turn," 11–12; Ahlstrom, "Traumatic Years," 512–13; Kyle, *Religious Fringe*, 185–86.

9. Ronald Enroth, Edward E. Ericson Jr., and C. Breckinridge, *The Jesus People* (Grand Rapids: Eerdmans, 1972) 182.

10. Enroth, *Jesus People*, 182.

11. Marty E. Marty, "As the New Religions Grow Older," in *Encyclopaedia Britannica, 1986 Book of the Year*, eds. Daphne Daume and J. E. Davis (Chicago: Encyclopaedia Britannica, 1986) 371; Kyle, *Religious Fringe*, 187.

are Western in origin. They differ from Eastern and occult groups in that they generally embrace the Judeo-Christian worldview or have some historic connection with the Christian church. But they are often deviant and bizarre. Some of these groups also believe that the world or this age will end soon.

In Chapter 3 we described apocalyptic groups that originated in nineteenth-century America. Several of them are alive and well in modern America—the Jehovah's Witnesses, Seventh-day Adventists, and Mormons. In this chapter we will note a few Western groups that have developed primarily since 1945: the People's Temple, the Jesus People, the Children of God, the Worldwide Church of God, the Unification Church, the Branch Davidians, and the Lubavitchers. We will focus on the apocalyptic characteristics of these contemporary bodies; more complete descriptions can be found elsewhere.[12] Moreover, the racist groups also have Western and even Christian roots but they will be noted in a different category in this chapter.

Nightmare at Jonestown

"Alert! Alert! Alert! Everybody to the pavilion." The Reverend Jim Jones was using the loudspeaker to summon the members of his People's Temple to their last communion. "Everyone has to die," said Jones. "If you love me as much as I love you, we must all die or be destroyed from the outside." And indeed they did die.[13]

Perhaps the most bizarre religion-based incident of the twentieth century occurred in Jonestown, Guyana, in November 1978. Here more than nine hundred people committed suicide or were murdered because of their involvement with the People's Temple and its leader, Jim Jones.[14]

---

12. For more general descriptions of fringe religions in Modern America see Kyle, *Religious Fringe*; Ruth Tucker, *Another Gospel* (Grand Rapids: Zondervan, 1989); J. Gordon Melton, *Encyclopedic Handbook of Cults in America* (New York: Garland, 1986).

13. Quoted in Tom Mathews, "The Cult of Death," *Newsweek*, 4 December 1978, 38.

14. For more on the Jonestown story see Judith M. Weightman, *Making Sense of the Jonestown Suicides* (Lewiston, NY: E. Mellon, 1983); Philip Kerns, *People's Temple, People's Tomb* (Plainfield, NJ: Logos, 1979); Marshall Kilduff and Ron Jovers, *The Suicide Cult* (New York: Bantam, 1978); Kenneth Wooden, *The Children of Jonestown* (New York: McGraw-Hill, 1981); Ethan Feinsod, *Awake in a Nightmare* (New York: Norton, 1981); Tim Reiterman, *Raven: The Untold Story of the Rev. Jim Jones and His People* (New York: Tarcher/Penguin, 1982).

Messiahs, Prophets, and End-Time Visions

What caused Jim Jones to go off the deep end? Why did over nine hundred people commit suicide?

Most government investigators and journalists interpret the Guyana situation psychologically. They say that Jones may have been insane, and the people may have been brainwashed to commit suicide by a charismatic personality who exercised immense control over them.[15] But behind the tragedy at Jonestown was also an ideology or theology. As John Hall points out, the People's Temple should be regarded as an apocalyptic movement. The apocalyptic mood of American society during the 1960s had made its impact on Jones, especially the racial strife, the political unrest, and the perceived impending nuclear holocaust.[16] A predisposing factor here was Jones's own social background. Born and raised in southern Indiana, a Ku Klux Klan stronghold, he had founded the People's Temple in the 1950s "as a reaction to a cultural situation that was extremely racist." Thus the struggle against racist persecution had been a part of Jones's life from an early stage.[17]

While the roots of the People's Temple can be traced to the revivalistic evangelical tradition, by the time of Jonestown the group had come to resemble an otherworldly apocalyptic cult. They shared with other apocalyptic groups a pessimism about reforming social institutions. Though Jones supported various progressive causes, he had little hope for their success.[18] Accordingly, his prophetic views were more radical than those of most millennial groups: "he focused on an imminent apocalyptic disaster rather than on Christ's millennial salvation." His eschatology set before him the choice of either fighting the beast (the American social and economic system) or collective flight from the impending disaster to set

---

15. James T. Richardson, "People's Temple and Jonestown: A Corrective Comparison and Critique," *Journal for the Scientific Study of Religion* 19/3 (1980) 240; Kyle, *Religious Fringe*, 351.

16. John R. Hall, "The Apocalypse at Jonestown," *In Gods We Trust*, eds. Thomas Robbins and Dick Anthony (New Brunswick, NJ: Transaction, 1981) 248; Kyle, *Religious Fringe*, 351; Stephen C. Rose, *Jesus and Jim Jones* (New York: Pilgrim, 1979) 93–94.

17. Richardson, "People's Temple and Jonestown," 241–42 (quote); H. Paul Chalfant, Robert E. Beckley, and C. Eddie Palmer, *Religion in Contemporary Society* (Sherman Oaks, CA: Alfred, 1981) 276; "Messiah from the Midwest," *Time*, 4 December 1978, 22.

18. Hall, "Apocalypse at Jonestown," 174–75; Kyle, *Religious Fringe*, 351; Richardson, "People's Temple and Jonestown," 249.

up a kingdom of the elect. The People's Temple was more "directed toward the latter possibility."[19]

Even while in Indiana, Jones had adhered to an apocalyptic worldview. He then moved his followers to Redwood Valley in California on the assumption that this area would survive a nuclear holocaust. During these years Jones's apocalyptic vision turned to predictions of "CIA persecution and Nazi-like extermination of blacks." Like many apocalyptic sects or cults, the People's Temple promised a theocratic heaven on Earth in which members could "escape the 'living hell' of society at large." Many of Jones's followers joined the People's Temple with such a hope in mind. For blacks in particular, the temple promised some immediate relief from persecution rather than some otherworldly hope. Gradually developing communal characteristics, "the People's Temple more and more [came] to exist as an ark of survival."[20]

In 1977 the People's Temple came under closer investigation by the media, which the church perceived as CIA persecution. As the scrutiny mounted and defectors from the temple increased, it became doubtful whether Jones could maintain his haven in the United States. He was "reduced to decrying the web of 'evil' powers" that had entrapped him and searching for another post-apocalyptic sanctuary—that is, one that would survive the impending catastrophe. He went to Jonestown hoping to find a haven. But he could not be sure that Jonestown was the promised land. Unable to "trust the Guyanese government," he was "considering seeking final asylum" in the Soviet Union or Cuba.[21]

But even this hope came unraveled when Jones became convinced that the church's enemies were about to descend on Jonestown. Without any prospect of victory over his enemies, Jones was convinced that the only recourse for the People's Temple was to "abandon the apocalyptic hell by an act of mass suicide." The opponents of the temple would then no longer be a threat: "there could be no recriminations against the dead." Moreover, this mass suicide "could achieve the otherworldly salvation Jones had promised his more religious followers."[22]

19. Hall, "Apocalypse at Jonestown," 175–76 (quote); Kyle, *Religious Fringe*, 351.

20. Hall, "Apocalypse at Jonestown," 175–76, 186–89 (quote); Kyle, *Religious Fringe*, 352, 354; "Messiah from the Midwest," 22; Robert S. Ellwood and Harry B. Partin, *Religious and Spiritual Groups in Modern America* (2nd ed.; Englewood Cliffs, NJ: Prentice-Hall, 1988) 300.

21. Hall, "Apocalypse at Jonestown," 186–89 (quote); Kyle, *Religious Fringe*, 354; Kenneth Labich, "Ghosts of Jonestown," *Newsweek*, 11 December 1978, 29.

22. Hall, "Apocalypse at Jonestown," 186–89 (quote); Kyle, *Religious Fringe*, 354;

The Last Days and the Jesus People

"The last days are upon us ... and I believe that it won't be long until we see the Second Coming of the Lord," proclaimed Chuck Smith, pastor of Calvary Chapel.[23] His words were echoed throughout the Jesus movement. Aside from the simple gospel, no doctrine characterized the Jesus People more than did the belief that the last days have arrived.

The Jesus movement refers to a social phenomenon involving numerous young people whose religious activities revolved around a strict literal interpretation of the Bible and other trappings of conservative Christianity. The phenomenon began in the mid-1960s and continued in a modified and reduced form into the 1980s. Though the Jesus movement falls largely within the framework of evangelical and fundamentalist Christianity, it has produced some deviant groups that have been labeled as cults.[24]

Coming out of the counterculture, the Jesus People had characteristics shaped by that movement, namely, a subjective approach to life, an alienation from the dominant culture, and an apocalyptic hope. Smacking of fundamentalism as well, their faith was Christ-centered, Bible-centered, and focused on the simple gospel—the message that Jesus saves.[25]

Everything in the Jesus movement—its views on evangelicalism, politics, culture, history, and the church—hinged on the belief that this world was in its last days. In fact, the Jesus People not only reflected the apocalyptic mentality so prevalent in the 1960s, but carried it further. Most of the Jesus People could not imagine themselves growing old and dying a natural death. They fervently believed that they were God's chosen instruments to give the world one last chance to repent.[26]

"Nightmare in Jonestown," *Time*, 4 December 1978, 19.

23. Quoted in Enroth et al., *Jesus People*, 179.

24. Chalfant, Beckley, and Palmer, *Religion in Contemporary Society*, 267. For a general description of the Jesus People see Enroth et al., *Jesus People*; Michael McFadden, *The Jesus Revolution* (New York: Harper & Row, 1972); Edward E. Plowman, *The Jesus Movement in America* (Elgin, IL: David C. Cook, 1971); Robert S. Ellwood Jr., *One Way: The Jesus Movement and Its Meaning* (Englewood Cliffs, NJ: Prentice-Hall, 1973).

25. James T. Richardson and Rex Davis, "Experiential Fundamentalism: Revisions of Orthodoxy and the Jesus Movement," *Journal of the Academy of Religion* 5 (1983) 398; Christopher R. Stones, "The Jesus People: Fundamentalism and Changes in Factors Associated with Conservatism," *Journal for the Scientific Study of Religion* 17/1 (1978) 155–58; Enroth et al., *Jesus People*, 161–64; McFadden, *Jesus Revolution*, 7–10; Jack Balswick, "The Jesus Movement: A Generational Interpretation," *Journal of Social Issues* 30/3 (23–27).

26. Ellwood, *One Way*, 186–93; Enroth et al., *Jesus People*, 179–87; "The New Rebel

While apocalyptic hope unified the Jesus movement, there were still many differences on how and when the world would end. The Jesus People overwhelmingly embraced premillennialism, but held to three premillennial views regarding the rapture: pretribulationalism, midtribulationalism, and posttribulationism. All three could be found within the Jesus movement. Yet profoundly influenced by Hal Lindsey's *Late Great Planet Earth*, most accepted the pretribulational view. However, a substantial number insisted that the church would go through the tribulation. Some even went so far as to call the pretribulational rapture a "damnable heresy."[27]

Prominent among the posttribulationists were the Children of God (COG), the most controversial of the Jesus People groups. Born of the counterculture, they sprang from the social crises of the late 1960s. Their founder, David Berg (1919-94), took them beyond the confines of orthodox Christianity into some deviant beliefs and practices. Consequently, the mainstream of the Jesus People ostracized them.[28]

Fervently apocalyptic, the Children of God, who in 1979 changed their name to the Family of Love, were driven by their belief in the imminent end of the world. "Probably the most important COG teaching is 'End Time Prophecy,'" says Jack Sparks. "This concept is their key to understanding every part of the Christian Life."[29] Indeed, contrary to most Jesus People, the Children of God even engaged in some date setting.

Expecting the return of Christ and his thousand-year rule to be soon, the Children of God saw the present system, especially that of the Western world, as so corrupt that no reformation was possible. It had to end before a new order could begin. In their view the final collapse "will come when communism takes over the western nations and paves the way for the anti-Christ," declared Ruth Tucker. Under this individual's rule, professing Christians will deny the faith and receive the mark of the beast mentioned

---

Cry: Jesus Is Coming," *Time*, June 1971, 59; Richardson and Davis, "Experiential Fundamentalism," 399-400.

27. Enroth et al., *Jesus People*, 186-88; Ellwood, *One Way*, 90-92; David Gordon, "The Jesus People: An Identity Synthesis," *Urban Life and Culture* 3/2 (1974) 162-63.

28. Melton, *Encyclopedic Handbook of Cults in America*, 154; Kyle, *Religious Fringe*, 361; Daniel Cohen, *The New Believers* (New York: Ballantine, 1975) 3. For a general description of the Children of God see David E. Van Zandt, *Living in the Children of God* (Princeton, NJ: Princeton University Press, 1991); Ellwood, *One Way*, 101.

29. Jack Sparks, *The Mindbenders* (Nashville: T. Nelson, 1979) 166; Ellwood, *One Way*, 101.

in the Book of Revelation. But the Children of God will stand "as God's faithful remnant of 144,000."[30]

Firmly convinced of the coming downfall of the United States, Berg had left the country by the early 1970s, and some of the Children of God followed him. One "Mo-letter" (as Berg's letters were called) warned that the comet Kohoutek would destroy America: "You in the U.S. have only until January [1974] to get out of the States before some kind of disaster." Typical of most apocalyptic groups, the Children of God went wild and insisted that the comet represented the final sign of America's doom and a fulfillment of prophecy. Though they believed that the whole world would end soon, they were obsessed with the downfall of America in particular, most likely through a communist takeover.[31]

The Children of God expected a posttribulational rapture: the saints would be persecuted during the tribulation and drawn up into heaven at the end. In some ways "Berg's eschatology resembled dispensational premillennialism," but he emphasized the coming tribulation and a subsequent rapture.[32] In still other ways his eschatology—especially his date setting and exclusivism—resembled the systems of the Jehovah's Witnesses and the Worldwide Church of God. Berg's countdown to the end began with the "End of the Time of the Gentiles" in 1968. In the mid-1980s, the Antichrist would reveal himself, and the rapture would occur around 1993. After Christ's return the Children of God would serve as important officials during the millennium.[33]

---

30. Tucker, *Another Gospel*, 240 (quote); Melton, *Encyclopedic Handbook of Cults in America*, 156; Roy Wallis, "Observations on the Children of God," *Sociological Review* 24/4 (1976) 818–19; Ellwood, *One Way*, 102.

31. Lowell D. Streiker, *The Cults Are Coming* (Nashville: Abingdon, 1978) 52 (quote); Roy Wallis, *Salvation and Protest* (New York: St. Martin's, 1979) 58–59; Wallis, "Observations on the Children of God," 814; Leon McBeth, *Strange New Religions* (rev. ed.; Nashville: Broadman, 1977) 51; Rex Davis and James T. Richardson, "The Organization and Functioning of the Children of God," *Sociological Analysis* 37/4 (1976) 325–26.

32. Tucker, *Another Gospel*, 240–41 (quote); Van Zandt, *Living in the Children of God*, 24; Kyle, *Religious Fringe*, 363.

33. David G. Bromley and Anson D. Shupe Jr., *Strange Gods* (Boston: Beacon, 1981) 29–31; Wallis, "Observations on the Children of God," 818–19; Tucker, *Another Gospel*, 240–41; Kyle, *Religious Fringe*, 366.

The End According to Herbert Armstrong

Founded in the 1930s by Herbert W. Armstrong (1892–1986), the Worldwide Church of God draws its ideas from Seventh-day Adventism, the Jehovah's Witnesses, Judaism, Mormonism, and British Israelism. Until recently the Worldwide Church of God was regarded as an unorthodox religion because of its rejection of many basic Christian doctrines. Since Armstrong's death, however, the church has moved toward orthodox Christianity.[34] Moreover, repudiating its prophecy-mongering past, it now refuses to speculate when the end will come. Thus our comments will relate to the Worldwide Church of God as it existed under Herbert Armstrong.

While the Worldwide Church of God maintained a number of distinctives—Sabbath keeping, Old Testament dietary practices, and rejection of the Trinity—its teachings revolved heavily around the end times. Among the marks of Armstrong's prophetic doctrines were British Israelism, a modified dispensationalism, the belief that world history spans six thousand years, pronouncements relating to nineteenth- and twentieth-century Britons and Americans, and an emphasis on the Old Testament.

Basic to the beliefs of the Worldwide Church of God was British Israelism (or Anglo-Israelism), which has been noted in chapter 7. The central idea was that after the dispersion of the ten lost tribes of Israel, they migrated to northern Europe, where they became the ancestors of the Saxons who invaded England. Thus the people of England (and by extension, the United States and the peoples of the British Commonwealth of Nations) are the literal descendants of the ten lost tribes of Israel. So Britain and the United States are special objects of God's promises and blessings.[35]

---

34. J. Gordon Melton, *The Encyclopedia of American Religions* (Wilmington, NC: McGrath, 1978) 1:471; William J. Whalen, *Strange Gods* (Huntington, IN: Our Sunday Visitor, 1981) 28–29; "Worldwide Church of God Edges toward Orthodoxy," *Christianity Today*, 9 November 1992, 57; Mark A. Kellner, "Move toward Orthodoxy Causes Big Income Loss," *Christianity Today*, 24 April 1995, 53; David Neff, "The Road to Orthodoxy," *Christianity Today*, 2 October 1995, 15: Ruth Tucker, "From the Fringe to the Fold," *Christianity Today*, 15 July 1996, 26–32. For general information on the Worldwide Church of God see Joseph Hopkins, *The Armstrong Empire* (Grand Rapids: Eerdmans, 1974); Herman Hock, *A True History of the Church* (Pasadena, CA: Ambassador College, 1959); Marion J. McNair, *Armstrongism: Religion ... or Rip-Off?* (Orlando, FL: Pacific Charters, 1977); David Robinson, *Herbert Armstrong's Tangled Web* (Tulsa, OK: Hadden, 1980).

35. Melton, *Encyclopedic Handbook of Cults in America*, 100; Hopkins, *Armstrong Empire*, 66–88; Tucker, *Another Gospel*, 207–8; Horton Davies, *Christian Deviations* (Philadelphia: Westminster, 1985) 74–85; Whalen, *Strange Gods*, 32–33; Robert Katz and Richard H. Popkin, *Messianic Revolution: Radical and Religious Politics to the End*

The Worldwide Church of God also "adopted the dispensational view of the history of the Church of God" drawn from the Book of Revelation. The seven churches of Revelation 2–3 were considered to be the seven church ages. "The Worldwide Church identifies itself as the Church at Philadelphia, which was to appear just before the end time events described in the Book of Revelation," asserts Gordon Melton. It was widely believed that the tribulation would start in 1972 and that the church would have to flee the United States.[36] This belief was based on Armstrong's view of history. Like most millennialists he equated each day of creation with a thousand years. God created the world in six days and rested on the seventh, thus establishing the pattern for human history. History would extend for six thousand years and be followed by a thousand-year millennial rest. From his belief that God had created the world in 4025 BCE, Armstrong concluded that the end would come around 1975. Though he denied setting dates, he did "suggest" that certain dates fit God's time schedule.[37]

A key element in Armstrong's prophetic scheme was based on Leviticus 26:18: "I will punish you seven times more for your sins." Dating the prophecy to 717 BCE, Armstrong concluded that God would withhold his blessings from his chosen people for 2,520 years (7 years of 360 days). Subtracting 717 from 2,520, Armstrong reached the early nineteenth century. Nothing prophetic happened around 1800. However, as Armstrong pointed out, America and Britain began to grow in power and size about this time.[38] He then milked the Old Testament for anything that might match current events. Micah 5 speaks of the remnant of Jacob (which Armstrong interpreted as Britain and America) being cut off. Armstrong noted that God continued to bless his chosen people—Britain and America—until about 1950; but after 1950 Britain's empire was nearly gone, and America did not fare well in the Korean and Vietnam Wars. "Why can't the United States whip little Vietnam?" Armstrong asked. He concluded that the decline of God's chosen people was under way, which was to take place

---

of the Second Millennium (New York: Hill and Wang, 1998) 170–204.

36. Melton, *Encyclopedic Handbook of Cults in America*, 100 (quote); Hopkins, *Armstrong Empire*, 89–100; "Worldwide Church of God Edges toward Orthodoxy," 57.

37. Herbert W. Armstrong and Garner Ted Armstrong, *The Wonderful World of Tomorrow* (Pasadena, CA: Ambassador College, 1966) 3; Tucker, *Another Gospel*, 208.

38. Herbert W. Armstrong, *United States and Britain in Prophecy* (New York: Everest House, 1980) 130–60; Tucker, *Another Gospel*, 208–9; Hopkins, *Armstrong Empire*, 84–85.

before the beginning of the tribulation and at the hands of the ten-nation European alliance.[39]

Another quirk of Armstrong's system was his fascination with the number nineteen. Noting that the Earth, moon, and sun come into near conjunction once every nineteen years, he concluded that God would work in nineteen-year cycles. That one of these cycles ended in 1972 is what led to the suggestion that the tribulation would begin in 1972. When this prediction failed, he adjusted his dates to a time in the near future. Nevertheless, the failure of this prophecy caused hardship among his followers and havoc in his empire.[40]

The Lord of the Second Advent

"We are living at a point in time unlike any since the beginning of history," declared the Unification Church. The church's leader, Sun Myung Moon (b. 1920), says that the last days are at hand. Humankind now has the opportunity to usher in the kingdom of God. Such opportunities have existed in the past, but humanity has bungled them. In terms of political power, converts, and finances, the second half of the twentieth century was a unique time to build God's kingdom on Earth.[41]

The Unification Church is one of the most controversial new religions to arrive on the contemporary American scene. Its beliefs are a syncretic mixture of many religious impulses. The recipe for Moon's religion combines ingredients from Eastern and Western systems, seasoned by mysticism from Moon's own revelations.[42]

Many millennial bodies withdraw from society and have few expectations for changing the world. Not so with the Unification Church. It is a messianic movement desiring to unite all people into one religion. The church aims to usher in a new age, a new moral order in which all religions

39. Armstrong, *United States and Britain in Prophecy*, 187–96; Tucker, *Another Gospel*, 210; Hopkins, *Armstrong Empire*, 84–85.

40. Herbert W. Armstrong, *The Incredible Human Potential* (Pasadena, CA: Worldwide Church of God, 1980) 123; Tucker, *Another Gospel*, 210–11; William Martin, "Waiting for the End," *Atlantic Monthly*, June 1982, 35; Tom Sine, "Bringing Down the Final Curtain," *Sojourners* 13/6 (June–July 1984) 12.

41. *Outline of the Divine Principle: Level 4* (New York: Holy Spirit Association for the Unification of World Christianity, 1980) 214 (quote); Bromley and Shupe, *Strange Gods*, 34.

42. John Newport, *Christ and the New Consciousness* (Nashville: Broadman, 1978) 122; McBeth, *Strange New Religions*, 11; Whalen, *Strange Gods*, 55.

Messiahs, Prophets, and End-Time Visions

are unified within itself. The church's objectives are theocratic—it seems to aspire to become, either overtly or covertly, the dominant religion in the world.[43]

Like many new religious groups in modern America, the Unification Church has placed considerable emphasis on doctrines of the end times. But most other groups have promoted a version of premillennialism. Moon's church has advocated a form of postmillennialism. Instead of looking for a cataclysmic end of history, the Unification Church sees the last days as a time when human beings will turn away from the selfishness of the past to a future of God-centeredness.[44]

J. Isamu Yamamoto divides the core teachings of the Unification Church into three eras: the first Adam, the Second Adam, and the Lord of the Second Advent. The first Adam and Eve were to establish the kingdom of heaven on Earth through their offspring. Instead, they fell into sin. The Second Adam, Jesus Christ, was to save humanity spiritually and physically, but his crucifixion frustrated God's plan for humanity. Jesus paid only for humankind's spiritual salvation.[45] Because Jesus failed to marry and produce the perfect family, another Messiah is needed to complete the physical aspect of salvation. This is the job of the Lord of the Second Advent, who must come to establish the kingdom on Earth. Although the *Divine Principle*, the church's scripture, does not state that Moon is the Messiah, it does establish conditions that only Moon fulfills. The Unification Church is, then, "a millennial Christian movement with the interesting twist that the anticipated Second Coming of Christ will have little to do with Jesus of Nazareth."[46]

---

43. Arthur S. Parsons, "Messianic Personalism: A Role Analysis of the Unification Church," *Journal for the Scientific Study of Religion* 25/2 (1986) 141–42; Whalen, *Strange Gods*, 57; Kyle, *Religious Fringe*, 330; Flowers, *Religion in Strange Times*, 105–6. See also David G. Bromley and David D. Shupe Jr., *Moonies in America* (Beverly Hills, CA: Sage, 1979) 243, 256.

44. Tucker, *Another Gospel*, 255; Mose Durst, *To Bigotry, No Sanction: The Reverend Sun Myung Moon and the Unification Church* (Chicago: Regnery Gateway, 1984) 42; Kyle, *Religious Fringe*, 337; Gordon L. Anderson, "The Unification Vision of the Kingdom of God on Earth," in *The Coming Kingdom*, eds. M. Darrol Bryant and Donald W. Dayton (Barrington, NY: International Religious Foundation, 1983) 209–20.

45. J. Isamu Yamamoto, "Unification Church," in *A Guide to Cults and New Religions*, ed. Ronald Enroth et al. (Downers Grove, IL: InterVarsity, 1983) 156–57; George Braswell Jr., *Understanding Sectarian Groups in America* (Nashville: Broadman, 1986) 113; Melton, *Encyclopedic Handbook of Cults in America*, 195; Newport, *Christ and the New Consciousness*, 122–23.

46. Bromley and Shupe, *Strange Gods*, 35 (quote); *Outline of the Divine Principle*, 199–214; Newport, *Christ and the New Consciousness*, 123–24; Yamamoto, "Unification

The *Divine Principle* also places great emphasis on the number two thousand. God took two thousand years from Abraham to Jesus to prepare the world for the first Messiah; for the last two thousand years God has been preparing the world for the second Messiah. The *Divine Principle* implies that the second Messiah could come at any moment, if he has not already.[47] For the kingdom of God will be ushered in when the Unification Church has brought sufficient change to the world. "The Kingdom of Heaven cannot be realized by supernatural miracles but only by man's fulfilling his responsibility to solve all of the problems in a realistic way." In the 1960s Moon predicted that the kingdom would be achieved in 1967. Later he revised this figure to 1981. Because the world was still not ready for the kingdom, Moon postponed the date to 2000.[48] Its coming will be an age of harmony, not a catastrophe.

The Messiah of Waco

"Fueled by kerosene," flames quickly consumed Ranch Apocalypse, killing "86 Branch Davidians—including 17 children."[49] How could this happen? In part, the religious freedom guaranteed by the First Amendment leads to such bizarre action. "If people want to follow Donald Duck, so be it. The First Amendment guarantees neither taste nor truth," says Leo Sandon, professor of religion at Florida State. But when Donald Duck turns out to be Jim Jones, Charles Manson, or David Koresh, people die—as they did at Waco in April of 1993.[50]

But religious freedom can account for only part of the story. Psychological explanations abound. David Koresh, the leader of the Branch Davidians, had obvious mental problems, especially a messianic delusion.

Church," 158–59; Tucker, *Another Gospel*, 251; Young Oon Kim, *Unification Theology* (New York: Holy Spirit Association for the Unification of World Christianity, 1980) 183; Braswell, *Understanding Sectarian Groups*, 120–21; James Bjornstad, *The Moon Is Not the Son* (Minneapolis: Bethany Fellowship, 1976) 58–59.

47. Yamamoto, "Unification Church," 158–59; Newport, *Christ and the New Consciousness*, 124; Braswell, *Understanding Sectarian Groups*, 120–21; Frederick Sontag, *Sun Myung Moon and the Unification Church* (Nashville: Abingdon, 1977).

48. *Outline of the Divine Principle*, 204 (quote); Bromley and Shupe, *Strange Gods*, 34–35.

49. "The Killing Ground," *Newsweek*, 3 May 1993, 20.

50. Kenneth L. Woodward, "Cultic America: A Tower of Babel," *Newsweek*, 15 March 1993, 60 (quote).

Others have used less charitable terms to describe him—"a religious psycho" or "the wacko from Waco."[51]

Koresh's chosen names and title betray his obvious messianic delusion. He changed his name from Vernon Howell to David Koresh, declaring himself to be prefigured by two kings mentioned in the Old Testament. From Koresh or Cyrus the Great, the leader of the Persian Empire, he gained his ruling authority. David, of course, referred to King David. This placed Koresh in the line of Christ. But the title "the Lamb of the Book of Revelation" is even more outrageous. Rather than identify the Lamb with Christ, he declared, "I am the Branch . . . the Lamb," thus reinforcing his claim to have ultimate truth.[52]

Koresh's puppet-like followers also had obvious psychological problems. They submitted themselves to the total control of a ninth-grade dropout with a charismatic personality and were willing to die for their cause.[53] That his followers were only a handful must have been a blow to the ego of someone who believed himself to be a prophet. This situation may have made it easier for him to lead his flock into a final inferno.

But psychology cannot provide all the answers. The Branch Davidians had a history and a theology. They were a split-off from a split-off. In 1959 the Branch Davidians splintered from the Davidian Seventh-day Adventists, who had broken from the mainline Seventh-day Adventists thirty years earlier.[54] The longstanding millennial tradition of Adventism significantly influenced the Branch Davidians and Koresh's ideas. Through the years, of course, the mainstream Seventh-day Adventists had lowered their expectations of an impending end-time and opted for institutional development instead. But some of the split-offs maintained and even accelerated the apocalypticism of earlier Adventism. In addition, from the time of William Miller and Ellen G. White, Adventism has housed a number of prophetic voices. In David Koresh the apocalyptic extremes of this

51. Stephen D. O'Leary, *Arguing the Apocalypse* (New York: Oxford University Press, 1994) 227; James Ridgeway, "Armies of God," *Valley Voice*, 14 May 1993, 16.

52. Kenneth R. Samples et al., *Prophets of the Apocalypse* (Grand Rapids: Baker, 1994) 60, 69–70 (quotes); James M. Wall, "Eager for the End," *Christian Century*, 5 May 1993, 475.

53. Barbara Kantrowitz, "The Messiah of Waco," *Newsweek*, 15 March 1993, 56–58; Melinda Beck, "Children of the Cult," *Newsweek*, 17 May 1993, 48–53; Mark E. DeVries, "David Koresh and the Apocalyptic Imagination," *Perspectives*, June 1993, 3.

54. William L. Pitts Jr., "Davidians and Branch Davidians, 1929–1987," in *Armageddon in Waco*, ed. Stuart A. Wright (Chicago: University of Chicago Press, 1995) 1995) 20–38; Samples et al., *Prophets of the Apocalypse*, 29–30; "Apocalypse in Waco," *America*, 22 May 1993, 3.

tradition came home to roost.[55] In all fairness, however, it must be noted that the Branch Davidians distorted the broader Adventist tradition. The cultic trademarks of the Branch Davidians—widespread intimidation and abuse, a perverted view of sex and marriage, and military-like discipline—cannot be found in mainstream Adventism.[56]

In professing his lineage from King David, Koresh had established himself as a messianic figure on a divine mission—namely, to open the seven seals of Revelation. These seals were the core of Koresh's eschatology. He embraced something resembling a premillennial posttribulational view of the end. Koresh believed that humanity had already entered the tribulation prophesied in Revelation. The tribulation was a necessary purging prior to the Second Coming of Christ and the millennium.[57] In addition, the opening of the seven seals would precede the end of the world. With the opening of each seal, the Lamb would unleash another judgment upon the world. His disciples saw themselves as God's remnant, chosen to rule with the Messiah during the millennium.[58]

More specifically, Koresh saw himself as carrying out the judgment of the sixth seal. The sixth seal of Revelation 6:12–17 involves several cataclysmic events. When government agents surrounded the Branch Davidians in their compound at Mt. Carmel, Koresh interpreted this confrontation with the government as one of the events associated with the opening of the sixth seal. The government agents, who were part of the evil world order (Babylon), were simply carrying out their prophesied role. Their attack on Mt. Carmel would trigger the end of the world.[59] We know the rest of the story. Koresh and his followers went to a fiery death. The confrontation may not have been the fiery seal destroying the world—but it certainly was for the Branch Davidians.

---

55. David G. Bromley and Edward D. Silver, "The Davidian Tradition," in *Armageddon in Waco*, 56–57; Samples et al., *Prophets of the Apocalypse*, 36–37, 98–119; Pitts, "Davidians and Branch Davidians," 30–36.

56. Raymond Contrell, "History and Fatal Theology of the Branch Davidians," *Adventist Today*, May–June 1993, 5–7; Samples et al., *Prophets of the Apocalypse*, 97.

57. Bromley and Silver, "The Davidian Tradition," 58; Paul Boyer, "A Brief History of the End of Time," *New Republic*, 17 May 1993, 30.

58. Bromley and Silver, "Davidian Tradition," 59; Samples et al., *Prophets of the Apocalypse*, 79.

59. Samples, et al., *Prophets of the Apocalypse*, 80–81; Kantrowitz, "Messiah of Waco," 57; George J. Church, "The End Is Near?," *Time*, 26 April 1993, 32.

Messiahs, Prophets, and End-Time Visions

A Jewish Messiah in New York

As we saw in chapters 4-9, many fundamentalist Christians believe in the impending return of Christ. They view the establishment of the Israeli state and the Six-Day War as the fulfillment of prophecy. Some even insist that the Jewish temple must be rebuilt in Jerusalem before Christ will return.

Orthodox Judaism maintains similar ideas. More liberal Jews depersonalize the messianic concept, seeing it as an era of peace rather than an individual. Not so with the Orthodox Jews. They view the Old Testament as literally as Christian fundamentalists do the entire Bible. Refusing to believe that Jesus Christ has fulfilled the Old Testament prophecies, they look for a future Messiah.[60]

Orthodox Judaism has its ultra-orthodox wing, the Hasidic Jews. A conservative branch of the Hasidic Jews is the Chabad Lubavitch movement. According to the Lubavitch tradition, during every generation there lives at least one righteous Jew who meets the qualifications for the Messiah. In recent years the Lubavitchers even went so far as to set up a toll-free Messiah hotline and to carry beepers so that they could be reached immediately when the Messiah arrives. They tapped their leader Menachem Mendel Schneerson of Brooklyn as the prime candidate for Messiah.[61]

A prominent rabbi, Schneerson had an outstanding Jewish pedigree: a brilliant scholar in Jewish law, math, and science; a student of seventeen languages; a descendant of the founder of Hasidism; and a rabbi's son. Like the Christian fundamentalists he saw current events—the establishment of the Israeli state, the collapse of the Soviet Union, and the first Persian Gulf War—as the final events preceding the Messiah's arrival.[62] In particular, he used the Persian Gulf War to stir up apocalyptic expectations, for according to a Midrashic prophecy the Messiah would come in the year of a great confrontation in the Arabian Gulf. In fact, Schneerson predicted that the Messiah would come by September 1991. Despite this misfire Lubavitchers still looked for the Messiah, probably Schneerson himself. But disaster struck—Schneerson died in 1994. Some Lubavitchers still did

---

60. Russell Chandler, *Doomsday* (Ann Arbor, MI: Servant, 1993) 214; Arthur Hertzberg, ed., *Judaism* (New York: George Braziller, 1962) 210-20.

61. "Zealots for the Television Age," *New Statesman and Society*, 15 May 1992, 21; Chandler, *Doomsday*, 213; Os Guiness, *Fit Bodies, Fat Minds* (Grand Rapids: Baker, 1994) 66.

62. Allen Lesser, "Waiting for the End of the World," *Humanist*, September 1992, 19; Chandler, *Doomsday*, 214.

not give up on Schneerson—they expected him to be raised from the dead as the Messiah.[63]

OCCULT AND NEW AGE PREDICTIONS

The end could come in any one of many forms. Occult prophets and New Age seers provide us with a variety of options. End-time predictions "range from a violent apocalypse, floods, pestilence, and utter chaos to utopian visions of technological breakthrough and peace for the Age of Aquarius."[64] On the whole, the occult prophets foresee an impending catastrophe, but many New Agers view the future as an era of enlightenment.

Prophets of Doom

"The future is frightening," said Marie Julie in 1880. "The Earth will be like a vast cemetery. Corpses of the impious and the just will cover it. The Earth will tremble to its foundations, then great waves will agitate the sea and invade the continents."[65] This view of the future, especially the years around 2000, as noted in chapter 6, is shared by many occult prophets. These doomsday seers could fill an entire volume, but we will note only three—Nostradamus, Edgar Cayce, and Jean Dixon.

Nostradamus may be the world's most famous prophet. (We have encountered him in chapters 1–6 and will do so again in chapter 13). Michel de Notredame (1503–66) may have lived in the sixteenth century, but his prophecies address issues ranging from his day to the late twentieth century and beyond. In particular, his predictions regarding the end of the twentieth century have intrigued millions, catapulting his writings to record sales.

How accurate are his predictions? Nostrdamus's vague quatrains are subject to varied interpretations. His supporters claim an 85–90 percent accuracy rate for his prophecies. But according to Daniel Cohen, "his followers usually credit the master with predicting whatever it is that they

---

63. Lesser, "Waiting for the End of the World," 19; Chandler, *Doomsday*, 214–15; "Zealots for the Television Age," 21; "Lubavitcher Rabbi Schneerson Dies," *Christian Century*, 29 June 1994, 636.

64. John Hogue, *The Millennium Book of Prophecy* (San Francisco: Harper, 1994) inside cover.

65. Quoted in ibid., 83.

Messiahs, Prophets, and End-Time Visions

already believe." Detractors such as James Randi claim his quatrains are either inaccurate or allegorical nonsense.[66]

Whether seer or charlatan, current interest in Nostradamus rests on his prophecies regarding the modern world. He has been credited with predicting communism, the creation of the state of Israel, nuclear warfare, the AIDS epidemic, and the first Persian Gulf War. But most important, his prediction of a cataclysm at the end of this millennium sent chills through the spines of those who believe his prophecies.[67]

> In the year 1999 and seven months
> The great King of terror will come from the sky.
> He will bring back to life the great king of the Mongols,
> Before and after war reigns happily unrestrained.

Nostradamus expected the world to go beyond 1999. Although the world will be shattered by global conflict, famine, and pestilence, despair will give way to hope. Eventually there will come a gradual reawakening and world peace. Nostradamus's end-time scenario bears some resemblance to Christian eschatology, namely, the destruction followed by a golden age. And he even refers to an Antichrist.[68] But on the whole, Nostradamus brings us an end without God; political and military activities—not divine intervention—determine the end-time events.

Edgar Cayce (1877–1945) is well known for many occult activities, including his prophecies. This so-called sleeping prophet founded the Association for Research and Enlightenment in 1931. It still continues his work, especially by promoting his writings on physical healing, astrology, diet, reincarnation, and prophecy, including interpretations of biblical prophecy. While in a self-induced trance, Cayce would make pronouncements on many subjects. Some events he predicted successfully include the Great Depression, the union of Austria and Germany, the death of two

---

66. Daniel Cohen, *Waiting for the Apocalypse* (Buffalo: Prometheus, 1983) 248; James Randi, *The Mask of Nostradamus* (Buffalo: Prometheus, 1993) 235–44; Chandler, *Doomsday*, 67.

67. Daniel Cohen, *Prophets of Doom* (Brookfield, CT: Millbrook, 1992) 71; Jean-Charles de Fontbrune, *Nostradamus into the Twenty-First Century* (New York: Holt, 1982) 133–54; A.T. Mann, *Millennium Prophecies* (Rockport, MA: Element, 1992) 63–64; Dava Sobel, "The Resurrection of Nostradamus," *Omni* 16/3 (December 1993) 48; Peter N. Stearns, *Millennium III, Century XXI* (Boulder, CO: Westview, 1996) 39–41.

68. Peter Lorie, *Nostradamus* (New York: Simon & Schuster, 1933) 66, 98–105; Cohen, *Prophets of Doom*, 71–72; *Prophecies on World Events by Nostradamus*, ed. Stewart Robb (New York: Liveright, 1961) 135–40.

American presidents while in office, the Russian-German clash, and the end of World War II in 1945.[69]

Before his death in 1945, Cayce prophesied many catastrophic events that would begin in 1958 and run to the end of the century. While he did not predict doomsday, the magnitude of the disasters he prophesied point in that direction. Much of the North American continent will break up and slide into the sea; Japan will experience a similar fate; rising oceans will inundate coastal areas throughout the globe; earthquakes and volcanoes will wreak terrible havoc; and the lost civilization of Atlantis will rise again, probably in the Caribbean Sea.[70]

While Cayce twisted prophetic scriptures, the Bible—especially Daniel and Revelation—heavily influenced his thinking. In fact, he put a Christian veneer on many of his prophecies. He believed that the natural disasters coming around 2000 point to the Second Coming of Christ and will be followed by the millennium and a new age.[71]

During the 1960s Jeane Dixon became an American legend, largely because she had forecast the assassination of John F. Kennedy. She had a number of other successful predictions, along with many misfires. Of particular interest is her disclosure relative to end-time events. On February 5, 1962, the day of the great Aquarian conjunction, a child of the East was born. Dixon saw this child as revolutionizing the world's religions and governments. His power would reach its zenith in 1999, "when a terrible holocaust will shock the world's peoples into a true renewal." At first Dixon regarded this child as a new Messiah, but then she decided that he was the Antichrist.[72]

---

69. See Jess Stearn, *Edgar Cayce: The Sleeping Prophet* (New York: New American Library, 1969) 16–32; Richard Woods, *The Occult Revolution* (New York: Herder, 1971) 160–65; James Bjornstad, *Twentieth Century Prophecy* (Minneapolis: Dimension, 1969) 84–89; Kyle, *Religious Fringe*, 269; John Godwin, *Occult America* (Garden City, NY: Doubleday, 1972) 100–111.

70. Mann, *Millennium Prophecies*, 86–88; Stearn, *Edgar Cayce, Modern Prophet* (New York: Gramercy, 1990) 39–62; Samuel McCracken, "Apocalyptic Thinking," *Commentary*, October 1971, 65–66; Moira Timms, *Prophecies and Prediction* (Santa Cruz, CA: Unity, 1980) 153–56; Marin Ebon, *Prophecy in Our Time* (New York: New American Library, 1986) 35–36.

71. Mann, *Millennium Prophecies*, 90–91; Cohen, *Prophets of Doom*, 73–74; Bjornstad, *Twentieth Century Prophecy*, 113–26; Charles Berlitz, *Doomsday: 1999 A.D.* (Garden City, NY: Doubleday, 1981) 52–53.

72. Woods, *Occult Revolution*, 165–68 (quote); Ruth Montgomery, *A Gift of Prophecy* (New York: Bantam, 1965) 103, 155, 164, 176; Kyle, *Religious Fringe*, 269–70; Jeane Dixon, *The Call to Glory* (New York: Bantam, 1971) 160–84; Bjornstad, *Twentieth Century Prophecy*, 46–54.

The predictions of many more prophets could be noted. But their message is basically the same, even a bit repetitious: "We are heading into a time of tremendous upheaval—what some seers have described as the 'end of the world.' . . . Yet along with this foreboding is the promise of a new and far better world to be built beyond."[73]

The New Age Movement

The New Age movement became visible in the early 1970s; during the 1980s New Age ideas penetrated American culture. The New Age can be seen as a cultural shift with social and religious dimensions. Gordon Melton regards it as "a social, religious, political, and cultural convergence between the new Eastern and mystical religious and the religious disenchantment of many Westerners."[74] The New Age is a meeting of three cultural forces: the Judaic and Christian traditions, Western occult mysticism, and Eastern religions.

The New Age is also a transformational or millennial movement. It regards humanity as standing between two ages in human history—the Age of Pisces and the Age of Aquarius.[75] The heart of the New Age vision is the spiritual and psychological transformation of individual people. But this is only the first step. The New Age, as the name indicates, envisions a new world, a new era in human history. For this change to begin, a number of influential individuals must experience transformation and then to actively work for social change.[76]

73. Joey R. Jochmans, *Rolling Thunder: The Coming Earth Changes* (Santa Fe, NM: Sun, 1980) 16.

74. Melton, *Encyclopedic Handbook of Cults in America*, 107-8. For general information on the New Age movement see Richard Kyle, *The New Age Movement in American Culture* (Lanham, MD: University Press of America, 1995); Russell Chandler, *Understanding the New Age* (Dallas: Word, 1988); Douglas Groothuis, *Unmasking the New Age* (Downers Grove, IL: InterVarsity, 1986); Karen Hoyt, ed., *The New Age Rage* (Old Tappan, NJ: Revell, 1987); James R. Lewis and J. Gordon Melton, eds., *Perspectives on the New Age* (Albany: State University of New York Press, 1992); Elliot Miller, *Crash Course on the New Age Movement* (Grand Rapids: Baker, 1989); Ted Peters, *The Cosmic Self* (San Francisco: Harper, 1989).

75. Tucker, *Another Gospel*, 335; Robert Burrows, "A Vision for a New Humanity," in *New Age Rage*, 33.

76. Ted Peters, "Post Modern Religion," *Update* 8/1 (1984) 23; J. Gordon Melton et al., *New Age Almanac* (Detroit: Visible Ink, 1991) 3; Richard Kyle, "The Political Ideas of the New Age Movement," *Journal of Church and State* 37/4 (Autumn 1995) 831-32; Kyle, *Religious Fringe*, 286; Martin Green, *Prophets of a New Age* (New York: Scribner, 1992) 213-26.

Barbara Hargrove sees New Age apocalypticism as different from that of similar post–World War II movements, namely the Jesus People and fundamentalist premillennialism. The Jesus People took a dim view of the future and were absolutely convinced that Jesus would come in their lifetime. Fundamentalist premillennialism, as represented in Hal Lindsey's *Late Great Plane Earth*, "holds that social and moral corruption will increase until Jesus returns to take up his faithful." Unlike this pessimistic apocalypticism, New Age millennialism is "characterized by love and light." More like postmillennialists than premillennialists, the New Age groups have a "more positive interpretation of the end of the Age."[77]

The writings of prominent New Age advocate David Spangler reflect this positive view. He contended that the world is entering a new age, a cycle when humanity will become the "world savior," a time when light will enter the planet and the world will experience an "occult redemption." The New Age is to be "the age of communication" when humanity, nature, Christ, and God effectively communicate and come to realize their unity and oneness.[78]

The coming New Age will be based not on some doomsday scenario, but on a paradigm shift. "A paradigm is a scheme for understanding and explaining certain aspects of reality," writes New Age spokesperson Marilyn Ferguson. "A paradigm shift is a distinctly new way of thinking about old problems." While a new paradigm will include old truth, a paradigm shift has taken place when people begin to think differently.[79]

New Ager Fritjof Capra believed that the Western world was in a state of crisis brought on by the old paradigm that was formed by the rationalism of Rene Descartes, Isaac Newton's physics, and the Judeo-Christian tradition. Cartesian rationalism promoted linear reason and pushed mysticism aside. Newtonian physics gave the West a mechanized worldview. The Judeo-Christian tradition desacralized creation by removing God from it and opened the door to the exploitation of nature. The old

---

77. Barbara Hargrove, "New Religious Movements and the End of the Age," *Iliff Review* 39/2 (Spring 1982) 42–46; Martin, "Waiting for the End," 34–36; Kyle, *New Age Movement*, 77.

78. David Spangler, *Reflections on the Christ* (Findhorn, Scotland: Findhorn, 1978) 11, 19. See also David Spangler, *Revelation: The Birth of a New Age* (Middleton, WS: Lorian, 1976); David Spangler, *Emergence: The Rebirth of the Sacred* (New York: Delta, 1984); Kyle, *The New Age Movement*, 57–58.

79. Marilyn Ferguson, *The Aquarian Conspiracy* (Los Angeles: J. P. Tarcher, 1980) 26–28. See also Thomas Kuhn, *The Structure of Scientific Revolutions* (Chicago: University of Chicago Press, 1962).

Messiahs, Prophets, and End-Time Visions

paradigm also produced a patriarchal order, an authoritarian and centralized political system, and a hierarchical social organization.[80]

Based on a new paradigm, the New Age will be different. While elements of the old order will be retained, there will be a convergence of East and West. Rationalism will be balanced by intuition. God, humanity, and nature will no longer be regarded as distinct entities. The environment will be nurtured because humanity will be one with nature. A holistic view of science will replace Newtonian physics. Men and women will have an equal status. Society will be less hierarchical and the political systems will be decentralized. Internationalism will replace nationalism in global relations. Crime and war will be greatly reduced. Also, there will be one world religion, based on common mystical assumptions drawn from the religions of the world. Finally, instead of competition which fragments the world, cooperation will reign supreme.[81]

While most New Agers are working toward a new world order, some connect the New Age with the coming of Christ. Of course, the Christ of the New Age is not the Jesus of orthodox Christianity. In fact, the New Age movement separates the human Jesus from the office of Christ or the divine Christ spirit, which has indwelt many great religious leaders throughout history (e.g., Rama, Krishna, Buddha, and Jesus). In fact, because Christ is divine and divinity indwells all people, Christ is within each person.[82]

When will this New Age arrive? When will the paradigm shift occur? On the whole, New Agers are vague about this issue, suggesting a range of several centuries. According to the astrologers, however, an equinox shift occurs about every two thousand years, and one is due anytime now. Such a change in the stars ushers in a new age in human history. Thus

---

80. Fritjof Capra, *The Turning Point* (New York: Bantam, 1982) 53-74, 101-22; Kyle, *New Age Movement*, 78; Robert J. L. Burrows, "Americans Get Religion in the New Age," *Christianity Today*, 16 May 1986, 18-19. See also Fritjof Capra, *The Tao of Physics* (3rd ed.; Boston: Shambhala, 1991); Michael Talbot, *Beyond the Quantum* (New York: Bantam, 1986); Paul Davies, *God and the New Physics* (New York: Simon & Schuster, 1983).

81. Many New Age sources promote these general views. Examples include Capra, *Turning Point*; Ferguson, *Aquarian Conspiracy*; and Spangler, *Emergence*. See also Kyle, *New Age Movement*, 78-79.

82. Spangler, *Reflections on the Christ*, 4, 6-10, 40-41; Benjamin Crème, *The Reappearance of Christ and the Masters of Wisdom* (North Hollywood, CA: Tara Center, 1980) 28, 46-48; Shirley MacLaine, *Out on a Limb* (New York: Bantam, 1983) 91. For a critique of the New Age view of Christ see Ron Rhodes, *The Counterfeit Christ of the New Age Movement* (Grand Rapids: Baker, 1990); Norman Geisler, "The New Age Movement," *Bibliotheca Sacra* 144/573 (1987) 91-92; Douglas Groothuis, "The Shamanized Jesus," *Christianity Today*, 29 April 1991, 20-23.

many New Agers expected a change around 2000. On the basis of Mayan and Aztec beliefs, David Spangler saw an age of harmony beginning about 2000. Ken Carey regarded 2000 as a kind of psychic watershed. On the other side lies a utopian society.[83]

Still, most New Agers do not specify when the golden age will arrive. They speak of the coming of Christ in only a very general sense—he manifests himself in all humanity.[84] However, other New Age teachers have become involved in specific predictions, date setting, and even doomsday forecasts. Many Theosophists believed that a world savior had come in the person of Jiddu Krishnamurti. When he renounced this role in 1929, Alice Bailey predicted the reappearance of the Christ, whom some called Lord Maitreya. Several groups and individuals emerging from her Arcane School continued this line of prediction.[85]

Most prominent of these individuals was Benjamin Crème (b. 1922). He said that in 1945 Christ announced that he would return if certain global conditions were met (peace, economic sharing, human goodwill, and reduction of authoritarianism). In July 1977 Maitreya informed Crème that he had taken a body and would descend from the Himalayas. Crème intensified his traveling and speaking on the matter, and in 1982 took out full-page ads in major newspapers to announce the coming of Maitreya.[86]

The Harmonic Convergence of 1987 was an event that prompted an end-of-the-world prediction. In his book *The Mayan Factor*, Jose Arguelles contended that according to ancient Mayan calendars August 17, 1987, would be the beginning of the end. On that day three planets would line up with the moon, and a twenty-five year period of trouble would begin, culminating in a catastrophe in 2012—a subject to be encountered in chapter 13. This period could be headed off only if 144,000 believers would gather at various sites around the world "to resonate in

---

83. Chandler, *Doomsday*, 183; Tucker, *Another Gospel*, 335; Robert Muller, *The New Genesis* (New York: Image, 1984) 186: Hillel Schwartz, "Fin-de-Siecle Fantasies," *New Republic*, 30 July, 6 August 1990, 22.

84. Spangler, *Reflections on the Christ*, 4–10; George Trevelyan, *Visions of the Aquarian Age* (Walpole, NH: Stillpoint, 1984) 137; Ron Rhodes, "The Christ of the New Age Movement," *Christian Research Journal* 12/1 (1989) 9–14; 12/ 2 (1989) 15–20.

85. Melton et al., *New Age Almanac*, 10; Tucker, *Another Gospel*, 335. See also Alice Bailey, *The Externalization of the Hierarchy* (New York: Lucis, 1957); Jonathan Adolph, "What Is New Age?," *Guide to New Age Living* 1 (1988) 9.

86. Crème, *Reappearance of the Christ*, 31–32, 55–56; Melton et al., *New Age Almanac*, 316; Tucker, *Another Gospel*, 336–37; Kyle, *New Age Movement*, 79.

Messiahs, Prophets, and End-Time Visions

harmony" for a new age of peace and unity. Thousands of people did meet on that date.[87]

The "11:11 Doorway" movement made a similar prophecy. Humankind was in a twenty-year period of opportunity to end the conflict on Earth. The doorway would open only once—from January 11, 1992, to December 31, 2011. During this timeframe a unified humanity could pass through the door into new realms of consciousness, perhaps opening a "major planetary activation."[88]

The New Age movement has several prophets who believe that violence and destruction will usher in the new era. One of the better-known doomsday prophets was Ruth Montgomery (1912–2001). In her view the Age of Aquarius will be a time of love and brotherhood, but the transition from the Piscean Age to the Aquarian Age will be a time of purging. The evils of the old age will be eradicated by wars and natural disasters, including a shift in the Earth's axis. Montgomery even contended that the Antichrist is currently alive and will reveal himself as the final shift in the axis occurs.[89]

Another New Age doomsday prophet was Elizabeth Clare Prophet (1939–2009), known as Guru Ma. She led the Church Universal and Triumphant, a syncretistic mixture of Western occult and Eastern spirituality. Prophet claimed to be "God's chosen earthly messenger for direct dictations [channeled messages] from a host of ascended masters including Buddha, Jesus, Saint Germain, [and] Pope John XXIII."[90]

Guru Ma came close to predicting the end of the world. On April 23, 1990, the world entered a twelve-year period of negative karma. Thus from 1990 to 2002 all kinds of disasters—including nuclear war and

---

87. Bill Barol, "The End of the World (Again)," *Newsweek*, 17 August 1987, 70–71; Martha Smiglgis, "A New Age Dawning," *Time*, 31 August 1987, 83; Tucker, *Another Gospel*, 335–36; Kyle, *New Age Movement*, 79–80; Dick Teresi and Judith Hooper, "The Last Laugh?," *Omni* 12/4 (January 1990) 82; Stearns, *Millennium III*, 12–13.

88. Charles B. Strozier, *Apocalypse* (Boston, 1994) 231; Ashtar Command, "11:11 Doorway," *Connecting Link*, n.d.; Chandler, *Doomsday*, 185; *Millennial Prophecy Report*, May 1994, 13–14.

89. Ruth Montgomery, *Strangers among Us* (New York: Fawcett, 1979) 30–35, 38, 52, 64, 191–205, 220–21; Strozier, *Apocalypse*, 230–31.

90. Chandler, *Understanding the New Age*, 63 (quote); Melton, *Encyclopedic Handbook of Cults in America*, 137; Kyle, *New Age Movement*, 71; Samples et al., *Prophets of the Apocalypse*, 153–54; Holger Jensen, "Trouble in Paradise," *Maclean's*, 7 May 1990, 34; Majorie Lee Chandler, "Churches Wary of 'New Age' Neighbors," *Moody Monthly*, September 1987, 95–96; Bill Shaw and Maria Wilhelm, "The Cloud over Paradise Valley," *People's Weekly*, 4 June 1990, 48–53.

earthquakes—would befall planet Earth. In particular, a Soviet nuclear strike would devastate the United States.[91]

The Church Universal and Triumphant's headquarters is a 63,000-acre ranch in Montana. Here Guru Ma's followers have built underground bunkers and stockpiled food, fuel, and weapons. She likened her shelter to Noah's ark in the Earth. Others feared another Jonestown was in the making. When Armageddon did not come as she anticipated and the Cold War ended, she denied making any specific predictions regarding a catastrophe. She even took some credit for the turn of events by attributing the lessening of international tensions to her church's rapid-fire prayer chants.[92]

The Apocalypse and Flying Saucers

William Ferguson claimed to have been picked up by a spacecraft. He described his conversation with the space beings, in this case the oligarchies of the planet Venus: "They [the oligarchies] told me to tell the people of planet Earth, that all unidentified flying objects are here to help planet Earth . . . at the time when it is approaching its next evolutionary step." During the 1980s unidentified flying objects (UFOs) became popular in the New Age subculture.[93]

The UFO movement, which began in the 1940s, can be divided into two categories. First are the ufologists, who believe that flying saucers are real and that the political establishments have suppressed evidence proving their existence. But the scientific proof being meager, what began as science has sometimes turned into religion. Out of this development came the UFO cults. Rather than discuss UFOs in a scientific framework, the

---

91. Chandler, Doomsday, 186; Samples et al., Prophets of the Apocalypse, 152–53; Jensen, "Troubles in Paradise," 33–35; Timothy Eagan, "Guru's Bomb Shelter Hits Legal Snag," New York Times, 24 April 1990, A16–17; "Weapons, Arrests and Doomsday Talk Shroud Church Universal and Triumphant," Christian Research Journal 12/3 (Winter-Spring 1990) 27; Walter Kirn, "Apocalypse Later," Village Voice, 14 August 1990, 45; Ron Rhodes, "Millennial Madness," Christian Research Journal 13/2 (Fall 1990) 39.

92. Jensen, "Trouble in Paradise," 33, 35; Chandler, Doomsday, 186; Samples et al., Prophets of the Apocalypse, 152–53; Eagan, Guru's Bomb Shelter," A16–17.

93. John A. Saliba, "Religious Dimensions of UFO Phenomena," in The Gods Have Landed, ed. James R. Lewis (Albany: State University of New York Press, 1995) 48 (quote); William Alnor, "UFO Cults Are Flourishing in New Age Circles," Christian Research Journal 13/1 (1990) 5.

Messiahs, Prophets, and End-Time Visions

cultists spiritualize the phenomena, relying on inward states of mind and occult information.[94]

It was in 1952, when George Adamski claimed that a UFO occupant met and talked with him, that the UFO sightings took on another dimension. Some of the people who claimed to have been contacted by UFO occupants sought scientific answers about the nature of UFO visitors. But a second group viewed the UFOs from an occult perspective. Having made contact with what they claimed to be extraterrestrial beings, they committed themselves to telling others the message of the space people. The movement had acquired a religious dimension.[95] While the message articulated by the space people varied in the specifics, the general thrust was the same. The space people were more highly evolved beings who were coming to aid the occupants of Earth. "They brought a message of concern about the course of man, whose materialism is leading him to destruction." But the space people also offered a means of salvation: humankind could avoid the coming destruction by following the message of love.[96]

On the whole, the UFO movement must be regarded as a world affirming religion. The message coming from the aliens from space is essentially redemptive. They will cure all diseases, deliver humanity from nuclear holocaust, and even provide transportation to another planet where there are happiness and security. In sum, salvation is to come though the intervention of the space beings, who will lead humanity to a higher state of evolution.[97]

Still, some UFO passages are starkly apocalyptic, predicting catastrophes that will bring an end to history. Some speak of an economic collapse;

---

94. David M. Jacobs, "UFO's and Scientific Legitimacy," *The Occult in America*, eds. Howard Kerr and Charles Crow (Urbana: University of Illinois Press, 1983) 219, 228–29; Alnor, "UFO Cults Are Flourishing in New Age Circles," 5–6; "UFO Believers Demand End to Cosmic Cover-Up," *Wichita Eagle*, 6 July 1993, 10A; Mark Albrecht and Brooks Alexander, "UFO's: Is Science Fiction Coming True?," *SCP Journal*, August 1977, 14–16; Elizabeth L. Hillstrom, *Testing the Spirits* (Downers Grove, IL: InterVarsity, 1995) 200–204.

95. Robert W. Balch and David Taylor, "Salvation in a UFO," *Psychology Today* 10/5 (October 1976) 58–66; Robert W. Balch and David Taylor, "Seekers and Saucers: The Role of the Cultic Milieu in Joining a UFO Cult," *American Behavioral Scientist* 20/6 (1977) 839–60; Jacobs, "UFO's and Scientific Legitimacy," 219, 22–29.

96. Melton, *Encyclopedia of American Religions*, 2:199 (quote); Chandler, *Understanding the New Age*, 92–93; Ted Peters, *UFOs—God's Chariots?: Flying Saucers in Politics, Science and Religion* (Atlanta: John Knox, 1977); Melton et al., *New Age Almanac*, 143.

97. Saliba, "Religious Dimensions of UFO Phenomena," 48; Ellwood and Partin, *Religious and Spiritual Groups in Modern America*, 126.

others point to natural disasters, perhaps a depletion of the ozone or pollution of the oceans. Yet humanity "will survive, either by being transplanted to some safe planet to live . . . or through becoming one with the aliens through their process of hybridization," writes John Whitmore. (Hybridization refers to the union of a space being with a human, a process through which the superior knowledge and moral strength of the alien raise humankind to a higher level.)[98]

Among the examples of UFO apocalypticism is Marian Keech, who, as the leader of a small saucer cult in the 1950s, claimed to have received channeled messages from space beings. These communications spoke of the world being destroyed by a great flood. Confident that flying saucers would rescue her group and transport them to another planet, she gathered her flock. Well, the deadline came, but the flying saucers did not. The only flood was one of tears. So the group disbanded.[99]

In true apocalyptic fashion Augusta Almeida brought disaster and triumph together. Merging the concepts of UFOs, Jesus, and the rapture, she claimed that Jesus was an extraterrestrial and the leader of a large space force. In what she called the "Grand Lift," the Earth was to be "evacuated" between 1993 and 1997 so it could be repaired. After the repairs Jesus would return, and Earth would again be a paradise: "People will then be returned to live in peace on it for a thousand years."[100]

The Aetherius Society also belongs to the apocalyptic wing of the flying saucer movement. The society has shifted its focus from saucer phenomena to direct communication with celestial beings. According to the society, the Earth is at a crisis point as it enters the Aquarian Age. There is a lot of negative karma around, and evil magicians from the lower astral realms are attempting to enslave humanity. They will employ bacterial and nuclear warfare as well as terrible mental illusions to do the job. But Operation Karmalight will save humanity. Interplanetary Adepts will come to Earth, even to the pits of hell, to battle the forces of darkness and free humankind.[101]

98. John Whitmore, "Religious Dimensions of the UFO Abductee Experience," in *The Gods Have Landed*, 73. See also Strozier, *Apocalypse*, 235.

99. John A. Saliba, "UFO Contactee Phenomena from a Sociopsychological Perspective: A Review," in *The Gods Have Landed*, 222-23; Chandler, *Doomsday*, 188; Cohen, *Prophets of Doom*, 91-94; Michael J. St. Clair, *Millenarian Movements in Historical Context* (New York: Garland, 1992) 331-35; Leon Festinger, Henry W. Riecken, and Stanley Schachter, *When Prophecy Fails* (New York: Harper & Row, 1964) 139-73.

100. Strozier, *Apocalypse*, 237-38.

101. Ellwood and Partin, *Religious and Spiritual Groups in Modern America*, 126-28.

Messiahs, Prophets, and End-Time Visions

In March 1997 UFO apocalypticism took a bizarre and deadly twist—thirty-nine members of the Heaven's Gate cult committed mass suicide in southern California. "Planet Earth [is] about to be recycled. Your only chance is to survive [is to] leave with us," said Marshall Herff Applewhite, the group's leader. In what was the worst mass suicide on American soil, his followers "killed themselves in order to hook up with a UFO."[102]

But this sad story began years earlier. It started in the 1970s with a UFO cult known by several names—the Human Individual Metamorphosis, the UFO People, and eventually Heaven's Gate. Its leaders, Applewhite and Bonnie Nettles, went by several names: Bo and Peep, Pig and Sow, Do and Ti. Borrowing from Gnosticism, Christianity, and Theosophy, they preached a "strange brew of Christian theology, castration, science fiction [and] belief in UFO's."[103] Convinced that they were the two witnesses prophesied by the Book of Revelation, Applewhite and Nettles proclaimed a flying saucer gospel for years, largely in the Western states. Their UFO gospel, which was never set in stone and which in fact underwent several shifts, claimed that Bo and Peep had come to Earth in a spaceship with a mission and a message: "Only escape from our planet, doomed by pollution and decay, [can] save the human race." Salvation meant moving up to the kingdom of God, which is a physical place outside the Earth's atmosphere. The saved will be "beamed up by a flying saucer and transformed into a higher level, that of resurrected people." But prospective members had to prepare themselves, that is, renounce their desires and possessions.[104]

During the 1970s and 1980s Applewhite and Nettles moved through the West, exhorting potential enlistees to give up friends, families, and jobs in hope of getting beamed up by a flying saucer to the next level. At one point Bo and Peep disappeared only to reappear and reinvigorate the UFO group with a new message: "the doors of the next level are closed,"

---

102. Elizabeth Gleick, "The Marker We've Been . . . Waiting For," *Time*, 7 April 1997, 30–31 (quote); "Toll at 39 in California Mass Suicide," *Wichita Eagle*, 27 March 1997, 1A, 4A; William Booth and William Claiborne, "Suicide the Final Step in Leaving It All Behind," *Wichita Eagle*, 29 March 1997, 1A, 6A.

103. Saliba, "Religious Dimensions of UFO Phenomena," 31; Evan Thomas et al., "The Next Level," *Newsweek*, 7 April 1997, 26–28 (quote); Stephen J. Hedges, "WWW.MASSSUICIDE.COM," *U.S. News and World Report*, 7 April 1997, 26; Richard Lacayo, "The Lure of the Cult," *Time*, 7 April 1997, 46: Kenneth Woodward, "Christ and Comets," *Newsweek*, 7 April 1997, 42.

104. Saliba, "Religious Dimensions of UFO Phenomena," 31 (quote); Robert W. Balch, "Waiting for the Ships," in *The Gods Have Landed*, 137–39; Hedges, "WWW.MASSSUICIDE.COM," 28; Thomas et al., "Next Level," 32.

and few will be eligible to enter God's kingdom. At this time the group became more regimented internally and isolated from the world.[105]

By the 1990s the message of the UFO cult evidenced a more dramatic apocalyptic tone. In 1985 Nettles had "left her human vehicle." By 1987 the practice of castration had been introduced. In the early 1990s the group believed that the lift-off might take place in the next two years. They even took out an advertisement in *USA Today* saying that "the Earth's present civilization is about to be recycled—spaded under."[106] They were making their final bid for recruits. As they awaited the end, along came Comet Hale-Bopp. For most people it was a celestial wonder. But to the Heaven's Gate group it signaled the end. The tail of Hale-Bopp, they believed, concealed the UFO that would lift them up. But to be beamed up to the next level they had to leave their human containers. And this they did by swallowing up a dose of lethal drugs.[107]

THE RACIST APOCALYPSE

According to the Bible, we are redeemed by grace. Several racist groups, however, both black and white, drop the "g." They say that we are saved by race. In particular, the Christian Identity movement and the Black Muslims take this tack. But while focusing on race, they are also millennial groups with an apocalyptic worldview.

The Christian Identity movement and the Black Muslims are obviously poles apart—one regarding non-Aryans as either subhuman or children of the devil, the other speaking of the Caucasian devils. Yet they have much in common. They are both world-rejecting movements, believing that society is hopelessly corrupt. Also, they fervently maintain an apocalyptic and dualistic worldview: the forces of good and evil are on a collision course. Exuding pessimism, both movements have adopted a twisted version of premillennialism. They also share other convictions—namely,

---

105. Balch, "Waiting for the Ships," 153–54 (quote); Joel Achenbach and Laurie Goodstein, "Web-Connected Doomsayers Left for the Next World," *Wichita Eagle*, 28 March 1997, 4A.

106. Howard Chua-Eoan, "The Faithful Among Us," *Time*, 14 April 1997, 45–46; Balch, "Waiting for the Ships," 163–64 (quote); Gleick, "Marker," 42; Thomas et al., "Next Level," 32–38; T. Trent Gegax, "The Unkindest Cut of All," *Newsweek*, 7 April 1997, 39.

107. Hedges, "WWW.MASSSUICIDE.COM," 26–30; Achenbach and Goostein, "Web-Connected Doomsayers Left for 'Next Level'"; Thomas et al., "Next Level," 35.

Messiahs, Prophets, and End-Time Visions

every government is by nature evil, they are the chosen people, and other races are inferior.

The Christian Identity Movement

The Jews are a "half-breed, race-mixed, polluted people not of God.... They are not God's creation." Rather, they are "the children of Satan," "the serpent seed line" that came from Cain.[108] Does this sound like something Adolf Hitler would say? Actually, these are the words of leaders of the Christian Identity movement.

What is Christian Identity? It is an extreme right-wing militant movement that believes only Caucasians are God's people. It is also an umbrella term for a number of independent religious groups and congregations most of which were at one time led by a "prominent minister who frequently combine[d] the roles of congregational leader, writer, and radio-TV spokesperson." However, the leadership of these groups rapidly passed to a number of extreme right-wing political organizations, the best-known being the Aryan Nations, the Order, Posse Comitatus, and the Ku Klux Klan.[109]

Founded after World War II, Christian Identity is a mutation of British Israelism, which we encountered when examining Herbert Armstrong's Worldwide Church of God. This ideology, which began in nineteenth-century Britain, maintained that "the Anglo-Saxon-Celtic peoples are in reality the 'ten lost tribes of Israel.'"[110] Though both movements insisted that the lost tribes of Israel migrated to northern Europe, where they eventually became the British people, Christian Identity constructed an elaborate anti-Semitic ideology that was totally foreign to British Israelism. While contending that the tribes of Israel migrated to northwest Europe and that nearly all non-Slavic European peoples are Israelites, Christian Identity denies that there is a link between the Jews and Israel.

---

108. Quoted in Michael Barkun, *Religion and the Racist Right* (Chapel Hill: University of North Carolina Press, 1994) 191. See also Jarah B. Crawford, *Last Battle Cry: Christianity's Final Conflict with Evil* (Knoxville: Jann, 1984) 7, 321, 333-40, 346.

109. Melton, *Encyclopedic Handbook of Cults in America*, 57 (quote); Barkun, *Religion and the Racist Right*, 3; John George and Land Wilcox, *American Extremists* (Amherst, NY: Prometheus, 1996) 340-49; Richard Abanes, *American Militias* (Downers Grove, IL: InterVarsity, 1996) 44, 154-55.

110. Harry Benjamin Gray, "Eschatology of the Millennial Cults," ThD diss., Dallas Theological Seminary, 1956, 11 (quote); Jeffrey Kaplan, *Radical Religion in America* (Syracuse, NY; Syracuse University Press, 1997) 1.

Instead, the Jews descended from the Khazars, a people from the Black Sea area who in the seventh century converted to Judaism but could not assimilate into Western culture.[111] In fact, Christian Identity contends that the Jews are ultimately the devil's offspring, the result of Satan's sex with Eve in the Garden of Eden. White Aryans are the true descendants of the tribes of Israel and have been chosen to do God's work on Earth; all other races were planted on Earth before the Aryans and are inferior.[112]

Christian Identity is also a millennial movement with an apocalyptic worldview. But its end-time perspective differs significantly from that of contemporary dispensationalism, which it holds in utter contempt. Both movements believe that the last days are upon us, but the similarity ends there. Dispensationalism points to the return of Israel, moral decay, apostasy, and certain events as signs of the times. While Christian Identity may mention such developments, its focus is on what it perceives to be the destruction of the white race. Because the white Aryans are God's chosen people, this is an apocalyptic event.[113] The assault on the white race is being led by a Jewish conspiracy, which controls the American government ("Zionist Occupation"). Remember, in dispensationalism the Jews are the centerpiece; they occupy the key position in God's future plans, especially the millennium. No wonder dispensationalism is anathema to the Christian Identity movement, which regards the Jews as the children of Satan, not as God's chosen people.[114]

Christian Identity utterly rejects the pretribulational rapture, which it regards as a cowardly notion. Christians will not be taken out of the tribulation. Instead, they must participate in the final apocalyptic struggle between good and evil, which will be a great racial conflict. The chosen of

---

111. Michael Barkun, "Racist Apocalypse," *American Studies* 31/2 (Fall 1990) 123; Melton, *Encyclopedic Handbook of Cults in America*, 55, 60; George and Wilcox, *American Extremists*, 340–42; "Freedmen's Beliefs Roadblock to Peace," *Wichita Eagle*, 3 April 1996, 8A; Abanes, *American Militias*, 155–56.

112. Barkun, "Racist Apocalypse," 123–24; George and Wilcox, *American Extremists*, 340–42; Barkun, *Religion and the Racist Right*, 188–89; Kaplan, *Radical Religion in America*, 2, 47–48; Richard Abanes, "America's Patriot Movement," *Christian Research Journal* 19/3 (1997) 15; Abanes, *American Militias*, 162–63.

113. Barkun, *Religion and the Racist Right*, 104–5; Barkun, "Racist Apocalypse," 126–28; Kaplan, *Radical Religion in America*, 4; Abanes, "America's Patriot Movement," 10–12.

114. Barkun, "Racist Apocalypse," 126–28; Barkun, *Religion and the Racist Right*, 103–5; John Coleman, "Who Are the Jews, and Where Do They Come From?," *Christian Vanguard* 131 (November 1982) 1–2; Abanes, *American Militias*, 166–67; Kaplan, *Radical Religion in America*, 48.

God, the white Aryans, must do battle against the forces of Satan, that is, Jews and other non-Aryans. Thus survival mentality pervades the Christian Identity movement. Its adherents have moved to remote areas and stockpiled guns and food for Armageddon, which will take place in the United States, not Israel.[115] In this struggle the destruction of the white race will be narrowly averted. The Jesus-led Aryan forces will defeat the Jewish and non-white armies. Following this violent struggle will come the New Order—the Christian Identity version of the millennium. Jesus Christ will return and establish his earthly rule in Jerusalem. During this golden age Jesus will reunite the twelve tribes of Israel, and the Aryans will rule as the spiritual and racial elite.[116]

The Black Muslims

The Black Muslims constitute a protest movement closely related to the urbanization of blacks, racial tensions, and the spirit of black nationalism. Though the group is also known as the Nation of Islam, Eric Lincoln regards it as more an expression of social protest than a religious movement. E. U. Essien-Udom sees the Black Muslims as primarily a black nationalist movement. To be sure, the Nation of Islam is both a social protest and a black nationalist movement.[117] But these two expressions are cast in an apocalyptic context. The primary drawing card of the Nation of Islam is the opportunity to identify with a group strong enough to cast off the domination of the white race—and perhaps even subordinate it in turn. This basic appeal has apocalyptic and millennial overtones. For Black Muslims, the end means the end of the present white civilization.[118]

The Black Muslims developed primarily in two periods: the 1920s and 1930s, which gave birth to the movement; and the 1950s and 1960s,

---

115. Barkun, "Racist Apocalypse," 126–27; Barkun, *Religion and the Racist Right*, 104, 106; Samples et al., *Prophets of the Apocalypse*, 154; Abanes, *American Militias*, 166–67; Kaplan, *Radical Religion in America*, 4.

116. Barkun, "Racist Apocalypse," 131–32; Barkun, *Religion and the Racist Right*, 108–11; Kaplan, *Radical Religion in America*, 4.

117. C. Eric Lincoln, *The Black Muslims in America* (rev. ed.; Boston: Beacon, 1973) 29; E. U. Essien-Udom, *Black Nationalism: A Search for an Identity in America* (Chicago: University of Chicago Press, 1962).

118. Perry E. Gianakos, "The Black Muslims: An American Millennialistic Response to Racism and Cultural Deracination," *Centennial Review* 23 (Fall 1979) 435–38; Sydney Ahlstrom, *A Religious History of the American People* (New Haven, CT: Yale University Press, 1972) 1068; Peter W. Williams, *Popular Religion in America* (Englewood Cliffs, NJ: Prentice-Hall, 1980) 52.

which provided the catalyst for its greatest growth. During the early years leadership came primarily from Timothy Drew and Wallace D. Farad. But after World War II, Elijah Muhammad (1897–1975) became the dominant figure and the primary source for Black Muslim apocalypticism.[119]

Because Black Muslims despise white society, they must be regarded as a world-rejecting movement. The Nation of Islam rejects "the whole value construct of white Christian society." Instead, it seeks to establish a new nation of blacks with a black God, new values, and a new creed.[120] This hatred for white society has fueled Black Muslim apocalypticism and provided the basis for regarding Caucasian civilization as the work of the devil. Black Muslims take two approaches to American society—separation and expectancy. They erect a rigid dualism between the devil society and themselves. Since the white civilization is evil and doomed to destruction, there is no need to integrate with it or to reform it. Rather, it must be destroyed. Allah will destroy this devilish Caucasian civilization and usher in a millennial age in which blacks dominate.[121]

In spelling out this millennial vision, Elijah Muhammad turned traditional American values upside down, namely, the belief in Anglo-Saxon superiority and the idea of America as the Redeemer Nation.[122] His writings teach that the Nation of Islam will lead the blacks of North America to their "true inheritance as members of the ancient tribe of Shabazz," of which Abraham was the patriarch and to which the non-white people of the world belong. "Caucasian people are an inferior, latter-day offshoot of the Black Asiatic Nation." Consequently, African-Americans' self-hatred and negative regard for black culture must be replaced with a strong positive image and a sense of triumphant nationhood.[123]

Despite shunning Christianity, the leaders of the Nation of Islam drew support for their eschatology from the Book of Revelation. According to Elijah Muhammad, Revelation prophesies the downfall of the white

119. Kyle, *Religious Fringe*, 240.

120. Lincoln, *Black Muslims*, xxvii–xxx (quote) Richard Kyle, "Black Muslims," in *Encyclopedia U.S.A.*, ed. Archie P. McDonald (Gulf Breeze, FL: Academic International, 1985) 6:137; Kyle, *Religious Fringe*, 242–43.

121. Gianakos, "Black Muslims," 435–39. See also Martha Lee, *The Nation of Islam: An American Millenarian Movement* (Syracuse, NY: Syracuse University Press, 1996).

122. Gianakos, "Black Muslims," 435, 439–42; Ernest Lee Tuveson, *Redeemer Nation: The Idea of America's Millennial Role* (Chicago: University of Chicago Press, 1968).

123. Ahlstrom, *Religious History*, 1068 (quote); Williams, *Popular Religion*, 50–52; Kyle, "Black Muslims," 138; Henry J. Young, *Major Black Religious Leaders since 1940* (Nashville: Abingdon, 1979).

Messiahs, Prophets, and End-Time Visions

devils. Their demise, he claimed, began in World War I, the "War of the Antichrists," but Allah gave them a fifty-year grace period. Furthermore, "the years 1965 and 1966 are going to be fateful for America." They will bring a "showdown to determine who will live on Earth. The survivor is to build a nation of peace to rule the people forever."[124] When America did not fall in 1965 or 1966, the Black Muslims responded to Elijah Muhammad's failed prediction with silence. References to America's fall disappeared from their publications. The subject did return in a few years, but in a much-subdued way. Elijah Muhammad gradually de-eschatologized Black Muslim doctrine by pointing to a distant date for the end.[125]

Still, Black Muslim doctrine—at least under Elijah Muhammad—must be regarded as millennial. It insists that God has already come. In addition, there is no life after death, and "heaven and hell are only two contrasting earthly conditions." The hereafter, which will begin about 2000 CE, is but the end of the present "civilization of the Caucasian usurpers, including the Christian religion." This age will be followed "by the redemption of the Black Nation" and its glorious dominion over the world.[126]

With the death of Elijah Muhammad in 1975, his son Wallace Muhammad assumed the Nation's leadership. He further de-eschatologized his father's doctrine and reduced his strident racism, in effect moving the Nation of Islam more toward the mainline Islamic tradition and American culture. The "white devil" doctrine was dropped, and the Nation's racist apocalypticism was significantly modified. The new leadership has also ignored Elijah Muhammad's designation of the year 2000 as the date for the end of white civilization.[127]

After Elijah Muhammad's death the Nation of Islam began to call itself the Bilalian Muslims, and in 1976 it adopted a new name, the World Community of Islam in the West. All of this Americanization and Islamization was too much for some Black Muslims. Louis Farrakhan left the organization and in 1978 formed his own Muslim movement, which still

---

124. Quoted in Martha Lee, "The Black Muslims and the Fall of America: An Interpretation Based on the Failure of Prophecy," *Journal of Religious Studies* 16/2 (1990) 145.

125. Ibid., 146.

126. Ahlstrom, *Religious History*, 1068 (quote); Gianakos, "Black Muslims," 436, 440–42; Elijah Muhammad, *Message to the Blackman in America* (Chicago: Muhammad Temple of Islam no. 2, 1965); Elijah Muhammad, *The Fall of America* (Chicago: Muhammad's Temple of Islam no. 2, 1973); Kyle, *Religious Fringe*, 242.

127. Gianakos, "Black Muslims," 436, 449–50; Kyle, *Religious Fringe*, 244–45; Lee, "Black Muslims," 147–48.

uses the original name, the Nation of Islam. Farrakhan has remained true to the literal teaching of Elijah Muhammad, including a combative racism and black separation. In recent years, however, Farrakhan has experienced health problems and is less active in the movement.[128]

AMERICAN CULTURE AND FRINGE APOCALYPTICISM

Most fringe religions have been shaped extensively by the cultural milieu out of which they arose. Some adopt the traits of the dominant culture. Others are influenced in a different way: they strongly reject the dominant culture. Whatever direction the influence runs, such fringe groups usually exaggerate cultural trends. And this response is reflected in how fringe groups view the end of the world. They exaggerate the various apocalyptic tendencies found in society.

Since World War II the end-time ideas of non-traditional religions have run in two directions—the catastrophic and the utopian. These differences are largely due to cultural shifts and to the orientations of the particular groups. The fringe religions coming out of the counterculture have quite naturally taken a doomsday outlook, for they were products of the turmoil ignited by the developments of the counterculture years—political assassinations; the civil rights, feminist, and environmental movements; and the Vietnam War. Added to the proliferation of nuclear weapons and the Cold War, these developments prompted considerable apocalyptic excitement among both non-traditional religions and Christian premillennialists. That is to say, what stirred up Christian fundamentalists also ignited the fringe religions—often in an exaggerated way.

Like similar groups throughout history, the non-traditional religions today usually exist on the margins of society and are subject to apocalyptic pressures. Most often they originated in the West, where apocalyptic ideas have been the strongest. The apocalyptic visions of such bodies often bear a vague resemblance to Christian eschatology, especially a twisted version of premillennialism.

---

128. Braswell, *Understanding Sectarian Groups*, 347–48; William J. Whalen, *Minority Religions in America* (New York: Alba, 1981) 30–31; Lawrence H. Mamiya, "From Black Muslim to Bilalian," *Journal for the Scientific Study of Religion* 21/2 (1982) 141–44, 149; David Gates, "The Black Muslims: A Divided Flock," *Newsweek*, 9 April 1984, 15; George and Wilcox, *American Extremists*, 320–21; Lee, "Black Muslims," 148–49.

Messiahs, Prophets, and End-Time Visions

Not all end-time ideas associated with fringe religions sprang from the counterculture. The counterculture had wound down by the mid-1970s, but end-time visions did not. Instead, they took a different shape—one more conductive to the therapeutic milieu of the 1980s and 1990s with its emphasis on self-improvement. Such end-time ideas were usually less apocalyptic and more utopian. If humankind will reverse their destructive behavior, a new age will dawn in the not-too-distant future. But if humankind fails to do so, dire consequences lie ahead. New Age and occult prognostications are a mixed bag containing both utopian and catastrophic elements.

It is clear that Christianity does not have a corner on apocalyptic visions. Some of the counterculture groups and nearly all New Age and occult bodies have drawn their end-time views from sources other than Scripture. At times their terminal visions resemble Christian eschatology, but usually in a muddled way. In other cases, end-time ideas approximate a secular millennialism or are closely connected with occult prophecies.

11

The Godless Apocalypse

How will the world end? With a bang or a whimper? asked writer T.S. Eliot. By fire or by ice? Wondered poet Robert Frost. "Is there hope for men?" asked economist Robert Heilbroner in *An Inquiry into the Human Prospect* (1980).[1] It is clear from *The Population Bomb* (1968) that doomsday ecologist Paul Ehrlich did not think so: "The battle to feed all humanity is over. In the late 1970s the world will undergo famines—hundreds of millions of people will starve to death." The population explosion, he contended, would be halted by "three of the four apocalyptic horsemen—war, pestilence, and famine."[2] Elsewhere Ehrlich was even more pessimistic. In a 1969 publication he pointed to a series of catastrophes that was to befall humanity during the 1970s. His hypothetical scenario envisioned the end of the oceans as coming in the summer of 1979: "By September 1979, all important animal life in the ocean was extinct. . . . Earlier in the year, the bird population was decimated." Humans do not escape these calamities—people die of malnutrition, pollution kills millions, diseases increase, and chaos breaks out.[3]

If this is not bad enough, consider what a few more scientists have said. In *Cosmos* (1980) astronomer Carl Sagan warned that "we may have

---

1. Robert L. Heilbroner, *An Inquiry into the Human Prospect* (rev. ed.; New York: Norton, 1980) 11. See also Cullen Murphy, "The Way the World Ends," *Wilson Quarterly* 14/1 (Winter 1990) 50.

2. Paul R. Ehrlich, *The Population Bomb* (New York: Ballantine, 1968) 11.

3. Paul R. Ehrlich, "Eco-Catastrophe," *Ramparts* 8/3 (September 1969) 24–31.

The Godless Apocalypse

only a few decades until Doomsday."[4] In 1975 biologist George Wald described himself as "one of those scientists who... still finds it difficult to see how the human race will get itself past the year 2000."[5] In *Famine—1975! America's Decision: Who Will Survive?* William and Paul Paddock painted a grim picture: "Catastrophe is foredoomed... now it is too late."[6]

Does all of this sound like something in a doomsday sermon? Well, it did not come from Hal Lindsey, Jerry Falwell, Pat Robertson, Jack Van Impe, or Tim LaHaye. Instead, by the 1950s members of the scientific and economic communities began to use apocalyptic rhetoric—"the last days," "day of judgment," "the horsemen of the apocalypse," "atonement," and more.[7] As with religious people, not all scientists believe that doomsday is approaching. Still, a number do. What's more, like prophets of the apocalypse, scientists differ over what the end will bring—total or limited destruction. Some see the end of all life on Earth; others see a more limited catastrophe—segments of humanity will survive. They see the world ending as we know it, not complete annihilation. Other scientists speak not so much about the end of days but of a modern anxious mood. Previously, disasters such as tsunamis, earthquakes, volcanoes, pandemics, hurricanes, comets, and UV radiation used to worry people. But they usually impacted only the people directly affected by them. With modern communication, however, people are instantly aware of them and doomsday has become "a state of mind." For example, the tsunami of Christmas 2004 in the Indian Ocean "washed up directly into our living rooms..."[8]

Thus in the late twentieth and early twenty-first centuries, the apocalyptic mindset is no longer "the fringe phenomenon of a few marginalized people which we can ignore." Instead, people who "sit in the seats of political power" are embracing an apocalyptic worldview.[9] Also, end-time ideas are being accepted by members of the scientific and literary communities. As noted in chapter 8, many fiction authors have produced a parade of books and films portraying the apocalypse in one form or another. And

---

4. Carl Sagan, *Cosmos* (New York: Random House, 1980) 328.

5. George Wald, "There Isn't Much Time," *The Progressive* 39 (December 1975) 22.

6. William and Paul Paddock, *Famine—1975! America's Decision: Who Will Survive?* (Boston: Little, Brown, 1967) 9.

7. Chris H. Lewis, "Science, Progress, and the End of the Modern World," *Soundings* 75/2 (Summer–Fall 1992) 307–8.

8. Marq De Villiers, *The End: Natural Disasters, Manmade Catastrophes, and the Future of Human Survival* (New York: St. Martin's, 2008) 3.

9. Paul D. Hanson, "The Apocalyptic Consciousness," *Quarterly Review* 4/3 (1984) 26.

many of these productions have nothing to do with religion and are the work of men and women of the literary mainstream.[10]

For at least two thousand years there have been countless predictions regarding the end of the world. But now such prognostications are taken more seriously, largely because they are thought to be grounded in science. Our age is different from previous ages: "predictions of imminent catastrophe are far more justified [because they] are based on scientific observation rather than on religious inspiration."[11] In fact, writing in the 1990s, Charles Krauthammer stated that in recent years the most significant apocalyptic outbursts have been secular.[12]

WHAT IS THE SECULAR APOCALYPSE?

Some scholars see great continuity between the sacred and secular apocalypses; others regard them as strikingly different. As a general statement, it would seem that the early secular apocalyptic grew out of the sacred, and that until the early twentieth century there existed considerable interaction between the two.[13] Even today the differences are not always clear. Consider, for example, that the end can come by any one of three causes—divine, natural, and human. Some prophets see God employing earthquakes and floods to punish humanity. Other people attach no eschatological significance to such events. Were a comet to destroy the Earth, they would say that it just happened; God did not cause it. To a lesser degree, the same dilemma applies to human disasters. Will God use nuclear weapons, environmental pollution, or overpopulation to destroy humankind? Or will humanity be foolish enough to do it to themselves?

In fact the line between natural and human disasters is often blurred. Or, in many cases both humans and nature are at fault. Natural disasters such as earthquakes, hurricanes, floods, and even diseases would have only a limited impact except for the fact of overpopulation, urbanization in

---

10. W. Warren Wagar, *Terminal Visions* (Bloomington: Indiana University Press, 1982) 10.

11. Michael, Emsley, "The Evolution and Imminent Extinction of an Avaricious Species," in *The Apocalyptic Vision in America*, ed. Lois Parkinson Zamora (Bowling Green, OH: Bowling Green University Popular Press, 1982) 183.

12. Charles Krauthammer, "Apocalypse with and without God," *Time*, 22 March 1993, 82.

13. For two different opinions see Michael Barkun, "Divided Apocalypse: Thinking about the End in Contemporary America," *Soundings* 66/3 (Fall 1983) 257–80; and Lewis, "Science, Progress, and the End of the Modern World," 307–31.

The Godless Apocalypse

problem areas, and globalization. For example, when cities have been built in low lying areas, hurricanes and floods have had a more catastrophic effect than they would otherwise. Who is at fault? Nature or humankind? Moreover, because of globalization and modern transportation, diseases can spread rapidly and turn a local problem into a widespread epidemic.

However, differences do exist between the sacred and secular apocalyptic. Religion no longer has a corner on eschatology. While new to the game, science has exerted considerable impact on end-time thinking. It has given us a depersonalized end: there will be no redemption, no survivors, and no paradise. Scientists warn us that forces are at work in the universe that can literally blow us out of existence.[14]

Like religious predictions, there is an extensive menu of scientific end-time projections. These doomsday scenarios wax and wane in popularity. In the 1950s and 1960s, nuclear destruction ranked first on the list. By the 1980s, environmental issues began to jump to the forefront. The greenhouse effect may melt the polar caps, flooding coastlines. Or perhaps the planet will experience another ice age. Another possibility is that doomsday may be brought on by pollution or the depletion of rain forests. The betting odds are that at some time Earth will be hit by another celestial body—this has happened before, and next time it may be catastrophic. Consider too that in the developing world humans are breeding like rabbits. As a result, overpopulation may bring famine. Or pestilence could do us in: something like AIDS, the Ebola virus, SARS, or the avian flu may get out of control, killing large numbers as did the bubonic plague. Others talk of a global financial disaster ushering humankind into hopelessness and despair.[15]

No matter how the end might come, secular prophets take a different approach. Strictly defined, apocalypse connects both disaster and triumph. Accordingly, most religious millenarians see doomsday as being followed by a golden age. At times they tend to get carried away with the impending calamity. Still, they maintain that recovery and victory will come. Secular prophets of doom, on the other hand, come up a bit short on the positive aspect. Their apocalyptic visions have "tended to be clear

---

14. Russell Chandler, *Doomsday* (Ann Arbor, MI: Servant, 1993) 127; Yuri Rubinsky and Ian Wiseman, *A History of the End of the World* (New York: Morrow, 1982) 133.

15. Such ideas are found in many sources, including Hanson, "Apocalyptic Consciousness," 24–27; Murphy, "Way the World Ends," 54–55; Chandler, *Doomsday*, 128–36; Peter Shaw, "Apocalypse Again," *Commentary*, 4 April 1989, 50–52; Dick Teresi and Judith Hooper, "The Last Laugh?" *Omni* 12/4 (January 1990) 43–44, 78.

and stronger on the coming catastrophe than on the new world that will arise from it." In fact, many scientists bleakly insist that the problems of the physical world are irreversible—no redemption will come forth. Some modern fiction writers have picked up on similar themes.[16]

Still, all is not gloom and doom. Some environmentalists have hope for a golden age, but not one that rises out of the ashes of a catastrophe. Rather, a millennium can come by means of care for Mother Earth. Some movements such as Earth First are rooted in a philosophy known as "deep ecology." This philosophy "demands that human beings revaluate their relationship with the environment in such a way as to acknowledge that both human and non-human life have an intrinsic moral worth." If such does not happen, a catastrophe will result. On the other hand, if the principles of deep ecology are adopted a new society will emerge, one that resembles a millennium. And adopting these principles will not result in personal deprivation, but in a new society and a joyous way of life. Of course, deep ecology is not strictly secular. It has religious implications, largely drawn from Eastern religions (Taoism, Buddhism, and Hinduism), witchcraft, other pagan forms of Earth worship, and Native American spirituality.[17]

Religious and secular thinkers also differ as to the cause of apocalyptic events. From a religious perspective, "the end of history will be brought about through external, divine intervention." The last days are tied to a divine design. Wars and natural disasters do not occur randomly, but are part of a divine plan "to separate good from evil."[18] Secularists move down a different path. Rather than regard a nuclear war, an environmental crisis, or natural disaster as being directed by God, secular prophets regard these events in themselves as potential causes of doomsday. Human beings and natural forces, not God, are behind these events. This secular apocalypticism "grows out of a naturalistic world view, indebted to science and to social criticism rather than to theology."[19]

16. Thomas R. DeGregori, "Apocalypse Yesterday," in *Apocalyptic Vision in America*, 214 (quote); Chandler, *Doomsday*, 127–28; Catherine Keller, *Apocalypse Now and Then* (Boston: Beacon, 1996) 142.

17. Martha Lee, *Earth First!: Environmental Apocalypse* (Syracuse, NY: Syracuse University Press, 1995) 15, 18 (quote); Lois Ann Lorentzen, "Phallic Millennialism and Radical Environmentalism, " in *2000: Essays on the End* eds. Charles B. Strozier and Michael Flynn (New York: New York University Press, 1977) 144–53; Martha F. Lee, "Environmental Apocalypse: The Millennial Theology of 'Earth First,'" in *Millennium, Messiahs, and Mayhem*, eds. Thomas Robbins and Susan J. Palmer (New York: Routledge, 1997) 119–37.

18. Barkun, "Divided Apocalypse," 271.

19. Lewis, "Science, Progress, and the End of the Modern World," 308 (quote);

The Godless Apocalypse

The secular apocalypse sprang from a growing disillusionment with the belief in progress, the notion that civilization would steadily advance. Sometime between the mid seventeenth and early nineteenth centuries, the modern world arrived. Along with it came great optimism. Scientists and philosophers believed that science and human reason could improve the lot of humanity. Advances in agriculture, science, commerce, and industry bolstered such contentions and countered arguments that the world would end because of human evil.[20] By the nineteenth century the belief in progress had taken root in the Western world. It helped to justify humankind's dominance and exploitation of nature. Intoxicated with tremendous improvements in living standards brought on by the Industrial Revolution, most people did not notice the downside, namely, the potential for environmental disasters.[21]

But this gradually began to change. By the 1930s scientists, theologians, philosophers, novelists, and social critics warned about uncontrolled industrial and population growth. Unless humanity put limits on economic development, they would face extinction. Life on Earth could be saved only by reinventing the idea of progress to include living with nature.[22]

Thus was born the secular apocalypse. A number of scientists and social critics in the 1960s and 1970s built on this beginning. They warned that humanity's faith in science and industrial development was actually irrational, not scientific. This misguided faith came from a faulty understanding of the relationship between humankind and nature, an understanding that allowed humanity to exploit the environment with impunity.[23]

In some ways the sacred and secular apocalypses mirror each other. Millennial movements grow out of disasters and social dislocations, and dashed expectations. The same seems to be true for the secular

---

Barkun, "Divided Apocalypse," 263, 271-72.

20. Wagar, *Terminal Visions*, 132-34; Lewis, "Science, Progress, and the End of the Modern World," 313. See also W. Warren Wagar, *The Idea of Progress since the Renaissance* (New York: Wiley, 1969); Ulrich H. J. Kortner, *The End of the World: A Theological Interpretation* (Louisville: Westminster John Knox, 1995) 2-3.

21. Lewis, "Science, Progress, and the End of the Modern World," 315-16; Wagar, *Terminal Visions*, 132-37.

22. Lewis, "Science, Progress, and the End of the Modern World," 325-26; Heilbroner, *Human Prospect*, 47. See also Herbert Marcuse, *One-Dimensional Man* (Boston: Beacon, 1964).

23. Barkun, "Divided Apocalypse," 274-75; Lewis, "Science, Progress, and the End of the World," 326-28; Shaw, "Apocalypse Again," 51-52.

apocalypse. The hopes that the progress of science and industry would usher in a golden age (a secularized version of the Christian millennium) were dashed—by increasing environmental degradation—and out of this disillusionment grew the secular apocalypse. Radical events in America during the 1960s and 1970s produced apocalyptic excitement that went beyond the religious community. Scientists and economists also joined in by depicting terrible end-time calamities—nuclear destruction, ecological disasters, financial collapse, and racial conflict. Indeed, many secular prophets were as gloomy as were some fundamentalists—but they did not have the rapture to bail them out.[24]

Some scientists came close to being date-setters. They insisted that life on Earth could not survive beyond a particular year. Fortunately for their reputations, most of their projected dates for the end still lie in the future. Also, the secular prophets have not been quite as specific as some Christian date-setters have. Nevertheless, some of the years designated by scientists for global destruction have come and gone. On the whole, society has been more charitable to such disconfirmations than it has to similar failures by religious prophets.

THE BIG BANG THEORY

The world may not have begun with a big bang, but it could certainly end with one. Consider what some people have to say: "As the bomb fell over Hiroshima and exploded, we saw an entire city disappear. . . . 'My God, what we have we done?" wrote Robert C. Lewis, an American aviator.[25] According to Andrei Sakharov, Soviet nuclear scientist, "All-out nuclear war would mean the destruction of contemporary civilization."[26] And as J. Robert Oppenheimer, father of the nuclear bomb, watched the first mushroom-shaped cloud over the New Mexico desert, he was heard to say, "I am become death, the destroyer of the world."[27] Indeed, the fear of

---

24. Debra Bergoffen, "The Apocalyptic Meaning of History," in *Apocalyptic Vision in America*, 33–34; Lewis, "Science, Progress, and the End of the Modern World," 308–9; Barkun, "Divided Apocalypse," 274–75; Wagar, *Terminal Visions*, 118–19. See also Charles Reich, *The Greening of America* (New York: Random House, 1970).

25. Quoted in Arthur M. Katz, *Life after Nuclear War* (Cambridge, MA: Ballenger, 1982) xxi.

26. Quoted in Carl Sagan, "Nuclear War and Climatic Catastrophe: Some Policy Implications," *Foreign Affairs* 62/2 (Winter 1983–84) 257.

27. Quoted in Anthony Hunter, *The Last Days* (London: Anthony Blond, 1958) 231. See also Chandler, *Doomsday*, 145; Richard Rhodes, *The Making of the Atomic*

The Godless Apocalypse

nuclear annihilation has not been limited to the scientific community. As noted in chapter 8, the theme of an atomic holocaust has captivated the imagination of fiction writers and has appeared in both novels and films.

Revelation 6 speaks of the four horsemen of the apocalypse. The red horse denotes war. Of course, war is not new, and today humans are not more evil or cruel. In fact, people have fought wars of unspeakable ferocity in ancient times. The nature of war has changed, however; weapons are far more efficient. The most sadistic Roman soldier could not have killed in a lifetime what a modern pilot can do on one mission. And on August 6, 1945, warfare became even more efficient as the United States dropped the first bomb on Hiroshima.[28]

In searing heat and a blinding light, the nuclear age opened with awesome destructiveness. From one to two hundred thousand people died directly or indirectly at Hiroshima. But even worse, these early bombs look like firecrackers when compared to modern weapons. Today, one bomb is from five to fifty times more powerful, and ten or more can be carried on a multiple-warhead missile.[29]

While everybody agrees that a nuclear war would be cataclysmic, the inevitability of nuclear war is subject to debate. The probability of such a conflict has waxed and waned since 1945. The bomb ended World War II in short order: we had won the war, and only we had the bomb; no one would attack us. But this sense of euphoria ended in 1949 when the Soviets tested their first nuclear weapon. The United States and the Soviet Union were already embroiled in the Cold War, and many thought a nuclear war inevitable. At various levels of intensity this feeling prevailed until the late 1980s. About fifty thousand nuclear weapons existed, enough to destroy the Earth many times over. And somebody was bound to use them—or so many people thought.[30]

Then came the end of the Cold War. The upheaval of 1989 ended Soviet rule in Eastern Europe, and the Soviet Union came unraveled in 1991. In the minds of many, nuclear war was no longer likely. The hands

---

Bomb (New York: Simon & Schuster, 1995).

28. W. Warren Wagar, *Next Three Futures: Paradigms of Things to Come* (New York: Praeger, 1991) 98–99; Daniel Cohen, *Waiting for the Apocalypse* (Buffalo: Prometheus, 1983) 165; Daniel Cohen, *Prophets of Doom* (Brookfield, CT: Millbrook, 1992) 123.

29. Wagar, *Next Three Futures*, 103; Paul R. Ehrlich et al., *The Nuclear Winter* (London: Sidgwick, 1984) 6–7.

30. Cohen, *Waiting for the Apocalypse*, 165–66; Sagan, "Nuclear War and Climatic Catastrophe," 260–61; Philip Morrison, "The Actuary of Our Species: The End of Humanity Regarded from the Viewpoint of Science," in *Visions of the Apocalypse*, 256–58.

of the Doomsday Clock in Chicago, where 12:00 symbolizes the dreaded nuclear apocalypse, were moved back from 11:58 to 11:43—the farthest the hands had been since the clock was introduced in 1947.[31]

The specter of a nuclear war has disappeared, so many believe. The red horse of the apocalypse has faded to a shade of pink. Yet even by 2010 the world still had about twenty-two thousand nuclear weapons, and the technology to make more continues to exist. To some extent the mushroom-shaped cloud still hangs over the world. Doomsday may only have been postponed. With all these weapons around, some madman will probably push the button.[32] The big questions are who, when, why, and where.

The most devastating nuclear holocaust, it was believed, would come in an American-Russian conflict. The old Soviet Union may be dead, but Russia still possesses thousands of nuclear weapons. In the late 1990s and the early twenty-first century, Russian nationalism has been on the rise. Also, Russia has tremendous natural resources and massive potential strength. While a resurgence of Russian power may not come in the near future, it is possible somewhere down the road. And along with this recovery will come a renewed possibility of a nuclear confrontation.

But Russia is merely the most obvious threat. A small power or a terrorist group could also provoke a nuclear confrontation. The technical know-how to build nuclear weapons is here to stay. Despite well-meaning arms control treaties and sanctions, this technology has spread. Officially, nine nations have the bomb, but many smaller nations either have secret nuclear weapons or the capability to build them in short order. And most frightening, nations like North Korea and Iran have very unstable rulers—modern-day Neros who might push the button with little regard for the consequences.[33] In *Thinking about the Unthinkable*, nuclear war expert Herbert Kahn presented a James Bond–type scenario in which a smaller power or even a terrorist group provokes the larger powers into a nuclear

---

31. "Hands of Doomsday Clock Are Moved Up Three Minutes," *Wichita Eagle*, December 1995, 7A; Chandler, *Doomsday*, 147; *National and International Religion Report*, 16 December 1991, 1.

32. Bruce W. Nelan, "How the World Will Look in 50 Years," *Time*, Fall 1992 (special issue), 37; Sagan, "Nuclear War and Climatic Catastrophe," 260–61; Apocalypse Right Now?," *Psychology Today* 27/1 (January 1994) 27–31.

33. Rubinsky and Wiseman, *End of the World*, 156; Ignace Lepp, "Fear of Collective Death," in *Endtime: The Doomsday Catalog*, ed. William Griffin (New York: Macmillian, 1979) 59: Chandler, *Doomsday*, 148–49; Nelan, "How the World Will Look in 50 Years," 37; Dominique Lagarde, "The Highest Bidder Gets the Weapons," *World Press Review*, December 1991, 11.

The Godless Apocalypse

exchange. The renegade launches a first-strike nuclear attack in the hope of drawing the major powers into the conflict. They go for the bait and proceed to demolish each other. Meanwhile, the rogue power is left standing and gains control after the war.[34]

Or a nuclear debacle could come by an accident or an act of nature. The world has seen a number of lesser episodes such as the 1979 partial meltdown at Three Mile Island, Pennsylvania. In 2011 Japan also experienced a nuclear crisis due to a tsunami. The worst nuclear disaster came in 1986 at the Chernobyl power plant in the Soviet Union. This and perhaps a future meltdown could have devastating consequences. Humanity lives in fear of such an accident. Even if such a catastrophe does not happen, we still have the problem of nuclear waste, the most dangerous pollutant on Earth. Currently we have no safe way to dispose of it, and it takes thousands of years to lose its radioactivity. Even in minute amounts, plutonium—the waste product of nuclear fuel—can be deadly to human, animal, and plant life.[35]

Still, the most likely scenario for the nuclear holocaust is war. War is endemic to the modern world system. Despite much idealism and efforts to curb belligerence, war will continue to be a fact of life. If a conflict escalates to merely the use of "low-yield 'tactical' or 'battlefield' nuclear weapons, limiting its further escalation up the ladder to thermonuclear doomsday" may be impossible.[36]

How destructive would a nuclear war be? This would depend on the nations involved, the number of warheads detonated, their destructive power, and the targets selected. Still, even the best-case scenarios are catastrophic. Moreover, students of nuclear war agree that the long-term effects will be at least as disastrous as the immediate destructiveness of the nuclear weapons themselves.[37]

In the first few days, millions of people will perish. The initial blast, firestorms, heat, radiation, hurricane-strength winds, and choking smoke and dust will cause an unprecedented number of casualties. Even if civilian centers are not targeted, the deaths will be in the millions, for military,

---

34. Herman Kahn, *Thinking about the Unthinkable* (New York: Horizon, 1962); Chandler, *Doomsday*, 148–49; Rubinsky and Wiseman, *End of the World*, 158.

35. David H. Hopper, *Technology, Theology, and the Idea of Progress* (Louisville: Westminster John Knox, 1991) 17; Cohen, *Waiting for the Apocalypse*, 184–85; Chandler, *Doomsday*, 149–50; Rubinsky and Wiseman, *End of the World*, 152.

36. Wagar, *Next Three Futures*, 103 (quote); Sagan, "Nuclear War and Climatic Catastrophe," 261–62.

37. Wagar, *Next Three Futures*, 104; Katz, *Life after the Nuclear War*, 41–68.

industrial, and government centers are often in densely populated areas.[38] In the worst-case scenarios far more people will die in the months and years thereafter. Almost all urban centers will be destroyed. While not everyone will perish, a large percentage of the total population will be burned or poisoned by radiation. The very fabric of life might unravel. With transportation and communication systems severed, power plants destroyed, governments incapacitated, and medical supplies unavailable, the necessities of life will be lacking in many regions. And if several industrial nations were destroyed, there would be little chance of aid from the outside, just as there was after World War II. Indeed, with farmers no longer growing food or unable to transport it to urban areas, the Western world would be threatened by famine, pestilence, and civil disorder not seen since the Middle Ages.[39]

But even worse is the "nuclear winter" scenario, which has come under attack by respected scientists. However, if the doomsday ecologists are on target, global temperatures would plunge, especially in the Northern Hemisphere, to at least negative ten degrees Fahrenheit. The world would be in an artificial winter from three months to two years. As a result, the food cycle would be disrupted and millions of people would die.[40]

THE WRATH OF MOTHER NATURE

"Oh, my God! Los Angles has vanished! . . .Wait a minute. There's more. Orange County is gone too. And most of San Diego. And . . ." So goes the

---

38. L.S. Stavrianos, *The Promise of the Coming Dark Age* (San Francisco: Freeman, 1976) 190; Wagar, *Next Three Futures*, 104: Sagan, "Nuclear War and Climatic Catastrophe," 262–63; Otto Friedrich, *The End of the World* (New York: Fromm, 1986) 344–47; Katz, *Life after the Nuclear War*, 41–78; Herman Kahn, *On Thermonuclear War* (Princeton, NJ: Princeton University Press, 1960) 40–54.

39. Stavrianos, *Coming Dark Age*, 190; Wagar, *Next Three Futures*, 104; Sagan, "Nuclear War and Climatic Catastrophe," 261–62; Katz, *Life after Nuclear War*, 48–68; Kahn, *On Thermonuclear War*, 57–74; Magus Clarke, *The Nuclear Destruction of Britain* (London: Croom Helm, 1982) 29–37; Jonathan Schell, *The Fate of Earth* (New York: Avon, 1982) 56–76; Paul R. Ehrlich et al., "Long Term Biological Consequences of Nuclear War," *Science*, 22 December 1983, 1293–97.

40. Wagar, *Next Three Futures*, 105; Ehrlich et al., *Nuclear Winter*, 3–43; Ehrlich, "Long Term Biological Consequences of Nuclear War," 1297–98; R. P. Turco et al., "Nuclear Winter: Global Consequences of Multiple Nuclear Explosions," *Science*, 22 December 1983, 1283–89.

The Godless Apocalypse

book *The Last Days of the Late Great State of California* (1968) by Curt Gentry, a California journalist.[41]

Will the end come at the hands of Mother Nature? Today very few scientists believe that natural causes—earthquakes, volcanoes, and floods—can precipitate a global catastrophe. To be sure, nature can still get angry and cause great havoc on a regional level. Thousands of people could still die because of one of these upheavals. And for others caught up in such a calamity, their world may in effect come to an end.

Throughout history people have viewed nature with great awe. Earthquakes, tsunamis, volcanoes, tidal waves, floods, and the like have roused terror. To religious people the forces of nature were viewed as the instruments of God, but some individuals saw nature as acting without God. Today a collection of scientists, prophets, psychics, astrologers, and eccentrics predict widespread natural catastrophes, if not the absolute end of humanity. The calamities that most frequently arouse an apocalyptic excitement include earthquakes, volcanoes, an ice age, and a polar shift.

Earthquakes head the list. Why? A sense of the havoc they can wreak is deeply imbedded in the human psyche. In the Middle East, where much of our thinking is rooted, earthquakes are the most common natural disaster. The Old Testament prophets, Jesus, and John of Revelation spoke of them, as did Nostradamus. And in the modern era, a host of soothsayers including Edgar Cayce and Jeane Dixon have predicted them. Semi-scientific seers like Jeffrey Goodman and Immanuel Velikovsky refer to them apocalyptically.[42]

History has witnessed a number of devastating earthquakes. The most deadly earthquake occurred in central China in 1556; approximately 830,000 people perished. The Lisbon earthquake of 1775 killed about 60,000 people. The 1811–12 quake in New Madrid, Missouri, killed few people because of the sparse population, but it shifted the topography of the entire area. Chile experienced a major earthquake in 1960, killing 3,000 people and sinking about 5,000 square miles of land. The worse natural disaster of the twentieth century occurred in 1976 in Tangshan, China, when 242,000 people perished. The quake that rocked Haiti in January of 2010 nearly equaled this number. Estimates say about 230,000 died.[43]

---

41. Curt Gentry, *The Last Days of the Late Great State of California* (New York: Putnam, 1968); Cohen, *Waiting for the Apocalypse*, 193.

42. Chandler, *Doomsday*, 138; Cohen, *Waiting for the Apocalypse*, 197; Charles Berlitz, *Doomsday: 1999 A.D.* (Garden City: NY, Doubleday, 1981) 57–59.

43. Berlitz, *Doomsday*, 41; Chandler, *Doomsday*, 139; Cohen, *Waiting for the Apocalypse*, 189; *The World Almanac and Book of Facts: 1992*, ed. Mark S. Hoffman (New

Could earthquakes endanger life on Earth? Probably not. But one theory conjectures that gigantic earthquakes could impact the rotation of the Earth. Scientists know that the Earth's rotation wobbles and that this wobble is related to earthquakes and volcanoes. Moreover, even minor variations in the rotation axis can affect climate on the Earth's surface and stresses within the Earth. But scientists do not know whether an axis shift causes earthquakes or earthquakes cause axis shifts, which could be catastrophic. If the latter, an earthquake might well be indirectly connected with the end of the world.[44]

Still, we do know that earthquakes can cause tsunamis. And while they may not bring an end to civilization, they can be catastrophic. "Technically, a tsunami is any set of ocean waves (tsunamis never come in singles, always in sets) caused by any abrupt disturbance of the sea surface." Most tsunamis are triggered by large earthquakes of a magnitude of at least seven on the Richter scale. While tsunamis may start locally and wreck regional havoc, they may travel thousands of miles and cause devastation in a distant place. On a destructive scale, tsunamis rank high. Since 1850 over 420,000 people have lost their lives to tsunamis. The seven most destructive tsunamis took place around Asia. By far the most deadly came after Christmas 2004 near Indonesia and several countries bordering the Indian Ocean. The death toll numbered around 300,000 plus thousands of missing people. While not as devastating, the earthquake and tsunami that rocked Japan in March of 2011 killed around 28,000 people plus damaging several nuclear reactors.[45]

Volcanoes may be nature's most spectacular expression, but they have not evoked much apocalyptic excitement. While they had a role in the end-time scenario of the Norseman, they play little role in the Christian and Western traditions. Moreover, unlike earthquakes, which strike without warning, volcanoes send a clear signal before erupting. Thus, if humans perish, it is usually because they failed to evacuate the area.[46]

York: Pharos, 1991) 546; Gordon Rattray Taylor, *The Doomsday Book* (Greenwich, CT: Fawcett, 1970) 39: Friedrich, *End of the World*, 179–212; Bill McGuire, *A Guide to the End of the World* (New York: Oxford University Press, 2002) 109–14.

44. Cohen, *Waiting for the Apocalypse*, 200–202; Chandler, *Doomsday*, 140–41; Moira Timms, *Prophecies and Predictions* (Santa Cruz, CA: Unity, 1980) 80.

45. De Villiers, *The End*, 175–77 (quote 176); McGuire, *Guide to the End of the World*, 114–18; Nancy Gibbs, "The Day the Earth Moved," *Time*, 28 March 2011, 24–32; Jeffrey Kluger, "Fear Goes Nuclear," *Time*, 28 March 2011, 34–38.

46. Cohen, *Waiting for the Apocalypse*, 206–7.

The Godless Apocalypse

Still, there have been at least two doomsday explosions in modern times. Perhaps the most devastating eruption took place in 1883 on Krakatoa, an island in what is now Indonesia. The explosion could be heard nearly 3,000 miles away, and about 37,000 people perished. In 1902 Mount Pelee blew up on Martinique in the Caribbean. About 40,000 died, largely because they failed to heed the ample warnings.[47]

A more likely but far more distant threat to world survival is ice. Scientists say that ice ages occur in cycles that last perhaps 100,000 years. Between these ice ages are balmy interludes, but they are the exception not the rule. Geologists insist that a new ice age is all but inevitable; sheets of ice will again spread over much of the Northern Hemisphere.[48] We are now about halfway through the warm interlude. In about 10,000–15,000 years a new cycle will begin. Ironically, there must first be warming for ice to soften and move south. Because the greenhouse effect may quicken the process, some scientists believe that a new ice age will be upon us within 2,000 years. They disagree, however, as to the effects of this new ice age. Some scientists believe it will be devastating, but humanity will survive. Others say no one will survive. Regardless, we ought not to lose any sleep over it—it's still thousands of years away.[49]

THE QUIET APOCALYPSE

The end of the world may be sneaking up on us, say some environmentalists. We are committing global suicide. Global warming, spilled oil, poisoned seas, ozone depletion, radioactive soil, acid rain, and toxic waste are "combining to bring the Earth to the brink of apocalypse." Thus the "coming end will be a strictly do-it yourself apocalypse."[50] No one is doing it to us; we are doing it to ourselves!

47. Chandler, *Doomsday*, 142; Edward O. Wilson, "The Discovery of Life," *Discover*, September 1992, 48–50; Cohen, *Waiting for the Apocalypse*, 207–8; John Zajac, *The Delicate Balance* (Lafayette, LA: Prescott, 1990) 92–93; Richard W. Noone, 5/52000 (New York: Harmony Books, 1983) 306.

48. Gregg Easterbrook, "Return of the Glaciers," *Newsweek*, 23 November 1992, 62–63; Cohen, *Waiting for the Apocalypse*, 216–17; Chandler, *Doomsday*, 142–43; Al Gore, *Earth in the Balance: Ecology and the Human Spirit* (Boston: Houghton Mifflin, 1992) 61–62.

49. Easterbrook, "Return of the Glaciers," 62–63; Chandler, *Doomsday*, 142–43; Cohen, *Waiting for the Apocalypse*, 216–17; Taylor, *Doomsday Book*, 62–63; Rubinsky and Wiseman, *End of the World*, 162.

50. Chandler, *Doomsday*, 163 (quote); "Doom Hotline: Hang It Up," *United Methodist Reporter*, 5 October 1990, 2.

Nearly all scientists view the rape of the environment with extreme concern. Unless we do an about-face in the near future, humanity will face serious problems. But there is disagreement as to whether the environmental damage can be reversed. The pessimists "warn of doom within a century unless mankind mends its ways. Pshaw, say the skeptics. But they too, see a need for change."[51] The doomsday environmentalists—those that believe the planet is near death—view the greatest threat as coming from three related problems. Global warming, deforestation, and the depletion of the ozone—especially global warming—could bring us to the brink of a secular Armageddon.

The greenhouse effect (or global warming) has many environmentalists up in arms. The Earth's temperature is rising because the upper atmosphere contains too much carbon dioxide and other greenhouse gases. These pollutants come from the burning of fossil fuels (oil, gasoline, and coal) and other causes such as agriculture. Such substances serve as a blanket trapping the Earth's heat. Up to a point this is normal. But excessive gases cause a gradual warming of the Earth's temperature.[52]

The greenhouse effect had its beginnings in the nineteenth century. With industrialization and later the automobile, tremendous amounts of fossil fuels were burnt, emitting enormous quantities of carbon dioxide into the atmosphere. Such emissions have accelerated rapidly in the twentieth and twenty-first centuries, bringing the world to a dangerous point.[53] Efforts to improve this situation by means of international agreements and quotas were attempted at Kyoto (1997) and Copenhagen (2009), both to little avail.

According to many environmentalists, global warming threatens the climate equilibrium. Temperatures could rise from three to thirty degrees

---

51. Sharon Begley, "Is It Apocalypse Now?," *Newsweek*, 1 June 1992, 37–42 (quote); William Lowther, "A Threat to Human Life," *Macleans's*, 30 June 1996, 43; Robert Silverberg, "The Greenhouse Effect: Apocalypse Now or Chicken Little?" *Omni* 13/10 (July 1991) 50–54, 86; Robert J. Samuelson, "The End Is Not at Hand," *Newsweek*, 1 June 1992, 43; Robert M. White, "The Great Climate Debate," *Scientific American*, July 1990, 36–37; Morrison, "Actuary of Our Species," 250–54.

52. George F. Sanderson, "Climate Change," *Futurist*, March–April 1992, 35–36; Michael Oppenheimer and Robert H. Boyle, *Dead Heat* (New York: Basic, 1990) 2–3; Wagar, *Next Three Futures*, 61; Silverberg, "Greenhouse Effect," 52–53; Burkhard Bilger, *Global Warming* (New York: Chelsea, 1992) 33–38; Bill McKibben, *The End of Nature* (New York: Random House, 1989) 11–12.

53. Wagar, *Next Three Futures*, 61; White, "Great Climate Debate," 37–38; Bilger, *Global Warming*, 14–15; Leslie A. Chambers, "Air Pollution in Historical Perspective," in *Environmental Decay in Historical Context*, ed. Robert Detweiler et al. (Glenview, IL: Scott, Foresman, 1973) 114–18.

The Godless Apocalypse

Fahrenheit. Even a change of a few degrees would dramatically affect life on Earth. Weather patterns in every part of the globe would change. Some areas would be drier, significantly reducing the food supply. Others would experience monsoons and floods. Even a rise in temperature of a few degrees would melt the polar caps; the oceans would rise, submerging coastal areas throughout the globe. Most of the world's major low-lying cities would be inundated. And we have said nothing about a rise of twenty to thirty degrees. This would be unimaginably disastrous.[54]

Doomsday by deforestation! Could it happen? In *Earth in the Balance*, former Vice President Al Gore said that the destruction of the rain forests and the living species found therein "represent[s] the single most serious damage to nature now occurring."[55] Forests and the plant and animal life they now house are the key to biodiversity. And without a hospitable ecosystem "the remaining tenure of the human race would be nasty and brief."[56]

What if we lose some species? Who needs these birds, insects, and plants anyway? We do! They perform services such as pollination. Indeed, our ecosystem cannot be altered significantly without impacting human life. On a more direct level, the forests provide humanity with pharmaceuticals, fibers, petroleum substitutes, timber, and other essential products.[57]

Deforestation is also an aspect of the greenhouse effect—it magnifies global warming. Carbon dioxide levels in the atmosphere are the highest because of the mass destruction of the world's forests. Trees consume much carbon dioxide, which they need for photosynthesis. Therefore, fewer trees result in more carbon dioxide in the atmosphere, which in turn produces greater global warming in a vicious cycle. And we know what a catastrophe this will cause.[58]

The third environmental problem with the potential for worldwide disaster is the depletion of the ozone. The Earth's atmosphere has a thin ozone layer, which protects us from harmful ultraviolet sunlight. Unfortunately, chlorofluorocarbons (CFCs), which are used in refrigeration

---

54. Lowther, "Threat to Human Life," 43; Wagar, *Next Three Futures*, 62; Sanderson, "Climate Change," 35–37; Oppenheimer and Boyle, *Dead Heat*, 8–17; McKibben, *End of Nature*, 23–32.

55. Gore, *Earth in Balance*, 116, 119; Chandler, *Doomsday*, 168–69.

56. Wilson, "Diversity of Life," 65–68 (quote); Chandler, *Doomsday*, 168.

57. Jamie Murphy, "The Quiet Apocalypse, *Time*, 13 October 1986, 80; Chandler, *Doomsday*, 168–69; Barry Commoner, *The Closing Circle* (New York: Bantam, 1971) 32–33.

58. Wagar, *Next Three Futures*, 61; Commoner, *Closing Circle*, 26–27.

systems, some aerosol sprays, fertilizers, jets, and the production of foam packaging, contain ozone-destroying chemicals.[59] Some governments have taken steps to greatly reduce CFCs. And to some extent, these steps have helped to arrest the problem and even repair the ozone.

Yet some scientists tell us that a hole in the ozone about the size of the United States still exists over Antarctica. Another one might be developing over the heavily populated Northern Hemisphere. Without this ozone shield all kinds of problems will develop—genetic abnormalities, skin cancers, cataracts, and damage to marine life. In fact, some scientists even contend that the increase in radiation could destroy all plant and animal life. Could a hole in the ozone bring doomsday? Probably not. But southern Chile, where an ozone hole exists, has experienced some ominous phenomena—blind cattle and sheep, withered trees and cacti, severe sunburns, and strange spots on animals. One farmer even tried to put sunglasses on his sheep.[60]

STANDING ROOM ONLY

Planet Earth is small, and at this time we have no place else to go. Eventually, we may run out of space and the ability to feed ourselves. The end will come because of overpopulation and lack of food. In *The Population Bomb* (1968), scientist Paul Ehrlich said we would cross this threshold by the 1970s: "At this date nothing can prevent a substantial increase in the world death rate." Despite crash programs to feed people, millions will starve. Such "programs will only provide a stay of execution" unless there are successful efforts to control the population.[61]

Ehrlich's first prediction misfired, but like many religious prognosticators he did not recant. He continued to make similar forecasts. His 1991 book *The Population Explosion* said that our runaway population will result in "a billion or more deaths from starvation and disease." Moreover, society as we know it will dissolve.[62]

59. McKibben, *End of Nature*, 132–34; Chandler, *Doomsday*, 166–67.

60. Begley, "Is It Apocalypse Now?," 42; Lowther, "Threat to Human Life," 43; "Evidence Points to Regeneration of Ozone Layer," *Wichita Eagle*, 31 May 1996, 5A; Chandler, *Doomsday*, 167–68.

61. Ehrlich, *Population Bomb*, prologue. See also Rubinsky and Wiseman, *End of the World*, 148; Paddock and Paddock, *Famine—1975!*

62. Paul R. Ehrlich, *The Population Explosion* (New York: Simon & Schuster, 1991). See also Chandler, *Doomsday*, 171; William F. Allman, "Fatal Attraction: Why We Love Doomsday," *U.S News and World Report*, 30 April 1990, 12; Shaw, "Apocalypse

The Godless Apocalypse

Of course, not all scientists agree with Ehrlich's doomsday predictions. Some starry-eyed optimists such as Julian Simon see the world supporting from twenty-five to thirty billion people. They see most of the world improving its agricultural productivity to something approximating that of North America and Western Europe. More realistic scientists set the limits at around fifteen billion.[63]

Scientists also disagree as to when, if ever, humanity will reach the limits of population growth. The optimists point to the slow population growth in the industrial nations and say that the whole world will emulate this pattern. The world's population should stabilize within tolerable limits, somewhere between ten and fifteen billion. Other scientists point to the runaway population growth in the developing world. Barring a nuclear war or a devastating plague, the upper limits will be reached around 2100. Mother Earth will snap. Billions will die from starvation and disease.[64] There will also be incredible tension, for lack of food brings out the animal instincts in humans. It will be survival of the fittest. With the lack of space prohibiting privacy, people will become unsociable and hostile. Poverty will run rampant. Even if humanity survives, much of the world will be crowded into metropolises like Mexico City, Sao Paulo, and Calcutta.[65]

Awareness of the population peril goes back as far as English economist Thomas Malthus and his 1798 *Essay on the Principle of Population*: "The power of population is indefinitely greater than the power in the Earth to produce subsistence for man." Malthus believed that the population would grow until checked by a lack of food. For a while, people accepted Malthus's ideas. But improved agricultural methods came along, allowing fewer people to produce more food on less land. Medical advances such as

---

Again," 51.

63. Taylor, *Doomsday Book*, 193–97; Colin Clark, "World Population," *Nature*, 3 May 1958, 1235–36; Kevin Kelly, "Apocalypse, Juggernaut, Goodbye," *Whole Earth Review* 65 (Winter 1989) 38–40.

64. Taylor, *Doomsday Book*, 194–209; McKibben, *End of Nature*, 144–45; Barry B. Hughes, *World Futures* (Baltimore: Johns Hopkins University Press, 1985) 58; Cohen, *Waiting for the Apocalypse*, 176; Wagar, *Next Three Futures*, 53–54; Tim Stafford, "Are People the Problem?," *Christianity Today*, 3 October 1994, 47–48; Ehrlich, *Population Bomb*, 69–71; Donnella H. Meadows et al., *The Limits of Growth* (New York: Universe, 1974) back cover.

65. Commoner, *Closing Circle*, 131–32; Rubinsky and Wiseman, *End of the World*, 148; Brian J. L. Berry, *The Human Consequences of Urbanization* (New York: St. Martin's, 1973).

antibiotics also prolonged life. As a result, the world population grew from about one billion in Malthus's day to about 6.9 billion in 2010.[66]

But Malthus may eventually prove to be right. Improved agricultural methods have increased the food supply—only to be outstripped by an exploding population. Today much of the world is not being fed properly and periodic famines in the developing world still occur. Unless the world's population is drastically limited in the next one hundred years, the crash will come. Indeed, the rider on the black horse (famine) may stalk humanity once again. And this is to say nothing about the environmental problems caused by overpopulation. The more people polluting nature and cutting down trees, the greater the chance for an environmental catastrophe.[67] Moreover, nearly all other disasters, whether caused by humankind or nature, are made worse by overpopulation.

PLAGUE AND PESTILENCE

The pale horse of the apocalypse—representing death by plague and disease—has stalked humanity through history. Quite often it has been associated with end-of-the-world panics or judgment. In Matthew 24:7 Jesus speaks of "famines, and pestilences, and earthquakes" as signs of the end. Revelation 8–16 tells of God's pouring out his judgment at the end of the world in the form of pestilences and plagues.

Horror of horrors, the Black Death terrified Western society as no plague ever has. During the Middle Ages it killed about one third of Europe's population. No one knew what caused it. "Some say it descended upon the human race through the influence of the heavenly bodies," wrote Giovanni Boccaccio in his *Decameron*. A grand conjunction of Saturn, Jupiter, and Mars in March 1345 was thought by some enlightened scientists of the day to have corrupted the Earth's atmosphere and caused the plague. Many said that it was "a punishment signifying God's righteous anger at

---

66. Hughes, *World Futures*, 55–58; Cohen, *Waiting for the Apocalypse*, 174–75 (quote); Wagar, *Next Three Futures*, 53; Meadows et al., *Limits to Growth*, 48–49; E. A. Wrigley, *Population and History* (New York: McGraw-Hill, 1969); Carlo M. Cipolla, *The Economic History of World Population* (New York: Penguin, 1972); Clark, "World Population," 1235; *The Global 2000 Report to the President of the U.S.*, ed. Gerald O. Barney (New York: Pergamon, 1980) 12.

67. Commoner, *Closing Circle*, 131–36; Cohen, *Waiting for the Apoclaypse*, 175; Meadows et al., *Limits to Growth*, back cover; Paddock and Paddock, *Famine—1975!*, 7–23.

The Godless Apocalypse

our iniquitous way of life." Still other Europeans blamed it on the Jews, insisting that they had poisoned the wells.[68]

Most people connected the Black Death with some form of divine judgment or end-of-the-world scenario. But when the plague continued for centuries, people gradually began to think in terms of natural causes. By the early twentieth century they figured out that bacilli from rat fleas had caused the epidemic.[69]

The Black Death illustrates how pestilences relate to end-of-the-world thinking. Religious people see plagues as a divine instrument for punishing humanity for its evil and as a sign of the end. To secular thinkers epidemics have natural causes—sometimes unknown. They may also view plagues apocalyptically, but not as the end of the world, for plagues are usually local in scope. Globalization and rapid international travel, however, has become a game changer. Even local outbreaks can spread rapidly throughout the globe. In addition, a new pestilence adds to the horror. People become particularly terrified when an unknown disease—one they don't understand—attacks.[70]

To a large extent modern medicine has curbed the specter of widespread epidemics, but not completely. During World War I more than three million Russians died of typhus. In 1918 an influenza epidemic killed twenty million people throughout the world. But this attack did not set off an end-of-the-world panic, for influenza was a known disease that could be treated.[71]

Then came AIDS. By the 1980s it had surfaced in America, largely among homosexuals. As long as it was confined to the gay community, it did not set off a major crisis. But when AIDS began to go mainstream, it stirred up considerable apocalyptic excitement, for until recent antiviral drugs the disease had no known cure. So until these advances, once contracted it usually proved fatal.[72]

68. Friedrich, *End of the World*, 116, 129–30.

69. Robert Lerner, "The Black Death and Western European Eschatological Mentalities," *American Historical Review* 86/3 (1981) 534; Philip Ziegler, *The Black Death* (New York: Harper & Row, 1969); Barbara W. Tuchman, *A Distant Mirror: The Calamitous 14th Century* (New York: Ballantine, 1978); Rubinski and Wiseman, *End of the World*, 87.

70. Cohen, *Waiting for the Apocalypse*, 179; "Why Viruses Push Our Hot Buttons," *Newsweek*, 22 May 1995, 54.

71. Cohen, *Prophets of Doom*, 128–29; Matthew Naythons, "Commandos of Viral Combat," *Newsweek*, 22 May 1995, 50. See also Frederick F. Cartwright, *Disease and History* (New York: Mentor, 1972).

72. Cohen, *Prophets of Doom*, 128–29; Larry Martz, "A New Panic over AIDS,"

The chief causes of AIDS are homosexual or promiscuous heterosexual activity and the exchange of needles for taking drugs, all of which most Christians consider immoral. Thus some Christians declared AIDS to be God's judgment for sin. By the mid-1980s the spread of AIDS had begun to arouse some apocalyptic excitement. Jerry Falwell said, "AIDS is God's judgment on a society that does not live by his rules."[73] Then Jack Van Impe really stirred matters up. Quoting Revelation 16, he related AIDS to the sin of bestiality. In Africa's jungles men committed sex with monkeys carrying the virus and thus catapulted the disease to global proportions. In the belief that AIDS could wipe out civilization, Van Impe declared that by 2020 the disease might kill the last human on Earth.[74] Citing a CIA study, Hal Lindsey estimated that by the mid-1990s 75 percent of sub-Saharan Africa could be infected by AIDS.[75]

But such apocalyptic talk is not confined to the doomsday preachers. Millions will obviously die if a cure is not found. In 1992 the World Health Organization estimated that forty million people will be HIV-infected by 2000. And as AIDS spreads among heterosexuals, the crisis will grow worse unless a cure is developed.[76] These figures were slightly off but the situation was still serious. In 2008, global estimates said from thirty-one to thirty-five million people had AIDS and that since 1981 twenty-five million had died from HIV infections.

Could much of the world wind up like Uganda? In the 1980s and early 1990s, Uganda represented the worst-case scenario. Estimates said half of Uganda's population of eighteen million had contracted HIV and that many could die in the near future. British journalist Dan Wooding feared that Uganda might become "so decimated that it will not be able to exist as a nation." Thanks to strong government leadership such a dire situation has not materialized. By 2008, however, 1.1 million people still had AIDS and 61,000 had died of the disease in that year alone. While AIDS is

---

Newsweek, 30 March 1987, 18–19; Brian K. Murphy, "Waiting for the Apocalypse," *Canadian Forum*, October 1989, 31.

73. Quoted in Chandler, *Doomsday*, 156.

74. Jack Van Impe, "The AIDS Cover-Up" (TV soundtrack) (Troy, MI: Jack Van Impe Ministries, 1986). See also Chandler, *Doomsday*, 157.

75. Hal Lindsey, *Planet Earth—2000 A.D.* (Palos Verdes Estates, CA: Western Front, 1994) 109.

76. *World Almanac: 1992*, 198; Chandler, *Doomsday*, 157; Bernard Gavzer, "What Keeps Me Alive," *Parade*, January 1993, 4; Martz, "New Panic over Aids," 18–19.

The Godless Apocalypse

not as bad elsewhere, it has destabilized other countries in the developing world by inflicting especially young adults in the prime of life.[77]

By the mid-1990s a measure of medical progress with HIV helped to reduce the hysteria over AIDS. But along came the gruesome Ebola virus. Having first surfaced in Sudan in 1976, it lay dormant for about sixteen years, only to arise in 1995 to kill again—this time in Zaire. It is one of the most elusive, mysterious, and deadly pathogens in the world. The Ebola virus ravages the human body by destroying the immune system and causing massive bleeding that usually ends in a horrible death.[78] True, but most scientists say that the Ebola virus is ill suited to bring about doomsday. It cannot be transmitted by a sneeze or cough; it kills its victims so quickly that they don't have much chance to infect others. In the twentieth-first century dire warnings came regarding the Avian flu and SARS. As of yet, these diseases have not wrecked the havoc once feared. Still, if a mysterious disease without a cure ever got loose in a major urban center, a catastrophe would result. Compounding this situation, bacteria are increasingly becoming resistant to antibiotics.[79]

Futurists envision two other plague-related nightmares—biological warfare and diseases from outer space. Even small powers can develop a stock of devastating bacteriological weapons. Such weapons could also be launched by a clandestine terrorist organization. However, for a global doomsday to be a real possibility, a major power with missiles and planes would probably have to get involved. More far-fetched is the possibility of unknown germs entering Earth from a spacecraft. If humans ever begin to explore other planets, such a scenario will be a realistic concern.[80]

---

77. Dan Wooding, "Former Football Player Aids Ugandan AIDS Victims," *Evangelical Press News Service*, 10 July 1992; Chandler, *Doomsday*, 159 (quote); "Massive AIDS Epidemic Festers in Latin America," *New York Times*, 25 January 1993, A1-8; Rod Nordland, "AIDS: Fear of Foreigners," *Newsweek*, 6 April 1987, 36.

78. Geoffrey Cowley, "Outbreak of Fear," *Newsweek*, 22 May 1995, 48-55; Geoffrey Cowley, "New AIDS Optimism," *Newsweek*, 22 July 1996, 68; Michael D. Lemonick, "Returning to the Hot Zone, *Time*, 22 May 1995, 62-63: Mark Jaffe, "Deadly Outbreak a Mystery," *Wichita Eagle*, 15 May 1995, 1A, 14A; Shannon Brownlee, "Horror in the Hot Zone," *U.S. News and World Report*, 22 May 1995, 57-61; "Drug Combinations Make Inroads on AIDS Virus," *Wichita Eagle*, 12 July 1996, 3A.

79. Lemonick, "Return to the Hot Zone," 63; Cowley, "Outbreak of Fear," 51-53; Brownlee, "Horror in the Hot Zone," 61. See also Richard Preston, *The Hot Zone* (New York: Random House, 1994).

80. Cohen, *Waiting for the Apocalypse*, 179, 181.

BIG SCARY THINGS FROM THE SKY

Suppose we come to our senses and eliminate nuclear, chemical, and biological weapons. Suppose we also solve our environmental problems, and medical science learns to control all communicable diseases. Would the possibility of doomsday then be eliminated? Not entirely! Planet Earth could still be bombarded by a comet or asteroid. Or we could experience some other cosmic disaster such as the sun exploding.[81]

"During a human lifetime, there's roughly a 1-in-10,000 chance that Earth will be hit by something big enough to wipe out crops worldwide and possibly force survivors to return to the ways of Stone Age hunter-gathers," writes Sharon Begley of *Newsweek*. Those odds are about the same as one dying in a car crash during any six-month period, getting cancer from breathing automobile exhaust in Los Angeles, or dying from anesthesia during surgery. The fact is that "killer asteroids and comets are out there. And someday, one will be on a collision course with Earth." The only question is when. If life on Earth goes on long enough, scientists believe that such a fate is inevitable.[82]

Before proceeding we need to define some terms. What is the difference between comets, meteors, meteorites, and asteroids? Comets consist of frozen gases. Like planets, they travel around the sun, but in irregular orbits. Meteors are small particles entering the Earth's atmosphere, where they burn up and are seen as shooting stars. The remains of these shooting stars are called meteorites—solid objects of metal and stone that actually reach the Earth. Asteroids are large meteoroids whose usual orbit lies between Mars and Jupiter.[83]

For several millennia people have watched cosmic objects—comets, meteor showers, and asteroids—with great fascination. They saw them as strange and unnatural events and as omens for good or ill. "These signs forerun the death or fall of kings," says a minor character in Shakespeare's *Richard II*. Early Christians more often viewed such cosmic activities as

---

81. John R. Albright, "The End of the World," *Dialog* 30/4 (Autumn 1991) 280–81.

82. Sharon Begley, "The Science of Doom," *Newsweek*, 23 November 1992 (quote); Melinda Beck, "And If the Comet Misses," *Newsweek*, 23 November 1992, 64; Frank Close, *Apocalypse When?: Cosmic Catastrophe and the Fate of the Universe* (New York: Morrow, 1988) 204–21; McGuire, *Guide to the End of the World*, 140–45.

83. Cohen, *Waiting for the Apocalypse*, 110–11; Chandler, *Doomsday*, 129; David Crystal, ed., *Cambridge Encyclopedia* (Cambridge: Cambridge University Press, 1992) 786.

The Godless Apocalypse

signs of God's wrath rather than his favor. But while they may be omens, they do not always point to the end of the world.[84]

Of the various astronomical phenomena comets have generated the most end-of-the-world excitement. The appearance of a comet in 1843 swelled the ranks of the Millerite movement, convincing many that Christ would return shortly. In 1910 Halley's Comet prompted an end-time panic. Many people believed that it would collide with the Earth and smash it to bits. To no avail scientists pointed out that Halley's movement had been known for two centuries and that it would miss the Earth by millions of miles. In 1910 Halley disappointed the doomsayers; its reappearance in 1986 prompted no apocalyptic excitement.[85]

Are the comets merely omens of doom, or could they become agents of doom? Could a collision with a large comet destroy planet Earth? This possibility has been the grist for many science fiction stories. And, in fact, some astronomers contend that a huge comet smashed into the Earth sixty-five million years ago, killing the dinosaurs and about two thirds of all life. (Other scientists believe that even worlds could collide.)[86]

In June 1908 a huge fireball streaked across the Siberian sky. What scientists believe was a comet leveled eighty million trees in a circle about twenty-five miles in diameter. Scientists theorize that the comet, which was several miles in diameter and about ten million tons in weight, exploded in the atmosphere right before reaching the ground. Thus it created no large crater. But the people in Siberia thought that the world had ended.[87]

In the late twentieth century the comet Swift-Tuttle concerned some scientists. Most comets originate in far space beyond Pluto. Gravity pulls some of them toward the sun, and at times they cross the Earth's orbit. About two hundred visit the Earth's environs every two centuries. Swift-Tuttle (named after the two astronomers who first saw it) passed within 110 million miles of Earth in 1992. Astrophysicist Brian Marsden

---

84. Cohen, *Waiting for the Apocalypse*, 91, 113; Bradley E. Schaefer, "Comets That Changed the World," *Sky and Telescope*, May 1997, 46–51.

85. Michael Barkun, *Crucible of the Millennium* (Syracuse, NY: Syracuse University Press, 1986) 54–56, 107–17; Cohen, *Waiting for the Apocalypse*, 85–86; Cohen, *Prophets of Doom* 108; Close, *Apocalypse When?*, 23, 35, 43, 59; Schaefer, "Comets That Changed the World," 49–50.

86. Begley, "Science of Doom," 56; Cohen, *Waiting for the Apocalypse*, 92; Close, *Apocalypse When?*, 53–69; Adam Rogers, "Attention: Incoming Object," *Newsweek*, 24 March 1997, 64–65.

87. Chandler, *Doomsday*, 115–16; Cohen, *Waiting for the Apocalypse*, 98–106; Begley, "Science of Doom," 59; Albright, "End of the World," 280; Close, *Apocalypse When?*, 9–10.

calculates that Swift-Tuttle will come much closer to Earth in August 2126. And if it goes slightly off course, it might even hit Earth. The odds are one in ten thousand.[88]

Meteorites constantly bombard Earth, but they are usually small and do little damage. Fortunately, the larger asteroids, which could devastate Earth, are fewer in number. But so much for the friendly skies. Earth has taken some major hits: scientists have verified 139 craters, and erosion has undoubtedly erased many more. Meteor Crater, which is near Winslow, Arizona, has a three-mile circumference. The thirty-mile-wide Vredefort Ring in South Africa may have been a meteorite. The largest meteorite in recent years struck Siberia in 1947.[89]

Actually, the near misses have caused more anxiety than have the hits. The asteroid Hermes passed Earth by five hundred thousand miles in October 1937. If it had crashed, Hermes would have packed more punch than all the nuclear weapons in the world. In August 1972 an asteroid with five times the power of the Hiroshima bomb passed over Wyoming. Another asteroid missed the Earth by seven hundred thousand miles in March 1989. Had it arrived six hours later, civilization might have been destroyed. In 1992 the asteroid Toutatis came within two million miles of Earth. In 2004 it came back, swooping less than one million miles away. Some doomsday projections say that Toutatis will approach the Earth in December 2012. In September of 2010 two asteroids—too small to do significant damage—came within forty-five thousand miles of the Earth, a distance closer than the moon.[90]

If the comets miss, the friendly skies have other ways to do us in. Scientists tell us that the days on Earth are getting one second longer every sixty thousand years because the moon is gradually pulling away from the Earth. As this occurs, the Earth's rotation slows down and oceanic tides are disrupted. In about ten million years, each day and night will equal

---

88. Begley, "Science of Doom," 58–59; Chandler, *Doomsday*, 131; Blaine P. Friedlander Jr., "Comet Could Collide with Earth in 2126," *Washington Post News Service*, 22 October 1992; Close, *Apocalypse When?*, 44; Marq de Villiers, *The End*, 106.

89. Begley, "Science of Doom," 58; Cohen, *Waiting for the Apocalypse*, 111–21; Close, *Apocalypse When?*, 13–20.

90. Begley, "Science of Doom," 56; Chandler, *Doomsday*, 130–31; Close, *Apocalypse When?*, 40; "Asteroid Making Close Pass," 28 November 1996, 3A; "Two Asteroids to Narrowly Miss Earth," http://www.australiangeographic.com.au/journal/asteroids-to-pass-cl; "Asteroid Toutatis Approaches Earth on December 12, 2012," http://ddig.wordpress.com/2008/07/07astroid-toutatis-approaches-e.

The Godless Apocalypse

fifty of our current days. Such a climatic change will have a drastic effect on plant and animal life.[91]

In addition, if a comet or asteroid doesn't strike this planet, a star might. Our Milky Way is hurtling toward its nearest neighbor—the galaxy Andromeda—at about seventy miles a second. In about five to ten billion years they will collide. And since Andromeda is two to three times larger, the Milky Way will get the worse of the collision. Our galaxy will be destroyed and consumed.[92]

But before Andromeda gets us, our own sun may do us in. Planet Earth may well get cooked by its own star. The sun is now about 4.5 billion years old, making it a middle-aged star. Its fuel supply is moving to its outer edges. As a result, the sun is gradually getting bigger and brighter. In about two billion years Earth will feel the effects; for example, winters in New England will hit about ninety degrees Fahrenheit. In about seven billion years, the oceans will boil, and the sun will get so large that it engulfs the inner planets of Mercury and Venus and chars Earth into a cinder. But this will be the last hurrah for the sun. It will run out of fuel and become a dwarf star. It will then be too cold for any form of life in our solar system to survive.[93]

THE SECULARIZATION OF THE FOUR HORSEMEN

The four horsemen portrayed in the Book of Revelation symbolize a catastrophic end of the world. For most of Western history, people have believed that the end would come at the hands of God. But God now has some competition—humanity might destroy itself. To be sure, the sacred and secular apocalypses overlap at points. In fact, given a particular view of divine providence, Christians can interpret secular disasters as being directed by God. Traditionally, natural calamities—earthquakes, volcanoes, and such—have been seen as the work of God. Some Christians

---

91. Beck, "And If the Comet Misses," 64; Chandler, *Doomsday*, 133; Rubinsky and Wiseman, *End of the World*, 163.

92. Beck, "And If the Comet Misses," 64; Chandler, *Doomsday*, 132–33; Close, *Apocalypse When?*, 111–12.

93. Beck, "And If the Comet Misses," 64; Chandler, *Doomsday*, 133–34; Close *Apocalypse When?*, 204–9; Albright, "End of the World," 281: Morrison, "Actuary of Our Species," 259.

even attribute manmade catastrophes—wars and the rape of the environment—to divine providence.

This chapter, however, has focused on a different perspective—that there will be a natural and secular end to the world. While the sacred and secular apocalypses are often muddled together, they differ at two points—the end results and the causes. In a strict sense, apocalyptic thinking entails both disaster and triumph. The secular apocalypse places little emphasis on triumph. No golden age will follow a nuclear war or an environmental catastrophe. At best, humankind will pull back from the edge of a precipice and avert a calamity. But this can hardly be viewed as a triumph, let alone a golden age.

The major point of divergence concerns causes. Who or what causes wars, earthquakes, famine, pestilence, and environmental crises? Or, should the ultimate disaster, a nuclear holocaust occur, who would be responsible? Christians may not say that God has caused these calamities, but they will say that he has permitted them. Conversely, secular thinkers look to natural or human causes. While they may not be irreligious people, they focus on secondary factors, that is, human beings or nature, rather than the ultimate cause, God. They emphasize what can be observed or scientifically validated. Such thinking has its roots in the late Middle Ages. While the vast majority of the people attributed the Black Death to divine judgment, some individuals began to look for natural causes. As the modern world emerged in the eighteenth and nineteenth centuries, the notion of a secular apocalypse began to gain momentum. But it was not until the post–World War II era that such thinking took off: humanity does not need God to destroy the world; they can do it themselves!

We have seen that the end without God can come in several ways. If doomsday comes via an environmental crisis or a plague, there will be a quiet apocalypse. Or, as T. S. Eliot put it, "This is the way the world ends, not with a bang but a whimper." On the other hand, if the end comes by means of a nuclear war or cosmic collision, it may come with a bang after all.[94]

---

94. D. E. Thomsen, "The End of the World: You Won't Feel a Thing," *Science News*, 20 June 1987, 391.

12

An Eschatological Hodgepodge

As we are moving toward the end-time events of 2012 in chapter 13, several eschatological subjects need to be addressed. And they do not fit into a cohesive package. They are diverse and unrelated, except for the fact that they point to the end of history. So this chapter will resemble a medley and be somewhat heterogeneous.

Roman Catholics make up about half of the world's Christians and nearly a quarter of the religious bodies in America. Still, the Catholic perspective regarding end-time events has received little attention, especially in contemporary America. Save for some coverage in chapter 2, this study has barely mentioned the subject. This situation has developed for several reasons. One, official Catholic teaching discourages apocalyptic speculation. Next, Catholicism emphasizes living in the present more than it focuses on the end of the world. Three, Catholics themselves have evidenced considerable apathy regarding this subject.[1]

What about mainline Protestantism in America? Such Christians focus on improving life in the here and now and have little to say about eschatological events. Seventh-day Adventists and their origins have been noted in chapter 3. While they are premillennialists, they take a unique

---

1. Carl E. Olson, *Will Catholics Be Left Behind?* (San Francisco: Ignatius, 2003) 34–36. See *Catechism of the Catholic Church* (2nd ed.; United States Catholic Conference—Libreria Editrice Vaticana, 1997) 1002, 1011; John A. Hardon, *The Catholic Catechism* (Garden City, NY: Doubleday, 1975) 254–80; Richard P. McBrien, *Catholicism* (San Francisco: HarperSanFrancisco, 1994) 1123–30, 1141–48.

approach to this issue. Pentecostals and charismatic Christians make up about a quarter of the world's Christians. On the whole they are dispensational premillennialists, but they give a new twist to this belief. And some charismatic groups even contradict this doctrine.

CATHOLICISM AND THE END OF DAYS

Despite being a non-millennial faith and minimizing an apocalyptic worldview, the Catholic Church has definite eschatological teachings. It believes that time will come to a definite end and history as we know it will cease. Yet contrary to official teachings, the church has pockets of end-time speculations. Before turning to this subject, however, standard Catholic doctrine must be noted.

The Catholic Church firmly believes Jesus Christ will return. At Mass Catholics recite the Nicene Creed, which states that Jesus Christ "will come in glory to judge the living and the dead and his kingdom will have no end." Indeed, they commonly proclaim the following words: "Christ has died. Christ has risen. Christ will come again." The Catholic Church affirms that on the "last day" the "Lord himself will descend from heaven with a cry of command, with the archangel's call, and with the sound of the trumpet of God. And the dead in Christ will rise first" (1 Thess 4:16).[2]

Still, the Catholic Church is very wary of date setting and rejects dispensationalism, which has been the driving force behind end-time thinking in contemporary America. As noted in chapter 2, since the time of Augustine in the late fourth and early fifth centuries, the church has rejected the notion of a literal millennium and frowned on the idea of saying the world will end at a specific time. The millennium began with Christ's first coming and will conclude with his return to Earth. Catholics believe that humanity is currently living in the millennium—"that long but indefinite period of time between the Incarnation and the Second Coming," writes William Whalen. The kingdom of God is not some future event, but has been established and is currently being worked out in the church.[3]

---

2. Russell Chandler, *Doomsday: The End of the World, A View through Time* (Ann Arbor, MI: Servant, 1993) 208 (quotes); William J. Whalen, "Why Some Christians Believe the End of the World Is Near," *U.S. Catholic*, February 1989, 35-36, 38; Pius Oyeniran Ahioje, "A Review of Catholic Eschatology," *Africa Theological Journal* 31/1 (2008).

3. Peter Brown, *Augustine of Hippo* (Berkeley: University of California Press, 1969) 140, 272; Gerald Bonner, "Augustine's Thoughts on This World and Hope for the Next," *Princeton Seminary Bulletin*, supplementary issue 3 (1994) 94-99; Paula

An Eschatological Hodgepodge

The Greek word *parousia* means "presence" or "arrival" and is used several times in the New Testament to describe Christ's glorious and victorious coming (e.g., Matt 24:27, 37, 39; 1 Cor 15:23; 2 Pet 3:4; 1 John 2:28; 1 Thess 2:19; 3:13: 4:15; 5:23; 2 Thess 2:1, 8). According to Catholic beliefs, the Parousia began with the incarnation of Christ and continues throughout the ages with the presence of the Holy Spirit. With the birth, death, and resurrection of Christ, "the most significant coming had already taken place . . ." For Catholics—thanks to their belief in transubstantiation—when the believer partakes of the actual body and blood of Christ in the Eucharist, the presence of Christ is most fully experienced.[4]

In part, Catholics arrive at this non-millennial position by means of their interpretation of the Book of Revelation. As noted in chapter 1, there are three ways to interpret this book—futuristic, historical, and preterist. While no repetition will be given here, some review is appropriate. The futuristic approach means nearly all of Revelation addresses future events. The historical interpretation argues that Revelation points to various ages throughout church history. The preterist method contends that the events described in Revelation occurred during the early years of the church. The Book of Revelation contains apocalyptic literature, which is rich in symbolism and speaks of developments in the first century. Radical preterism contends that all events mentioned in New Testament occurred in the early church. A more moderate or partial form of preterism insists that while most predictions found in the New Testament have been fulfilled, there are still some crucial events to occur. While there is no official Catholic position regarding these interpretations of the Book of Revelation, an increasing number of Catholic scholars have adopted a moderate form of preterism. This allows them to arrive at a non-millennial view of Revelation while still prompting them to look for some significant events to occur in the future.[5]

Fredriksen, "Tyconnius and Augustine on the Apocalypse," in *The Apocalypse in the Middle Ages*, eds. Richard K. Emmerson and Bernard McGinn (Ithaca, NY: Cornell University Press, 1992) 1992) 24; Whalen, "Why Some Christians Believe the End is Near," 38 (quote); Chandler, *Doomsday*, 209; Christopher Howard, "Roman Catholic Teaching on Eschatology," *Theologia*, http://theologia.indicium.us2009/02/roman-catholic-teaching-on-esc.

4. Olson, *Will Catholics Be Left Behind?*, 35–36; Joseph Ratzinger, *Eschatology, Death, and Eternal Life* (Washington, DC: Catholic University of America Press, 1988) 44–45 (quoted in Olson).

5. Olson, *Will Catholics Be Left Behind?*, 81–86; R. C. Sproul, *The Last Days According to Jesus: When Did Jesus Say He Would Return?* (Grand Rapids: Baker, 1998) 24.

This flexibility permits Catholics to deal with the tension of believing in the imminent return of Christ in the face of delays regarding this event. Catholic theology approximates the amillennial view of end-time events and rejects the dispensational premillennial perspective. Still, these two approaches have some things in common: "Christ's Second Coming could happen in the near future" and the end of history will not result in global peace and happiness. But the premillennial dispensationalists say no event must occur before the return of Christ. Conversely, Catholics believe at least three developments must precede the return of Christ.[6]

One, the Catholic Catechism states, "Before Christ's second coming the Church must pass through a final trial that will shake the faith of many believers." This time of testing will witness apostasy, religious deception, and rise of the Antichrist. Such developments will come because God and Christ are denied and humankind is deified. Have such events already occurred? Catholic theology allows for this possibility. They note the following. More Christians have been killed in the twentieth century than in all previous centuries combined. Disbelief is rampant and many nations have abandoned Christianity because of secular humanism, paganism, and the rise of communism. The future, of course, could even be worse, but this cannot be known. Of importance, Catholic doctrine rejects the notion that the church will be spared from this coming turmoil by means of a secret rapture.[7]

Two, Catholics take seriously Jesus' statement that "this gospel of the kingdom will be preached throughout the whole world, as a testimony to all nations and then the end will come." (Mt. 24:14). Whether this has occurred is difficult to say. "Certain nations have had the gospel preached to them in the past but not in the present." Still, the church believes that the gospel must continually be preached.[8]

A third event has not happened. Catholic teaching says that prior to the Second Advent Israel will recognize Jesus as Messiah. Ethnic Israel will be merged into the church. How this will happen is unclear. Such an

---

6. Olson, *Will Catholics Be Left Behind?*, 37 (quote); "Catholic Community Forum," 1.

7. *Catechism of the Catholic Church*, 675; Olson, *Will Catholics Be Left Behind?*, 37 (quote); Howard, "Roman Catholic Teaching on Eschatology," 1; "Catholic Community Forum," http://www.catholicforum.com/forms/showthread.php?22074-Cathol.

8. Ralph Martin, *Is Jesus Coming Soon?: A Catholic Perspective on the Second Coming* (San Francisco: Ignatius, 1997) 63; Olson, *Will Catholics Be Left Behind?*, 38 (quote). See also, Ralph Martin, *The Catholic Church at the End of an Age* (San Francisco: Ignatius, 1994).

An Eschatological Hodgepodge

inclusion may have even begun, but it is certainly not completed. In looking at these three events, it is obvious that at least one—the conversion of Israel—is still in the future. Catholic doctrine thus has difficulties with the idea of Christ's imminent return. In looking for persecution, turmoil, and the rise of the Antichrist at the end of time, Catholicism has not ignored the apocalyptic and catastrophic element of eschatology.[9]

THE VIRGIN MARY AND APOCALYPTIC APPARITIONS

Official Roman Catholic doctrine discourages speculation regarding the end of the world. Still, among the Catholic laity and on a popular level, end-time visions are common. This apocalyptic undercurrent is usually associated with Marian apparitions. The word *apparition* means appearance or presence. Most often, it refers to the sudden appearance of a supernatural being to individuals or groups of people. Within a Catholic context, such apparitions are often appearances by the Virgin Mary. Throughout church history, there have been at least twenty-one thousand claimed sightings of the Virgin Mary. Since the 1930s, there have been two hundred observances alone, and some have had apocalyptic overtones. The connection between prophecy and Marian visitations has gone on for centuries. But it has been only in the last one hundred fifty years or so that these prophecies have had apocalyptic implications.[10]

This increase in sightings with catastrophic predictions can be attributed to a number of factors. We live in an age in which people value experience over doctrine. And this trend has produced a strong undertone in the Catholic world, one that is supported by popular literature. In addition, the modern world is fraught with many dangers that contribute to an apocalyptic mood: world wars, the threat of nuclear annihilation, communism, terrorism, and more. Also, the church has sanctioned several of these Marian visitations, and when it has not many laity have followed their own instincts. The messages connected with these unapproved apparitions have been quite influential in certain sectors of American Catholicism.

9. Olson, *Will Catholics Be Left Behind?*, 38–39; Martin, *Is Jesus Coming Soon?*, 62; Howard, "Roman Catholic Teaching on Eschatology," 1; "Catholic Community Forum," 2.

10. Miriam Lambouras, "The Marian Apparitions: Divine Intervention or Delusion?," http:///www.inplainsite.org/html/apparitions_of_the_virgin_mary.html; Daniel Wojcik, *The End of the World As We Know It* (New York: New York University Press, 1997) 60–62.

The end-time visions of many prophets and mystics have also significantly impacted Catholic apocalyptic thinking. The prophecies of people such as Anna-Katarina Emmerick (1774–1824) and Michel de Notredame run through the centuries and are open-ended and thus susceptible to many interpretations, including apocalyptic catastrophes.

Moreover, the apocalyptic mood generated by dispensational premillennialism has often spilled over into the Catholic world. For example, estimates claim that about 11 percent of the readers of the *Left Behind* series have been Roman Catholics. More significantly, like the dispensationalists, some Catholics believe they will be raptured out of the trouble that will visit Earth. Lastly, the conspiracy culture associated with America's extreme political right has made inroads into Catholic apocalyptic thinking. The notions of a one-world government and America becoming a police state can be detected.[11]

The messages associated with the Marian apparitions have not been uniform. Still, some common characteristics emerge. One, chastisement is approaching. Because of its evil transgressions the world stands on the brink of catastrophic damnation. Two, certain spiritual elites have been called to warn the world of this impending judgment. Next, aside from the message of repentance, Catholic apocalypticists generally withdraw and ignore other pressing social issues. Four, Catholic apocalyptic movements in the United States were staunchly anti-communist. Moreover, closely connected with this strident anti-communism is a conspiracy mindset. Beneath the surface lurk forces or people who will do us in. Six, without exception Catholic apocalypticists believe the institutional church has fallen into a crisis following the Second Vatican Council. Closely related, since Vatican II the popes have been either extremely weak or imposters. Eight, the authority for such Catholic apocalypticists has not been the traditional church but the information provided by the Marian apparitions. Lastly, Catholic apocalyptic movements have tended to be sectarian, setting themselves apart from the institutional church.[12]

11. Richard Kyle, *Evangelicalism: An Americanized Christianity* (New Brunswick, NJ: Transaction, 2006) 277–78; Bruce David Forbes and Jeanne Halgren Kilde, "Rapture, Revelation, and the End Times," in *Rapture, Revelation, and the End Times*, eds. Bruce David Forbes and Jeanne Halgren Kilde (New York: Palgrave, 2004) 1; Bruce David Forbes, "How Popular Are the Left Behind Books . . . and Why?," in *Rapture, Revelation, and the End Times*, 8–9,21–22; Cathleen Falsani, "Bishops Warn Catholics about 'Left Behind' Books," *Chicago Sun Times*, 6 June 2003, 5.

12. Michael W. Cuneo, "The Vengeful Virgin: Case Studies in Contemporary American Apocalypticism," in *Millennium, Messiahs, and Mayhem*, eds. Thomas Robbins and Susan J. Palmer (New York: Routledge, 1997) 178–80.

An Eschatological Hodgepodge

The theological justification for the Marian apparitions—whether officially sanctioned by the Church or those unofficially embraced by the laity—rests on two pillars. First, Mary's role as a divine intercessor between God and humanity is one of her primary functions in the apparitions. In Catholic theology, Mary's intercessory role has its basis in the wedding at Cana (John 2:1-11), where Mary influenced Jesus to transform the water into wine. Second, Revelation 12 refers to "a woman clothed with the sun, with the moon under her feet" in conflict with "a huge red dragon." She gives "birth to a son, a male child destined to rule all nations with an iron rod." After the woman flees into the desert, a great war breaks out and Michael and his angels defeat the dragon. Catholic theologians generally interpret the women as a symbol of the early church while the dragon represents the Roman Empire. However, millions of Catholics throughout the globe with an interest in prophecy say the women refers to the Virgin Mary, who is now appearing to warn humanity of an impending catastrophe.[13]

Bad News from the Virgin in Europe

Our primary concern is with apocalypticism in modern America. Thus our attention must turn to the apparitions of the Virgin Mary in New York City. But before doing so, something should be said about the more noteworthy Marian sightings elsewhere in the world. Several of these visitations, indeed, have had shrines established at their sites. Millions of people visit annually the shrines at places such as Fatima, Lourdes, Guadalupe, and Medjugorie. And in each of these cases, the Virgin appeared to poor, humble, uneducated, and theologically unsophisticated individuals.

In eighteenth- and nineteenth-century France, many believed that the return of Christ would be preceded by an age of Mary. This dramatic devotion to the Virgin Mary was reinforced in the 1840s and 1850s by two Marian sightings.[14] In 1846 there had been a major crop failure in southeastern France. The Virgin appeared in that year to two shepherd children on the mountain of LaSalette. She criticized humanity's sinful behavior and predicted further calamities if people did not mend their ways.[15]

13. Wojcik, *The End of the World*, 64-65. The quotations come from the St. Joseph Edition of *The New American Bible*.

14. McBrien, *Catholicism*, 1089-90; Michael J. St. Clair, *Millenarian Movements in Historical Context*. (New York: Garland, 1992) 233-34.

15. McBrien, *Catholicism*, 1092; St. Clair, *Millenarian Movements*, 234-35.

One of the most famous Marian visitations occurred in 1858 in the small village of Lourdes in southwestern France. Here the Virgin appeared eighteen times to Bernadette Soubirous, a fourteen-year-old illiterate girl. In one of her messages Mary announced to Bernadette, "I am the Immaculate conception." The immaculate conception of Mary soon became official Catholic doctrine. And with a reputation for the miraculous, Lourdes became a major shrine for pilgrims. Also, the Marian appearances convinced many that the age of Mary and the end times had arrived.[16]

But the Marian appearances with the strangest end-time messages occurred at Fatima in central Portugal. Between May and October 1917, Mary is claimed to have appeared six times to ten-year-old Lucia dos Santos and two of her cousins.[17] Lucia revealed the contents of three special revelations to Catholic authorities, who wrote them down. Ten years later the church permitted Lucia to disclose the contents of two of these messages. They contained prophecies regarding the end of World War I (which was raging in 1917), the rise and collapse of Russian Communism, and the coming of World War II.[18]

There was, however, the third and presumably more terrifying revelation, which was sealed and kept secret in the archives of the local bishop. Supposedly, Pope John XXIII opened and read the document in 1960. Yet he and the succeeding popes have refused to discuss its contents. What did it say? Few people know for sure. But the most common story says that the message predicts a catastrophic end to the world during the tenure of the fifth pope after the opening of the document. Benedict XVI is the fourth pope since 1960. This story explains why the church has kept the contents secret—it fears the masses would become immoral or suicidal if they knew the end was at hand.[19]

While not as catastrophic as some previous apparitions, the visitations of Mary at Medjugorie were more recent and internationally celebrated. In 1981 Mary appeared to six children in the former Yugoslavia, at

16. Mary Lee Nolan and Sidney Nolan, *Christian Pilgrimage in Modern Western Europe* (Chapel Hill: University of North Carolina Press, 1989) 199; St. Clair, *Millenarian Movements*, 235; McBrien, *Catholicism*, 1092; Elliot Miller and Kenneth R. Samples, *The Cult of the Virgin* (Grand Rapids: Baker, 1992) 90-92.

17. McBrien, *Catholicism*, 1093; Chandler, *Doomsday*, 2005; Yuri Rubinsky and Ian Wiseman, *A History of the End of the World*, (New York: W. Morrow, 1982) 122; Miller and Samples, *Cult of the Virgin*, 93-97.

18. Rubinsky and Wiseman, *End of the World*, 122; Chandler, *Doomsday*, 205-6; Kenneth L. Woodward, "Going to See the Virgin Mary," *New York Times Book Review*, 11 August 1991, 22.

19. Chandler, *Doomsday*, 211; Rubinsky and Wiseman, *End of the World*, 122.

An Eschatological Hodgepodge

a place that became the largest Marian apparition site in Eastern Europe. To this point the Roman Catholic Church has not officially sanctioned this visitation, though the case still remains open. On the third evening of visitations, the six children were joined by five thousand people. After flashes of light, however, only the six children could see her. Her ten "secret" messages consisted of blessings for the obedient and punishment for the wicked. The children were shown visions of heaven, hell, and purgatory. And people believed that Medjugorie would be the last time the Virgin would appear and all future visitations must be regarded as false.[20]

The Virgin Brings Bad News to New York

Perhaps the best-known American Catholic prophetess of the apocalypse was Veronica Lueken (1923–95). For over twenty years, Veronica of the Cross (as her loyal followers often called her) made pronouncements regarding sin, salvation, killer comets, UFOs from hell, vampires, and—most important—an imposter pope. Some of these declarations were unique to her, but she focused on a theme common to Catholic mystics for years: because of human sin the entire world stood on the brink of a terrible judgment. In a short while, millions of people would perish in a nuclear holocaust and the surviving sinners would be destroyed by a "cleansing ball of redemption."[21]

The story of Mrs. Lueken's contacts with the Virgin Mary began in April of 1970. The Virgin appeared to Mrs. Lueken—a working-class housewife from Queens, New York—and instructed her to establish a shrine at the Saint Bellarmine Church in Bayside, New York. For over two decades Mrs. Leuken would function as a voice box for the Virgin Mary, relaying her messages to people. In a short time, the apparitions drew a sizeable audience, ranging from five hundred to two thousand pilgrims. But after investigating these apparitions, the Roman Catholic diocese of Brooklyn concluded that these appearances were the product of a "highly fertile imagination." Moreover, they would not permit such vigils on church property so Mrs. Leuken and her followers regularly met elsewhere, eventually at Flushing Meadows Park. Still, the visitations are referred to as the "Bayside apparitions" and her followers as the "Baysiders."[22]

20. Chandler, 204; Wojcik, *The End of the World*, 62; Lambouras, "Marian Apparitions," 7.
21. Cuneo, "The Vengeful Virgin," 175.
22. Wojcik, *The End of the World*, 68–69; Cuneo, "The Vengeful Virgin," 187; Philip

Over the next twenty years a pattern developed. Upon arriving at the shrine, Mrs. Leuken would function as a medium, relaying messages from heavenly beings and saints. She would fall into an ecstatic trance and receive communications from Jesus, Mary, Saint Paul, Saint Joseph, Saint John the Evangelist, Saint Francis of Assisi, Saint Teresa of Avila, and many more. These messages would be tape-recorded and sent out to the growing number of Mrs. Leuken's followers throughout the country.[23]

The centerpiece of these vigils was the sacred messages sent by the Virgin to Mrs. Leuken. These pronouncements followed a predictable pattern: the condemnation of specific sins and the coming judgment. Differing from previous Marian apparitions were the specific transgressions and the corresponding punishments. They connected more or less with the contemporary American scene. The Virgin Mary railed against homosexuality, abortion, modern biblical criticism, UFOs coming from hell, the United Nations and the threat of a one-world government, and much more.[24]

A particular target of her condemnation was the earthshaking changes within the Catholic Church after Vatican II. Most startling, the Virgin said the current Pope Paul VI was not the real Pope Paul VI, who was being held prisoner in the Vatican. Thanks to plastic surgery, an imposter now occupied the papal throne. While this allegation may seem preposterous, it did much to explain to Mrs. Leuken's followers the monumental changes that the Catholic Church was undergoing. After all, the real Pope Paul VI would not dismantle the Tridentine Mass and traditional Catholicism. Such was being done by a "cosmetically enhanced stooge who had taken his place on the papal throne."[25]

According to the Virgin, such transgressions would result in divine judgment. This chastisement would come in two phases. The apocalyptic scenario would began with a global conflict, namely World War III, in which countless people would die. Second, the entire world would be destroyed by a great comet, a God-sent "Fireball of Redemption." Prior to this punishment, humanity would receive a warning: "There will be a tremendous explosion and the sky shall roll back like a scroll.... There will

---

Nobel, "Our Lady of Bayside," *New York*, 11 December 1978, 57–60; Roberta Grant, "War of the Roses," *Rolling Stone*, 21 February 1980, 43–46.

23. Cuneo, "The Vengeful Virgin," 187; Wojcik, *The End of the World*, 79; *Our Lady of Roses, Mary Help of Mothers: A Book about the Heavenly Apparitions to Veronica Leuken at Bayside New York* (Lansing, MI: Apostles of Our Lady, 1986) 81.

24. Cuneo, "The Vengeful Virgin," 188; Wojcik, *The End of the World*, 71.

25. Cuneo, "The Vengeful Virgin," 188 (quote); Our Lady of Roses Shrine, *Roses from Heaven* (Orange, TX: Children of Mary Inc.) 116–29.

An Eschatological Hodgepodge

be tremendously high waves roaring and taking with them cities . . . the atmosphere shall spew forth currents of great heat; a darkness of spirit and a darkness of atmosphere shall settle in a deadly quiet upon mankind."[26]

There was a slim chance that these catastrophes might be avoided or the severity of them reduced. And this small possibility rested with Mrs. Leuken and her followers. They were given the task of preaching repentance to the entire world. In effect, they would function as the disciples of the last days and if the world rejected their efforts, they would be miraculously raptured prior to the great apocalypse. To complete this task, Mrs. Leuken and her followers developed an organizational hierarchy. The inner circle consisted of Mrs. Leuken, her husband, and a few close followers. Next came several young men who worked full-time in promoting the Bayside ministry. They lived in a community called the Lay Order of St. Michael. Third in line were the organizers who usually arranged activities outside of New York City. Last were the rank-and-file supporters.[27]

While the Bayside apparitions had many precedents, several unique aspects come to the forefront. As noted earlier, Mrs. Leuken received messages not only from the Virgin Mary but also from Michael the Archangel, Christ's disciples, and many saints. The appearance of these saints was due in part to Leuken's desire to restore the "cult of the saints," which modernists in the church desired to eliminate. She also communicated with recently deceased church leaders, including Pope Pius X, who opposed modernist trends in the church.[28]

Vast differences exist between the Bayside apparitions and dispensational fundamentalism. Still, the influence of popular premillennial dispensationalism can be detected in the Bayside movement. Perhaps even Hal Lindsey's books—which were popular during the decade when Mrs. Leuken began to receive messages—had an impact. Still, her message in this regard is muddled. On one hand, Mrs. Leuken's messages encourage her followers to prepare for future sufferings and catastrophes. On the other, her prophecies imply that a select group will be raptured before the end-time horrors hit the Earth. Or in her words: "I give you grace of heart, My children, to know that many shall be taken from Earth before the great chastisement."[29]

26. *Our Lady of Roses Book*, 44–45 (quote); Wojcik, *The End of the World*, 72.
27. Cuneo, "The Vengeful Virgin," 189.
28. Wojcik, *The End of the World*, 79; *Our Lady of Roses Book*, 81.
29. *Our Lady of the Roses, Mary Help of Mothers: An Introductory Booklet on the Apparitions of Bayside* (Bayside, NY: Our Lady of Roses, Mary Help of Mothers Shrine, n.d.) 2 (quote); Wojcik, *The End of the World*, 78.

Mrs. Leuken's followers were not unique in using photography to prove the miraculous nature of certain events. But they carried it to a new level. The photography began as soon as she went into a trance. Her messages explicitly encouraged observers to employ Polaroid technology because it could be developed instantly. Such a step would eliminate the claim that people had tampered with the negatives and thus created miraculous events. Baysiders have a twofold purpose for examining these photographs. The pictures give revelations regarding the coming apocalypse. They also offer people information pertaining to their personal lives. The streaks and marks of light on the photos were interpreted as supernatural symbols relaying both end-time and personal messages to the faithful. Rather than interpret such imperfections as mistakes such as double exposures, the Baysiders viewed them as miraculous messages. The photos thus became a form of divination and a means to interpret God's will.[30]

The Bayside apparitions represent a reaction to the modernist trends within the Catholic Church that developed after the Second Vatican Council. Along with much of traditional Roman Catholicism, the Bayside movement rejected the reforms initiated by this council and in the process developed a conspiratorial mindset. Traditionalists regarded these liberalizing trends as a betrayal of the historic Catholic faith. They condemned Pope Paul VI, who sanctioned these changes. In fact, they believed him to be an imposter who, along with his satanic allies, had brought these modernist changes as a plot to destroy the church. The church had indeed been infiltrated by evil forces intent on its demise.[31]

In linking a conspiratorial mindset with an apocalyptic catastrophe, Mrs. Leuken was building on previous Marian visitations, especially the one at Fatima. Because of the secret nature of the third message, all kinds of apocalyptic rumors circulated. The Catholic Church, according to Mrs. Leuken, did not reveal this secret because it had been infiltrated by satanic forces. These sinister imposters wanted the major powers to arm themselves with nuclear weapons and thus destroy the world in a great conflagration. As with other Catholic traditionalists (and even Protestant fundamentalists), the Baysiders developed a Manichaean mindset. They viewed global issues in polarized black-and-white terms. In particular, they saw the struggle to restore "traditional Catholic doctrines and rites

30. Cuneo, "The Vengeful Virgin," 187; Wojcik, *The End of the World*, 81–88; *Our Lady of Roses Book*, 22.

31. Wojcik, *The End of the World*, 86–88.

An Eschatological Hodgepodge

as a conflict between good and evil, an eschatological battle between the sinister minions of Satan and the righteous army of Christ."[32]

MAINLINE APATHY

Mainline Protestants have little to say about the world coming to an end, especially in any catastrophic way. As James Moorhead says, "In mainstream Protestantism, apocalypticism was the dog that did not bark." Or in a more precise analogy he states, "it was the dog whose barking, muted from the outset, became ever fainter until it was little more than a whimper." This should be understood in the context of what is meant by the "end of the world." At the end of the nineteenth century, many mainline Protestants still believed the world would come to an end, but in a gradual way. As the twentieth century unfolded, in evangelical circles this sense of progression was displaced by a more catastrophic view of end-time events. Thus much of mainstream Protestantism ceased to participate in end-of-the-world discussions.[33]

What do I mean by "mainline Protestantism"? By the early twentieth century, it came to refer to the churches that had engaged the major issues of American life and came to identify with the mission of the nation. Included would be the Presbyterians, Congregationalists, Episcopalians, Disciples of Christ, many Methodists, and the major Lutheran bodies.[34] By the late twentieth and early twenty-first centuries, it came to denote most Protestant bodies not categorized as evangelical, Pentecostal, or African-American.

If mainline Protestants do not embrace an apocalyptic world view, just what do they believe regarding the Second Coming of Christ, the end of the world, and the judgment? Each Sunday most mainline Protestants recite the historic Apostles' Creed. This early faith statement declares that Jesus Christ, who sits at the right hand of God, "shall come to judge the quick and the dead." This creed also affirms a belief in "the resurrection of the body; and the life everlasting. Amen." In summary, this statement affirms the main outlines of historic Christian eschatology: the physical

---

32. Ibid., 87–88.

33. James H. Moorhead, "Apocalypticism in Mainstream Protestantism, 1800 to the Present," in *The Continuum History of Apocalyptism*, eds. Bernard McGinn, John J. Collins, and Stephen J. Stein (New York: Continuum, 2003) 467.

34. Ibid., 468.

return of Christ, the final judgment of humankind, and the beginning of the eternal order.[35]

Mainline Tendencies

But the mainline denominations do not get upset about end-time events nor do they place much emphasis on such subjects. Actually, among such Christians one can find three tendencies regarding eschatology. One, they have little to say about the end of the world. Few books have been written by mainline Protestants on the subject of prophecy. And what has been written in the twentieth century has been from the perspective of amillennialism, which currently is the prevailing view among mainline scholars. Seldom would one hear a sermon concerning eschatological events coming from the pulpit of a mainline denomination. Such Protestants focus on issues and problems in the here and now and do not speculate about future events. In fact, many of them are apathetic regarding eschatology.[36]

Two, many liberal scholars openly attack the premillennialists who see current events through the lenses of eschatology. They dump more on the "doomsday mongers" than they articulate their own beliefs. They see such evangelicals and fundamentalists as adopting a literal interpretation of the biblical prophecies, which they reject. Worse than that, these mainline Protestants believe many premillennial dispensationalists have pandered to popular fears and view them with thinly veiled contempt, perhaps even as charlatans. After all, much of the noise regarding end-time events comes from uneducated populists.

Three, in a more constructive way such liberal scholars set forth their own position regarding eschatology. Premillennial dispensationalists have incorrectly embraced a literal interpretation of apocalyptic literature, they contend. Instead, writes Whalen, mainline Protestants often say apocalyptic literature is "a literary form that uses rather unusual imagery to convey a consoling message to people undergoing some form of persecution." The peak for writing Jewish apocalyptic literature was from 200 BCE to 200 CE. According to liberal scholars, these writers intended the genre of apocalyptic literature to bolster the faith of beleaguered people in the face of persecution. Through images and symbols, apocalyptic literature told the faithful that God would sustain them in times of trial. Contrary to what

---

35. *The Worship Services* (Louisville: Westminster John Knox, 1970) inside cover (quote); Chandler, *Doomsday*, 242.

36. Chandler, *Doomsday*, 236–38.

An Eschatological Hodgepodge

many prophecy buffs contend, these ancient writers were not describing the events of the late twentieth and early twentieth-first centuries.[37]

More specifically, liberal scholars contend that the Book of Daniel was written in the second century BCE and not the sixth century BCE as conservative scholars say. Rather than predicting a revival of the Roman Empire at the end of time, the writer of Daniel is encouraging faithful Jews in the face of the persecution by Antiochus Epiphanes of Syria. Turning to the prophecies of Matthew 24, liberal scholars assert that Christ's words have been fulfilled by the destruction of Jerusalem in 70 CE. The events described are fulfilled history, not prophecy.[38]

Mainline commentators date the Book of Revelation at about 90-95 CE and say it was written to support Christians living under the threat of Roman persecution. Near the end of the first century, Roman authorities revived and enforced worship of the emperor. Thus John's Revelation called "for resistance to all demands of the cult of emperor worship." He thus glorifies the "privileges of martyrdom" throughout the book. Liberal scholars often look at the description of the battle of Armageddon as written for a specific time and culture and not a future battle. Similarly, the beast of Revelation (or Antichrist) was an amalgam of evil and "a worldly power that aligns itself against God." They believe modern Antichrist hunters who are in search of an individual are on a wild goose chase.[39]

But all of this is not to imply that mainline scholars dismiss the apocalyptic passages of the Bible as having no relevance for the modern age or that they do not point to the end of history. Rather, they contend that biblical symbolism "cannot be applied literally to random events in the twentieth [and twenty-first centuries] without causing vast confusion and misunderstanding." The biblical prophets could not foretell the distant future. Instead, liberal scholars say the prophets were "forthtelling the truth

---

37. Whalen, "Why Some Christians Believe the End of the World Is Near," 37-38; Russell Chandler and John Dort, "Visions of the Apocalypse Rise Again," *Los Angeles Times*, 26 July 1976, A1; Chandler, *Doomsday*, 238; David Briggs, "Predicting War to End All Wars Is Risky Business," Associated Press, 27 September 1991.

38. John Dart, "Armageddon—Threat or Bunk?," *Los Angeles Times*, 3 March 1984, I-A6; Chandler, *Doomsday*, 238; Gary DeMar, *Last Days Madness: The Folly of Trying to Predict When Christ Will Return* (Brentwood, TN: Wolgemuth and Hyatt, 1991) 24.

39. Chandler, *Doomsday*, 237 (quote); Chandler, S. MacLean Gilmour, "The Revelation to John," in *The Interpreter's Concise Commentary: Revelation and the General Epistles* (Nashville: Abingdon, 1983) 142, 145; Robert Fuller, *Naming the Antichrist: The History of an American Obsession* (New York: Oxford University Press, 1995).

of God's Word in the context of their own time rather than foretelling future events . . . ," writes Russell Chandler.[40]

What Happened to Apocalyptic Thinking?

How did the dog lose its bark? How did mainline Protestantism lose its interest in end-time events and its apocalyptic worldview, mild as it was? This story is closely related to the decline of postmillennialism as the dominant eschatology among Protestants. As noted in chapter 3, in the late nineteenth century, mainline Protestantism had embraced a postmillennial eschatology. Such an end-time view saw a gradual improvement of the human state by means of divine and human efforts. Moreover, postmillennialism reinforced the notion of America as a millennial nation. God had indeed blessed America and chosen it for a special mission. Postmillennialism, however, has not completely vanished as a viable eschatology. In recent years it has witnessed a resurgence among several conservative groups, but that is a story for elsewhere in this study.[41]

But all of this would undergo a change in the late nineteenth and early twentieth centuries. Postmillennialism saw the catastrophes predicted in the Bible—wars, earthquakes, famines, pestilences, and more—as not reserved for the end times but as running the course of history. So they did not completely dismiss a catastrophic view of history but balanced it with human progress. This tenuous balance between the apocalyptic and progressive elements in eschatology came to an end, however. And with the rise of premillennialism, the catastrophic components became increasing important in Protestant thinking.[42]

---

40. Clifford Hill, *Prophecy Past and Present: An Exploration of the Prophetic Ministry in the Bible and the Church Today* (Ann Arbor, MI: Servant, 1991) 187; John Wiley Nelson, "The Apocalyptic Vision in Popular Culture," in *The Apocalyptic Vision in America*, ed. Lois Parkinson Zamora (Bowling Green, OH: Bowling Green University Popular Press, 1982) 161; Chandler, *Doomsday*, 239 (quote).

41. Moorhead, "Apocalypticism in Mainline Protestantism," 468–71. See also James H. Moorhead, "Engineering the Millennium: Kingdom Building in American Protestantism, 1880–1920," *Princeton Seminary Bulletin*, supplementary issue 3 (1994) 104–28; James H. Moorhead, "Searching for the Millennium in America," *Princeton Seminary Bulletin* 8/2 (1987) 17–33.

42. James H. Moorhead, "Between Progress and Apocalypse: A Reassessment of Millennialism in American Religious Thought, 1800–1850," *Journal of American History* 71/3 (1984) 524–42; Moorhead, "Apocalypticism in Mainstream Protestantism," 472–74.

An Eschatological Hodgepodge

On top of this, a series of developments facilitated postmillennialism's decline. Higher criticism came to dominate many mainline seminaries. Among many other things, higher criticism downplayed the notion that books such as Daniel and Revelation contained literal predictions regarding the future. In addition, mainline Protestants embraced a new kingdom theology and decisively oriented the kingdom of God to this world. The kingdom of God now became a present reality and operated according to natural laws. This new theology came to be known as the social gospel. The church became concerned with establishing God's justice and righteousness in this world and subduing the world for Christ. This focus on the here and now totally contrasted with the perspective of the rising premillennialism, which regarded "the current age world as hopelessly corrupt and incapable of redemption until the supernatural advent of Christ inaugurated a new heaven and new Earth . . ."[43]

A series of events compounded such developments. The fundamentalist-modernist conflict erupted in the 1920s and continued in various forms for several decades. In the course of this battle, mainstream Protestantism cut itself off from the apocalyptic discourse associated with fundamentalism and premillennialism. Also, the rapid rise of Pentecostalism in the 1920s and 1930s, with its emotionalism and embrace of premillennialism, contributed to the decline of apocalypticism among mainline Protestants. Secure in their own denominations, mainline Protestants had little inclination to engage these more conservative and emotional groups in a conversation regarding many issues. Thus, the gap between mainline Protestantism and the growing evangelical movement contributed to the decline of end-time thinking among liberal Protestants.[44]

PENTECOSTAL AND CHARISMATIC VISIONS

Pentecostalism is a mass religious movement, perhaps the largest in the twentieth century. Along with its more recent outgrowth—neo-Pentecostalism, or the charismatic movement—Pentecostalism is the most significant of the new or innovative religious movements in the twentieth century, even being designated as the "third force in Christendom." No

43. James H. Moorhead, "The Erosion of Postmillennialism in American Religious Thought, 1865-1925," *Church History* 53/1 (1984) 61-77; Moorhead, "Apocalypticism in Mainstream Protestantism," 487 (quote).

44. James H. Moorhead, *The World Without End: Mainstream Protestant Visions of the Last Things*, 1880-1925 (Bloomington: University of Indiana Press, 1999) 170-202; Moorhead, "Apocalypticism in Mainstream Protestantism," 488-89.

one knows just how large the movement is, but from inauspicious beginnings at the turn of the century Pentecostalism claimed more than five hundred million adherents globally by the end of the century.[45]

The distinguishing mark of Pentecostalism is a religious experience, usually called the "Pentecostal experience," which often entails receiving the gift of speaking in an unknown tongue as a sign of the baptism of the Holy Spirit. In Pentecostalism, this baptism usually comes as an experience subsequent to conversion and is regarded as the Holy Spirit's coming to indwell an individual believer. From the idea of this baptism of the Holy Spirit and speaking in tongues emerged the belief in the current operation of the gifts of the Holy Spirit as manifested in the New Testament church. Included would be miraculous healing, speaking in tongues, the interpretation of tongues, personal prophecy, discernment of spirits, and expressions of knowledge and wisdom. In addition, Pentecostals fervently believed that they were living in the last days, evidenced by the outpouring of the Holy Spirit.[46]

Rising from humble origins, Pentecostal and charismatic individuals became the leading figures on Christian television. Examples included Oral Roberts, Kathryn Kuhlman, Pat Robertson, Rex Humbard, Jim Bakker, Jimmy Swaggart, Kenneth Copeland, and Kenneth Hagin. Some have either reached the highest levels of American government or aspired to these offices. Pat Robertson sought the presidency in 1988; James Watt was Ronald Reagan's Secretary of the Interior; and John Ashcroft served as George W. Bush's Attorney General.[47]

The charismatic movement is an outgrowth of Pentecostalism. By the 1960s, Pentecostalism was becoming more middle class. Pentecostals had shed much of their excesses. Some had joined the National Association

---

45. For general information on Pentecostalism see Walter J. Hollenweger, *The Pentecostals* (Minneapolis: Augusburg, 1972); Vinson Synan, *The Holiness-Pentecostal Movement in the United States* (Grand Rapids: Eerdmans, 1971); John Thomas Nichol, *The Pentecostals* (Plainfield, NJ: Logos, 1966); Jessyca Russell Gaver, *Pentecostalism* (New York: Award Books, 1971); Robert Mapes Anderson, *The Vision of the Disinherited: The Making of American Pentecostalism* (New York: Oxford University Press, 1979); Vinson Synan, ed., *Aspects of the Pentecostal-Charismatic Origins* (Plainfield, NJ: Logos, 1975); James R. Goff Jr. and Grant Wacker, "Introduction," in *Portraits of a Generation: Early Pentecostal Leaders*, eds. James R. Goff and Grant Wacker (Fayetteville,: University of Arkansas Press, 2002) xi, xii.

46. Grant Wacker, *Heaven Below: Early Pentecostalism and American Culture* (Cambridge, MA: Harvard University Press, 2001) 12; Dennis J. Bennett, "The Gifts of the Holy Spirit," in *The Charismatic Movement*, ed. Michael P. Hamilton (Grand Rapids: Eerdmans, 1975) 16-20.

47. Kyle, *Evangelicalism*, 92-93.

An Eschatological Hodgepodge

of Evangelicals, and many of their teachings were even accepted by mainline Protestants and Catholics. The charismatic movement can be seen and even defined as Pentecostal beliefs and practices going outside of the Pentecostal denominations and penetrating other Protestant and Catholic groups.[48]

The most prominent figure in the charismatic movement was southern California dairyman Demos Shakarian. He founded the Full Gospel Business Men's Fellowship International (FGBMI). This organization provided the catalyst for the Pentecostal experience penetrating other Protestant and Catholic groups. Other classical Pentecostals who assisted in this effort were Oral Roberts and David DuPlessis.

The movement began when Dennis Bennett, rector of St. Mark's Episcopal Church in Van Nuys, California, experienced Holy Spirit baptism. From this initial event the movement began to penetrate mainline Protestantism (though evangelicals were more resistant) and Catholicism. Episcopal, Presbyterian, and Methodist churches felt the impact of the movement. Soon many non-aligned churches embraced the Pentecostal experience. By the end of the twentieth century, many mega churches can be regarded as charismatic. Gradually, some of these independent churches began to acquire denominational characteristics—e.g., John Wimber's Vineyard Christian Fellowship and Chuck Smith's Calvary Chapel.[49]

Pentecostalism via the charismatic movement has had a tremendous impact on Christianity in the modern era. It prompted and connected well with the religious mood of America for spiritual experience and not doctrine. It has been a huge factor in the movement toward non-rational, experiential, and emotional religion. Expressive worship styles have been the result of the charismatic movement. Its greatest growth, however, has come in Asia, Africa, and Latin America. Why? In the developing world, Christianity is growing more rapidly than in the industrialized world and Pentecostalism is part of that growth. In part, this growth is because supernaturalism and more emotional worship styles are better received there than in the West. By 2025 some researchers predict there will be one billion Pentecostals in the world.

---

48. H. D. Hunter, "Charismatic Movement," in *Dictionary of Christianity in America*, ed. Daniel G. Reid et al. (Downers Grove, IL: InterVarsity, 1990) 241–43.

49. Ibid. 241–44.

Premillennialism with a Twist

Pentecostals substantially borrowed their eschatology from dispensationalism and fundamentalism. Their dependence on the *Scofield Reference Bible* can hardly be overstated. They followed the usual dispensational line except in a few areas that shall be noted shortly. Pentecostals embraced the pretribulational and premillennial return of Christ. Believers will be raptured prior the tribulation and return to rule with Christ during the millennium. They saw the return of Israel in 1948 and its capture of Jerusalem in 1967 as marking the end of the times for the Gentiles. On nearly every issue since then, the Pentecostals have supported Israel.[50]

Like most dispensationalists, Pentecostals viewed Russia as the "Gog and Magog" of Ezekiel 38–39. Moreover, they saw the Cold War as a harbinger of Armageddon. They viewed most moments of crisis between the West and the Soviet Union as end-time events. They interpreted the rise of the European Union and the formation of NATO through the lenses of dispensationalism. Such events portended the revival of the Roman Empire and the rise of the Antichrist.[51]

Premillennial doctrines have dominated Pentecostal thinking since its origins in Topeka, Kansas. Still, at points Pentecostal eschatology differed from dispensationalism and acquired a new twist. The early Pentecostals believed that the events happening in the early twentieth century were showers of God's "latter rain." They based this understanding of the latter rain on Joel 2:23–28. The former rain was fulfilled in Acts 2 at Pentecost. The latter rain would come in the days immediately preceding Christ's Second Coming. Verse 28 says, "I will pour out my spirit upon all flesh; and your sons and your daughters shall prophesy, your old men shall dream dreams, your young men shall see visions." This latter rain would fully restore New Testament Christianity with all its signs and wonders, including speaking in tongues and faith healing. This fully restored church would in turn spark a great revival in the last days. Thus Pentecostals saw this outpouring of the Holy Spirit as an important sign of the end.[52]

---

50. D. J. Wilson, "Pentecostal Perspectives on Eschatology," *International Dictionary of Pentecostal and Charismatic Movements*, eds. Stanley M. Burgess and Edward M. Van Der Mass (rev. ed.; Grand Rapids: Zondervan, 2002) 601–2; Patrick Alexander, "Scofield Reference Bible," in *International Dictionary of Pentecostal and Charismatic Movements*, 1044.

51. Wilson, "Pentecostal Perspectives on Eschatology," 601–2.

52. Margaret Poloma, "The Millenarianism of the Pentecostal Movement," in *Christian Millenarianism*, ed. Stephen Hunt (Bloomington: Indiana University Press, 2001) 167; Wilson, "Pentecostal Perspectives on Eschatology," 604; F. L. Arrington,

An Eschatological Hodgepodge

Paralleling the work of the Holy Spirit at the end of time would be an increase in demonic activity. The outpouring of the gifts of the Spirit signaled the second return of Christ and prepared believers for this event and a great struggle at the end of history. This conflict would be against Satan. Pentecostals regarded this increase in evil as heralding the appearance of the Antichrist. Satan and his demons would "unleash a full scale assault against true believers and the world as a kind of warm-up session for the End of Days."[53]

At yet another crucial point, Pentecostalism distanced itself from dispensational eschatology. And in fact, Pentecostalism and dispensationalism can be regarded as strange bedfellows. Dispensationalism insists that the miraculous gifts of the Spirit such as tongues speaking and healing are not for the post-apostolic age and should be rejected. How did Pentecostals handle this rejection of their distinctive, namely, the baptism of the Holy Spirit and the Pentecostal experience? In general they glossed over this subject and still embraced the dispensational view of the church and end-time events. But as the twentieth century moved to a close, Pentecostal scholars appeared to be less dependent on the dispensational system.[54]

On another issue, Pentecostalism and dispensationalism parted company. They had a different understanding of prophecy. Some Pentecostals joined their dispensational and fundamentalist cousins in focusing on the doomsday aspects of prophecy as found in the Book of Revelation. Many more, however, tended to downplay the catastrophic elements of prophecy and viewed prophecy from a practical perspective.[55]

Along with the gifts of tongues speaking and healing, the outpouring of the Holy Spirit in the last days restored the office of the prophet. The office and gift of prophecy had now been democratized. The Holy Spirit came on people and used them "as a human vehicle to speak a divine word." Such prophetic revelations came in several ways: "visions, dreams, impressions, divine coincidences or verbal proclamations." Rather than

---

"Dispensationalism," in *International Dictionary of Pentecostal and Charismatic Movements*, 585.

53. W. Scott Poole, *Satan in America* (Lanham, MD: Rowman & Littlefield, 2009) 102.

54. Arrington, "Dispensationalism," 585; E. L. Blumhofer, *Restoring the Faith: The Assemblies of God, Pentecostalism, and American Culture* (Urbana: University of Illinois Press, 1993) 4.

55. Damian Thompson, *Waiting for Antichrist: Charisma and Apocalypse in a Pentecostal Church* (New York: Oxford University Press, 2005) 57–58; Poloma, "The Millenarianism of the Pentecostal Movement," 169; Arrington, "Dispensationalism," 585–86.

predict the future, these prophetic utterances usually served "to edify, encourage and comfort; [and] to provide correction and warning..."[56]

Shades of Postmillennialism

In chapter 9 we saw the resurrection of postmillennialism via the Christian Reconstruction movement. For the most part, Reconstructionism has been associated with the Reformed or Calvinist tradition. To a lesser extent, it can also be found in the Pentecostal and charismatic movements. As noted in chapter 9, despite being a Pentecostal, Pat Robertson flirted with postmillennialism. On one hand, he maintained his premillennial stance. On the other, his vision for restoring America to its Christian roots contained and implicit postmillennialism.

Along with the Christian Right, other Pentecostal and charismatic bodies have evidenced a similar ambivalence and tension between pre- and postmillennialism. Their premillennialism emerged in the belief that Christ could return at any moment. Yet such groups desired to restore the kingdom of God on Earth as much as possible prior to the Second Advent. Such ambivalence can be seen in John Wimber's Vineyard movement and its emphasis on "signs and wonders." Taking a similar approach, the "Toronto Blessing" stressed revival and the arrival of the kingdom of God.[57]

In yet another way, postmillennial charismatic Christians have evidenced dualistic tendencies. The charismatic movement contains both world-affirming and world-rejecting movements. Such tendencies can be seen in Christian Reconstructionism and Restorationism. Reconstruction teachings understand current social trends and say Christians should engage the world and reform its evil ways. But they do not separate themselves from the world. Conversely, while desiring to change society, Restorationism detaches itself from society.[58]

Restorationism has sectarian tendencies. The Restorationists are charismatics who see themselves in tune with God's plans to restore the world. This restoration would be implemented by an outpouring of the Holy Spirit in the last days. The kingdom of God would be established,

56. Poloma, "The Millenarianism of the Pentecostal Movement," 170–71 (quotes); C. Jacobs, *The Voice of God: How God Speaks Personally and Corporately to His Children Today* (Ventura, CA: Regal, 1995).

57. Stephen Hunt, "The Rise, Fall and Return of Post-Millennialism," in *Christian Millenarianism*, 56–57; Thompson, *Waiting for the Antichrist*, 43; John Wimber, "John Wimber Calls It Power Evangelism," *Charisma*, September 1985, 26–34.

58. Hunt, "The Rise, Fall, and Return of Postmillennialism," 57–59.

An Eschatological Hodgepodge

but it would be an alternative society operating on God's rules. In the end times, denominations would be abolished, God's people would prosper, and a restored church would usher in the kingdom of God before Christ's return. Some examples of Restorationism include a network of churches known as the People of Destiny International, and the National Leadership Conference based in North Carolina.[59]

ADVENTISM AND END-TIME EVENTS

In chapter 3 we have encountered the origins of Seventh-day Adventism and its intense apocalypticism. The movement emerged out of the Great Disappointment of 1844 and in respect to eschatology it focused on two distinctives: the spiritualization of Christ's return and sabbatarianism. Christ did not return to Earth in 1844 because Christians failed to keep the Sabbath. Since then he has been in the holy sanctuary cleansing the remaining sins of repentant believers. Adventism is now over 150 years old and several eschatological trends can be noted. It has lost much its apocalyptic urgency; it advocates a distinctly different premillennialism; and it has muddled pre and postmillennialism.

It is difficult for any movement to maintain urgent end-time beliefs. And the Seventh-day Adventists have been no exception. Despite having some beliefs and practices that have set them apart, they have moved from being an apocalyptic sect to an established denomination. Their numbers have grown; they have prospered; they have put down roots in society and established many institutions.[60]

All of this development does not mean that Adventists have abandoned their eschatology. While end-time beliefs have often been placed on the back burner, they are still being taught. In fact, while the church has not made any recent official predictions, Adventist evangelists have focused on certain events as signs of the end. Developments that have stirred up end-time excitement include the following: the two World Wars; the Great Depression; the election of John F. Kennedy, the first Catholic president; the Cuban Missile Crisis; the Cold War; the first moon landing;

---

59. Ibid. 57–58.
60. Gary Land, "Coping with Change," in *Adventism in America*, ed. Gary Land (Grand Rapids: Eerdmans, 1986) 208–30; Ronald Lawson, "The Persistence of Apocalypticism within a Denominationalizing Sect," in *Millennium, Messiahs, and Mayhem: Contemporary Apocalyptic Movements*, 208.

the Persian Gulf War; the sexual revolution of the 1960s; and society's increased acceptance of homosexuality.[61]

Since the collapse of the Soviet Union in 1989, Adventist evangelists have pointed to other trends as signs of the end—especially as they concern the Catholic Church. What they perceive as growing papal influence has caused anxiety. Opposed by the Catholic Church, the Soviet Union and communism collapsed. Thus the United States has emerged as the sole superpower and it could push the world into religious conformity. Adventist evangelists point to the alliance of the Christian Right and Catholicism over social issues. They fear that this will erode the separation of church and state. They also take alarm over the growth of spiritualism in the form of the New Age movement. (Spiritualism is feared because Adventists hold to soul sleep. Thus any communication with the dead must be with satanic beings).[62]

Despite these end time anxieties, hardline apocalypticism has declined in mainstream Adventism—especially in academic circles and official church agencies. Over the years, Adventism has been less separationist—interacting more with the world and building considerable institutions. As a result of being more world affirming, its end-time views have become less intense. Rather than seeing itself as the remnant about to be rescued from this world, it is helping to make the world a better place in which to live. In viewing itself as a godly remnant, Adventism has traditionally opposed other religions. It has maintained a virulent anti-Catholicism, viewing the papacy as the Antichrist, and Protestants as apostate and the whore of Babylon. (Protestants have been regarded as such because they followed Catholicism in worshipping on Sunday). In recent years, such perceptions have been modified.[63]

Seventh-day Adventists still maintain a unique version of premillennialism, one that is distinctly different from dispensationalism. As noted in chapters 4 and 5, dispensationalism believes Christ will rapture the saints prior to the great tribulation. The Earth now goes through horrible calamities, including the battle of Armageddon. The saints will stay with

---

61. Lawson, "The Persistence of Apocalypticism," 213–14; Jon Paulien, *What the Bible Says about the End-Time* (Hagerstown, MD: Review and Herald, 1994) 24.

62. Lawson, "The Persistence of Apocalypticism," 214–15; Mark Finley, "How Near Is Near?," *Adventists Affirm* 6/1 (1992) 12–24, 40; Marvin Moore, *The Crisis of the End of Time* (Boise, ID: Pacific, 1992).

63. Kenneth Newport, "The Heavenly Millennium of Seventh-day Adventism," in *Christian Millenarianism*, 137; *Seventh-day Adventist Bible Commentary* (Washington, DC: Review and Herald, 1957) 7:851–82.

An Eschatological Hodgepodge

Christ in heaven during these seven years of trial. After these catastrophic events, Christ returns to Earth with the saints for the thousand-year millennium. At the close of this golden age, Satan is released and rebels against God for the last time. God casts him into the lake of fire and creates the new heaven and Earth.

Unlike the dispensationalists, Seventh-day Adventists believe in a "heavenly millennium." It is a literal thousand years, but it takes place in heaven, not Earth. They have a different interpretation of Revelation 19–21, which is central to their understanding since 20:1–7 is the only passage in the Bible to mention the millennium. They read these chapters in simple chronological sequence. Prior to Christ's return there is a time of intense turmoil on Earth but not what they call the tribulation. Adventists maintain neither a pre- nor posttribulational version of premillennialism. Upon the premillennial return of Christ (which is symbolized by the white horse), God raises the righteous dead and the whole company of saints. The saints then tour the universe with Christ and remain in heaven with him for the duration of the thousand-year millennium, which is a time of preparation for eternal life on Earth. After the millennium, evil is banished and the returning saints become "citizens of the eternal city, the new Jerusalem." After one last rebellion by Satan, God "purifies the Earth with fire" and "recreates the Earth in its original edenic state."[64]

Seventh-day Adventists continue to affirm the premillennial Second Coming of Christ. Yet the situation is somewhat muddled. Adventism contains elements of pre- and postmillennialism. On a theological level, the Earth is not purified until after the millennium, which bears some resemblance with postmillennialism. But the major confusion comes on the practical level. Seventh-day Adventism is a church that is premillennial but behaves as if it is postmillennial. Premillenialism is a world-rejecting movement with a pessimistic view of human nature. But Seventh-day Adventism also maintains an impressive global presence. Its numbers are increasing significantly. Globally, it has established many educational institutions, including universities, seminaries, high schools, and over 4,500 primary schools.[65]

---

64. Newport, "The Heavenly Millennium of Seventh-day Adventism," 139–44 (quotes from 140); Ellen G. White, *The Great Controversy between Christ and Satan* (Mountain View, CA: Pacific, 1911) 653–61.

65. Newport, "The Heavenly Millennium of Seventh-day Adventism," 131, 142–44. See also Malcolm Bull and Keith Lockhart, *Seeking Sanctuary: Seventh-day Adventism and the American Dream* (San Francisco: Harper & Row, 1989) ch. 4.

Even more impressive are Adventism's contributions to healthcare. They place a major focus on healthy dietary practices, which are often drawn from Old Testament restrictions. Moreover, they not only prohibit the use of alcohol and tobacco products but also of caffeine. And, for the most part, they are vegetarians. Throughout the world, Adventists operate over five hundred hospitals, clinics, nursing homes, orphanages, and retirement homes. In addition, they maintain international humanitarian and development agencies.[66]

How do we explain this situation? What is the purpose of this vast humanitarian institutional structure? At one point in their history, Seventh-day Adventists attempted to opt out of society. Are they now attempting to clean up the world? Most of their institutional activities are not directed toward members of the Adventist church. Like some other premillennial movements, they uphold a premillennial doctrine but function as postmillennialists. But some difference can be detected. While they do not ignore evangelism, Adventists appear to place more emphasis on humanitarian efforts than do some other groups.[67]

This chapter contains some eschatological odds and ends. Still, some threads relate these religious groups to dispensational fundamentalism, a major source of end-time ideas in America. The movements noted in this chapter have either mirrored, modified, or rejected dispensationalism. Despite being non-millennial, Catholicism contains an apocalyptic, reactionary movement in the Baysiders—one that saw a catastrophic judgment coming and wished to turn the Catholic Church's clock back. In addition to believing that calamitous times were at hand, the Baysiders rejected the modern trends in Catholicism. Conversely, mainline Protestantism, while believing Christ will return, has categorically rejected the dispensational approach to Scripture and focused on living the Christian life in the present. While embracing premillennialism, both the Seventh-day Adventists and Pentecostals have each given a new twist to the doctrine. Seventh-day Adventists believe they will spend the millennium in heaven, not on Earth. Pentecostals see their distinctive, the out pouring of the Holy Spirit, as pointing to the latter days and the return of Christ.

66. Newport, "The Heavenly Millennium of Seventh-day Adventism," 131.
67. Ibid. 131, 146.

13

The Next Great Turning Point?

WHEN WILL THE NEXT great turning point occur? Will the world end in 2012? Or will it end on a less advertised date? During the first decade of the twenty-first century, many apocalyptic speculations paraded across the American religious landscape. Many people thought that such conjectures would subside after the year 2000. But never underrate America's appetite for conspiracy thinking, including end-time predictions. In the years following the turn of the millennium, the hoof beats of Armageddon could once again be heard.[1]

Take your choice. Prognosticators have earmarked nearly every year from 2005 to 2012 and beyond for catastrophic events. In addition habitual augurs such as Pat Robertson and Jack Van Impe have made predictions for this time period. The followers of Nostradamus insist that his writings contain predictions for the years from 2003 to 2025.[2] And several years into his presidency, Barrack Obama still conjures up visions of the Antichrist.

---

1. Americans have had a fascination with conspiracy theories. See Kathryn S. Olmsted, *Real Enemies: Conspiracy Theories and American Democracy, World War I to 9/11* (New York: Oxford University Press, 2009); David Aaronovitch, *Voodoo Histories: The Role of the Conspiracy Theory in Shaping Modern History* (New York: Riverhead, 2010); Martha F. Lee, *Conspiracy Rising: Conspiracy Thinking and American Public Life* (Santa Barbara, CA: Praeger, 2011).

2. See Peter Lorie, *Nostradamus 2003-2025: A History of the Future* (New York: Pocket Books, 2002).

319

Two movements and dates have aroused the most attention, however. One centers around Harold Camping, president of Family Radio. He was at it again. The end did not come in 1994 as he had predicted so he then said 2011 was the date. The most well-known date is December 21, 2012, when the Mayan calendar ends. Will the world end or will it be ushered into a new age of harmony? Believers in the Mayan chronology offer differing interpretations regarding this date.[3] And the Mayan calendar is not the only source of speculation for 2012. Other sources also predict worldwide upheavals for the year 2012.

A FEW PREDICTIONS

Many predictions place great emphasis on numbers, giving them almost a magical quality. Modern-day prophets such as Ron Patterson and F. M. Riley believed 2005 would witness the fulfillment of prophecy. They saw great significance in the number 38. John 5 tells us that at the pool of Bethesda Jesus healed a man who had been an invalid for 38 years. At the end of 38 years of wandering in the wilderness, the Israelites entered the Promised Land. But they still had to fight a seven-year war to subdue their enemies. How does 38 relate to prophecy? In the Six-Day War of 1967, God delivered the Temple Mount into the hands of the Jews. Add 38 to 1967 and you get the year 2005. Yet, the great tribulation was still to come. Israel will have to fight a seven-year war to subdue their enemies. The number 12 also held considerable significance and relates to 2005. Matthew 9 tells us that Jesus healed a menstruating woman who had an issue of blood. They saw this woman as a type of Jerusalem. In 1993, Rabin of Israel and Arafat of the PLO signed the Oslo Accords, which Patterson and Riley regarded as horrible and deceitful. Subtract 12 from 2005 and you get 1993.[4]

The year 2006 conjured up many more apocalyptic speculations. Aside from June 6, 2006—which had a special significance—several prophets pointed to catastrophic events. In May a comet would hit the Atlantic Ocean and generate a massive tsunami 650 feet high. July witnessed an escalation of tension in Lebanon, which many saw as the beginning of the end. For others August 22 held significance for a clash between Islam

---

3. See Marie D. Jones, 2013: *The End of Days or a New Beginning?* (Franklin Lake, NJ: New Page, 2008).

4. "Patterns pointing to the year A.D. 2005," http://www.choicesforliving.com/spirit/Prophecy0/020Updates/2005.htm.

The Next Great Turning Point?

and Christianity. Glenn Beck, then of CNN Headline News, said that on August 22 Israel would be wiped off the map. He then backtracked and claimed he was quoting someone else. Others insisted that on this date the Hidden Imam would return and the end-time struggle would begin. September would bring more bad news. A nuclear bomb would hit the UN Plaza in New York. According to the House of Yahweh—a religious movement based in Texas—a nuclear war would begin in September.[5]

June 6, 2006, with its resemblance to 6/6/6 caused considerable end-time anxieties. The speculators linked this date with both individuals and events. The "rapture index," which measures the likelihood of Christ's return, hit 156, which means, "fasten your seatbelts, for the time is near." Some people could not wait for June 6. They believed that the Antichrist had already arrived in the person of George W. Bush. After all, he began his presidency under the violence and fear of September 11. And they pointed out that George (six letters) Walker (six letters) and Bush Jr. (six letters) adds up to 666. But President Bush was not alone. Using biblical letter-numeric codes, countless political leaders have been designated as their generation's Antichrist. In modern America the list would include Franklin Delano Roosevelt, John F. Kennedy, Ronald Reagan, and Bill Clinton.[6] (Two years later Obama would be added to this list).

Then we have Jose Luis de Miranda, or "Daddy" as his followers call him. While he may not have earmarked June 6, he is a pastor with a 666 tattoo who claims to be divine. De Miranda is a former heroin addict and convict who believes he is the living incarnation of Jesus Christ, the Second Coming of Christ. De Miranda describes himself in seemingly contradictory terms, namely as both "God on Earth" and the Antichrist who will destroy all other religions. In particular he had made Catholicism a target of his denunciation, calling it "a doctrine of devils." He has thousands of followers worldwide who believe they are God's chosen people, predestined to salvation.[7]

---

5. "15 Failed Predictions That the End of the World Would Happen in 2006," http://www.religioustolerance.org/end_wrl.htm.

6. Tony Allen-Mills, "Mothers Expect Damien on 6/6/6," *Times Online*, http://www.timesonline.co.uk/tol/news/uk/article711393.ece?print=yes; Seth Borenstein, "Curiosity, Humor Surround June 6, 2006," *ABC News*, http://abcnews.go.com/US/print?id=2038673.

7. John Zarrella and Patrick Oppmann, "Pastor with 666 Tattoo Claims to Be Divine," *CNN.com* http://cnn.usnews.printthis.clickability.com/pt/cpt?action=cpt&title =Pastor+with=666=tatto; "Jose Luis de Jesus Miranda-Million Dollar Messiah," http://www.allaboutcults.org/jose-luis-de-jesus-miranda.htm.

Something about 666 brings out the worry in people. Others have capitalized on the date for financial reasons. One pregnant woman, Francesca Renouf, booked a medical appointment to insure that her child would not be born on June 6. Another woman said she would name her child Damon, after the satanic boy in the movie *Omen*. Actually, Twentieth Century Fox scheduled its remake of the horror film *Omen* to appear on June 6. In America on June 6, Slayer—the heavy metal rock group—started its Unholy Alliance tour, subtitled Preaching to the Perverted. June 6 also witnessed the publication of Tim LaHaye's new *Left Behind* series book and Ann Coulter's polemic called *Godless: The Church of Liberalism*. In the latter book the only demons were the Democrats.[8]

Not to be left out, Pat Robertson made a number of predictions for the years 2006–2010. And none of them improved his prophetic batting average. In 2006 "the coasts of America will be lashed by storms," including a terrible tsunami that would strike the Pacific Northwest. God told him that a terrorist attack would hit the United States in 2007 and there would be a "mass killing," possibly numbering in a million deaths. The year 2008 would be a year of violence and a recession in America, followed by a major stock market crash by 2010.[9]

With a succession of failed predictions, it would seem that Pat Robertson's hotline to God is a bit defective. His alleged dialogues with God go back to at least the 1960s. In the 1980s his prognostications included a worldwide economic depression and a major war in the Middle East. Of significance, Robertson claimed to have received the following words from God: "I have something else for you to do. I want you to run for president of the United States." Robertson clearly flunks the Bible's test for measuring whether one is a true prophet or not. According to Deuteronomy 18:22, "When a prophet speaketh in the name of the Lord, if the thing follow not, nor come to pass, that is the thing which the Lord hath not spoken..."[10]

The year 2007 aroused other dire prognostications, most on the level of tabloid journalism. According to some interpretations, the Bible Code

---

8. Borenstein, "Curiosity, Humor Surround June 6, 2006."

9. "Pat Robertson's 2008 Predictions," Law and Magic blog, http://lpcprof.typepad.com/law_and_magic_blog/2008/01/pat-robert. See David Edwin Harrell Jr., *Pat Robertson: A Life and Legacy* (Grand Rapids: Eerdmans, 2010).

10. "God Is Warning of Big Storms, Robertson Says," *Seattle Times*, http://community.seattletimes.nwsource.com/archive/?date=20060519&slug=pat19 (quote); "Pat Robertson's Defective Hotline to God," http://www.humanismbyjoe.com/Pat_Robertson_Prophecies.htm (quote); Harrell, *Pat Robertson*, 91–124.

The Next Great Turning Point?

forecasted a horrific Ebola attack on Philadelphia, killing thousands of people and resulting in a quarantine of the area. The CIA in turn would blame Iran and President Bush would launch a massive attack on Iran. In yet another way, Iran generated considerable prophetic speculation. Since Ahmadinejad became president of the country in 2005, anticipation of the arrival of the Mahdi ("the Islamic Messiah") has intensified. This event, it is speculated, could spark an apocalyptic war with America and Israel.[11]

Ronald Weinland regarded 2008 as the beginning of the final events that would thrust the world into the great tribulation. Weinland is a minister in the Church of God. This denomination is a split off from the Worldwide Church of God (WCG) founded by Herbert Armstrong. When the WCG moved toward historic Christianity, Weinland broke from it and formed the United Church of God (UCG) and then renamed it Church of God. Weinland insists that in 1997 he became a prophet and says God speaks through him. He claims to be one of the two witnesses spoken of in Revelation 11 and hinted that his wife Laura was the second witness.[12]

Weinland's first book, *The Prophesied End-Time* (2004), is what God has given to him regarding the events that have already begun to be fulfilled. His next book, *2008—God's Final Witness* (2006), is a revelation of the Book of Revelation. It pinpoints the timing of the end time-events mentioned in Revelation. The Apostle John, as he claims, recorded the prophetic events reserved for the end of history. Weinland in turn has been given the task of revealing the truth about what John wrote.[13]

According to Weinland, *2008—God's Final Witness* reveals truths unknown to humankind for thousands of years. In fact, this book discloses the seven thunders of the Book of Revelation, which the Apostle John was not permitted to reveal. The year 2008 would mark the beginning of the end. The final tribulation would strike with destructive power, crippling world governments and destroying the world economy. These

---

11. "Iranian Cataclysm Forecast August 22," *WorldNetDaily*, http;//www.wnd.com/news/article.asp?Article_ID=51445; "Iranian TV Special—The Mahdi Could Return This Spring—Iran Preparing for Apocalyptic War with the U.S.," http://www.injesus.com/index.php?module=message&task=view&MID=CB007BGB&GroupID=AA006SGW#1; "Bible Code: Terror Attack on Philadelphia [USA] Will Crash the Stock Market and Trigger the Apocalypse," http://www.satansrapture.com/maycode2.htm.

12. Ronald Weinland, "The Prophesied End-Time Revealed," http://the-end.com/RonaldWeinland.asp; "False Prophet Ronald Weinland," http://ronaldweinland.info.

13. See Ronald Weinland, *The Prophesied End-Time* (n.p.: the-end.com, inc., 2004); Ronald Weinland, *2008:God's Final Witness* (n.p.: the-end.com, inc., 2008); Weinland, "The Prophesied End-Time Revealed."

events would usher in World War III, the death of billions, and the return of Jesus Christ.[14]

Any list of end-time predictions would not be complete without words of wisdom from Jack Van Impe and his wife Rexalla. Van Impe first forecasted 2011 as the time for the rapture, then revised it to 2012. Matthew 1:17 lists 40 generations from Christ to Abraham. Based on his arithmetic, this is a historical period of 2,160 years. Then divide 42 into that number and you come up with 51.4 years. The countdown begins with 1967, when the Jews captured Jerusalem. Add 51.4 to 1967 and you arrive at 2018. Subtract the 7-year tribulation from 2018 and you get 2011, the date of the rapture. But what do you with the extra 4/10 of a year? The capture of Jerusalem occurred in June 1967 so one can add it to that date and come out to 2019. Then subtract 7 and you have 2012. By using this formula, Van Impe brought his Christian math into harmony with the date set by what he calls the Inca and Aztec calendars. Still, he resisted the temptation of linking these calendars with his Christian timetable and only asks the question: could this have any bearing on the return of Jesus Christ?[15]

HAROLD CAMPING IS AT IT AGAIN

We met Harold Camping in chapter 5. As noted there, he is not a dispensational premillennialist—the frequent avenue for conveying end-time ideas in modern America. Rather, he describes himself as a Reformed amillennialist but one with an elaborate and different system for calculating the return of Christ. Camping is a retired civil engineer by trade but has no formal theological training. Like some other end-of-the-world forecasters, he has a mathematical or engineering background and believes that he can predict God's time schedule by means of numerical formulas.[16]

As president of the California-based Family Radio, he has a vehicle for projecting his ideas. This network broadcasts his messages over 150 stations in America, and satellites take it to many countries in the world.

14. Weinland, 2008: *God's Final Witness*, 84–113; Weinland, "The Prophesied End-Time Revealed."

15. "The Date-Setting of Jack Van Impe," *The Heresy Hunter*, http://heresyhunter.blogspot.com/2006/10date-setting-ofjack-vanimpe; "Jack Van Impe Soothsaying Again," *Apostasy Alert*, http://www.apostasyalert/vanimpee.com.

16. Perucci Ferraiuolo, "Could '1994' Be the End of Family Radio?," *Christian Research Journal* 16/1 (Summer 1993) 5–6; Joe Maxwell, "Camping Misses End-Times Deadline, *Christianity Today*, 24 October 1994, 84.

The Next Great Turning Point?

Thus, he has attracted a substantial number of followers worldwide. In addition, his ministry has a website named WeCanKnow.com, meaning that Christians can know exactly God's schedule for end-time events. His followers have also erected about five thousand billboards all over the nation and handed out T-shirts and bumper stickers.[17]

In addition Camping has published several books articulating his ideas. The first of these books—*1994?* and its sequel, *Are You Ready?: Much More Evidence That 1994 Could Be the End of World*—presented an elaborate system of dating pointing to 1994 as the end of days. The prediction of September 1994 obviously did not come about. How did Camping explain this prophetic failure? We find his explanations in his latest book, *Time Has an End: A Biblical History of the World 11,013 B.C.–2011 A.D.*[18]

First, like Hal Lindsey and other prophets, he downplayed his previous prognostication, insisting that it was a suggestion not a prediction. He claimed the Bible, "suggested very strongly that there was a high likelihood that the world would come to an end sometime in the year A.D. 1994." Two, like the Seventh-day Adventists and Jehovah's Witnesses, he contended that an eschatological event did occur on the designated date. Also, like them he spiritualized it. Indeed, "it was the year 1994 in which Christ came a second time to begin the completion of the evangelization of His true people." On September 7, 1994, God began to evangelize people outside the churches because they had become apostate. Third, God gave him new information, which he integrated into the projections previously set forth in the book *1994?*. When combined with what he had said earlier, this new information pointed to the "high likelihood that the year 2011 will be the year in which the end will come."[19]

Actually, Camping's movement bears a superficial resemblance to the Millerite movement, which we encountered previously. Basing his

---

17. David R. Reagan, "Harold Camping: Date-Sitting Madness," *Religious Trojan Horse*, http://www.worldviewweekend.com/worldview-times/article.php?articleid=6956; Tom Breen, "End of Days in May?: Christian Groups Spreads Word," http://www2.tbo.com/news/breaking-news/2011/jan/03/end-of-days-in-may-christian-group-spreads-word-ar-18337/.

18. Harold Camping, *1994?* (New York: Vantage, 1992); Harold Camping, *Are You Ready?: Much More Evidence that 1994 Could be the End of the End of the World* (New York: Vantage, 1993). See also Harold Camping, *The End of the Church Age*, (Oakland, CA: Family Radio Stations, 2002); Harold Camping, *We Are Almost There!* (Oakland, CA: Family Radio Stations, 2008); Harold Camping, *To God Be the Glory* (Oakland, CA: Family Radio Stations, 2008).

19. Harold Camping, *Time Has An End: A Biblical History of the World 11,013 BC–2011 AD* (New York: Vantage, 2005) xiv–xv.

prediction on Daniel 8:14, Miller believed Christ would return by March 21, 1844. When this did not happen his followers pressured him into issuing a new date, October 22, 1844. As noted, this failure became know as the Great Disappointment. Disillusioned, many of his followers dispersed. But like Camping, one group—which became the Seventh-day Adventists—contended that an eschatological event did occur in 1844. Christ entered the Holy of Holies in heaven and began to cleanse the remaining sin of repentant believers.

We Can Know

The Bible admonishes people not to speculate regarding the time of the Second Advent and the end of the world. In reference to his return, Christ said, "But of that day and hour knoweth no man, no not the angels of heaven, but my Father only" (Matt 24:36). In 1 Thessalonians 5:2–3, Paul tells us "that the day of the Lord so cometh as a thief in the night. For when they shall say, Peace and safety; then destruction cometh upon them . . ." Despite such verses, Harold Camping and many others have predicted specific eschatological events.

What does Camping do with these verses? Before earmarking May 21, 2011, as the judgment day, he had to come to grips with the exhortations to not speculate regarding end-time events. He acknowledged that the Bible contains such verses. But he goes to great lengths to demonstrate scriptural passages supporting the notion that Christians can know the timing of the end of the world. According to Camping, other biblical passages allow for God's people to learn the date when the world will end. He insists the churches of the modern day have fallen far from the truth. As a result they teach the lie that Christians cannot know the date of the judgment day.[20]

While Camping brings up many verses, primarily from the Old Testament, the theme is largely the same: God has always warned his people regarding the coming judgments. He points out that Noah knew about the judgment day and prepared an ark. God told Abraham about his plan to destroy Sodom and Gomorrah, allowing his nephew Lot to escape. The

---

20. "The Bible Reveals WE CAN KNOW May 21, 2011 Is Judgment Day!," http://www.ebilefellowship.com/wecanknow/index.html; Camping, *Time Has an End*, xviii–xiv; "We Can Know! Christ's Return on Judgment Day: May 21, 2011," http://www.wecanknow.com.

The Next Great Turning Point?

Ninevites were not God's people; still he sent Jonah to them with a message of warning and the opportunity to repent.[21]

Camping said people could know that May 21, 2011, would be the judgment day only if God had opened their eyes. The majority of the world's population have not been chosen to salvation. Thus, the Second Advent will surprise billions of people. Another factor is that many people trust their churches or pastors, whose message is the old lie that people cannot know the date of the judgment day.[22]

May 21 and October 21, 2011

Harold Camping firmly believed that the end would come on May 21, 2011, but this time he left himself wiggle room and utilized some conditional terms. In *Time Has an End* he says, "We find more and more evidence of the likelihood that 2011 could well be the end-time year." But, "If this world is still in existence after the end of 2011, we will know that there is still much more we can learn from the Bible."[23]

Camping arrived at the date of 2011 by a prophetic methodology based on his strange and complicated (too complicated for this study) numerology. His calculations begin with creation, which is ground zero. God created the world in six 24-hour days in 11013 BC. Camping arrived at the date of 2011 by claiming the end would come 7,000 years after the Noahic flood, which he dated at 4990 BC. (The transition between BC and AD is the year zero. This accounts for the missing number).[24]

Closely related to the end-time date is the termination of the church age in 1988. Camping calculated that the church age—beginning at Pentecost—lasted 1,955 years and ended in 1988, 40 years after the beginning of the nation of Israel in 1948. The year 1988 also marked the beginning of the great tribulation. Christians are now to leave their spiritual homeland, namely, the local church, as Jacob left Canaan for Egypt. The local churches have become apostate and "true" Christians must abandon them. Camping accorded great importance to the number 23, which normally signifies God's wrath being poured out. Rather than the usual seven-year duration for the tribulation, Camping said it would last 23 years. Add 23

---

21. "The Bible Reveals WE CAN KNOW"; Camping, *Time Has an End*, xix–xxi, 15–17, 93–96; "We Can Know! Christ's Return on Judgment Day: May 21, 2011."
22. "The Bible Reveals WE CAN KNOW"; Camping, *Time Has an End*, 355.
23. Camping, *Time Has an End*, xxii.
24. Ibid., 88–89, 101, 147.

to 1988 and you arrive at 2011, the year of great eschatological significance for Camping. In *We Are Almost There* and *To God Be the Glory*, he projected May 21, 2011, as the date for Christ's return and the rapture and October 21, 2011, as the time when the world would end.[25]

Camping arrived at these conclusions and others by according great (almost magical) significance to numbers. He believes God dictated the Bible and so every word and number carries a spiritual importance. In fact, this study has only noted the numbers Camping has most frequently employed. He has noticed the context in which certain numbers occurred and endowed them with a similar spiritual meaning.[26]

According to Camping, judgment would begin on May 21 at 6:00 p.m. with a huge earthquake in New Zealand and make its way across the Earth's time zones. Those who remained would face destruction in October. May 21 came and went with no fierce earthquake or rapture. How did Camping react? He was depressed but also unbowed and defiant. Once again, and like the Seventh-day Adventists and Jehovah's Witnesses, he spiritualized the event. Judgment day indeed came on May 21 but it was spiritual and not visible. He had the correct day but misread its meaning. "We were convinced that, on May 21, God would return in a very physical way by bringing an earthquake and ushering in the final five months of judgment. When we look at it spiritually, we find he did come." On May 21 God decided humanity's fate and the sentence would come on October 21. And it would not be spiritual. Rather the entire world would be destroyed.[27]

What about all of the money donated to proclaim the coming of doomsday? Family Radio and its supporters spent millions to inform humanity that Jesus would return on May 21, thus marking the end of the world as we know it. Would Camping return this money? Absolutely not.

---

25. Camping, *Time Has an End*, 291, 299, 331, 344, 357, 369–72, 380, 396, 400–405, 410.

26. "Harold Camping's Teachings about the End of the World Do Not Agree with the Bible," http://www.cogwriter.com/haroldcamping-May-21-2011.htm.

27. Zondra Hughes, "Harold Camping's New Rapture: October 21, 2011. Do You Believe?" http://rollingout.com/news-politics/harold-camping's-new-rapture-oc (5/24/2011) (quotes). See also Michael Sheridan, "Harold Camping: May 21 Was 'Invisible Judgment Day,' the REAL Rapture Comes on October 21," *Daily News*, http://www.nydailynews.com/news/national/2011/05/24/2011-05-24; Antonio Prado, "Harold Camping Breaks His Silence: Judgment Day Is October 21," http://www.mexicoledger.com/lifestyle/x1495161448/Harold-Camping; "Shameless Harold Camping's New Prediction: World Will End Quickly on Oct. 21," http://www.ibtimes.com/art/services/print.php?articleid=150770.

The Next Great Turning Point?

"We're not at the end. We're not out of business. We still have to go another five months," he said. But Family Radio would not be putting up any more billboards or passing out more tracts. The world had been warned and now stands under judgment. Family Radio, however, was not broke, for in 2009 it reported its assets to the IRS as totaling $104 million.[28] Still, the organization did experience some financial difficulties after May 21.

October 21 came and went with less fanfare than May 21. Camping had "cried wolf" once too often and was dismissed as a discredited nut or a false prophet. He said God had declared his final judgment on May 21 and there was no need to warn the world regarding his impending wrath. On May 21 the door of salvation had closed and, except for the elect, no one could be saved. Moreover, Camping had a stroke on June of 2011 and, while partially recovered, he has not returned to full-time broadcasting. His message, however, has still reached 65 stations in the United States, but it was more moderate than his previous declarations regarding the coming judgment.

2012: DESTRUCTION OR TRANSFORMATION

The great Oxford literary critic Frank Kermode spoke of "the sense of an ending" in his book by that name. The year 2012 evokes a similar feeling. The tagline for the movie 2012 captures this emotion: "Never before has a date in history been so significant to so many cultures, so many religions, scientists, and governments." While the end of the Mayan calendar on December 21, 2012, has seized the spotlight, 2012 is not just about one day in 2012. Rather, it is about many predictions for that year. And if they come about, 2012 will witness a sea change—either positive or negative—for the future of humanity.[29]

Throughout history a chorus of voices have predicted the end of the world. Still, the year 2012 is different. It has evoked a wider range of responses. Traditions as diverse as the Christian, Chinese, Mayan, Indian,

---

28. "Harold Camping Breaks His Silence," (quote); Hughes, "Harold Camping's New Rapture"; Garance Burke, "For Rapture Believers, It's a New Doomsday," *Wichita Eagle*, 22 May 2011, 12A.

29. Mark Hitchcock, 2012: *The Bible and the End of the World* (Eugene, OR: Harvest House, 2009) inside cover (quote); Frank Kermode, *The Sense of an Ending: Studies in the Theory of Fiction* (New York: Oxford University Press, 1967); Lawrence E. Joseph, *Apocalypse 2012: An Investigation into Civilization's End* (New York: Broadway, 2007) 213; John Major Jenkins, *The 2012 Story: The Myths, Fallacies, and Truth behind the Most Intriguing Date in History* (New York: Tarcher/Penguin, 2009) 282.

Native American, and New Age, plus some scientists, believe something big is going to happen. Perhaps much of this can be attributed to a sense of doom in contemporary culture, or at least to the belief that major changes must happen for civilization to survive. Yes, as the world approached 2012 apocalyptic thinking was in the air.[30]

Many people have talked about the year 2012. Some have feared it, believing that it will mark the end of time. Others have waited with great anticipation, believing that 2012 will bring the great transformation, a whole new world, and a new way of being. Still, others have wondered if anything will happen. Will 2012 be a big bust as was Y2K? Many believe the winds of change are blowing. Will these winds obliterate humanity or bring the world into a new tomorrow?[31]

In part, this interest in 2012 can be measured by the marketplace. Thousands of people are purchasing 2012 survival kits, T-shirts, and shelters. At least one movie, *2012*, is out and several more are in progress. The websites are too numerous to name. Several examples are survive2012.com, 2012predictions.net, apocalypse2012.com, and december212012.com. A number of television programs have featured the year 2012. A few examples include: the History Channel, "Decoding the Past—Doomsday 2012: The End of Days"; ABC News, "Will the World End in 2012?: Thousands Worldwide Prepare for the Apocalypse, Expected in 2012"; and Fox and Friends, "It's the End of the World: Mayan Calendar Ends in 2012." The print news media also has a long list. Noted are the following: *U.S. News & World Report*, "Are the Final Days Coming Soon?; New Doomsdayers Adapt a Mayan Prediction"; *Newsweek*, "2012: A Y2K for the New Age"; and *USA Today*, "Does Maya Calendar Predict 2012 Apocalypse?" Books regarding 2012 are too numerous to list. Suffice it to say that there is even *The Complete Idiot's Guide to* 2012.[32]

How did the year 2012 gain such visibility? Jose Arguelles put 2012 "on the map." As noted earlier, in 1987 he authored the best-selling book *The Mayan Factor: Path beyond Technology*. He coined the term *harmonic convergence* and helped turn it into a global network and a defining component for the New Age movement. Harmonic Convergence was a

---

30. Joseph, *Apocalypse* 2012, 214; Christine Brouwer, "Will the World End in 2012?: Thousands Worldwide Prepare for the Apocalypse Expected in 2012," *ABC News*, 3 July 2008, 1–3.

31. Marie D. Jones, *2013: The End of Days or a New Beginning? Envisioning the World after the Events of* 2012 (Franklin Lakes, NJ: New Page, 2008) 19–20.

32. Hitchcock, *2012: The Bible and the End of the World*, 19–20; Synthia Andrews and Colin Andrews, *The Complete Idiot's Guide to* 2012 (New York: Alpha, 2008).

The Next Great Turning Point?

peace initiative that occurred on August 16 and 17, 1987, at sacred sites throughout the world. It was based on the notion that an exceptional planetary alignment would help start a global transformation. People gathered to awaken the "energy grid" and set in motion a twenty-five-year era of spiritual growth culminating in 2012. After the Harmonic Convergence in 1987, an apocalyptic subculture began to emerge. Thus began a twenty-five-year countdown to 2012. For almost twenty years the movement remained somewhat submerged. But in recent years it has exploded and the year 2012 has become nearly a household word.[33]

The Mayan Calendar

As noted previously, a number of civilizations earmarked the year 2012 as a time for significant change. Also, the time for these developments is not limited to December 21, but encompasses the entire year. Nevertheless, the spotlight has zeroed in on the Mayan calendar as the date for an earthshaking transformation. And whether this upheaval will be a disaster or the beginning of something positive is subject to debate. Of course, other observers say the Mayans meant nothing cataclysmic but simply the end of a life cycle.

Who are the Mayans? The Maya Empire was a Mesoamerican civilization stretching from the southern states of Mexico to the current Central American countries of Belize, Guatemala, El Salvador, and some of Honduras. They had much in common with other Mesoamerican civilizations such as the Aztec, Toltec, Zapata, Mixtecs, and Teotihuanacos. The Mayans exhibited advanced writing skills, an amazing understanding of astronomy and mathematical knowledge, plus an incredible ability when constructing cities and pyramids. Their civilization began approximately 1800–1900 BCE and peaked about 250–900 CE. Today they are most famous for their pyramids and calendars.[34]

What is the Mayan calendar all about? The Mayans utilized approximately twenty different calendars and saw time as coming in spiritual cycles. Their calendars had many practical functions relating to agricultural, commercial, social, and administrative tasks. But very important was the

---

33. Matthew Restall and Amara Solari, *2012 and the End of the World: The Western Roots of the Mayan Apocalypse* (Lanham, MD: Rowman & Littlefield, 2011) 42–43; Hitchcock, *2012: The Bible and the End of the World*, 16–17.

34. Jones, *2013: The End of Days or a New Beginning?* i, 24; Jenkins, *The 2012 Story*, 13–17; Restall and Solari, *2012 and the End of the World*, 1–13.

religious component. Each day had a patron spirit, signifying the specific use for that day. In contrast, our modern Gregorian calendar largely focuses on economic, administrative, and social dates.[35]

For the most part, the Mayans relied on three of these calendars and two of these were short. The solar calendar, known as the *Haab,'* was based on the celestial cycle. It contained 365 days divided into 18 months of 20 days. Each year then had one five-day period left over. Because the Mayans considered the number 20 to be sacred, each month contained 20 days. The Mayans called the second calendar the *Tzolk'in* or "sacred calendar." This ceremonial or sacred calendar contained 260 days, known as the "sacred cycle." It utilized a 13-day count and a 20-day cycle with a different sign ascribed to each day. The Maya and other Mesoamerican cultures used this calendar until the rise of the Gregorian calendar in 1582.[36]

These two calendars, however, could only measure short durations of time. With need of another calendar, they devised the Mayan Long Count Calendar. This calendar could last 5,126 years and is most associated with the changes predicted for 2012. The Mayans divided this calendar into five units or cycles that extend backward and forward from August 11, 3114 BCE, which they believed to be the date for the creation of the Maya. In the Mayan Long Count Calendar that date is represented as 0.0.0.01 (Day One). This fifth cycle is to end on 13.0.0.0.0 (Day Last), which happens to be December 21, 2012.[37]

But what will happen on December 21, 2012? One must remember that the Mayan calendar makes no predictions, either positive or negative, for December 21. It simply stops on that date. What that means is subject to interpretation. There seem to be, more or less, four schools of thought. One prediction contends that December 21 will witness a global catastrophe, perhaps even the end of the world. A modification of this view says that during the year 2012—not just on December 21—humanity will experience a series of disasters.

A third opinion sees December 21 as ushering in a time of transformation. Yes, there might be some terrible problems or even a purification surrounding this transition, but the world will become a better place. Humanity will enter an age of enlightenment. A fourth perspective

---

35. Jones, 2113: *The End of Days or a New Beginning?*, 24–26; Jenkins, *The 2012 Story*, 59–81.

36. Joseph, *Apocalypse 2012*, 23–25; Hitchcock, 2012: *The Bible and the End of the World*, 32–33; Jones, 2013: *The End of Days or a New Beginning?*, 27–30.

37. Jenkins, *The 2012 Story*, 56–57; Hitchcock, 2012: *The Bible and the End of the World*, 32–33; Jones, 2013: *The End of Days or a New Beginning?*, 28–30.

The Next Great Turning Point?

argues that the Mayan calendar has nothing to do with either a disaster or transformation. Such an apocalyptic perspective is rooted in Western culture, not the Mayan civilization. Instead, this apocalyptic and doomsday interpretation has been imposed upon the Mayan calendar by Western millennial thinkers.[38]

2012 Global Predictions

The first three perspectives regarding 2012 have something in common—the world as we know it will end. It could be a doomsday disaster or it could be a series of catastrophic events leading to the humankind's transformation. If a new age arrives it will be accompanied, as are all new births, "by blood and agony as well as hope and promise." In either case, proponents of these views say the world will face calamities "to a degree unmatched in human history."[39]

What are some of these developments? There will be a sunspot surge. Scientists say this latest sunspot cycle will be much stronger than any in recent years. What does this have to do with life on Earth? A much stronger solar cycle could be catastrophic, producing multiple Katrina-like storms. The result might be ruined economies, energy shortages, and massive loss of life. Such sunspots could have a significant impact on technology including satellites, GPS systems, cell phones, and the Internet.[40]

Planet Earth might experience a pole reversal, that is, the North and South Poles shift positions. The cause of this is not known for certain. Some scientists say a pole reversal might follow a decline in the Earth's magnetic field strength. Another view is that an intense influx of energy from the sun can produce a pole reversal. The results of such a situation could obviously be cataclysmic—volcanic activity, earthquakes, floods, and the destruction of agriculture and the ecosystem.[41]

---

38. Restall and Solari, 2012 *and the End of the World*, 113–32.

39. Joseph, *Apocalypse* 2012, 16 (quotes); John Kehne, "Is the World Really Going to End on December 21, 2012," http://www.december212012.com/articles/editors-notes/Is-the-world.

40. Patrick Geryl, *How to Survive* 2012 (Kempton, IL: Adventures Unlimited, 2007) 79–84; Joseph, *Apocalypse* 2012, 16; Jones, 2013: *The End of Days or a New Beginning?*, 101–3.

41. Geryl, *How to Survive* 2012, 26–33; Joseph, *Apocalypse* 2012, 16; Jones, 2013: *The End of Days or a New Beginning?*, 106–8; Patrick Geryl, "Pole Shift & Pole Reversal in 2012," http://survive2012.com/geryl11.php.

Some scientists conjecture that a super volcano has the potential to destroy vast areas of Earth. A super-volcano contains the destructive power of one thousand Hiroshima-type nuclear bombs. Unlike a regular volcano, which can kill thousands and wreck havoc over a local area, a super volcano can have a global impact, perhaps even sending the planet into a mini ice age. The largest super-volcano hotspot is at Yellowstone National Park. It is fueled by underground accumulations of uranium. While there is no evidence that such an eruption is imminent, if such were to happen it would spew radioactive lava across the adjacent states and parts of Canada. Some 2012 prognosticators believe such an eruption will occur on December 21.[42]

The Milky Way is central to Mayan mythology. They regarded it as the main component to the Sacred Tree of Life. The Milky Way contained "the womb of the world," that is, the place where the Maya believed all stars were born. Modern science has since confirmed this belief. On December 21 our solar system—for the first time in twenty-six thousand years—will eclipse the view from Earth of the center of the Milky Way.

What does this have to do with doomsday? The energy streaming to Earth from the center of the Milky Way will be disrupted on December 21 for the first time in thousands of years. Some believe that even this slight disruption will have significant consequences for planet Earth and its people. They contend, as did the Mayans, that such a break will throw out of kilter mechanisms vital to our body and planet.[43]

While not as pronounced, several other doomsday predictions are associated with 2012. Death might come from the sky. The Planet X Hypothesis claims that an unnamed planet will either hit the Earth or come close enough to cause a global catastrophe. A similar prognostication says that the asteroid Toutatis will come close enough to Earth on December 12, 2012, to cause a disaster. Gamma rays are high-energy radiation beams, the most explosive known in the universe. According to one scientist, Gamma waves come in waves and will hit the Earth in 2012. One effect would be to increase earthquakes.[44]

To this point the prognostications regarding 2012 have been catastrophic. But remember, the predictions regarding the Mayan calendar

42. Geryl, *How to Survive 2012*, 85–92; Joseph, *Apocalypse 2012*, 17; Jones, *2013: The End of Days or a New Beginning?*, 114–16.

43. Joseph, *Apocalypse 2012*, 32–33, 161; Jenkins, *The 2012 Story*, 138–47.

44. Jones, *2013: The End of Days or a New Beginning?*, 108–13; "Asteroid Toutatis approaches Earth on December 12, 2012," Doomsday Information Guide, http://ddig.wordpress.com/2008/07/07astroid-toutatis-approache-e.

The Next Great Turning Point?

are like a two-sided coin, one with both physical disasters and spiritual enlightenment. As the Earth moves into celestial alignment, tremendous energy will be released, wrecking both physical havoc and a spiritual awakening. The year 2012 will mark a shift in the collective consciousness. It will usher in a new golden age, a new beginning for humankind, and a gentler time of transformation. In a different sense, 2012 will mark the end of a chapter in human history and the beginning of a new era of human growth. John Major Jenkins, an expert on Mesoamerican culture and 2012, "identifies A.D. 2012 as a time of tremendous transformation and opportunity for spiritual growth [and] transition from one World to another."[45]

Some Related Prophecies

There are other prophecies fitting the general pattern of the Mayan calendar but do not earmark the year 2012. The Hopi are a Native American tribe living in the Four Corners area of the southwestern United States. Like the Mayan, the Hopi speak of four or five previous worlds that have been destroyed as part of the purification process. A huge volcano destroyed the first world. The second Hopi world ended because of a pole shift. Like many religious traditions, the Hopi believe a great flood destroyed their third world. The fourth world, which is the present era, will end in fire. This destruction will come from the sky, which could refer to a nuclear device or impact from space. The final stage of this fourth world is the great purification, a theme common with many cultures. After this purification humankind enters a period of peace and returns to balance. As with many apocalyptic scenarios, there are catastrophic events followed by a time of bliss.[46]

Nostradamus has been noted previously, so little will be said at this point except for a few predictions relevant to the early twenty-first century. His quatrains, of course, are subject to many interpretations. One explanation claims the early twenty-first century will experience considerable turmoil that gives rise to the third Antichrist—the first two being Napoleon and Hitler. Some interpretations say this third Antichrist may not

---

45. John Major Jenkins, *Maya Cosmogenesis 2012* (Rochester, VT: Bear & Co.) xl–xli; Hitchcock, *2012 The Bible and the End of the World*, 57–59; Jenkins, *The 2012 Story*, 167–70; Geryl, *How to Survive 2012*, 182–87; Lisa Miller, "2012: A Y2K for the New Age," *Newsweek*, 11 and 18 May 2009, 12.

46. "Hopi Indian Predictions & Prophecies," http://www.ezpowell.com/armageddon/?p=13; Jones, 2013: *The End of Days or a New Beginning?*, 50.

be a person but the evil of our time. Whether a person or the force of evil, he or it rules for twenty-five years and then humankind is delivered and a golden age commences around 2024. This date would coincide with the time many see as a popular date for the beginning of the Age of Aquarius (2023). Still, the end of the world for Nostradamus is 3797, a long way off from 2012.[47]

Some see *The Bible Code* as forecasting the end of the world, first in 2006 and then possibly in 2010 or 2012. Dr. Eli Rips, an Israeli mathematician, discovered the "Bible Code." He claimed that the first five books of the Hebrew Bible, known as the Torah, contain encoded messages. Michael Drosin, an investigative reporter, popularized Rips' work and in 1997 published *The Bible Code*. Drosin went on to write two sequels: *The Bible Code II*, and *The Bible Code III: The Quest*. The last book indicates that the origin of the Bible Code is extraterrestrial and that it only suggests probabilities and not exact dates. Here is the process. Letters of the passages of the Torah are placed at equal intervals formatted to fit into boxes like graph paper. Then high-powered computers look for sequences. The process is called "Equidistant Letter Sequences" (ELS). Using this process, Drosin used the Bible Code to predict the apocalypse, which he said would most likely be in 2006, with 2010 or 2012 as the latest dates. On these dates the Earth would be annihilated by comets.[48]

And if all of these dates prove incorrect, people may have to wait until 2060, the date Isaac Newton (1642–1727) set for the end of the world. Known as a great scientist, Newton also had a passion for biblical prophecy—something difficult for many people to believe. In part this catches people by surprise because Newton hated date-setting and his predictions were private and not discovered until 1936. He was a historic premillennialist and used the day-for-a-year principle. Thus he equated the 1,260 days of Daniel 7:25 with 1,260 years. Newton strongly disliked Catholicism and regarded 800 CE as a significant moment in history. On this date, Charlemagne was crowned emperor of Rome in the west by Pope Leo III. To 800 Newton added 1,260 and arrived at 2060 for the "fall of Babylon." After that Christ would return and establish his millennial kingdom.[49]

---

47. Lorie, *Nostradamus*, 35–38; Jones, 2013: *The End of Days or a New Beginning?*, 51–53.

48. Jones, 2013: *The End of Days or a New Beginning?*, 60, 61; Joseph, *Apocalypse 2012*, 178.

49. Stephen D. Snobelen, "Statement on the Date 2060," http://www.isaac-newton.org/update.html.

The Next Great Turning Point?

The prophetic misfires of the late twentieth century have not dampened the urge to make end-time speculations. The early twenty-first century has witnessed several predictions, especially for the years 2011 and 2012. Few of these prognostications, however, have related to dispensational premillennialism, which has shaped much of the apocalyptic thought in modern America. Harold Camping's movement spoke of no millennium, only judgment and destruction. The possible catastrophic or transformational date of December 21, 2012, mentioned by the Mayan calendar, stands outside of the Christian tradition. And surprisingly, few evangelical prophets have Christianized this date. In fact, a number of well-known premillennial spokespersons have repudiated 2012, saying it has no biblical basis. The closest thing to a millennium is that many New Age interpretations of the Mayan calendar say humanity will enter a golden age of harmony. One common thread running through the various Christian predictions concerns an almost magical obsession with numbers. Numbers, of course, can be adjusted to whatever date end-time prophets desire. And they have taken great spiritual and prophetic liberties with the numbers and dates in Scripture. Indeed, some of these calculations border on the bizarre.

14

Why Do We Love Doomsday?

DOOMSDAY HAS A WIDE appeal. What is the attraction? To this question there is no simple answer. As we move into the second decade of the twenty-first century, Chicken Little is still with us. The sky is still falling. Predictions regarding the end of time are common. Many religious traditions—Christian, Moslem, Jewish, Hindu, Buddhist, Mayan, Native American, Rastafarian, and more—plus occultists, New Agers, and even some scientists believe the world faces a catastrophe of some sort. Such doomsday and millennial thinking runs the course of Western civilization. Nevertheless, apocalyptic and millennial visions are perhaps more prevalent in America, especially in the modern era. Figures vary but about 35–40 percent of Americans look for the return of Christ or some disastrous event. While one cannot describe the apocalypse as "made in America," one can say end-time thinking is tailor made for American culture.

Specific predictions even for the modern United States are numerous so only a few examples will be recounted. Charles Laughead, a respected physician in Michigan, shocked people by saying doomsday will occur on December 20, 1954. The planetary alignment of February 4, 1962, sparked fears regarding a global destruction. In 1975 Charles Taylor, a Christian prophecy extremist, made the first of a string of end of the world predictions. He followed with prognostications for 1976, 1980 through 1989, and then 1992 and 1994. Herbert W. Armstrong of the Worldwide Church of God said the end would come sometime from 1975 to 1977. The Jehovah's Witnesses made another end-time prediction, this time for 1975.

Why Do We Love Doomsday?

While Hal Lindsey claims to have only made a suggestion, most readers of his *Late Great Planet Earth* believe he predicted the rapture for 1981.

Some people thought a planetary alignment in 1982 called the "Jupiter Effect" would bring doomsday. Pentecostal preacher Lester Sumrall claimed the end would come in 1985 and then revised the date to 2000. Christian preacher Edgar Whisenant said the rapture would occur in 1988. In 1991, Nation of Islam leader Louis Farrakan contended the Gulf War would become the battle of Armageddon as foretold in the Bible. The Korean *Hyoo-go* movement believed the rapture would come on October 28, 1992.

Then 1994 brought us to Harold Camping's first date for the Second Advent. California psychic Sheldon Nidle said that a million spaceships would arrive on December 17, 1996, thus ending the world. Another psychic selected August 18, 1999, as the date for the end of the world as we know it. The year 2000 brought too many end of the world predictions to list. Only one example will be given, namely that of Christian prophecy teacher Grant Jeffrey. He suggested October 9, 2000, as the probable date. Edgar Cayce prophesied 2001 as the year for a devastating pole shift. Jack Van Impe placed Christ's return sometime from 2003 to 2012. Camping returned to the prophetic scene and earmarked 2011 as the year for end-time events. And as is well known, many people believe the Mayan calendar points to December 21, 2012, as the end of time.[1]

On a lighter note, deep in the rain forest on the Belize and Guatemalan border there is a small hotel or bed and breakfast called duPlooy's. This hotel specializes in serving visitors to the Mayan ruins. For the days of December 18–22 they are offering an "Apocalypto" special complete with tours of the Mayan sites. If the world is still here on the 22nd, the night is free. If the world is not here, at least you have not paid for it. Bookings are filling up, and people from many places in the world, including Americans, are making reservations.[2]

---

1. This brief chronological survey of end-time dates in modern America has been drawn from two sources. Richard Abanes, *End-Time Visions: The Road to Armageddon?* (Nashville: Broadman & Holman, 1998) 337–42; and "The Next Great Turning Point" (source unknown).

2. Matthew Restall and Amara Solari, *2012 and the End of the World: The Western Roots of the Maya Apocalypse* (Lanham, MD: Rowman & Littlefield, 2011) 114.

WESTERN INFLUENCES

This study has focused on end-time ideas in modern America. But there is considerable continuity between apocalyptic thinking throughout two thousand years of Western history and such beliefs in modern America. Chapter 1 has noted how Western ideas have laid the foundation for America's fascination with doomsday and only a brief summary will be given here. First, historic Christianity teaches that Jesus Christ will return personally and visibly and the world as we know it will end. The Bible plus a number of other religious traditions also note that the world was once destroyed by water.

Third, the Western view of history promotes end-time speculations. Western thinking regards history as being linear, not cyclical. History is thus moving on a straight line with a definite end somewhere in the future. Conversely, the cyclical view of history, found in most Eastern religions, minimizes cataclysmic thinking because human events are repeatable. The Western view of history also encourages optimism and determinism, two characteristics of apocalyptic thinking. The end is determined by God but after the cataclysmic events comes a golden age. Four, until the modern age, the traditional Western concept of history viewed the Earth as relatively young, about six thousand years old. When linked to biblical teaching that "one day is with the Lord as a thousand years," many people believe the end of time will come shortly.

Conditions in Western history have also ignited considerable end-time thinking. Again, at this point the more detailed discussion found in chapter 1 will only be summarized. And even this information is subject to debate because apocalyptic and millennial movements are so complex as to defy any simple explanations. Some scholars have contended that end-time movements thrive with lower social and economic classes who live on the margins of society. Any kind of natural, social, or economic disaster can significantly disrupt their lives and influence them to embrace millennial visions. If these disasters occur in rural areas and the people have charismatic leaders to lead them, an apocalyptic movement is even more likely to develop.

Other scholars challenge such theories. They contend that millennial movements are more widespread than once believed. Middle- and even upper-class people have embraced end-time movements, and such individuals have not always experienced a disaster. To support this contention, they point to the Millerite movement of the nineteenth century and the modern-day fundamentalists, who often occupy seats of political and

Why Do We Love Doomsday?

economic power. Such fundamentalists are often out of sync with modern thinking and values and thus long for a change in the current situation.

In glancing at millennial visions in Western civilization two concepts rise to the surface: apocalyptic thinking has been highly adaptable, and as a result, it has persisted through over two thousand years of Western history. These two characteristics—elasticity and persistence—have marked end-time thinking in the West for over two millennia. Both the great minds and rank and file of the Christian church have thought about how the world will end—often with strikingly different conclusions. Such apocalyptic expressions show no sign of abating; they are alive and well as we enter the early decades of the twenty-first century.

THE PERSISTENT APOCALYPSE

To be sure, apocalyptic expressions have had their peaks and valleys. "Endism," as Charles Strozier calls it, "has ebbed and flowed in significance within the self and culture, depending on historical circumstances." At times it has been repressed by church and society only to break out in full fury on other occasions. Peter Stearns has likened the persistence of apocalyptic thinking to a dormant virus—it resides in the body only to break out periodically, especially in sectarian groups.[3]

"The crowding out of apocalyptic [beliefs and actions] into sectarian circles has characterized church history since its beginnings," writes Ulrich Kortner. Apocalyptic expressions can be found in the New Testament, the Didache, and other writings of the early church. Groups such as the Montanists anticipated that the world would end soon. The early church even had a date-setter in Hippolytus, who said the world would end in 500 CE.[4]

But when the church became incorporated into the Roman Empire, the situation changed. Thanks to Augustine's rejection of crass millennialism and his identification of the church on Earth with the kingdom of heaven, the church now worked to serve the world—not to oppose it

---

3. Charles B. Strozier, *Apocalypse* (Boston: Beacon, 1994) 249; Peter N. Stearns, *Millennium III, Century XXI* (Boulder, CO: Westview, 1996) 54–55. See also Ulrich H. J. Kortner, *The End of the World* (Louisville: Westminster John Knox, 1995) 12–13; Amos Funkenstein, "A Schedule for the End of the World: The Origins and Persistence of the Apocalyptic Mentality," in *Visions of Apocalypse*, ed. Saul Friedlander et al. (New York: Holmes and Meir, 1985) 44–60.

4. Kortner, *End of the World*, 12–13. See also Robert W. Thompson, "2001: A Millennial Odyssey?," *Military Chaplain's Review* 18/4 (Fall 1989) 36.

and separate from it. The secular state and the church now cooperated to restrain evil and further God's kingdom. Such thinking dominated the medieval church. Still, apocalyptic expression remained alive, usually underground. It burst forth in the prophetic vision of Joachim of Fiore and in groups such as the Hussites and Taborites.[5]

During the Reformation the official churches attempted to stifle apocalyptic thinking. Nevertheless, it did play an important role during this time, even with Martin Luther; Radicals such as Thomas Müntzer, Melchior Hofmann, and the people at Münster who behaved recklessly in the belief that the end was at hand and they were God's instruments to purge a fallen world. Apocalyptic thinking may have reached new heights in seventeenth-century England as the turmoil of the English Civil War ignited an explosion of end-time excitement.[6]

Apocalyptic expressions came to a standstill by the eighteenth century, however. The Enlightenment and the notion of progress repressed the apocalypse, although it did remain alive. End-time thinking was then awakened by events like the Lisbon earthquake and the French Revolution, and would later erupt in the Millerite movement and other nineteenth-century fringe groups.[7]

In our day apocalyptic thinking has roared back, says Stephen O'Leary: "The appeal of apocalyptic prophecy has endured through the ages; but its popularity has undergone a remarkable resurgence in the latter half of the twentieth century." He gives two reasons for this revival—the development of nuclear weapons and the establishment of the state of Israel.[8] Charles Strozier puts it in a different way: "It takes an act of imagination *not* to ponder end-time issues" in a day when human history could end by nuclear destruction or environmental degradation.[9]

Several theories have attempted to explain the ups and downs of apocalyptic ideas, but as Bernard McGinn notes, none fully accounts for the phenomenon. The ascendancy of end-time thinking has been variously seen as an attempt to understand the meaning of disasters, as a way for people to deal with social and economic deprivation, as a form of

---

5. Kortner, *End of the World*, 13–14.

6. Ibid., 14; Stephen D. O'Leary, *Arguing the Apocalypse* (New York: Oxford University Press, 1994) 7.

7. Kortner, *End of the World*, 14–15; Stearns, *Millennium III*, 45.

8. O'Leary, *Arguing the Apocalypse*, 7.

9. Strozier, *Apocalypse*, 249, 290.

paranoia, and as the response of a cognitive minority.[10] What is clear is that a crisis mentality seems to promote an apocalyptic mindset. And in the modern world, anxiety is certainly in the air. The twentieth century has seen two World Wars, a depression, the Holocaust, the advent of the nuclear age, a tense Cold War, the threat of environmental disaster, and the social upheavals of the 1960s. As Hillel Schwartz notes, the twentieth century "has often been regarded as a century less to celebrate than to survive." The early twenty-first century, with September 11, the war against terrorism, the "great recession," and economic uncertainties, has not been much better. The anxieties brought on by this turmoil have produced a doomsday mindset and even a belief that the world might end.[11]

Catherine Keller sees the apocalyptic pattern emerging today as entailing four basic beliefs: One, the world is "unacceptable and pervasively corrupt;" two, "an imminent and unavoidable catastrophe" will bring it to an end; three, individuals "proclaiming the end" have a prophetic calling; and four, the "final showdown" will be followed by a new age in which justice reigns and nature is renewed.[12]

THE ELASTIC APOCALYPSE

The second concept rising to the forefront is the adaptability of apocalyptic ideas. Indeed, end-time thinking has been incredibly elastic. It has been molded and shaped to the events of over two thousand years of Western history. Prophets and soothsayers have predicted the end countless times. And their batting average has been a perfect zero. But apocalyptic thinking has withstood many disconfirmations and is still going strong.

"Apocalypse can be disconfirmed without being discredited," explains Frank Kermode. It has an extraordinary resilience; it can "absorb changing interests [and] rival apocalypses." The apocalypse is "patient of change" and "allows itself to be diffused." When a prediction misfires, the failure "can be attributed to an error of calculation, either in arithmetic or allegory." With such freedom the prophet can "manipulate data" in order to achieve a desired result. Thus the end can "occur at pretty well

---

10. Bernard McGinn, *Visions of the End* (New York: Columbia University Press, 1979) 3; O'Leary, *Arguing the Apocalypse*, 10; Robert Fuller, *Naming the Antichrist* (New York: Oxford University Press, 1995) 8-9.

11. Hillel Schwartz, *Century's End* (New York: Doubleday, 1990) 201; Fuller, *Naming the Antichrist*, 8; Stephen J. Patterson, "The End of Apocalypse," *Theology Today* 52/1 (1995) 33.

12. Catherine Keller, "Why Apocalypse Now?" *Theology Today* 49/2 (1992) 184-85.

any desired date." Similarly, Peter Stearns sees the apocalyptic vision as having "proved immune to repeated failures in predictions" because "it provides[s] people with an alternative to the rigid, rationalistic scientific framework that dominates our culture."[13]

Shifting Millennial Interpretations

Although millennial and apocalyptic ideas are not identical, they are related, and the various millennial views often connect with how people perceive the end of the world. Not surprisingly, then, Christian millennial patterns generally approximate the ebb and flow, and elasticity, of apocalyptic expressions. Most millennial ideas roughly fit into one of three positions—premillennialism, amillennialism, and postmillennialism. End-of-the-world speculations are generally most at home with, though not limited to, premillennialism. And most contemporary apocalyptists thus tend to be premillennialists. But it must be remembered that pre-, post-, and amillennialism are relatively modern terms. Thus these expressions can be used only as rough approximations of earlier millennial positions.

While most millennial interpretations can be found throughout Christian history, certain positions predominated at various times. During the first three centuries of Christian history, an end-time expectancy was commonplace. Thus a version of premillennialism prevailed. Its adherents included Justin Martyr, Papias, Tertullian, Irenaeus, Hippolytus, and Lactantius.[14]

By the fourth century the church became incorporated into the Roman Empire. Visions of an impending end had largely waned, for Christians reinterpreted the millennium to refer to the church. Their equating of Christ's thousand-year rule with the entire history of the church on Earth negated the hope of a future millennium. The allegorical or amillennial position became the official position of the medieval Catholic Church. Its

---

13. Frank Kermode, *The Sense of an Ending* (New York: Oxford University Press, 1967) 8-9; Stearns, *Millennium III*, 57.

14. This general survey of different millennial views in various historical periods has been drawn largely from Robert G. Clouse, ed., *The Meaning of the Millennium* (Downers Grove, IL: InterVarsity, 1977) 9-13. For similar material see Stanley J. Grenz, *The Millennial Maze* (Downers Grove, IL: InterVarsity, 1992); J. C. De Smidt, "Chiliasm: An Escape from the Present into an Extra-Biblical Apocalyptic Imagination," *Scriptura* 45 (1993) 79-95.

Why Do We Love Doomsday?

most famous spokesperson was Augustine. But chiliasm continued on the fringes of society, usually associated with apocalyptic movements.

Despite some apocalyptic inclinations, the Protestant Reformers largely embraced a form of the amillennial position. At the same time medieval millennialism spilled over into the sixteenth century, energizing some radical groups to lash out at society. Such extremes encouraged the Reformers to condemn millennial beliefs, but versions of millennialism came back in the seventeenth century. In the chaos of the English Civil War, some radical Puritan groups espoused premillennialism.

Still, the situation would change in the eighteenth century. Radical Puritanism had discredited premillennialism, and the Enlightenment fostered an optimistic view of the world contrary to premillennialism. Thus in came postmillennialism, the eschatological interpretation that would dominate during the eighteenth and nineteenth centuries. According to this perspective, the world would be converted to Christ, and peace, happiness, and righteousness would reign for a thousand years.

But along came John Nelson Darby and the birth of a new version of premillennialism. As the nineteenth century progressed, this dispensational premillennialism gained steam and came to dominate the older variations of premillennialism. In the twentieth century, thanks to popularizers such as Hal Lindsey and Tim LaHaye, it is the dominant view within evangelical circles, although a significant number of evangelicals embrace amillennialism. Postmillennialism with its optimistic view of the world has to a substantial degree been stilled by the wars, turmoil, and atrocities of the twentieth century. Yet in the Reconstructionist or Dominion movement it is staging a comeback.[15] Indeed, apocalyptic expressions have been similarly repressed through much of Western history only to break out at certain times. The late twentieth and early twentieth-first centuries have been such occasions. Thanks to the persistence and chameleon-like quality of the apocalypse, end-time thinking has surged in America during the last fifty years or so.

AN AMERICAN TWIST TO DOOMSDAY

While apocalyptic thinking is a global phenomenon, it is most at home in America. It connects well with American culture. Its roots run deep

---

15. See Rousas J. Rushdooney, *Thy Kingdom Come: Studies in Daniel and Revelation* (Philadelphia: Presbyterian and Reformed, 1971); Rousas J. Rushdooney, *God's Plan for Victory: The Meaning of Post-Millennialism* (Tyler, TX: Thoburn, 1977).

in American history. From the very colonial period we have viewed ourselves as a millennial nation, meaning that God has a special mission for America. Or as Peter Marshall and David Manuel say in *The Light and Glory*: "This nation was founded by God with a special calling. The people who first came here knew that they were being led here by the Lord Jesus Christ, to found a nation where men, women and children were to live in obedience to Him . . ." God had a corporate relationship with America, specifically calling the nation into a covenant relationship with him.[16] Developing out of this chosen nation concept is the belief that America is a "redeemer nation" with a millennial mission. By the early nineteenth century, as Ernest Tuveson notes, many Americans believed that God had called the United States to be "a chief means of world-wide redemption, and that as a chosen people it was assigned a new promised land," namely a large part of the North American continent.[17]

Related to the redeemer nation concept was the dominant millennial view of the nineteenth century, namely, postmillennialism, the least apocalyptic of the various millennial views. But religious freedom produced a free market in religion and many other end-time views—some of them quite unconventional and much more catastrophic—have come to the surface. This religious freedom has also helped to make America a very religious nation, one in which the evangelical/fundamentalist brand of Christianity has flourished. And end-time views have thrived in the evangelical/fundamentalist subculture, which constitutes about 25–30 percent of the United States population. Moreover, evangelicalism is the most dynamic and growth orientated of all the major religious types in America. In addition to numerical growth, evangelicals have also acquired considerable political and economic power.[18]

Within the evangelical/fundamentalist subculture the dominant eschatology is dispensational premillennialism. Indeed, many evangelicals are only vaguely aware of other views regarding the end of time. While

---

16. Peter Marshall and David Manuel, *The Light and the Glory* (Grand Rapids: Revell, 1977) 16–26 (quote on 16). See also Peter Marshall and David Manuel, *From Sea to Shinning Sea* (Grand Rapids: Revell, 1993).

17. Ernest Lee Tuveson, *Redeemer Nation: The Idea of America's Millennial Role* (Chicago: University of Chicago Press, 1968) 91, 157 (quotes); Lefferts A. Loetscher, *The Problem of Christian Unity in Early Nineteenth-Century America* (Philadelphia: Fortress, 1969); 15; Richard T. Hughes, *Myths America Lives By* (Urbana: University of Illinois Press, 2004) 107–8, 110.

18. Paul Boyer, *When Time Shall Be No More: Prophecy Belief in Modern American Culture* (Cambridge, MA: Harvard, 1992) 293–94; Richard Kyle, *Evangelicalism: An Americanized Christianity* (New Brunswick, NJ: Transaction, 2006) 167–209.

Why Do We Love Doomsday?

they may not understand the details of dispensational theology, they accept it as biblical truth. Having a secure home in a dynamic and growing subculture has given dispensationalism a solid base from which to propagate its beliefs. Evangelicals are the most entrepreneurial of all the major religious bodies. By means of television and paperbacks they vigorously market their views, including dispensational eschatology. In doing so, they reach a large audience. Some of the best selling books in the last fifty years, such as Hal Lindsey's *The Late Great Planet Earth* and the *Left Behind* series, have embraced premillennial doomsday predictions. Moreover, the same end-time messages can be heard on most Christian cable television programs.

The doomsday message strikes a strong cord with America's populist impulse. While evangelicalism and even dispensationalism have reputable scholars, it is not the academics who are driving the end-time messages. Most of the prophets of doom have little or no theological training, and they are not denominational leaders. Quite often, they have no church or denominational structure to restrain their excessive and irrational pronouncements. Rather, they flourish on the margins of even the evangelical subculture, especially on the airwaves and in the paperback markets. The doomsday prognosticators are often TV preachers, freelance writers, or evangelists. As such they frequently exhibit distain for intellectuals and trained theologians. Popular dispensational premillennialism has become in Paul Boyer's words, "A Theology of the People."[19]

In commenting on some of our mediocre political leaders, the president of DePauw University often said, "The World is being run by 'C' students." In politics (except for a bachelor's degree), education counts for little. If the United States is a nation being run by C students, what can be said about the evangelical popularizers, especially the prophets of doom? Perhaps their grade would be a D-. Unfortunately, the thinking and behavior of millions of evangelicals, particularly in respect to end-time matters, is being driven by uneducated popularizers.[20]

Closely related to this populist inclination is a conspiratorial mind set and Manichaean worldview. Fundamentalists in particular often see the world in black-and-white terms. In respect to the great issues facing

---

19. Boyer, *When Time Shall Be No More*, 304–5. See Kyle, *Evangelicalism*, 250–55; Richard Kyle, "The Electronic Church: An Echo of American Culture," *Direction* 39/2 (2010) 162–76.

20. Quoted in Kenneth J. Heineman, *God Is a Conservative: Religion, Politics, and Morality in Contemporary America* (New York: New York University Press, 1998) 155. See also Kyle, *Evangelicalism*, 317–18,

the world, there is no gray. Human events are caused by either God or the devil and one must choose sides. Even natural disasters have been determined by God for his purpose. And behind many human activities lurks a conspiracy, some hidden evil plot hatched by those in league with Satan. In particular, these doomsday prophets earmark specific individuals as the predicted Antichrist or "man of sin" and believe that global developments all point to the end-time events forecast in Scripture.

The events of the late twentieth and early twenty-first centuries did not disappoint doomsday forecasters. The fundamentalist mindset also needs an enemy or a looming catastrophe and one did not have to look very far to find them. For starters try wars, terrorism, diseases, communism, economic crises, natural disasters, religious apostasy, occult activities, New Age mysticism, Islam, energy shortages, environmental crises, the threat of nuclear annihilation, terrorism, and much more. When one problem comes to an end, another must replace it. If not the doomsday mentality is ill at ease.

Indeed, as Randall Balmer asserts, evangelical leaders have long recognized the need for enemies because "we define ourselves in contradistinction to them, whether they be the cultured laity and the intellectual preachers or the godless Communists." For example, ever since 1917 and for most of the twentieth century, the most "durable" enemy has been communism. Since the end of the Cold War and the collapse of the Soviet Union, evangelicals have been adrift. They have been searching for a durable enemy to satisfy their dualistic worldview.[21]

On a domestic level they have pointed to socialism, big government, secular humanism, the New Age movement, gays and lesbians, and some individuals such as Bill and Hillary Clinton and Barack Obama. Internationally, evangelicals have earmarked Islam and terrorism as the threats to be feared. As evangelicals read "the tea leaves of Daniel and Revelation," they do not do so "wearing blinders." Rather, they are acutely aware of current events, which they match up with the apocalyptic literature of Scripture. As we know, Daniel, Ezekiel, and Revelation are very malleable and can be shaped and interpreted to suit one's inclinations.[22]

Of paramount importance, prophecy must be seen as being fulfilled right in front of one's eyes. One must remember that many prophetic predictions rest on apocalyptic literature, a literary genre that is highly

---

21. Randall Balmer, "Thy Kingdom Come: Apocalypticism in American Culture," *Union Seminary Quarterly Review* 49 (1995) 27–28.

22. Ibid.

Why Do We Love Doomsday?

symbolic and adaptable. Thus the apocalyptic books of Scripture have been interpreted to reflect current events throughout 2000 years of Christian history. Indeed, global developments in the late twentieth and early twenty-first centuries have provided ample material for prophetic interpretation. The birth of the Israeli state in 1948, the Six-Day War of 1967 and the capture of Jerusalem, the spread of communism, the growth of Soviet power, the invention of nuclear weapons, the organization of the European Union, the rise of China, and the threat of Islam all have been seen as the fulfillment of prophecy. Dispensationalism has indeed encountered some disconfirmations, namely, the collapse of the Soviet Union and the growth of the European Union well beyond ten nations. But remember, in the mind of the faithful, one apparent confirmation counts for more than several disconfirmations.[23]

The events of the modern era also stir up the fear factor, a necessary ingredient in doomsday thinking. The specter of fear and its cousin fatalism often shape the worldview of end-time prognosticators and their followers. In general, premillennialism lends itself to a catastrophic view of the future. Yes, there will a golden age of bliss, but this must be preceded by the tribulation, Armageddon, and much destruction. What saves many dispensationalists from being depressed regarding the future is their belief in the rapture or "blessed hope." They expect to be removed from planet Earth before all of this "hell" breaks loose.

Premillennialists are not alone in this negative estimate of the future. Some secular apocalyptic thinkers can be just as pessimistic and perhaps more fatalistic. In fact, they do not envision a future golden age. Their enemies, however, are different. Their global list would include environmental catastrophes, overpopulation, nuclear disasters, disease, widespread famine, a polar shift, and energy shortages. Only a dramatic change in human behavior can avert doomsday, and for most of humankind this is too late. While they certainly do not embrace a secular view of the end of time, the visions of the Virgin Mary offer little hope for humanity unless drastic changes are made soon.[24]

The cognitive and psychological make up of many evangelicals, especially the fundamentalist variety, promotes doomsday thinking. As noted

---

23. Timothy P. Weber, "Dispensationalism and Historic Premillennialism as Popular Millennial Movements," in *A Case for Historic Premillennialism* (Grand Rapids: Baker, 2009) 17–18, 21; Boyer, *When Time Shall Be No More*, 295, 311; O'Leary, *Arguing the Apocalypse*, 17.

24. Daniel Wojcik, *The End of the World As We Know It: Faith, Fatalism, and Apocalypse in America* (New York: New York University Press, 1997) 60–96, 133–47, 209–11.

several times in this work, modern day fundamentalists do not necessary come out of the lower social orders. Some are wealthy and politically powerful, and they thrive in America's populist culture. They are, however, out of step with modernity. While they may embrace up-to-date technology, they reject many modern values and the direction of contemporary society. In doing so, they have become a cognitive minority and are out of sync with modern thinking. Fundamentalists of nearly any stripe, including the premillennial variety, represent a reactionary force in American society. They wish to turn the clock back on many religious, social, political, and economic issues.

But Protestant fundamentalists are not alone in being a conservative force. Catholics who embrace the apocalypticism associated with the Marian apparitions also wish to return the Catholic Church to its pre–Vatican II values and liturgy. They are part of the traditionalist movement that developed in response to the liberalizing trends in Catholic doctrine and policy. Moreover, they view many developments in contemporary Catholicism through the conspiratorial lenses. Satanic forces have indeed hijacked the papacy and are taking the Church in the wrong direction. Such conspiratorial theories stem from the "secrets" revealed by Mary at Fatima concerning the end of time—secrets the church has never disclosed.[25]

In spite of rejecting aspects of modern science, many evangelicals and fundamentalists regard prophecy as a "scientific" or at least "a quasi-empirical" validation of the Christian faith, writes Boyer. Since the mid-nineteenth century, Christianity has felt the "corrosive effects of Darwinism and other non-theistic explanations of the physical order . . ." Prophecy, however, stepped in and filled the intellectual gap for many premillennialists. Global events in the early twentieth century—World War I, the birth of the Soviet Union, the Balfour Declaration, the collapse of the Ottoman and Austro-Hungarian Empires—seemed to dovetail with the dispensational interpretations of Daniel and Revelation. Events in the post–World War II era surrounding Israel, communism, the Soviet Union, and the Common Market have added to this evidence. The flow of history, indeed, seemed to offer tangible proof that "the Bible is the inspired and infallible Word of God."[26]

Also feeding the doomsday attitude among many evangelicals is their escapist attitude. The world may be going to hell, many say, but we

25. Ibid. 86–87.

26. Boyer, *When Time Shall Be No More*, 293–95 (quotes); Timothy Weber, *Living in the Shadow of the Second Coming: American Premillennialism, 1875-1925* (New York: Oxford University Press, 1979) 105–15.

Why Do We Love Doomsday?

will be rescued from the impending doom by the rapture. Through history most Christians regard the Second Coming of Jesus Christ as one single event. Dispensational theology teaches that the Second Advent will come in two stages: Christ appears before the tribulation to rapture Christians and fully returns before the millennium to rule on Earth. Such a scenario allows Christians to escape the turmoil that the world will experience. This escapist attitude dovetails with how many evangelicals approach salvation. They have in effect "McDonaldized" salvation. They like their salvation (including the rapture) like their fast food—quick and cheap.[27]

This study has looked at end-time views in modern America from several perspectives—dispensational premillennialism, postmillennialism, amillennialism, Catholicism, fringe religions, Islam, the Y2K threat, fiction, the occult and New Age, science, natural disasters, nuclear annihilation, environmental destruction, and the Mayan calendar. While there are vast differences in these views, a few threads connect them. Most embrace a sense of crisis and a loss of confidence in the ability of governments and human institutions to resolve our current problems. There is a growing stress on "cultural pessimism and an increasing emphasis on evil conspiracies." With this deep fatalism, people are more willing to embrace an apocalyptic worldview.[28]

In the opposite direction, a second common thread is the redemptive side of the apocalypse. Except for the secular apocalypse, most end-time views envision some kind of new era or golden age. Christianity calls this golden age a millennium and interprets it several ways. Most fringe religions, especially the New Age movement and some interpretations of the Mayan calendar, see the dawning of a new era of cooperation in which human problems are solved. While Islam has no future millennium, it desires to see the establishment of a worldwide Islamic rule termed a Caliphate. In such an era justice would prevail.

Even this positive aspect of the apocalyptic mindset has its downside. People believe current problems are so serious that only forces beyond human control can cleanse the world and usher in an earthly paradise. Or as William Allman has said, "Ultimately the allure of the Apocalypse may lie in the very human trait of wanting simple solutions to complex problems."

---

27. Kyle, *Evangelicalism*, 313; Richard Kyle, "Inconsistent Evangelicals," *Christian Leader*, June/July 2010, 18.

28. Wojcik, *The End of the World as We Know It*, 175.

Some people believe that abandoning this world for another is easier than working to improve human existence in the here and now.[29]

A third common thread centers on the resemblance of several end-time views with Christian eschatology, especially the premillennial variety. To be sure, this resemblance is superficial. Nevertheless, it can be detected. A variety of end-of-the-world expressions evidence the following traits: a clash between good and evil, a coming judgment, a Manichean and conspiratorial mindset, a reactionary and populist impulse, a means of salvation, and a coming golden age. In part, these similarities can be attributed to the influence of Christian apocalyptic literature, especially the Book of Revelation.

This study has not been kind to the doomsday prophets, or Chicken Littles, as I have called them. Such criticism, however, is not to minimize belief in the Second Advent. Scripture and the historic Christian faith clearly teach that Jesus Christ will return personally and visibly. But this faith is not a license to speculate on the time of this event or to encourage an escapist attitude. People must live in the present and endeavor to solve current human problems.

---

29. William F. Allman, "Fatal Attraction: Why We Love Doomsday," *U.S. News & World Report*, 30 April 1990, 13.

Bibliography

Abanes, Richard. *End-Time Visions: The Road to Armageddon?* Nashville: Broadman & Holman, 1998.
Alnor, William A. *Soothsayers of the Second Advent*. Old Tappan, NJ: Revell, 1989.
Anderson, Robert. *The Coming Prince*. Grand Rapids: Kregel, 1975 [reprint].
Baigent, Michael. *Racing toward Armageddon: The Three Great Religions and the Plot to End the World*. New York: HarperCollins, 2009.
Balmer, Randall. "Thy Kingdom Come: Apocalypticism in American Culture," *Union Seminary Quarterly* 49 (1995) 17–33.
Barkun, Michael. "Divided Apocalypse: Thinking about the End in Contemporary America." *Soundings* 66/3 (Fall 1983) 257–80.
———. *Crucible of the Millennium: The Burned-Over District of New York in the 1840s*. Syracuse: Syracuse University Press, 1986.
———. *Disaster and the Millennium*. New Haven, CT: Yale University Press, 1974.
Barron, Bruce. *Heaven on Earth?: The Social and Political Agendas of Dominion Theology*. Grand Rapids: Zondervan, 1992.
Blomberg, Craig L., and Sung Wook Chung, editors. *A Case for Historic Premillennialism: An Alternative to "Left Behind" Eschatology*. Grand Rapids: Baker, 2009.
Boyer, Paul. *When Time Shall Be No More: Prophecy Belief in Modern American Culture*. Cambridge, MA: Harvard University Press, 1992.
Butler, Jonathan M. "From Millerism to Seventh-day Adventism: Boundlessness to Consolidation." *Church History* 55/1 (1986) 50–64.
Camping, Harold. *1994?* New York: Vantage, 1992.
———. *Time Has an End: A Biblical History of the World 11,013 B.C.–2011 A.D.* New York: Vantage, 2005.
Chandler, Russell. *Doomsday: The End of the World, A View through Time*. Ann Arbor, MI: Servant, 1993.
———. *Understanding the New Age*. Dallas: Word, 1988.
Clark, Victoria. *Allies for Armageddon: The Rise of Christian Zionism*. New Haven, CT: Yale University Press, 2007.
Close, Frank. *Apocalypse When?: Cosmic Catastrophe and the Fate of the Universe*. New York: Morrow, 1988.
Clouse, Robert G. "The New Christian Right, and the Kingdom of God," *Christian Scholar's Review* 12 (1983) 3–16.
———, editor. *The Meaning of the Millennium: Four Views*. Downers Grove, IL: InterVarsity, 1977.

Bibliography

Clouse, Robert G., Robert N. Hosack, and Richard V. Pierard. *The New Millennium Manual: A Once and Future Guide*. Grand Rapids: Baker, 1999.
Cohen, Daniel. *Waiting for the Apocalypse*. Buffalo: Prometheus, 1983.
Cohn, Norman. *The Pursuit of the Millennium: Revolutionary Millenarians and Mystical Anarchists of the Middle Ages*. Rev. ed. New York: Oxford University Press, 1974.
Cook, David. *Contemporary Muslim Apocalyptic Literature*. Syracuse: Syracuse University Press, 2005.
Cumbey, Constance E. *The Hidden Dangers of the Rainbow: The New Age Movement and Our Coming Age of Barbarism*. Lafayette, LA: Huntington House, 1985.
Curry, Melvin D. *Jehovah's Witnesses: The Millenarian World of the Watch Tower*. New York: Garland, 1992.
Davidson, James West. *The Logic of Millennial Thought: Eighteenth-Century New England*. New Haven, CT: Yale University Press, 1977.
DeMar, Gary. *Last Days Madness: The Folly of Trying to Predict When Christ Will Return*. Brentwood, TN: Wolgemuth and Hyatt, 1991.
Doan, Ruth Alden. *The Miller Heresy, Millennialism, and American Culture*. Philadelphia: Temple University Press, 1987.
Durham, Martin. *The Christian Right, the Far Right, and the Boundaries of American Conservatism*. Manchester, UK: Manchester University Press, 2000.
Dyer, Charles H. *The Rise of Babylon: Sign of the End of Times*. Wheaton, IL: Tyndale, 1991.
Ehrlich, Paul R. et al. *The Nuclear Winter: The Cold and the Dark*. London: Sidgwick, 1984.
———. *The Population Bomb*. New York: Ballantine, 1968.
———. *The Population Explosion*. New York: Simon and Schuster, 1991.
Ellwood, Robert S., Jr. *One Way: The Jesus Movement and Its Meaning*. Englewood Cliffs, NJ: Prentice Hall, 1973.
Evans, Michael. *Showdown with Nuclear Iran: Radical Islam's Messianic Mission to Destroy Israel and Cripple the United States*. Nashville: Nelson Current, 2006.
———. *The Final Move beyond Iraq*. Lake Mary, FL: Front Line, 2007.
Fackre, Gabriel. *The Religious Right and the Christian Faith*. Grand Rapids: Eerdmans, 1982.
Falwell, Jerry. "The Twenty-First Century and the End of the World." *Fundamentalist Journal* 7/5 (May 1988) 10–11.
Ferguson, Marilyn. *The Aquarian Conspiracy: Personal and Social Transformation in the 1980s*. Los Angeles: J. P. Tarcher, 1980.
Filiu, Jeane-Pierre. *Apocalypse in Islam*. Berkeley, CA: University of California Press, 2011.
Forbes, Bruce David, and Jeanne Halgren Kilde, editors. *Rapture, Revelation, and the End Times: Exploring the Left Behind Series*. New York: Palgrave, 2004.
Friedrich, Otto. *The End of the World: A History*. New York: Fromm, 1986.
Fuller, Robert C. *Naming the Antichrist: The History of an American Obsession*. New York: Oxford University Press, 1995.
Gianakos, Perry E. "The Black Muslims: An American Millennialistic Response to Racism and Cultural Deracination." *Centennial Review* 23 (Fall 1979) 430–45.
Goen, C.C. "Jonathan Edwards: A New Departure in Eschatology." *Church History* 28/1 (1959) 25–40.

Bibliography

Goldberg, Michelle. *Kingdom Coming: The Rise of Christian Nationalism*. New York: Norton, 2006.
Gore, Al. *Earth in Balance: Ecology and the Human Spirit*. Boston: Houghton Mifflin, 1992.
Graham, Billy. *Approaching Hoofbeats: The Four Horsemen of the Apocalypse*. New York: Avon, 1983.
Green, Martin. *Prophets of a New Age: The Politics of Hope from the Eighteenth through the Twenty-First Centuries*. New York: Scribner, 1992.
Grenz, Stanley J. *The Millennial Maze: Sorting Out the Evangelical Options*. Downers Grove, IL: Intervarsity, 1992.
Gribben, Crawford. *Writing the Rapture: Prophecy Fiction in Evangelical America*. New York: Oxford University Press, 2009.
Hagee, John. *Beginning of the End: The Assassination of Yitzhak Rabin and the Coming Antichrist*. Nashville: Nelson, 1996.
———. *In Defense of Israel*. Lake Mary, FL: Front Line, 2007.
———. *Jerusalem Countdown: A Warning to the World*. Lake Mary, FL: Front Line, 2007.
Hanegraaff, Hank. *The Millennium Bug Debugged: The Facts behind All the Y2K Sensation*. Minneapolis: Bethany House, 1999.
Hardon, John A. *The Catholic Catechism*. Garden City, NY: Doubleday, 1975.
Harrison, J. F. C. *The Second Coming: Popular Millenarianism, 1780–1850*. New Brunswick, NJ: Rutgers University Press, 1979.
Hendershot, Heather. *Shaking the World for Jesus: Media and Conservative Evangelical Culture*. Chicago: University of Chicago Press, 2004.
Hitchcock, Mark. *2012, the Bible, and the End of the World*. Eugene, OR: Harvest House, 2009.
———. *Iran: The Coming Crisis*. Sisters, OR: Multnomah, 2006.
———. *The Apocalypse of Ahmadinejad: The Revelation of Iran's Nuclear Prophet*. Colorado Springs, CO: Multnomah, 2007.
———. *The Late Great United States: What Bible Prophecy Reveals about America's Last Days*. Colorado Springs, CO: Multnomah, 2009.
Hogue, John. *The Millennium Book of Prophecy: 777 Visions and Predictions from Nostradamus, Edgar Cayce, Gurdjieff, Tamo-San, Madame Blavatsky, the Old and New Testament Prophets and 89 Others*. San Francisco: Harper, 1994.
Hunt, Stephen, editor. *Christian Millenarianism: From the Early Church to Waco*. Bloomington, IL: University of Indiana Press, 2001.
Hutchings, N. W., and Larry Spargimino. *Y2K = 666?* Oklahoma City: Hearthstone, 1998.
Hyatt, Michael S. *The Millennium Bug: How to Survive the Coming Chaos*. Washington, DC: Regnery, 1998.
———. *The Y2K Personal Survival Guide: Everything You Need to Know to Get from This Side of the Crisis to the Other*. Washington, DC: Regnery, 1999.
Jeffrey, Grant R. *Armageddon: Appointment with Destiny*. Toronto: Frontier Research, 1988.
———. *The Millennium Meltdown: The Year 2000 Computer Crisis*. Toronto: Frontier Research, 1998.
Jenkins, John Major. *The 2012 Story: The Myths, Fallacies, and Truth behind the Most Intriguing Date in History*. New York: Tarcher/Penguin, 2009.

Bibliography

Jones, Marie D. *2013: The End of Days or a New Beginning?* Franklin Lake, NJ: New Page, 2008.
Joseph, Lawrence E. *Apocalypse 2012: An Investigation into Civilization's End.* New York: Broadway, 2007.
Kahn, Herman. *On Thermonuclear War.* Princeton, NJ: Princeton University Press, 1960.
Kaplan, Jeffrey. *Radical Religion in America: Millenarian Movements from the Far Right to the Children of Noah.* Syracuse University Press, 1997.
Katz, Robert, and Richard H. Popkin, *Messianic Revolution: Radical and Religious Politics to the End of the Second Millennium* .New York: Hill and Wang, 1998.
Keller, Catherine. *Apocalypse Now and Then: A Feminist Guide to the End of the World.* Boston: Beacon, 1996.
Kermode, Frank. *The Sense of an Ending: Studies in the Theory of Fiction.* New York: Oxford University Press, 1967.
Kerns, Philip. *People's Temple, People's Tomb.* Plainfield, NJ: Logos, 1979.
Kirban, Salem. *666.* Wheaton, IL: Tyndale, 1970.
Kortner, Ulrich H. J. *The End of the World: A Theological Interpretation.* Louisville: Westminster John Knox, 1995.
Kyle, Richard. *Evangelicalism: An Americanized Christianity.* New Brunswick, NJ: Transaction, 2006.
———. *The Last Days Are Here Again: A History of the End Times.* Grand Rapids: Baker Books, 1998.
———. *The New Age Movement in American Culture.* Lanham, MD: University Press of America, 1995.
———. *The Religious Fringe: A History of Alternative Religions in America.* Downers Grove, IL: InterVarsity, 1993.
LaHaye, Tim, and Jerry B. Jenkins. Left Behind Series. 18 vols. Wheaton, IL: Tyndale, 1995–2007.
LaHaye, Tim. *Rapture under Attack: Can We Still Trust the Pre-Trib Rapture?* Sisters, OR: Multnomah, 1992.
Lahr, Angela M. *Millennial Dreams and Apocalyptic Nightmares: The Cold War Origins of Political Evangelicalism.* New York: Oxford University Press, 2007.
Land, Gary, editor. *Adventism in America: A History.* Grand Rapids: Eerdmans, 1986.
Lee, Martha. *Earth First!: Environmental Apocalypse.* Syracuse: Syracuse University Press, 1995.
———. *The Nation of Islam: An American Millenarian Movement.* Syracuse: University Press, 1996.
Lewis, James R. editor. *The Gods Have Landed: New Religions from Other Worlds.* Albany: State University of New York Press, 1995.
Lindsey, Hal. *Planet Earth—2000 A.D.* Palos Verdes Estates, CA: Western Front, 1994.
———. *The Late Great Planet Earth.* Grand Rapids: Zondervan, 1970.
Livingston, Robert. *Christianity and Islam: The Final Clash.* Enumclaw, WA: Pleasant Word, 2005.
Lorie, Peter. *Nostradamus 2003–2025: A History of the Future.* New York: Pocket Books, 2002.
———. *Nostradamus: The Millennium and Beyond.* New York: Simon and Schuster, 1993.
Marsden, George M. *Fundamentalism and American Culture: The Shaping of Twentieth Century Evangelicalism, 1870-1925.* New York: Oxford University Press, 1980.

Bibliography

McAlvany, Donald S. *The Y2K Tidal Wave: Year 2000 Economic Survival.* Toronto: Frontier Research, 1999.
McCain, Alva. *Daniel's Prophecy of Seventy Weeks.* Grand Rapids: Zondervan, 1940.
McGinn, Bernard. *Antichrist: Two Thousand Years of the Human Fascination with Evil.* San Francisco: Harper, 1994.
———. *Visions of the End: Apocalyptic Traditions in the Middle Ages.* New York: Columbia University Press, 1979.
McGinn, Bernard, John J. Collins, and Stephen J. Stein, editors. *The Continuum History of Apocalypticism.* New York: Continuum, 2003.
McGuire, Bill. *A Guide to the End of the Earth: Everything You Never Wanted to Know.* New York: Oxford University Press, 2002.
Melton, J. Gordon. *Encyclopedic Handbook of Cults in America.* New York: Garland, 1986.
Miller, Elliot. *Crash Course on the New Age Movement: Describing and Evaluating a Growing Social Force.* Grand Rapids: Baker, 1989.
Missler, Chuck. *Prophecy 20/20: Profiling the Future through the Lens of Scripture.* Nashville: T. Nelson, 2006.
Moorhead, James H. "Searching for the Millennium in America." *Princeton Seminary Bulletin* 8/2 (1987) 17–33.
———. "The Erosion of Postmillennialism in American Religious Thought, 1865–1925." *Church History* 53/1 (1984) 61–77.
———. *The World without End: Mainstream Protestant Visions of the Last Things, 1880–1925.* Bloomington: University of Indiana Press, 1999.
Newport, Kenneth G. C., and Crawford Gribben, editors. *Expecting the End: Millennialism in Social and Historical Context.* Waco, TX: Baylor University Press, 2006.
Numbers, Ronald L., and Jonathan M. Butler, editors. *The Disappointed: Millerism and Millenarianism in the Nineteenth Century.* Knoxville: University of Tennessee Press, 1993.
O' Leary, Stephen D. *Arguing the Apocalypse: A Theory of Millennial Rhetoric.* New York: Oxford University Press, 1994.
Olson, Carl E. *Will Catholics Be "Left Behind"?: A Catholic Critique of the Rapture and Today's Prophecy Preachers.* San Francisco: Ignatius, 2003.
Penton, M. James. *Apocalypse Delayed: The Story of the Jehovah's Witnesses.* Toronto: University of Toronto Press, 1985.
Peretti, Frank. *This Present Darkness.* Eastbourne, UK: Minstrel, 1986.
Poole, W. Scott. *Satan in America: The Devil We Know.* Lanham, MD: Rowman & Littlefield, 2009.
Randi, James. *The Mask of Nostradamus: The Prophecies of the World's Most Famous Seer.* Buffalo: Prometheus, 1993.
Ratzinger, Joseph. *Eschatology, Death, and Eternal Life.* Washington, DC: Catholic University Press, 1988.
Restall, Matthew, and Amara Solari. *2012 and the End of the World: The Western Roots of the Mayan Apocalypse.* Lanham, MD: Rowman & Littlefield, 2011.
Richardson, Joel. *Antichrist: Islam's Awaited Messiah.* Enumclaw, WA: Pleasant Word, 2006.
Robbins, Thomas, and Susan J. Palmer, editors. *Millennium, Messiahs, and Mayhem: Contemporary Apocalyptic Movements.* New York: Routledge, 1997.

Bibliography

Robertson, Pat. *The New Millennium*. Dallas: Word, 1996.
Rowe, David L. *God's Strange Work: William Miller and the End of the World*. Grand Rapids: Eerdmans, 2008.
Rubinski, Yuri, and Ian Wiseman. *A History of the End of the World*. New York: Morrow, 1982.
Rushdooney, Rousas J. *Thy Kingdom Come: Studies in Daniel and Revelation*. Philadelphia: Presbyterian and Reformed, 1971.
Samples, Kenneth R., et al. *Prophets of the Apocalypse: David Koresh and Other American Messiahs*. Grand Rapids: Baker, 1994.
Scofield, C. I., editor. *Scofield Reference Bible*. New York: Oxford University Press, 1909.
Shuck, Glenn W. *Marks of the Beast: The Left Behind Novels and the Struggle for Evangelical Identity*. New York: New York University Press, 2005.
Smith, Wilbur M. *Israeli/Arab Conflict and the Bible*. Glendale, CA: Regal, 1967.
St. Clair, Michael J. *Millenarian Movements in Historical Context*. New York: Garland, 1992.
Stearns, Peter N. *Millennium III, Century XXI: A Retrospective on the Future*. Boulder, CO: Westview, 1996.
Stice, Ralph W. *From 9/11 to 666: The Convergence of Current Events, Biblical Prophecy and the Vision of Islam*. Nashville: ACW, 2005.
Stozier, Charles B. *Apocalypse: On the Psychology of Fundamentalism in America*. Boston: Beacon, 1994.
Stozier, Charles B., and Michael Flynn, editors. *The Year 2000: Essays on the End*. New York: New York University Press, 1997.
Tucker, Ruth. *Another Gospel: Alternative Religions and the New Age Movement*. Grand Rapids: Zondervan, 1989.
Tuveson, Ernest Lee. *Millennium and Utopia: A Study in the Background of the Idea of Progress*. New York: Harper, 1964.
———. *Redeemer Nation: The Idea of America's Millennial Role*. Chicago: University of Chicago Press, 1968.
Underwood, Grant. *The Millenarian World of Early Mormonism*. Urbana, IL: University of Illinois Press, 1993.
Van Impe, Jack. *2001: On the Edge of Eternity*. Dallas: Word, 1996.
Villers, Marq de. *The End: Natural Disasters, Manmade Catastrophes, and the Future of Human Survival*. New York: St. Martin's, 2008.
Wacker, Grant. *Heaven Below: Early Pentecostalism and American Culture*. Cambridge, MA: Harvard University Press, 2001.
Wagar, W. Warren. *The Next Three Futures: Paradigms of Things to Come*. New York: Praeger, 1991.
———. *Terminal Visions: The Literature of the Last Things*. Bloomington: Indiana University Press, 1982.
Walvoord, John F. *Armageddon, Oil and the Middle East Crisis*. Rev. ed. Grand Rapids: Zondervan, 1990.
———. *Israel in Prophecy*. Grand Rapids: Zondervan, 1962.
Weber, Timothy P. "Happily at the Edge of the Abyss: Popular Premillennialism in America." *Ex Auditu* 6 (1991) 87.
———. *Living in the Shadow of the Second Coming*. Rev. ed. Chicago: University of Chicago Press, 1987.

Bibliography

———. *On the Road to Armageddon: How Evangelicals Became Israel's Best Friend.* Grand Rapids: Baker, 2004.
Wilcox, Clyde. *Onward Christian Soldiers: The Religious Right in American Politics.* Boulder, CO: Westview, 1996.
Williams, George H. *The Radical Reformation.* Philadelphia: Westminster, 1962.
Wilson, Dwight. *Armageddon Now!: The Premillennial Response to Russia and Israel Since 1917.* Grand Rapids: Baker, 1977.
Wójcik, Daniel. *The End of the World as We Know It: Faith, Fatalism, and Apocalypse in America.* New York: New York University Press, 1997.
Wright, Stuart A., editor. *Armageddon in Waco: Critical Perspectives on the Branch Davidian Conflict.* Chicago: University of Chicago Press, 1995.
Zamora, Lois Parkinson, editor. *The Apocalyptic Vision in America: Interdisciplinary Essays on Myth and Culture.* Bowling Green, OH: Bowling Green University Popular Press, 1982.

Index

1994, 325
1000, 26
11:11 Doorway" movement, 253
2008-*God's Final Witness,* 323
2012 global predictions, 2-3, 329-335
666, 194
700 Club, 102
88 Reasons Why the Rapture Will Be in 1988, 109, 195

Abortion, 127, 160, 179, 210
Adamski, George, 253
Adventism, 48, 67-70, 78, 229, 232, 244, 293, 315-18, 325, 327
Aetherius Society, 256
Afghanistan, 4, 158, 174
Africanus, Sixtus Julius, 24
Age of Aquarius, 4, 246
Age of Reason, 35
Ahmadinejad, 2, 167-70, 323
AIDS, 1, 7, 18, 112, 144, 247, 269, 285, 286-87
Albanese, Catherine, 47, 58
Ali Khamenei, Ayatollah Mohammed, 169
All Aboard for Ararat, 184
Allah, 164
Allegorical interpretation, 11-12, 25-26
Allenby, General Edmund, 95
Allies for Armageddon, 218
America in prophecy, 175-79
American Israel Political Affairs Committee (AIPAC) 222-23
American Revolution, 49, 52-53

American Vision Organization, 211
Amillennialism, 10-11, 110, 230, 296, 306, 324, 343-44, 351
Anabaptists, 37-39
Anderson, Robert Sir, 87-88
Andromeda, 291
Angley, Ernest A. 194
Ankerberg, John, 127
Antarctica, 282
Antichrist, 2, 6, 28-32, 35, 39-41, 47, 49, 53, 83, 96, 109, 111, 120-29, 146, 151, 157, 165, 167-69, 173, 175, 177, 179, 186, 191, 198-99, 219, 248, 261, 296-97, 307, 312-13, 316, 335.
Antioch, 25
Antiochus Epiphanes, 125, 307
Anti-Semitism, 35, 95
Apocalypse 2000, 143
Apocalypse Dawn, 201
Apocalyptic literature, 8, 22
Applewhite, Marshall, 257
Are You Ready? 110, 325
Arguelles, Jose, 145, 330
Armageddon, Battle of, 3-4, 72-73, 92-98, 106, 108-9, 121, 130, 145, 168, 218-19, 254, 307, 316, 319, 339, 349
Armageddon, Oil and the Middle East Crisis, 105, 118
Armstrong, Herbert, 5, 176, 238-40, 259, 338
Artaxeres, 88
Aryan Nations, 259-61
Ashcroft, John, 216, 310

Index

Asteroid, 188
Asteroids, 288–91
Atlantis, 13, 248
Atomic bomb, 102, 112–14, 117, 193, 231, 272–76, 348–49
Augustine, 25–28, 31, 294, 342, 345
Australia, 149
Aztecs, 6, 252, 324

Bailey, Alice, 145, 252
Bakker, Jim, 102, 224, 310
Balfour Declaration, 94–95, 115–17, 220, 350
Balmer, Randall, 348
Barkun, Michael, 16
Barnes, Bruce, 198–99
Barnhouse, Donald Grey, 111
Batra, Ravi, 143
Bayside apparitions, 301–5, 318
Be Thou Prepared for Jesus Is Coming, 193
Bear, Sun, 145
Beck, Glenn, 321
Begin, Menachem, 222
Bell, Daniel, 143
Bellamy, Edward, 142
Beneath the Planet of the Apes, 186
Benedict of Nursia, 32
Benedictine XVI, Pope, 300
Ben-Judah, Rabbi Tsion, 199
Bennett, Dennis, 311
Berg, David, 236–37
Berlitz, Charles, 143
Bible belt, 218
Bible Code, 322–23, 336
Bible Institute of Los Angeles, 89
Black Death, 30, 34, 284–85, 292
Black Muslims, 258, 261–64. (See also Nation of Islam)
Blackstone, William E. 94, 220
Blavatsky, Madame, 145
Blood Moon, 201
Bob Jones University, 200
Bock, Darrell, 103
Book of Eli, The, 187
Book of Mormon, 57
Boyer, Paul, 125, 153, 191, 347

Branch Davidians, 5, 18, 228, 232, 242–46
Britain (England) 52–53, 62, 98
British Empire, 176, 238–39
British Israelism (Anglo-Israelism) 238, 259
Brooke, James, 89
Buddhism (Buddhists) 6–7, 134, 146, 215, 253, 270, 338
Bullinger, Heinrich, 39
Burkett, Larry, 124
Burnt-Over District, 57
Burroughs, Joseph Birbeck, 192
Bush, George W. 215, 224–25, 310, 321, 323
Byers, Marvin, 141

Caliphate, 164, 351
Calvary Chapel, 108
Calvin, John, 39, 213
Calvin's Geneva, 213
Cambridge University, 42–43
Camisard prophets, 41–42
Camping, Harold, 110, 320, 324–29, 337, 339
Canada, 149, 334
Canticle for Liebowitz, A, 187
Capra, Fritjof, 250
Carpathia, Nicole Jetty, 198–99
Carter, Jimmy, 126, 132, 221–23
Catholic Catechism, 296
Catholic eschatology, 40, 294–97
Cayce, Edgar, 5, 135, 145–46, 246–48, 277, 339
Chafer, Lewis Sperry, 103
Chalcedon Foundation, 211
Chameleon-like character, 80, 112, 129, 157
Charismatic movement, 294, 311–15
Charlemagne, 30
Charles I, King, 41
Cheney, Dick, 225
Chernobyl, 18, 275
Children of God, 232, 235–37
Chilton, David, 211–12
China, 98, 119, 131, 135, 149, 172, 178, 277, 349

362

Index

Chosen nation concept, 207, 239, 346 (See also Christian nation)
Christadelphians, 60–61, 78
Christian Coalition, 224
Christian Identity, 18, 258–61
Christian nation concept, 207, 209, 262, 346
Christian Right, 203–10, 316
Christian Right and Israel, 209
Christian Right theology, 204–8
Christian Right's inconsistencies, 208–10
Christian Zionism, 218
Christian Zionism, 203, 217–27
Church of England, 40, 53
Church of God, 5, 323
Church of Ireland, 43
Church Universal and Triumphant, 18, 253–54
Church, J.R. 140
CIA (Central Intelligence Agency) 286, 323
City of God, The, 26
Civil Religion, 207, 210
Civil Rights Movement, 186
Civil War, 47, 62, 81, 85, 87, 90, 99
Civilizations Last Hurrah, 194
Clash of Civilizations and the Remaking of the World Order, 162, 225
Clinton, Bill, 140, 147, 149, 152, 154–55, 224, 321, 348
Clinton, Hillary, 155, 348
Clock Strikes, The, 194
Clouse, Robert, 209
Cognitive minority, 17–18, 343, 350
Cohen, Daniel, 194
Cohen, Gary, 104, 246
Cohn, Norman, 16
Cold War, 7, 118, 129–30, 158, 160, 193–94, 203, 220, 264, 273, 312, 315, 343, 348
Columbus, 36
Comets, 288–91
Coming Prince, The, 87–88
Common Market (European Union) 117–21, 127, 132, 350
Communalism, 54–60

Communism, 11, 95, 97, 127, 129–30, 135, 143, 179, 193–94, 237, 296, 300, 348–49
Computer bug, 135
Comte, Auguste, 32
Conditions in Western history, 15–18, 340–41
Congress, United States, 147, 221
Congregationalists, 91, 305
Conversion experience, 206
Convulsionaries, 138
Copeland, Paul, 102
Copenhagen, 280
Counterculture, 230–32
Covenant principles, 214, 219, 287, 346
Creationism, 24, 206–7
Crème, Benjamin, 252
Cromwell's England, 213
Crusades, 29
Cuba, 234, 315
Cumbey, Constance E. 128, 195
Cyclical view of history, 14–15

Dajjal, 160, 163–66
Dallas Seminary, 103, 105–6
Dami sect, 228
Daniel, Book of, 22, 32, 36, 65,74,80, 85–86, 119, 121, 124,137, 154, 189, 219, 248, 307, 309, 336, 348, 350
Daniel's sixty-ninth week, 44, 141
Darby, John Nelson, 41, 43–44, 73, 82–83, 87–89, 116–20, 345
Darwinsim, 79, 182, 214
Day of the Tiffids, 185
Day the Earth Caught Fire, The, 186
De Mar, Gary, 211
De Miranda, Jose Luis, 321
December, 21, 2012 2–3, 186, 320, 324, 337, 339
Decentralized political systems, 214–15
Defense of Israel, 169
Deforestation, 280–81
DeHaan, M.R. 220
Democracy, 62, 213
Department of Defense (DOD) 148

363

Index

DePauw University, 347
Descartes, Rene, 250
Desmond, Shaw, 185
Devil's Bride, The, 192
Disciples of Christ, 305
Dispensationalism, 4, 19-20, 43-44, 82-133, 141, 154, 167, 171, 173, 175, 177, 189-92, 201, 205, 209, 214, 217-27, 230, 239, 260, 294, 296, 306, 312-13, 318, 337, 346-47, 349, 351
Dispensationalism, early, 84-92
Dispensationism, varieties of, 103-4
Divine Principle, 241-42
Dixon, Jeanne, 5, 145, 246, 248, 277
Dobson, James, 153
Dominion theology, 210-17
Doomsday clock, 274
Drew, Timothy, 262
Dualism (See Manichean worldview)
Duguet, Jaques-Joseph, 138
DuPlessis, David, 311
Durham, Hattie, 198
Dwight, Timothy, 53, 138
Dyer, Charles, 130, 158, 179

Earth First Movement, 270
Earth in Balance, 281
Earthquakes, 5, 160, 277-79, 291, 308, 328
East Germany (Gomer) 119
Eastern Europe, 119, 129-30, 149, 157, 182, 273, 300
Eastern Orthodox Church, 99
Eastwood, Clint, 166
Ebola virus, 269, 287
Edwards, Jonathan, 51-52, 78, 138
Ehrlich, Paul, 142, 266, 282-83
Eiffel Tower, 135
Elastic apocalypse, 341, 343-45
Elias, Prophecy of, 137
Emmerick, Anna-Katarina, 298
End of State, 201
End of the Age, The, 197
End-time Christian novels, 188-200
End-time films, 185-88
End-times secular novels, 182-85
English Civil War, 41, 342-43, 345

Enlightenment, 22, 342, 345
Environmental degradation, 186, 189, 269, 272, 279-82, 292, 343, 346, 349, 351
Environmentalism, 230
Ephesus, 23, 25
Epicenter, 170
Episcopalians, 305
Escapism, 349, 351
Eschatological fiction, 182-202
Essay on the Principle of Population, 283
Eucharist, 295
European currency (EURO) 141
European Union (Common Market) 4, 96-97, 117-18, 120, 157, 132, 172, 194, 203, 220, 349,
Evangelical media, 132-33, 151, 347
Evangelical prophecy fiction, 188-202
Evans, Michael D. 140
Ezekiel (Book of) 2, 22, 32, 80, 98, 119, 167, 169-71, 174, 176, 189, 219, 348

False Prophet, 167
Falwell, Jerry, 5, 17, 102, 106, 112, 116, 153, 205, 216, 223-24, 226-67, 286
Family Radio, 110, 320, 324, 328-29
Famine, 283-84
Famine-1975! 267
Farad, Wallace, 262
Farrakhan, Louis, 263-64, 339
Fatima, 299-300, 304
Feast of the Trumpets, 110
Federal Deposit Insurance, 148
Feminism, 127, 160, 148, 215, 230
Ferguson, Marilyn, 250
Fichte, Johann, 32
Final Victory: The Year, 2000? The, 141
First Great Awakening, 51-52, 138
Flagellants, 32
Food of the Gods, 187
Ford, Gerald, 230
Fourth, Reich, The, 201
France, 52, 62
Francis, Saint, 302
Franciscan Spirituals, 30-31

Index

Frederick II, 30–31, 125
French and Indian Wars, 52
French Revolution, 41–42, 62, 342
Frost, Robert, 266
Fundamentalism (Christian) 2, 5, 17–18, 81–82, 89–90, 93, 101, 235, 272, 304, 340, 346, 350
Fundamentals, The, 89
Futuristic interpretation, 11–12, 85–86

Gaebelein, Arno, 89, 94, 120, 220
Gamma-rays, 324
Garden of Eden, 56
Gas War of, 1940 185
Gaza, 115, 177
Genesis account of creation, 206
George III, King, 53
Germany, 38, 97, 98, 131, 141, 247
Global economy, 121–23
Global Positioning Satellite (GPS) 148, 155, 333
Global Warming (greenhouse effect) 279–82
Globalization, 285
Gnosticism, 23, 257
Gog and Magog, 28–29, 39, 92, 118–20, 131, 171–72
Golden Plates, 57
Gorbachev, Mikhail, 126
Gore, Al, 155, 281
Graham, Billy, 105, 114
Graham, Franklin, 226
Grant, George, 201, 211
Great Depression, 99, 152, 179, 193, 247, 315
Great Disappointment, 67–68, 72, 85, 326
Great Parenthesis, 43–44, 86, 88, 141
Great Recession of, 2008 124
Great Wall of China, 135
Greatest Sign, The, 115–17
Gregorian calendar, 165, 332
Grosso, Michael, 137
Guadalupe, 299
Gulf War, First (1991) 4, 129, 157, 245, 247
Gulf War, Second, 159

Hagee, John, 5, 17, 109, 168–71
Hale-Bopp Comet, 258
Halley, Edmund, 42
Halley's Comet, 183, 289
Hargrove, Barbara, 250
Harmonic Convergence, 252–53, 330
Hart, D. G. 206
Hasidic Jews, 245
Heaven's Gate, 257–58
Heavenly millennium, 316–18
Hegel, Georg, 32
Heilbroner, Robert, 144, 266
Herzl, Theodor, 94, 220
Hidden Dangers of the Rainbow, 128, 195
Hidden Imam, 162, 321
Himalayas, 252
Himes, Joshua, 65–66
Hinduism, 6–7, 146, 215, 270
Hippolytus, 24, 341, 344
Hiroshima, 113, 272–73, 290, 334
Historic premillennialism, 12, 62–68, 85–87
Historicist interpretation, 11–12, 64, 294
Hitchcock, Mark, 1, 5, 168–69, 172, 179
Hitler, Adolf, 45, 97–99, 125, 170, 335
Hofmann, Melchoir, 38, 292
Holy Land, 168, 222, 226
Holy Spirit, outpouring of, 300–15, 318
Holy Spirit, baptism of, 310–11
Home school movement, 216
Homosexuality, 160, 179, 210, 214, 286, 302, 316
Hopi predictions, 6, 335
House of Yahweh, 321
Howell, Vernon, 243
Humbard, Rex, 102, 310
Hunt, David, 127, 129
Huntington, Samuel, 162, 225
Hussein, Saddam, 126, 129–30, 157–58
Hutchings, N.W. 154
Hyatt, Michael, 150, 152–53

I Am Legend, 188

365

Index

IBM, 147
ICBM missiles, 148
Idealist interpretation, 11
Image of the Beast, 101, 195
Imam, 162
In the Twinkling of an Eye, 193
Independence Day, 188
Indiana, 234
Inerrant Bible, 206
Inquiry into the Human Prospect, An, 266
Institute for Holy Land Studies, 222
Institute of Christian Economics, 211
International Monetary Fund, 122
Interplanetary Adepts, 256
Invasion of the Body Snatchers, 188
Iran, 1, 158, 160, 165, 168–69, 171, 274, 323
Iraq, 4, 130, 158
Ironside, H.A. 98, 118, 120, 220
Irrationalism, 347–49
Islam and apocalypticism, 159–67
Islamic Antichrist, 163–66
Islamic eschatology, 161–66
Islamic terrorism, 1–2, 5, 92, 158–59, 166–67, 169
Israel, return in, 1948 4, 102, 106–7, 115–17, 157, 194, 245, 247, 260, 348
Israeli-Hezbollah conflict, 159
Italy, 97
Jansenism, 138
January, 1, 2000 135, 147
Japan, 97, 119,123, 129, 131, 149, 178, 202, 228–29, 248, 275, 278
Jeffrey, Grant R. 108, 130, 140, 153, 339
Jehovah's Witnesses, 5, 71–76, 78, 229, 232, 237, 325, 327–38
Jenkins, Jerry, 199–200, 202
Jenkins, John Major, 335
Jericho, 187
Jerusalem Countdown, 169
Jesuits, 40
Jesus People, 232, 235–37, 250
Joachim of Fiore, 31–34, 342
John of Leiden, 38
John Paul II, Pope, 126, 197
John XXIII, Pope, 126, 253, 300
Johnson, Lyndon, 231
Jones, Jim, 232–34, 242
Jonestown, Guyana, 232–34
Joseph, Saint, 302
Judgment Day, 188, 193
June, 6, 2006 6, 321
Jung, Carl, 145
Jupiter, 143

Kahn, Herbert, 274
Kalki, 146
Katrina, Hurricane, 177, 333
Keech, Marian, 256
Keller, Catherine, 343
Kennedy, James, 153, 216
Kennedy, John F. 126, 230, 248, 315, 321
Kennedy, Paul, 144
Khrushchev, Nikita, 186
King James Bible, 91
King Philip's War, 49
Kirban, Salem, 5, 109, 113, 118–19, 194
Kissinger, Henry, 126, 166
Kohoutek, 237
Korean War, 239
Koresh, David, 242–46
Kortner, Ulrich, 137, 341–42
Krauthammer, Charles, 168, 225, 268
Ku Klux Klan, 233, 259
Kyoto, 280

Ladd, George, 111
LaHaye, Tim, 5, 17, 108, 112, 199–200, 204, 224, 267, 345
Lancaster, Burt, 166
Last Man, The, 183
Late Great Planet Earth, The, 4, 101, 103, 107, 109, 161, 189, 194–95, 221, 250, 336, 346
Latter Rain, 312–13
Lay Order of St. Michael, 303
League of Nations, 97
Lebanon, 143
Left Behind series, 1, 104, 191, 197–200, 298, 322
Leo III, Pope, 336

Index

LeSEA Broadcasting, 139
Lessing, Gotthold, 32
Liberalism, 89–90, 97, 112, 122, 127, 191, 206
Libertarian economics, 214
Light and Glory, The, 346
Likud Party, 222–24
Lindsey, Hal, 2, 4, 17, 101, 104, 106–7, 112, 119–20, 139, 157, 159, 161, 189, 201, 224, 250, 267, 325, 338, 345–46
Linear view of history (See Western view of history)
Lisbon earthquake, 42, 79, 277, 342
Livingston, Robert, 173–74
Lord of the Second Advent, 240–42
Lord of the Flies, 188
Louis VII, King, 30
Lourdes, 299
Lubavitch movement, 245–46
Lueken, Veronica, 301–5
Luther, Martin, 34, 36–37, 138, 342

Maastricht Treaty, 121
Mad Max movies, 187
Madhi, 2, 134, 160, 163–69, 173–75, 323
Mainline Protestant eschatology, 305–9
Maitreya, 146, 252
Malthus, Thomas, 182, 283–84
Manichean worldview, 177, 202, 205, 208, 304, 347–48, 351
Manson, Charles, 242
Manuel, David, 346
Marian apparitions, 297–305
Mark of the Beast (666) 6, 83, 86, 126–28, 162, 167, 189–90
Mark of the Beast, The, 97, 193
Marsden, George, 81, 219, 227
Marshall, Peter, 346
Martinique, 279
Marx, Karl, 32
Mary's intercessor role, 299
Masque of the Red Death, The, 183
Mather, Cotton, 48, 50, 78
Mather, Increase, 49
Matthys, Jan, 38

May, 21, 2011 327–29
Mayan calendar, 2, 5, 81, 134, 186, 320, 329–35, 337–38, 351
Mayan Factor, The, 252, 330
Mayan prophecies, 252, 329–35, 339
McAlvany, Don, 152, 155
McDonald's, 190, 351
McGinn, Bernard, 8, 16, 342
McKeever, James, 140
Medieval millennialism, 30–34
Medjugorie, 299–301
Mega-churches, 218
Melanchthon, Philip, 399
Melton, Gordon, 68, 239, 249
Merchants of Tarshish, 176–77
Merlin the Seer, 31
Meteors, 288–91
Methodist churches, 305, 311
Mexico, 100, 283, 331
Michael the Archangel, 303
Middle Ages, 16, 18, 28–34, 80, 113, 188, 276, 284, 292
Middle East, 2, 5 167, 170, 172, 190, 218, 226, 277, 322
Midtribulationism, 10, 236
Milky Way, 291, 334
Millennial anxieties, 134–56
Millennial celebrations, 134–36
Millennial mission of America, 308, 47–53, 79, 84, 346
Millennium Bug, The, 152
Miller, William, 61–68, 78, 243, 326
Millerite movement, 17, 48, 61–68, 86, 94, 105, 289, 325, 340, 342
Mind at the End of Its Tether, 184
Missler, Chuck, 153, 172, 177
Montanists, 341
Montgomery, Ruth, 144–46, 253
Moody Bible Institute, 89
Moody, Dwight, 88–90
Moon, Sun Myung, 240–42
Moorhead, James, 305
Moral Majority, 106
Mormonism, 57–59, 204, 229, 232, 238
Mosaic Law, 212
Movement for the Restoration of the Ten Commandments, 229

367

Index

Moynihan, Daniel Patrick, 147, 149
Mt. Carmel, 244
Muhammad, 162–63
Muhammad, Abu'l-Qasium, 162
Muhammad, Elijah, 262–64
Münster, 37–38
Müntzer, Thomas, 37–38, 342
Mussolini, 97–98, 125
Myer, John, 194

Nagasaki, 113
Napoleon, 125, 335
National Association of Evangelicals, 224, 310–11
National Council of Churches, 122
National Recovery Administration, 97
Native American religions, 76–78, 99, 140, 330, 335
Native-American spirituality, 76–78, 99, 134, 270, 330, 338
Natural disasters, 30, 276–79
Nazism, 11, 117, 168, 234
Neptune, 143
Nero, 11, 125, 274
Netanyahu, Benjamin, 224
New Age millennialism, 249–54
New Age movement, 3–5, 18, 127, 129, 135, 137, 140, 195, 231, 246, 249–54, 316, 330, 337–38, 348, 351
New Deal, 97
New Jerusalem, 48, 83
New Millennium, The, 196
New Testament, 22, 39, 295, 312, 341
New World Order (one world government) 117–23, 140–41, 190, 195, 202
New World Order, The, 196
New York City, 127, 166, 176, 245, 299, 301–5
New York Times, 101, 152
New Zealand, 328
Newton, Isaac, 3, 41, 336
Newtonian physics, 250
Nicene Creed, 294
Night of the Lepus, 187
Nixon, Richard, 231
Noah (and the flood) 13, 42

North Atlantic Treaty Organization, 118, 120, 155, 172, 312
North Pole, 6
North, Gary, 155, 211, 215–16
Northwestern Bible School, 89
Nostradamus, 2, 5, 134, 146, 246–47, 277, 298, 319, 335–36
Noyes, John Humphrey, 59–60
Nuclear holocaust, 112–14, 272–76
Nuclear war, 112–14, 272–76
Nuclear winter scenario, 276
O'Leary, Stephen, 342
Obama, Barack, 2, 5, 81, 158, 319, 348
Occult activities, 246–58
Odom, Mel, 201
Oilar, Loman, 193
Old Believers, 41–42
Old Testament, 4, 22, 211, 215, 238, 243, 277, 318
Omega Code, The, 198
Omen, The, 188, 322
On the Road to Armageddon, 218
Oneida Community, 59–60, 229
Operation Rescue, 216
Oppenheimer, J. Robert, 272
Orthodox Jews, 245–46
Orwell, George, 122
Oslo Peace Accord, 224, 320
Ottoman Empire, 63, 95–98, 159, 350, *Outbreak*, 188
Owen, Robert, 60
Ozone depletion, 281–82

Paepke, C. Owen, 144
Palestine Liberation Movement, 129–30
Pandemics, 269, 284–87
Paradigm shift, 249–52
Patterson, Ron, 320
Paul VI, Pope, 302, 304
Paul, Apostle, 302
Peasant's War, 38
Pentecost, Dwight J. 104, 111
Pentecostalism, 93, 218, 294, 305, 309–15, 339
People of the Ruins, 185
People's Temple, 232–34
Peretti, Frank, 195–96

368

Index

Peres, Shimon, 224
Perfectionism, 50–52, 54, 59–60
Persistent apocalypse, 341–43
Piercing the Darkness, 195–96
Planet Earth—2000 A.D. 159, 161
Planet of the Apes, The, 107, 186
Planet X Hypothesis, 334
Planetary realignment, 143
Plymouth Brethren, 43
Poe, Edgar Allan, 183
Popularizers, 111–13, 116, 125–26, 129, 132, 139–40, 153, 159, 167, 190, 345, 347
Population Bomb, The, 282–84
Population explosion, 282–84
Populism, 19, 111, 190–91, 199–200, 347, 351
Portugal, 299–300
Posse Comitatus, 259
Post-Christian era, 17
Postmillennialism, 10, 35, 41–43, 46–53, 62, 84–85, 96, 138, 192, 209–10, 214, 227, 230, 241, 308–9, 314–15, 344–46, 351
Postponement theory, 43–44, 86, 88, 141
Postribulational view, 10, 236–37, 260, 316
Premillennialism, 4, 19–20, 31, 41, 62, 80–133, 191, 196, 236, 241, 258, 264, 293–94, 306, 308, 337, 341, 344–5, 349
Premillennialism, propagation of, 10, 99–100
Presbyterians, 305, 311
Preterist interpretation, 1–12, 26–28, 294
Prophecy novels, 183–85, 188–202
Prophesied End-Time, The, 323
Prophet, Elizabeth Clare, 5, 145, 253
Prophet, office of, 9, 313
Prophets of the apocalypse, 11, 104–111, 246–49
Protestant Reformation, 12, 29, 34–42, 45, 98
Psychics and, 2000 144–47
Public Faces, 185

Puritans, 41, 48–50, 78, 207–8, 211, 213, 345

Qur'an, 175

Rabin, Yitzhak, 109, 224, 320
Racism, 230, 260
Radical Reformers, 36–39, 342
Rafsanjani, 171
Ragnarok, 185
Randal, Terry, 216
Rapp, George, 60
Rappites, 59–60
Rapture, 44–45, 83, 93, 103, 114, 179, 272, 296, 350
Rapture Index, 158–59, 321
Rapture, The, 101
Raptured, 194
Reagan, Ronald, 4, 102, 126, 221, 223–24, 321
Reconstructionism, 141, 155, 203, 210–17, 314
Red Square, 135
Redeemer nation, 346
Redwood Valley, 234
Reed, Ralph, 224
Reeves, Marjorie, 16
Reformed amillennialist, 110, 324
Relfe, Mary Stewart, 109
Religious Right (see Christian Right) 17, 196, 204
Replacement theology, 94
Republican Party, 199
Restoration movement, 314–15
Revelation, Book of, 4, 9, 11–12, 25–26, 32, 36, 39–40, 43–44, 62, 64, 70, 74, 80, 85, 121, 124, 137, 154, 160, 172–73, 189, 201, 219, 237, 239, 244, 248, 257, 273, 284, 291, 295, 299, 307, 309, 313, 323, 348, 350–52
Revivalism, 48
Ribeira, Franciscus, 40
Richard the Lion-Hearted, 32
Richardson, Joel, 173
Rightly Dividing the Word of Truth, 91
Riley, F.M. 320

369

Index

Rise and Fall of the Great Powers, The, 144
Road, The, 187
Roberts, Oral, 102, 310–11
Robertson, Pat, 5, 17, 102, 106, 114, 196–97, 204–5, 215, 224, 226, 267, 310, 319, 322
Roman Catholicism, 27, 29, 34, 36–37, 63, 70, 99, 122, 127, 129, 142, 192, 197, 293–99, 321, 350–51
Roman Empire, 11, 25, 98, 98, 119, 125, 127, 167, 173, 299, 307, 312, 344
Romantic Movement, 182
Rome, 25, 183
Roosevelt, Franklin, 97, 152, 321
Rosenberg, Joel C. 2, 168, 170–71
Rumsfeld, Donald, 225
Rushdooney, Rousas John, 211, 213, 216
Russell, Charles Taze, 72–73
Russia, 1, 63, 92, 95, 115, 117–18, 130, 149, 158–59, 167–73, 179, 274, 285
Russia and Islam, 167–73
Russian Revolution, 117
Rutherford, Joseph Franklin, 74–75
Ryrie, Charles, 104, 111

Saint Germain, 253
Sale-Harrison, Leonard, 98
Samaria, 176
Sandeen, Ernest, 47, 61
SARS, 269, 287
Satanists, 212, 219
Saturn, 143
Scarlet and Purple, 193
Schilling, Friedrich, 32
Schneerson, Menachem Mendel, 245–46
Schwartz, Hillel, 134, 343
Scofield, Cyrus Ingerson, 90–92
Scofield Reference Bible, 90–92, 103, 312
Second Advent (Second Coming) 3, 5, 13, 26, 30, 41–43, 56, 69, 70, 81, 86–87, 103, 112, 118, 137–39, 141–42, 212, 219, 241, 244, 248, 294, 296, 305, 312, 327, 339, 351–52
Second Great Awakening, 53, 56
Secular apocalypse, 34, 42, 268–72, 292
Secular humanism, 296
September, 11, 2001 7–18, 81, 158, 166, 202, 218, 321, 343
Shakarian, Demos, 311
Shakers, 55–57, 229
Shape of Things to Come, 184
Shariah law, 164–65
Shelley, Mark, 183
Shifting sands of prophecy, 129–31
Shiites, 162–63
Siberia, 289–90
Simpson, A. B. 95
Sinai Peninsula, 115
Sino-Soviet Alliance, 119
Six Day War of, 1967 107, 115–16, 132, 163, 221, 224, 245, 320, 349
Six-day creation, 15, 24, 136, 194
Skolfield, Ellis, 175
Smith, Chuck, 108, 235, 311
Smith, Joseph, 57–60
Smith, Wilbur, 111
Social Darwinism, 214
Social Security, 214
Socialism, 122, 127, 155
Society of the Public Friend, 54–55
Soon, 202
South Pole, 6, 145
Southern Baptist churches, 218, 221
Southwold, Stephen, 185
Soviet Union, 47, 95, 99, 103, 115, 118, 127, 129–30, 141, 157–59, 171, 179, 203, 234, 275, 350
Spangler, David, 250
Spanish Armada, 41
Spargmino, Larry, 154
Stalin, Joseph, 45, 97
Stanley, Ann Lee, 55–56
Stearns, Peter, 341, 343–44
Steele, Rayford, 198
Stice, Ralph W. 173–75
Stonehenge, 135
Strasbourg, 38

Index

Struggle between good and evil, 17–18, 181–82
Sumrall, Lester, 139, 339
Sunday, Billy, 88
Sunnis, 162
Supreme Truth, The, 18, 228
Swaggart, Jimmy, 102, 224, 310
Swift-Tuttle Comet, 289–90
Switzerland, 228
Syria, 176

Taliban, 166
Tangshan, China, 277
Taoism, 270
Tatford, Frederick Albert, 194
Taylor, Charles, 110, 338
Temple Mount, 320
Teresa of Avila, 302
Texas, 321
Them, 187
Theocracy, 213
Theological liberalism (See liberalism)
Theonomy, 210–17 (See Reconstructionism)
Theosophists, 252
They That Remain, 193
Thief in the Night, A, 101, 195
Thinking About the Unthinkable, 274
Thirty Years War, 41
This Present Darkness, 195
Thomas, John, 60
Thompson, Donald W. 195
Three Mile Island, 275
Time Has an End, 325, 327
Time Machine, The, 184
Time/CNN poll, 19, 81
Titan, Son of Saturn, 192
Tokyo, 228
Tongues speaking, 310–11
Torrey, Reuben A. 88, 92, 220
Totalitarian rulers, 184
Toth, Max, 145
Toutatis asteroid, 290, 334
Tribulation Force, 198–99
Trilateral Commission, 123
Trinity Broadcasting Network (TBN) 198
Trinity College, 43

Trumbull, Charles, 89
Trumpet Sounds, The, 194
Tsunamis, 267, 275, 277–78, 322
Turkey, 23, 39, 117, 172
Tuveson, Ernest Lee, 27, 346
TV preachers, 1, 4, 19, 151, 347
Twelvers, 162
Tyconius, 26, 28
Tyndale House, 200

UFO movement, 18, 103, 134, 254–58, 302
Uganda, 229, 286
Unification Church, 232, 240–42
United Nations, 123, 153, 194–95, 198, 202, 222, 302, 321
United States (America) 2, 7, 21, 46–78, 61, 98
Uranus, 143
USA Today, 258, 330
Ussher, Archbishop James, 15, 65, 72, 138–40

Van Impe, Jack, 5, 108, 113, 128, 140, 153, 176, 267, 286, 319, 324, 339
Van Kampen, Robert, 201
Van Til, Cornelius, 211
Vatican II, 298, 302, 304, 350
Vietnam War, 186, 194, 231, 239, 264
Vineyard Christian Fellowship, 311, 314
Virgin Mary, 42, 297–305, 349
Volcanoes, 267, 278–79, 291
Vredefort ring, 290

Waco, 242–43
Wahhabism, 174
Walvoord, John, 104–5, 111, 116, 118
War in the Air, The, 185
War of the Worlds, The, 184
Watergate, 231
Waterworld, 187
Watt, James, 4, 310
WE CAN KNOW movement, 325–27
Weber, Timothy, 19, 105, 115, 139
Weinberger, Caspar, 4
Weinland, Ronald, 323
Wells, H.G. 184–85.

371

Index

West Bank, 115
Western Europe, 21, 29–30, 45, 120–23
Western view of history (see linear view) 7–8, 13–15, 339–40
When Time Shall Be No More, 153
Whisenant, Edgar, 109, 195, 339
Whiston, William, 41
White Aryans, 259–61
White, Ellen G. 69–70, 243
White House, 147
Wilcox, Clyde, 204
Wilkinson, Jemima, 55
Williams, Roger, 204
Wimber, John, 311, 314
Witchcraft, 270
Wolfowitz, Paul, 225
World- affirming movements, 229–30, 240–42, 249–54
World Bank, 122
World Community of Islam, 263
World -rejecting movements, 229–45, 314
World Set Free, The, 184
World War I, 87, 93, 95–96, 100–101, 116–17, 182, 263, 285, 350
World War II, 92, 99, 112, 117, 119–20, 124, 131–32, 148, 189, 231, 248, 262, 284, 262, 264, 273, 276, 292, 300
World War III, 109, 113, 302
Worldwide Church of God, 5, 176, 232, 237–40, 259, 338
Wrath of nature, 276–79
Wyndham, John, 185

Y2K as a Christian apocalypse, 137–42
Y2K as a secular apocalypse, 142–44
Y2K meltdown (computer bug) 3, 135, 142, 147–57, 152, 330, 351
Y2K: The Day the World Shut Down, 152, 201
Yamamoto, J. Isamu, 241
Yellowstone National Park, 334

Zakaria, Fareed, 177
Zion's Christian Soldiers? 218
Zionism, 217–27
ZOG (Zion Occupation Government) 260
Zorastrianism, 7
Zwingli, Huldrych, 36, 39

www.ingramcontent.com/pod-product-compliance
Lightning Source LLC
Chambersburg PA
CBHW020606300426
44113CB00007B/522